SAILOR'S CREEK:

Major General G. W. Custis Lee, Captured with *Controversy*

SAILOR'S CREEK:

Major General G. W. Custis Lee, Captured with *Controversy:*

by
Frank Everett White Jr.

Foreword by
Patrick A. Schroeder

SCHROEDER PUBLICATIONS
2008

Published by
SCHROEDER PUBLICATIONS
131 Tanglewood Drive
Lynchburg, VA 24502
www.civilwar-books.com
civilwarbooks@yahoo.com

Printed by
McNaughton & Gunn, Inc.
Saline, Michigan

ISBN 1-889246-40-9

DEDICATED TO:
<u>DAVID DUNNELLS WHITE</u>
1844-1924
37TH MASSACHUSETTS INFANTRY
Infantryman
Pioneer Corpsman
Hospital Train Corpsman
Private/Corporal

<u>ABOUT THE AUTHOR</u>

<u>Frank Everett White Jr:</u>

Frank E. White Jr. is a life long resident of NJ. He is a graduate of Montclair State University in Montclair, NJ, with a B.S. degree in pre-medicine biology. He obtained his certification in professional genealogy and family history research from Brigham Young University in Provo, UT. Frank Jr. is married to Susan Slusarczyk White of NJ. Susan is also a graduate of Montclair State University, with a B.A. degree in communication sciences and disorders. Frank Jr. and Susan have three sons. Frank III is a graduate of Harvard University, is employed by Deutsche Bank in New York, NY, and is married to Elizabeth Briggs White of MA. Jared is a graduate of Beacon College in Leesburg, FL, and is employed by Utah County Sheriff's Department in Spanish Fork, UT. Ethan is a student of North Hunterdon Regional High School in Annandale, NJ, is an honor roll student and active in church and sports. Ethan loves his dog, Daisy. Frank Jr. is employed by Accenture LLC in their New York, NY, office as a Senior Executive working in the field of consulting. Frank Jr. has always had a life long passion for history, genealogy and historical archaeology, with a special emphasis on the Civil War. This is Frank Jr.'s first published work, blending together the events of the Battle of Sailor's Creek with the lives of the men who desperately fought it. This work, and the in-depth research that went into it, was a perfect blend of genealogy and history coming alive for the author.

TABLE OF CONTENTS:

Photographs:

Acknowledgements:
All proprietary photographs are noted above, with the owners' names. The author has received, with gratefulness, permission from these owners to publish these photographs in this book.

ACKNOWLEDGEMENTS

The author wishes to express his deep appreciation to a number of individuals that have made this work possible:

- First, my dear wife Sue, and our three sons, Frank III, Jared and Ethan, for their unfailing support, love, encouragement, and patience. Especially to Sue for her many hours of proofreading and editing the manuscript.
- Frank White III, our son, for compiling a comprehensive name and unit index for this work, which required many long hours of difficult work.
- Charles Thayer, for graciously sharing a wealth of Thayer family material and for thoroughly proofreading the manuscript.
- The late Mr. Jim Parsons, for his in-depth knowledge of the local history of the Northampton, MA, area and his willingness to help with every request asked of him.
- Denise Adams, Stephanie Poluhovich, Tamika Hare, Debbie Fagel and Michael Christensen for the many hours they spent typing and retyping this work.
- Chris Calkins, for his friendship and technical content guidance, being a renowned expert on the Battle of Sailor's Creek.
- Dave Borne, for photographing and measuring the Sailor's Creek battlefield.
- Eve Mahogany, for sharing her family Civil War letters.
- Donna Gibney, for her help and support.
- Edward Stanard, for sharing his collection of 37th Massachusetts materials and for proofreading the manuscript.
- Lance Herdegen, Pat Karr and Miles Butterfield for providing Butterfield family information.
- Greg Eanes, for his assistance and advice on local history.
- Salvatore Cilella, for sharing with me his in-depth research on the 121st New York.
- John Thillmann, for his expert advice on Civil War swords.
- Marie Panik, curator of Historic Northampton, Northampton, MA, for the many hours of research she performed on their Civil War sword collection and the records of the Northampton Historical Society.
- For all the employees and volunteers at the National Archives, Washington, DC; Civil War Library in Philadelphia, PA; Library of Congress, Washington, DC; Historic Northampton, Northampton, MA, and the many other repositories that have provided invaluable assistance.
- Donna Zentmayer, director of the inter-library loan program for the Hunterdon County, NJ, library, for all her assistance in acquiring resource material throughout the country, effectively using the inter-library loan program.
- Patrick Schroeder, my publisher, for his expert advice on the required steps needed to prepare my manuscript for publication and sharing with me his in-depth knowledge of the Appomattox Campaign and the Civil War.
- Last, but surely not least, for the good Lord who has blessed me with so many rich blessings in this life. The Lord has blessed me yet again, with the ability to complete this work and fulfill an obligation I have felt to my great, great grandfather, David Dunnells White. Though David White and I have not walked on the earth at the same time, I have come to know him through this work. I have come to deeply love and respect him as my great, great, grandfather, and I am grateful for the opportunity to try to live my life in such a way as to bring honor to his name and express thanksgiving for the legacy he has left behind for our family.

Thanks to all.

FOREWORD

With Frank White's work on the battle of Sailor's Creek focusing on the capture of Confederate Major General George Washington Custis Lee, eldest son of the famed General Robert E. Lee, new light is shed on this often overlooked pivotal battle during the final days of the Civil War.

Indeed, one could easily argue that the Confederate defeat at Sailor's Creek was more disastrous to the Confederacy than at Gettysburg. After the Battle of Gettysburg, the Army of Northern Virginia continued to fight for nearly another two years. After the Battle of Sailor's Creek on April 6, 1865, Lee's army ceased to exist as a combat force within three days. The loss of more than 8,000 men and nine generals (one-fifth of Lee's army, with 7,700 being captured, the largest field surrender of the Civil War without terms following) directly affected Lee's ability to combat Grant's pursuing legions.

Among those nine Confederate generals captured was Robert E. Lee's son, a former aide to Jefferson Davis, in his first combat action. However, controversy quickly developed over Custis Lee's capture. Mr. White is out to set the record straight.

Was a Congressional Medal of Honor for the capture of Custis Lee awarded to a man undeserving of that honor? In a style different from your typical Civil War manuscript, Mr. White compiled and reviewed the evidence, much of it previously untapped material, to determine the facts in the matter.

The question is answered by using the evidence presented in a fashion as if it was a court case. Did Private Harris S. Hawthorn of the 121st New York Infantry, or David D. White of the 37th Massachusetts Infantry (the author's great-great-grandfather), actually capture Custis Lee? Through this study, White aptly reveals the answer, and as a Historian, I certainly agree with his conclusion. By doing such thorough research, Mr. White has added to the history of the Battle of Sailor's Creek and also calls for an in-depth review of the award in this case, "for the integrity of the esteemed Congressional Medal of Honor."

Illustrated by more than 70 photos and maps, this well-indexed study breaks the mold of the typical Civil War book. White presents the detailed account of the capture of General Custis Lee at the Battle of Sailor's Creek and the controversy that surrounds it drawing on a myriad of sources, which allows the reader to make their own determination. With the tome of Civil War volumes being added to on a daily basis, it is refreshing to come across a piece that is developed in such a unique manner on a distinct subject. The topic of Custis Lee's capture has certainly been a largely ignored event, seldom receiving more than a mention by historians. Thanks to White's diligent and copious research, this is no longer the case.

Patrick A. Schroeder
Lynchburg, Virginia

PREFACE

"There having been some controversy about the matter"
The capture of Major General George Washington Custis Lee at the Battle of Sailor's Creek, VA, April 6, 1865

The author clearly recalls the day, while researching his family history; when he stumbled upon James Bowen's book entitled, "Thirty Seventh Regiment Massachusetts Volunteers in the Civil War, 1861–65." He was amazed to find an entry concerning his 2nd great grandfather, David Dunnells White. The entry read, "General Custis Lee, who directed the charge upon the Thirty-Seventh had till shortly before filled a clerkship at Richmond, but finally laid down the pen to take up the sword, surrendering the latter at the muzzle of the Spencer rifle to Corporal David White of Company E." Bowen was writing about the Battle of Sailor's Creek, VA, April 6, 1865. The author also recalls the day, about a year later, when he stumbled upon a book written by Chris Calkins entitled, "Thirty-Six Hours before Appomattox." Eagerly reading this book for additional references to David D. White capturing General Custis Lee, the author discovered the following entry; "There is some contention over the credit for capturing General Custis Lee. Both Privates Harris S. Hawthorn of Co. F, 121st New York Infantry, and David D. White of Co. E, 37th Massachusetts Infantry, claim they were the captors; Hawthorn's statement is officially recorded in the Regimental report–reference: O. R. p. 937 and 947." Astounded at this new revelation, the author made a quick appeal to the Official Records that were cited. What the author found in the Official Records was a statement by Col. Olcott, the commander the 121st New York at the Battle of Sailor's Creek, which reads, **"there having been some controversy about the matter."** Col. Olcott was referencing the capture of Major General George Washington Custis Lee, son of the famed Robert E. Lee, at the Battle of Sailor's Creek, VA. The author chose to use Olcott's statement as the main theme for this work. What exactly was this controversy? How far reaching was it? Who was involved? Was it of any importance? Who cares? In an attempt to answer these questions, the author embarked on a vigorous quest to answer a simple question first; "who within the Federal forces was responsible for the capture of Confederate Major General George Washington Custis Lee at the Battle of Sailor's Creek, VA, on April 6, 1865." What the author soon discovered was that this was not a simple question at all. This matter not only involved Hawthorn and White, it involved two other claimants as well. It also involved the awarding of a Congressional Medal of Honor for this heroic feat, followed by a formal protest case initiated by a 37th Massachusetts Veterans Association. This was followed by a controversial decision on this protest case by the Secretary of War. This matter is bathed in perplexity, intrigue, "material" mistakes and political maneuverings. It affects the very integrity of the esteemed Congressional Medal of Honor. The author structured and presented this work as a "court case." The author clearly argued on behalf and in favor of the 37th Massachusetts' position. A wealth of evidence is presented which the author believes is both accurate and complete. Readers should judge for themselves the veracity of the author's arguments and his resulting concluding verdict in favor of the 37th Massachusetts. By prosecuting this case, the author believes that he has now definitively answered the question that has remained unanswered since the year 1865; "who within the Federal forces was responsible for the capture of Confederate Major General George Washington Custis Lee at the Battle of Sailor's Creek, VA, on April 6, 1865. By definitively answering this question, however, the author has discovered a whole new set of questions that must be answered. The author has left these new questions, and any answers, to a future champion who, it is hoped, will one day come forth and work with the United States Government to correct the past mistakes made in this important matter. The very integrity of the esteemed Congressional Medal of Honor depends on it.

The reader is encouraged to carefully read and ponder all the evidence presented in this book. The reader is also encouraged to challenge every aspect of this work, especially the conclusion developed by the author. At the end of this book, if the reader happens to reach the same conclusion as the author, it is bound to leave the reader with an unfinished, yearning type of feeling. A yearning to know the answer to this singular question; "what must be done to make this matter right?" Enjoy reading.

CHAPTER ONE:

Introduction:

George Washington Custis Lee (circa 1864):

As stated previously, this report is structured like a "court case." It contains a wealth of evidence and testimony. The main objective of this "court case" is to definitively answer the question: "who within the Federal forces was responsible for the capture of Confederate Major General George Washington Custis Lee at the Battle of Sailor's Creek, VA, on April 6, 1865?" There are four claimants. Chapter **2** presents evidence for claimant **Brevet Lieutenant Colonel Miles L. Butterfield** of the 5th Wisconsin Infantry Volunteer Infantry. Chapter **3** presents evidence for claimant **Brevet Major General J. Warren Keifer**, commanding the 2nd Brigade, 3rd Division, 6th Army Corps. Chapter **4** presents evidence for claimant **Sergeant Harris S. Hawthorn** of the 121st New York. Chapter **5** presents evidence for the claimant being the **37th Massachusetts Veterans Association** and **Corporal David D White** of 37th Massachusetts. Each chapter of chapters 2-5 contains the following sections:

- Evidence Overview: a brief description of the nature of the line of evidence that will be introduced.
- Exhibit Identifier: a unique alpha/numeric identifier for each piece of evidence in this report.
- Evidence: the actual documented evidence; transcribed verbatim from the identified sources (all sources are well documented and the citation follows each piece of evidence).
- Comments and Supporting Evidence: the author's comments and arguments on the evidence and the introduction of any supporting evidence.

In **Chapter 6-Verdict**, after a careful examination of all the evidence for all four claimants, the author offers a definitive verdict. The author believes this verdict can withstand the closest scrutiny and the most rigorous challenge. It allows for the final resolution of the question concerning the capture of Major General George Washington Custis Lee at the Battle of Sailor's Creek. This topic in the great "book of Civil War history" has remained open and unresolved since April 6, 1865. It can now be closed.

In **Chapter 7-Call to Action**, although the author was not anticipating writing this chapter at the start of the report, the process of answering the original question concerning who captured Custis Lee has brought to light a whole new set of issues and questions. This chapter seeks to address these issues and questions and puts forth a specific call to action. The very integrity of the Congressional Medal of Honor depends upon this action being taken.

WHO CARES?

As an aside, one might question the historical significance of the capture of Major General G. W. Custis Lee at the Battle of Sailor's Creek, VA, April 6, 1865. Does this event really matter with in the overall context of the Civil War? The answer is maybe. The historical significance of the capture of Major General G. W. Custis Lee can best be measured by gauging the effect that it might have had on his father, Robert E. Lee, during the final days of the Civil War and leading up to his surrender at Appomattox. The following write-up concerning a little known communication that took place between Ulysses S. Grant and Robert E. Lee the morning after the Battle of Sailor's Creek serves as a good introduction to this interesting topic:

… Robert Lee was in Farmville before the sun rose, and got a few hours of sleep in the home of Patrick Jackson. Mrs. Jackson gave him tea for breakfast as he left. The commander also made a call on the widow of Colonial John Thornton, who had been killed in the Sharpsburg campaign, and then rode to inspect the work of quartermaster clerks at the depot, who were giving out the scanty rations to troops….Just outside the town, pushed by a heavy Federal force, was the 35th Virginia Cavalry Battalion, with Captain Frank Myers commanding the lead squadron. A bluecoat came up with a white flag. "Letter from General Grant to General Lee," he said. "Nothing doing," Myers said. "I won't take it unless that line of infantry stops where it is." The Federal rider went back, and the troops were halted half a mile away. Myers sent a rider into Farmville with the dispatch. It was good news for Robert Lee—Custis was a Federal prisoner, alive, unwounded and well.

[Source: "To Appomattox, Nine April Days, 1865" by Burke Davis, Rinehart & Co., NY, 1959 pages 279 & 280]**Manuscript 69**

Captain Frank M. Myers of Company A, 35th Virginia Calvary, further describes this event in his own writings written in the year 1871:

…About sunrise (Friday April 7, 1865) the enemy became very troublesome and as not more than one mile could be marched without a halt to wait for the wagons to be pulled out of the mud, which in many places was hub-deep, the position of the rear guard became a very exciting one, especially as it was found that the enemy's infantry had left the road and was out marching them through the fields and open pine woods to the left. During one of the halts, about nine o'clock, as the battalion was, as usual, drawn up in line facing the left, and Capt. Myers, with a few pickets, was a half mile from his people down a road that led towards the enemy, a party of four Yankees were seen approaching through the woods, and as they came very confidently along making no sign to the two Confederates, who were standing in full view, it was decided best to halt them with a shot from a Sharpe's rifle, which resulted in the killing of the foremost Yankee, and in falling he displayed a white flag, which, until that moment, had not been seen, because of the pines. Both parties hastily retired, and it being now discovered that the army was moving again, the battalion also marched quietly, but in the distance of two miles another halt was called, and now the country being open the thousands of men in blue could be seen, drawing close along the flank and rear, but what puzzled the Confederates was the total absence of cavalry, in any force, with Grant's army. While standing here, a mounted Yankee was observed galloping along the road waving a white flag, and being met by one of the battalion, he presented a letter addressed to General Lee, but Capt. Myers refused to forward it unless the line of infantry, now within half a mile, would halt, which the bearer of the flag communicated to the enemy's officers, and a halt was immediately ordered, the command distinctly heard by the Confederate rear-guard. The letter was now sent forward to Gen. Lee, and in half an hour an answer, directed to Gen. Grant, was returned, with a request from Gen. Lee that one or two of the best dressed officers in the battalion be sent in company with the truce-bearer to the enemy's line, and this mission fell upon Capt. French and Lieut. James, who rode back to Grant's headquarters and met with his Chief-of-Staff, Gen. Williams, who treated them handsomely, gave them a drink of whiskey, and talked, as James said, "exactly like a gentleman." He asked them a number of questions, and informed them that they (the Yankees) had taken thirty-two thousand prisoners since the capture of Petersburg. Capt. French asked him the meaning of the correspondence between the Generals, to which he replied that Gen. Custis Lee had been taken prisoner, and his father, Gen. Lee, had merely inquired if he was killed or wounded, and that Gen. Grant had replied, telling him that his son was unhurt. Another letter was dispatched to Gen. Lee, and the well-dressed Confederates returned to their own lines, with no idea that they were aiding the negotiations for the surrender of Lee's army by carrying the letters on the subject back and forth, and as the wagons were again out of the mud the rear-guard resumed its march, as also did the Federal army. About 3 o'clock the battalion was relieved from its perilous position in the rear.

[Source: "The Comanches: A History of White's Battalion Virginia Calvary" Laurel Brig., Hampton Div. A. N. V. C. S. A. by Frank M. Myers, Late Capt., Co. A, 35th VA Cav. Approved by all the Officers of the Battalion, 1871]**Manuscript 75**

It would appear that General Robert E. Lee, being very concerned for the safety on his beloved son, Custis Lee, sent a dispatch to Grant shortly after the Battle of Sailor's Creek inquiring as to the welfare of his son   In support of this fact, it would appear from the following write up that Robert E. Lee was very active in creating dispatches on the evening of April 6, 1865:

Lee rode at nightfall (April 6, 1865) to Rice's Station, and in a field beside the railroad tracks, with only an orderly or two and a staff officer, made headquarters as the army moved toward Farmville in retreat. He handled many dispatches during the night…. Wise found Lee in the field, standing by a fire. Colonel Charles Marshall was in a headquarters wagon, writing dispatches on a lap desk as Lee dictated.
[Source: "To Appomattox: Nine April Days 1865" by Burke Davis, Rinehart & Co., NY, 1959]Manuscript 69****

Robert E. Lee sent a dispatch to Grant on the evening of April 6 or early on the morning of April 7 and Grant replied on the morning of April 7. This first exchange of dispatches between Lee and Grant was centered exclusively on the welfare of General Custis Lee after the Battle of Sailor's Creek. A second exchange of dispatches occurred between Grant and Lee. This second exchange was centered exclusively on the surrender of Robert E. Lee's Army of Northern Virginia. As the first exchange between Lee and Grant occurred most likely late on the evening of April 6th, this second exchange concerning surrender was initiated by Grant at 5 P.M. on April 7th, as noted below:

April 7, 1865 – 5 P.M.   To: General R. E. Lee, Commanding C. S. Army:
General: The results of the last week must convince you of the hopelessness of further resistance on the part of the Army of Northern Virginia in this struggle. I feel that it is so, and regard it as my duty to shift from myself the responsibility of any further effusion of blood, by asking of you the surrender of that portion of the C. S. Army known as the Army of Northern Virginia.
Very respectfully, your obedient servant,
U. S. Grant, Lieutenant General, Commanding Armies of the United States

In this letter, it should be noted, Grant addressed General Lee as the Commander-in-Chief of the Confederate Armies and said that he was asking of him the surrender, without making mention of President Davis or any other Confederate authorities. Since Grant claimed that he himself would not be responsible for any further effusion of blood, he obviously meant to say that the sole responsibility of making a decision was now in the hands of General Lee. This letter was entrusted to Grant's adjutant general, Seth Williams, who had been Lee's old friend and former adjutant at West Point. Williams carried the letter through Meade's lines, and tried to present it on Mahone's front, but had considerable difficulty in getting it through to Lee. There was evidently some anxiety on the Union side about getting Grant's letter through the lines. C. A. Whittier, A. A. G., wrote to General N. A. Miles: "It is desired to get this through the lines tonight." Miles replied that he believed it would be possible to send a communication through the picket line that night. Captain H. H. Perry of Sorrel's Brigade left a detailed account of the efforts to get the letter through the Confederate lines. He said that a flag of truce was presented from the Union lines about 5 P.M., and that he attempted to answer it, but he claimed he could not do so because he was fired upon by a number of Federal sharpshooters. As the top of the earthworks was reached, a number of Federal sharpshooters fired to me, and two balls passed through the uniform coat I wore, and one ball wounded a Confederate soldier in the hand, who had risen up with others from behind the works, out of curiosity to see what was going to take place. That ended the truce business for that afternoon. About 9 P.M., when the moon was about to rise, a flag of truce was again presented from the Union lines and Perry again made an attempt to answer it. Passing by the bodies of Federal dead and wounded lying between the front lines, he made contact with a handsomely dressed Federal officer. "The officer spoke first, introducing himself as Gen. Seth Williams, of General Grant's staff." Perry said that Williams first offered him a drink of fine brandy, which Perry politely refused. Then Williams handed Grant's letter and asked for it to be delivered to General Lee immediately. Perry estimated that the letter reached General Lee within twenty minutes after it passed through the Confederate lines. This would have caused it to reach Lee about 10 P.M.

[SOURCE: "The Proceedings Connected with the Surrender of the Army of Northern Virginia, April 9, 1865" by Frank P. Cauble, Research Historian, Appomattox Court House National Historic Park, 1962, Revised 1975]**Manuscript 94**

To add support that a first exchange of dispatches occurred between Lee and Grant late on April 6th, or early on April 7th, concerning the welfare of Custis Lee after the Battle of Sailor's Creek, the author notes that Colonel Charles Marshall, Aide-De-Camp of Robert E. Lee, records in his writings an event that happened at the surrender at Appomattox Court House, VA:

General Lee was standing at the end of the room opposite the door when General Grant walked in. General Grant had on a sack coat, a loose fatigue coat, but he had no side arms. He looked as though he had had a pretty hard time. He had been riding and his clothes were somewhat dusty and a little soiled. He walked up to General Lee and Lee recognized him at once. He had known him in the Mexican war. General Grant greeted him in the most cordial manner, and talked about the weather and other things in a very friendly way. Then General Grant brought up his officers and introduced them to General Lee. I remember that General Lee asked for General Lawrence Williams, of the Army of the Potomac. That very morning General Williams had sent word by somebody to General Lee that Custis Lee, who had been captured at Sailor's Creek and was reported killed, was not hurt, and General Lee asked General Grant where General Williams was, and if he could not send for him to come and see him. General Grant sent somebody out for General Williams, and when he came, General Lee thanked him for having sent him word about the safety of his son.

[SOURCE: "Lee's Aide-De-Camp: Being the Papers of Colonel Charles Marshall, edited by Frederick Maurice, Little, Brown and Co., 1927, pages 269-270]**Manuscript 95**

There is a high probability that Colonel Charles Marshall was a little confused on some points in his recollection of this event. His reference to a General Lawrence Williams is most certainly General Seth Williams. To further validate this notion, the author consulted the reference work "Civil War Generals" by James Spencer. This work is a comprehensive listing of all Civil War Generals who fought on both the Federal and Confederate sides. Only a General David Henry Williams, General John Stuart Williams, General Seth Williams and General Thomas Williams exist for the surnames starting with W.

[SOURCE: "Civil War Generals – Categorical Listings and a Biographical Directory" Compiled by James Spencer, Greenwood Press, NY]**Manuscript 115**

Marshall may have also been confused about other particulars surrounding the events at Appomattox. The most important point, however, is that Colonel Marshall's recollection of this event substantiates in large measure the account given by Captain Frank M. Myers. That is, an early exchange took place between Grant, Seth Williams, and Robert E. Lee, concerning the welfare of Custis Lee shortly after the Battle of Sailor's Creek. This event surely took place before the surrender at Appomattox Court House, VA, according to the Marshall account. For Robert E. Lee, the news that Custis Lee was unhurt and a prisoner of war had to be both comforting and concerning. It was comforting in the fact that Custis was alive and uninjured. It was concerning in the fact that Custis was now a prisoner of war destined for a harsh Federal prison. This concern must have weighed on Robert E. Lee's mind to some degree. How much, will never be known. Grant must have detected a trace of concern in Robert E. Lee's communication on April 6th or early morning April 7th. Grant must have intuitively felt that the thought of Custis being a prisoner of war would be a very difficult thought for Robert E. Lee. Robert E. Lee deeply loved his son Custis. Did Grant now view this as a good opportunity to continue the communication that was opened by Robert E. Lee? Did Grant now view this as a good opportunity to ask Lee for the surrender of the Army of Northern Virginia? The answer to these questions will never be known. Grant's second communication to Lee did, however, ask for the surrender of his army. Did Lee surrender the Army of Northern Virginia on April 9, 1865, because Custis Lee was now destined for a Federal prison? The answer is absolutely no. Was it just one small factor leading up to Robert E. Lee's decision? The answer to this question is, maybe. It would have been one of Robert E. Lee's more personal reasons contributing to his decision. If the capture of Custis Lee at the Battle of Sailor's Creek played some small part in Robert E. Lee's decision to surrender the Army of Northern Virginia on April 9, 1865, then the capture of Custis Lee does have some historical significance. The degree of this historical significance should now be carefully studied and documented by scholars of the Civil War.

CHAPTER TWO:
Captain Miles T. Butterfield
(PHOTO: COURTESY CARROLL COLLEGE)

Exhibit Category
Claimant One:

Code Key
B

Captain Miles T. Butterfield
5th Wisconsin Infantry
3rd Brigade, 1st Division, 6th Army Corps

Evidence Type:

(1) Miscellaneous Records, including
regimental histories, publications,
personal reminiscences, journal
entries, diary entries, books, etc. (1-3)

MR

EVIDENCE OVERVIEW
EXHIBITS-B-MR-(1-3)

The purpose of this line of evidence is to introduce to the reader a claim made by a Captain Miles L. Butterfield that he captured Major General Custis Lee at the Battle of Sailor's Creek April 6, 1865.

EXHIBIT-B-MR-1

Introduction:

This "Reminiscence" by Butterfield was read to an audience on April 15, 1905. Miles L. Butterfield was a member of the 5th Wisconsin and is writing about the Battle of Sailor's Creek. This work appears to be some recollections given by Mr. Butterfield to a "Mr. Commander," possibly associated with a local Wisconsin G. A. R. He does make mention, however, of consulting his diary entries when creating these "Reminiscences."

Evidence:

… And now, Mr. Commander, I would like to give an account of an incident that occurred at that battle (Sailor's Creek). It is a little personal, I admit, but nevertheless I think it ought to be made on behalf of the 6th Corps. When our division arrived at the creek, and found that they could not cross at that point, (the water being very deep and running very swift) they were obliged to march a mile to the left, as before stated. General Wheaton, in command of our division, was stationed about the center of the division and in the rear of it, on somewhat elevated ground, so as to see the whole battlefield. I was the only officer of his staff left with him, the others having been sent with orders to the different brigade commanders. When the bugle sounded the advance, General Hamblin, being on the extreme left, with a thicket of small timber between his brigade and the 3rd, did not see the movements of the troops to his right, and did not move his brigade with the rest of the corps, which left a big gap between the two brigades, and the left flank of our regiment exposed to a cross fire from the enemy. As General Wheaton saw this, he turned to me and said: "Major, for God's sake, start General Hamblin's brigade." I dismounted, and, leaving my horse with the orderly, plunged into the stream which was about to my waist and running very swift. By the aid of the willows and witch hazel, I managed to reach the other side of the creek, where General Hamblin's brigade was awaiting orders. On receiving the order, the brigade was immediately put in motion and I joined the 37th Massachusetts in the charge. When we reached the crest of the ridge, we found that the enemy had made breastworks of an old rail fence and were lying behind the piles of rails. As we charged up to them, I heard one say, "We will surrender. Cease firing." If my memory is correct, there were only five men of the 37th Massachusetts and myself in front of that pile of rails. I said, "Get up then," and there arose from behind that pile of rails, six rebel officers. I then shouted as loud as I could, "Cease firing;" I had to shout loud so as to be heard, as there was considerable noise and confusion about there. I took charge of them and one of their numbers asked to whom he had the honor of surrendering. When told, he said that he was General Custis Lee, son of General Robert E. Lee, and would like to be taken to General Sheridan. With two men of the 37th Massachusetts, I took them to the rear where Generals Sheridan and Wright were found, and turned them over to General Sheridan. General Wright had been Lee's tutor at West Point, and recognizing General Wright, Lee extended his hand to the General, who did not take it, but turning to Colonel Franklin, Chief of Staff, said, "Colonel, take these men to the rear." Mr. Commander, I think it due to the 6th Corps that this statement should be made, as the 6th Corps is as much entitled to the credit for the capture of the rebel Generals Custis Lee, Kershaw, Barton, Due Boise, Hunter and Corse, as it was for the capture of General Ewell ….

[Source: "Personal Reminiscences with the Sixth Corps, 1864 – 1865" by M. L. Butterfield, Bvt. Lieutenant Colonel (1905) Wisconsin War Papers, MOLLUS-Vol. 4, pages 85-93]**Manuscript 5**

Comments and Supporting Evidence:

1. It is interesting to note that Butterfield gave orders to General Hamblin's Brigade to close the big gap at the right of their Brigade. Butterfield then joined the 37th Massachusetts troops in the charge of the Confederates. Butterfield describes a "thicket of small timbers between Hamblin's Brigade and troops to their right (Edwards' Brigade). This thicket was large enough to conceal the movements of Edwards' Brigade from Hamblin's Brigade. This thicket separated the two brigades for most of the battle.

2. It is interesting how this account describes the manner in which Custis Lee was taken to the rear by Butterfield, along with two men of the 37th Massachusetts, and how Custis Lee wanted to be taken to General Sheridan. It is also interesting how this account describes the alleged interaction between Custis Lee and General Wright. It should be noted here, however, that General Wright does not corroborate Butterfield's account, as will be seen from Wright's testimony contained in the 37th Massachusetts Protest File which is found later in this report.

3. It would appear from Custis Lee's own report dated April 25, 1865, of the Battle of Sailor's Creek, that Custis Lee did not take an active, first-hand roll in surrendering his command as alleged by Butterfield. It would also appear from Custis Lee's report that the surrender of Custis Lee's troops was initiated by some of his subordinate officers. Custis Lee's report follows:

REPORT OF GENERAL G. W. C. LEE
From 2nd to 6th April, 1865
RICHMOND, VA, April 25, 1865
Lieutenant-Colonel W. H. Taylor, A. A. G.:

Colonel:--In obedience to instructions, I have the honor to submit the following report of the operations of my command, from the time of its leaving the lines at Chaffin's Farm on Sunday night, April 2, 1865, to its capture on the afternoon of the following Thursday, April 6, 1865.

....General Gordon having filed off to the right after the wagon-trains, the enemy's cavalry followed closely upon General Kershaw's rear, driving it across Sailor's Creek, and soon after the enemy's infantry (said to be the 6th corps) massed rapidly in our rear. To meet this movement General Kershaw's division formed on the right and mine on the left of the road upon which we were moving, our line of battle being across the road facing Sailor's Creek, which we had not long passed. Before my troops got into position, the enemy opened a heavy fire of artillery upon our lines, which was continued up to the time of our capture. After shelling our lines and skirmishing for some time, an hour or more, the enemy's infantry advanced and were repulsed, and that portion which attacked the artillery brigade was charged by it and driven back across Sailor's Creek. This brigade was then brought back to its original position in line of battle under a heavy fire of artillery. Finding that Kershaw's division, which was on my right, had been obliged to retire in consequence of the enemy having turned his right flank, and that my command was entirely surrounded, to prevent useless sacrifice of life the firing was stopped by some of my officers aided by some of the enemy's and the officers and men taken as prisoners of war.

Very respectfully your obedient servant,

G. W. C. Lee, Major-General.

P. S. I was told after my capture that the enemy had two corps of infantry and three divisions of cavalry opposed to us at Sailor's Creek; and was informed by General Ewell that he had sent me an order to surrender, being convinced of the hopelessness of further resistance. The order was not received by me. G. W. C. L.

[Source: Southern Historical Society Transactions, Volume One, 1874, pages 118-121]**Manuscript 64**

4. Butterfield's Civil War pension records indicate that he received a gunshot wound to the left leg on May 10, 1864, at the battle of the Wilderness. The wound was not severe and Butterfield does not appear to have lost any active service time as a result of this wound. The pension record also states that Miles Butterfield contracted severe rheumatism "caused by exposure and hardship incident to a soldiers' life." Butterfield claims to have contracted this ailment starting in September 1863. This disease appears to be so debilitating that he was not able to work or leave his house immediately upon his return home from the Civil War. If this statement is true, one has to question Butterfield's ability to physically participate in the strenuous charge at the Battle of Sailor's Creek as described by his own account.

[Source: Civil War pension record # 545.392 for Miles L. Butterfield at the National Archives, Washington, DC]**Manuscript 116**

EXHIBIT-B-MR-2

Introduction:
On February 10, 1904, Miles L. Butterfield wrote Personal Sketches of his Civil War experiences. In this work he wrote of the following about the Battle of Sailor's Creek:

Evidence:
... At Little Sailors' Creek, Apr. 6, 1865, on the arrival of our Division commanded by Gen'l Frank Wheaton—we found the bridge burned and the troops went a mile upstream to cross (as the water was very swift and deep) and down on the opposite side and then formed line of battle. The Gen'l and most of the staff were still on the East side of the creek—and as the formation of the troops was completed—

the order was given for the charge – but Gen'l Hamblin's Brigade was to the left of some small Pine timber, could not see balance of the Division as it advanced and did not move his Brigade. Gen'l Wheaton seeing this, turned to me (as I was the only officer of his staff left) the others had all been sent with orders, and said, "Major, for God's sake, start Gen. Hamblin's Brigade." I dismounted and leaving my horse with my orderly – plunged into the swift stream, which was about waist deep and by the aid of Willows reached the opposite side, and started Gen'l Hamblin's Brigade – and I went in the charge with them and behind a pile of Rails, myself and five men of the 37th Mass. Captured five Rebel Officers including Gen'l Custis Lee, son of Gen'l Rob't E. Lee.

[Source: "Personal War Sketches"–Wm. B. Cushing Post No. 19, Waukesha County, WI, by Miles L. Butterfield Co. F, 5th Reg. Wis. Vol. Infantry–typescript in the possession of the Institute for Civil War Studies, Carroll College, Waukesha, WI]**Manuscript 117**

COMMENTS AND SUPPORTING EVIDENCE:

1. In this 1904 writing, Miles L. Butterfield is much tamer about his claim that he captured Custis Lee. The author can not reconcile this discrepancy between the Butterfield 1904 and 1905 versions.
2. In this 1904 version Butterfield states that he, together with five men of the 37th Massachusetts, captured Custis Lee. He is not claiming the sole capture for himself in this version.
3. Miles L. Butterfield kept a very consistent diary throughout the Civil War. His diary entry for Thursday, April 6, 1865 reads as follows in its entirety:

Weather very pleasant was up at 4 and went out on the line and got the Brigade in position and we made advance at 7 found no enemy then marched down the Danville R about 12 miles and found the enemy and had very hard fight Captured Genl Ewell, Custis Lee and other large number of Prisoners. Got in camp at 12 o'clock Battle of Sailor Creek

[Source: Diary of Miles L. Butterfield at the Institute for Civil War Studies, Carroll College, Waukesha, WI]** Manuscript 118 **

This is an extremely important piece of evidence in that Butterfield does not reference in his April 6, 1865 diary entry that he personally captured Custis Lee. He just mentions the overall capture of Ewell, Custis Lee and a large number of prisoners. As an aside note, Butterfield often references in his diary entries the time in the evening that he gets into camp. In this case, he got into camp at twelve o'clock (most probably midnight) on April 6, 1865.

4. General Frank Wheaton, commanding the 1st Division, 6th Army Corps writes about the following concerning Miles L. Butterfield in his Official Report dated April 20, 1865:

"Soon after daylight (April 2, 1865) Capt. M. L. Butterfield, acting engineer officer of the division, while inspecting the picket-line, was met by the Mayor of Petersburg, under flag of truce, and handed by him a letter to Lieutenant-General Grant, or any other commander, surrendering the town."

[Source: Official Records, Appomattox Campaign–Volume 46–Part One Page 913]**Manuscript 119**

In Miles L. Butterfield's 1904 "Personal War Sketches," he writes the following concerning this incident:

I had already ordered my horse and at that time the orderly came with it and we started to the front and on the Picket line – just in front of the inner lines of the Rebels' Works – I advanced the lines about thirty (30) rods and could see in the Morning light a Carriage and a flag of truce on the Rebels' Works. Halting the line, I advanced with the Division Officer of the day, Col. Naylar – and then met the Mayor of the City, W. W. Towns – and members of the city council – when the Mayor handed me a letter addressed to Gen'l Grant or any Union Gen'l, commanding the forces before Petersburg. I returned with the letter to Gen'l Wright, who was in command, as Gen'l Grant was on the opposite side of the city. The letter proved to be the surrender of the City of Petersburg. I returned by orders from Gen'l Wright to the Mayor and entered the city with him in advance of the troops who soon followed. – At the Home of Mr. W. R. Malory, one of the members of the city Council – I met Roger A. Pryor (Rebel Gen'l) who was sick – and he said to me that he was glad the war was about over as he was tired of it. So I claim the surrender of the City of Petersburg from the Mayor.

It would appear that Miles L. Butterfield can make claims that can not be exactly substantiated by the Official Records, like in this case claiming that he received the surrender of the City of Petersburg from the Mayor of that City. Though Miles Butterfield was indeed handed the letter of surrender, General Wheaton was very clear in his Official Report that General Hamblin, not Miles Butterfield, was the first commander to enter the city of Petersburg with his Brigade and caused this city to surrender. To further examine this event, the reader is encouraged to read General Frank Wheaton's Official Report where he addresses the surrender of the City of Petersburg.

5. Only two other references are made about Miles L. Butterfield by General Wheaton in Wheaton's April 20, 1865, Official Report. The first is one thanking him and all his staff for gallant service. The second is one recommending Butterfield and all his staff for promotions for gallantry at Petersburg and Sailor's Creek. It is important to note that Miles L. Butterfield receives no mention by General Wheaton for capturing Custis Lee.

[Source: Official Records, Appomattox Campaign, Volume 46 Part One pages 915 and 918]**Manuscript 119**

EXHIBIT-B-MR-3

Introduction:
In Miles L. Butterfield's Personal Sketches dated February 10, 1904, Butterfield writes the following:

Evidence:
Fifteen years after the close of the War – in 1880 – I made an application to the war department and was awarded one of the Medals (awarded) voted by Congress to be given to soldiers who had assumed extra and hazardous duties which were almost certain to result in capture or death.

[Source: "Personal War Sketches"–Wm B. Cushing Post No. 19 Waukesha County, WI, by Miles L. Butterfield Co. F 5th Reg. Wis. Vol. Infantry–typescript in the possession of the Institute for Civil War Studies, Carroll College, Waukesha, WI]**Manuscript 117**

COMMENTS AND SUPPORTING EVIDENCE:
1. In this paragraph, Miles Butterfield is claiming that he received a medal for his actions on April 6, 1865, at the Battle of Sailor's Creek and other military actions performed by him.
2. The author performed research at the National Archives to validate this claim and perhaps shed additional light on Butterfield's actions at the Battle of Sailor's Creek. The author received the following letter from the National Archives:

NATIONAL ARCHIVES AND RECORDS ADMINISTRATION
Washington, D.C. 20408-0001

March 28, 2003
Dear Mr. White:
The following is in reply to your inquiry concerning medals which Miles L. Butterfield applied for following his military service during the Civil War. We have examined the War Department records in our custody including the Quartermaster Departments' Index to Decorations and Awards (R. G. 92, Entry 256) but did not locate evidence that Butterfield applied for a Civil War Campaign Badge. The only medal officially awarded during the Civil War was the Medal of Honor, which our records indicate was not issued to Butterfield. We did locate a Volunteer Service File (5787-VS-1884) concerning this officer. It concerns his request for a correction of muster rather than an application for a medal. We can provide you with an electrostatic (paper) copy of this file for the price quoted.
DAVID H. WALLACE
Old Military and Civil Records, Textual Archives Services Division
[Source: Letter in the possession of the author]**Manuscript 120**

It would appear from this letter from the National Archives that Miles L. Butterfield did not apply for a medal and did not receive a medal. His "correction of muster" file referenced in his letter was examined by the author and contains no information relevant to our matter. In this "correction of muster" file, Butterfield was merely trying to document the timing of his advancements in rank.

3. Several interesting points can be learned from examining Miles L. Butterfield's military service record. First, he appears to be a good soldier capable of receiving promotions. He mustered into service as a 2nd Lieutenant on December 25, 1862, and he mustered out as a captain in 1865. He was brevetted a Major for gallantry in the Wilderness Campaign and brevetted a lieutenant colonel for gallantry in the services at Petersburg and Sailor's Creek. He was appointed to the Staff of General Wheaton as Division Engineer in 1865, which is consistent with his account of the Battle of Sailor's Creek. Second, we can also learn from his military service record housed at the National Archives and from the 5th Wisconsin papers housed at the University of Wisconsin in Milwaukee, WI, that Miles Butterfield must have had a deep personal need to receive proper recognition for his military service. This is demonstrated by the following letter:

Camp 5th Regt – Wis. Vols. Infty. Before Petersburg VA
December 13, 1864
I have the honor hereby to tender my resignation as Captain of Company "C" 5th Regt – Wis. Vols. Infty. For the following reasons; Lieut. Col. Bull who has recently been appointed to said position in this Regiment from Captaincy in the 23rd Wis., who was at the same time my junior in rank and in my opinion no better qualified to fill the said position than myself, and I therefore feel it my duty as any officer and a gentleman to adopt this method, knowing if I leave the service at this time, I can procure a far better and higher position than I now hold. Hoping that this may meet with the approval of the Commander General.
I have the honor to be, Very Respectfully, Your Obedient Serv't
M. L. Butterfield, Captain Co. C: 5th Regt., Wisconsin Vols. Infty.
[Source: Butterfield, Miles b. 1837 Papers, 1864-1865, University of Wisconsin, Milwaukee, WI, (U. W. M.) Manuscript Collection 77, University Manuscript Collections, U. W. M. Libraries, University of Wisconsin, Milwaukee, WI]Manuscript 121 ****

Third, it would also appear that in the years 1864-1865, Miles Butterfield was tired of military service and was repeatedly trying to get out. His military service record in the National Archives and the 5th Wisconsin papers at the University of Wisconsin, Milwaukee, WI, contain several attempts by Miles L. Butterfield to secure leaves of absence and several submissions of resignation. The most dramatic of these attempts is best depicted in the following three letters, two dated April 14, 1864 and one dated April 28, 1864:

(1) *Camp 5th Wis. Vols .Infty., April 14, 1864*
I have the honor through you to tender my Resignation under the following circumstances:
1st Because I am incompetent to fill the position I now hold. 2nd Because the men under me do not respect me as their commanding officer, knowing that I am inefficient. 3rd Because my present position can be filled to far better advantage by my immediate inferior in rank! And therefore in my opinion, by taking this step I am working for the interest and welfare of the service. Taking into consideration the above circumstances, I can but hope that this will meet with a full approval of the commanding General.
I have the honor to be Very Resp'ly Your Obt. Servant,
M. L. Butterfield, Capt. Co. 5th Wis. Vols. Infty.

(2) *1st Lieut. Wm. H. Keis, Adgt., 5th Wis. Vols., Head Qrs.*
I have the honor to Respectfully forward this approved; and would further state that it would be beneficial to the Service that Capt. Butterfield be discharged, as the vacancy so caused can be filled by a more competent and efficient officer from the same Company.
Theo B. Catlin, Lt. Col. Comdg. 5th Wis. Vols.

(3) *Camp 5th Wis. Vols. Infty., April 28, 1864.*

I have the honor through you to tender my Resignation as I am incompetent to fill the position that I now hold. Taking into consideration the above circumstances I can but hope that this will meet with the full approval of the Commanding General. I have the honor to be Very Resp'ly You Obt. Servt
M. L. Butterfield, Capt. Co. 5th Wis. Vols.

CHAPTER THREE:
Brevet Brigadier General J. Warren Keifer

Exhibit Category
Claimant Two:

Code Key
K

Brevet Brigadier General J. Warren Keifer
2ⁿᵈ Brigade, 3ʳᵈ Division, 6ᵗʰ Army Corps

Evidence Type:

(1) <u>M</u>iscellaneous <u>R</u>ecords, including
regimental histories, publications,
personal reminiscences, journal
entries, diary entries, books, etc. (1-2)

MR

EVIDENCE OVERVIEW
EXHIBITS-K-MR-(1-2)

The purpose of this line of evidence is to introduce to the reader a claim by J. Warren Keifer that his command was responsible for the capture of Major General G. W. Custis Lee at the Battle of Sailor's Creek April 6, 1865.

EXHIBIT-K-MR-1

Introduction:

In the book entitled, "More Civil War Curiosities"—Chapter Ten, "Claims to Fame," author Webb Garrison describes a claim made by Bvt. Major-General J. Warren Keifer of the State of Ohio, that his "command" was responsible for the capture of General Custis Lee. This claim by Keifer was made on December 6, 1911.

Evidence:

CHAPTER 10
Claims to Fame

At least one out of every ten Confederate soldiers alive after Appomattox seems to have claimed to have been involved in the last gasp of the Lost Cause. Some of these doings show up in official documents, but many do not. Practically all of them have produced historical markers that were erected by state or local organizations. This subject is a challenge. To deduce the truth, the language used to describe a last military encounter has to be analyzed and the evidence sifted. On December 6, 1911, Bvt. Maj. Gen. J. Warren Keifer of Ohio addressed a band of veterans. In his closing remarks he modestly indicated that his command was responsible for the capture of Robert E. Lee's oldest son. Powerfully built and standing six feet, two inches tall, Confederate Maj. Gen. George Washington Custis Lee was made a prisoner three days prior to his father's surrender to U. S. Grant. Describing the capture of the high-ranking prisoner, Keifer said that it took place on April 6 "at Sailor's Creek, Virginia, the last field battle of the war." No matter what terminology is used to label it, the fracas that occurred at Sailor's Creek was a lot more than a skirmish. Federal forces suffered about twelve hundred casualties before forcing nearly eight thousand men in gray to surrender. Keifer was a colonel on April 18, 1865, when he compiled his official report at Burkeville, Virginia. In it he does not mention capturing Lee, saying only that the division of Custis Lee was "known to have participated in the battle."

Four days earlier at the same village, Pvt. Harris S. Hawthorn, Company F, 121st New York Volunteers, appeared before Judge Advocate H. E. Hindmarsh of the First Division, Sixth Corps, to sign a sworn statement. According to it, Hawthorn was "the first person [officer or enlisted man] who seized or captured General Custis Lee, of the Confederate Army, in the engagement of the 6th of April" His regiment, known as the Orange and Herkimer, was attached to the Second Brigade, First Division, Sixth Corps. When Lee was captured during the "last field battle," Keifer was a brevet brigadier at the head of the Second Division, Sixth Corps.

[Source: "More Civil War Curiosities," by Webb Garrison, Rutledge Hill Press, Nashville, TN, 1995. ISBN # 1-55853-366-4, Chapter 10 pages 128–129, "Claims to Fame"]**Manuscript 66**

Comments and Supporting Evidence:

1. To test the validity of Keifer's claim as described in the above reference, the author appealed to Keifer's Official Report written shortly after the Battle of Sailor's Creek. The Report is as follows:

   HDQRS. SECOND BRIG., THIRD DIV., SIXTH ARMY CORPS,
   Camp at Burkeville, VA, April 18, 1865

   MAJOR: In obedience to orders, I have the honor to forward a report of movements and operations of this brigade from the 3rd to the 13th of April, 1865, inclusive. An attack was ordered to be made by Maj. Gen. H. G. Wright, commanding corps, with the troops already upon the ground. A concentrated artillery fire was directed upon the enemy's center, under cover of which the troops advanced through and across the swamp, and at once charged up the steep hills upon which the enemy was posted. A severe conflict ensued as the lines of the opposing forces came together. A number of men were bayoneted on both sides. The enemy had a heavy column massed in the rear of his center, with which he charged upon our troops. Owing to the fact that our troops could only be fought in one line, the enemy succeeded in breaking through the center and gaining a momentary success. The troops on the right and left continued the advance until the enemy's column in the center was enveloped and cut to pieces and captured. The enemy was soon routed at all points, and many general officers and many thousands of prisoners threw down their arms and surrendered. The rebel Marine Brigade fought with most extraordinary courage, but was finally cut off and captured. Commodore Tucker, Commander Hunter, Captain Semmes, and about twenty-five naval officers, with the brigade, surrendered to me. It is impossible to give the number of prisoners captured by troops of this brigade. Two battle flags were taken from the enemy during the conflict ….

   J. Warren Keifer, Brevet Brigadier-General, Commanding

   [Source: Official Records, Appomattox Campaign, Volume 46 Series 1, pages 997-999]**Manuscript 67**

General Keifer absolutely makes no claim to capturing General Custis Lee at the Battle of Sailor's Creek in his Official Report dated April 18, 1865. He does, however, claim the capture of Commodore Tucker, Commander Hunter, Captain Semmes and about 25 Confederate Naval officers.

EXHIBIT-K-MR-2

Introduction:

The author was able to discover Keifer's original claim in a paper written to the Ohio Commandery of the Loyal Legion, December 6, 1911. The important excerpt is as follows:

Evidence:

… Another memorable incident not connected with the Rich Mountain battle will be mentioned. General R. E. Lee assembled (August, 1861) in Western Virginia, at Big Springs, Valley Mountain, well up Tygart's Valley River, a somewhat formidable Confederate Army with the purpose of driving our forces out of that region. He advanced early in September, 1861, down the valley to the front of General Reynolds's command at Camp Elk Water. On the 12th of September, I was posted, in the advance, with companies of my own and other regiments and some artillery on grand guard, outpost and picket duty, near the mouth of Elk Water, a position commanding the Elk Water and Brady's Gate road, the main pike and the whole then narrow valley of the Tygart's. Lee's advance was then in my immediate front. A preliminary fight was expected to take place there. On the afternoon of September 13th, a report came to me that a body of Confederate cavalry was rapidly approaching from Brady's Gate (near the place of DeLagnel's capture) down the Elk Water, which would bring it into my rear. I made some necessary dispositions, but, being incredulous about cavalry undertaking to maneuver in a narrow mountain road, I went personally to my advance picket post to make observations and to obtain first-hand information. Some soldiers of the 17th Ind. (Col. Haskell's) were there on picket. While there two richly caparisoned and well-mounted officers rode into full view from around a point of a mountain spur, followed, not closely, by a cavalry force. On seeing us, the two officers halted and hastily wheeled their horses about to escape. They were distant about 150 yards. Sergeant Weller and three or four others, by my command, fired on them. The leading officer fell from his horse, and the other officer's horse fell with him, but he arose, and, by mounting the fallen officer's horse, fled and escaped, as did the cavalry, for other pressing reasons. I hastened to the side of the fallen officer raised him on one elbow, and, though gasping and dying, he (as usual with the wounded) called for "water." When brought from the nearby stream he was dead. At least three balls penetrated from his back through his left breast. A few years since Rev. John T. Rose, an Episcopal minister, son of Captain George S. Rose of General Reynolds's staff, showed me a common-sized letter envelope taken from this officer's breast pocket showing three bullet holes through it. I readily recognized it with the dried blood on it. This officer was John Augustine Washington, then serving as aid-de-camp, with the rank of lieutenant colonel, on General Robert E. Lee's staff. He was probably the then nearest living relative of George Washington, and great-grandson of General Washington's brother, John Augustine Washington, and, on his mother's side, a great-grandson of Richard Henry Lee, of Revolutionary fame. He had owned Mount Vernon, but had sold it to an association of patriotic ladies, who still own it. He fell in his first military campaign. His body was taken the day after his death, under a flag of truce, and delivered to his great chief—Lee. It was buried on his "Waveland" plantation, near Marshall, Fanquier Co., V. His eldest son, Lawrence Washington, a friend of mine, is a resident of Washington, D. C., has a large family and is a clerk in the Congressional Library. The officer who escaped was Major W. H. F. Lee, son of General R. E. Lee. He became a major-general in the Confederate Army; was wounded and captured at Brandy Station, VA, 1863; was exchanged and surrendered at Appomattox. His brother [cousin], George Washington Custis Lee, was a West Point graduate, who left the United States Army, after his illustrious father, and served with distinction through the Civil War, reached the rank of major-general, and was captured by my command at Sailor's Creek, VA, the last field battle of the war, April 6th, 1865, three days before his father surrendered his sword and the army of Northern Virginia to Grant at Appomattox.

[Source: Sketches of War History 1861–1865, A Compilation of Miscellaneous Papers Compiled for the Ohio Commander of the Loyal Legion February 1885–February 1909, Wilmington, OH, 1993 "Battle of Rich Mountain and Some Incidents" by J. Warren Keifer, Major General U. S. V.]**Manuscript 123**

Comments and Supporting Evidence:

1. Keifer is relating an episode that occurred on September 13, 1861, in Western VA. Keifer's troops which were posted on picket duty, fired upon two richly "caparisoned" and well-mounted Confederate officers who rode into full view from around a point of a mountain spur. Keifer relates that his men killed one of them and the other escaped. The one killed was John Augustine Washington, aid-de-camp to Robert E. Lee. The officer who escaped was W. H. F. Lee. In his concluding remarks in this writing, it is difficult to ascertain if Keifer is making the assertion that troops directly under his command captured Custis Lee at Sailor's Creek.

2. The above question can best be answered by appealing to a work that Keifer wrote in 1888 on the Battle of Sailor's Creek. An excerpt is as follows:

… As the gloom of approaching night settled over the field, covered with dead and dying, the fire of artillery and musketry ceased, and General Ewell, together with eleven of his general officers, and about all his gallant army that survived, were prisoners. Commodore Tucker and his Marine Brigade, numbering about 2,000, surrendered to me a little later. They were under cover of a dense forest, and had been passed by in the first onset of the assault.
[Source: "A Forgotten Battle Sailor's Creek, April 6, 1865," Cincinnati, 1888, by Joseph Warren Keifer]** Manuscript 124 **

In this earlier 1888 writing, Keifer is making no claim to the capture of Major General George Washington Custis Lee. He does, however, make a claim of capturing "Commodore Tucker and his Marine Brigade." The author believes that Keifer was not making a claim to the direct capture of Custis Lee in his 1911 writings. Keifer most likely was referencing the 6th Corps as the command that captured Custis Lee, that Keifer's Brigade was a part.

CHAPTER FOUR:
Sergeant Harris S. Hawthorn

H. SMITH HAWTHORNE.

Exhibit Category   **Code Key**
Claimant Three: **H**

Sergeant Harris S. Hawthorn
121st New York Infantry
2nd Brigade, 1st Division, 6th Army Corps

Evidence Types

    (1) <u>O</u>fficial <u>R</u>ecords of the War of the   **OR**
       Rebellion with Supplement (1 – 6)

    (2) <u>P</u>ension <u>R</u>ecords on file at the National   **PR**
       Archives, Washington, DC, (1 – 3)

    (3) <u>M</u>iscellaneous <u>R</u>ecords, including regimental histories,   **MR**
       publications, personal reminiscences, journal entries,
       diary entries, books, letters, etc. (1 – 7)

    (4) <u>A</u>pplication <u>F</u>ile for the Medal of Honor on file at   **AF**
       the National Archives, Washington, DC,
       file number 401673 (1 – 10)

EVIDENCE OVERVIEW
EXHIBITS-H-OR-1-6

The purpose of this line of evidence is to introduce to the reader a claim made by Harris S. Hawthorn of the 121st New York to the capture of Major General Custis Lee at the Battle of Sailor's Creek April 6, 1865. The specific purpose of the H-OR evidence is to show in various Official Reports of the Civil War that Hawthorn was indeed credited with capturing Major General G. W. Custis Lee at the Battle of Sailor's Creek, VA, April 6, 1865. Hawthorn was also recommended to receive a medal for this act. Private Dennis Moore of the 2nd Connecticut Heavy Artillery was credited with assisting in the capture of Major General G. W. Custis Lee at the Battle of Sailor's Creek.

EXHIBIT-H-OR-1

Introduction:

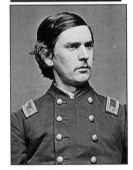

Egbert Olcott:

Brevet Colonel E. Olcott, commanding the 121st New York, which was within Brevet Brigadier General Joseph E. Hamblin's 2nd brigade of General Frank Wheaton's 1st Division, 6th Army Corps, reports on his Regiment's participation in the Battle of Sailor's Creek, VA, on April 6, 1865.
Report is dated April 14, 1865.

Evidence:

Headquarters 121st New York Volunteers, April 14, 1865
FROM: E. OLCOTT, Brevet Colonel, Commanding
Report of the part taken by the One hundred and twenty-first New York Volunteers in the Battle of Sailor's Creek, April 6, 1865. The One hundred and twenty-first New York having checked the enemy, who were endeavoring to get into the rear of the brigade, was ordered to charge, which it did, driving the enemy in confusion, capturing General Custis Lee and several other officers of high rank, together with two stands of colors. General Lee was captured by Private Harris S. Hawthorn, Company F, the proofs of which, there having been some controversy about the matter, accompany this report marked
(Inclosure A)
Camp in the Field, VA, April 14, 1865
Private Harris S. Hawthorn, Company F, One hundred and twenty-first New York Volunteers, being duly sworn, says, that he knows of his own knowledge that he is the first person (officer or enlisted man) who seized or captured General Custis Lee, of the Confederate Army, in the engagement of the 6th of April; and that he never lost sight or control of said General Custis Lee until he delivered him up to Colonel Olcott, commanding One hundred and twenty-first New York Volunteers; and that he, Hawthorn, was one of the men detailed by Colonel Olcott, on account of such capture, to conduct General Custis Lee to the headquarters of General Wheaton, commanding First Division, Sixth Army Corps.

H. S. HAWTHORN
Subscribed and sworn to, at Malvern, near Burkeville, VA, this 14th day of April, 1865, before me.
H. E. HINDMARSH, Lieutenant, Judge-Advocate, First Division, Sixth Army Corps.

CAMP OF 121ST NEW YORK REGIMENT,
April 14, 1865
I hereby certify that for more than two years I have well known Harris S. Hawthorn, Company F, One hundred and twenty-first New York Regiment, as a professed Christian, and have always regarded him worthy of confidence, by the uniform consistency of his religious life. I regard his testimony on any

subject as unimpeachable, and that no assurance can be stronger than his affirmation under the sanctity of an oath.

JOHN R. ADAMS, *Chaplain of 121st New York Regiment.*

[Source: War of the Rebellion: A Compilation of the Official Records of the Union and Confederate Armies (Official Records), Volume 46, Series 1, "The Appomattox Campaign," Folio No. III, pages 936-938]**Manuscript 3**

Comments and Supporting Evidence:

It is interesting to note that Brevet Colonel Olcott states in his Official Report that there has been some controversy surrounding the person who actually captured General Custis Lee.

1. The author questions why Brevet Colonel Olcott goes through so much time and trouble in his Official Report trying to establish proof that Hawthorn captured Custis Lee. This is made manifest by Olcott including addendums in his Official Report from the 121st New York's Chaplain and Hawthorn himself which was then witnessed by a Lieutenant Judge Advocate.

2. Olcott's proof would have been much more powerful in his Official Report if it was given by another eyewitness of the event, instead of Hawthorn giving his own statement about his actions and then having a character testimonial by his Regimental chaplain. Hawthorn's Medal of Honor application file, which will be examined later in this report, states that there were three eye witnesses to Hawthorn's capture of Custis Lee, namely Colonel Olcott, First Lieutenant Thomas J. Hassett, and Captain Josh Heath, all of the 121st New York. The question that this begs is, why were the testimonies of these three eye witnesses not included in Olcott's Official Record? Surely these soldiers were available on April 14, 1865, when Olcott's Official Report was written. Once again, the author believes that the testimony of these other eye witnesses would have been much more compelling proof for Olcott's Official Report than Hawthorn's own testimony.

3. It is interesting to note that Brevet Colonel Olcott, commanding the 121st New York at the Battle of Sailor's Creek, most likely did not author the Official Report dated April 14, 1865, of his regiment's actions on April 2 and April 6, 1865 (Folio III). Sentences in the Official Report that reference Olcott in the third person such as, "The Regiment, by order of Colonel Olcott, rapidly changed front, forming on the road that, crossing the creek, runs nearly perpendicular to the original line of battle," would indicate that someone other than Olcott authored the Official Report. If this is true, it would raise the question whether or not Olcott himself supported the statement made by Hawthorn that he captured Custis Lee, or was this just the viewpoint of the Report's actual author.

4. Brevet Colonel Olcott not writing his own Official Report (which would appear to be somewhat unusual after examining the other Official Reports written by Regimental commanders for April 2 and 6, 1865) can possibly be explained by documents found in Olcott's military pension record. **[Source: Egbert Olcott Pension File, National Archives File Designation Number 213381 National Archives, Washington, DC]** Manuscript 16**** Brevet Colonel Olcott was severely wounded in the battle of the Wilderness on May 5, 1864. He received a bullet to the brain. He returned to service in the latter part of the war. In the year 1872, "he was consigned as a lunatic in the Kings County Asylum" in NY. He remained in asylums, "not having lucid intervals so that he was incapable of the government of himself," until he died on February 23, 1882. He died at the Willard Asylum for the Insane, Willard, NY. An autopsy of his brain is found in his pension record and it would indicate that Olcott suffered from extensive brain damage due to his war injury. His severe brain injury in May 1864, could possibly explain why Olcott did not author his own Official Record for his Regiment's actions on April 2nd and 6th, 1865. Perhaps he was physically or mentally incapable of doing so. Olcott's death in 1882 would explain why Hawthorn did not attempt to contact him for support during his 1894 Medal of Honor application process, or Hawthorn's 1897 defense of that medal as a result of the 37th Massachusetts' Protest Case which is contained later in this report.

5. The following narrative is interesting in that it offers an opinion of Col. Egbert Olcott by the 121st New York's assistant surgeon, Daniel Holt. It also discloses an incident involving Olcott.

Daniel M. Holt:

On the surface Olcott's career seems encouraging and unsullied. But if our curiosity is stirred to further investigate what sort of man Egbert Olcott was, the glimpses we find are apt to be contradictory. Letters and diaries give the perception of a military man as a strict disciplinarian, respected but by no means idolized by his men. They with some affection referred to him as "Daddy Olcott." But what we find of Olcott's personal nature seems largely incongruous with his military self. While Assistant Surgeon Holt had been glad to see the return of Olcott's discipline, and even praised him as "a first rate officer," he also criticized Olcott as being morally inadequate. In one letter home Holt described him by stating, "...his character as a man is bad enough. He is, I am sorry to say, anything but a temperate, virtuous man. Wine and women are his gods, and to indulge his appetite, in the manner he has taken to the card table to supply an empty purse. Not an officer in the reg't. and sometimes even enlisted men, have not been put under torture to supply money in the shape of "loans" to keep his bottle full and satisfy his lust while on leave of absence." That there was some basis in truth for Holt's complaints is apparent in view of charges filed against Olcott in January of 1864. Olcott was brought before a court martial following a series of incidents which had taken place during a post-Christmas bacchanal the previous month. According to the trial transcript, Olcott, in company with Sutler Sam Miller and Captain Cleveland Campbell, engaged in assorted drunken antics in the presence of enlisted men. At one point Miller held Campbell down while Colonel Olcott forced whiskey into him. Olcott poured the liquor down Campbell's throat shouting, "Will you take it Captain? Drink it! Drink it!" Campbell protested vehemently and, once released, retired to his quarters to sleep off his intoxication. Olcott, on the other hand, seems not to have finished with the hapless captain. Perhaps thinking him a spoilsport, Olcott used Campbell's indisposed condition as grounds to have him forcibly removed from his tent. He told the sergeant of the guard that he wanted Campbell brought to his quarters, telling him, "Sergeant, Captain Campbell is Officer of the Day and he has got his sword and belt off. I authorize you to get the men and bring Captain Campbell to my quarters. If ten men are not sufficient you may call out your whole company, and if that is not sufficient I authorize you to call out the whole regiment. If you bring Captain Campbell to my quarters, I will make you Orderly Sergeant. The sergeant of the guard, understandably hesitant at taking such action, even though authorized to do so, was unsuccessful. Olcott next summoned the corporal of the guard and gave him the same instructions. Corporal Covell, with two privates, forcibly removed Campbell from his bed and delivered him to the colonel. For his conduct, Olcott received a severe reprimand."

[Source: Joseph Covais, Middlebury, VT, June 1995, as a Forward in the reprint of the History of the 121st New York State Infantry, reprint 1996, Butternut and Blue, Baltimore, MD]**Manuscript 152**

This event might lead one to conclude that Olcott could have been somewhat liberal in handing out credit or advancements, given the fact that he was willing, in this instance, to advance a sergeant of the guard to an orderly (1st) sergeant for accomplishing a personal act that Olcott wanted done.

BIOGRAPHY:

Hawthorn, Harris S.: Age, 30 years. Enlisted, August 11, 1862, at Otsego, to serve three years; mustered in as private, Co. F, August 23, 1862; promoted sergeant, May 1, 1865; mustered out with company, June 25, 1865, near Hall's Hill, VA; awarded medal of honor.

Olcott, Egbert: Age [blank] years. Enrolled at Herkimer to serve three years, and mustered in as major, August 23, 1862; as lieutenant-colonel, April 10, 1863; wounded in action, May 6, 1864, at the Wilderness, VA; mustered out, to date December 13, 1864; mustered-out revoked and restored to his command, January 10, 1865; mustered in as colonel, April 18, 1865; mustered out with the regiment, June 15, 1865, near Hall's Hill, VA; prior service as private, Co. C, Forty-Fourth Infantry, and captain, Co. B, Twenty-fifth Infantry.

Holt, Daniel M.: Age 43 years. Enrolled at Albany, to serve three years, and mustered in as assistant surgeon, September 2, 1862; discharged, October 16, 1864.

[Source: Annual Report of the Adjutant-General of the State of New York for the Year 1903, Serial No. 36, Albany, NY, Oliver A. Quayle; 1904]** Manuscript 127**

EXHIBIT-H-OR-2

Introduction:

Joseph E. Hamblin:

Brevet Brigadier-General Jo. E. Hamblin, commanding the 2nd Brigade of General Frank Wheaton's 1st Division, 6th Army Corps – reports on his Brigade's participation in the Battle of Sailor's Creek, VA, April 6, 1865, as follows: **Author Note:** Within General Hamblin's 2nd Brigade were the 121st New York and 2nd Connecticut Heavy Artillery, along with several other regiments.

Evidence:

HDQRS. SECOND BRIGADE, FIRST DIVISION, SIXTH CORPS,
FROM : JO. E. HAMBLIN

Report of operations of Second Brigade in the Battle of Sailor's Creek, April 6, 1865:
… Two colors, a large number (exceeding 1,000) prisoner, wagons, forges, battery wagons, and a profusion of small-arms were the results of this charge….
… I beg your attention to the following statement of gallant and meritorious conduct by officers and men of this brigade…Private Dennis Moore, Company K, Second Connecticut Heavy Artillery, assisted in capturing Brig. Gen. Custis Lee…Private Harris S. Hawthorn, Company F, One hundred twenty-first New York State Volunteers, captured Brig. Gen. Custis Lee on the 6th instant…. I earnestly recommend that a medal be awarded to each of the above-mentioned enlisted men.
[Source: Official Records, "The Appomattox Campaign," Volume 46, Series 1, Folio 109, pages 931-935.]Manuscript 3****

Comments and Supporting Evidence:

1. This Official Report is, in essence, the 121st New York regimental report getting rolled up and consolidated at the higher Brigade level. The awarding of medals is now being introduced within this higher Brigade report, with Private Dennis Moore of the 2nd Connecticut Heavy Artillery and Private Harris S. Hawthorn of 121st New York being recommended for medals in connection with the capture of General G. W. Custis Lee at the Battle of Sailor's Creek.

2. Unfortunately, the Official Reports do not contain a Regimental report from Colonel Hubbard, commanding the 2nd Connecticut Heavy Artillery at the Battle of Sailor's Creek. So other than the mention of Dennis Moore assisting in the capture of Custis Lee reported at this higher Brigade level report, there is no other mention or description on how Moore assisted in this act. The missing 2nd Connecticut Heavy Artillery Regimental Official Report would have been nice to examine to shed some additional light on the manner in which Custis Lee was alleged to be captured by Hamblin's 2nd Brigade with the assistance of Dennis Moore of the 2nd Connecticut Heavy Artillery.

EXHIBIT-H-OR-3

Introduction:

Bvt. Major-General Frank Wheaton, commanding the 1st Division of the 6th Army Corps, reports on his Division's participation in the Battle of Sailor's Creek, VA, April 6, 1865.

Author Note: Within General Wheaton's Division were Hamblin's 2nd and Edwards' 3rd Brigades.

Evidence:

HEADQUARTERS FIRST DIVISION, SIXTH CORPS,
April 20, 1865

...The number of prisoners taken is not known. I understand that the result of our attack was the capture of nearly all the rebel troops in our front, which consisted of Ewell's two divisions and the Confederate Marine Brigade. This division took Lieutenant General Ewell and General G. W. Custis Lee and several battle flags....The following named enlisted men of the Second Brigade are recommended to the general commanding the corps as deserving special mention and reward for conspicuous bravery and good conduct: ... Private Dennis Moore, Company K, Second Connecticut Heavy Artillery Volunteers, assisting in the capture of Brig. Gen. Custis Lee.... Private Harris S. Hawthorn, Company F, One hundred and twenty-first New York Volunteers, captured Brig. Gen. (G. W.) Custis Lee, on the 6th instant.

Very respectfully, your obedient servant,

F. WHEATON, Brevet Major-General, U.S. Volunteers.

[Source: Official Records: "The Appomattox Campaign," Volume 46, Series 1, Folio 106, pages 913-926.]**Manuscript 6**

Comments and Supporting Evidence:

1. This Official Report is, in essence, the 2nd Brigade report now getting rolled up and consolidated at the higher Division level.

EXHIBIT-H-OR-4

Introduction:

This is a listing of all Companies within the 121st New York and their entries in the "Record of Events" section of their Muster Rolls Reports for April 6, 1865.

Evidence:

121ST NEW YORK REGIMENT
RECORD OF EVENTS
Company **A**

April 6 – Were engaged at Sailor's Creek. Loss in company one wounded, a large number of prisoners captured.

Company **B**

April 6 – In the engagement at Sailor's Creek, in which the regiment captured a large number of prisoners including General [George Washington] Custis Lee, also two battle flags. Loss of one officer killed.

Company **C**

April 6 – In the engagement at Sailor's Creek, in which the regiment captured a large number of prisoners including General Custis Lee and two battle flags. Loss in company was one first lieutenant and one private killed.

Company **D**

No record for April 6, 1865.

Company **E**

April 6 – In the engagement of Sailor's Creek, in which the regiment captured a large number of prisoners including General Custis Lee and also two battle flags.

Company F (Pvt. Harris Hawthorn's Company)

April 6 – Also captured General Custis Lee and two battle flags. Lost two men wounded.

Company **G**

April 6 – Lost three privates killed, one private and one corporal wounded.

Company **H**

April 6 – We had two corporals killed. The regiment captured General Custis Lee and a large number of prisoners, also two flags.

Company I

No records are available for this company.

Company K (Lt. T. J. Hassett's Company)

April 6 – We were engaged near Sailor's Creek and broke the enemy's line. Captured a large number of prisoners. Their battle flags were taken by the regiment. Followed the enemy.
[Source: Supplement to the Official Records, Part II, Records of Events Series, Volume 46 "Record of Events for One Hundred Twenty-First New York Infantry, August 1862-May 1865," pages 457-513.]**Manuscript 7**

Comments and Supporting Evidence:

1. An observation by the author is that the members of the 121st New York were meticulous and copious record keepers, especially when compared to the 37th Massachusetts. The 121st New York had many completed entries for the "Record of Events" while the 37th Massachusetts had very few.
2. These entries by the various 121st New York companies show their well justified spirit of pride in their accomplishments. These Company records not only contained accomplishments for their respective Companies, but often contained entries or accomplishments made by the entire Regiment as a whole.
3. It should be noted that the "Morning Reports" for all of the companies of the 121st New York for the month of April 1865, do not note the capture of Major General Custis Lee.

[Source: The 121st NY Infantry: Record Group 94: Records of the Adjutant General's Office, Entry 112-115: Book of Records of Union Volunteer Organizations: 121st NY Infantry, Morning Reports for Companies A to K, Vol. 6 of 6, National Archives, Washington, DC]**Manuscript 153**

EXHIBIT-H-OR-5

Introduction:

This is a nice Company "Muster Roll" and "Record of Events" report for the 121st New York, Company F, for the months of March and April, 1865.

Evidence:

F Co., 121 N.Y. Inf.
Company Muster Roll
For: March and April, 1865,
Station of company, Danville VA
Record of Events

From March 1 to March 25 in camp in front of Petersburg time employed in drilling fatigue and picket duty Mch. 25 attacked and carried the enemies outer works capturing a number of prisoners returned to camp remaining until April 2 took an active part in breaking the enemies lines in front of Fort Fisher Apr. 6 engagement at Sailor's Creek in which the Regt. Captured a large number of prisoners also Gen. Custer Lee and two battle Flags, lost two men wounded. April 9 present at the surrender of the army of Northern VA, April 11 – 12 and 13. Returned to Berksville Junction and went into camp–Apr. 23 Marched to Danville arriving on the 27 Mustered for pay on the 30 by Col. Hobart G. Smith

[Source: Company F 121st New York Infantry – Company Muster Roll for March and April, 1865, Record of Events, National Archives Record of Events Book in National Archives, Microfilm Publication M-594, #2702769]**Manuscript 8**

Comments and Supporting Evidence:

1. This book was researched by the author via microfilm in the National Archives. Once again, members of the 121st New York were copious note takers and record keepers. This is evidenced by this nice entry in their Records of Events section of their Muster Rolls.
2. In contrast, the 37th Massachusetts was a poor record keeping regiment, and their whole Record of Events sections of their Muster Rolls are either blank or very brief.
3. It would have been powerful testimony for Hawthorn if the commanding officer of Company F of the 121st New York, when he wrote this report for Company F, affirmatively stated that Private Hawthorn within his Company F captured Custis Lee. Instead, he just vaguely reported that the

121st New York captured Custis Lee. The commanding officer of Company F of the 121st New York during the Battle of Sailor's Creek was most likely First Lieutenant Charles H. Barr. Captain Albert A. Tyler of Company F, who would have normally commanded the Company, was acting as Assistant Adjutant-General of the 1st Division, 6th Corps during the Battle of Sailor's Creek. One would think that the capture of Custis Lee is something that Lt. Barr would have known about and would have wanted to report in his Company's Record of Events to highlight the heroic accomplishments of his Company F. In addition, as will be seen later in this report, it is puzzling why First Lieutenant Hassett of Company K witnessed Hawthorn's capture of Custis Lee and then was in a position to testify about it many years later. One would think that this should have been First Lieutenant Barr of Company F (Hawthorn's Company) and not T. J. Hassett of Company K. The only plausible explanation is that during the battle the companies of the 121st New York somehow got all jumbled up and Hawthorn of Company F got mixed in with Hassett's troops of Company K.

EXHIBIT-H-OR-6

Introduction:
This document contains the continuing paperwork process of awarding special recognition for acts performed on April 2 and 6, 1865.

Evidence:

(Extract from Enclosure LIII 314 P. C. B. W. V. 1865)
Headquarters, 1st Division, 6th Army Corps
April 18, 1865

TO: *Maj. C. A. Whittlesey   AAr 6th Corps*
I have the honor to submit the following list of recommendations for promotion of Officers in this Division for conspicuous gallantry and meritorious services in the assault on Petersburg, April 2, 1865, and at the Battle of Little Sailor's Creek, VA, April 6, 1865 and the names of Enlisted men deserving mention for conspicuous bravery and good service in the same engagements…. The following named Enlisted men of the 2nd Brigade are recommended to the General Commanding the Corps as deserving of special mention and reward for conspicuous bravery and good conduct…. Private Dennis Moore, Co. K, 2nd Conn, Hvy. Art. Vol. (Noted in rolls register April 18/19, 1878) assisting in the capture of Brig. Gen. Custis Lee…. Pvt. Harris S. Hawthorne, Co F. 121st N.Y. Vol., captured Brig. Gen. Custis Lee, on the 6th inst. (Noted).
Very Resp.
Frank Wheaton, Bt. Maj. Gen. U.S. Vol.

Author Note: On the original of this document the Adjutant General checked off the names of those who were entitled to have Medals of Honor whenever they make special application for them, or when their whereabouts and identity become known. These names on the list are checked off with red ink.
[Source: National Archives File Mark 3963B1878 "Medals of Honor for Enlisted Men," Recommendation for Medals of Honor for Men in the Battles of Petersburg, April 2 and Sailor's Creek, April 6, 1865, 1st Division, 6th Corps, original being coupled with recommendations for Brevet filed in the Commission Branch April 5, 1878]Manuscript 9****

Comments and Supporting Evidence:
1. It would appear that in 1878, Private Dennis Moore and Private Harris Hawthorn both qualified for Medals of Honor based on entries in the Official Records as submitted by their Brigade commander, Joseph Hamblin. Their names were not checked off in red ink, indicating they did not make any special application for the Medals as of the compiling of this Report dated April 5, 1878.

EVIDENCE OVERVIEW
EXHIBITS-H-PR-(1-3)

The purpose of introducing this line of evidence is to show injuries sustained by Privates Harris Hawthorn and Dennis Moore during the Civil War and the probable state of their physical condition at the Battle of Sailor's Creek, April 6, 1865. In addition, this line of evidence will also show an injury sustained by a Sergeant Thomas J. Hassett during the Civil War. Hassett was an alleged eye witness to Harris Hawthorn capturing Major General Custis Lee at the Battle of Sailor's Creek. Thomas J. Hassett's actual eye witness account will be found later in this report. This evidence will also show the probable state of Hassett's physical condition at the Battle of Sailor's Creek.

EXHIBIT-H-PR-1

Introduction:
This is an affidavit written October 5, 1882, by W. J. Spencer, former Captain of Company K, 2nd Connecticut Heavy Artillery, attesting to the origin of a disability for Private Dennis Moore of Company K, 2nd Connecticut Heavy Artillery. Dennis Moore was recommended for a Medal by Col. Joseph E. Hamblin, Commander of the 2nd Brigade, for assisting in the capture of Brig. Gen. Custis Lee at the Battle of Sailor's Creek, April 6, 1865, according to Hamblin's Official Record.

Evidence:

AFFIDAVIT TO ORIGIN OF DISABILITY 1882
Dennis Moore Pension File
Private, Company K, Second Reg't Conn H. Arty, October 5, 1882
... that on or about the First day of May, 1864...at or near Fort Worth, state of Virginia, said soldier incurred typhoid fever and was sent to Regt Hospital near Fort Williams, Virginia, which rendered him totally unfit for duty. When the Regt left to join the Army of the Potomac, he was left in Hospital and did not report to his Regt for duty until the latter part of August, 1864, after which he was crippled with disease in his eyes which rendered him unfit for duty most of the time until he was mustered out of the service August 18, 1865...the above fact came to my knowledge as Capt of Co K 2 Regt CT H A at the time his disability was incurred.
W. J. Spencer, Independence, Iowa
[Source: Dennis Moore's Civil War Pension File, National Archives, Washington, DC]**Manuscript 10**

Comments and Supporting Evidence:
1. It would be surprising to think that Dennis Moore who was "crippled with disease in his eyes which rendered him unfit for duty most of the time until he was mustered out of the service," could have participated in any significant way in the capture of Custis Lee at the Battle of Sailor's Creek.
2. Dennis Moore's eyesight disability, as described above, should have rendered him completely debilitated on April 6, 1865.
3. This raises the question of what did Hamlin's Brigade specifically mean when they used the words "assisted in the capture" to describe Moore's participation in the capture of Custis Lee.
4. **Author Note:** The 2nd Connecticut Heavy Artillery's report for the Battle of Sailor's Creek does not appear in the Official Records, and the author's unsuccessful appeal to the National Archives would indicate that this report is lost.

EXHIBIT-H-PR-2

Introduction:
The pension record of Harris Hawthorn shows that he sustained an injury on July 2, 1863, while on a forced march to Gettysburg, PA.

Evidence:
...On or about the 2nd day of July, 1863, while on a forced march from West Minister to Gettysburg, PA, he received an injury causing rupture, as he was informed at the time by said claimant, and was received from jumping a ditch, and greatly aggravated by continuation of the march. That I recollect

distinctly the circumstance of the claimants falling out of the ranks at the time and helped administer to his wants at said time.
Horatio L. Perry of Cooperstown, NY
[Source: Harris Hawthorn Pension File, National Archives, Washington, DC, #724261 and #327492]**Manuscript 96**

Comments and Supporting Evidence:

1. One has to ask what effect, if any, this serious rupture had on Harris Hawthorn's physical abilities during the Battle of Sailor's Creek on April 6, 1865. From these pension records it does not appear that Harris Hawthorn had this disabling rupture treated or repaired prior to the Battle of Sailor's Creek.

EXHIBIT-H-PR-3

Introduction:

Thomas J. Hassett's, pension file contains an interesting application process. Hassett is applying for an invalid pension as a result of a neck injury he suffered at the battle of Spotsylvania Court House, May 10, 1864.

Evidence:

… on this 10th day of February, A.D., one thousand eight hundred and eighty six personally appeared before me, L. F. McCoy, Clerk, of the Jackson County Circuit Court, a court of record in and of the county and state aforesaid, Thomas J. Hassett, aged forty years, a resident of Kansas City, County of Jackson, State of Missouri, who being duly sworn according to law declares…. In the State of Virginia, on or about the tenth day of May, 1864, he received a bayonet wound of the right side of neck causing stiffness of the muscles of the neck and deafness of the right ear and lock in jaw and pain in using same and extreme sensitiveness to the touch…. That since leaving the service his occupation has been that of school teaching. That prior to his entry to the service above named he was a man of good, sound, physical health, being then enrolled a farmer. That he is now totally disabled from obtaining his subsistence by manual labor by reason of his injuries above described, received in the service of the United States and he therefore makes this declaration for the purpose of being placed on the invalid pension roll of the United States….
Thomas J. Hassett
[Source: Thomas J. Hassett Pension File, acquired from a Maryland repository by the Veteran's Administration in Newark, NJ, #1059890 and 568455]**Manuscript 137**

COMMENTS AND SUPPORTING EVIDENCE:

1. It would appear from this declaration made in the year 1886 by Thomas J. Hassett that the bayonet wound he suffered to his neck during the battle of Spotsylvania left him totally disabled from obtaining his subsistence by manual labor at the age of 40.
2. As part of the standard process to qualify a veteran for a disability pension, the Surgeon General's Office conducted a thorough medical examination of Thomas J. Hassett as documented below.

Rest, Pension Claim No. 350043, Thomas J. Hassett, Rank, Sgt, Company F, 121 Reg't NY Inf. Birmingham, Ala. State, August 12, 1896. We hereby certify that in compliance with the requirements of the law we have carefully examined this applicant, who states that he is suffering from the following disability, incurred in the service, viz: Bayonet wound of right side of neck and resulting stiffness of the neck and deafness of right ear. He makes the following statement upon which he bases his claim for restitution. On account of injury to neck can do only about one half work. Upon examination we find the following objective conditions: Pulse rate, 85; respiration 20; temperature 98 ½; height, 5 feet 11 inches; weight, 190 pounds; age 52 years. Upon examination of this man we find a small scar on right side of neck; flesh wound which gives no trouble, no stiffness of neck. No deafness—can hear ordinary conversation at any point of room. There is no disability found to exist. No rating.
LG Gooson, Pres. John A. Moore, Secy Saml Perry, Treas.

[Source: Thomas J. Hassett's pension file as cited above]** Manuscript 137**

The reason that these documents, which are contained in Hassett's pension file, are included as evidence in this report is that it demonstrates that Thomas J. Hassett is not above of the realm of bending the truth a little to accomplish certain objectives. In this case, it was to receive a military pension. This point is important to keep in mind when reading Hassett's testimony which is found later in this report.

EVIDENCE OVERVIEW
EXHIBITS H-MR-(1-5)

The purpose of introducing this line of evidence is to show the various individuals who state, in a written form, that Harris S. Hawthorn, or the 121st New York Infantry, captured Major General G. W. Custis Lee at the Battle of Sailor's Creek, April 6, 1865.

EXHIBIT-H-MR-1

Introduction:

John R. Adams:

This is a write-up from the memoirs of Rev. John R. Adams, chaplain of the 121st New York. The evidence below is an excerpt of a letter that Adams wrote to a C. A. Lord Esq. on April 20, 1865. It should be noted that Rev. Adams was well known to the men of the 121st New York and often led the men in religious services.

Evidence:

…. It was not till four P.M. on Thursday that our division was put into line. Though wearied with the march, the last part "double quick," they waded through Sailor Creek and moved over the opposite crest to meet the foe. The conflict was short but severe. Many a stalwart man fell in death that day. A captain and lieutenant and several men were killed in our regiment, and one officer and thirteen men wounded. The limb of the officer (Major Cronkite) has since been amputated. Our regiment captured two colors, and General Custis Lee (son of General R. E. Lee) was made prisoner by Private H. S. Haythorn, Company F, and our colonel has receipts for more than five hundred additional prisoners.
[Source: Memorial and Letters of Rev. John R. Adams, Chaplain of the Fifth Maine and the One hundred and Twenty-First New York Regiments During the War of the Rebellion, Serving from the Beginning to its Close, privately printed, Cambridge, MA, University Press, 1890]**Manuscript 11**

Comments and Supporting Evidence:

1. This is the same chaplain of the 121st New York who provided a character reference for Harris Hawthorn as recorded in the April 14, 1865, entry of the Official Records. Chaplain Adams appears to carry the same overall enthusiasm exhibited by the members of the 121st New York when reporting their War time activities. Adams also appears to have a good recollection of the items claimed to be captured by his Regiment during their various engagements.
2. The author's research indicates that chaplain Adams was well liked by his regiment and was a man of strong character.
3. In this letter, Adams is stating to his friend, C. A. Lord Esq., what Adams believed were the results of his regiment's participation in the Battle of Sailor's Creek on April 6, 1865.
4. On April 15, 1865, Adams wrote a letter to the editor of the New York Otsego Republican, and this letter was published in the newspaper on April 29, 1865. A portion of this letter references the Battle of Sailor's Creek and the capture of Custis Lee. This portion is as follows:

…The march was resumed and continued without interruption, till the enemy made a stand at Sailor's Creek. Though wearied with the march on that day (Thursday) yet the 121st went bravely into the fight

and covered itself with new laurels… In their charge they broke the enemy's line and then gathered the trophies of the day. Two battle flags were secured by two privates of this regiment by the names of B. Gifford and W. Dockum. Gen. Custis Lee (son of R. E. Lee) was captured by private H. S. Haythorn of Company F. This regiment secured about 500 additional prisoners.
[Source: Otsego Republican, Otsego County, New York, April 29, 1865]**Manuscript 189**

BIOGRAPHY:
Adams, John R.: Age, 62 years. Enrolled in the field, to serve three years, and mustered in as chaplain, September 15, 1864; mustered out with regiment, June 25, 1865, near Hall's Hill, VA; prior service, chaplain Fifth Maine Volunteer Infantry.
[Source: Annual Report of the Adjutant-General of the State of New York for the Year 1903, Serial No. 36; Albany, NY; Oliver A. Quayle; 1904]**Manuscript 127**

EXHIBIT-H-MR-2

Introduction:
In the 121st New York's regimental history by Isaac O. Best, the account on the Battle of Sailor's Creek was taken from the diary entries of Corporal Clinton Beckwith of the 121st New York. This regimental history was published in the year 1921. In the forward of the book, the author, Isaac O. Best, states the following:

Evidence:

Isaac O. Best:

"In compiling a History of the 121st Regiment of New York Volunteers, the writer feels handicapped by two facts: He is not an original member of the regiment, but was transferred from the 16th N.Y. in the spring of 1863; and after his transfer, he did not serve in the regiment, having previously been detailed for clerical duty in the office of the Adjutant General of the Brigade. Consequently he never had that close personal relation with the members of the regiment that would give to his writing the intimate character of a fellow soldier. On the other hand, however, his position gave him the advantage of a close observer; for all the orders from the higher authorities and all the reports of the brigade and regimental commanders passed under his hand, and he was able to estimate more fully the character of the services rendered, and the estimation in which those services were held by the superior officers."

Best's account of the Battle of Sailor's Creek is as follows:

Dewitt Clinton Beckwith:

… Of the next day's march Beckwith says…. These last troops we encountered were Marines, or land soldiers, and had never before been in battle. They were mostly boys and were commanded by G. W. Custis Lee who fell into our hands with a large number of prisoners and several stands of colors. One of these was a beautiful silk banner belonging to the 8th Savannah Guards, whose organization dated back to 1804. This was captured by H. S. Hawthorne of Company F and by him turned over to Colonel Olcott. The inscription on this flag was a follows: "To the Defenders of Our Altars and Our Hearths. Presented by the Ladies of Savannah, Ga., to the Eighth Savannah Guards."
[Source: "History of the 121st New York State Infantry" by Isaac O. Best, published by Lieut. Jas. H. Smith, Chicago, IL, 1921]**Manuscript 12**

Comments and Supporting Evidence:

1. Isaac Best states in this work that Harris Hawthorn captured the Savannah Guard's flag, not Custis Lee. Isaac Best relied on the memoirs of Clinton Beckwith to a degree when compiling the history of the 121st New York. Mr. Sal Cilella, currently President and CEO of the Atlanta Historical Society, recently discovered the actual memoirs of Clinton Beckwith that were published in the Herkimer County, NY, "Herkimer Democrat" newspaper. They were published as a 52 part series running from July 12, 1893, to July 4, 1894, and were entitled "Three Years with the Colors of a Fighting Regiment in the Army of the Potomac, by a Private Soldier." In the June 6, 1894 edition of the Herkimer Democrat, Beckwith states the following in his memoirs:

These last troops we encountered were Marines, or land sailors, and had never been in battle before. They were mostly boys, and were commanded by G. W. Custis Lee, who fell into our hands, with a large number of prisoners and several stands of colors, one a beautiful silk flag belonging to the Savannah Guards, whose organization dated back to 1804. General Lee was captured by H. S. Hawthorn, of Company F, and turned over to Colonel Olcott. Our captures numbered at least five hundred, and our little regiment had again covered itself with glory.

[Source: Herkimer County, New York, "Herkimer Democrat"; Articles Entitled "Three Years with the Colors of a Fighting Regiment in the Army of the Potomac, by a Private Soldier," by Clinton Beckwith, June 6, 1894, published in the July 4, 1894 edition]Manuscript 160****

Given the close similarities between the writings of Best and Beckwith, one would have to assume that Isaac Best just copied from Beckwith's 1893-1894 memoirs when Best wrote the History of the 121st New York many years later. The question that this begs is: "did Isaac Best just misquote from Beckwith when coping, or did Isaac Best make a deliberate attempt to correct Beckwith?" No one will ever know definitively the answer to this question. Sal Cilella offers the following opinion; "Best had written about the three large campaigns, Beckwith's manuscript with details of the common soldier was handy, Best asked Beckwith if he could use portions, Beckwith probably said no problem, just give me credit. Even though Best takes full credit for the work in the end, he does say that he asked Beckwith, Smith and Wescott to act as a committee to examine and criticize the manuscript, ascertain the cost of publication and report to the association at its next meeting. I get the impression that Beckwith had no final input on the final document, and because Best is listed as the author and not a co-author with Beckwith, the work is indeed Best's."

[Source: Letter from Mr. Sal Cilella, April 19, 2006, in the author's possession]Manuscript 160****

BIOGRAPHY:
Best, Isaac O.: *Private, Co. A, Sixteenth Infantry; transferred to Co. A, 121st New York Regiment, May 11, 1863; mustered out with company, June 25, 1865, near Hall's Hill, VA.*
Beckworth, Dewitt Clinton: *Age, 18 years. Enlisted, July 31, 1862, at German Flats, to serve three years; mustered in as corporal, Co. B, August 23, 1862; returned to ranks, September 28, 1864; promoted to corporal, May 1, 1865; mustered out with company, June 25, 1865, near Hall's Hill, VA; as Dewitt C. Beckworth*
[Source: Annual Report of the Adjutant-General of the State of New York for the Year 1903; Serial No. 36; Albany, NY; Oliver A Quayle, 1904]Manuscript 127****

EXHIBIT-H-MR-3

Introduction:
In the early 1900's, there was an important book published entitled, "Deeds of Valor." This book was published to highlight the various feats performed by the recipients of the Medal of Honor. Harris Hawthorn appears in this book describing his feat of the capture of Custis Lee. The following write up provides a good introduction into the nature of this book entitled "Deeds of Valor."

DEEDS OF VALOR…The highly embellished portraits shown in this account, like others shown in this and the next two chapters are taken from Deeds of Valor, a collection of Medal of Honor stories published in

1906 by the Perrien-Keydel Company. The book contained extensive graphic treatments of Medal of Honor feats, along with accounts drawn from "records in the archives of the United States government" and "personal reminiscences and records of officers and enlisted men who were rewarded by Congress for most conspicuous acts of bravery." Flags, outspread wings, and other devices surrounding the portraits are typical of the romantic illustrations of the time.

[Source: "Above and Beyond" A History of the Medal of Honor from the Civil War to Vietnam, Boston Publishing Company, Boston, MA, 1985, ISBN Number: 0-939526-19-0]**Manuscript 13**

Evidence:

The preface to the "Deeds of Valor" Book is found below:

DEEDS OF VALOR is a compendium of the personal reminiscences and records of Civil War soldiers who were awarded the Congressional Medal of Honor. First published in 1901, this exciting and well-illustrated historical work is filled with action-packed accounts and vivid first-hand descriptions of the harrowing exploits of men and women under almost unimaginable wartime stress. This book recounts 293 of the most incredible war stories in American history. The events reported occurred during the course of 185 different battles and engagements....Some of the remarkable stories in this book are told in the simple language of the heroes themselves, who have minimized their own merits—partly out of modesty, but also because of their lack of literary and reportorial skills. On the other hand, many of the incidents have been related by officers who were witnesses to the deeds of their subordinates, and who had the facility to describe them in the manner they deserved, but without exaggeration or embellishment.

INTRODUCTION

The official record of these stories of heroic deeds in the service of the Republic is of the most meager character, a mere line, with the name of the individual, his company and regiment, and a brief phrase designating the character of his achievement, without any of the details which would give it life and dramatic interest. It scarcely rises above the form of a tabular statement. As time passed, the heroes of these deeds were rapidly disappearing from the stage of life, and soon all recollection of the essential features of their achievements, would be buried in the graves of those who performed and witnessed them. The design of this work was to gather these details together, verified by the medal bearers, their superior officers, or other witnesses, and present them to the American public in a form worthy of the subject. The work has been by no means an easy one. It involved several years of arduous pursuit by the compilers, voluminous correspondence and exhaustive search; but it has been accomplished with a degree of completeness which was hardly to be expected. The compilers have had the advantage of the zealous assistance of every officer of the army to whom they applied, access to the official reports of the War Department, and written reports of the incidents from the medal holders themselves. So far therefore, as historical accuracy is concerned, there is little apology to be made for the work. As to its literary merit, it may be said that much of it is in the simple and modest language of the heroes themselves, who have minimized their own merits, and taken from their narratives much of the dramatic interest which a disinterested witness would have found in the deeds they performed. Many of the incidents, on the other hand, have been related by officers who were witnesses of the deeds of their subordinates, and who had the literary skill to mark and describe them in the manner they deserved, but without exaggeration for embellishment. The editing of the work was committed to competent hands, whose chief purpose was to eliminate crudities, and to avoid extravagant expressions to which such a work was easily liable. Whatsoever may be its demerits, its publishers may at least fairly claim that it is a truthful and modest narration of the most heroic personal achievements of our soldiers during the past half century, verified by competent officers, and sustained by proofs which have been accepted by the Government of the United States as evidence of the facts which deserved the distinguishing acknowledgement of the Medal of Honor.

COMPILER'S PREFACE

The pages of our country's history abound with instances of the most lofty courage, which thrill the pulse and kindle the spirit of every true patriot. Congress itself has singled out many of these instances and given them special recognition. It has provided for a medal, known as the "Medal of Honor." It is the nation's grateful acknowledgement of a great and heroic deed, a reward for such gallant services in action as make him who renders them conspicuous among his comrades. The heart beats faster and the blood courses through the veins more rapidly, as one reads these simple stories published in the heroes' own modest words. These narrations speak for themselves. Editorial embellishment could only detract from their value.

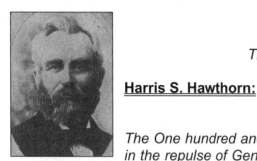

Harris S. Hawthorn:

The entry for Harris Hawthorn is as follows:
Harris S. Hawthorn
Private, Co. F. 121st NY Inf.
Born at Salem, NY, 1832
Humor, Persistency, Gallantry
The One hundred and twenty-first New York Volunteer Infantry took an active part in the repulse of General Ewell's forces when they were endeavoring to recapture the wagon train Custer had taken only a few hours before, and one of its members, Private Harris S. Hawthorn, of Company F, greatly distinguished himself in the charge by capturing, single-handed, General Custis Lee. Because of the conspicuous nature of this capture Colonel Egbert Olcott, commanding the regiment, detailed Hawthorn as one of the men to conduct the noted rebel general to the headquarters of General Wheaton.

[Source: "Deeds of Valor," edited by W. F. Beyer and O. F. Keydel, Longmeadow Press, 1992 ISBN 0-681-41567-3, 1992, originally published in 1903]Manuscript 14****

Comments and Supporting Evidence:

1. This is a valuable piece of evidence because there is a high probability that the description of the capture of Custis Lee by Hawthorn was either written by Hawthorn himself or Hawthorn directly communicated his recollections to a writer. This suggestion is supported by the following facts: (1) this work contains Hawthorn's photograph, most probably submitted by himself; (2) it uses very brief and simple language, which was typical of Hawthorn's writing style; and (3) Col. Olcott, Hawthorn's commanding officer at the Battle of Sailor's Creek, died before 1903, so he was not able to write this narrative for Hawthorn. Once again, the compliers of *"Deeds of Valor"* preferred that the commanding officers write the descriptive accounts of the acts that yielded Medals of Honor for their soldiers. In Hawthorn's case, however, this was not possible due to the death of Col. Olcott.

2. An analysis of the key points of Hawthorn's statement is as follows:

   A. Hawthorn's statement, "the 121st New York Volunteer Infantry took an active part in the repulse of General Ewell's forces when they were endeavoring to recapture the wagon train Custer had taken only a few hours before," is somewhat correct if interpreted in a certain manner. At Marshall's Crossroads, which crossroads are south of Sailor's Creek, Custer and his Federal Calvary made an attack on a portion of the Confederate wagon train. This took place about late morning on the day of the Battle of Sailor's Creek, April 6, 1865. This Federal Calvary was temporarily successful in capturing and burning some of the Confederate artillery wagons of Frank Huger's 1st Artillery Corps, before being pushed back by the main body of General Anderson's Confederate Infantry troops. As substantiation for this point that the Federal Calvary was successful in capturing some of the Confederate wagons late in the morning on April 6th, Federal General Phil Sheridan has the following observation recorded in his Official Report. Just prior to the start of the battle of Hillsman Farm late in the afternoon on April 6, Sheridan noticed a long line of smoke coming from the burning Confederate wagons at Marshall's Crossroads. At this time Sheridan was positioned at the Hillsman Farm, a relatively short distance away from Marshall's Crossroads on the other (north) side of Sailor's Creek. During this initial Federal Calvary attack at Marshall's Crossroads late in the morning of April 6, Confederate General Ewell, together with his Infantry troops, was still some distance away at Hott's Corner. When he was informed of the Federal Calvary attack on the Confederate wagon train at Marshall's Crossroads he stated in his Official Report that, he hurried to the aid of General Anderson who was at Marshall's Crossroads. When you put all these many events together, to Private Hawthorn it could have appeared to him that when he was taking part in the Hillsman Farm battle, he was actually taking part in repelling "General Ewell's forces when they were endeavoring to recapture the wagon train Custer had taken only a few hour before." The reality was that General Ewell had no interest in recapturing any of the lost Confederate wagons that the Federal Calvary captured earlier in the day. Ewell was totally preoccupied with holding off the Federal Infantry in his rear, to allow General Anderson enough time to break through the Federal Calvary in his front at Marshall's Crossroads. This was Ewell's sole objective, so that his Infantry troops could continue marching and be reconnected with the strength of the main body of the Confederate army of Robert E. Lee and Longstreet. Both Robert E. Lee and Longstreet got disconnected from Ewell and had traveled well in front of Ewell.

B. Hawthorn states that he distinguished himself "in the charge." This would indicate that Hawthorn captured Custis Lee while charging Custis Lee's troops.

C. Hawthorn states that he captured Custis Lee single-handedly, making an obvious rebuttal at the time of this publication (1903) to the fact that this claim was disputed by others (as will be seen in the 37th Massachusetts Protest Case which they filed in the year 1897, which is outlined later in the report).

D. Hawthorn's use of the words, "conspicuous nature of this capture," would indicate that Hawthorn was well versed in the regulations regarding the requirements for the awarding of the Medal of Honor. One of the requirements for the Medal of Honor was the "conspicuous nature" of a military act that qualified for a Medal.

E. Hawthorn states that, as his reward for capturing Custis Lee, he was one of the men detailed by his commanding officer, Col. Egbert Olcott, to conduct Custis Lee to the headquarters of General Wheaton. It would have been nice if Hawthorn offered more concrete proof of the capture, like the act being witnessed by others. Instead, he rests his claim on having the privilege of escorting Custis Lee to the Federal rear.

3. Given the nature of the *"Deeds of Valor"* work, and the opportunity it afforded Medal of Honor recipients to tell their heroic story, it is a shame that Hawthorn did not provide us with a more fact filled and less aggrandized account of his capture of Major General Custis Lee.

EXHIBIT-H-MR-4

Introduction:

John James Ingraham: (PHOTO: COURTESY EDWARD C. INGRAHAM)

This is a letter written by John James Ingraham of Company D of the 121st New York, on April 16, 1865, to his parents back home in NY.

Evidence:

Head Quarters 121st N.Y. near Berksville Hills Station, April 16th, 1865
.... We marched from 15 to 20 miles every day and finally overtook them on the 6th Inst. Our Div and 3d Div of our Corps and Sheridan's cavalry fought them that day. Our Regt took two stands of Rebel colors that day. Our stand was the prettiest I ever saw. It was captured from the 18th Georgia Battalion. It was presented to them by the ladies of Savannah. It was a very pretty silk flag with bead work. It had a very large bead castle to represent the capitol of Georgia. There was inscribed on it our hearts and our homes. Our Regt also captured Maj. Gen Custan Lee, Gen Bob Lee's son. Gen Sheridan captured Lieut Gen Ewell. We captured a large amount of wagon trains, mules and ambulances & c. The Rebels burned a large train besides blew up their ammunition. They were in a perfect rout. Night came on, which ended the pursuit.

[Source: Dolgeville-Manheim Historical Society, Dolgeville, NY, Publication of Civil War Letters by the Phoenix Printing Corporation, Frankfort, NY, January 1992]Manuscript 157****

Comments and Supporting Evidence:

1. On the surface, this looks like a compelling piece of evidence for the Harris Hawthorn case. A closer examination of this letter in its entirety, however, indicates that Ingraham is merely relaying to his parents back home the basic statistics recorded by his Regiment for the Battle of Sailor's Creek. This includes the capture of two stands of colors, Custis Lee, a wagon train, mules and ambulances & c. Though it appears that he personally observed the "pretty" 18th Georgia flag that was captured by the 121st New York, there is no indication that he eye-witnessed the capture of Custis Lee by his regiment. He was just simply writing home and sharing some documented official statistics, just like he did with other events that Ingraham described in this April 16, 1865, letter.

BIOGRAPHY:

Ingraham, John J.: Age, 18 years. Enlisted, August 12, 1862, at Manheim, to serve three years; mustered in as private, Co. D, August 23, 1862; mustered out with company, June 25, 1865, near Hall's Hill, Va.

[Source: Annual Report of the Adjutant-General of the State of New York for the Year 1903, Serial 36; Albany, NY; Oliver A. Quayle, 1904]**Manuscript 127**

EXHIBIT-H-MR-5

Introduction:

John S. Kidder:

This is a letter written on April 10, 1865, by Captain John S. Kidder of Company I of the 121st New York, to his wife back home in NY.

Evidence:

Camp of the 121st N. Y. V., April 10, 1865

… came up to the rebs in the afternoon of the 6th at Saylor Creek. Here we had a hard fight but we succeeded in driving them. I lost one Capt E. W. Lewis killed and G. Roberts and Wm Olin slightly wounded. We lost 7 men killed and 2 officers Capt Howland and Lieut Martin. We lost 12 others wounded in the Regt. We captured Genl Custer Lee and 2 stands of colors and over 1000 prisoners. This the 121st did, the men fought well, never done better. We marched day and night ever since ….

[Source: Original letter in the possession of Mr. Harrie Kidder Washburn of Sharon Springs, NY, who is a descendant of Captain John S. Kidder. A photocopy of this letter was provided to the author by Mr. Sal Cilella, formally President of the Indiana Historical Society, Indianapolis, IN, currently President of the Atlanta Historical Society, Atlanta, GA]**Manuscript 156**

Comments and Supporting Evidence:

1. As with the Ingraham letter found in the preceding Exhibit-H-MR-4, on the surface this Kidder letter looks like a compelling piece of evidence for the Harris Hawthorn case. But just like the Ingraham letter, Kidder is simply writing home and relaying the basic official statistics of his Regiment's participation in the Battle of Sailor's Creek. Kidder follows this "reporting type" style throughout this entire letter. There is no indication that Kidder eye-witnessed the capture of Custis Lee by the 121st New York. Kidder was merely writing back home informing his wife what others in his Regiment have reported to him concerning the capture of Custis Lee. The Ingraham and Kidder letters would have been much more powerful pieces of evidence for the Hawthorn case if they were actual eye-witness accounts. Through these letters, however, it is quite apparent that the 121st New York is laying claim to the capture of Major General George Washington Custis Lee.

EXHIBIT-H-MR-6

Introduction:

John M. Lovejoy:

These are two letters written by John M. Lovejoy of the 121st New York; one to his mother dated April 14, 1865, and the other to his cousin Cynthia dated April 15, 1865. Below are the references in these letters to the Battle of Sailor's Creek and the capture of Custis Lee.

Evidence:

(1) *Camp 121st Regt N. Y. S. Vols   Near Burkes Junction Va.   April 14, 1865*

Dear Mother,
Our Corps the 2nd of April captured 3000 prisoners 24 pieces of Artillery the 6th inst we Captured 4000 prisoners and a train of Wagon about 3 miles in length our Regt in the last fight lost 9 Killed 17 wounded Captured 960 prisoners among them Gen. Ewell and Custer Lee and three Rebel Battle flags. We have done a great work and every Soldier feels as cheerful as can be.

(2) *Camp 121st Regt N. Y. S. Volunteers   Near Burkes Junction Va.   April 15, 1865*

Dear Cousin Cynthia,
…There we took 7,000 prisoners, the 6th Corps took 4,000, Custors Div of Cavalry took 3,000, the 121st had receipts for over 700, and 2 Battle flags, a man in Co F took Gen. Custor Lee prisoner, then we followed the rebs as fast as we could follow them ….

[Source: Photocopies of these letters were provided to the author by Mr. Sal Cilella, currently President of the Atlanta Historical Society, Atlanta, GA]**Manuscript 190**

Comments and Supporting Evidence:

1. These two Lovejoy letters appear to be very similar to the Ingraham and Kidder letters above. Like Ingraham and Kidder, Lovejoy also writes about the results of battles. The results written by Lovejoy for the battle of Sailor's Creek on April 6th are as Lovejoy understood them on April 14th and 15th (note: differences exist in Lovejoy's battle results between his two letters of April 14th and April 15th). There is no evidence from these two letters, however, that Lovejoy actually eye-witnessed the captured of Custis Lee by "a man" in his regiment's Company F. It appears that Lovejoy was just merely reporting back home on what he believed the results were for the Battle of Sailor's Creek.

2. In the year 1892, John M. Lovejoy sent the following cover letter to the Otsego Republican newspaper, suggesting a reprint of the Adams newspaper article found in Exhibit-H-MR-1:

The following letter written by Chaplain Adams, 121st N. Y., was printed in the Otsego Republican in April, 1865, and is republished by request of survivors of that Regt. as it is proof, in regards to honors, which are now subject to dispute by present writers of War History…J. M. Lovejoy…Sec 121st NY Asso.

[Source: Otsego Republican, Otsego County, New York, January 6, 1892]**Manuscript 193**

Since Lovejoy wrote this cover letter in 1892, Lovejoy is probably referring to on-going disputes of the honors that the 121st New York had received for actions in the Civil War, up to the year 1892.

3. On December 2,1895, Lovejoy, acting as treasurer and secretary of the 121st New York Veterans Association, completed a State of New York Adj. Gen. questionnaire asking for various pieces of information including the following question, which Lovejoy gave the following response:

Q: The names of Medal of Honor men of your command and the circumstances that led to its award?
A: Private Harris S. Hawthorn Co. F for capturing Genl. Custis Lee

BIOGRAPHY:
Lovejoy, John M.: Age, 19 years. Enlisted, August 7, 1862, at Roseboom, to serve three years; mustered in as private, Co. G, August 23, 1862; wounded in skirmish, August 21, 1864; promoted corporal, Jan 1, 1865; mustered out with company, June 25, 1865, near Hall's Hill, Va.
[Source: Annual Report of the Adjutant-General of the State of New York for the Year 1903; Serial No. 36; Albany NY; Oliver A Quayle, 1904]Manuscript 194****

EXHIBIT-H-MR-7

Introduction:
This is a diary entry on April 6, 1865, written by Lieutenant Philip Woodcock of Company E, 121st New York, which has reference to the Battle of Sailor's Creek and the capture of Custis Lee.

Evidence:
...we captured 2 stands of colors, all the prisoners vis. Gen Ewell & staff & General Custar Lee surrendered to us...
[Source: Philip Woodcock Civil War Diary, archived in the U. S. Army War College, Carlisle Barracks, PA]Manuscript 192****

Comments and Supporting Evidence:
1. Woodcock's diary entry appears to be more narrative in nature when compared to the statistical reporting nature of the letters above. In his entry on April 6, 1865, Woodcock describes marching all day, still in pursuit of General Lee and how the enemy "stood well" at the battle. He does not appear to be an eye-witness to the capture of Custis Lee. Once again, there is absolutely no doubt that the 121st New York is laying claim to the capture of Custis Lee. The author likes this diary entry in that it clearly shows that the 121st New York is laying claim to the capture of Custis Lee as early as the Woodcock's diary entry on April 6, 1865. His use of the word "us" must refer to the 121st New York.

BIOGRAPHY:
Woodcock, Philip, R.: Age, 22 years. Enrolled, July 23, 1862, at Springfield, to serve three years; mustered in as sergeant, Co. E, August 23, 1862; promoted first sergeant, no date; wounded in action, September 22, 1864, at Fisher Hill, Va; mustered in as first lieutenant, Co I, February 22, 1865; mustered out with company, June 25, 1865, near Hall's Hill, Va.
[Source: Annual Report of the Adjutant-General of the State of New York for the Year 1903; Serial No. 36; Albany NY; Oliver A Quayle, 1904]Manuscript 194****

EVIDENCE OVERVIEW
EXHIBITS-H-AF-(1-10)

The purpose of introducing this line of evidence is to outline a claim made by Harris S. Hawthorn that he single handedly captured Major General G. W. Custis Lee at the Battle of Sailor's Creek, April 6, 1865. This line of evidence is primarily in the form of an application for a Medal of Honor that was created and submitted by Hawthorn, with the help of others, in the year 1894.

EXHIBIT-H-AF-1

Introduction:
In the year 1894, approximately 29 years after the Battle of Sailor's Creek, Harris S. Hawthorn submitted an application for a Medal of Honor. He claimed the capture of Confederate Major General G. W. Custis Lee at this battle. The following is a letter from Thomas J. Hassett to Harris S. Hawthorn, dated September 9, 1894. This would appear to be a response from Mr. Hassett to a letter sent to him from Harris Hawthorn, dated September 6, 1894, requesting Hassett to provide Hawthorn with

information on the capture of Major General George Washington Custis Lee at the Battle of Sailor's Creek.

Evidence:

AMERICAN BOOK COMPANY
Birmingham, Alabama,
Sept 9, 1894

My Dear Comrade Hawthorn:

Your favor of Sept 6 is duly received. I assure you it gives me more than ordinary pleasure to hear from you. Time has made great ravages in the ranks of those who, in the vigor of young manhood, joined the ranks of the great army of the Potomac thirty years ago. We are growing old, brother Hawthorn, and very soon we too will add to that other great army and be forgotten. I have always had a great desire to meet again those old comrades who served with me in those historic battles of the war. I rejoice to hear that you are well and hope you have prospered in the battle of life. "In regard to your request to give you a statement regarding the capture of General Custis Lee, I will say it gives me pleasure to do so, knowing that you must have some special reason for wanting me to do so. Perhaps you are not aware that I received a commission from Congress for services at the battle of Little Sailor's Creek as a memorial. But to your question. In marching towards the scene of the battle, we passed General Sheridan's Headquarters beside the road, about a mile and a half from the creek. We opened fire as soon as our ranks were forward in line on the north bank of the creek, and in charging the enemy we became somewhat mixed up with a part of another regiment of infantry but pressed on and in a short time got so close to the enemy that we could easily distinguish their officers. Just at the critical moment General Lee rushed in front of his corps shouting to his men to stand firm. But just at that moment another brave man rushed in front of his comrades of Company K̶ (F) [**Author note:** K was crossed out and F inserted by Hawthorn in his own handwriting] *121ˢᵗ New York Volunteers and at the point of his bayonet demanded and received the surrender of the young general. The name of the soldier was H. S. Hawthorn. Colonel Egbert Olcott and myself both witnessed the scene. General Lee requested to be allowed to return and surrender his corps but Colonel Olcott who was also on foot refused the request – but ordered Comrade Hawthorn to conduct General Lee to Sheridan's Headquarters. No sooner had he started, however, when an officer in the other regiment (37ᵗʰ Mass.)* [**Author note:** the (37ᵗʰ Mass.) entry was inserted here by Hawthorn in his own handwriting] *referred to attempted to take charge of the prisoner. My orderly sergeant Tom Smith reported the fact to me and I called Colonel Olcott's attention to it. When the Colonel raised his sword as if to strike the officer down when the latter quickly got away. The Colonel then ordered me to take charge of the prisoner. With orderly Tom Smith and Private H. S. Hawthorn we conducted the prisoner to where we supposed General Sheridan's headquarters to be but found they had been removed two miles to the front. But we met one of his staff officers who kindly furnished General Lee a horse to ride and with that staff officer as a guide we started back to find General Sheridan. We re-crossed Little Sailors Creek and about half a mile from the creek we met the Major of the 121ˢᵗ and was glad enough to turn our prisoner over to him. We soon found the regiment and Hawthorn and Smith joined the company which had bivouacked for the night and I reported all that had transpired to Colonel Olcott in his tent. The battle practically ended with the surrender of Lee. The enemy fell back and night came on. The above are the facts in the case and I have always felt that the horse was furnished to the wrong man. Lee was more exalted in the eyes of that contemptible staff officer than the tired soldiers who had captured him. I would like to even the score with that staff officer if I should be fortunate enough to ever meet him. I say staff officer because that was what he said he was. But he may never have been on General Sheridan's staff, but simply an officer of some squad of cavalry. If due credit has never been given you for the capture of Custis Lee, the fault has been with our Major to whom we turned over the prisoner. Please write me again and often.*

Yours sincerely,

T. J. Hassett, Late Captain Co., "K" 121 N. Y. V.

[Source: National Archives File 401673, Medal of Honor Application File for Harris Hawthorn]Manuscript 15****

Comments and Supporting Evidence:

It is interesting to note that Mr. Hassett does not appear to know why Harris Hawthorn wants his statement regarding the capture of Custis Lee. Hassett then goes on to state that he received a commission from Congress "for services at the battle of Little Sailor's Creek as a memorial." This is an interesting statement by Hassett and deserves some clarification. In this statement, Hassett must have been referring to his commission to the rank of a captain. His reference to a "memorial" must have been Hassett's way of stating two ideas, that his promotion to captain was by brevet and it occurred after the Civil War was over.

1. The following letter from Michael Pilgrim of the National Archives sheds some light on an Adjutant General's Office (AGO) correspondence file at the National Archives which provides information on Thomas J. Hassett's Commission and war time recognitions:

May 25, 2000

Dear Mr. White:

This is in response to your recent request for information on the Civil War service of Thomas J. Hassett. Enclosed for your information is a copy of a small Adjutant General's Office correspondence file relating to Hassett's promotion to Captain. Additional information will be found in his compiled service record and pension application case file. If you have not done so already, you should request copies of those files by completing and returning the enclosed NATF Forms 80. Hassett's promotion to Captain was by brevet, in recognition of his actions at Sailor's Creek, Virginia. Hassett did not receive the Congressional Medal of Honor, but did apply for and received the Civil War Campaign Medal which was presented to all Civil War veterans.

Sincerely,

MICHAEL E. PILGRIM, Old Military and Civil Branch, Textual Archives Services Division

[Source: National Archives Adjutant General's Office Correspondence File Numbers 994910 and 2187969 for Thomas J. Hassett] Manuscript 17****

A close examination of this AGO correspondence file brings to light the fact that Thomas J. Hassett, through his attorney William A. Saxton of Albany, NY, applied for an "amendment of muster." It would appear that Hassett was undertaking this action to receive additional monetary compensation from the Government. Hassett's application was initiated on March 27th, 1905. In this "amendment of muster" application, Hassett states that he was commissioned a 1st Lieutenant from February 22nd, 1865, and then a Captain from April 29th, 1865. At first, the War Department disagreed with Hassett's claim. The War Department auditor initially stated that, "the records show that he (Hassett) did not enter upon duty as 1st Lieutenant prior to May 21st, 1865, the date of his muster into service as such. He is not entitled to recognition as of that grade from an earlier date under existing law." With persistence and new evidence, Hassett ultimately prevailed in this matter and received his "amendment of muster." In addition to his "amendment of muster" application, this AGO correspondence file also contains the following interesting letter written by Hassett:

July 18, 1914

The Honorable Sec. of War, Washington D.C.

I respectfully apply for myself a Congressional medal such as are given to the old soldiers of both armies of the civil war period. I enlisted in August 1862 in Co. F 121st N.Y.-Upton's regiment. Was commissioned 1st Lieutenant in March, 1865 and Captain later, was transferred to 65 N. Y. V. reg, when the 121st was discharged. I was discharged in July, 1865. I also received a memorial Commission as Captain by brevet U. S. V. at the close of the war.

Very respectfully,

Thomas J. Hassett

[Source: National Archives Adjutant General's Office Correspondence File Numbers 994910 and 2187969]Manuscript 17****

It is unusual that Hassett applied for a Congressional Medal on Honor for "himself." This casual application in the year 1914 suggests that Hassett was unfamiliar with the qualifications for a Medal of Honor and the rigors of the application process. This "unfamiliarity" to precise military detail is uncharacteristic for Hassett. Hassett wrote several in-depth articles on the Civil War for his local home town newspaper in the years 1912 and 1913. In these articles, written for the West Winfield Star, West Winfield, NY, Hassett demonstrates good authorship skills and a command of precise Civil War facts. In his last article in the Star, published on February 7, 1913, Hassett concludes the article by stating several detailed facts, such as: that his Regiment "had at different times seven regimental commanders, none of whom are now living. Four private soldiers won Medals of Honor for bravery on the battlefield, one line officer won a memorial from Congress for services in battle and on one occasion three privates were promoted lieutenants on the battlefield." Given this kind of understanding in the year 1913 of the various types of recognitions that members of his Regiment received, and what was required by these members to receive them, i.e.: bravery on the battlefield, his statement one year later in 1914 that, "I respectfully apply for myself a Congressional medal such as are given to the old soldiers of both armies of the civil war period," seems odd. Surely Hassett must have known in the year 1914 that Medals of Honor were earned and secured through a rigorous process, not just merely given to the old soldiers of both armies of the Civil War period. This disparity in the command of details between Hassett's newspaper articles and his 1914 letter is unexplainable. It does call into question whether or not the detailed and "fact rich" Civil War newspaper articles alleged to have been written by Hassett were in fact written by him. Were these articles written for Hassett by another person like an interviewer? Were they only partially written by Hassett? The answer may never be known. One has to question the authenticity of these newspaper articles instead of the letter because the July 18, 1914, letter contains Hassett's signature and is penned with his handwriting. The newspaper articles are typeset and could have been written by anybody.

[Source: West Winfield Star, West Winfield, New York, editions November 15, 1912, December 27, 1912 and February 7, 1913. Photocopies of T. J. Hassett articles in the possession of the author]**Manuscript 147**

The following letter shows Hassett did qualify for a Civil War Campaign Badge:

NATIONAL ARCHIVES AND RECORDS ADMINISTRATION
December 16, 2003

Dear Mr. White:

Thank you for your note of December 12 regarding Capt. Thomas J. Hassett, 121st New York Infantry, Civil War…. As evidenced by the enclosed copy of the "record card" to part of the AGO document file I sent you the other year, Hassett was authorized to purchase a Civil War Campaign Medal on July 21, 1914. Whether or not he did cannot be determined. For information on the Civil War Campaign Medal you should consult your local library or various on-line bibliographies.

Sincerely,

MICHAEL E. PILGRIM, Senior Archivist for Records Control, Records Control Staff

Enclosures (RECORD CARD)
July 20 1914

To: War Department

Thomas J. Hassett, Late Co. F, 121st N.Y. Brevet Capt., U. S. V. Civil War, From: Self, West Winfield, N.Y., Date of communication: July 19, 1914, Purpose of communication: To Secy. Of War

Makes application for a "Congressional Medal"

And incloses 50 cts. Silver, (Civil War Campaign Badge)

[Source: Written communication and "Record Card" photocopy in the possession of the author; Adjutant General's Office Correspondence File for T. J. Hassett; #994910 and 2187969; National Archives, Washington, DC]**Manuscript 136**

It is clear from this "Record Card" found in the National Archives that Thomas J. Hassett applied for a "Congressional Medal" on July 19, 1914, but was awarded instead a Civil War Campaign Badge. Civil War Campaign Badges were offered to all Civil War veterans with documented proof of service in the Civil War.

2. Thomas J. Hassett was a First Lieutenant during the Battle of Sailor's Creek and Harris Hawthorn was a Private. It should be noted that Hassett was a member of company **K** and Hawthorn was a member of company **F** of the 121st New York. This could explain the "cross out" found in this Hassett letter. This "cross out" is where Hassett wrote that Hawthorn was of Company **K** and then Hawthorn subsequently corrected the text and crossed **K** out and wrote the letter **F**. Hassett must have believed at the time of his writing this letter that Hawthorn was in his own company **K**. This is a very important point which will be expounded upon shortly in this report.

3. Hassett's account of passing General Sheridan's headquarters about a mile and a half from the creek, with the Union ranks forming on the other side of the creek and charging the enemy, are all consistent with other reliable accounts of the Battle of Sailor's Creek.

4. This part of the Hassett's account is most interesting. "Got so close to the enemy that we could easily distinguish their officers. Just at the critical moment, General Lee rushed in front of his corps shouting to his men to stand firm. But just at that moment another brave man rushed in front of his comrades of Company **K (F)** 121st New York Volunteers, and at the point of his bayonet demanded and received the surrender of the young General. The name of the soldier was H. S. Hawthorn." This statement would indicate that the battle was still very active at this point in time and Custis Lee's troops were still a well organized unit when Custis Lee was captured by Hawthorn. If this is true, it would have been extremely unusual for Major General Custis Lee to rush unprotected in front of his troops when the Federal enemy was so close by. This is particularly true if the battle was still well organized with well defined Confederate and Federal lines, as suggested by this Hassett account. Harris Hawthorn is extremely lucky he did not get shot by Custis Lee's troops who would have been immediately behind their General when Custis Lee rushed forward. Custis Lee's troops would have been tenaciously dedicated to protecting Custis Lee as their Division commander when Hawthorn made his move to capture Custis Lee. It is impossible to imagine why Custis Lee's troops immediately behind Custis Lee did not try to desperately wrest their Major General away from Hawthorn's grasp. It should have been very easy to do since Hawthorn was by himself with a pointed bayonet as described by Hassett in his account of a "one-on-one" (Hawthorn vs. Custis Lee) type of capture.

5. Concerning Hassett's account that General Custis Lee was actively involved in trying to secure the surrender of his troops once he was captured by Hawthorn, it is necessary to review again Custis Lee's own words as contained in his Official Battle Report on the Battle of Sailor's Creek. Custis Lee created his Report shortly after the battle and his memory should have been somewhat fresh concerning the events. An excerpt is as follow:

Finding that Kershaw's division, which was on my right, had been obliged to retire in consequence of the enemy having turned his right flank, and that my command was entirely surrounded, to prevent useless sacrifice of life the firing was stopped by some of my officers aided by some of the enemy's, and the officers and men taken as prisoners of war.

[Source: "Report of General G. W. C. Lee from 2nd to 6th April, 1865, Southern Historical Society Transactions (1874) page 118-121 and Official Records, Volume 46, Series 1, "The Appomattox Campaign"; Pages 1296-1298] Manuscript 64****

If Custis Lee is giving an accurate account in his Official Report of the cease fire that took place and the subsequent surrender of his troops, Custis Lee does not appear to have been actively involved in this cease fire and surrender. It would appear that some of his officers, not Custis Lee, initiated the cease fire and surrender. If this is a correct interpretation of Custis Lee's account in his Official Report, then this would contradict Hassett's account where Hassett states that Custis Lee was very much involved in the negotiations of the surrender of his Troops with Col. Olcott of the Federal army.

6. Hassett's account that, "Colonel Egbert Olcott and myself both witnessed the scene," is also interesting. This begs the following question: As eyewitnesses to this event, why were Olcott's and Hassett's testimonies not given to Lieutenant Judge Advocate H. E. Hindmarsh and recorded in the Official Records? Surely their testimonies would have been much more powerful than Hawthorn's own testimony in establishing proof of the capture of Custis Lee. This can not be explained that perhaps Col. Olcott was not aware that Hawthorn was giving his written testimony about this matter to Judge Hindmarsh. In fact, Colonel Olcott, or the person writing the Official Report for Colonel Olcott, was well aware that Hawthorn was giving his own testimony to Judge Hindmarsh. This is due to the fact that Olcott's Official Report references Hawthorn's written testimony as a definitive attachment to this Report. If Olcott really did eyewitness this event, and if he knew that Hawthorn was giving his own written testimony on the capture of Custis Lee, surely Olcott would have given his own testimony to supplement Hawthorn's. This would have made his Official Report much more "iron clad" concerning the capture of Custis Lee and could have "put to bed" the controversy concerning the matter, with the use of the word "controversy" being Olcott's own word in his Report.

7. Colonel Olcott died February 23, 1882, and naturally was not available to support Hawthorn in his application for the Medal of Honor in 1894.

8. The account goes on to state, "General Lee requested to be allowed to return and surrender his corps – but Colonel Olcott, who was also on foot refused the request but ordered comrade Hawthorn to conduct General Lee to Sheridan's Headquarters." This account would once again suggest that Custis Lee's troops were still organized at this stage of the battle. The fact is, Custis Lee would have had to have an organized force on the battlefield for Custis Lee to have wanted to return to them and tender their surrender. If this is all true, it is hard to believe that this type of negotiations would have taken place on an active bullet flying battlefield between Custis Lee, Harris Hawthorn, and Egbert Olcott. It is even more surprising that Custis Lee would have even made such a request. How could Custis Lee possibly think that Col. Olcott would have granted him such a request? If Custis Lee were to return to his troops, he would have never come back to surrender his troops to Col. Olcott. Surely Custis Lee would have kept on fighting with the full protection of his men now with him. Custis Lee would have known that Col. Olcott would have been of this mindset, and surely would have been loath to ask this embarrassing question of Olcott.

9. Hassett's account indicates a tussle after the capture; "No sooner had he started, however, than an officer in the other regiment (**Author Note:** "37th Mass." was inserted here by Hawthorn) referred to attempted to take charge of the prisoner. My orderly, Sergeant Tom Smith, reported the fact to me and I called Colonel Olcott's attention to it. When the Colonel raised his sword as if to strike the officer down, when the latter quickly got away. The Colonel then ordered me to take charge of the prisoner. With orderly Tom Smith and Private H. S. Hawthorn, we conducted the prisoner to where we supposed General Sheridan's Headquarters to be." It would appear from these statements that T. J. Hassett's attention got diverted between the time that he eye witnessed the capture of General Custis Lee by Hawthorn and the time that the other Regiment attempted to take charge of the prisoner. This is manifested by the fact that Tom Smith had to call Hassett's attention to the matter. It is also very unusual that Colonel Olcott would raise his sword "as if to strike down" another Union officer within his own Division. This act of attempting to strike down, or perhaps even mortally wound, a fellow Union officer most assuredly would have created a much bigger controversy for Olcott within the Federal elite hierarchy than the controversy that later ensued around who really captured of Custis Lee.

10. Hassett's account of meeting a staff officer of General Sheridan's, the horse given to Custis Lee and the turning over of General Custis Lee to a Major of the 121st New York, is all interesting. T. J. Hassett appears to be very bitter toward this staff officer, to the point of wanting to "even the score" with him, what ever that might mean.

11. The following statement is interesting, "If due credit has never been given you for the capture of Custis Lee, the fault has been with our Major to whom we turned over the prisoner." The author is not sure why T. J. Hassett might believe at this point in time, when Hawthorn was just simply requesting a statement from Hassett, that Hawthorn might not been given "due credit' for the

capture of General Custis Lee. Did Hassett know at this early stage in the process that Hawthorn was actively pursuing a Medal of Honor? In addition, if Colonel Olcott eye witnessed the event as suggested by Hassett, how could this Major have been at fault for Hawthorn not receiving proper credit for the capture of Custis Lee? The fault would have had to reside with Col. Olcott, who should have personally risen to the defense of Hawthorn and given his own personal written testimony that Hawthorn did indeed capture Custis Lee, not the Major who took custody of Custis Lee from Hassett.

12. It is surprising that Harris Hawthorn did not secure the testimony of Sergeant Tom Smith during his application process, given Smith's close involvement in the matter. Tom Smith lived in Springfield and Middlefield, Otsego County, NY, after the Civil War. Smith was living in Middlefield in 1911 at the age of 75. It would appear that Tom Smith was alive and would have been available to Hawthorn to provide invaluable supporting testimony during Hawthorn's initial application process and surely during the 37th Massachusetts Protest Case which was to come three years later. As an interesting aside, Tom Smith suffered a very severe foot injury at the battle of Spotsylvania, VA, May 12, 1864. He was hospitalized from that date through December, 1864. His injury is described as follows:

… His disability arises from a gunshot wound in the left foot, the ball striking the big toe and severing the Phalanges, and passed along the Metatarsus bone and escaping by the internal malleolus, leaving this foot permanently disabled.

[Source: Thomas Smith Pension File, numbers 261599 and 409897; National Archives, Washington, DC]** Manuscript 97**

Given the severity of this injury and permanent disablement of his left foot, he must not have been able to travel very far from his Regiment's original position on the Sailor's Creek battlefield. One has to question how a disabled Tom Smith was able to get into the middle of this altercation of bringing Custis Lee to the Federal rear, when the location of Custis Lee's capture was a considerable distance from Tom Smith's 121st New York original battlefield position.

BIOGRAPHY:

SMITH, THOMAS—Age, 25 years. Enlisted, August 5, 1862, at Butternuts, to serve three years; mustered in as private, Co. K, August 23, 1862; promoted corporal and First sergeant, no dates; mustered out with company, June 25, 1865, near Hall's Hill, VA; also borne as Thomas H. Smith.
[Source: Annual Report of the Adjutant-General of the State of New York for the Year 1903, Serial No. 36, Albany, NY Oliver A. Quayle; 1904]** Manuscript 127**

14. Given the importance of Hassett's testimony for Harris Hawthorn, being for all intents and purposes the corner stone of credible eye witness testimony for Hawthorn's Medal of Honor application file, the author was extremely fortunate to uncover another version of Hassett's testimony. This version was created many years after his 1894 version and was found in the February 7, 1913 newspaper edition of the West Winfield Star, West Winfield, NY, as cited earlier. This account of the Battle of Sailor's Creek and Harris Hawthorn is as follows:

… our corps reached the line in front of Ewell on the afternoon of the 6th. It was 4 o'clock when our lines were completely formed and the order to advance was given. A low wooded ridge extends along the north bank of the Little Sailor's creek. On the brow of the ridge Ewell's corps was deployed in line of battle awaiting our approach. Slowly and steadily our column moved forward up the wooded ridge, in face of a galling fire from the enemy, with bayonets fixed—this being our favorite way of going into battle. When close up to the enemie's line the order came to "charge bayonets." As we advanced the Confederates retreated in order and kept up a desperate fusillade until nightfall. This was the last desperate fusillade until nightfall. This was the last desperate effort of Lee to save his army. Our regimental loss in the battle was eight men killed and many more wounded of the 121st. Just as the enemie's lines began to waver and fall back a Confederate general in command of a division appeared in front of my company and about midway between the lines, attended by one or two orderlies. He was noticed by a private soldier of the company, H. S. Hawthorn, who dashed forward in the midst of a rain

of minnie balls and ordered the General to surrender. Single handed and alone Hawthorne brought his prisoner and his companions into our lines. He proved to be Charles Custiar Lee, a nephew of Robert. For this daring feat Hawthorne received a "Medal of Honor" from Congress. Lee was held on the firing line until the battle was over and then conducted to Sheridan's headquarters. The regiment captured also about 200 other prisoners in this action and the corps captured besides these a whole division of Ewell's command with Ewell himself. They were taken the next day under guard to City Point and the Sixth Corps pushed on westward toward Appomattox County on a road parallel to the one taken by Lee's army as they retreated from Amelia Court House after the Battle of Sailor's Creek.

[Source: Feb. 7, 1913 edition of the West Winfield Star, West Winfield, New York. The title of the column is entitled: Written for the Star. "INITIATION INTO THE WAYS OF WARFARE," by T. J. Hassett, late Capt. Co. K, 121st N. Y. V. and Co. I, 65th NY Veterans]**Manuscript 125**

There are many important points contained in this version of T. J. Hassett's account of the Battle of Sailor's Creek. These important points are:

A. Hassett describes the 121st New York charging the Confederate line with "bayonets fixed." He also describes the Confederates retreating in order to maintain a desperate fusillade until nightfall. As will be seen later in this report, this account differs significantly from an account given by a Major Basinger who commanded the 18th Georgia Battalion which directly opposed the 121st New York at the Battle of Sailor's Creek. In this account, Basinger describes his 18th Georgia pushing the 121st New York back to Sailor's Creek with a charge of their own.

B. This Hassett statement is interesting, "just as the enemie's lines began to waver and fall back, a Confederate general in command of a division appeared in front of my company and about midway between the lines, attended by one or two orderlies." It is most difficult to see how this Confederate General, Custis Lee, got stuck with his orderlies midway between the Confederate and Federal battle lines. Reason would dictate that he would have been one of the first to fall back from the Federal bayonet charge, remaining behind his own lines and orchestrating the retreating fusillade. It is hard to imagine that a Division commanding Major General like Custis Lee would have gotten himself so isolated from his troops, even in a wooded area, that he would not be aware of his troop's total retreat. It is also difficult to imagine that his troops would have abandoned their Division commander in such a way as to leave Major General Custis Lee in such a precarious and isolated position that he could be easily captured by a lone advancing Federal Private like Hawthorn.

C. This statement by Hassett is also interesting, "he was noticed by a private soldier **of the company**, H. S. Hawthorn, who dashed forward in the midst of a rain of minnie balls and ordered the General to surrender." Hassett is again mistaking in this newspaper article, like he was in his original testimony, that Hawthorn was a member of his own Company. Hassett was a First Lieutenant of Company **K** and Hawthorn was a Private of Company **F** during the Battle of Sailor's Creek, with both Companies belonging to the 121st New York. With the repeat of this mistake by Hassett, first made in 1894 and now repeated in 1913, Hassett must have really believed that Hawthorn was a part of his own Company **K** during the Battle of Sailor's Creek. If Custis Lee was indeed directly in front of Company **K** during the battle when he was captured as stated by Hassett, one has to now question whether or not Hawthorn was actually in close enough proximity to Custis Lee to capture him, since Hawthorn was in Company **F**. The distance between Company **K** (Hassett's Company) and that of Company **F** (Hawthorn's Company) could have been significant as components of an organized Federal battle line as described by Hassett. However this event might have happened, it does underscore the question posed earlier in this report. Why did an officer of Company **K** (Lt. Thomas J. Hassett) witness Hawthorn's capture of Custis Lee and not an officer of Hawthorn's own Company **F** (Lt. Charles Barr, commander of Company **F** at the Battle of Sailor's Creek according to the "Morning Report"). Once again, the only reasonable explanation for this event is that Hawthorn somehow got mixed into Hassett's Company **K** during the initial charge by the 121st New York on Custis Lee's troops.

D. It would appear from Hassett's statement about a "rain of minnie balls" that Custis Lee's troops where firing within close range of Custis Lee in a battle that was still very much active. This has to beg the question once again why Custis Lee did not fall back with the rest of his troops who were still very much firing their guns at the Federals in an organized fusillade? Why was Custis Lee, a Division commander, stuck so isolated midway between two battle lines? This does not seem like something that a capable Major General like Custis Lee, who was responsible for an entire Confederate Division, would have allowed to have happened. One has to also question how Hawthorn single handedly ordered General Custis Lee to surrender, when Custis Lee had one or two of his orderlies by his side that would have had an obligation to protect him. In addition, Custis Lee's Confederate troops were raining minnie balls all around, indicating they were in close proximity to Custis Lee. Hawthorn would have been tremendously out numbered by active Confederate troops while attempting this single handed capture of Custis Lee.

E. Hassett's reference to, "single handed and alone Hawthorne brought his prisoner and his companions into our lines," is an obvious rebuttal to a 37th Massachusetts Protest Case that was filed in the year 1897 and will be described in detail later in this report. Bottom line, this just seems like an unbelievable feat for Hawthorn to accomplish. Not only was Hawthorn able to single handedly capture an enemy General, but also all his orderlies who were presumably well armed, and all this was all done on an active battlefield with minnie balls flying all around.

F. Hassett's statement that, "he proved to be Charles Custiar Lee, nephew of Robert," is a little disturbing to the author. Robert E. Lee had a brother, Charles Carter Lee, but he was not a soldier in the Civil War nor did he have a son Charles Carter Lee, which would have been a nephew of Robert E. Lee, if such a person existed. Surely Hassett must have been referring to George Washington Custis Lee, son of Robert E. Lee. Hassett must have been just confused on this important point so many years after the fact, from 1865 to 1913. Still, if Hassett felt that this fact was important to include in his newspaper article, and all of his other facts in his newspaper articles appear to be highly accurate, the author is somewhat bothered that Hassett would be so confused on the exact name and relationship to Robert E. Lee of the person Hawthorn captured. Especially when Hassett was espousing the heroic nature of the act which was performed for his Company K of the 121st New York.

G. This Hassett statement is insightful, "Lee was held on the firing line until the battle was over and then conducted to Sheridan's headquarters." In an active battle like the one portrayed by Hassett, it is difficult to understand why Confederate Major General Custis Lee, son of Robert E. Lee, was kept on the firing line where he could have been easily shot and killed. Why was Custis Lee not immediately conducted to the rear, particularly given his importance? The only possible answer to this question is that perhaps the 121st New York wanted to showcase the capture of Division commander Custis Lee so that his remaining Confederate troops would give up and surrender. The author believes this scenario is highly unlikely.

H. It is a little disturbing that there are some significant differences between Hassett's 1894 and 1913 versions of the capture of Custis Lee. The versions are consistent in two respects in that Hassett describes charging the enemy and Custis Lee being conducted to Sheridan's Headquarters. The versions are inconsistent in two significant respects in that Hassett's 1894 account describes Custis Lee rushing to the front of his Corps shouting to his men to stand firm, while the 1913 account describes Custis Lee being isolated with one or two orderlies in a desperately retreating fusillade of his troops. In addition, the 1894 account describes Hawthorn capturing Custis Lee and then Colonel Olcott refusing Custis Lee's request to return to his troops and surrender his Corps, while the 1913 account states that Hawthorn captured Custis Lee together with his orderlies and brought them directly into the Federal lines. These inconsistencies cannot be reconciled. Perhaps they can be attributed to the passing of time and the fading of precise memories. For the purpose of this report, Hassett's earlier 1894 account, which was written approximately 29 years after the fact as opposed to 48 years after the fact, will be assumed to be a more accurate reflection of Hassett's memory of the actual events.

I. An important question that must be asked concerning Hassett's testimony for Harris Hawthorn, both Hassett's 1894 and the 1913 accounts, is; "did Hassett have any other motive for offering this testimony for Hawthorn other than desiring to tell the complete truth about the matter"? A possible answer might lie in the "Morning Report" of Company **K** of the 121st New York written the morning after the Battle of Sailor's Creek. This April 7, 1865, "Morning Report" for Company **K** clearly states that Thomas J. Hassett, First Lieutenant, commanded Company **K** at the Battle of Sailor's Creek. A company was normally commanded by a Captain, but in the absence of a Captain, devolved to a First Lieutenant like T. J. Hassett. With Hassett commanding Company **K** at the Battle of Sailor's Creek, and with Hassett insisting in both of his accounts that Hawthorn captured Custis Lee and Hawthorn was a member of his own Company **K** (Hawthorn was actually a member of Company **F**), was Hassett trying to capture some of the glory for himself as the commander of the Federal Company that ultimately captured Major General George Washington Custis Lee, eldest son of the famous Robert E. Lee? The answer will never be known, but the possibility surely exists and this can not be lightly dismissed.

[Source: The 121st NY Infantry: Record Group 94: Records of the Adjutant General's Office, Entry 112-115: Book Records of the Union Volunteer Organizations-121st NY Infantry, Morning Reports for Companies A-K, Vol. 6 of 6, National Archives, Washington, DC]**Manuscript 153**

13. It is learned from Thomas J. Hassett's military service record that he received a severe bayonet wound to the neck in the battle of the Wilderness on May 5th, 1864. He was hospitalized until March, 1865, when he was promoted to 1st Lieutenant and assigned to the command of Company K (coming from Company F) of the 121st New York. He was brevetted for "gallant and meritorious services before Petersburg and at the battle of Little Sailor's Creek, VA." From all accounts from his military service record, Hassett was a solid soldier for the Federal Army.

[Source: Military Service Record of Thomas J. Hassett in the National Archives, Washington, DC]**Manuscript 126**

BIOGRAPHY:

HASSETT, THOMAS J.—Age, 18 years. Enrolled, August 12, 1862, at Exeter, to serve three years; mustered in as private, Co. F, August 23, 1862; promoted sergeant and first sergeant, no dates; mustered in as first lieutenant, Co. K, March 21, 1865; as captain, May 21, 1865; transferred to Co. I, Sixty-fifth Infantry, June 24, 1865. Commissioned First Lieutenant, March 14, 1865, with rank from February 22, 1865, vice T. E. C. Howland promoted; captain, May 16, 1865, with rank from April 29, 1865, vice T. C. Howland killed in action.

[Source: Annual Report of the Adjutant, General of the State of New York for the Year 1903, Serial No. 36, Albany, NY, Oliver A. Quayle; 1904]**Manuscript 127**

EXHIBIT-H-AF-2

Introduction:

Mr. S. D. Locke of Hoosick Falls, NY, appears to be championing the application for a Medal of Honor for Harris Hawthorn. Mr. Locke appears to be using House of Representative Charles D. Haynes of Kinderhook, NY, to influence the government concerning this application. This is a letter from Sylvanus D. Locke to Honorable Charles D. Hayes.

Evidence:

FROM: Sylvanus D. Locke, Automatic Binding Harvester
Hoosick Falls, NY, Oct. 17, 1894
TO: Hon. Chas. D. Haynes, Kinderhook, N.Y.

I would like, in the Hawthorne matter, to ascertain the address of General (G. W.) Custis Lee and General Wheaton. If you can aid me and will do so soon I shall be much obliged.

Hastily Yours,   S. D. Locke

[Source: National Archives file 4O1673, Medal of Honor Application File for Harris Hawthorn]**Manuscript 15**

Comments and Supporting Evidence:

1. Sylvanus D. Locke was a well known figure in Hoosick Falls, NY. This was also Harris Hawthorn's home town. Locke invented a harvester machine and developed a successful business. The exact connection between Mr. Locke and Mr. Hawthorn is unknown.
2. It is interesting that Hawthorn and Locke were trying to get a hold of General Custis Lee and General Frank Wheaton to help substantiate their claims made in Hawthorn's Medal of Honor application. Hawthorn had consistently maintained that he was one of several men detailed by Colonel Olcott to deliver the captured Custis Lee to the headquarters of General Wheaton. Given this claim by Hawthorn, it makes sense that Hawthorn and Locke would try to get a hold of General Wheaton for proof of this event. This is, however, totally contrary to Hassett's account for Hawthorn, which states that only Hawthorn was ordered by Col. Olcott to bring General Custis Lee to the headquarters of General Sheridan.
3. One has to wonder why Hawthorn waited such a long time, from 1865 to 1894, to file an application for Medal of Honor. Perhaps he was prompted to do so by his local G. A. R. group.

EXHIBIT-H-AF-3

Introduction:
This is a letter from Mr. S. D. Locke to Honorable Chas. D. Haynes pursuing a Medal for Harris Hawthorn.

Evidence:

FROM: Sylvanus D. Locke, Automatic Binding Harvester
Hoosick Falls, NY, Nov. 22, 1894
TO: Hon. Chas. D. Haynes, Kinderhook, Col. Co. N.Y.

Mr. Hawthorne has been trying to get into communication with General Wheaton but has so far failed. He thinks the General will remember the fact that Major Stiles (he may have the name wrong) was delivered to him as a prisoner with General Custis Lee by a private soldier on the sixth of April 1865. Mr. Hawthorne also fails to get further communication from Captain T. J. Hassett. For this reason, I think it best to rest Hawthorne's claim for a medal on the official records in the War Department, with possibly the letter from Captain Hassett which I showed you in Kinderhook and which I enclose herewith to you. You can use your judgement about using it. If you desire to see me further about this matter, I will run down to Kinderhook; or, if you are to visit Troy or Albany before returning to Washington, I can meet you there if you think best. In any event, I would like to meet you. It is too bad that you were beaten, but you were not without good company. I hope you will find time to take an early opportunity to secure a medal for Mr. Hawthorne and so put both him and myself under great obligations to you. Please let me hear from you soon.
Truly Yours,
S. D. Locke

[Source: National Archives File 401673, Medal of Honor Application File for Harris Hawthorn]**Manuscript 15**

Comments and Supporting Evidence:

1. It would appear that Mr. Locke and Hawthorn could not locate and get any communication from General Wheaton, commander of the 1st Division, 6th Army Corps, at the Battle of Sailor's Creek.
2. It is very important to note the following statement by Locke, "He thinks the General will remember the fact that Major Stiles (he may have the name wrong) was delivered to him as a prisoner with General Custis Lee by a private soldier of the sixth of April 1865." This statement could suggest that Major Stiles and General Custis Lee were captured approximately at the same time and place. This supposition can be corroborated by Major Stiles' own account of his capture as found in Exhibit W–PF–23 outlined latter in this report. If indeed Major Stiles and General Custis Lee were captured approximately at the same time and place, was the 37th Massachusetts or the 121st New York in the

best battlefield position to produce these two captures? This author will attempt to definitively answer this question later in this report.

3. In the six volumes of the Regimental books for the 121st New York Infantry in the National Archives, there is the following record: *"Private Harris Hawthorn of Company F was promoted to Corporal, Vice Chas Metcalf being promoted."* According to this record, this promotion was retroactively effective to March 1, 1865. So Hawthorn is correct when he states that he was a private at the Battle of Sailor's Creek, having been promoted to a corporal after the Battle of Sailor's Creek on April 20, 1865. **[Source: 121st New York Regimental Books; Record Group 94, Stack Area 9W3, Row 9, Compartment 30, Shelf A, Special Order No. 29 from Headquarters 121st Regt. N. Y. S. Vols., dated April 20, 1865]**Manuscript 49****

4. Hawthorn's claim that he delivered Major Stiles and General Custis Lee to Federal General Wheaton is in direct contradiction to Thomas J. Hassett's account that states Hawthorn was ordered by Colonel Olcott to deliver Custis Lee to General Sheridan's headquarters. This occurred only after Colonel Olcott refused General Custis Lee's request to return to his troops to surrender them to Colonel Olcott. This Hawthorn claim also contradicts Hassett's account which states Hassett, Tom Smith, and Hawthorn ultimately delivered General Custis Lee to a Major of the 121st New York when they could not locate Sheridan's headquarters.

5. Hawthorn's account seems to make more sense to the author than the Hassett account. General Wheaton was in charge of the Federal Infantry Division of which Hawthorn was a part. One would think that if Hawthorn was ordered by his immediate superior to bring Custis Lee to the rear, it would have been to Wheaton headquarters, not Sheridan's. It is worth mentioning here the role of General Sheridan at the Battle of Sailor's Creek. General Sheridan was a higher ranking officer when compared to General Wheaton, and General Wheaton reported to General Wright who in turn mostly reported to General Sheridan during this battle. General Sheridan was, however, primarily involved in directing the Federal Cavalry assault, while General Wheaton and General Wright were primarily involved in directing the Federal Infantry assault. The Federal Cavalry, under Sheridan's direction, galloped in front of a segment of the retreating Confederate army, severing the Confederates' escape route into North Carolina along the Richmond and Danville Railroad. General Sheridan's Calvary was primarily engaged against Confederate General Richard H. Anderson's Corps. General Wheaton's and General Wright's Infantry was primarily engaged against Confederate General R. S. Ewell's Corps, of which General Custis Lee's Division was a part. General Wright commanded the Federal 6th Infantry Corps and General Wheaton commanded the 1st Division within this Corps.

6. It is interesting to note and causes one to ask the question why Hawthorn, "fails to get further communication from Captain T. J. Hassett" (presumably after Hassett's original September 9, 1894, letter to Hawthorn). Perhaps Hawthorn was attempting to contact Hassett again to ask Hassett to correct some points in his original letter.

7. It is also very interesting to note that Mr. Locke seems to be questioning the use of Hassett's September 9, 1894, letter in Hawthorn's application. Locke states that it can be "possibly" submitted with Hawthorn's Medal of Honor application and that the Honorable Chas. D. Haynes should "use his judgment about using it." It would appear that Locke and Hawthorn might have had some concerns with the accuracy of the letter's content. They could have been concerned that the inconsistencies between the Hawthorn and Hassett accounts could have been brought to light at this critical time of application.

8. Once again, Mr. Locke is clearly championing this application for Harris Hawthorn by trying hard to meet with the Hon. Chas D. Haynes in Troy or Albany. This strenuous effort on the part of Mr. Locke is underscored by his statement, "I hope you will find the time to take an early opportunity to secure a medal for Mr. Hawthorn and so put both him and myself under great obligation to you."

EXHIBIT-H-AF-4

Introduction:

This is the official application document for a Medal of Honor for Harris Hawthorn and it is dated November 26, 1894. This is a Record and Pension document forwarded to the War Department on December 4, 1894.

Evidence:

CASE OF: *H A R R I S   S.   H A W T H O R N E.*
Late of Company F, 121st New York Volunteers
Application for a Medal of Honor

Under date of November 26th, 1894, the Honorable Charles D. Haines, M. C., forwarded to this Department an application from Mr. S. D. Locke, of Hoosick Falls, NY, for a medal of honor in behalf of Mr. Harris S. Hawthorne, of that place, for gallantry in action at the battle of Sailors Creek, VA, April 6, 1865, while serving as a member of Company F, 121st New York Volunteers, he having captured the Confederate general, Custis Lee, in that engagement. In support of the application, Mr. Locke submits a letter from Mr. T. J. Hassett of Birmingham, Ala., late captain, Company K, 121st New York Volunteers, from which the following is an extract: "In regard to your request to give you a statement regarding the capture of General Custis Lee, I will say it gives me pleasure to do so, knowing that you must have some special reason for wanting me to do so, perhaps you are not aware that I received a commission from Congress for services at the battle of Little Sailors Creek, as a memorial. But to your question. in marching towards the scene of the battle we passed General Sheridan's Head Quarters beside the road about a mile and a half from the creek. We opened fire as soon as our ranks were formed in line on the north bank of the creek, and in charging the enemy we became somewhat mixed up with a part of another regiment of infantry but pressed on and in a short time got so close to the enemy they we could easily distinguish their officers. Just at the critical moment General Lee rushed in front of his corps shouting to his men to stand firm. But just at that moment another brave man rushed in front of his comrades of Company F, 121st New York volunteers and at the point of his bayonet demanded and received the surrender of the young general. The name of the soldier was H. S. Hawthorn, Colonel Egbert Olcott and myself both witnessed the scene. General Lee requested to be allowed to return and surrender his corps but Colonel Olcott who was also on foot refused the request but ordered Comrade Hawthorn to conduct General Lee to Sheridan's Head Quarters. No sooner had he started, however, than an officer in the other regiment [37th Mass.] referred to attempted to take charge of the prisoner. My orderly sergeant – Tom Smith – reported the fact to me and I called Colonel Olcott's attention to it, when the Colonel raised his sword as if to strike the officer down when the latter quickly got away. The Colonel then ordered me to take charge of the prisoner. With Orderly Tom Smith and Private H. S. Hawthorn we conducted the prisoner to where we supposed General Sheridan's Head Quarters to be but found they had been removed two miles to the front. But we met one of his staff officers who kindly furnished General Lee a horse to ride and with that staff officer as a guide we started back to find General Sheridan. We recrossed Little Sailors Creek, and about half a mile from the creek we met the Major of the 121st and was glad enough to turn our prisoner over to him. We soon found the regiment and Hawthorn and Smith joined the company, which had bivouacked for the night and I reported all that had transpired to Colonel Olcott in his tent. The battle practically ended with the surrender of Lee. The enemy fell back and night came on." The records show that Harris S. Hawthorne was enrolled, August 11, 1862, as a private in Company F, 121st New York Volunteers, to serve three years; was appointed corporal March 1, 1865, sergeant May 1, 1865, and was mustered out with the company, June 25, 1865. The following are extracts from the official reports of the capture of General Lee, as appears in Vol. 46, Part 1, of the Rebellion Records:

Head Quarters Sixth Army Corps,
Danville, VA, April 29, 1865, Sailors Creek

The First and Third Divisions charged the enemy's position many general officers were captured by the combined forces of the infantry and cavalry, and of those who surrendered to the Sixth Corps were Lieutenant General Ewell and Major General Custis Lee.

H. G. Wright, Major General Commanding.

Headquarters First Division, Sixth Corps.
April 20, 1865

The Second Brigade was ordered to charge and the battle of Sailors Creek was won. This Division (First) took Lieutenant General Ewell and General G. W. Custis Lee.

F. Wheaton, Brevet Major General, U.S. Volunteers

Headquarters First Division, Sixth Corps.
April 18, 1865

The following named enlisted men of the Second Brigade are recommended to the general commanding the corps as deserving special mention and reward for conspicuous bravery and good conduct: Private Harris S. Hawthorne, Company F, One hundred and twenty-first New York Volunteers, captured Brig. Gen. (G. W.) Custis Lee, on the 6th instant.

F. Wheaton, Brevet Major General, U.S. Volunteers

Hdq'rs. Second Brig., First Division, Sixth Army Corps
April 15, 1865

I beg your attention to the following statement of gallant and meritorious service by officers and men of this brigade: Private Harris S. Hawthorne, Company F, One hundred and twenty first, New York State Volunteers, captured Brig. Gen. Custis Lee on the 6th instant.

J. E. Hamblin, Brevet Brigadier General, U.S. Volunteers, Comdg. Brigade

Headquarters 121st New York Volunteers,
April 14, 1865

The one hundred twenty first New York having checked the enemy who were endeavoring to get into the rear of the brigade, was ordered to charge, which it did, driving the enemy in confusion, capturing Gen. Custis Lee and several other officers of high rank, together with two stand of colors. General Lee was captured by private Harris S. Hawthorne, Company F, the proofs of which, there having been some controversy about the matter, accompany this report marked A.

[inclosure A]
Camp in the Field, VA, April 14, 1865

Private Harris S. Hawthorne, Company F, One hundred twenty first New York Volunteers, being duly sworn, says that he knows of his own knowledge that he is the first person (officer or enlisted man) who seized or captured General Custis Lee, of the Confederate Army, in the engagement of the 6th of April; and that he never lost sight of or control of the said General Custis Lee until he delivered him up to Colonel Olcott, commanding One hundred and twenty first New York Volunteers, and that he, Hawthorne, was one of the men detailed by Colonel Olcott on account of said capture, to conduct General Custis Lee to the Headquarters of General Wheaton, commanding First Division, Sixth Army Corps.

H. S. Hawthorne.

Subscribed and sworn to, at Malvern, near Berkesville, VA, this 14th day of April, 1865, before me.

E. Hindmarch, Lieutenant, Judge Advocate, First Division, Sixth Army Corps Camp.

Camp of 121st New York Volunteers,
April 14, 1865

I hereby certify that for more than two years I have well known Harris S. Hawthorne, Company F, one hundred twenty first New York Regiment, as a professed Christian, and have always regarded him worthy of confidence, by the uniform consistency of his religious life. I regard his testimony on any subject as unimpeachable and that no assurance can be stronger than his affirmation under the <u>sanctity</u> of an oath.

John R. Adams, Chaplain of the 121st New York Regiment
[Source: National Archives File 401673, Medal of Honor Application File for Harris Hawthorn]**Manuscript 15**

Comments and Supporting Evidence:

1. It is worth noting that the Record and Pension Office of the War Department received Hawthorn's application from the Honorable Charles D. Haines, M. C., who received it from Mr. S. D. Locke of Hoosick Falls, NY, who sent it in behalf of Mr. Harris S. Hawthorn of Hoosick Falls, NY.

2. It is also interesting to note that the Honorable Charles D. Haines decided to use in support of Hawthorn's application, only a portion of the letter and testimony of T. J. Hassett of Birmingham, AL.

3. The Official Record entries cited in this application once again show a roll-up from E. Olcott (commanding the 121st New York) to J. E. Hamblin (commanding the 2nd Brigade) to F. Wheaton (commanding the 1st Division) to finally H. G. Wright (commanding the 6th Army Corps). As an aside, the Official Records also show that T. J. Hassett was a 1st Lieutenant during the Battle of Sailor's Creek

4. As stated before, there is a disturbing discrepancy between Hassett's accounts which states that General Custis Lee was delivered to General Sheridan's headquarters, and Hawthorn's account and the account in the Official Records, which states that Hawthorn delivered General Custis Lee to the headquarters of General Wheaton, who commanded the 1st Division of the 6th Army Corps at the Battle of Sailor's Creek.

EXHIBIT-H-AF-5

Introduction:

This is a letter dated November 26, 1894, by House of Representative Charles Haines taking Hawthorn's Medal of Honor application to the Secretary of War.

Evidence:

Kinderhook, NY, Nov 26, 1894
TO: Hon. D. S. Lamont, Sec'y of War, Wash DC
Mr. Harris S. Hawthorne, Hoosick Falls, N.Y., late of Co. F. 121st NY Vols., is very anxious to have you grant him a medal. See below letters. Please advise me if you can grant the request.
Yrs Very Truly
Charles D. Haines, M. C.
As to Mr. Hawthorne's capture of Gen'l Custis Lee. See pages 907, 914, 925, 933, 937, 938. Operations in northern and southeastern VA, NC (Jan 1 to 31), W. VA, MD, and PA
[Source: National Archives File 401673, Medal of Honor Application File for Harris Hawthorn]**Manuscript 15**

Comments and Supporting Evidence:

1. Charles D. Haines is apparently a member of the United States House of Representatives, residing in Kinderhook, NY.

2. Mr. Haines is writing, on his official U.S. House of Representatives letterhead, to the Honorable D. S. Lamont who, at the time, is the U.S. Secretary of War residing in Washington, DC. Haines is promoting the award of a Medal of Honor for Mr. Harris Hawthorn.

3. It is interesting to note that Mr. Haines states that Harris Hawthorn "is very anxious to have you grant him a medal." Hawthorn appears to have been very proactive at this stage in his life in trying to obtain a Medal of Honor for himself for the capture of Major General Custis Lee.

EXHIBIT-H-AF-6

Introduction:

The United States Government is acknowledging Hawthorn's application.

Evidence:

December 1st, 1894
TO: Hon. Chas. D. Haines, M. C.,
I have the honor to acknowledge the receipt yesterday of your letter of the 26th ultimo, enclosing papers in connection with an application for a medal of honor in behalf of Mr. Harris S. Hawthorne of Hoosick Falls, N.Y., for meritorious conduct while serving as a member of Company F, 121st New York Volunteers and to inform you that the record of the soldier will be made up and the case prepared for the decision of the Secretary of War. As soon as the case is decided, you will be promptly notified of the result.
Very respectfully,
From: F. C. Ainsworth, Colonel, U.S. Army, Chief, Record and Pension Office
[Source: National Archives File 401673, Medal of Honor Application File for Harris Hawthorn]**Manuscript 15**

Comments and Supporting Evidence:

1. The Honorable Chas D. Haines, MC, is from Kinderhook, NY, which is in close proximity to Hoosick Falls, NY, the homes of S. D. Locke and Harris Hawthorn. This close geographic proximity could account for their personal relationships.
2. The Secretary of War will be deciding the merits of the application for Harris Hawthorn.

EXHIBIT-H-AF-7

Introduction:
These are five letters from the United States Government awarding Harris Hawthorn the Medal of Honor (letters dated December 12, 1894, and December 29, 1894).

Evidence:

(1) *FROM: War Department*
December 12, 1894
By direction of the President let a medal of honor be presented to Harris S. Hawthorne, late Sergeant Co. "F," 121st New York Volunteers. This non-commissioned officer while serving as a Private in the same Company and regiment captured General G. W. Custis Lee of the Confederate Army on April 6, 1865.
Joseph B. Doe, Asst. Secretary of War

(2) *FROM: Record and Pension Office,*
December 12, 1894
M E M O R A N D U M The Assistant Secretary of War has directed the issue of a medal of honor to Sergeant Harris s. Hawthorne, Company F, 121st New York Volunteers, the medal to be engraved as follows:

The Congress to
Sergt. Harris S. Hawthorne,
Co. F. 121 N. Y. Vols.
For Gallantry at Sailors Creek, VA,
April 6, 1865

(3) *FROM: Record and Pension Office*
December 12, 1894
TO: Hon. Charles D. Haines, House of Representatives.
I have the honor to inform you that, by direction of the President and in accordance with the act of Congress approved March 3, 1863, providing for the presentation of medals of honor to such officers, non-commissioned officers and privates as have most distinguished themselves in action, the Assistant Secretary of War has awarded a medal of honor to Harris S. Hawthorne of Hoosick Falls, New York,

late sergeant, Company F, 121st New York Volunteers, for gallantry at Sailors Creek, Virginia, April 6, 1865. The medal will be forwarded to Mr. Hawthorne as soon as suitably engraved.
Very respectfully,
FROM: F. C. Ainsworth, Colonel, U. S. Army, Chief, Record and Pension Office

(4) FROM: Record and Pension Office,
December 29, 1894

TO: Mr. Harris S. Hawthorne, Late sergeant, Company F, 121st New York Volunteers:
I have the honor to inform you that, by direction of the President, and in accordance with the act of Congress approved March 3, 1863, providing for the presentation of medals of honor to such officers, non-commissioned officers and privates as have most distinguished themselves in action, the Assistant Secretary of War has awarded you a medal of honor for gallantry at Sailor's Creek, Virginia, April 6, 1865. The medal has been forwarded to you by registered mail. Upon receipt of the medal please advise this office thereof.
Very respectfully,
FROM: F. C. Ainsworth, Colonel, U. S. Army, Chief, Record and Pension Office.

(5) FROM: Record and Pension Office
December 29, 1894

TO: The Adjutant General, State of New York, Albany.
I have the honor to inform you that, by direction of the President and in accordance with the act of Congress approved March 3, 1863, providing for the presentation of medals of honor to such officers, non-commissioned officers and privates as have most distinguished themselves in action, the Assistant Secretary of War has awarded a medal of honor to Harris S. Hawthorne, late sergeant, Company F, 121st New York Volunteers, for gallantry at Sailor's Creek, Virginia, April 6, 1865.
Very respectfully,
FROM: F. C. Ainsworth, Colonel, U. S. Army, Chief, Record and Pension Office.

[Source: National Archives File 401673, Medal of Honor Application File for Harris Hawthorn]**Manuscript 15**

Comments and Supporting Evidence:

1. Harris Hawthorn is awarded the Medal of Honor by direction of the President in accordance with the Act of Congress which was approved March 3, 1863.
2. This is the first time in the application process that Harris Hawthorn is referenced as a Sergeant. This rank is validated by Special Order Number 39, dated June 10, 1865, at the Headquarters of the 121st New York, which states that Corporal Harris S. Hawthorn, Company F, was promoted to Sergeant, Vice J. S. Scott being discharged.

[Source: 121st New York Infantry Regimental Books, 6 volumes, Record Group 94, Stack Area, 9W3, RCW9, Compartment 30; National Archives, Washington, DC]** Manuscript 49 **

EXHIBIT-H-AF-8

Introduction:

Harris Hawthorn is keeping current with the changes in the ribbon and knot associated with the Medal of Honor (these two letters are dated April 12, 1897, and April 16, 1897).

Evidence:

(1) April 12th/97
Will you please send to me the ribbon and knot as prescribed by act of Congress approved May 2, 1896
Yours Truly,
FROM: Harris S. Hawthorn, Member of the Medal of Honor Legion
The above is the said Harris S. Hawthorn as I have known him for more than five years.
Henry Harrison Post Com. Post W. A. WOOD, Daniel W. Eddy, Quartermaster

(2) *April 16th, 1897*

I am directed by the Secretary of War to inform you that a ribbon of the pattern prescribed and established by the President under the provisions of the Joint Resolution of Congress approved May 2, 1896, to replace the ribbon to which the medal of honor heretofore awarded to you is attached, and a knot to be worn in lieu of the medal, have been forwarded to you by registered mail today. Upon receipt of the ribbon and the knot please advise this office thereof.

Very respectfully,   FROM: F. C. Ainsworth, Colonel, U.S. Army, Chief of Office

[Source: National Archives Files 401673, Medal of Honor Application File for Harris Hawthorn]**Manuscript 15**

Comments and Supporting Evidence:

1. Harris Hawthorn is apparently literate, or at least able to sign his own name, as this document appears to contain his original signature.
2. It would appear that Harris Hawthorn was a member of the W. A. Wood G. A. R. Post (probably located in Hoosick Falls, NY) as early as April 12, 1897. This Post could have initiated Hawthorn's interest in a Medal of Honor back in 1894, when Hawthorn submitted his application. G. A. R. Posts were noted for their involvement in generating a sizeable amount of Medal of Honor applications for Civil War veterans during this 1890's period.

EXHIBIT-H-AF-9

Introduction:

Hawthorn is applying for and did receive the new design and rosette for the Medal of Honor in the year 1907 (there are two documents, one (1) dated May 6th and the other (2) June 19th, 1907).

Evidence:

(1) *Application for Medal of Honor of new design and for Rosette:*

Under the provisions of the Act of Congress approved April 23, 1904, as modified by the Joint Resolution approved February 27, 1907, State of New York, County of Rensl, on this 6th day of May personally appeared before me, a Notary Publick, of the County and State aforesaid, Harris S. Hawthorn, aged 75 years, a resident of Hoosick Falls, in the County of Rensselaer and State of New York, who, being duly sworn, declares that he is Harris S. Hawthorn, the identical person of that name who was in the military service of the United States as a member of Company F, in the 121st Regiment of New York Inf Vol., that a Congressional Medal of Honor was awarded him on or about the [blank] day of between the Years of 1890 and 1895 at which time he was residing at Hoosick Falls, in the State of New York; that he received the Medal at Hoosick Falls, on or about the [blank] day between year of 1890 and 1895; that the Medal was awarded him for capture of Confederate Gen. Custis Lee, Battle of Sailors Creek, April 6th, 1865; and is inscribed as follows: The Congress to Sergt Harris S. Hawthorn, Co F 121st N.Y. Vol. for Gallantry at Sailor's Creek, VA, April 6, 1865. This declaration is made for the purpose of securing the Congressional Medal of Honor and the rosette provided for in the Act of Congress approved April 23, 1904, as modified by the Joint Resolution approved February 27, 1907, and the applicant desires that the new medal and the rosette be sent to him at No. 73 Elm Street, in the Village of Hoosick Falls, County of Rensselaer, State of New York.

Harris S. Hawthorn

Also personally appeared before me Alonzo Lohnes, aged 71 years, now a resident of the Village of Hoosick Falls, in the County of Rensselaer and State of New York, and Joseph Hale, aged 65 years, now a resident of the Village of Hoosick Falls, in the County of Rensselaer and State of New York, to me well known as credible persons, who, being duly sworn, declare that they have been for 40 years, and 40 years, respectively, personally acquainted with the applicant hereinbefore named; that they saw him sign his name to the foregoing application; that they have every reason to believe that he is the identical person he herein represents himself to be and that the foregoing affidavit by him subscribed is correct and true.   *Alonzo Lohnes, Joseph Hale*

Walter A. Wood Post, No. 294, G. A. R, Hoosick Falls, N.Y., May 25, 1907
I have known the applicant (Harris S. Hawthorn) for 25 years as an honest upright citizen. For particulars as to the reasons for awarding the Medal of Honor to Comrade Hawthorn see Official Records War of the Rebellion series 1 vol 46 Page 925 also pages 937 and 938. Capture of Brig Gen G. W. Custis Lee, C. S. A. at the Battle of Sailors Creek, VA,, April 6, 1865. The two witnesses to affidavit Alonzo Lohnes, Co L 6th N. Y. Cav and Joseph Hale Co D 21st N. Y. Cav are Veterans of the Civil War.
I remain yours respectfully,
Lawrence E. Buckley, Chaplain

(2) *The Secretary of War has directed the issue of a medal of honor of new design to Harris S. Hawthorn, sergeant, Company F, 121st New York Infantry Volunteers, to whom a medal of honor of the old design was issued December 28, 1894. The new medal is to be engraved as follows:*

The Congress
To Sergeant Harris S. Hawthorn,
Co. F., 121st N.Y. Inf. Vols.
Sailor's Creek, VA, April 6, 1865

I am directed by the Acting Secretary of War to inform you that, under the provisions of the act of Congress approved April 23, 1904, as modified by the join resolution of Congress approved February 27, 1907, a medal of honor of new design and a rosette to be worn in lieu thereof have this day been issued to you. The medal, the rosette and the Medal of Honor ribbon have been sent to you under separate cover by registered mail. Please acknowledge their receipts.
Very respectfully,
F. C. Ainsworth
[Source: National Archives Files 401673, Medal of Honor Application File for Harris Hawthorn]**Manuscript 15**

Comments and Supporting Evidence:
1. In the year 1907 Hawthorn applies for and receives from the Adjutant General's Office the new design and the rosette for his Medal of Honor. Mr. Hawthorn appears to be very active in keeping up to date on the regulatory changes to the Medal of Honor, all the way up to the year 1907.
2. It is worth noting now in this report, that it would appear that the Adjutant General's Office of the War Department was not aware, or chose to ignore, a determination made by the Secretary of War as a result of a 37th Massachusetts Protest Case filed in the year 1897. This determination had a significant bearing on Hawthorn's Medal of Honor and it will be disclosed in complete detail later in this report.

EXHIBIT-H-AF-10

Introduction:
Hawthorn is acknowledging receipt of his Medal of Honor.

Evidence:
Harris S, Hawthorn acknowledges receipt of the New Medal of Honor
Received A. G. O. June 24, 1907
[Source: National Archives Files 401673, Medal of Honor Application File for Harris Hawthorn]**Manuscript 15**

Comments and Supporting Evidence:
1. This is the last piece of documentation in Hawthorn's Medal of Honor application file. As will be seen later in this work, it is surprising that Hawthorn still has a valid Medal of Honor in 1907.

CHAPTER FIVE:
Corporal David D. White

Exhibit Category	**Code Key**
Claimant Four:	**W**

Corporal David D. White
37th Massachusetts Infantry
3rd Brigade, 1st Division, 6th Army Corps

Evidence Types

(1) Official Records of the War of the   **OR**
Rebellion with Supplement (1 – 5)

(2) Pension Records on file at the National   **PR**
Archives, Washington, DC, (1–3)

(3) Miscellaneous Records, including regimental histories,   **MR**
publications, person reminiscences, journal entries,
diary entries, books, etc. (1–9)

(4) Protest File of the 37th Massachusetts concerning   **PF**
the Hawthorn Medal of Honor, on file at the
National Archives, Washington, DC,
file number 476510 (1–29)

(5) Charles W. Thayer collection of family letters,   **CT**
accounts, family history and civil war relics (1–4)

EVIDENCE OVERVIEW
EXHIBITS W-OR-(1-5)

The purpose of introducing this line of evidence is to introduce to the reader a claim made by David D. White, and the 37th Massachusetts of which he belonged, to the capture of Major General Custis Lee at the Battle of Sailor's Creek, April 6, 1865. The specific purpose of the W-OR evidence is to show in various Official Reports of the Civil War that White was credited for capturing Major General G. W. Custis Lee at the Battle of Sailor's Creek, April 6, 1865. This line of evidence also describes the role that a Lt. William Morrill, White's commanding officer, played in the capture of Custis Lee and the credit he received for this capture.

EXHIBIT-W-OR-1

Introduction:

Captain Archibald Hopkins, commanding the 37th Massachusetts, within Colonel Oliver Edwards' 3rd Brigade, General Frank Wheaton's 1st Division, 6th Army Corps, reports on his Regiment's participation in the Battle of Sailor's Creek, VA, April 6, 1865.

Evidence:

HDQRS. THIRTY-SEVENTH MASSACHUSETTS VOLUNTEERS
March [April] 7, 1865
SIR: I have the honor to state that there were 3 officers and 28 men wounded and 8 men killed in the engagement of yesterday. The officers were Capt. Walter B. Smith, First. Lieut, and Adjt. John S. Bradley, and Second Lieut. Harrie A. Cushman. There were 360 officers and men, and General C. Lee, captured by my command. General Lee was captured by Private D. D. White, Company E, of this regiment, and he formally surrendered his sword to Lieut. W. C. Morrill, of this regiment, who now wears it. At least one battle flag was captured by the Thirty-seventh Regiment, and one other is claimed, although the capture of it is claimed by another command.
Very respectfully,
A. HOPKINS, Captain, Commanding Regiment.

No. 115

Report of Capt. Archibald Hopkins, Thirty-seventh Massachusetts Infantry
HDQRS. THIRTY-SEVENTH MASSACHUSETTS VOLUNTEERS
In the Field, April 15, 1865
SIR: In compliance with circular from headquarters Third Brigade, of April 14, 1865, I have the honor to submit the following report of the part taken by my command in the operations of the late campaign:
...At the Battle of Sailor's Creek, we immediately opened again with redoubled energy, and in a few moments they surrendered in earnest. More than 390 were taken and sent to the rear. General Custis Lee, who commanded their line, surrendered and gave up his sword to Private David D. White, of Company E; and Private Charles A. Taggart, of Company B, captured their battle-flag. Corpl. Richard

Welch, of Company E, was overpowered by numbers and taken prisoner in a desperate attempt to capture a battle-flag in advance of our line. He was afterward retaken.

[Source: War of the Rebellion: A Compilation of the Official Records of the Union and Confederate Armies (Official Records), Volume 46, Series 1: "The Appomattox Campaign," Folio No. 115, pages 945 – 948]**Manuscript 4**

Comments & Supporting Evidence:

1. This Official Report written by Archibald Hopkins for David D. White/William Morrill differs in one significant way from the Official Report written by Egbert Olcott for Harris Hawthorn. It states that physical evidence was involved in the capture, the sword of Major General George Washington Custis Lee.

2. The following two statements are unique and important: "General Custis Lee, who commanded their line, surrendered and gave up his sword to Private David D. White, of Company E (report dated April 15, 1865)." "General Lee was captured by Private D. D. White, Company E, of this Regiment, and he formally surrendered his sword to Lieut. W. C. Morrill, of this Regiment, who now wears it (report dated April 7, 1865)."

3. On a different but interesting topic, one might question why a Captain (typically a Colonel) was commanding the 37th Massachusetts and a Lieutenant (typically a Captain) was commanding Company E within that Regiment at the Battle of Sailor's Creek. Archibald Hopkins refused promotion on March 4, 1865, because he felt that he was with the Regiment a short time, having served as an aide to General Briggs for two years. William Morrill was due for promotion about September 18, 1864, but was wounded so severely at the Battle of Winchester, that his return to the Regiment was delayed along with his promotion to a higher rank. The following two executive letters will show the delay in the promotions for both Hopkins and Morrill.

(1) HOPKINS:
Head Quarters 37th Mass Vols, March 4th 1865
TO: Brig. Gen'l Wm. Schouler, Adjutant General-State of Mass.
I also recommend Capt. M. W. Tyler (Brevet Major) to be promoted to Major 37th Mass. Vols. Vice Lincoln recommended for promotion. Brevet Major Tyler is senior captain of the Reg't except one Capt Hopkins who resigns his claim to promotion in favor of Bvt. Major Tyler in consideration of his (Hopkins) having been in the field with the Regiment but a short time.

Williams College Aug. 23 1862
TO: Governor Andrew:
At the request of Gen. Briggs, Mr. White wrote you in regard to delaying the commission of my son Archibald that he might be able to have him as one of his aides. I should prefer to have him with Gen. Briggs, but there is an unexpected delay in his receiving his command, and you will please consider that request as withdrawn if its continuance would in any way embarrass your actions.
With Great Respect Yours,
FROM: Mark Hopkins

(2) MORRILL:
Brig. Genl. William Schouler, Adjutant General, State of Massachusetts
I have the honor to make the following recommendations for promotion in this regiment. 2nd Lieut. William C. Morrill of Northampton to be 1st Lieut Oct. 6th 1864 vice Bardwell died of wounds. 1st Sergt Joseph D. Calahan of Tarinton to be 2nd Lieut. Oct. 13th 1864 vice Stockwell promoted. Lieut. Morrill is one of the ten officers who were recommended for promotion to the grade of 2nd Lieut. about Sept. 18th 1864. He was wounded in the Battle of Winchester Sept. 19th 1864, so severely as to prevent his return to the regiment and thus delayed his muster until Nov. 1st. I consider him the most efficient officer of those now remaining in the grade to which he belongs, and I do not deem it just that the fact of his having been wounded in battle should be a bar to his merited advancement.
Very Respectfully, Your Obt. Servt.,   G. L. Montague, Lt. Col. Commdg. Reg't.

[Source: Executive Letters to the Governor, Massachusetts State Archives, Boston, MA, Bound Volume 66]**Manuscript 37**

EXHIBIT-W-OR-2

Introduction:

Colonel Oliver Edwards, commanding the 3rd Brigade, which was a part of General Frank Wheaton's 1st Division, 6th Army Corps–reports on his Brigade's participation in the Battle of Sailor's Creek, VA, April 16, 1865. Reports are dated April 10, 1865 (addenda) and April 17, 1865. Within Colonel Edwards' Brigade were the 37th Massachusetts and the 5th Wisconsin.

Evidence:

No. 114

Report of Col. Oliver Edwards, Thirty-seventh Massachusetts Infantry,
HDQRS. THIRD BRIG., FIRST DIV. SIXTH ARMY CORPS
April 17, 1865

SIR: I have the honor to submit the following report of the part taken by this brigade in the late operations…. On the 6th my brigade led the division, following in rear of the Third Division. …The enemy were finally forced back and then taken in flank; their line being swept by the fire of the Spencers they surrendered. Amongst the captures were Brig. Gen. Custis Lee and a rebel stand of colors. Lieutenant-General Ewell and staff surrendered to the Fifth Wisconsin. A large number of prisoners were taken by the brigade, the number I cannot accurately state.

… I have the honor to be, very respectfully, your obedient servant.

O. EDWARDS, Colonel, Commanding.

ADDENDA:

HDQRS. THIRD BRIDG., FIRST DIV., SIXTH ARMY CORPS, April 10, 1865
Maj. GEORGE CLENDENIN, Jr., Asst. Adjt. Gen., First Division, Sixth Army Corps:

MAJOR: In compliance with orders from headquarters Sixth Army Corps, of April 3, 1865, I have the honor to forward a list of commissioned officers in my command who particularly distinguished themselves for gallantry and meritorious services on the 2d and 6th of April, and who I would recommend for promotion; also the names of enlisted men, including those who captured colors, who, by their conduct on that day, are entitled to receive medals…. First Lieut. William C. Morrill, Thirty-seventh Massachusetts Volunteers, to be brevet captain, for conspicuous bravery on April 2 and gallantry in capturing a General officer April 6.

O. Edwards, Colonel, Commanding

[Source: Official Records, Volume 46, Series 1, "The Appomattox Campaign," Folio 114, pages 941-945]Manuscript 4****

Comments & Supporting Evidence:

1. These reports are now the Regimental reports getting rolled up and consolidated at the higher Brigade level. Recommendations for promotion for commissioned officers for gallantry, as well as, recommendations for medals for enlisted men for their conduct, are getting introduced at this time.
2. Colonel Oliver Edwards in his 3rd Brigade report takes credit for the capture of General Custis Lee.
3. He looks to promote First Lieutenant William C. Morrill to Brevet Captain for gallantry in capturing a general officer, which in all likelihood was Major General G. W. Custis Lee.
4. Colonel Edwards is silent in his report on David White's role in capturing General Custis Lee and recommending him for a medal for this action. Based on Captain Hopkins' Regimental reports, it is difficult to see why Lieutenant Morrill, a commissioned officer, is being recommended by Edwards for promotion for capturing Custis Lee and Private David White, an enlisted soldier, is not being recommended by Edwards for a medal for capturing Custis Lee. Captain Hopkins' report seems to be quite clear concerning the manner on how Custis Lee was captured. Perhaps this was simply an oversight on Oliver Edwards' part when constructing his Official Report.

EXHIBIT-W-OR-3

Introduction:

Frank Wheaton:

Bvt. Major General Frank Wheaton, commanding the 1st Division of the 6th Army Corps, reports on his Division's participation in the Battle of Sailor's Creek, VA, April 6, 1865. Reports are dated April 20, 1865, and April 18, 1865. Within General Wheaton's Division were Hamblin's 2nd Brigade and Edwards' 3rd Brigade.

Evidence:

HEADQUARTERS FIRST DIVISION, SIXTH CORPS,
April 20, 1865

SIR: I have the honor to submit a report of the operations of my command from the 3d to the 13th instant, inclusive.

April 6, 1865

The number of prisoners taken is not known. I understand that the result of our attack was the capture of nearly all the rebel troops in our front, which consisted of Ewell's two divisions and the Confederate Marine Brigade. This division took Lieutenant General Ewell and General G. W. Custis Lee and several battle flags.

ADDENDA:

SIR: I have the honor to submit the following list of recommendations for promotion of officers in this division for conspicuous gallantry and meritorious services in the assault on Petersburg, April 2, 1865, and at the battle of Little Sailor's Creek, VA, April 6, 1865, and the names of enlisted men deserving mention for conspicuous bravery and good service in the same engagements:

... First Lieutenant William C. Morrill, Thirty-seventh Massachusetts Volunteers, to be captain by brevet for conspicuous bravery and meritorious services in the assault on the enemy's works near Petersburg, April 2, 1865, and at the battle of Little Sailor's Creek, April 6, 1865;

Very respectfully, your obedient servant
F. WHEATON, Brevet Major-General, U. S. Volunteers

[Source: Official Records, Volume 46, Series 1, "The Appomattox Campaign," Folio 106, Pages 908-926]**Manuscript 6**

Comments & Supporting Evidence:

1. These are the Brigade reports now getting rolled up and consolidated at the higher Division level.
2. Lieutenant William C. Morrill's promotion to Captain by brevet for meritorious service is, in all likelihood, for the capture of General Custis Lee at Sailor's Creek. His promotion is now being recommended at the higher Division level.
3. Private David White's Regimental recognition as the enlisted man who captured Custis Lee, as recorded by Captain Archibald Hopkins in the 37th Massachusetts report, is now lost at the higher Division level, not having been introduced at the Brigade level from the lower Regimental level by Oliver Edwards.

EXHIBIT-W-OR-4

Introduction:

The following are "roll – ups" of the Official Reports; first, the 37th Massachusetts to the 3rd Brigade and then to the 1st Division; second, the 121st New York to the 2nd Brigade and then to the 1st Division. These roll – ups generate the following three important questions that must be answered:

1. Lieut. William C. Morrill was cited for "capturing a General Officer," most probably Custis Lee, at the 37ᵗʰ Massachusetts and 3ʳᵈ Brigade reporting levels. Why then, was it dropped at the 1ˢᵗ Division reporting level?
2. Private Harris Hawthorn was cited for the "capture of Brig. Gen. Custis Lee" at the 121ˢᵗ New York, 2ⁿᵈ Brigade and 1ˢᵗ Division reporting levels. Why did this citation get preserved at the 1ˢᵗ Division reporting level?
3. Since the 1ˢᵗ Division report was the consolidation of Hamblin's 2ⁿᵈ Brigade and Edwards' 3ʳᵈ Brigade reports, did General Wheaton, who commanded the 1ˢᵗ Division, definitely decide the issue of who captured Custis Lee by including in his Division report only the Hawthorn citation and not the White/Morrill citation?

The answers to these three very important questions are as follows in A-C below:

A. For some reason, General Frank Wheaton dropped from his Division's Official Report all descriptions of acts of bravery performed by all commissioned officers in the 1ˢᵗ, 2ⁿᵈ and 3ʳᵈ Brigades for the actions performed on April 2ⁿᵈ and April 6ᵗʰ. William Morrill's act of "capturing a general officer" was dropped, not because Wheaton decided that Morrill did not do it, but because Wheaton dropped all actual descriptions for all acts of bravery for all commissioned officers. He replaced these actual descriptions of their specific acts of bravery with general "one size fits all" statements like, "conspicuous bravery and distinguished service in the assault on the enemy works near Petersburg, April 2, 1865, and/or at the battle of Little Sailor's Creek, April 6, 1865." Since Wheaton credits Morrill with conspicuous bravery at the Battle of Sailor's Creek within his Division Official Report, and Wheaton based this on Edwards' statement found in Edwards' Brigade Official Report that Morrill's conspicuous bravery was based on Morrill "capturing a general officer" at the Battle of Sailor's Creek, then Wheaton did indeed, indirectly, acknowledge that Morrill captured G. W. Custis Lee in his Division's Official Report.

B. Unlike commissioned officers, General Frank Wheaton did retain in his Division Report all specific descriptions of acts of bravery for all enlisted men rolling up from the Brigade commanders. This is why Hawthorn's description "captured Brig. General G. W. Custis Lee," which was recorded in Olcott's Regimental report and Hamblin's Brigade report, got preserved in Wheaton's Division report.

C. In conclusion, it is perfectly clear after a careful examination of these reports, that General Frank Wheaton did not decide the issue of who captured General G. W. Custis Lee at the Battle of Sailor's Creek when he created his Division's report. When Wheaton created his Division's report, Morrill's specific citation for capturing Custis Lee was dropped from Wheaton's report due to a standard format that Wheaton was using. Once again, Wheaton's format did not describe the specific acts of bravery for commissioned officers. Hawthorn's citation for the capture of Custis Lee was retained in Wheaton's report due to the standard format that Wheaton was using which did describe the specific acts of bravery for all enlisted solders. Since Wheaton cited Morrill with bravery at Sailor's Creek in his report, and this bravery was a result of capturing Custis Lee according to his Brigade Commander's (Edwards) report, then Wheaton was crediting Morrill with the capture of Custis Lee. Naturally, Wheaton also credited Hawthorn with the capture of Custis Lee by retaining this description in his report from Hawthorn's Brigade commander (Hamblin). In summary, both Morrill and Hawthorn got credited with the capture of Custis Lee in Frank Wheaton's 1ˢᵗ Division Official Report. It was cited differently because Wheaton used different reporting formats for commissioned officers and enlisted men.

Evidence:

The following pages depict representative examples of how these commissioned officer and enlisted men "roll – ups" occurred from the Brigade commanders, which were Edwards and Hamblin, to the common Division commander, which was Frank Wheaton. Please compare the descriptions of acts of bravery for each officer and enlisted soldier as recorded in the Brigade and the Division reports:

Officers
Hamblin's 2nd Brigade
2nd Brigade Report

I beg your attention to the following statement of gallant and meritorious conduct by officers and men of this brigade:

A: ***Bvt. Col. E. Olcott****, commanding the One Hundred and Twenty-First, distinguished himself by abilities and gallantry which are beyond praise. The success of the 6th instant is largely due to the prompt and splendid manner in which he maneuvered his regiment, changing front under a heavy fire, and driving the enemy from our right flank. I earnestly recommend that he be appointed brigadier-general U.S. Volunteers.*

B: ***Capt. Michael Kelly****, Second Connecticut Heavy Artillery, on the 2d instant turned the guns of a captured battery on the retiring foe and fired them with great effect; he also took a battle-flag inside the enemy's works.*

C: ***Capt. Michael Devine****, Capt. Fred J. Volks, Sixty-Fifth New York Volunteers, on the 2d instant displayed great coolness and ability in handling their men on the Boydton plank road, where they advanced immediately after the charge.*

D: ***Capt. Deane****, turned the guns of a captured fort, and with a detachment from the Second Connecticut Heavy Artillery, fired them on the enemy, until no enemy was in range. I earnestly recommend that all the above-named officers be promoted by brevet.*

Enlisted Men
Hamblin's 2nd Brigade
2nd Brigade Report

E: ***Private Dennis Moore****, Company K, Second Connecticut Heavy Artillery, assisted in capturing Brig. Gen. Custis Lee.*

F: ***Private Warren C. Dockun****, Company H, One Hundred and Twenty-First New York State Volunteers, and Private B. Gifford, Company H, One Hundred and Twenty-First New York State Volunteers, each captured a flag.*

G: ***Sergt. Redford Dustin****, Company F, One Hundred and Twenty-First New York State Volunteers, on the 2d instant, turned, loaded and fired a captured gun upon the enemy.*

H: ***Private Harris S. Hawthorn****, Company F, One hundred and Twenty-First New York State Volunteers captured Brig. Gen. Custis Lee on the 6th instant.*

I earnestly recommend that a medal be awarded to each of the above-mentioned enlisted men.

Jo. E. Hamblin, Brevet Brigadier-General, U.S. Volunteers, Comdg. Brigade.

Author Note: Hamblin frequently described the brave acts of his officers and enlisted men when recommending them for promotion or medals for the acts they performed on April 2nd and 6th, 1865 (see the examples above).

Officers
Hamblin's 2nd Brigade
Wheaton's 1st Division Report

Sir: I have the honor to submit the following list of recommendations for promotion of officers in this division for conspicuous gallantry and meritorious services in the assault on Petersburg, April 2, 1865, and at the battle of Little Sailor's Creek, VA, April 6, 1865, and the names of enlisted men deserving mention for conspicuous bravery and good service in the same engagements:

A: ***Col. Egbert Olcott****, One hundred and Twenty-First New York Volunteers, to be brigadier-general by brevet for distinguished gallantry at the assault on the enemy's works near Petersburg, April 2, 1865, and to be brigadier-general for bravery and meritorious services at the battle of Little Sailor's Creek, VA, April 6, 1865.*

B: ***Capt. Michael Kelly****, Second Connecticut Heavy Artillery Volunteers, to be major by brevet for conspicuous gallantry and distinguished services in the assault on the enemy's works near Petersburg, VA, April 2, 1865, and at the battle of Little Sailor's Creek, April 6, 1865.*

C: **Capt. Michael Devine**, *Sixty-Fifth New York Volunteers, to be major by brevet for conspicuous gallantry and distinguished services in the assault on the enemy's works near Petersburg, VA, April 2, 1865, and at the battle of Little Sailor's Creek, VA, April 6, 1865.*

D: **Capt. James Deane**, *Second Connecticut Heavy Artillery Volunteers, to be major by brevet for conspicuous gallantry and distinguished services in the assault on the enemy's works near Petersburg, VA, April 2, 1865, and at the battle of Little Sailor's Creek, VA, April 6, 1865.*

Enlisted Men
Hamblin's 2nd Brigade
Wheaton's 1st Division Report

E: **Private Dennis Moore**, *Company K, Second Connecticut Heavy Artillery Volunteers, assisting in the capture of Brig. Gen. Custis Lee.*

F: **Private Warren C. Dockun**, *Company H, One hundred and Twenty-First New York Volunteers, capturing a rebel battle-flag.*

G: **Sergt. Redford Dustin**, *Company F, One hundred and Twenty-First New York Volunteers, firing a captured gun upon the enemy.*

H: **Private Harris S. Hawthorn**, *Company F, One Hundred and Twenty-First New York Volunteers captured Brig. Gen. [G. W.] Custis Lee, on the 6th instant.*

F. Wheaton, Commanding

Author Note: Wheaton did not use any of Hamblin's descriptions of the acts of bravery performed by his commissioned officers, but did use all of Hamblin's descriptions of the acts of bravery performed by his enlisted men (compare the Hamblin and Wheaton reports).

Officers
Edwards' 3rd Brigade
3rd Brigade Report

Major: In compliance with orders from headquarters Sixth Army Corps, of April 3, 1865, I have the honor to forward a list of commissioned officers in my command who particularly distinguished themselves for gallantry and meritorious services on the 2d and 6th of April, and who I would recommend for promotion; also the names of enlisted men, including those who captured colors, who, by their conduct on that day, are entitled to receive medals.

1: **Bvt. Maj. E. A. Landell**, *captain, One hundred and Nineteenth Pennsylvania Volunteers, brigade inspector, to be brevet lieutenant-colonel, for meritorious services in being one of the first in the enemy's works April 2, and also to the brevet colonel for conspicuous gallantry at the battle of Little Sailor's Creek, April 6.*

2: **First Lieut. William C. Morrill**, *Thirty-Seventh Massachusetts Volunteers, to be brevet captain, for conspicuous bravery on April 2 and gallantry in capturing a General officer April 6.*

Enlisted Men
Edwards' 3rd Brigade
3rd Brigade Report

3: **Private William Railton**, *Company E, Second Rhode Island Volunteers, for gallantry in being one of the first in the enemy's works April 2.*

4: **Corpl. Richard Welch**, *Company E, Thirty-Seventh Massachusetts Volunteers, for conspicuous bravery April 2, 1865, capturing a stand of colors and shooting a man at the guns, and for conspicuous bravery on the 6th of April.*

5: **Private Charles A. Taggart**, *Company B, Thirty-Seventh Massachusetts Volunteers, for capturing a stand of colors from enemy April 6.*

6: **Corpl. Patrick Kelly**, *Company E, Thirty-Seventh Massachusetts Volunteers, for bravery and bayoneting a rebel soldier in act of shooting his commanding officer April 2, 1865.*

7: **Sergt. George W. Johnson**, *Company K, One hundred and Nineteenth Pennsylvania Volunteers, for being one of the first of the regiment to enter the enemy's works and secure two pieces of artillery, April 2, 1865.*

Very respectfully, your obedient servant,
O. Edwards, Colonel, Commanding

Author Note: Edwards occasionally described the acts of bravery performed by his commissioned officers and frequently described the acts of bravery performed by his enlisted men when recommending them for promotion or for medals for the acts they performed on April 2nd and 6th, 1865 (see examples above).

Officers
Edwards' 3rd Brigade
Wheaton's 1st Division Report

1: **Bvt, Maj. Edwin A. Landell**, *One hundred and Nineteenth Pennsylvania Volunteers, to be lieutenant-colonel by brevet for conspicuous gallantry and meritorious services in the assault on the enemy's works near Petersburg, April 2, 1865, and the battle of Little Sailor's Creek, VA, April 6, 1865.*

2: **William C. Morrill**, *Thirty-Seventh Massachusetts Volunteers, to be captain by brevet for conspicuous bravery and meritorious services in the assault on the enemy's works near Petersburg, April 2, 1865, and at the battle of Little Sailor's Creek, VA, April 6, 1865.*

Enlisted Men
Edwards' 3rd Brigade
Wheaton's 1st Division Report

3: **Private William Railton**, *Company E, Second Rhode Island Volunteers, for gallantry, being one of the first of his regiment to enter the enemy's works on the 2d instant.*

4: **Corpl. Richard Welch**, *Company E, Thirty-Seventh Massachusetts Volunteers, for conspicuous bravery in capturing a rebel stand of colors.*

5: **Private Charles A. Taggart**, *Company B, Thirty-Seventh Massachusetts, for capturing a rebel stand of colors.*

6: Corpl. Patrick Kelly did not make it to Wheaton's report. This was either an accidental omission or Wheaton was doing some filtering out of what he thought were unjustified claims for a medal.

7: **Sergt. George W. Johnson**, *Company K, One hundred and Nineteenth Pennsylvania Volunteers, for being one of the first of the regiment to enter the enemy's works and secure two pieces of artillery, April 2, 1865.*

Very respectfully, your obedient servant,
F. Wheaton, Brevet Major-General, U. S. Volunteers.

Author Note: Wheaton did not use any of Edwards' descriptions of the acts of bravery performed by his commissioned officers but did use all of Edwards' descriptions of the acts of bravery performed by his enlisted men. (Compare the Edwards and Wheaton reports).

[Source: Official Records, Volume 46, Series 1, "The Appomattox Campaign," for all the references cited above in this exhibit]**Manuscripts 3, 4, and 6**

Comments & Supporting Evidence:

1. An interesting note concerning the Brigade to Division "roll-ups" of the Official Reports; Hamblin's 2nd Brigade report does not mention that his Brigade captured General Custis Lee. He only mentions it in Hawthorn's and Dennis Moore's recommendations for medals.

2. By way of contrast, Edwards' mentions that his Brigade, and specifically the 37th Massachusetts within his Brigade, captured Brigadier General Custis Lee. He also mentions that his Brigade, and specifically the 5th Wisconsin within his Brigade, captured Lieutenant General Ewell. Please read Edwards' report below:

Thirty-seventh Massachusetts advanced at the same time with the brigade, driving the enemy slowly, but soon found both flanks exposed and a column of the enemy coming in on their left. Their left was thrown back to meet this attack, which they admirably repulsed. By this time they discovered the enemy on their right flank and some 100 yards in the rear. The regiment faced about, and a desperate hand-to-hand fight ensued. The enemy were finally forced back and they taken in flank; their line being swept by the fire of the Spencers they surrendered. Amongst the captures were Brig. Gen. Custis Lee and a rebel stand of colors. Lieutenant-General Ewell and staff surrendered to the Fifth Wisconsin. A large number of prisoners were taken by the brigade, the number I cannot accurately state.

I have the honor to be, very respectfully, your obedient servant.

O. Edwards, Colonel, Commanding

3. In Wheaton's 1st Division report, he simply states the following concerning Custis Lee's and Ewell's capture:

I understand that the result of our attack was the capture of nearly all the rebel troops in our front, which consisted of Ewell's two divisions and the Confederate Marine Brigade. This division took Lieutenant-General Ewell and General G. W. Custis Lee and several battle flags – eight have been turned over to the assistant adjutant-general of the corps, and four more are known to have been taken within the four days preceding and including that.

[Source: Official Records, Volume 46, Series 1, "The Appomattox Campaign" for all the references cited above in this exhibit]Manuscripts 3, 4 and 6****

EXHIBIT-W-OR-5

Introduction:

This is a "Record of Events" recorded by the 37th Massachusetts for the March – April 1865 time period.

Evidence:

37th Massachusetts Regiment Record of Events

Company **A**	Stationed at Danville, Virginia, March – April, 1865
Company **B**	April 6 – [In action] at Sayler's Creek.
Company **C**	April 6 – The company took part in a spirited engagement. From Clover Hill, they returned to Burkeville.
Company **D**	April 6 – The company participated in an engagement at Sayler's Creek. Also participated in the marches of the Sixth Corps to Appomattox Court-House; thence back to Burkeville Junction and from thence to Danville, Virginia.

Company **E** (David White's Company)

Stationed at Danville, Virginia, March –April 1865

Stationed at Hall's Hill, Virginia, June 21, 1865

June 21 – Muster-out roll of First Lieutenant William C. Morrill's Company E, in the Thirty-seventh Regiment of Massachusetts Volunteers, commanded by Colonel Oliver Edwards, called into the service of the United States by the President at Pittsfield, Massachusetts (the place of general rendezvous) on September 4, 1862 to serve for the term of three years from the date of enrollment, unless sooner discharged, from April 30, 1865 (when last mustered) to June 21, 1865 when discharged. The company was organized by Captain A. Hopkins at Pittsfield, Massachusetts in the month of August 1862

Company **F**	Stationed at Danville, Virginia, March – April 1865
Company **G**	April 6 – Participated in the engagement at Sayler's Creek.
Company **H**	Stationed near Danville, Virginia, March – April, 1865
Company **I**	Stationed near Danville, Virginia, March – April, 1865
Company **J**	No records available
Company **K**	Stationed at Danville, Virginia, March – April, 1865

(Note: The entries that list Danville show where the regiment was when the report was made at the end of April 1865. On April 6, 1865, the regiment was engaged at Sailor's Creek).

[Source: Supplement to the Official Records, Part II, Record of Events Series, Volume 29]Manuscript 18****

Comments & Supporting Evidence:

1. The 37th Massachusetts was very brief in recording their Record of Events. This is especially true when compared to the 121st New York, who had men that were enthusiastic and copious record keepers.
2. The 37th Massachusetts companies are completely silent on their accomplishments and losses in the Battle of Sailor's Creek, April 6, 1865.
3. Of note is the June 21, 1865, 37th Massachusetts, Company E, "Record of Events" entry which states that First Lieutenant William C. Morrill's Company E, David White's Company, was mustered out of service. This record could indicate that David White's commanding officer at the Battle of Sailor's Creek was William C. Morrill; however, the 37th Massachusetts' "Morning Report" for the Battle of Sailor's Creek (April 7, 1865) has Captain Francis Greys as the commander of Company E. Like the 121st New York, the 37th Massachusetts' "Morning Reports" for April 1865, make no mention of the capture of Custis Lee.

[Source: 37th MA Infantry: Record Group 94: Records of the Adjutant General's Office, Entry 112-115: Book Records of Union Volunteer Organizations 37th MA Infantry, Morning Reports for Companies A to K]**Manuscript 153**

EVIDENCE OVERVIEW
EXHIBITS-W-PR-(1-3)

The purpose of introducing this line of evidence is to show the injury that White sustained during the Battle of Sailor's Creek, April 6, 1865. This fact is pertinent to the case. This line of evidence also discloses unsolicited testimonials by White's fellow 37th Massachusetts soldiers that White captured Major General G. W. Custis Lee.

EXHIBIT-W-PR-1

Introduction:

An affidavit given by John Grace for the David White pension case, dated November 8, 1884.

Evidence:

Adams, Mass. Nov. 8, 1884.

Sir: On April 6, 1865 White and I were together in the afternoon at the battle of "Sailors Creek" where he took young General Lee prisoner, shortly after which White and myself were detailed to go to the rear after ammunition, and it was while returning each with a box of ammunition, that in jumping the creek, White fell, and was unable for some time to get up and was obliged to leave the box of ammunition there. He said to me, "Jack, I am hurt" and held his hand to his groin. It was about for a day or two until he got a furlough home but could not do duty–I know he was injured in the groin but never saw the rupture that I remember–When I came home I saw him and he then told me that this hurt he received and have above mentioned caused a rupture.

Witness F. H. B. Nussison

John Grace (his mark)

Berkshire SS: Commonwealth of Massachusetts

On this eighth day of November, AD 1884, personally appeared John Grace above named to me well known and made oath to the truth of the above statement by him signed in my presence.

J. H. Nussison Justice of the Peace

Certificate of qualification on file in Pension Office

[Source: David D. White Pension File, Claim 210739, National Archives, Washington, DC]**Manuscript 19**

Comments & Supporting Evidence:

1. It is interesting to note that shortly after David White captured "young General Lee," he was detailed with fellow soldier, John Grace, "to go to the rear after ammunition." If this is true, it would appear

that David White was not involved in any significant degree in delivering General Custis Lee to the Federal rear or to a Union General's headquarters as was stated in Harris Hawthorn's account. If White and Grace were bringing up ammunition from the rear, they were still actively engaged in fighting the battle and not involved in the processing of General Custis Lee as a prisoner of war. This retrieval of ammunition is also an indication that the battle was still being actively fought after the capture of Custis Lee, if White and Grace were detailed to get ammunition from the rear.

2. It is easy to understand how this event could occur. The Spencer rifle ammunition was extremely heavy due to its copper casing. White was injured so badly that he had to leave the ammunition box.
3. It also appears that White's injury disabled him for some time after this incident.
4. This injury, and his subsequent disablement, could be one of several factors that would explain why White did not actively claim the capture of General Custis Lee after the Battle of Sailor's Creek. Harris Hawthorn, in comparison, took very proactive steps in claiming Custis Lee's capture after the Battle of Sailor's Creek by producing a sworn statement to field Judge Advocate Hindmarsh on April 14, 1865.

EXHIBIT-W-PR-2

Introduction:
Another affidavit of John Grace dated 1884.

Evidence:

AFFIDAVIT TO ORIGIN OF DISABILITY
In the matter of the Pension claim of David D. White, Corporal, Company E, 37th Reg't, Mass Vols: personally came before me, a Justice of the Peace in and for the aforesaid County and State, John Grace, of Adams, County of Berkshire, State of Massachusetts, who, being duly sworn, declares in relation to the aforesaid claim that his age is 42 years; that he is the identical person who served as a private in Company E, 37th Reg't, Mass Vols, and knows the above-named soldier, who was a member of Co. E, 37th Reg't Mass Vols that on or about the 6th day of April, 1865, while in the line of duty, and without fault or improper conduct on his part, at or near Sailor's Creek, State of Virginia, said soldier incurred a rupture on both sides of body. We were both detailed to bring ammunition to the front. White had charge of the Squad. This about 5 or 6 o'clock on the day of the fight. While returning from the rear with box of ammunition on his shoulder, in jumping the creek, slipped and fell, causing the rupture. He said to me, "Jack, I am hurt." He had to leave the box; was hardly able to straighten up. He went to Regt'l Surgeon that night and in the morning was sent to the rear. I came home July 3, 1865, and saw White a short time after. Up to the time he was hurt he was a sound able bodied man, always able to do duty. He was sound before enlistment. I was acquainted with him for several years. I enlisted at same time he did; was for three years in same Company with him, saw him almost daily until he was hurt and sent back.
John Grace
[Source: David D. White Pension File, Claim # 210739, National Archives, Washington, DC]**Manuscript 19**

Comments & Supporting Evidence:
1. John Grace testifies once again to the injury sustained by David White "during the fight."
2. Once again, it would appear that David White had little or no involvement in bringing Custis Lee to the rear of the Federal lines. He was busy bringing ammunition to the battlefront from the rear.
3. With David White "being in charge of the squad" detailed to bring ammunition up from the rear, it sounds like White, Grace and the other squad members were still engaged in an active battle at this point in time.

BIOGRAPHY:
Grace, John – Priv. – Res. Cheshire; 22; laborer, enl. Aug. 12, 1862; must. Sept. 2, 1862; mustered out June 21, 1865.

[Source: "Massachusetts Soldiers, Sailors and Marines in the Civil War," Volume 3, Compiled and Published by the Adjutant General, Norwood Press; 1932]**Manuscript 68**

EXHIBIT-W-PR-3

Introduction:

Jonas A. Champney: (PHOTO: COURTESY U. S. ARMY WAR COLLEGE)

An affidavit given by Jonas A. Champney dated November 27, 1889. This affidavit was given by Champney for the David White's pension case and is totally unrelated to the upcoming 37th Massachusetts' Protest Case.

Evidence:

Berkshire County, Massachusetts

In the matter of the Pension Claim of David D. White, late Corporal of Co. "E," 37th Regt. Mass. Vols.: Personally came before me, a Justice of the Peace within and for said County and State, Jonas A. Champney, aged 59, of Adams, Berkshire County, Massachusetts, whose post office address is Adams, Berkshire Co. Mass.–late Captain of Co. "H," 37th Regt. Mass. Vols–of lawful age, who, being duly sworn, declares in relation to said claim as follows–I knew the claimant, David D. White, before his enlistment and all through his service, part of the time being in Command of his Company; knew him to be a strong, able bodied man. On April 6, 1865, at Sailor's Creek, VA, he was ordered to bring ammunition to the front. The road was all was washed out and, while crossing the gully with box of ammunition, he fell striking on the box and injuring himself so as to cause a rupture of the right side. He was picked up and helped to an ambulance and was confined to the same all the time the regiment was on march for about fourteen days. I have known and seen him frequently ever since his discharge and know he has always been a sufferer from the injuries then received, often being laid up, entirely, unable to do any manual labor. I further know that he was always a good, faithful soldier, and that he captured General Custis Lee, forcibly taking him prisoner upon his refusal to surrender except to a commissioned officer. All the above is of my personal knowledge. I further declare that I have no interest in said case and am not concerned in its prosecution.

Jonas A. Champney

Sworn to and subscribed before me this twenty seventh day of November, AD, 1889, and I hereby certify that the contents of the foregoing affidavit were fully made known and explained to the affiant before swearing thereto; that the affiant is to me well known and is respectable and worthy of full faith and credit and that I have no interest in the said claim and am not concerned in the prosecution of the same.

J. H. Nussison, Justice of the Peace, Certificate of Qualification on file in Pension Office

[Source: David D. White Pension File, Claim # 210739, National Archive, Washington, DC]Manuscript 19****

Comments & Supporting Evidence:

1. This account by Captain Jonas Champney is very consistent with the account given by John Grace.
2. In Captain Champney's account, David White appears to be more significantly disabled from his injury, having been confined to an ambulance while his Regiment was on the march, for approximately fourteen days after April 6, 1865.

3. It would appear that when Harris Hawthorn was giving his sworn statement to Judge-Advocate Hindmarsh on April 14, 1865, concerning his capture of General Custis Lee, White was quite disabled and confined to an ambulance. If this is true, White was not around to contest the issue or probably in a state of health to make a big counter-claim in his behalf. This is assuming that David White even had a desire to do so.

4. It could also be true that David White did not view, at the time, his capture of Custis Lee as anything extraordinary. He could have simply viewed it as an act in line with his duty. Hence, he did not make an issue of it.

5. It is interesting to note that both Grace (1884) and Champney (1889) reference White's capture of Custis Lee without any prompting. Their affidavits had the objective of testifying to White's injury and disability. It is compelling evidence to see these unsolicited "capture" references many years before the 37th Massachusetts' Protest Case in the year 1897.

BIOGRAPHY:
Champney, Jonas A.–1st Lieut.–Res. South Adams; 30; machinist; comm. Aug 27, 1862; must. Sept. 4, 1862; wounded May 12, 1864; Spotsylvania, VA; comm. Captain, May 15, 1865; must. July 1, 1864; must. out June 21, 1865, as Captain of Co. "H," Brevet Major U. S. Vols., to date April 6, 1865.
[Source: "Massachusetts Soldiers, Sailors and Marines in the Civil War," Volume 3, Compiled and Published by the Adjutant General, Norwood Press, 1932]**Manuscript 68**

EVIDENCE OVERVIEW
EXHIBITS-W-MR-(1-9)

The purpose of introducing this line of evidence is to show the various individuals who state, in a formal written instrument, that David D. White of the 37th Massachusetts, captured Major General G. W. Custis Lee at the Battle of Sailor's Creek, April 6, 1865.

EXHIBIT-W-MR-1

Introduction:
The Regimental history of the 37th Massachusetts contains a brief description of the capture of Major General Custis Lee.

Evidence:

… General Custis Lee, who directed the charge upon the Thirty-seventh, had till shortly before filled a clerkship at Richmond, but finally laid down the pen to take up the sword, surrendering the latter at the muzzle of the Spencer rifle to Corporal David White of Company E.
[Source: "History of the Thirty-Seventh Regiment Massachusetts Volunteers in the Civil War of 1861–1865, With a Comprehensive Sketch of the Doings of Massachusetts as a State, and the Principal Campaigns of the War," by James L. Bowen, Clark W. Bryan & Company, Publishers, Holyoke, Mass. and New York City; 1884]**Manuscript 20**

Comments & Supporting Evidence:
1. The important point in this regimental history description is that of David White capturing General Custis Lee and Custis Lee surrendering his sword at the muzzle of David White's Spencer rifle.

BIOGRAPHY:
White, David D.–Private–Res. Cheshire; 18 laborer; enl. Aug. 21, 1862; mustered in Sept. 2, 1862; mustered out June 21, 1865, as Corporal.
[Source: Massachusetts Soldiers, Sailors and Marines in the Civil War, Volume 3, Compiled and published by the Adjutant General, Norwood Press; 1932]** Manuscript 68**

EXHIBIT-W-MR-2

Introduction:

Hazard Stevens:

This is a brief description of the Battle of Sailor's Creek by Hazard Stevens. Steven's last brevet promoted him to a Brigadier General on April 2, 1865, for heroism at Petersburg and Richmond, VA.

Evidence:

... The left of our line, Edwards' brigade, or Wheaton's First Division, had met with equal success. Encountering first scattered skirmishing fire and then heavy musketry, it forced its way upwards through the woods, and after a brief struggle broke the enemy's line in its front. Thus almost simultaneously both flanks of the Sixth Corps broke the enemy's line, and its center was repulsed and driven back by them. Many prisoners surrendered to the corps, among them Generals Ewell and Custis Lee. The latter surrendered to Corporal David White of Company E, 37th Regt. Mass. Vols. But the bulk of the enemy fled back through the woods and fell into the hands of the cavalry on the other side.

[Source: Stevens, Hazard, 1842-1918. "The Battle of Sailor's Creek," Papers of the Massachusetts Historical Society Magazine, Volume 6 (1884) pages 437-448]**Manuscript 21**

Comments & Supporting Evidence:

1. It is interesting to note that Hazard Stevens states that the, "bulk of the enemy fled back through the woods." This shows that the Confederates made some escape attempts during the battle.
2. This is an important account due to the fact that Stevens performed his duties at the Battle of Sailor's Creek at a Division and Corps level. He was not associated with either 121st New York or 37th Massachusetts. With his writings on the Battle of Sailor's Creek based on his vantage point of the broader Division and Corps level, it is interesting that he definitively states that Custis Lee surrendered to Corporal David White of Company E, of the 37th Massachusetts.

EXHIBIT-W-MR-3

Introduction:

Mason Tyler:

Mason Tyler of the 37th Massachusetts gives an account of the Battle of Sailor's Creek.

Evidence:

… Late in the afternoon of April 6th, the rear guard of the Rebel army made a stand at Sailor's Creek. The Sixth Corps had now to face about ten thousand of Lee's veterans, but not even the fatigue of this strenuous campaign had dampened their ardor. As a result, they took or put hors de combat some six thousand of the enemy, and among those taken prisoners were Lieutenant-General Ewell and Brigadier-General Custis Lee (son of General Robert E. Lee), the latter being captured by Corporal David White of Company E of the Thirty-seventh Massachusetts Regiment.

[Source: Tyler, Mason Whiting, 1840–1907, "Recollections of the Civil War with Many Original Diary Entries and Letters, Written from the Seat of the War, and with Annotated References," by Mason Whiting Tyler, late Lieut.-Colonel and Brevet-Colonel 37th Reg't. Massachusetts

Volunteers, edited by William S. Tyler, New York, G. P. Putnam's Sons, 1912, 379 pgs. with plates]**Manuscript 22**

Comments & Supporting Evidence:

1. It would be interesting to know if Mason Whiting Tyler is describing the capture of General Custis Lee from his own personal recollections or if he is basing this description on his original diary entry that was created at the time of the actual event.

BIOGRAPHY:

Tyler, Mason. – 1st Lieut. – Res. Amherst; 22; student; comm. Aug. 3, 1862; must. Sept. 4, 1862; comm. Captain, Jan. 17, 1863; must, to date Jan. 17, 1863; wounded Sept. 19, 1864, Winchester, VA; comm. Major, March 4, 1865; must. March 21, 1865; muster as Major revoked; wounded March 25, 1865, Petersburg, VA; comm. Lieut. Colonel, May 19, 1865; not must.; comm. Colonel,, June 26, 1865, no must. ; must. out June 21, 1865, as Captain Co. F. Brevet Major U. S. Vols., to date Sept. 19, 1864.
[Source: Massachusetts Soldiers, Sailors and Marines in the Civil War, Volume 3 Compiled and Published by the Adjutant General, Norwood Press; 1932]Manuscript 68**

EXHIBIT-W-MR-4

Introduction:

These are the words of David D. White on the capture of Custis Lee as recorded in two newspaper articles. They are most likely the result of an interview of David White by a local (North Adams, MA) newspaper reporter.

Evidence:

(1) *Charlemont Veteran Captured a General*

Among the visitors which the circus brought to this City on Friday was David D. White of Charlemont, who was on the street a part of the morning. Mr. White formerly lived here and has many acquaintances. As a soldier in the Union Regiment when the war was nearly ended the likes of which probably fell to the lot of no other Private soldier in the war. Mr. White was a member of Company E, 37th Reg. Massachusetts, one of the fighting regiments. He was in the Battle of Sailor's Creek near Appomattox April 6, 1865, and had got out beyond his own lines. He noticed a Confederate officer who was also alone and who had got separated from his command. Without knowing exactly what the impulse was that prompted him, Mr. White ordered the officer to halt. He was making for the creek but did not stop. "Halt" ordered White again, and the stranger turned. "What do you want?" he demanded. "Do you think I'm going to surrender to any Yankee, Private?" "Yes, sir," said White "or you'll get what's in this gun." He had an old seven shooter musket and had pointed it at the officer. In disgust, the officer reluctantly gave up and White triumphantly marched him into camp as a prisoner. He did not know the game he had bagged until the name of the distinguished prisoner was none other than Custis E. Lee, a general in the Confederate Army and son of the Commander in Chief, Robert E. Lee. He had been in the War Department at Richmond until that city was taken by the Union troops and had been given command of a brigade of marines and infantry men on Sailor's Creek. The prisoner was paroled but in three days his father surrendered at Appomattox to Grant and the war was over. White never saw his prisoner again. William Morrill, who was in command of his company, took Lee's sword and sent it later to the Smithsonian Institution at Washington. The Haversack which the officer had been carrying with him, White brought back from the war and gave [it] to Dr. Duncan of Williamstown and it is believed to be in [the] possession of Williams College.

(2) *David White Super Soldier of Civil War is still active*
Resident of Charlemont captured rebel General single handed.
Born in Cheshire, Mass., once lived here in North Adams

Over in Charlemont living a placid life on a small farm with a lack of change and excitement that might almost be considered a deadly monotony, is Dave White. But life is not monotonous for Dave when he gets time to take things easy and sit about. He does not seek excitement elsewhere for stored in his mind are memories of exciting days in which he prominently figured. For be it known that he is the only man living or dead for a radius of many miles that ever captured a general single handed. The said general was no less a personage than Custis E. Lee of the Confederate forces in the Civil War. Needless to say White was of the Northern Forces. Other exciting things happened to him during his long and useful life and recalling them when he gets time provides him with sufficient amount of amusement and recreation. He is satisfied that in his younger days he had his share of excitement that was going around and is content to sit back and live on its memories today leaving actual excitement to the younger blood. <u>Native of Cheshire Mass.</u> Dave is a native of Cheshire and being at the same time youthful, patriotic, courageous and of a somewhat adventurous turn of mind, he could not let the Civil War pass without having a personal and direct part in it. Hence he was a member of the 37th Massachusetts regiment and more particularly of Company E of that organization. His Regiment figured prominently in the Battle of Sailor's Creek in April, 1865. "They gave us quite a rassle there too before we got through with that little scrap," he declared impressively. Anyway, things got pretty hot with shot and shell screaming." When Dave spotted close to him an officer of the rebel forces who had got lost in the shuffle, without any idea as to his identity, Dave commanded him to surrender. The rebel sized up the situation and finding no aid in sight gave up his sword with a weary face. Dave marched to headquarters with his prisoner and was thunderstruck when he learned that it was no less a personage then General Custis E. Lee. He kept the General's sword which is now in the Smithsonian Institute in Washington. The General's Haversack he brought back with him and presented [it] to Dr. Duncan of Williamstown. After the war, Mr. White immediately returned to this City and with his brother-in-law took the contract to dig the cellar for the old Wilson Hotel in three weeks. They deposited a bond of $500 and were to pay a forfeit for every day beyond the three weeks that it required to complete the work. At the time, they didn't even have a place engaged to dump the dirt and set out to rent one. The next day, however, they were saved for Rufus Walden, a Selectman of the town, went to them and in behalf of the town offered them 25 cents for every load of dirt he would dump on State and Marshall Streets, the town to do the leveling. Mr. White laughs when he recalls this incident. "We made money going and coming," he declared. The money he made however did not stick with him long. Saw mills were responsible. White claims to have been razzled in his first saw mill venture. The second one burned down and left him completely stranded for a time. He did not loose courage however and recalls the days when he lived here with relish, declaring he had many good times in the old town. Eventually, he located in Charlemont and although he doesn't visit this city as often as he used to he still retains a feeling of deep regard for it.

[Source: Two handwritten transcriptions (undated but probably late 1800's or early 1900's) most likely from North Adams, MA, newspapers (probably the "North Adams Transcript") interviewing David White on his recent trip to North Adams. Transcriptions provided to the author by Margaret Hitchcock, granddaughter of David White, provided on July 17, 1979, transcriptions currently in the possession of the author]**Manuscript 24**

Comments & Supporting Evidence:

1. Other than a brief affidavit written by David White as will be seen in the 37th Massachusetts Protest Case file in Exhibit W–PF–7, these newspaper articles are the only first-hand accounts found by the author that originated directly from David White describing his capture of Major General Custis Lee. There are many important and distinguishing facets of this account that are different from the account given by Thomas J. Hassett for Harris Hawthorn:

   A. **First:** Hassett states that Hawthorn "rushed in front of his comrades of Company K (F) of the 121st New York Volunteers and at the point of his bayonet demanded and received the surrender of the young general." White simply states that General Custis Lee was alone, that he was separated from his command and was making his way toward the creek when White captured him. That Custis Lee was alone at the time of his capture is supported by a very similar account given Confederate Major Robert Stiles. Major Robert Stiles, commanding a battalion under Custis Lee, describes the final moments of the Battle of Sailor's Creek and his own capture as follows:

… I managed to get my men into some line sort of formation and their guns loaded, and then charged the Federal line, driving it back across the creek, and forming my command behind a little ridge, which protected it somewhat. I ran back up the hill and had a brief conversation with General Custis Lee–commanding the division, our brigade commander having been killed–explaining to him that I had not ordered the advance and that we would be cut off if we remained long where we were, but that I was satisfied I could bring the battalion back through a ravine, which would protect them largely from the fire of the enemy's artillery, and reform them on the old line, on the right of the naval battalion, which had remained in position. He expressed his doubts as to this, but I told him I believed my battalion would follow me anywhere, and with his permission I would try it. I ran down the hill again and explained to my men that when I got to the left of the line and shouted to them they were to get up and follow me, on a run and without special formation, through a ravine that led back to the top of the hill. Just because these simple-hearted fellows knew only enough to trust me, and because the enemy was not so far recovered as to take advantage of our exposure while executing the movement to the rear and reforming, we were back in the original lines in a few moments–that is, all who were left of us. It was of no avail. By the time we had well settled into our old position we were attacked simultaneously, front and rear by overwhelming numbers, and quicker than I can tell it the battle degenerated into a butchery and a confused melee of brutal personal conflicts. I saw numbers of men kill each other with bayonets and the butts of muskets, and even bite each others' throats and ears and noses, rolling on the ground like wild beasts. I saw one of my officers and a Federal officer fighting with swords over the battalion colors, which we had brought back with us, each having his left hand upon the staff. I could not get to them, but my man was a very athletic, powerful seaman, and soon I saw the Federal officer fall. I had cautioned my men against wearing "Yankee overcoats," especially in battle, but had not been able to enforce the order perfectly–and almost at my side I saw a young fellow of one of my companies jam the muzzle of his musket against the back of the head of his most intimate friend, clad in a Yankee overcoat, and blow his brains out. I was wedged in between fighting men, only my right arm free. I tried to strike the musket barrel up, but alas, my sword had been broken in the clash and I could not reach it. I well remember the yell of demoniac triumph with which that simple country lad of yesterday clubbed his musket and whirled savagely upon another victim. I don't think I ever suffered more than during the few moments after I saw that nothing could possibly affect or change the result of the battle. I could not let myself degenerate into a mere fighting brute or devil, because the lives of these poor fellows were, in some sense, in my hands, though there was nothing I could do just then to shield or save them. Suddenly, by one of those inexplicable shiftings which take place on a battle-field, the fighting around me almost entirely ceased, and whereas the moment before the whole environment seemed to be crowded with the enemy, there were now few or none of them on the spot, and as the slaughter and the firing seemed to be pretty well over, I concluded I would try to make my escape. By the way I had always considered it likely I should be killed, but had never anticipated or contemplated capture. I think it was at this juncture I encountered General Custis Lee, but it may have been after I was picked up. At all events, selecting the direction which seemed to be most free from Federal soldiers and to offer the best chance of escape, I started first at a walk and then broke into a run; but in a short distance ran into a fresh Federal force, and it seems the most natural and easy thing in the world to be simply arrested and taken in. My recollection is that General Lee asked to be carried before the Federal general commanding on that part of the line, who, at his request, gave orders putting a stop to the firing, there being no organized Confederate force on the field. Thus ended my active life as a Confederate soldier, my four years' service under Marse Robert, and I was not sorry to end it thus, in red-hot battle, and to be spared the pain, I will not say humiliation, of Appomattox.

[Source: Robert Stiles, "Four Years under Marse Robert, Neale Publishing Company, New York, 1903, pages 329-335]Manuscript 2**

This Stiles account brings out four important points bullet pointed below:

- Like David White's account where Custis Lee was alone and making his way towards the creek when White captured him, Major Stiles was also alone and making an escape attempt when he was captured by Federal forces.
- Stiles might have encountered Custis Lee at the moment Stiles was making his escape attempt, suggesting as well that General Custis Lee was making an escape attempt to avoid capture. It would have been nice if Robert Stiles had a more definitive recollection of this important fact. Some scholars might argue that Robert Stiles', "Four Years under Marse Robert," is filled with this type of uncertainty and can not be relied upon to be accurate. The author argues that Stiles' account is extremely valuable and most likely accurate, and offers the following editorial in support of this viewpoint.

The primary shortcoming of Four Years Under Marse Robert *lies in its origins in a discouragingly imprecise instrument – the human mind, unguided by contemporary records, and separated from the event to be chronicled by four decades. There are some twenty separate instances in the book in which Stiles frankly confesses forgetfulness. The more critical instances are on pages 42, 156, 181, 227, 231, 320 and 331. The third entry listed is a good example, as the author discusses with himself in print whether he attended Jackson's funeral in Richmond – or whether someone else told him of seeing it! These admissions are more noteworthy for their honesty than for the uniqueness of the problem. Many authors in the same straits flailed away to the same end, without acknowledging the difficulty. Stiles' intent in the matter was impeccable (p. 302), and he recognized the situation frankly (p. 44)…. Robert K. Krick, Chancellorsville, VA, 1977*

[Source: "Four Years under Marse Robert" by Robert Stiles, Major of Artillery in the Army of Northern Virginia, Introduction and Index by Robert K. Krick, Press of Morningside Bookshop, 1977]**Manuscript 2**

- Major Stiles had a sword during the battle.
- General Custis Lee asked to be brought to a Federal General at the time of his capture.
- B. **Second:** Hassett states that Hawthorn rushed in front of his comrades and at the point of his bayonet captured General Custis Lee, suggesting that Custis Lee was in front of his line unprotected by his men. In contrast, Major Stiles' states in his account that he (Stiles) placed himself <u>behind</u> his line at very critical moments of the Federals' advance:

… My men were lying down and were ordered not to expose themselves. I was walking backward and forward just <u>back</u> of the line, talking to them whenever that was practicable, and keeping my eye upon everything, feeling that such action and exposure on my part were imperatively demanded by the history and condition of the command and my rather peculiar relations to it.... The Federal infantry had crossed the creek and were now coming up the slope in two lines of battle. I stepped in <u>front</u> of my line and passed from end to end, impressing upon my men that no one must fire his musket until I so ordered…. The enemy showed no disposition to break into the charge, but continued to advance in the same deliberate and even hesitating manner, and I allowed them to approach very close—I should be afraid to say how close—before retiring <u>behind</u> my men. I had continued to walk along their <u>front</u> for the very purpose of preventing them from opening fire, but now <u>I stepped through the line</u>, and, stationing myself about the middle of it, called out my orders deliberately—the enemy, I am satisfied, hearing every word. "Ready!" To my great delight the men rose, all together, like a piece of mechanism, kneeling on their right knees and their faces set with an expression that meant— everything. "Aim!" The musket barrels fell to an almost perfect horizontal line leveled about the knees of the advancing front line. "Fire!"

[Source: Robert Stiles, "Four Years under Marse Robert," Neale Publishing Company, New York, 1903, pages 329-335]**Manuscript 2**

One would definitely think that General Custis Lee, being a Division commander, would have been even more careful than Stiles to place himself behind the protection of his line during the critical moments of the battle.

C. **Third:** This David White account distinguishes itself from the T. J. Hassett account in that White's account describes two events that the Hassett account does not: **(1)** the giving up of a sword with surrender, **(2)** the reluctance of an officer to surrender to a Private, together with the desire of an officer to surrender to another officer. The following are just a few examples to show that there is clear precedence for surrendering one's sword when captured, and the desire of an officer to surrender only to another officer when captured.

Sword Surrender Examples: (A – J)

Example A:
HOW I RECOVERED BY SWORD
By Brevet Major HENRY S. BURRAGE
The circumstances connected with my capture November 1, 1864, on the left of our line at Petersburg, VA, I have already recorded in a paper read before the Commandery March 7, 1888. The sword which I carried at the time of my capture was one which I especially valued, as it was the sword which I held in my hand, inclosed in the scabbard, when I was wounded at the battle of Cold Harbor, June 3, 1864. The blood stains on the scabbard were not removed at the time, and when later I discovered them I let them remain, it being my purpose to preserve the sword as a memorial of a day which would have for me life-long memories. But the officer who was in command of the Confederate picket line at the point where I was captured demanded my sword – this sword which I desired so much to keep. I reluctantly handed it to him, and at the same time I expressed my mind somewhat freely on account of what I regarded as bad faith on the part of the Confederates in making the capture. Believing that I would be returned to our own lines as soon as I should reach an officer of higher rank, and state the circumstances of the capture, I asked the name of the officer who demanded my sword in order that I might secure it on my return to our lines. He gave his name as Captain James A. Summers, Company A, 33d North Carolina Troops. As it was finally determined that I should be held as a prisoner of war, my expectation of a release was not realized, and consequently I did not then recover the sword that was taken from me at the time of my capture. On Major Burrange's quest to recover his sword after the war, he received a more detailed account of his capture and sword as follows:

Major Henry S. Burrage,
Portland, Me.
MY DEAR SIR: -- Replying to your very kind letter of the 24th inst., I wish to repeat somewhat more fully my first statement, that First Lieutenant R. H. Teague, Company K, 7th North Carolina Regiment, captured a Federal officer in front of the picket of his regiment on the Petersburg lines in the vicinity of the Jones house in the early winter of 1864. Lieutenant Teague stated that the officer came within easy range of his line and displayed a newspaper, and not being aware of any previous arrangement in regard to swapping papers, he very naturally supposed that the officer approached for purposes of observation, and acting on that belief he demanded an immediate surrender. Captain Summers, Company A, 33d North Carolina Regiment, was the commanding officer of Lane's Brigade picket and happened to be present, and assumed charge of the captured officer and his arms by virtue of his rank. Lieutenant Teague, finding that Captain Summers was disposed to retain the sword, made a formal demand for it, and to decide the ownership, as between them, a commission was called, and in accordance with its judgment, and very properly so, as Captain Summers had neither demanded nor compelled the surrender, the sword was given to Lieutenant Teague and by him sent to his home in Alexander County, North Carolina, with the expressed determination of keeping it as long as he lived. The affair was by many at the time regretted, and there was some disposition to censure Lieutenant Teague for seemingly acting in bad faith, but when it transpired that he had in no way enticed the Federal officer to his line, then his action was approved by his comrades in arms, and also by his regimental commander. As before stated, Lieutenant Teague has been dead for several years. I hope

you will succeed in recovering your sword, for I can well imagine that it has a value to you that could not possibly attach to any other person.
Yours sincerely,
J. S. Harris

This account shows the importance of surrendering a sword during a capture. It is also interesting to note that an officer would, by virtue of his rank, take control of a captured enemy officer along with any side arms that the captured enemy officer might possess.

[Source: War Papers. Read before the Commandery of the State of Maine, Military Order of the Loyal Legion of the United States, Vol II, Portland, ME; Lefavor Tower Company; 1902]**Manuscript 34**

Example B:

With regard to General Robert E. Lee's surrender to General Grant, the following terms applied as pertaining to the "turning over" of swords and side arms during the surrender:

Headquarters, Armies of the United States
Appomattox Court House, VA, April 9, 1865
To: General R. E. LEE, Commanding C. S. Army
In accordance with the substance of my letter to you…. I propose to receive the surrender of the Army of Northern Virginia on the following terms, to wit: Rolls of all the officers and men to be made in duplicate….; the officers to give their individual paroles not to take up arms against the Government of the United States until properly exchanged…. The arms, artillery, and public property are to be parked and stacked, and turned over to the officers appointed by me to receive them. This will not embrace the side-arms of the officers, nor their private horses or baggage. This done, officers and men will be allowed to return to their homes, and not be disturbed by United States authority so long as they observe their paroles and the laws in force where they may reside.
Very respectfully,
U.S. GRANT, Lieutenant-General
Since it was specifically mentioned that side arms were allowed to be retained by the officers, it meant the men would not have to suffer the humiliation of turning over their swords. This also relieved Lee from tendering his sword to Grant which was customary in a situation like this.

It would appear from this example that surrendering a sword was not a unique event during a formal surrender, but was in fact a customary protocol.

[Source: "Great Campaigns, the Appomattox Campaign, March 29–April 9, 1865," by Chris Calkins, Combined Books, PA; 1997]**Manuscript 36**

Example C:

Near the close of the battle of Ball's Bluff, October 21, 1861, 1st Lieut. J. Evarts Greene of the 15th Mass., found himself surrounded by the enemy so that to fight longer was useless, and to run away impossible. At this moment a gray coated gentlemen stepped forward, and, raising his cap courteously, said: "I am Captain Singleton of the 13th Miss. I must ask you to surrender." Mr. Greene returned the salute, mentioned his name and rank, and handed Captain Singleton his sword.

There does not seem to be any question in Lieut. Greene's mind that he needed to surrender his sword, and there does not seem to be any question in Captain Singleton's mind to demand the sword from Greene.

[Source: "Camp Fire Sketches and Battlefield Echoes" W. C. King & Co 1887. Story entitled on page 488, "Interesting War Relic, a Sword Returned to its Owner after Twenty-Two Years"]**Manuscript 82**

Example D:

This is an account from the Official Records that highlights the importance of swords and their relation to prisoners of war.

Office Commissary-General of Prisoners,
Detroit, Mich., August 29, 1862
Capt. H. M. Lazelle, U. S. Army
Agent for Delivery of Prisoners of War, Vicksburg, Miss.

CAPTAIN: In my letter this morning I omitted to mention that a box of swords belonging to the officers of the Confederate Army will be forwarded to you by the quartermaster at Columbus, and you will please return [them] to their owners when you turn the prisoners over to the agent who is to receive them. Some of the swords belong to officers who have taken the oath of allegiance and been released. These you should bring back with you to be returned to their owners. Capt. William Peyton is one of them. Other swords belong to officers who were at Fort Warren, and if they are marked so as to be distinguished you may turn them over to the agent and take his receipt. Swords which are without marks you will bring back with you to be held subject to the order of the owners. Pistols are not considered side-arms and will not be returned. If there are any in the box you will bring them back with you.

Very Respectfully, your obedient servant,
W. HOFFMAN, Colonel Third Infantry, Commissary-General of Prisoners

[Source: Official Records of the Union and Confederate Armies, Volume 4, Series 2; "Prisoners of War"]**Manuscript 92**

Example E:

Federal Lieutenant George Peck of the 2nd Rhode Island describes the following incident that happened during the Battle of Sailor's Creek.

…With the third dash came the words: "Now close on them—Go for them!" I always had a horror of stepping on the wounded, especially my own; besides this was my first charge, and that over anything but smooth ground; so naturally I devoted considerable attention to seeing where I was going. At length I imagined I had about reached the summit, and must be ready to close on the hostiles, so I looked up; but lo! No one was before me. Surprised and perplexed, I turned to the left and no one was there. The colors were already half way down the hill and moving deliberately to the rear; the soldiers on the extreme left had already reached the creek. Glancing now to the right, I found the nearest man, eight or ten feet away, was wheeling about. As I did not care to present any Confederate with either sword, watch or revolver, and could offer but slight resistance when single-handed, I concluded to retrace my steps also, and accordingly commenced a march in common time to the rear.

It appears from this account that Lt. Peck was fully aware that if he were captured by a Confederate, he would have to give up his sword, watch and revolver.

[Source: "The Appomattox Campaign, March 29–April 9, 1865" by Chris M. Calkins, Combined Books, 1997]**Manuscript 35**

Example F:

Confederate Lieutenant-Colonel R. T. Duke of the 2nd Battalion Virginia Reserves writes the following account of surrendering his sword at the Battle of Sailor's Creek.

… All things were quiet for a time; then I observed a flag of truce on the opposite ridge. General Barton directed me to meet it. I did so, and proceeded to the bottom of the ravine, where I met a mounted officer, who proved to be General (or Colonel) Oliver Edwards. He informed me that Generals Ewell, Lee, and all of the command who were not killed, had surrendered, and he desired us to surrender in order to prevent the further useless effusion of blood. This proposition I declined, on the grounds that we had received no orders from our commanders to surrender. I reported the interview to General Barton and about that time a squadron of Virginia cavalry rode up from the rear and we surrendered. I surrendered my sword, which had been the dress-sword of my great-grandfather, a Dr. Thomas

Walker, of Castle Hill; to a lieutenant, taking down his name, and some years since I recovered it by paying $25 (C. O. D.).
[Source: Southern Historical Society Papers, Volume 25, "Burning of Richmond," by R. T. W. Duke, page 138]**Manuscript 38**

Example G:

Confederate Captain Blake, of the 10th Virginia Artillery in Colonel Crutchfield's Artillery Brigade, wrote about the Battle of Sailor's Creek with regard to surrendering his sword.

… In the meanwhile the infantry, which had been driven across the creek, had reformed and were advancing in force. Our men then threw down their arms, and we were prisoners of war. I remember that in the hot blood of youth, I broke my sword over a sapling, rather than surrender it.
[Source: Southern Historical Society Papers, Volume 25, "Retreat from Richmond," by Thomas Ballard Blake, page 142]**Manuscript 38**

Example H:

The following account, concerning General Kershaw surrendering to a Corporal of the Federal Calvary, is unique in two respects. First, a Federal Lieutenant Cavalryman, seeing that one of his subordinate Corporals captured General Kershaw, demanded Kershaw's sword. Second, General Kershaw's captor wore Kershaw's sword on his belt as a trophy. This account bears remarkable resemblance to the David White/William Morrill account in the Official Records where Morrill wore Custis Lee's sword after Custis Lee's capture. General Kershaw himself is giving this account.

… Then, lead the way, Corporal' said I and we rode away together. Emerging from the wood into the open ground, we passed along the line of a regiment of Union cavalry. We had not proceeded far, before a smart, brusque young officer galloped across the field, and joined the party. "Who is it you have there, Corporal," he asked. "General Kershaw," said Lanham. The officer then addressed me. "I see you have a sword by your side," said he. "Yes," I replied. "I will trouble you for it," said he. I turned to Lanham and said "Corporal, I surrendered to you upon your pledge of honor that I should be conducted to General Custer's headquarters without molestation or insult and I call upon you to redeem your pledge." He replied, "General, I did make you this promise, and this gentleman has no right to your sword, but he is my superior officer, and I cannot protect you." I then handed my sword to the officer after obtaining his name, and charging Lanham to remember it. He was a Lt. R [blank] of the [blank] 8th Illinois Cavalry…. When I awoke, the sun shone brightly, and all was bustle and activity. Our host was already up, and gave me a cheery greeting as I arose and joined him, standing near the fire. He wore an air of thought upon his face, betokening the work of the day that lay before him—and received and sent many brief communications. Whilst at breakfast, one after another, some thirty troopers rode up within a few rods, each dismounting, and aligning himself, and holding his horse by the bridle. Each also carried a Confederate Battle Flag, except my captor of the previous day, whom I recognized in the ranks, and he bore two of our Flags. He also, as he caught my eye and bowed, pointed to my own saber, worn at his belt with an air of pride and pleasure. My curiosity was greatly excited by this group, and I asked Custer what it meant. "That," said he, "is my escort for the day. It is my custom after a battle to select for my escort a sort of garde du honeur, bearing, for the time, the trophies which they have taken from the enemy. These men are selected as the captors of the flags which they bear." I counted them. There were thirty-one captured banners, representing thirty-one of our regiments, killed, captured or dispersed the day before. It was not comforting to think of. Lanham's possession of my sword was easily accounted for. I had told Custer of the conduct of the officer who had taken it, and requested that Lanham should have it. He said nothing in reply, but, nonetheless, had done the right thing. May Lanham's descendants wield that sword in defense of their country, whenever called upon, as honestly as its old master sought to do his duty, according to the dictates of his conscientious convictions.
[Source: Black Day of the Army, April 6, 1865. The Battles of Sailor's Creek, by Greg Eanes, E & H Publishing Company, Inc., 2001]**Manuscript 98**

Example I:

The following account is relevant in that it deals specifically with Col. Archibald Hopkins, the 37th Massachusetts commander at the Battle of Sailor's Creek, and his taking of a Confederate sword at the Battle of Sailor's Creek.

… Yesterday, as Col. Hopkins sat in his home at 1826 Massachusetts Avenue, looking back over fifty-eight years to those three days of culminating strife, pursuit and victory, his eyes rested upon two crossed swords, while his old commander and friend, Gen. Phil Sheridan, looked down from a large autographed photograph. One of the swords was carried at Sailor's Creek and Appomattox, by Col. Hopkins; the other belonged to a Texas colonel, and was taken from him in hand-to-hand fighting on April 6. In the hilt is wrought a "lone star," showing the vanquished foe was a Texan. "If I knew where his relatives are I would be glad to restore it to them," said Col. Hopkins, showing that the war has left in his breast none but tender and sympathetic feelings toward those who were even his bitterest foes, while both sides were fighting for what they honestly believed to be right. … "We opened fire again with deadly effect and they gave up in earnest. Gen Custis Lee surrendered at the muzzle of Corp. David White's rifle."

[Source: An unknown and undated (probably 1923) newspaper article that was pasted and bound into a volume that had information about specific alumni, Williams College, Williamstown, MA, Archives and Special Collections, Citation Number: 63.W1862, Class of 1863, Volume VI, Griffin to Lewis]**Manuscript 148**

It is interesting to note that Colonel Hopkins, like his Lieutenant William Morrill (Custis Lee's sword), took possession of a sword from an enemy Confederate officer that was captured during the hand to hand battle at Sailor's Creek. It is also interesting and important that Hopkins puts forth a statement in this newspaper article that Custis Lee was captured by David White.

Example J:

This final account is interesting in that it shows that John R. Tucker, commander of a Confederate unit which was comprised of a mixture of sailors and marines, had in his possession during the Battle of Sailor's Creek a sword. He surrendered this sword when he was captured by the Federals.

… The battle was essentially over, and dusk was beginning to set in, when word reached General J. Warren Keifer, commander of the 2nd Brigade, 3rd Division, 6th Corps, that a force of Confederates was still in this patch of woods. Two efforts to communicate with the Confederate command failed. Keifer began to have doubts of the unit's existence and rode alone into the woods to investigate. Running head on into the Naval Battalion, Keifer was able to escape with his life only by the actions of Tucker and Marine Captain John D. Simms in using their swords to strike the rifle barrels of their men causing their aim to be poor. Upon making his escape, Keifer returned under a white flag to meet Tucker and explain to him his untenable situation following Ewell's surrender of his entire command. Tucker surrendered his sword to Keifer, the same one he had used to save Keifer's life moments earlier…. In 1878, Keifer, who was speaker of the U.S. House of Representatives, returned the sword to Tucker who, after the war, became an admiral in the combined navies of Peru and Chile in a war with Spain. The sword is now in the possession of Mrs. St. George Tucker Arnold of Oakridge, TN., widow of Tucker's great-grand-nephew.

[Source: "The "Aye, Ayes" At Sayler's Creek," "Alabama Confederate," Newsletter of the Alabama Division of the Sons of Confederate Veterans, January, 1998, Volume 17 Number 1]**Manuscript 158**

These examples of Confederate officers surrendering their swords to Federal officers, particularly at the Battle of Sailor's Creek, can lend credence to the story that Custis Lee surrendered his sword to Lieutenant William Morrill of the 37th Massachusetts as described in their accounts.

Officers Surrendering Examples (A-D)

In addition to the sword surrender accounts above, the following accounts give a nice description of how difficult it was for an officer to surrender to an enemy non-commissioned enlisted soldier.

Example A:

This account was taken from diary entries of William. H. Shaw, of the 37th Massachusetts, relating to the Battle of Sailor's Creek.

… In the midst of the battle when we were using our bayonets and the butts of our guns, and shouting to them to surrender, a private of our regiment came face to face with a colonel of a South Carolina regiment, the private says: surrender, the colonel says I cannot, my pride will not allow me to surrender my sword to a private, where is your colonel? I will surrender my sword to him." The private says: he is somewhere in the field, but you must surrender to me or I will shoot you down. The Colonel says: I cannot, the private shot him. As the colonel fell, the private bent over him and says: Do you think I done wrong to shoot you? The Colonel says: No, you did not; I was a fool to throw away my life for my pride. He asked the private if he was a Christian. He answered yes! Then said the Colonel; won't you pray for me, I cannot die like this, and while the tempest of battle was raging the soldier knelt by his side and offered up a short fervent prayer for the departing spirit, and at its close the dying officer joined in the Amen. He gave his sword to the soldier, also his gold watch a few keepsakes and a message for his wife, asking him to send them to her at the first opportunity giving him her address, the soldier said he would, he then picked up his rifle and continued on in the battle.
[Source: William H. Shaw: A Diary as kept by Wm. H. Shaw during the Great Civil War, from April 1861 to July 1865, by William H Shaw, 76 pp]**Manuscript 39**

Example B:

This is an account given by Charles Stevens Dwight, a Confederate Captain of the Corps. of Engineers and Staff of Major General J. B. Kershaw. It underscores how difficult it was for a Confederate officer to surrender to a Federal Private. It also highlights the desire of Confederate officers to surrender to Federal officers. Captain Dwight's narrative below is describing the Battle of Sailor's Creek

… I was riding rapidly back from the right to join the general and find out the situation. Suddenly I saw blue in every direction, but still hoped it might be some stray cavalry of ours, for many wore blue overcoats. In another moment a Yankee cavalryman riding towards me locked knees with me and said, "Halt!" Now, comrades, as these are personal reminiscences, and as many versions of this story have gotten out among my friends, I venture at the risk of glaring egotism to tell just how it happened. "Who are you?" said I. "Oh, I am a Yankee soldier and you are my prisoner." "I am not so sure of that," said I, fighting for time and looking about for one chance in a hundred to make a dash. "Oh, you needn't look around, we've got you tight." Just then a Confederate private was running across a little bare space. The Yankee called to him to halt; the soldier kept on running; the Yankee aimed and fired his seven-shooter carbine; the poor fellow fell in his tracks, hardly twenty yards off, dead, I supposed. Then the Yankee said, "That's the way I'd have done you if you had run. I guess you'll have to surrender." Our knees were still locked and his carbine rested on his thigh. I said, "You are a private, aren't you?" "Yes, I am a private." "Well, I'll be damned if I will surrender to a private," said I. "The hell you won't–then I'll have to shoot you." "Shoot and be damned, I will not surrender to a private, bring an officer and I will surrender to him," said I. "Well, you are a hell of a fellow." During this parley had I seen any chance to dash, and, having no side arms (staff officers often left them off on long marches), I fully intended giving my enemy a staggering blow in the face with my gauntleted hand–I could have escaped that fellow certainly; but there was not the shadow of a chance. Luckily, just then a major was passing and my Yankee hailed him saying, "Major, here is a rebel officer who says he'll be damned if he will surrender to a private." The major saluted and said, "He is perfectly right. Captain, I see you are a staff officer; upon whose staff are you?" "If you wish to know, find out; I do not give information to the enemy." "You

are right again, Captain, I beg pardon, I should not have asked. You see the situation; it is hopeless, will you give me your parole?" "There is no alternative, I give you my parole," said I. "Well, just ride aside, dismount if you choose, and await events," said he.

[Source: "A South Carolina Rebel's Recollections, Personal Reminiscences of the Evacuation of Richmond and the Battle of Sailor's Creek, April, 1865," read before Camp Hampton, U. C. V. Columbia S.C., by Charles Stevens Dwight, Captain Corps of Engineers, Staff of Major General J. B. Kershaw, the State Company, Columbia SC, 1917]**Manuscript 40**

Example C:

This is another version of the incident described by William H. Shaw on the preceding page, but it highlights more vividly a Confederate officer's refusal to surrender to a Federal corporal who became separated from his main command and inadvertently came upon the Confederate officer.

Thumbnail Sketches

During the fight, a corporal, who was noted for his quiet promptitude and unvarying good behavior, becoming a little separated from the main command, found himself confronted by a Confederate officer, whose surrender he demanded. The officer refused and the corporal fired, shooting him through the body. As he fell, the corporal bent over him and told him he was sorry he had to shoot him, and that he was a Christian, and, if he wished it, would pray with him. The officer eagerly assented, and the corporal knelt by his side amidst the drifting smoke and flying missiles, undisturbed by the roar of musketry and the shouts and groans of the combatants, and offered a fervent prayer for the parting soul of his dying foeman, hostile no longer. When he had finished, they shook hands, and the officer gave the corporal his sword as a memento, and asked him to write to his wife and tell her what had befallen him.

[Source: "The Battle of Sailor's Creek" by Archibald Hopkins, Late Colonel, 37th Massachusetts Volunteers as found in "The Military Engineer, Volume XIX, May-June, 1927, No. 105]**Manuscript 85**

Example D:

It would appear from the following entry in the Official Records that General Ewell himself had difficulty surrendering to a non-commissioned Federal officer at the Battle of Sailor's Creek.

… These men soon got into their rear, when, seeing further retreat useless, Lieutenant General Ewell surrendered himself and staff to Sergt. Angus Cameron, in charge of squad, remarking that he surrendered himself and 5,000 men, and inquired for an officer; none being present at the moment, he surrendered unconditionally. Soon after a squad of cavalry came up and claimed the prisoners and took possession of them.

[Source: Colonel T. S. Allen's Report of the 5th Wisconsin, on the Battle of Sailor's Creek, Official Records, "The Appomattox Campaign" Volume 46, Series 1, Folio 120, page 952]**Manuscript 4**

General Oliver Edwards in his own writings describes the surrender of Ewell and highlights Ewell's desire to surrender to a Federal commissioned officer at the Battle of Sailor's Creek.

Richard Ewell:

… Cameron ordered his men to lie low, and Ewell rode up close, when Cameron and his men unmasked, and with their guns (pointed) demanded the surrender of Ewell and staff. Ewell replied: "I am Lieut General Ewell. I desire to surrender to a commissioned officer, to which Sergt. Cameron responded: "I am Sergt. Cameron, get off that horse," and Ewell explained that he had but one leg, and was fastened by a strap to his horse. Sergt. Cameron sent in his prisoners and they spent the night at (Gen. Wright's) headquarters.

2. David White's account references the confiscation of two pieces of physical evidence from Custis Lee, his sword and his haversack. In an attempt to validate the newspaper accounts given by David White concerning Custis Lee's sword, the author's uncle contacted the Smithsonian Institute to see if they were in possession of the sword of General Custis Lee as stated in these articles. The following was their response.

NATIONAL   MUSEUM   OF   AMERICAN   HISTORY
SCIENCE, TECHNOLOGY, AND CULTURE
Smithsonian Institute Washington, D.C. 20560, December 3, 1991

Dear Mr. White:
Your letter dated August 28, 1991, requesting assistance in locating a sword, once the property of your great grandfather, has come to me for reply. I have tried to reach you by telephone but no luck. I would like to know the source, and time period, of the article you attached to your letter. As a matter of record I would like to correct one or two mistakes in your letter and the article. The "CUSTIS" Lee referred to was actually Major General George Washington Custis Lee, CSA; the eldest son of Robert E. Lee. Most often called Custis. He was captured on the sixth of April, 1865 at the battle of Sayler's Creek along with a number of General Officer's including Lt. Gen. Ewell. The sword referred to in your letter and article is not in the collections of the Smithsonian Institution. During the period 1880-1930 a number of biographical objects were at one time or the other brought here for special study and/or exhibit. These objects were normally returned to their owners. I have contacted Mrs. Agnes Mullins of the Staff at Arlington House and indicated to her your desire to locate the sword. She promised to get in touch with you and to do some research in trying to determine the whereabouts of the sword if possible. Good luck with your endeavor in locating the sword.
Sincerely, Harry Hunter, Museum Specialist, Armed Forces History
[Source: Personal letter in the possession of the author]Manuscript 41**

3. In an attempt to validate the account given by David White concerning the haversack of Custis Lee, the author conducted a search to determine if the Custis Lee haversack was ever at Williams College, as stated in the newspaper articles. Williams College, located in Williamstown MA, was contacted by the author in March, 1994, with the following reply.

WILLIAMS COLLEGE
Williamstown, MA, Archives and Special Collections, March 11, 1994
Dear Mr. White:
Unfortunately I can find neither hide nor hair of a haversack, which your records say was captured from Custis Lee and donated to Williams by a Dr. Duncan, in either our files or our collections. The College Art Museum has likewise come up empty handed. Rest assured that, if we ever run across an artifact of this description, we will contact you straight away.
Yours sincerely,
Sylvia B. Kennick, College Archivist: Special Collections Librarian
[Source: Personal letter in the possession of the author]Manuscript 42**

4. In an additional attempt to validate the accounts given by David White in these newspaper articles, the author conducted research to determine if a Dr. Duncan of Williamstown, MA, ever existed, as stated by David White. This avenue of research yielded good results. A brief sketch of Dr. Samuel Duncan of Williamstown, MA is as follows.

A Samuel Duncan was born in Williamstown February 1, 1820, to Samuel and Sarah Surgeon Duncan. He mustered into the Civil War April 29, 1863, and was appointed by President Lincoln as surgeon of

the Board of Enrollment for the 10th Congressional District of Massachusetts. He was honorably discharged June 15, 1865.
[Source: An excerpt of a letter from Nancy Burstein, Curator, Williamstown, MA, House of Local History, dated March 24, 1994, in the possession of the author]**Manuscript 42**

The obituary of Dr. Samuel Duncan was located by the author and it reads, in part, as follows.

The death of this prominent Williamstown man, who was widely known and respected in Western Massachusetts, on account of his remarkable force of character and conspicuous qualities, occurred at his office in Williamstown, on Friday…. The doctor was ever industrious in his profession, but during the war was prominent in public affairs. His headquarters were in Springfield and the Republican says: "The chief public work of Dr. Duncan's life was done in the city during the war period, from 1863-5, as examining surgeon for this Congressional district. He was loyal, intelligent and devoted, and Capt. H. M. Morehouse, who was then provost marshal, bears hearty testimony to the thorough work done by Dr. Duncan. He probably passed upon some 6000 cases, and was a difficult man to deceive."… The doctor was a member of the Massachusetts Constitutional Convention in 1853.
[Source: "The Adams Transcript," North Adams, MA, March 2, 1882 Edition]**Manuscript 161**

There is another interesting aspect to Dr. Samuel Duncan, which was his keen interest in Civil War history and the veterans of the Civil War. On March 7, 1863, the Commonwealth of MA passed an act entitled, "An Act to Preserve a Record of our Soldiers and Officers." This act required that the, "clerk of every city and town within the Commonwealth, as soon as may be after the passage of this act, to make out a full and complete record of the names of all soldiers and officers who compose his town's quota of the troops furnished by the Commonwealth to the United States during the present rebellion." The Williamstown, MA, "House of Local History" is currently in possession of this record book for the town of Williamstown. On the second page of this record book it lists the individuals who helped create it. It states: "It is commenced by the undersigned Town Clerk, in the month of October 1863; Daniel Dewey. It is continued by the undersigned Town Clerk; B. F. Mather Jr.; 1866. Saml Duncan completed this record in 1878, having been authorized to do so by vote of the Town." A small article in the Adams Transcript newspaper states the following:

A complete record of the participation of Williamstown in the war of the rebellion has been completed and presented to the town by Dr. Duncan. Dr. Duncan's position as examining surgeon in Springfield during the last three years of the war gave him especial knowledge of the matter required, but the work has nevertheless been one of great labor, covering a period of four years. The record contains the name, place of birth, year of birth, names of parents, time of enlistment, company, regiment, length of service, promotion and time of death of those already dead, of every soldier from Williamstown, with remarks on the deportment and character of each man. No other town in the state has so complete a record, and the doctor has performed an inestimable service in preparing it. The town, in recognition of the service, has voted Dr. Duncan $100. A copy of the record is to be placed in the town library and one also in the college library."
[Source: "The Adams Transcript," North Adams, MA, March 28, 1878 Edition]**Manuscript 162**

In a book entitled, "Williamstown and Williams College," by Arthur L. Perry, on page 24, it states, "Dr. Samuel Duncan was one of the most intellectually gifted boys ever born and bred in this town (Williamstown) and became correspondingly accomplished in the medical profession. In a book entitled, "Origins in Williamstown," page 40, also by Arthur L. Perry, there is an account of interest that states, "George Kidder was three years in the war as a private soldier in the 37th Massachusetts, with Colonel Richards, and was ruptured in the service, wore a truss ever after, never got any pension…. If Dr. Duncan had lived, he would have helped me get it." It would appear from all this evidence that there was, in fact, a Dr. Duncan of Williamstown. He was a prominent man, active in the Civil War and in post war veteran affairs, and he had some acquaintances with the veterans of the 37th Massachusetts. The 1865 MA State Census shows Samuel Duncan, physician, age 45, living in Williamstown with his wife, Francis, age 37, and his daughter, Eleanor, age 1. In the 1880 Federal Census for Williamstown, Dr. Samuel Duncan, age 60, is living with his wife, Francis, age 52, daughter Eleanor, age 16, and son, Richard, age 15. Dr. Samuel Duncan's Williamstown estate was probated July 30, 1883. An inventory of his possessions was examined by the author and it did not list the haversack. Francis Duncan's Williamstown, MA, estate was probated on December 19, 1892, and her will leaves all her estate to her daughter, Eleanor, and to her son, Richard, with no specific mention of the haversack. Eleanor Duncan's Williamstown, MA, estate was probated on November 17, 1937 and an inventory of her possessions did not list the haversack. Richard Duncan moved to Providence, RI, in 1906, and married Ida Howard in 1928. In Richard Duncan's will, he mentions wife, Ida, and a daughter, Mary Francis Duncan Stevenson, wife of George B. Stevenson of Loch Haven, PA. Richard does not mention the haversack in his will. Ida Duncan died in Providence, RI, in 1958, with no direct heirs, and her will does not mention the haversack. Mrs. Mary Duncan Stevenson died in Loch Haven, PA, September 18, 1973, with no heirs. In summary, a thorough search by the author for the current location of the General G. W. Custis Lee haversack through this Dr. Samuel Duncan family line ended with no success.

The author, however, would like to put forth a possible scenario concerning this haversack of Major General Custis Lee. David White married his first wife, Maria McVee, on July 12, 1866, at North Adams, MA. North Adams is a bordering City to Williamstown. At the time of her marriage, Maria McVee and her entire family resided in Williamstown. In fact, in the 1865 MA State Census, Maria's uncle, Richard Welch, a veteran of the 37th Massachusetts and a Medal of Honor recipient, was listed as a next-door neighbor to Dr. Samuel Duncan. On June 5, 1867, Maria White gave birth to twins who died shortly thereafter of illness in North Adams. On October 25, 1869, David White's wife Maria died in North Adams after suffering from typhoid fever. Did Dr. Samuel Duncan, neighbor to the McVee family in Williamstown, provide medical care for David White's family during these difficult times of family illness? Did David White pay Dr. Duncan for his medical services by giving him the prized Custis Lee haversack? David White was a lowly paid factory mill worker at this time and would not have had the financial means to pay Dr. Duncan for the extensive medical services rendered by him. With Dr. Duncan being a prominent Civil War veteran, and being actively interested in the history of the Civil War through his work on the Williamstown Veterans Record Book as cited above, he would have valued this haversack immensely. He might have easily considered it as a payment in full for the medical services he rendered to David White and his family. Hence, David White "presented" the haversack to the well known and prominent Dr. Duncan of Williamstown, as stated in the newspaper article.

5. Given the success of positively identifying a Dr. Duncan of Williamstown, MA, which validated this particular point of the David White newspaper article, Williams College was contacted again by the author in June, 1994. This was the author's last attempt to locate the Custis Lee haversack and determine its past whereabouts within Williams College. This was their reply:

WILLIAMS COLLEGE
Williamstown, MA, Archives and Special Collections, June 24, 1994

Dear Mr. White,
I have given another look for any information regarding the haversack of General Custis Lee being donated to, or being on display at, Williams College between 1865 and 1883. Unfortunately, I can find no mention of this item at all. Collections I have checked include: the Board of Trustee's minutes, donation and bequest ledgers of the Treasurer's Office, Library gift records, and presidents' papers from this period. This does not mean, of course, that the haversack was never on campus; only that we can find no documentation in our records of its having been here. I am forwarding your correspondence on to the curator of our local historical society, Nancy Burstein, in the hopes that she may be able to track some leads regarding Dr. Samuel Duncan. Perhaps if we look at this problem from another angle, we'll be able to find an answer.
Yours sincerely,
Sylvia B. Kennick, College Archivist: Special Collections Librarian
[Source: Personal letter in the possession of the author]Manuscript 42****

EXHIBIT-W-MR-5

Introduction:

Edward P. Bridgman: (PHOTO: COURTESY U. S. ARMY WAR COLLEGE)

Edward P. Bridgman was a soldier and war time correspondent for the 37th Massachusetts. He wrote letters back home to the editor of his local newspaper, the "Northampton Gazette and Courier," in MA. He reported exclusively on the various activities of his 37th Massachusetts. The following are two letters written by Bridgman to the editor. One is dated April 10, 1865, and the other is dated July 11, 1865. Both describe the 37th Massachusetts' activities at the Battle of Sailor's Creek and are written shortly after the events of this battle.

Evidence:

(1) From the 37th Regiment
Correspondent of the Gazette & Courier
30 Miles East of Lynchburg, VA, April 10, 1865

Messrs Editors,
… A portion of the 3rd division broke, that joined our brigade, which caused us [37th] to be flanked, and for a few moments a portion of our regiment had a hand to hand fight; a few men received bayonet wounds; some men said it was the closest and hottest engagement they were in…. At this battle many prisoners were taken [by the 37th], among them Gen. Lee's son.
E. P. B.

(2) Last Letter from the 37th Regiment
Correspondent of the Gazette & Courier
Northampton, July 11, 1865

Messrs Editors,
Although the 37th no longer exists as an organization, yet we wish to write one more letter under its heading, and briefly mention its efforts during its term of service…. Four days later occurred the last battle of the 6th corps, that of Sailor's Creek. The brunt of this fell to our brigade, and the heaviest to our regiment. In no engagement has so large a proportion of its loss been among the killed, 8 were killed instantly and as many more died shortly after from wounds. One flank of the regiment came into such close action that bayonets were used. Such an event seldom occurred during the war. A member of Co. D was thrust through the body and yet he recovered; but he can show a wide scar in the breast and another, two inches from the backbone. In this battle, the 37th alone, captured the greater part of a brigade, with their commander, Gen. Custis Lee; also one stand of colors was taken.
[Source: <u>First letter</u>: "Northampton Gazette and Courier," Northampton, MA, Tuesday, April 25, 1865 edition; <u>Second letter</u>: Tuesday, July 18, 1865 edition]**Manuscript 99**

Comments and Supporting Evidence:

1. These Bridgman letters, of the 37th Massachusetts, are just like the Kidder and Ingraham letters, of the 121st New York. At first glance, they appear to be compelling evidence for the capture of Custis Lee by their respective units. Reading the letters in their entirety; however, it is apparent that these men did not physically witness the capture of Custis Lee but were just merely writing back home the statistics as officially reported by their regiments in their "Official Reports."

2. As an aside, Bridgman appears to be a gifted writer. His description of the night of the Battle of Sailor's Creek is extremely moving, as found in his first letter cited above. It reads: "That night we were dressing wounds till a late hour. At 2 o'clock went over the battle ground where lay the dead and dying in every direction and position, in several instances the "army blue" and "grey coats" lay side by side. Some of our men were killed while charging through the swale, and there they lay half

under water, or more strictly speaking, mud. The sight witnessed by moonlight was truly awful. Then further on, at the top of the hill, was seen the line of battle, or where it had been, for it could be traced by the dead and dying. It was a sad sight too horrible to describe. In several instances half of the head was taken off, a half a leg mangled to a jelly; no words can convey to you an idea of the horribleness of that moonlight scene. Here and there was a man dying or piteously calling for water, or pleading to be taken off the field." His training as a school teacher could account for his ability to express himself in this descriptive and interesting writing style.

BIOGRAPHY:
Bridgman, Edward P.: Priv.; Res. Northampton; 28; teacher; enl. Aug. 5, 1862; must. Aug. 30, 1862; must. out June 21, 1865.
[Source: Massachusetts Soldiers, Sailors and Marines in the Civil War, Volume 3, Published by the Adjutant General, Norwood Press, 1932]**Manuscript 68**

EXHIBIT-W-MR-6

Introduction:
Harrie A. Cushman, a member of the 37th Massachusetts, claims the following in his own writings.

Evidence:
… At this time Lieut. Cushman was wounded, while Gen. Custis Lee was in the act of surrendering to him, by a marine who had thrown down his gun, the rebel thinking that he was about to shoot the general, having him covered by a revolver near his left cheek. Corporal White of Lieut. Cushman's company afterwards captured the general.
[Source: "History of the Seventh Massachusetts Volunteers Infantry in the War of the Rebellion of the Southern States Against Constitutional Authority 1861–1865," By Nelson V. Hutchinson: Taunton, MA, Published by Authority of the Regimental Association 1890, Chapter "Veterans and Recruits, 7th Massachusetts Volunteers, Transferred to the 37th Massachusetts Volunteers" compiled by Harrie A. Cushman]**Manuscript 83**

Comments and Supporting Evidence:
1. This is an interesting account in that it describes how Custis Lee was almost captured by Harrie Cushman before Custis Lee was finally captured by David White. This could indicate that Custis Lee was very much in the middle of the active battle during its final moments.

EXHIBIT-W-MR-7

Introduction:
An account of the capture of Custis Lee given by Archibald Hopkins, who was commanding the 37th Massachusetts at the Battle of Sailor's Creek.

Evidence:
… After this, of course, we opened fire again, with deadly effect, and they gave up this time in earnest. General Custis Lee surrendered at the muzzle of Corporal David White's rifle, and we sent to the rear with him, his staff and nearly three hundred prisoners, and a silk flag belonging to a crack Savannah battalion, besides the battle flag already spoken of.
[Source: "The Battle of Sailor's Creek" by Archibald Hopkins, Late Colonel, 37th Massachusetts Volunteers found in "The Military Engineer" Volume XIX, May-June, 1927 No. 105]**Manuscript 85**
Author Note: This article was first printed in the Janaury 30th, 1897, edition of the Harper's Weekly magazine. This article published in Harper's Weekly was entitled; "Incidents of Lee's Last Struggle-The Battle of Sailor's Creek." Archibald Hopkins' statement about David White's capture of Custis Lee was made several months before the filing of the 37th Massachusetts Protest Case on April 15, 1897.

Comments and Supporting Evidence:

1. This is an important piece of testimony from David White's direct regimental commander at the Battle of Sailor's Creek, Captain Archibald Hopkins.
2. It is interesting to note that Hopkins claims to have "sent" Custis Lee to the rear with many other prisoners.
3. If actually intended, Hopkins is mistaken in this writing when he states that his Regiment captured the 18th Georgia (Savannah) silk flag. This flag was captured by the 121st New York, not the 37th Massachusetts. Hopkins was most likely referring to the Federal forces "in general," capturing the Savannah flag, which did indeed send large numbers of Confederate prisoners and flags to the rear.

EXHIBIT-W-MR-8

Introduction:

This is an account of the capture of Custis Lee given by Oliver Edwards, commanding the 3rd Brigade at the Battle of Sailor's Creek. The 37th Massachusetts was a part of Edwards' 3rd Brigade.

Evidence:

... Gen. Custis Lee (**Author Note:** this was crossed out at this point in the sentence: *"surrendered to C")* was really captured by (Corporal) David White of Co. E, though his reply to the demand for his surrender was tut tut man, I wish to surrender to a commissioned officer.

[Source: "My Recollections of the Civil War" by General Oliver Edwards pages 228-247, loose paper manuscript undated at the Illinois State Historical Library, Old State Capitol, Springfield, IL, Note: Oliver Edwards' lifespan, was 1835-1904]Manuscript 84****

Comments and Supporting Evidence:

1. This is an important piece of testimony from White's immediate Brigade commander at the Battle of Sailor's Creek, Oliver Edwards.
2. Edwards' was most likely going to write; "surrendered to Corporal David White." Instead, he used the words, "really captured," in a probable attempt to differentiate the roles that White and Morrill played in the capture of Custis Lee. For example, David White, not William Morrill, "really captured" Custis Lee.
3. Edwards validates that Custis Lee wanted to surrender to a Federal commissioned officer.

EXHIBIT-W-MR-9

Introduction:

On an annual basis, the Adjutant-General of MA made a report to the Governor of MA outlining in detail all the activities of MA troops involved in the Civil War. This is an important excerpt from the MA Adjutant-General's report for the year of 1865.

Evidence:

... Among the prisoners who fell into our hands was Major-General Custis Lee, the son of the commander-in-chief of the rebel armies.

[Source: Annual Report of the Adjutant-General of the Commonwealth of MA for the Year Ending December 31, 1865, Boston, MA, 1866] Manuscript 133 ****

Comments and Supporting Evidence:

1. It is not known what original source was used by the Adjutant-General's Office to make this definitive statement in their official annual report concerning the capture of Custis Lee.
2. It is clear from this official annual report that the 37th Massachusetts is definitively laying claim to the capture of Custis Lee at the Battle of Sailor's Creek.

EVIDENCE OVERVIEW
EXHIBITS-W-PF-(1-29)

The purpose of introducing this line of evidence is to examine a counterclaim, made in the form of an official Protest Case, filed by the 37th Massachusetts Veterans' Association contesting Harris Hawthorn's award of a Medal of Honor for capturing Custis Lee. The 37th Massachusetts claims that David D. White, not Harris Hawthorn, captured Major General G. W. Custis Lee at the Battle of Sailor's Creek, April 6, 1865. A detailed point, counterpoint, debate occurred between the 37th Massachusetts Veterans' Association and Harris Hawthorn during this Protest Case, which proves to be most insightful. In addition, the Secretary of War makes a final decision in this Protest Case to resolve this intriguing matter.

EXHIBIT-W-PF-1

Introduction:

James L. Bowen:

James L. Bowen, secretary and historian of the 37th Massachusetts Veterans' Association, submits a letter dated April 15, 1897, to the Chief of the Record and Pension Office, contesting the award of a Medal of Honor to anyone else but David White of the 37th Massachusetts for the capture of Major General G. W. Custis Lee at the Battle of Sailor's Creek, VA. The letter below initiates the official Protest Case.

Evidence:

37th Massachusetts Regiment Veterans' Association
Secretary's Office, Springfield, Mass.
To: Chief, Record and Pension Office, April 15, 1897

My attention was recently called to a newspaper paragraph stating that some soldier (from Pennsylvania if I mistake not, but the item is not at hand for verification) had been granted a medal of honor for the capture of Gen. Custis Lee at Sailor's Creek. This is very surprising to us of the 37th Mass. Vols., which regiment fought hand to hand with the command of Custis Lee at said battle. Gen. Lee himself surrendered to Corporal David White (now of Charlemont, Mass.) of my own Co. E, after Lieut. Harrie A. Cushman, now of Taunton, Mass., had been wounded while demanding the surrender of Gen. Lee. I inclose the leaf from History of the 37th Mass. which states the fact, agreeing with the reports of our Massachusetts Adjutant General. Col. Archibald Hopkins, who commanded the 37th on this occasion, and was brevetted for gallantry, is Clerk of the Court of Claims in your city. My only desire in this matter is that justice be done, and I shall be very glad to cooperate with you to that end, as I am sure, sir, that you will share my feeling in this respect.
Very respectfully yours,
From: James L. Bowen, Historian 37th Mass., Author of Mass. In the War 1861–1865

[Source: 37TH Massachusetts Protest Case file at the National Archives: AGO Record & Pension Office, Document File #476510, File for David D. White, 37th Massachusetts, Volume 8W3 ROW16 COM 17, Shelf F, Box #699]Manuscript 24****

Comments & Supporting Evidence:

1. James. L. Bowen starts the 37th Massachusetts Protest Case with this letter dated April 15, 1897, which he sent to the Record and Pension Office of the War Department. James Bowen is stating that David D. White captured Custis Lee at the Battle of Sailor's Creek.

2. Bowen states that, "my only desire in this matter is that justice be done." It would appear that Bowen is not seeking a Medal of Honor for David D. White at this point in time, but is just seeking to "set the record straight."

BIOGRAPHY:
Bowen, James, L.: Priv.; Res. Adams; 20; operative; enl. July 25, 1862; must. Sept. 2, 1862; wounded July 3, 1863, Gettysburg, Penna; disch. for wounds, April 17, 1864.
[Source: Massachusetts Soldier, Sailors and Marines in the Civil War, Volume 3, Compiled and Published by the Adjutant General, Norwood Press; 1932]**Manuscript 68**

EXHIBIT-W-PF-2

Introduction:

F. C. Ainsworth:

A response from a Colonel F. C. Ainsworth, Chief of the Record and Pension Office, dated April 20, 1865, acknowledging receipt of James Bowen's letter and stating the matter is being turned over to the Office of the Secretary of War.

Evidence:
From: RECORD AND PENSION OFFICE, WAR DEPARTMENT, Washington City, April 20, 1897
To: Mr. James L. Bowen
Referring to your letter of the 15th instant, in which, with reference to the medal of honor which has been awarded to a late member of the 121st New York Volunteers for the capture of General Custis Lee, C. S. A., at Sailors Creek, Virginia, April 6, 1865, you state that, as shown by the history of the 37th Massachusetts Volunteers, and the reports of the Adjutant General of the State of Massachusetts, General Lee surrendered to Corporal David White of Company E of the 37th Massachusetts Volunteers, I beg leave to inform you that your letter, together with the papers upon which the award of the medal to the New York soldier was based, has this day been submitted to the Secretary of War, and that as soon as a decision is reached you will be promptly advised.
Very respectfully,
F. C. Ainsworth, Colonel, U.S. Army, Chief Record and Pension Office.
[Source: 37th Massachusetts Protest Case file at the National Archives: AGO Record & Pension Office Document File #476510, File for David D. White, 37th Massachusetts, Volume 8W3 Row 16 COM 17, Shelf F, Box #699]**Manuscript 24**

Comments & Supporting Evidence:
1. This is the official initiation at the Federal Government level of the comprehensive and complex 37th Massachusetts Protest Case which caused the Secretary of War much difficult deliberation.
2.

EXHIBIT-W-PF-3

Introduction:
An introductory (summary) report generated by Colonel F. C. Ainsworth, Chief of the Record and Pension Office, to the Secretary of War, dated April 20, 1897, concerning the 37th Massachusetts Veterans' Association's dispute with Harris Hawthorn over the capture of General Custis Lee.

Evidence:

From: RECORD AND PENSION OFFICE, WAR DEPARTMENT, April 20, 1897

Respectfully returned to: The Honorable Secretary of War,

With testimony disputing this man's right to the Medal of Honor awarded him, and supplemental report:

SUPPLEMENTAL REPORT:

The application for the award of a medal of honor to this soldier, having been submitted to the Secretary of War, was returned to this office under date of December 12, 1894, with remarks of the Assistant Secretary of War as follows: "By direction of the President let a medal of honor be presented to Harris S. Hawthorne, late Sergeant, Co. F, 121st New York Volunteers." "This non-commissioned officer, while serving as a private in the same company and regiment, captured General G. W. Custis Lee of the Confederate Army, on April 6, 1865." A medal of honor was accordingly engraved "The Congress to Sergeant Harris S. Hawthorne, Company F, 121st New York Volunteers, for gallantry at Sailor's Creek, VA, April 6, 1865," and was sent to Mr. Hawthorne by registered mail, December 29, 1894. Following is a copy of a letter dated April 15, 1897, from James L. Bowen, Historian 37th Massachusetts Volunteers, addressed to the Chief of this office, where it was received April 17, 1897; "My attention was recently called to a newspaper paragraph stating that some soldier (from Pennsylvania if I mistake not, but the item is not at hand for verification), had been granted a medal of honor for the capture of Gen. Custis Lee at Sailor's Creek. This is very surprising to us of the 37th Mass. Vols., which regiment fought hand to hand with the command of Custis Lee at said battle. Gen. Lee himself surrendered to Corporal David White (now of Charlemont, Mass.) of my own Co. E, after Lieut. Harrie A. Cushman, now of Taunton, Mass., had been wounded while demanding the surrender of Gen. Lee. I enclose the leaf from History of the 37th Mass., which states the fact, agreeing with the reports of our Massachusetts Adjutant General. Col. Archibald Hopkins, who commanded the 37th on this occasion, and was brevetted for gallantry, is Clerk of the Court of claims in your city. My only desire in this matter is that justice be done, and I shall be very glad to cooperate with you to that end, and I am sure, sir, that you will share my feelings in this respect." The leaf from the history of the 37th Massachusetts Volunteers referred to in the foregoing letter, contains the following statement:

"General Custis Lee, who directed the charge upon the Thirty-seventh, had till shortly before filled a clerkship at Richmond, but finally laid down the pen to take up the sword, surrendering the latter at the muzzle of the Spencer rifle to Corporal David White of Company E." The official records show that David D. White was a corporal in Company E, 37th Massachusetts Infantry Volunteers,-enrolled August 21, 1862, and mustered out with company June 21, 1865,-and he is reported present on the muster roll of the company covering April 6, 1865. Following are extracts from reports of Captain Archibald Hopkins, 37th Massachusetts Infantry, commanding that regiment at Battle of Sailor's Creek, VA, April 6, 1865: Extract from report dated April 7, 1865: "There were 360 officers and men and General C. Lee captured by my command. General Lee was captured by Pvt. David D. White, Co. E, of this regiment, and he formally surrendered his sword to Lieut. W. C. Morrill, of this regiment, who now wears it." Extract from report of April 15, 1865: "General Custis Lee, who commanded their (enemy's) line, surrendered and gave up his sword to Private David D. White, of Company E."

F. C. Ainsworth

Colonel, U. S. Army, Chief, Record and Pension Office, Record and Pension Office,

[Source: National Archives File 401673, Medal of Honor Application file for Harris Hawthorn. Some paperwork from the 37th Massachusetts Protest Case file (National Archives File 476510) made its way into Hawthorn's 401673 Medal of Honor Application file. This is one such instance]**Manuscript 15**

Comments & Supporting Evidence:

1. This letter with its supplemental report is the Protest Case being turned over from the Record and Pension Office by its chief, F. C. Ainsworth, to the Office of the Secretary of War. Ainsworth nicely summarizes the matter for the Office of the Secretary of War.

EXHIBIT-W-PF-4

Introduction:

(1) A letter from James Bowen dated April 22, 1897, asking Harrie A. Cushman, Esq., to write a letter to the Secretary of War stating what he knows about the capture of General Custis Lee at the Battle of Sailor's Creek. (2) A letter from Harrie A. Cushman dated April 26, 1897, to R. A. Alger, Secretary of War, stating what he knows about the capture of Custis Lee at the Battle of Sailor's Creek.

Evidence:

(1) *37th Massachusetts Regiment Veterans' Association:*
From: SECRETARY'S OFFICE, Springfield, Mass. April 22, 1897.
To: Harrie A. Cushman, Esq., Taunton, Mass.:

Dear Comrade—Agreeable to my promise to you, I have taken up the matter of the medal for the capture of Gen. Custis Lee, and my claim that this was done by Corporal David White, Co. E, 37th Mass., is now in the hands of the Hon. Secretary of War. With it has gone the papers on which the medal was awarded to the member of 121st New York, and probably the matter will be thoroughly looked up. I wish you would write to the Secretary of War, telling him what you know about the matter, as I have made reference to your part and your being wounded at the time; of course it will be well if this can be done right away, so as to make sure of our ground.
Yours most sincerely,
From: James L. Bowen

(2) *From: F. C. Ainsworth, Colonel, U. S. Army*
April 26, 1894
To: Hon. R. A. Alger

Harris A. Cushman claims that the honor of the capture of General Custis Lee belongs to this man and Mr. White should have been awarded the Medal of Honor for the capture instead of a member of the 121st New York. Secy of War, please find herewith a letter from James L. Bowen Historian of the 37th Mass. Vols (from Harrie H. Cushman) relating to capture of General Custis Lee, Confederate Army, April 6th, 1865.

Harrie H. Cushman: (PHOTO: COURTESY U. S. ARMY WAR COLLEGE)

On said day, my Company "E" of the 37th Mass. Vols was on the left of the regiment. I was 2d Lieut. of the Company. As we advanced on the Confederate line, I approached General Lee with revolver and said to him, "you are my prisoner, surrender," he said, "I surrender." At that time I was struck by a bullet which went through my scrotum, ticked the left testicle, hit left buttock and came out about two inches from end of spine in buttock – upon which, I withdrew to the rear. I learned after that Corp'l David White of my Co. "E" 37th Mass. Vols captured General Custis Lee. Did not see it, but have every reason to believe Gen'l Lee was taken prisoner by White. The 121st New York was, when the advance was made, more than 4 companies distance from me, just before I was shot, and I think the honor should go to whom it belongs. Corp'l White I think is still living in Charlemont, Mass. He was an excellent soldier and will tell the truth regarding the matter.
Very Truly Yours
Harris H. Cushman

[Source: 37th Massachusetts Protest Case file at the National Archives: A60 Record and Pension Office Document File #476510 (477608), File for David D. White, 37th Massachusetts, Volume 8W3 ROW16, COM17, SHELF F, Box #699]Manuscript 24****

Comments & Supporting Evidence:

1. James Bowen most likely contacted Harrie A. Cushman, Esq. first because it would appear that Lt. Cushman made an initial attempt to capture General Custis Lee, and Cushman was right in the

middle of all the action at the battle. Lieut. Cushman does not have any first-hand knowledge of Custis Lee's capture by David D. White, due to Cushman being severely wounded.

2. It is not possible to determine from this account where Custis Lee was when Cushman made his capture attempt. It was, most likely, in the final moments of the battle when both the Federal and Confederate troops were commingled in a desperate hand to hand fight as will be seen later in this report. The mere fact that Cushman was quickly shot during this attempted capture of Custis Lee could indicate that this event occurred in the middle of the fierce hand to hand fight.

3. Cushman indicates that the 121st New York was more than four companies distant from his Co. E of the 37th Massachusetts when the Federal advance was made, and that his Company E was on the extreme left of the 37th Massachusetts.

BIOGRAPHY:
Cushman, Harrie A.: 1st Sergt.; Res. Taunton; 19; clerk; trans. June 1864, from 7th Mass. Inf.; comm. 2d Lieut., Oct. 13, 1864; must. March 7, 1865; wounded April 6, 1865; Sailor's Creek, VA; disch for wounds to date May 15, 1865, S. O. #357, War Dept., as 2d Lieut. of Co. A. See Co. F, 7th Mass. Inf.
[Source: Massachusetts Soldiers, Sailors and Marines in the Civil War, Volume 3, Compiled and Published by the Adjutant General, Norwood Press; 1932]**Manuscript 68**

EXHIBIT-W-PF-5

Introduction:

Oliver Edwards:

A letter from Oliver Edwards, Brvt. Major General, dated April 24, 1897, to Russell Alger, Secretary of War, stating what he knows about the capture of General Custis Lee at the Battle of Sailor's Creek. Oliver Edwards commanded the 3rd Brigade, of which, the 37th Massachusetts was a part during this battle.

Evidence:
Genl Oliver Edwards states circumstances under which this man captured Genl Custis Lee:
From: RECORD AND PENSION OFFICE, Washington, April 29, 1897.
Respectfully submitted to the Honorable Secretary of War, in connection with the papers upon which was based the award of a medal of honor to Harris S. Hawthorne, late private, Co. F, 121st New York Volunteers, and the testimony disputing his right to the medal; which papers and testimony were submitted on the 20th instant.
F. C. Ainsworth, Colonel, U.S. Army, Chief of Office

EXAMPLE: CIVIL WAR ERA MEERSCHAUM PIPE

To: Hon. Russell Alger U.S. Secretary of War
Warsaw, Illinois, April 24th, 1897
My attention is called to the report that the War Dept. has awarded a medal of honor to a Private of the 121st New York for capturing General Custis Lee. This is a great injustice to the 37th Mass Vols and to Corporal David White Co. E, 37th Mass Vols, the actual captor of Gen. Custis Lee. In the Battle of Sailor's Creek, April 6, 1865, I commanded my brigade, the 3rd of the 1st Div 6th Corps and the 37th Mass Vols was my left regiment. Major General Custis Lee commanded Gen Ewell's left division formed in two lines with the left and center in my front resisting my attack formed in one line without supports. As my brigade advanced up the Heights, the 49th Penna Vols connecting with the right of the 37th Mass Vols came under a fire of canister from our own batteries posted on the heights in our rear, and by the unauthorized orders of its Colonel Hickman fell back to the base of the hill, and the regiment

on its right conformed to the movement. Though these regiments obeyed my orders with alacrity and charged up the hill again, yet for some minutes there was a gap in my line on the right of the 37th Mass Vols – of the front of these two regiments. General Custis Lee charged with one of his brigades into this gap; his lines being closed en masse. The 37th Mass. were armed with Spencer magazine rifles which made them equal in fighting strength to a good brigade, and they seeing the coming charge, changed front forward on their right which brought them in contact with the right flank of General Lee's charging column and the bayonet was used freely. It was right here and then that Corporal David White, Co. E, 37th Mass. Vol. Inft captured Major General Custis Lee and when he disarmed him, he took from him his haversack and this fact would probably enable General Wright, commander of the 6th Corps, to remember that General Lee was captured by my command as Corporal White found in General Lee's haversack a marchaum pipe and an embroidered silk tobacco bag which he gave to me. At the close of the next day's march, I was at General Wright's headquarters smoking this pipe and I told General Wright that it was General Lee's pipe and tobacco and how it was taken. General Wright said that Custis Lee was his pupil at West Point and that he would like to send the pipe and bag of tobacco back to him. I gave them to General Wright, who sent them to General Lee. The 37th Mass. Vols., in contact with General Lee's charging column on their right flank, with their bayonets and the terrible fire of their repeating rifles enfilading Lee's lines en masse; killed, wounded or captured the entire charging column. No other regiment or command had anything to do with this part of the fight or with the capture of Major General Custis Lee. The Private of the 121st New York has probably mistaken some officer captured by him for General Lee. I have written in detail of the facts relating to the capture of General Lee in order to show clearly the circumstances of the capture.
Very Respectfully, Your Obt. Serv't
From: Oliver Edwards, Brevt Major General U. S. V.

EXAMPLE: CONFEDERATE HAVERSACK:

[Source: 37th Massachusetts Protest Case file at the National Archives: AGO Pension and Record Document File # 467510, File for David D. White, 37th Massachusetts Volunteer 8W3 Row 16, Com 17, Shelf F, Box #699]**Manuscript 24**

Comments & Supporting Evidence:

1. This is a powerful piece of testimony supporting the claim that David D. White captured General Custis Lee. Brvt. Major General Oliver Edwards writes, in detail, about the events leading up to the capture. It is compelling that Edwards' testimony corroborated the account given by David White, where White stated that he took General Custis Lee's haversack. Meerschaum pipes were owned by the aristocracy during the Civil War. Jefferson Davis owned such a pipe. Given Custis Lee's heritage and close association with Jefferson Davis, it is not unreasonable to think that Custis Lee also owned such a pipe, and was carrying it. It is also likely that White could have given these items to Edwards as his Brigade commander. It is interesting and important to note that General Edwards states that when David White captured General Custis Lee, he disarmed him. It would appear that the haversack could have been taken by White while he was in the process of disarming General Custis Lee. It would be nice to know what Edwards meant when he used the word "disarming." Did disarming to Edwards mean relieving Custis Lee of a sword, a revolver, or both items?

2. If General Custis Lee's and Major Stiles' troops were charging on the right flank of the 37th Massachusetts, and this according to Edwards' testimony was the area where Custis Lee was captured, and the 121st New York was separated by a significant distance from the left flank of the 37th Massachusetts, this would indicate that the 121st New York was a sizeable distance away from Custis Lee on the battlefield. The distance could have been the entire width of the 37th Massachusetts and then some. This distance probably lead General Edwards to state, "no other Regiment or command had anything to do with this part of the fight or with the capture of Major General Custis Lee."

Oliver Edwards: Colonel; Res. Springfield; 27; machinist; comm. Aug. 27, 1862; must. Sept. 4, 1862; must. Out June 21, 1865. Brevet Brig. Genl. U.S. Vols, to date Oct. 19, 1864; and brevet Major Genl U. S. Vols, to date April 5, 1865. See F. & S. Tenth Mass. Inf.; and Officer U. S. Vols.
[Source: Massachusetts Soldiers, Sailors and Marines in the Civil War, Volume 3, Compiled and Published by the Adjutant General, Norwood Press; 1932]**Manuscript 68**

EXHIBIT-W-PF-6

Introduction:

Darwin R. Field: (PHOTO: COURTESY OF U. S. ARMY WAR COLLEGE)

(1) A letter from James Bowen dated May 3, 1897, to the Secretary of War and the Chief of the Record and Pension Office, stating that he is now forwarding two affidavits from two Sergeants of Company E of the 37th Massachusetts, concerning the capture of Custis Lee. (2) Both affidavits are dated May 1, 1897, one from Sergeant Frederick L. Wheelock and the other from Sergeant Darwin R. Field.

Evidence:

(1) *37th MASSACHUSETTS REGIMENT VETERANS' ASSOCIATION:*
From: SECRETARY'S OFFICE, Springfield, Mass. May 3, 1897
Since writing you earlier in the day regarding the matter of capture of Gen. Custis Lee, C. S. A., I have received the inclosed affidavit of two sergeants of Co. E, 37th Mass. Inf. Vols., which I take the liberty of forwarding. Very respectfully yours,
From: James L. Bowen, Historian 37th Mass

(2) *To: Chief of Record and Pension Office, War Department, Washington.*
GENERAL AFFIDAVIT
State of Massachusetts, County of Berkshire, SS. In the matter of Medal of Honor for capture of Gen. Custis Lee, C. S. A. On this first day of May, AD, 1897, personally appeared before me, a Justice of the Peace, within and for the County of State aforesaid, duly authorized to administer oaths, Frederick L. Wheelock aged 55 years, a resident of Adams, in the County of Berkshire, and State of Massachusetts, whose Post Office address is Adams, Mass, and Darwin R. Field, aged 68 years a resident of Adams in the County of Berkshire and State of Massachusetts, whose Post Office address is Adams, Mass., well known to be reputable and entitled to credit, and who being duly sworn, declared in relation to the aforesaid case as follows: That I, the said Frederick L. Wheelock, saw General Custis Lee in the possession and under guard of David D. White of Co. E, 37th Massachusetts, at Sailors Creek, VA, April 6, 1865. That he had General Lee's marchaum pipe, diary, dictionary and haversack. And that I, Darwin R. Field, saw the same as above stated and that I had in my possession for a number of years a 50 cents Confederate script taken from the diary of the said General Lee. We further declared that we have no interest in said case and we are not concerned in its prosecution.
From: Frederick L. Wheelock, From: Darwin R. Field   **EXAMPLE: 50 CENT CONFEDERATE SCRIPT:**
(Signatures of affiants)
[Source: 37th Massachusetts Protest Case file at the National Archives: AGO Record & Pension Office, Document File #476510, File for David D. White, 37th Massachusetts Vol. 8W3, Row 16, Com 17, Shelf F, Box #699]**Manuscript 24**

Comments & Supporting Evidence:

1. These two affidavits are important because they corroborate the story concerning Custis Lee's haversack. They also confirm the Meerschaum pipe as reported by General Oliver Edwards. These affidavits go on to report that David White also had possession of Custis Lee's diary and dictionary (presumably all from General Custis Lee's haversack).

2. It is important to note that the two Sergeants, Wheelock and Field of Company E of the 37th Massachusetts, saw David White guarding Custis Lee, presumably, immediately after Custis Lee's capture.

3. It is interesting that Field states that he had for a number of years, a Confederate script taken from the diary of Custis Lee. This would indicate that Field was in possession of an item taken from Custis Lee after his capture.

BIOGRAPHIES:

Wheelock, Frederick L.: Priv.; Res. Adams; 21; machinist; enl. Aug 17, 1862; must. Sept. 2, 1862; must. out June 21, 1865; as Sergt.

Fields, Darwin R.: 1st Sergt.; Res. Adams; 34; operative; enl. July 20, 1862; must. Sept 2, 1862; wounded July 3, 1863; Gettysburg, Penna.; must. Out June 9, 1865.

[Source: Massachusetts Soldiers, Sailors and Marines in the Civil War, Volume 3, Compiles and Published by the Adjutant General, Norwood Press; 1932]**Manuscript 68**

EXHIBIT-W-PF-7

Introduction:

(1) A letter from James Bowen dated May 3, 1897, to the Secretary of War and Col. F. C. Ainsworth, Chief of the Record and Pension Office, Washington, DC, giving more of his own testimony and attaching an affidavit from David D. White. (2) This affidavit from David D. White, dated April 31, 1897, addresses the capture of General Custis Lee at the Battle of Sailor's Creek, VA.

Evidence:

(1) *37th MASSACHUSETTS REGIMENT VETERANS' ASSOCIATION*
From: SECRETARY'S OFFICE, Springfield, Mass., May 3, 1897

In pursuance of correspondence already opened in regard to the capture of Gen. Custis Lee at Sailor's Creek and Medal of Honor awarded for same, I have the honor to inclose herewith an affidavit of Corporal David D. White, Co. E, 37th Mass., Inf. Vols, and would ask that the same be taken into consideration. I was a member of the same company with Corporal White, and up to the time that I was wounded and disabled from further military service at Gettysburg, July 3, 1863, knew him well. He was an exceptionally modest, straightforward, unpretentious young solder, attentive and faithful. The affidavit which is inclosed is characteristic of him. I should say that he would be the last man to claim anything which was not his due. The reports of the regiment and brigade, made at the time (Vol. 46, pp. 940 et seq., Official Records), might be adduced, but I do not suppose it necessary. Col. Hopkins, commanding the regiment in that engagement, and Gen. Edwards, commanding the brigade (than whom there were no braver soldiers in the service) are not the men to claim honors for their commands to which they were not entitled; and their statements, in addition to their official reports, I believe that you have. It would be a simple matter, I believe, to furnish the testimony of scores of officers and men who witnessed the capture or knew the facts at the time so intimately as to make their testimony valuable. I do not suppose it necessary to do this; if it is necessary, kindly advise me and allow time for the collection of affidavits. We only wish to have the matter settled right. Corporal White has never made any request for a medal of honor or other special recognition in behalf of what he did, nor does he now. I do not suppose it has ever occurred to him that he did any more than his duty as a soldier in the matter. But if it is recognized by the Hon. Secretary of War that the capture of Gen. Lee was worthy a Medal of Honor, I would respectfully ask that a Medal of Honor may be given to Corporal White.
I am, Sir, very respectfully your obedient servant,
From: James L. Bowen, Historian 37th Mass. Inf. Vols.

(2) *GENERAL AFFIDAVIT:*

State of Massachusetts, County of Berkshire, SS. In the matter of Medal of Honor for capture of Gen. Custis Lee, C. S. A. Affidavit of Corporal David D. White, Co. E, 37th Massachusetts Inf. Vols.

On this 30th *day of April, 1897, personally appeared before me, a Notary Public, within and for the County and State aforesaid, duly authorized to administer oaths, David D. White, aged 55 years, a resident of Charlemont, in the County of Franklin, and State of Mass., whose Post Office address is Charlemont, Mass., well known to be reputable and entitled to credit and who being duly sworn, declared in relation to the aforesaid case as follows: On April 6, 1865, at about three o'clock in the afternoon, I captured General Custis Lee at Sailor's Creek, VA, and afterwards delivered him to the Provost Marshall in the rear. At the time of his capture he wore a sword, which I delivered to William C. Morrill, Commander, and his pipe and haversack I delivered to General Edwards.*
David D. White

[Source: 37th Massachusetts Protest Case file at the National Archives: AGO Record & Pension Office Document File #476510, File for David D. White, 37th Massachusetts, Volume 8W3, Row 16, Com 17, Shelf F, Box #699]**Manuscript 24**

Comments & Supporting Evidence:

James Bowen raises the following interesting points in this submission:

1. It would appear that Bowen could have acquired legal affidavits from many other 37th Massachusetts soldiers concerning the capture of Custis Lee, if requested to do so by the Secretary of War, who was currently reviewing this case.

2. Unlike Harris Hawthorn, who took very deliberate actions to secure a Medal of Honor for himself for the capture of Custis Lee and provided his own personal testimony to Judge Advocate H. E. Hindmarsh on April 14, 1865, David White took no action at all. As stated by Mr. Bowen, "Corporal White has never made any request for a Medal of Honor or other special recognition in behalf of what he did, nor does he now. I do not suppose it has ever occurred to him that he did any more than his duty as a soldier in the matter."

3. David White's testimony states that he delivered General Custis Lee to the Provost Marshall in the rear and that Custis Lee wore a sword at the time of his capture which he delivered to his commander, William C. Morrill. White's testimony also corroborates the pipe story as reported by General Oliver Edwards and others.

4. David White's statement that, "he afterwards delivered him to the Provost Marshall in the rear," is an important one. One has to question how David White was able to deliver Custis Lee to the Provost Marshal in the rear of the Federal lines, and also lead a detail of men to secure ammunition from the rear of the Federal lines for use at the battle front as was described in White's Pension Record. The two Hawthorn accounts, where Hawthorn states that he delivered Custis Lee by orders of Colonel Olcott to General Wheaton's headquarters and where Hassett states that he and Hawthorn were ordered by Colonel Olcott to deliver Custis Lee to General Sheridan's headquarters, differ substantially from White's account. In White's two newspaper articles, found in Exhibit W–MR–4, it states, "White triumphantly marched him into camp a prisoner" and "Dave marched to headquarters with his prisoner and was thunderstruck when he learned that it was no less a personage than General Custis E. Lee." The two sergeants of the 37th Massachusetts, Frederick L. Wheelock and Darwin R. Field, state in their affidavit (Exhibit W–PF–6) that they "saw General Custis Lee in the possession and under the guard of David D. White'. John Grace, a private of Company E, 37th Massachusetts, states in the upcoming Exhibit W–PF–10, "White then ordered him to the rear where he went." Jerome King, a member of Company F, 37th Massachusetts, states in the upcoming Exhibit W–PF–15, "White brought a Confederate officer into our lines, said to have been General Custis Lee. That the officer refused to deliver to said White his sword, his person then being under White's charge, and was then conveyed to the presence of a commissioned officer of said regiment and handed over to him." From these accounts, it is likely that White could have brought Custis Lee into his Regimental headquarters or the "lines" of the 37th Massachusetts. The author is less convinced that White had the time to personally deliver Custis Lee to the

headquarters of either the 1ˢᵗ Division or 6ᵗʰ Army Corps. Having said this, however, the statement by White that he, "afterward delivered him (Custis Lee) to the Provost Marshall in the rear," does have some merit. Custis Lee would have wanted to be delivered to the Provost Marshal to receive protection. In addition, this is where Custis Lee, as a Federal prisoner of war, should have been delivered following proper military protocol. To substantiate this point, the following is a partial description of the duties of a Provost Marshal:

General Orders, No. 23}   Hdqrs. Department of the Missouri,
Saint Louis, Mo. December 1, 1862.

VII. Officers of the provost-marshal's department during the existence of civil war are especially intrusted with the peace and quiet of their respective districts, counties and sections, and to this end may cause the arrest and confinement of disloyal persons, subject to the instructions and orders of the department. They will have charge of all prisoners taken from the enemy; the keeping of the records, as far as possible of the prisoners taken by the enemy, that the proper data for an exchange may be at any time obtained; the arrest and return or imprisonment of deserters, and in general all duties relating to prisoners of war or state.
[Source: Official Records, Volume 5, Series 2, Prisoners of War, page 9]**Manuscript 93**

The following is a good example of how a military Command, following proper military protocol, should turn over captured property and prisoners to a Provost Marshal:

No. 209
Report of Brig. Gen. Henry E. Davies. Jr., U. S. Army, commanding First Brigade.
HDQRS. FIRST BRIG., SECOND DIV., CAVALRY CORPS,
Nottoway Court House, April 14, 1865

…In this engagement (Sailor's Creek) 750 prisoners, 2 guns, and 2 flags were captured and turned over to Captain Harper, division provost-marshal. Some 300 prisoners were inadvertently turned over to another command by the officer in charge, and two guns captured by the Twenty-fourth New York, which they were unable to bring off at the time, were taken by some other command.
…I annex copy of receipt from Captain Harper, division provost-marshal, of prisoners and property turned over to him from this command:

HEADQUARTERS SECOND DIVISION, CAVALRY CORPS,
OFFICE OF PROVOST-MARSHAL, April 14, 1865

Received from the provost-marshal First Brigade, Second Division, Cavalry Corps, during the campaign from March 29, 1865, to April 14, 1865:

Date	Location	Captures	
		Character	Number
April 5	Farmville…………………….….	Prisoners of War……………..…….320 Colored teamsters…………………..……310 Battle-flags…………………..…… 11 Guns and teams………………….….5 Caisson……………………..……..1 Mules……………………..……….310	
April 6	Sailor's Creek…………………...	Prisoners of war……………..……750 Battle-flags………………….……….2 Guns……………………..…….…………….2	

W. M. Harper, Captain and Acting Provost-Marshal, Second Division, Cavalry Corps

[Source: Official Records, Volume 46, Series 1, Part 1, Reports: pages 1143-1147]**Manuscript 91**

The following account, given by Confederate Capt. Thomas Ballard Blake of Company E, 10th Virginia Battalion of Heavy Artillery in Custis Lee's Division, describes how he, Blake, wound up in the hands of the Provost Guard after his capture by the Federal Infantry at the Battle of Sailor's Creek.

… When the infantry which we had so recently repulsed, came up to us again, it was with smiling faces. They commenced opening their haversacks, offering to share their "hard tack" with us, which in our famished condition we most eagerly and gratefully accepted. They, moreover, complimented us on the gallant fight we had made. In this connection, I will add that we were always treated with every consideration by the veterans at the front. It was only when we fell into the hands of the provost guard that any harshness was shown.
[Source: "Retreat from Richmond," T. B. Blake, Southern Historical Society Papers, Volume 25 page 142]**Manuscript 38**

The following account given by R. Stiles shows how Custis Lee himself reported back to a Federal Provost Marshal after his leave to Richmond following his capture at the Battle of Sailor's Creek:

… Just before the surrender, on my way to Petersburg as a prisoner of war, I was standing on the roadside near General Custis Lee when he was shocked by a report of the death of his mother. I reminded him that, at such times, the wildest rumors were apt to be in circulation, and suggested his applying, by field telegraph, to Grant for leave to go to Richmond to ascertain the truth. He did so, and at once received leave, with transportation to Richmond. Upon finding there was nothing in the rumor, he reported promptly at the office of the provost marshal, but was there told that orders had been sent by General Grant that General Custis Lee should not be received as a prisoner of war, and he never succeeded in getting back into prison or any sort of captivity, though he made earnest efforts to do so.
[Source: "Four Years under Marse Robert," Robert Stiles, pages 238-239]**Manuscript 2**

Confederate General Rufus Barringer was captured by Federal spies on April 3, 1865, near Namozine Church, VA. That evening, he and his orderlies were taken to *"General Sheridan's Headquarters." "The next morning, most of the Confederate officers were invited to a breakfast of biscuits and coffee with Sheridan."* This sounds very similar to the treatment that Custis Lee received after the Battle of Sailor's Creek. *"As the captured officers began their trip to City Point, they were riding and walking against the procession of Union Infantry'.* This is also similar to Custis Lee's experience in that Custis Lee was taken to City Point after his capture at Sailor's Creek. *"Meade noticed that Sheridan had placed only a corporal over the Confederate officers and immediately ordered a general officer to take his place, instructing him to tell the provost marshall in City Point that Barringer could reach anybody he wanted."* This shows that Confederate General Barringer was in the custody of the Provost Marshall group, most likely immediately after his capture, during his march as a prisoner to City Point and once at City Point. This also shows that a Confederate General was not above the military protocol of the time, which was to be in the custody of a Federal Provost Marshal once becoming a prisoner of war.
[Source: "The Appomattox Campaign, March 29-April 9, 1865," Chris M. Calkins, Combined Books, PA, pages 82-83]**Manuscript 149**

The author was fortunate to uncover a book at the National Archives that appears to be an accounting ledger for the Provost Marshal General Army of the Potomac. The book's cover has the following prelude recorded:
Old Book No. 200 Provo. Marshal General Army of Potomac
Feb. 1/65 to Apl. 14/65
This appears to be a continuation of Book 194 which ends with the date Tuesday, Jan. 31, 1865, while this (No. 200) begins with Wednesday Feby 1, 1865 and ends with Friday Apl. 14, 1865. It contains about 1750 names, nearly all of which are Confederate Soldiers, a few being Citizens. No Federals are shown.

From Feby 1 to Mch. 31, 1865, the names under each date are given, after which the number of prisoners only is shown. These numbers indicate that for the period from April 1 to 14, 1865, about

15,000 Confederate prisoners of war were received. Under those dates where the names are given, the items shown are rank, organization, by whom sent in and how disposed. Names and all material information in this book are shown in two books numbered 201 and 202 covering from Feb 1 to Apl 1/65 and covering from Apl 1 to Apl 13/65. They are labeled on back in handwriting, "Records of Prisoners of War, Rebel Deserters, etc. received at and forwarded from Office Provost Marshal General Armies Operating against Richmond"; #202 shows City Point on label.

With 15,000 Confederate prisoners of war being processed between the dates of April 1-14, 1865, no wonder this ledger stopped recording the specific names of the Confederate prisoners of war during this time period and instead just recorded bulk numbers. The actual and complete entry for Thursday April 6, 1865, is as follows:

Name:	Rank:	Regiment:	Co.:	By whom sent in
Hugh Tower	Priv.	4th N. Cav.		Pro. Mar. 6th Corps
97 Com. Officers		Miscellaneous		"
1400 Enlisted Men		"		"
13 Com. Officers		"		"
420 Enlisted Men		"		"

The deserters from the enemy and Prisoners of War: Sent to Capt. Potter, Pro. Mar., City Point on April 7th.

[Source: National Archives and Records Administration-Record Group 393-Records of the U.S. Army Continental Commands, 1821-1920, Part One, Entry 4065, Vol. 73/200 (Army of the Potomac) List of Confederate Prisoners Received by the Provost Marshal, Feb.-Apr. 1865]**Manuscript 150**

This record is a clear indication that the Provost Marshals were very much in control of Confederate prisoners of war and deserters. There is a very good likelihood that Custis Lee was accounted for in the 97 and 13 commissioned officers listed above as being captured by the 6th Corps on April 6, 1865. So David White's statement that he "afterwards delivered him (Custis Lee) to the Provost Marshall in the rear," is once again exactly what David White should have done with Custis Lee after capturing him. Given this report, it is highly likely that this is exactly what happened to Custis Lee, if White did indeed capture him as stated in his affidavit above.

5. James L. Bowen is now asking the Secretary of War that a Medal of Honor be granted to David D. White as the true soldier who captured Custis Lee at the Battle of Sailor's Creek.

EXHIBIT-W-PF-8

Introduction:
A letter from F. C. Ainsworth, Chief of the Record and Pension Office, dated May 5, 1897, to James Bowen, acknowledging receipt of the affidavits of White, Wheelock, and Field and informing Bowen that these affidavits have been forwarded to the Secretary of War "in connection with previous papers in the case already submitted.

Evidence:
From: Record and Pension Office, War Department, Washington City, May 5, 1897
To: Mr. James L. Bowen,
I beg leave to acknowledge the receipt of your letters of the 3rd instant in the matter of the award of a medal of honor to David D. White, late corporal, Company E, 37th Massachusetts Infantry Volunteers, for the capture of General Custis Lee, C. S. Army, at Sailor's Creek, Virginia, April 2, 1865, and the affidavit of Messrs. White, Wheelock and Field, therewith inclosed, and to inform you that your letters and the inclosures have this day been submitted to the Secretary of War in connection with previous papers in the case already submitted.
Very respectfully,
From: F. C. Ainsworth, Colonel, U. S. Army, Chief, Record and Pension Office.

Comments & Supporting Evidence:

1. A central file consisting of many documents is now starting to accumulate at the office of the Secretary of War, via, F. C. Ainsworth, Chief of the Record and Pension Office. This is the direct result of Bowen's ongoing efforts.

EXHIBIT-W-PF-9

Introduction:

(1) A letter from James Bowen dated May 14, 1897, to the Secretary of War and the Chief of the Record and Pension Office, giving more of his testimony and attaching an affidavit from Adjutant Samuel E. Nichols of the 37th Massachusetts. (2) This affidavit from Samuel E. Nichols is dated May 11, 1897, and addresses the capture of General Custis Lee at the Battle of Sailor's Creek, VA.

Evidence:

(1) *From: RECORD AND PENSION OFFICE, Washington, May 17, 1897.*
Respectfully submitted to the Honorable Secretary of War,

In connection with the papers upon which was based the award of a medal of honor to Harris S. Hawthorne, late private, Company F, 121st New York Volunteers, and the testimony disputing his right to the medal, which papers and testimony were submitted on April 20, and May 5, 1897. Samuel E. Nichols, whose letter is herewith submitted, was formerly a 2d lieutenant of Company B, 37th Massachusetts Infantry Volunteers. He is reported present on the company muster roll, dated April 6, 1865, and on that date signed the regimental return as adjutant.
From: F. C. Ainsworth, Colonel, U.S. Army, Chief of Office.

(One inclosure)

37th MASSACHUSETTS REGIMENT VETERANS' ASSOCIATION
SECRETARY'S OFFICE, Springfield, Mass. May 14, 1897

In the matter of "Capture of General Custis Lee," now in the hands of the Honorable Secretary of War, I have the honor to submit herewith the statement of Lieut. Samuel E. Nichols, now U.S. Pension Agent at Buffalo, N.Y. Lieut. Nichols had been promoted from private to second lieutenant, on account of distinguished services, and was serving as such in this battle. Adjutant John S. Bradley of the 37th (now living at Bridal Veil, Or.) was wounded by the "reopening of fire" mentioned by Lieut. Nichols, when the latter was detailed by Capt. Archibald Hopkins, commanding the regiment, to serve as adjutant, and filled that position till the muster out of the regiment. Captain Morrill, of whom mention is made as receiving the sword of General Lee—and this is stated by several persons, died a few years since. I trust this declaration may be placed with the other papers in the case, and that I may be allowed to continue furnishing proof, or putting the War Department in position to obtain proof without my assistance, till satisfied of the truth of our claim in this matter. Personally, I would prefer that the War Department—which has certainly been imposed upon by somebody—should take names which we will furnish, and investigate through their own channels, for we invite and desire the fullest investigation of all that we claim.
Very respectfully yours, James. L. Bowen, Historian 37th Mass. Inf.

(2) *UNITED STATES PENSION AGENCY*

Samuel E. Nichols: (PHOTO: COURTESY U. S. ARMY WAR COLLEGE)

Buffalo, N.Y., May 11, 1897, To: James L. Bowen, Esq.
Concerning the capture of General Custis Lee and some of his staff at the Battle of Sailor's Creek I have positive knowledge to the following extent: Company "E," 37th Mass. Vols was thrown to the left of Edwards' brigade, of which it was a part, at

the ending portion of the fight on that day, April 6, 1865, in order to preserve the connection as closely as possible with the next brigade. Yet, considerable space intervened. At the time that the battle was properly closed and when some of our officers advanced to gather the fruits of success, there was resumption of firing by the Confederates–unauthorized probably–the result being the wounding of some of our best officers and men. A counter fire, general and destructive in character, was at once made by our brigade. To stop this murderous fire and to declare the non-resistance of the Confederate force opposite us, General Custis Lee and certain members of his staff came to our lines at the open space, above referred to, and approached the left of our brigade line where Co. "E" was placed. On General Lee's near approach, Corporal David E. White, of that company, called upon Lee to surrender. The response of General Lee in substance was as follows: "Tut, tut, my man, show me to an officer, I do not surrender to an enlisted man." With great emphasis Corporal White, bringing his rifle to a poise, declared he would see whether he (Lee) would surrender or not. Thereupon General Lee was about to yield his sword when Captain William C. Morrill, in command of the company, came up and General Lee had the privilege which he had asked for of yielding his sword to "an officer." One of the horses accompanying the party–whether Lee's or that of one of his staff I know not–was also taken possession of by Captain Morrill. One of our surgeons removed a small piece of shell from a fetlock joint and Captain Morrill, who was a wounded officer, rode the horse through the balance of the campaign. On reaching Washington, Captain Morrill turned the horse over to me in order that I might, as a staff officer, secure transportation to his home in Massachusetts. In the final review of the Sixth Corps at Washington, I rode this horse which afterwards went with us to Massachusetts, living and dying in Hadley, a town in the Connecticut River valley of Massachusetts. The heirs of Captain Morrill are in possession of the sword of General Custis Lee. They can best be communicated with, I think, by addressing Miss Harriet Richardson, care of Mr. Charles Thayer, Hockanum, Northampton, Massachusetts. Probably this statement, filed with your other papers will be all you may need in this connection from me. If, however, a sworn statement, more concise in character, should be desired, I will gladly give it.
Yours fraternally,
From: S. E. Nichols, Formerly Adjutant 37th Mass. Vols.
[Source: 37th Massachusetts Protest Case file at the National Archives: AGO Record & Pension Office, Document File #476510, File for David D. White, 37th Massachusetts, Volume 8W3, Row 16, Com 17, Shelf F, Box #699]**Manuscript 24**

Comments & Supporting Evidence:

1. Samuel Nichols' testimony corroborates many points found in David White's North Adams, MA, newspaper accounts and the testimony given by several others concerning the capture of Custis Lee. Custis Lee did not want to surrender to a Private or an enlisted man, but wanted to be shown to an officer for surrender. General Custis Lee had a sword which he surrendered, at the point of David White's rifle, to David White and William Morrill.

2. Samuel Nichols' testimony raises two new important points which will be corroborated by evidence presented later in this report:

   A. Morrill took possession of a horse somehow associated with Custis Lee's troops. Perhaps it was actually Custis Lee's horse. Nichols brought this horse back to Morrill's Hadley/Hockanum, MA, farm at the end of the War. To substantiate this point, the author was able to discover two references that will show that General Custis Lee was mounted at the beginning of the Battle of Sailor's Creek.

      • R. T. W. Duke, late Lieutenant Colonel of the 2nd Battalion Virginia Reserves, states: *"After going a short distance further, I came to a group of mounted officers, consisting of Generals Ewell, Custis Lee, Barton and others.* **[Source: Southern Historical Society Papers, Volume 25, page 137]**Manuscript 38****

      • (2)-Charles Stevens Dwight, Captain and of the Corps of Engineers and Staff of Major General J. B. Kershaw, states that *"when I reported to General Kershaw, he and General Ewell and General Lee with their staffs were watering their horses in Sailor's Creek, and the Generals* were consulting earnestly about their plans." **[Source: "A South Carolina Rebel's Recollections," the State Company, Columbia, SC; 1917]**Manuscript 40****

    B. Nichols states, "The heirs of Captain Morrill are in possession of the sword of General Custis Lee. They can best be communicated with, I think, by addressing Miss Harriet Richardson, care of Mr. Charles Thayer, Hockanum, Northampton, Massachusetts."

3. William Morrill died at the age of 51 in Rochester, NY, January 20, 1892. **[Source: Death Record of William Morrill, Rochester, NY]**Manuscript 43**** This is why Nichols refers to the "heirs" of William Morrill in his letter dated May 11, 1897. On the May 25, 1892, his wife, Mate Morrill, age 31, filed for a widow's pension. In this pension application record, she states that she married William Morrill as Mate Marshall on May 24, 1889, at Bolivar, NY. She also states that neither she, nor William Morrill, was married previously, nor did they have children. **[Source: William Morrill's Pension File, National Archives, Washington, DC]**Manuscript 43****

4. It was determined in a telephone interview conducted by the author with a member of the William Morrill family (Exhibit W–CT–2) that William Morrill has the following documented genealogy. A Jeddediah Morrill and Mable Richardson married in the year 1836 in Williamsport, ME. Their son, William Morrill, was born in ME in the year 1841. "William Morrill had come down from Williamsburg, ME, in the spring of the year 1860 when he was just past 19 years old to work on the Hockanum farm for his maternal uncle, William Richardson, who was a brother of his mother Mable Richardson." **[Source: "The Old Pomroy House at Hockanum and the Civil War" by Charles Hiram Thayer, 1962, 140 pp bound transcript, Amherst, MA]**Manuscript 27**** William Morrill enlisted into the Civil War and the 37th Massachusetts from the Hockanum home of his uncle, William Richardson. William Richardson and his wife, Sarah Clark, had a number of children at Hockanum. Miss Harriet Richardson, the person referred to in Nichols' testimony, is one of these children and a first cousin to William Morrill. The Charles Thayer referenced in Nichols' testimony married a sister of Harriet Richardson, a Miss Abbie Clark Richardson. Charles and Abbie Clark Thayer lived in the Hockanum home for a period of time.

5. It should be noted that this Richardson home in Hockanum, MA, served as the home for William Morrill as well. He wrote many letters during the Civil War to his cousins in Hockanum. When he returned from the Civil War, he went to this home in Hockanum. This is why Nichols, in his testimony, suggests that the Secretary of War contact Miss Harriet Richardson, in care of Charles Thayer, for the whereabouts of the Custis Lee sword that Morrill brought back home to Hockanum from the Civil War.

BIOGRAPHIES:

Morrill, William C.: Priv.; Res. Northampton; 21; farmer; enl. July 15, 1862; must. August 30, 1862; comm. 2d Lieut. from Sergt., Dec. 5, 1863; must. Nov. 1, 1864; wounded Sept. 19, 1864, Winchester, VA; comm. 1st Lieut., Oct. 7, 1864; must. Feb. 17, 1865; must. out June 21, 1865, as 1st Lieut. of Co. E. Brevet Captain U.S. Vols., to date April 6, 1865.

Nichols, Samuel E.: Priv.; Res. Northampton; 20; student; enl. July 15, 1862; must. Aug. 30, 1862; comm. 2d Lieut., Aug. 30, 1864; must. Sept. 18, 1864; comm. 1st Lieut., May 15, 1865; not must.; must. out June 21, 1865; as 2d Lieut. of Co. B.

[Source: Massachusetts Soldier, Sailors and Marines in the Civil War, Volume 3, Compiled and Published by the Adjutant, General Norwood Press; 1932]**Manuscript 68**

EXHIBIT-W-PF-10

Introduction:

This is an affidavit of John Grace, Private of Co. E, 37th Massachusetts, dated June 3, 1897, concerning the capture of General Custis Lee at the Battle of Sailor's Creek.

Evidence:

GENERAL AFFIDAVIT, State of Mass., County of Berkshire:
In the matter of Medal of Honor for Capture of Gen. Custis Lee, C. S. A, at Sailor's Creek, VA, April 6, 1865. On this third day of June, AD 1897, personally appeared before me, a Notary Public within and for the County and State aforesaid, duly authorized to administer oaths, John Grace, aged 57, a resident of Cheshire, in the County of Berkshire, and State of Mass., whose Post Office address is Cheshire aforesaid, well known to me to be reputable and entitled to credit, and who being duly sworn, declared in relation to the aforesaid case as follows: I was a Private in Co. E, 37th Mass Vols. was present at the capture of General Custis Lee at Sailor's Creek, April 6, 1865. I stood but a few feet from him when Corporal D. White of Co. E. called upon him to surrender. Lee replied," I'll never surrender to a d---d private." White pointed his gun at him when Lee became very much frightened and threw down saber, haversack, menschaum pipe and other articles that he had about him. White then ordered him to the rear where he went. This affidavit was written in my presence at Cheshire, Mass., by F. C. Brown of Cheshire, Mass. On the 3rd day of June, 1897, only from my oral statements then made and in making such oral statements, I did not use and was not aided or prompted by any written or printed statement or recital prepared or dictated by any other person and not attached as an exhibit hereto. I further declare that I have no interest in said case and am not concerned in its prosecution.
From: John Grace, (Affiant's Signature)

[Source: 37th Massachusetts Protest Case file at the National Archives: AGO Record & Pension Office, Document File #476510, File for David D. White, 37th Massachusetts, Volume 8W3, Row 16, Com 17, Shelf F, Box #699]**Manuscript 24**

Comment & Supporting Evidence:

1. John Grace was a Private in the 37th Massachusetts and was a resident of Cheshire, MA, as was David White. One could assume they were acquainted with one another, having similar backgrounds and home towns.

2. John Grace also testified in David White's pension application process about the injury White sustained during the Battle of Sailor's Creek as described in Exhibits W–PR–1 and W–PR–2.

3. Some of the familiar points Grace corroborates in his testimony concerning the capture of Custis Lee are:
   B. Custis Lee did not want to surrender to a Federal Private
   C. David White compelled General Custis Lee to surrender at the point of White's rifle.
   D. Custis Lee "had about him" and yielded up during his capture a saber, haversack, Meerschaum pipe and other articles.
   E. White took Custis Lee to the rear of the Federal lines.

4. An extremely important aspect of Grace's testimony is the statement that he was, "but a few feet," from David White when David White demanded the surrender of Custis Lee. This would indicate that Grace was an eyewitness of the capture of Custis Lee at a very close range.

EXHIBIT-W-PF-11

Introduction:

A letter from the Chief of the Record and Pension Office, dated May 17, 1897, to James L. Bowen, acknowledging receipt of the S. E. Nichols' letter and informing Bowen that it has been sent to the Secretary of War.

Evidence:

RECORD AND PENSION OFFICE, Washington City, May 17, 1897.
To: Mr. James L. Bowen
I beg leave to acknowledge the receipt of your letter of the 14th instant in the matter of the award of a medal of honor to David White, late corporal, Company E, 37th Massachusetts Infantry Volunteers, for the capture of General Custis Lee, Confederate States Army, at Sailor's Creek, Virginia, April 7, 1865,

and the letter of Mr. S. E. Nichols, Pension Agent at Buffalo, New York, therewith inclosed, and to inform you that your letter and its inclosure have this day been transmitted to the Secretary of War in connection with previous papers in the case already submitted.
Very respectfully,
From: F. C. Ainsworth, Colonel, U.S. Army, Chief, Record and Pension Office.

[Source: 37th Massachusetts Protest Case file at the National Archives: AGO Record & Pension Office, Document File #476510, File for David D. White, 37th Massachusetts, Volume 8W3, Row 16, Com 17, Shelf F, Box #699]**Manuscript 24**

Comments & Supporting Evidence:

1. The 37th Massachusetts Protest Case file is really starting to grow at the office of the Secretary of War, due to the dedicated efforts of James Bowen and others.

EXHIBIT-W-PF-12

Introduction:

George Washington Custis Lee (circa 1897):
(PHOTO: COURTESY WASHINGTON AND LEE UNIVERSITY)

(1) A letter from James Bowen dated May 19, 1897, to the Secretary of War, giving the Secretary of War more of his testimony and attaching a letter from the private secretary of Custis Lee that was written to Archibald Hopkins, who was the commander of the 37th Massachusetts at the Battle of Sailor's Creek. (2) This letter was from Thomas E. Marshall, Jr., and is dated May 12, 1897. It addresses the capture of Major General Custis Lee at the Battle of Sailor's Creek.

Evidence:

(1) *37th MASSACHUSETTS REGIMENT VETERANS' ASSOCIATION*
From: SECRETARY'S OFFICE, Springfield, Mass. May 19, 1897
I have the honor to file, herewith, a letter from General G. W. Custis Lee to Col. Archibald Hopkins of your city, referring to the capture of said Gen. Lee, C. S. A., at Sailor's Creek, April 6, 1865. It will be seen by this letter that Gen. Lee has not a clear recollection, if he ever knew, to whom he surrendered, but you will notice that his statement corroborates our claim to this extent, that the person to whom he surrendered wore chevrons, which he thinks were those of a sergeant. Now, in fact, Corporal White wore his uniform as a Corporal, and it would be much more natural to have mistaken a Corporal's chevrons for those of a sergeant, than to have mistaken the plain uniform of the other man (121st New York) who wore no chevrons. I would, therefore, ask that you file this letter with the other papers in the case, and give it such weight as may seem to be proper.
Fraternally yours,
From: James L. Bowen, Historian 37th Mass. Vols.
(2) *To: Honorable Sec. of War, May 20/94, Inclosure 1.*
Letter of the private Secretary of General. G. W. C. Lee, dated at Lexington, VA, May 12, 1897, relative to the person to whom Gen'l Lee surrendered at Sailor's Creek, VA, April 6, 1865. Submitted in the matter of the disputed right of Harris S. Hawthorne, late Pvt., Co. F, 121st N.Y. Vols. to the award of a medal of honor.

WASHINGTON & LEE UNIVERSITY, Lexington, Virginia, May 12, 1897
To: Archibald Hopkins Esq., Washington, D.C.:

The President of this institution (G. W. C. Lee), who is prevented from writing by a disabled hand, desires me to answer your letter of the 10th inst. He surrendered to a soldier who said he belonged to the 6th Corps, and who wore, as far as he can recollect, sergeant's chevrons; and he surrendered to this soldier because the latter said it would insure him (Custis Lee) a furlough. Genl. Lee did not wear a sword on the occasion, and consequently, did not surrender it; and did not ride a sorrel horse during the whole of the war. With regard to the hair-brush, it may have been taken from Genl. Lee's valise, which was in the wagon train; but he does not recollect anything about it. The printed matter is returned to you as requested.

Respectfully, From: Thos. E. Marshall, Jr., Pvt. Secty.

[Source: 37th Massachusetts Protest Case file at the National Archives: AGO Record & Pension Office, Document File #476510, File for David D. White, 37th Massachusetts, Volume 8W3, Row 16, Com 17, Shelf F, Box #699]**Manuscript 24**

Comments & Supporting Evidence:

1. First, we must take a look a close look at the physical and mental condition of Custis Lee at the time of this communication. Custis Lee suffered from severe depression and related ill health during his entire administration as President of Washington College, now Washington and Lee University, from the years 1870 to 1897. This is accurately documented in the following work: **[Source: "General Lee's College, the Rise and Growth of Washington and Lee University" by Ollinger Crenshaw, Random House, New York]**Manuscript 44**** In Chapter 15 entitled, "<u>Decline, Depressions, and Discouragement, 1870–1897</u>," which covered the period of Custis Lee's administration, the chapter notes many instances of ill health. As college president, he frequently submitted resignation requests that were denied. In June 1894, Custis Lee *"bluntly and pathetically stated that he did not think he should ever be good for anything."* On December 29, 1896, he resigned again, telling the University Board plainly what he had said many times before, *"that he was utterly useless here, with but little probability of ever being useful to the University."* This writing states, *"At long last, his resignation was accepted."* **[Source: "General Lee's College" by Ollinger Crenshaw, page 180]**Manuscript 44**** Custis Lee's successor, Mr. William Lyne Wilson, visited the College in March and April, 1897. Ollinger Crenshaw states in his book, *"a visit to President Custis Lee's darkened sick room must have been far from inspiring."* **[Source: General Lee's College by Ollinger Crenshaw, page 241]**Manuscript 44**** Mr. Wilson recorded in his diary the March 10, 1897 visit he made to Custis Lee. This diary entry reads as follows: *"Today at noon I called at Gen. Lee's, and was soon shown into the darkened bedroom where he lay. He told me his decision was irrevocable to vacate the house by July 1, spoke most despondingly of his health and even intimated that his physical ailments were so great that he would welcome a release by death…. Miss Mildred is bright, and unusually clean, but I felt a pang in anticipating the occupancy of a house, endeared to her by so many sacred memories of parents, and now darkened by the ill health and despondency of her brother."* **[Source: "The Perfect Gentleman, the Life and Letters of George Washington Custis Lee," Volume 2, Bernice-Marie Yates; 2003]**Manuscript 143**** This information provides some accurate insight into Custis Lee's probable state of mind from the time period of June, 1894 to May 12, 1897. In this poor health condition, one would have to assume that Custis Lee had very little interest in answering questions concerning his capture at the Battle of Sailor's Creek.

2. In a paper read at an annual meeting of the Virginia Historical Society on February 24, 1914, by its President, W. Gordon McCabe, entitled "Major-General George Washington Custis Lee," this paper contains the following quotes concerning Custis Lee:

George Washington Custis Lee (after father's death, circa 1870):
(PHOTO: COURTESY WASHINGTON AND LEE UNIVERSITY)

A. *"So long had he lived the life of a recluse, so persistently, in his later years, did he guard his seclusion from the outer world, that it is not improbable that few of the general public, outside his native State, knew that he was still alive."*

B. *"His habitual reticence was never pierced, save, perhaps, by one, and that one his father."*

C. *"But his constancy shone out as brightly in the gloom as did his daring, and, though it was the irony of fate that his first battle should be his last (and that battle a combat rather than a pitched fight), he fought his Division in the disastrous affair at "Sailor's Creek" with such skill and audacity as drew from Ewell (dear "Old Dick," hero of a hundred fights!), in his official report, most emphatic and enthusiastic commendation."*

D. *"Though it is not unlikely that the recollection of the untoward stroke of fate, that, in his younger days, had shattered his dream of military distinction, never faded from his mind, casting in no mean measure a shadow over his whole life."*

E. *"Owing to his inbred shrinking from publicity of every kind and to his almost impenetrable reserve, which not even the most persistent "interviewer" ever pierced, these few poor remarks will probably constitute the sole memorial of him, though, of course, his name will live, in some measure, in the memoirs of his contemporaries, and especially in the intimate domestic letters of his father, in many of which, still unpublished, there is (as some few of us know, who have had the privilege of reading them), constant mention of him.*

[Source: Southern Historical Society Papers, Volume 39]**Manuscript 45**

This paper clearly adds more insight into the life and the general state of mind of Custis Lee.

3. It would appear that Archibald Hopkins was trying to confirm some points by having a direct correspondence with Custis Lee in 1897. Mr. Hopkins probably undertook this endeavor at the request of Samuel Bowen, confident that Custis Lee would substantiate the 37th Massachusetts' claims. Custis Lee's remarks, however, did not help Archibald Hopkins.

4. Custis Lee's statement that he surrendered to someone in the 6th Corps supports the versions of all four claimants.

5. Custis Lee's claim that he surrendered to someone wearing chevrons, perhaps Sergeant's chevrons, does not support either the White, Hawthorn or Butterfield claims. Addressing White first, he was a Private at the Battle of Sailor's Creek and would not have worn chevrons. He was promoted to Corporal on May 19, 1865, after the Battle of Sailor's Creek, with Corporal Luther Tanner of the 37th Massachusetts having died of wounds. White's promotion was most likely a reward for his capture of General Custis Lee. **[Source: David White's Military Service Record in the National Archives]**Manuscript 47**** It should be noted that chevrons were worn by non-commissioned officers above the elbow of both sleeves of the uniform coat and overcoat to designate the rank of non-commissioned officers. In the Union army, the following non-commissioned officers were chevrons: Sergeant Major, Q. M. Sergeant, Ordinance Sergeant, Hospital Steward, First Sergeant, Sergeant, Corporal, and Pioneer. It should be noted that for most of David White's military service in the Civil War, he was detached to the Division's Pioneer and Ambulance Corps. **[Source: David White's Military Service Record in the National Archives]**Manuscript 47**** It is possible that David White could have been wearing a uniform at the Battle of Sailor's Creek that contained his Pioneer or Hospital Steward chevrons, which could have been mistaken as Sergeant's chevrons by Custis Lee.

6. Hawthorn was also a Private at the Battle of Sailor's Creek and would not have worn chevrons. Harris Hawthorn was promoted to Corporal on April 29, 1865 after the Battle of Sailor's Creek, with Corporal Metcalf of the 121st New York having been promoted to a higher rank. Like David White, Hawthorn's promotion was most likely as a reward for his capture of General Custis Lee. Corporal Hawthorn was promoted to Sergeant on June 10, 1865, with Sergeant Scott of the 121st New York having being discharged. **[Source: Harris Hawthorn's Military Service Record and 121st New York Regimental Books in National Archives, Washington, DC]**Manuscripts 48 and 49****

7. Butterfield was a commissioned officer at the Battle of Sailor's Creek and would not have worn chevrons.

8. William Morrill was a First Lieutenant at the time of the Battle of Sailor's Creek and would not have worn chevrons.

9. It is difficult to say who would have promised General Custis Lee a furlough if Custis Lee promised to surrender. The following four points concerning this specific matter are relevant:

   A. Custis Lee was in no position to negotiate the terms of his surrender with anyone, given the desperate state of his troops and the fact that he was physically apprehended.

   B. Custis Lee would not have negotiated a furlough with either Private White or Private Hawthorn. What authority would a Federal Private have in such matters? Custis Lee would have known this. If Custis Lee did attempt this, perhaps he did this jokingly or tauntingly.

   C. If Custis Lee did attempt to negotiate a furlough on the battlefield, it would have been with either Morrill or Butterfield, who were commissioned officers. A strong desire for a furlough could account for the fact that Custis Lee wanted to surrender to an officer, as stated in White's account. Custis Lee would have wanted to negotiate his furlough with someone having authority to grant one.

   D. It is interesting to note, however, that *"because of the illness of his mother, he was almost at once paroled and thus did not join his contemporaries at Fort Warren"* **[Source: Generals in Gray, page 179]**Manuscript 50****

10. With regard to the statement, "Gen'l Lee did not wear a sword on the occasion and consequently did not surrender it," the following comments and information are critically important:

    A. First, it must be remembered that Custis Lee was trying to remember events that happened over 37 years ago. A difficult task for someone suffering from ill health as he was.

    B. It is highly probable that Custis Lee possessed a sword like all Confederate officers of his rank. Given his hasty evacuation of Richmond, however, he might have left his sword in his Confederate wagon train and was not wearing it during the Battle of Sailor's Creek. It must be noted that other Confederate officers surrendered their swords at the Battle of Sailor's Creek, which would indicate that they were wearing them during the battle and did not store them in the wagon train. Most important, however, is that Custis Lee's statement is in direct contradiction with the following visual account given by Confederate Captain Charles Stevens Dwight, which states:

Charles Stevens Dwight: (PHOTO: COURTESY UNIVERSITY OF SOUTH CAROLINA)

"I must pay a passing tribute to Gen. C. W. Lee and his command. These naval officers and men had marched the fifty miles from Richmond most painfully, suffering with blistered feet and sore muscles—for sailors are not trained to marching—yet they kept up, took position in line of battle, and held it splendidly to the end. I saw Gen. Lee often. He was afoot passing up and down his line, his sheathed sword lying upon his left arm. His face and manner indicated perfect dignity and composure; his noble presence and bearing cheered and encouraged both officers and men."

[Source: "A South Carolina Rebel Recollections, Personal Reminiscences of the Evacuation of Richmond and the Battle of Sailor's Creek, April, 1865," Read before Camp Hampton, V. C. V., Columbia, SC., by Charles Stevens Dwight, Captain, Corps of Engineers, Staff of Major General J. B. Kershaw, the State Company, Columbia, SC, 1917]Manuscript 40****

If true, this visual observation by Charles Stevens Dwight <u>definitively</u> places Custis Lee with his sword at the Battle of Sailor's Creek. The author likes Dwight's description of the sheathed sword lying upon Custis Lee's left arm. This adds to the credibility of Dwight's account. A dismounted officer who was actively transversing a battlefield on foot would often cradle his sheathed sword, which was hooked to the left side of his belt, in his left arm to basically keep it out of the way and enhance his mobility. This account given by Captain Dwight is compelling.

11. Archibald Hopkins' initial inquiry to Custis Lee was most likely trying to jog Custis Lee's memory concerning his sword and how he surrendered it. Hopkins was hoping that Custis Lee would substantiate the account that Hopkins gave in his Official Report concerning the Battle of Sailor's Creek and that Custis Lee's sword was taken from him during the battle and was in the possession of the 37th Massachusetts. As stated before, this direct communication from Hopkins to Custis Lee did not yield the results that Hopkins was hoping for.

12. With regard to any military requirement, which would have required Major General Custis Lee to have carried a sword at the Battle of Sailor's Creek, please see the following:

THE COMMONWEALTH OF MASSACHUSETTS
MASSACHUSETTS NATIONAL GUARD, MILITARY MUSEUM & ARCHIVES

3 March 2001
Dear Mr. White:
This is in reply to your letter of 29 Mar 2001. All officers, in both the Union and Confederate Armies, were required to wear swords. All officers also carried pistols. There was no requirement but all officers up to and including major generals did carry sidearms. LT Morrill would have purchased his sword and revolver in Boston. MG Custis was required to carry a sword and, without a doubt, armed himself with a pistol. I hope that this answers your questions. We hope that you enjoyed your visit to our institution.
Sincerely,
From: Leonid Kondratiuk, Colonel, US Army (Ret), Director
[Source: Personal letter in the possession of the Author]Manuscript 102****

13. With regard to the statement that Custis Lee, "did not ride a sorrel horse during the whole of the war," the following comments are relevant:

   A. Webster's dictionary gives the following definition to the word "sorrel": "A sorrel colored animal, especially a light, bright, chestnut horse often with a white mane and tail."

   B. It is unclear whether Custis Lee was taking issue with the use of the word sorrel to describe his horse, or was Custis Lee denying that he had a horse at all during the Battle of Sailor's Creek. There are at least two accounts that state Major General G. W. Custis Lee was mounted at the time of the Battle of Sailor's Creek (see references in Exhibit W-PF-9). In addition, in Major General Custis Lee's Military Service Record there is a memorandum created in 1863 by Custis Lee to his Quartermaster where Custis Lee requested a "handsomer" bridle for his horse, which horse was used in Custis Lee's military service. There is also a requisition on May 31, 1864, for forage for the personal horse in the service of Custis Lee. The order was for 60 pounds of corn and 60 pounds of oats. Custis Lee did in fact have a private horse for his use in his military service in 1863 and 1864. These records directly challenge the statement made by Custis Lee that he did not ride a (sorrel) horse for the whole of the war. There is also a high probability that Custis Lee rode this same horse at the Battle of Sailor's Creek, since Custis Lee was not engaged in an active battle until Sailor's Creek, where an active battle prior to Sailor's Creek could have caused this horse to have been killed or wounded.

[Source: Military Service Record of George Washington Custis Lee; General and Staff Officers, Corps, Division and Brigade Staffs, Confederate, National Archives, Washington, DC]Manuscript 144****

C. Archibald Hopkins was evidently aware and agreed with the account given by Adjutant Samuel E. Nichols in Exhibit W-PF-9 where Nichols stated that Custis Lee had a horse at the Battle of Sailor's Creek. Hopkins was probably trying to jog Custis Lee's memory concerning this horse. This attempt to jog Custis Lee's memory did not work for Hopkins.

D. It is interesting to note the following account given by Confederate Major Basinger concerning the Battle of Sailor's Creek:

FOOTNOTE:

When we began to form our line of battle, I sent the mules, the ambulance with some sick men, and the man who had charge of my horse, to the rear to get them out of harm's way.
[Source: Southern Historical Collection, University of North Carolina, Chapel Hill, NC, "Personal Reminiscences of William Starr Basinger"]**Manuscript 77**

If one of Custis Lee's Majors had a horse at the Battle of Sailor's Creek, then one would have to assume that a Major General like Custis Lee also had a horse at the Battle of Sailor's Creek.

14. With regard to the last statement concerning a hairbrush, it would have been nice if we had Archibald Hopkins' original letter of inquiry to Custis Lee. Hopkins was trying to get at something concerning a hairbrush and was trying to jog Custis Lee's memory concerning this point. As this is the only mention of the hairbrush, we have to assume that it was in Custis Lee's haversack along with many other personal items belonging to Custis Lee. These items were distributed amongst the soldiers of the 37th Massachusetts after Custis Lee was captured according to the several 37th Massachusetts accounts. It would appear from his statement that Custis Lee was specifically disputing the fact that he had a valise with him, it being off with the wagon train in a different direction. A valise would have been on the rear of the saddle of his horse. If Custis Lee did indeed have valise containing personal items like a hairbrush, and these were physically extracted from him during his capture at the Battle of Sailor's Creek, this would have been a painfully humiliating experience for him. An experience that he would not want to remember or recall.

15. It must be remembered that Custis Lee was being asked to recall events that happened approximately 32 years before. This is a tremendous feat for someone in good health, let alone someone who was in failing health like Custis Lee. In a letter dated March 26, 1878, Custis Lee wrote to Jefferson Davis about some War time recollections that Custis Lee had, in response to a certain line of questioning from Jefferson Davis who was writing a book about the War. Custis Lee's letter was replete with phases like: (1) *"finding the incidents of the several raids on Richmond somewhat confused in my memory,"* (2) *"All I distinctly remember of the raid in question is this"* (3), *"I can not recollect being on the Brook turnpike, or to the right of it, during this raid,"* (4) *"I do not recollect any incident, which would enable me to say positively whether or not I was with you any time during the raid under consideration,"* and in his conclusion he states (5) *" Notwithstanding the trouble you have taken to refresh my memory in regard to the attack on the Brook turnpike by Kilpatrick, I can not recall any of the incidents mentioned with distinctness, though I have a sort of shadowy recollection of them, as if I had heard something of them with regard to someone else. My memory is very bad, however, I have no doubt that yours is to be more relied on, though it is possible that Johnson, or Wood or some other of your aides, was with you at the time."* **[Source: The Perfect Gentleman, The Life and Letters of George Washington Custis Lee-Volume 2, Bernice-Marie Yates; 2003]**Manuscript 143**** Custis Lee was characteristically humble and honest in this letter about the short comings of his memory. This self critique of his memory was offered by Custis Lee in the year 1878, nineteen years before trying to recollect another series of Civil War events for Hopkins in the year 1897. One would have to assume that Custis Lee's recollections of the events surrounding the Battle of Sailor's Creek were poor when he responded to Archibald Hopkins, through his private secretary, in the year 1897.

16. Lastly, research in the various medical journals indicates that there is a strong tie between depression/melancholia and memory deficits. As an example, the Neuroscience Institute, a division of GlaxoSmithKline, in their study entitled "Cognitive Symptoms of Depression" by Elizabeth P. Goodale, 2004, states, "a battery of memory tests found that depressed patients demonstrated

deficits in psychomotor speed and in free recall of material (both immediate and delayed recall)."
One would have to question if Custis Lee's depression and melancholia had a detrimental effect on
his ability to recall information about the Battle of Sailor's Creek in the year 1897 when his
symptoms were particularly severe.

BIOGRAPHIES:
*Tanner, Luther M.: Priv.; Res. Adams; 18; farmer; enl. July 15, 1862; must. Sept. 2, 1862;
wounded April 2, 1865, Petersburg, VA; died of wounds, May 18, 1865, at Washington, DC, as
Corpl.*
*Hopkins, Archibald: Captain; Res. Williamstown; 19; student; Comm. Aug. 27, 1862; must. Sept.
4., 1862; Comm. Major, May 19, 1865; not must.; Comm. Lieut. Colonel, June 26, 1865; not must.;
must. Out June 21, 1865, as Captain of Co. C. Brevet Major U. S. Vols., to date April 6, 1865;
and brevet Lieut. Colonel U. S. Vols., to date March 13, 1865.*
**[Source: Massachusetts Soldiers, Sailors and Marines in the Civil War, Volume 3, Compiled and
Published by the Adjutant General, Norwood Press; 1932]**Manuscript 68****

EXHIBIT-W-PF-13

Introduction:
A letter from the Chief of the Record and Pension Office, dated May 20, 1897, to James Bowen,
acknowledging receipt of the letter from the private secretary of Custis Lee and informing Bowen that it
has been forwarded to the Secretary of War.

Evidence:

RECORD AND PENSION OFFICE, Washington City, May 20, 1897.
To: Mr. James L. Bowen

*I beg to acknowledge the receipt of your letter of the 19th instant in the matter of the award of a medal
of honor to David White, late corporal, Company E, 37th Massachusetts Infantry Volunteers, for the
capture of General Custis Lee, Confederate States Army, at Sailor's Creek, Virginia, April 6, 1865, and
the letter of the private secretary of General Lee, dated May 12, 1897, therewith inclosed, and to inform
you that your letter and its inclosure have this day been transmitted to the Secretary of War in
connection with previous papers in the case already submitted.*
Very respectfully,
F. C. Ainsworth, Colonel, U.S. Army, Chief, Record and Pension Office.
**[Source: 37th Massachusetts Protest Case file at the National Archives: AGO Record & Pension
Office, Document File #476510, File for David D. White, 37th Massachusetts, Volume 8W3, Row
16, Com 17, Shelf F, Box #699]**Manuscript 24****

Comments & Supporting Evidence:
1. The War Department acknowledges receipt of Bowen's letter dated May 19th containing Archibald
   Hopkins' correspondence with Custis Lee. This Protest Case file continues to grow and is getting
   quite large, complex and perplexing.

EXHIBIT-W-PF-14

Introduction:

Harriett Richardson: (PHOTO: COURTESY CHARLES W. THAYER)

This important letter is from Harriett Richardson, who is a first cousin to William Morrill. It is dated May 26, 1897, and is addressed to James Bowen. Harriett Richardson mentions the sword of Major General Custis Lee in this letter.

Evidence:

In reply to yours of the 15th, I would say that the Custis Lee sword was, some years ago, by order of Captain Wm. Morrill of the 37th Mass. Reg't., delivered to Frank Abbott, brother of H. M. Abbott of Northampton. Of its present whereabouts, I have no knowledge, nor is our family informed of any facts regarding its capture.
Very Respectfully,
From: Harriet Richardson, Hadley, May 26 '97

[Source: 37TH Massachusetts Protest Case file at the National Archives: AGO Record & Pension Office, Document File #476510, File for David D. White, 37th Massachusetts, Volume 8W3 ROW16 COM17, Shelf F, Box #699]**Manuscript 24**

Comments & Supporting Evidence:

1. This is an extremely important piece of evidence. Harriet Richardson is a first cousin to William Morrill. In Exhibit W–PF–9, Adjutant Samuel S. Nichols suggests that James Bowen contact Miss Harriet Richardson, care of Mr. Charles Thayer, of Hockanum, MA, regarding the whereabouts of the sword of General Custis Lee. James Bowen must have contacted Harriet Richardson about the Custis Lee sword and this was her reply.

2. This evidence is important because she is a non-biased, non-military eyewitness to a sword, a sword that she references as the sword of Custis Lee and a sword that was in her family's possession. Her testimony is based upon her own personal knowledge and first hand observations.

3. Harriett Richardson's letter states that William Morrill ordered the sword to be delivered to a Frank Abbott. As later testimony will show, William Morrill did not stay at his uncle's home in Hockanum, MA, for a very long period of time after returning from the Civil War. He went to PA to pursue his interest in the oil industry. This could explain why Morrill "ordered" his cousin Harriet, who was still living at the Hockanum farm when Morrill was not, to deliver the Custis Lee sword to a Frank Abbott, brother of H. M. Abbott.

4. H. M. Abbott of Northampton, referred to by Harriet Richardson in her letter to James Bowen is Hubbard M. Abbott. Hubbard M. Abbott mustered into the 37th Massachusetts from Northampton, MA, and served in the capacity of first lieutenant. He was a life-long resident of Northampton, MA, and served as the Register of Probate in Northampton in 1889 and Treasurer of the 37th Massachusetts Veterans' Association. Due to Hubbard Abbott's close proximity to the Richardson family who resided at Hockanum, Harriet Richardson most likely was acquainted with Hubbard M. Abbott.

5. Hubbard M. Abbott had three brothers according to his father's (Moses Abbott) obituary published on January 4, 1889, in Andover; MA. The brothers were at the time of the obituary article: Oramel G. Abbott, who died October, 1888 in Milford CT; William Frank Abbott, residing in Lynn, MA; and

George B. Abbott residing in East Saginaw, MI. **[Source: Andover MA, Historical Society letter, dated December 12, 1995, letter in the possession of the author]**Manuscript 51****

6. From the pension records of William Frank Abbott, brother of Hubbard M. Abbott, the following information was obtained:
   A. William F. Abbott enrolled in the Civil War from South Hadley, MA. (Hockanum, MA, is the town of Hadley, MA, today) on July 21, 1862.
   B. William Frank Abbott mustered into the Civil War as a Private in Company G, 37th Massachusetts.
   C. He mustered out as a Sergeant June 21, 1865.
   D. Was wounded at the Battle of Winchester on September 19, 1865.
   E. He married Ellen Coville on February 25, 1869, at South Boston
   F. His places of residence after serving in the Civil War were: South Hadley, MA, 4 years; Andover MA, 5 years; Chelsea MA, 5 years; Neponset MA, 5 years; Milton MA, Lower Mill, 2.5 years; Lynn MA, 2.5 years; and Boston MA, 25 years.
   G. William F. Abbott died November 27, 1914, in a soldier's home in Chelsea, MA.
   H. On September 24, 1879, Hubbard M. Abbott of Northampton, MA, testified to injuries that his brother William Frank Abbott sustained at the battle of Winchester, VA. On September 26, 1879, Samuel E. Nichols of Pittsfield, MA, testified to the same.

[Source: Hubbard M. Abbott Pension File, records numbers 313624 and 1038996, National Archives, Washington, DC]**Manuscript 52**

7. When Harriet Richardson wrote her letter to James Bowen in 1897, it would appear that William Frank Abbott was then living in Boston. This could explain why it does not appear from her letter that Harriet personally knew William Frank Abbott like she did his local Northampton, MA, brother, Hubbard Abbott. James Bowen should have tried to contact William Frank Abbot in Boston and secure his testimony regarding his taking the Custis Lee sword from the Richardson home. Bowen, most likely, at the time did not think this kind of action was necessary to resolve the 37th Massachusetts Protest Case.

8. Testimony presented later in this work will corroborate the fact that Civil War buddies of William Morrill came and got the sword of Custis Lee from the Richardson family for use at a Grand Army Republic (G. A. R.) celebration. According to the letter of Harriett Richardson above, this was done with the full permission of William Morrill.

9. It would appear that when William Frank Abbott picked up the sword from the Richardson family in Hockanum, now Hadley, MA, that was the last time the Richardson family saw the sword. It was never returned. From the Harriett Richardson letter, it appears as if William Morrill never intended the sword to be returned to the Richardson family. William Frank Abbott died on November 27, 1914, with his residence at 21 Milford Street, Boston. A check of his probate record shows he died intestate. An inventory of his personal estate lists only his cash holdings, with no listing of any physical items like the sword of Custis Lee. **[Source: William Frank Abbott, Suffolk County, MA, Probate File #167460]**Manuscript 53****

BIOGRAPHY:
Abbott, William F.: Corpl.; Res. South Hadley; 25; farmer; enl. July 21, 1862, must. Aug. 30, 1862, wounded Sept. 19, 1864, Winchester, VA, as Sergt, must. Out June 21, 1865
[Source: Massachusetts Soldiers, Sailors and Marines in the Civil War, Volume 3, Compiled and Published by the Adjutant General, Norwood Press; 1932]**Manuscript 68**

EXHIBIT-W-PF-15

Introduction:

This is an affidavit from Jerome E. King of Company F, of the 37th Massachusetts, dated May 31, 1897, concerning the capture of General Custis Lee at the Battle of Sailor's Creek, VA.

Evidence:

GENERAL AFFIDAVIT, State of Maine, County of Kennebec,
In the matter of Medal of Honor for Capture of Gen. Custis Lee, C. S. A., at Sailor's Creek, VA, April 6, 1865. On this 31st day of May, A. D. 1897, personally appeared before me, a Notary Public within the County and State aforesaid, duly authorized to administer oaths, Jerome E. King, aged 61 years, a resident of National Home, Togus, in the County of Kennebec, and State of Maine, whose Post Office address is Natl. Home, Togus, ME, well known to me to be reputable and entitled to credit, and who being duly sworn, declared in relation to the aforesaid case as follows: That he was well acquainted with David White, late Corporal of Company E, 37th Mass Inf. Vols. and that he (King) as a member of Co. F. of same regiment. That at the Battle of Sailor's Creek, VA, on April 6, 1865, Corporal White brought a Confederate officer into our lines, said to have been General Custis Lee. That the officer refused to deliver to said White his sword, (his person then being under White's charge) and was then conveyed to the presence of a Commissioned officer of said regiment and handed over to him. He further declared that he has no interest in said case and is not concerned in its prosecution.
From: Jerome E. King, (Affiant's Signature)
[Source: 37TH Massachusetts Protest Case file at the National Archives: AGO Record & Pension Office, Document File #476510, File for David D. White, 37th Massachusetts, Volume 8W3 ROW16 COM17, Shelf F, Box #699]**Manuscript 24**

Comments & Supporting Evidence:

1. This testimony by Jerome E. King corroborates accounts given by many others that Custis Lee refused to surrender his sword to David White. Custis Lee eventually handed his sword over to a Federal commissioned officer (most likely William Morrill.)
2. It would appear that King was as an eyewitness to some of the events he related. He must have observed firsthand the following events: "Corporal White brought a Confederate officer into our lines, said to have been Custis Lee," and "this officer being under the charge of White."

BIOGRAPHY:

King, Jerome E.: Priv.; Res. Hatfield; 26; farmer; enl. Aug. 1, 1862; must. Aug. 30, 1862; must. Out June 21, 1865.
[Source: Massachusetts Soldiers, Sailors and Marines in the Civil War, Volume 3, Compiled and Published by the Adjutant General, Norwood Press; 1932]**Manuscript 68**

EXHIBIT-W-PF-16

Introduction:

Letter from James Bowen dated June 10, 1897, to the Chief of the Record and Pension Office of the War Department, stating that he has enclosed sundry affidavits and statements concerning the capture of Custis Lee.

Evidence:

37th MASSACHUSETTS VETERANS' ASSOCIATION, June 10, 1897
I have the honor to enclose you, herewith, sundry affidavits and statements in regard to the capture of General Custis Lee, C. S. A. I do not know whether it is desirable or necessary to continue piling up evidence of this nature, in order to establish our case. It would seem to me that we had already supplied as much as would be necessary. In some cases, I have sent simply letters, and in some

cases, sworn statements. The substance of all these letters could be embodied in affidavits, if necessary. Trusting that these papers may be filed with the Hon. Sec'y of War, with other papers already furnished in the case, I am,
Very respectfully yours,
From: James L. Bowen, Historian, 37ᵗʰ Mass. Inf.

[Source: 37ᵀᴴ Massachusetts Protest Case file at the National Archives: AGO Record & Pension Office, Document File #476510, File for David D. White, 37ᵗʰ Massachusetts, Volume 8W3 ROW16 COM17, Shelf F, Box #699]Manuscript 24****

Comments & Supporting Evidence:

1. James Bowen is quite correct when he states that he has piled up a voluminous file of letters.
2. It is interesting to note that James Bowen felt he could convert into legal sworn affidavits all the various testimonies that he had accumulated in the War Department up to this point in time (June 10, 1897). This would leave one to believe that the various 37ᵗʰ Massachusetts affiants felt very certain about their testimonies and statements in this matter.

EXHIBIT-W-PF-17

Introduction:

Archibald Hopkins: (PHOTO: COURTESY WILLIAMS COLLEGE)

A letter from Archibald Hopkins, the commander of the 37ᵗʰ Massachusetts at the Battle of Sailor's Creek, dated June 17, 1897, to Russell A. Alger, Secretary of War. Hopkins wants to be heard, most likely with a face to face meeting with Alger, on the matter concerning the capture of General Custis Lee.

Evidence:

Court of Claims, Washington, DC June 17, 1897
To: Hon. Russell A. Alger, Secretary of War

There is a dispute pending in the War Department in regard to the issue of a medal for the capture of Gen. G. W. C. Lee at the Battle of Sailor's Creek. One of the claimants was a member of the regiment I commanded at that time and I should like to be heard when you take the matter up for decision. It would be a favor to me could you do so at an early day as I expect to leave the city for some time in about ten days.
Yours very respectfully, From: Archibald Hopkins

[Source: 37ᵀᴴ Massachusetts Protest Case file at the National Archives: AGO Record & Pension Office, Document File #476510, File for David D. White, 37ᵗʰ Massachusetts, Volume 8W3 ROW16 COM17, Shelf F, Box #699]Manuscript 24****

Comments & Supporting Evidence:

1. Based on the letter found in Exhibit W–PF–12, it would appear that Archibald Hopkins is an attorney (Esq.) working for the Court of Claims in Washington, DC, in 1897. More in-depth research has discovered that Archibald Hopkins was a Williams College graduate prior to the Civil War, a Columbia University Law School graduate after the Civil War, a practicing attorney in New York, NY, for six years after graduating Columbia and was then appointed Chief Clerk of the Court of Claims, which was established by Congress in 1855, and served as the Chief Clerk for the Court of Claims from 1873 to 1914.

2. Archibald Hopkins might have had a personal or professional relationship with Secretary of War Alger, stemming from mutual Government associations. This is manifest by Hopkins asking Alger for a "favor." Archibald Hopkins was asking Alger "to be heard," most likely during a face to face meeting, before Hopkins left Washington, DC, for an extended period of time.

3. Since Archibald Hopkins wrote very specific Official Reports on April 10, 1865, and then again on April 17, 1865, concerning the capture of Custis Lee and his sword, it would have been desirable to have his written testimony concerning this matter in the 37th Massachusetts Protest Case file. Unfortunately, none could be found by the author. It does appear from Hopkins' letter that Archibald Hopkins had something very definitive he wanted to say to Alger. So much so that he wanted a personal meeting with Alger. Archibald Hopkins' enthusiastic desire to provide face to face support for the position of the 37th Massachusetts in this Protest Case is an important point given the fact that he commanded the 37th Massachusetts at the Battle of Sailor's Creek and eye witnessed many of the events, particularly those surrounding Custis Lee's capture and the surrender of his sword.

4. There is no written documentation in the 37th Massachusetts Protest Case file that Alger ever "heard" Archibald Hopkins on this matter during any personal meeting between the two men. This is unfortunate because Alger would have gained revealing insight into the Case that could have only come from a face to face, interactive meeting with Hopkins.

EXHIBIT-W-PF-18

Introduction:

Hubbard M. Abbott: (PHOTO: COURTESY U. S. ARMY WAR COLLEGE)

This is an affidavit from Hubbard M. Abbott, a Lieutenant in command of Company F within the 37th Massachusetts during the Battle of Sailor's Creek, which affidavit is dated July 9, 1897. This affidavit addresses the capture of General Custis Lee at the Battle of Sailor's Creek.

Evidence:

GENERAL AFFIDAVIT:
State of Massachusetts, County of Hampshire
In the matter of Medal of Honor for Capture of General G. W. Custis Lee, C. S. A., April 6, 1865
On this 9th day of July, A. D. 1897, personally appeared before me, a Clerk of the Superior Court within and for the County and State aforesaid, duly authorized to administer oaths, Hubbard M. Abbott, aged 58 years, a resident of Northampton, in the County of Hampshire, and State of Mass., whose Post Office is Northampton, County of Hampshire, State of Mass., well known to me to be reputable and entitled to credit, and who being duly sworn, declared in relation to the aforesaid case as follows:
I was on the 6th day of April A. D. 1865, Lieut. in Command of Co. F, 37th Mass. Vols. In the afternoon of said day, said Regiment was ordered into action at Sailor's Creek, Virginia. Lieut. William C. Morrill was in command of the Co. on the right of my Command. During the action I saw a squad of soldiers about 30 yards to the right of my Co. about a Confederate officer. I could not hear what was said but saw them bring their guns to charge Bayonet [**Author Note:** this means that the gun is gripped at the wrist of the gun, gun is then brought to the right hip and then leveled]. *I started towards there intending to take the officer's sword but Lieut. Morrill was nearer than I and the officer delivered his sword and*

other equipments to him. The officer who surrendered was Gen. Custis Lee, son of Robert E. Lee. The sword and belt were in the possession of Lieut. Morrill until his death. There were no troops in front of us at Sailor's Creek, ours was a single line of battle and we could not have held our position had we not been armed with the Spencer repeating rifle. We had seven killed or wounded with the bayonet. It was a hand to hand engagement and it seemed to me that the Regiment was fighting in defense of others. In the haversack of Gen. Lee was a pipe which Lieut. Morrill gave to Gen. Oliver Edwards, our Brigade Commander. Gen. Edwards gave the pipe to General H. G. Wright, 6th Corps commander. This affidavit is written by one Hubbard M. Abbott, Late First Lieut. Commanding Co. F, 37th Mass. Vols, and in its preparation I was not asked or prompted by any written or printed statement dictated or presented by any other person. That engagement is so stamped on my memory that I shall never forget it.
From: Hubbard M. Abbott, Late First Lieut. Commanding Co. F, 37th Mass. Vols.

[Source: 37TH Massachusetts Protest Case file at the National Archives: AGO Record & Pension Office, Document File #476510, File for David D. White, 37th Massachusetts, Volume 8W3 ROW16 COM17, Shelf F, Box #699] Manuscript 24 ****

Comments & Supporting Evidence:

1. This is a powerful piece of testimony from a close eyewitness that General Custis Lee surrendered his sword to Lt. William Morrill, who was the Federal officer nearest to Custis Lee when captured.
2. It is very important to note that Hubbard M. Abbott states that Custis Lee not only delivered his sword to Lt. William Morrill, but Custis Lee also delivered his "other equipment."
3. Another important item Abbott states is that Custis Lee's sword and belt were in the possession of Lt. Morrill until his death. William Morrill died in 1892. Custis Lee's belt, referenced by Hubbard above, will corroborate important Thayer family testimony that is presented later in this report.
4. Abbott's testimony corroborates nicely other testimony that a haversack was taken from General Custis Lee. It also corroborates General Oliver Edwards' testimony concerning Custis Lee's pipe, that it was taken from Custis Lee and given to General H. G. Wright after the battle.
5. Though this text was very difficult to translate and subsequently transcribe, the author managed to do so accurately through the use of a professional handwriting translator.

BIOGRAPHY:

***Abbott, Hubbard M.:** Sergt.; Res. Northampton; 23; clerk; enl. July 15, 1862; must. Aug. 30, 1862; prom. Sergt. Major, June 4, 1863; Comm. 2d Lieut. Oct 31, 1863; must. Sept. 18, 1864; wounded May 18, 1864; Spotsylvania, VA; Comm. 1st Lieut. Sept 23, 1864; must. Nov. 27, 1864; Comm. Captain May 24, 1865; not must., must. Out June 21, 1865; as 1st Lieut. of Co. H.*

[Source: Massachusetts Soldiers Sailors and Marines in the Civil War, Volume 3, compiled and published by the Adjutant General, Norwood Press; 1932] Manuscript 68 ****

EXHIBIT-W-PF-19

Introduction:

Horatio G. Wright:

This is a letter dated July 15, 1897, from George W. Davis, Major in the War Department, to General H. G. Wright, commander of the 6th Corps at the Battle of Sailor's Creek, asking General Wright to review the 37th Massachusetts Protest Case file. This initial letter **(1)** is then followed by the three communications listed below **(2-4)**:

(2)-A letter dated July 17, 1897, from General H. G. Wright to Major George W. Davis stating that he, General Wright, would be willing to look over and review the papers in the 37th Massachusetts Protest Case.

(3)-A letter dated July 23, 1897, from Major George W. Davis of the War Department to General H. G. Wright acknowledging Wright's letter of July 15, 1897, and then stating that he, Davis, is now forwarding to General Wright the papers of the 37th Massachusetts Protest Case. **(4)**-A letter dated July 30, 1897, from General H. G. Wright to Major George W. Davis of the War Department, outlining his, Wright's, recollections of this matter after reviewing the papers in the 37th Massachusetts Protest Case file.

Evidence:

(1) *WAR DEPARTMENT, To: General H. G. Wright,*
Dear General:
There is a peculiar case pending in the Department, consisting of a contest respecting which of two men is entitled to a medal of honor for the capture of General Custis Lee at the Battle of Sailor's Creek, April 6, 1865, by the troops of your Sixth Corps. The Secretary of War wishes me to ask if you would be willing to look over the papers in the case and to favor him with your best judgment as to the merits of the case. Upon the original presentation, several years ago, the medal was awarded to one of the men but now a rival for the honor insists that a mistake has been made. Upon receipt of a note to the effect that you would be disposed to look into the matter, I shall send the papers.
Respectfully,
From: George W. Davis, Major, U. S. A.

(2) *July 17, 1897, Washington, D.C.*
Dear Major,
Your letter of the 15th instant finds me here. I do not know that I can help you in the matter to which it refers, but shall willingly do all I can on my return to Washington, which will be by the 26th inst . if nothing occurs to occasion delay. At Sailor's Creek, General Custis Lee was forced back upon our cavalry by the attack of the 6th Corps and I found him, after the fight was over, at Gen'l Sheridan's Hdqrs. I did not see him afterwards. The details connected with his capture or surrender I did not know or, at any rate, do not now remember. But a perusal of the papers in the case may possibly refresh my memory. I will advise you of my return to Washington.
Very Respectfully,
From: H. G. Wright, Brig & Bvt. Major Gen'l U.S.A.

(3) *July 23, 1897, To: General H. G. Wright*
My Dear Sir:
The Secretary of War wishes me to acknowledge the receipt of your favor of the 17th instant, and to send you herewith the papers in the case of <u>Hawthorne vs. White</u> *for the Medal of Honor. You will see from the papers that the medal was some time since awarded to Hawthorne, but probably the fact that the credit for the capture of General Custis Lee was disputed was not known to the Department when Hawthorne's case was decided. I also enclose a copy of recent regulations issued by the President respecting awards of medals, and in this connection I will say that the propriety of giving a medal at all for this incident would seem to be questionable at least. Extracts from your own and General Wheaton's reports are in the brief, from the records. You will also see a letter from General Lee himself, in which he declares he was not riding a horse at the time, nor wearing a sword. The Secretary would be very glad to have an expression of opinion from you in this matter.*
Very sincerely yours,
From: George W. Davis, Major, U.S.A.

[Enclosure]
WAR DEPARTMENT, Washington, June 26, 1897:
By direction of the President, the following regulations are promulgated respecting the award of Medals of Honor, and paragraph 177 of the Regulations is amended to read as follows:
177: *Medals of Honor, authorized by the Act of Congress, approved March 3, 1863, are awarded to officers and enlisted men in the name of The Congress, for particular deeds of most distinguished gallantry in action.*

1. In order that the Congressional Medal of Honor may be deserved, service must have been performed in action of such a conspicuous character as to clearly distinguish the man for gallantry and intrepidity above his comrades—service that involved extreme jeopardy of life or the performance of extraordinarily hazardous duty. Recommendations for the decoration will be judged by this standard of extraordinary merit, and incontestable proof of performance of the service will be exacted.

2. Soldiers of the Union have ever displayed bravery in battle, else victories could not have been gained; but as courage and self-sacrifice are the characteristics of every true soldier, such a badge of distinction as the Congressional Medal is not to be expected as the reward of conduct that does not clearly distinguish the soldier above other men, whose bravery and gallantry have been proved in battle.

3. Recommendations for medals on account of services rendered in the Volunteer Army during the late war, and in the Regular Army previous to January 1, 1890, will, if practicable, be submitted by some person other than the proposed recipient, one who is personally familiar with all the facts and circumstances claimed as justifying the award, but the application may be made by the one claiming to have earned the decoration, in which case it will be in the form of a deposition, reciting a narrative description of the distinguished service performed. If official records are relied on as evidence proving the personal service, the reports of the action must be submitted or cited; but if these records are lacking the testimony must embrace that of one or more eyewitnesses, who, under oath, describe specifically the act or acts they saw, wherein the person recommended or applying clearly distinguished himself above his fellows for most distinguished gallantry in action.

4. Recommendations for medals on account of service rendered subsequent to January 1, 1890, will be made by the Commanding Officer at the time of the action or by an officer or soldier having personal cognizance of the act for which the badge of honor is claimed, and the recommendation will embrace a detailed recital of all the facts and circumstances. Certificates of officers or the affidavits of enlisted men who were eyewitnesses of the act will also be submitted if practicable.

5. In cases that may arise for service performed hereafter, recommendations for award of medals must be forwarded within one year after the performance of the act for which the award is claimed. Commanding officers will thoroughly investigate all cases of recommendations for Congressional Medals arising in their commands, and indorse their opinion upon the papers, which will be forwarded to the Adjutant General of the Army through regular channels.

From: R. A. ALGER, Secretary of War

(4) To: Major Geo. W. Davis – U.S.A., War Department

My Dear Major–I find on my return to Washington your letter of the 23rd inst, with the papers in the case of Hawthorne vs. White for Medal of Honor. These papers I have looked over with much care and find myself quite unable to reconcile the inconsistencies and contradictions contained therein, unless one or both parties were mistaken in the person of General G. W. C. Lee. My personal knowledge in the matter is confined to having met General Lee at Gen'l Sheridan's HQrs. After the battle was over and having a short conversation with him, in which, however, no references were made to the manner of his capture so far as I remember. I presume I looked upon it as a matter of no importance as he was a part of the entire command engaged against us and which we had captured. I distinctly remember that Gen'l Sheridan suggested that I might like to take Lee with me as he was an old friend of mine and that I was unable to do so as my HQrs were already overcrowded with Confederate officers, Generals, Admirals etc.–while his (Sheridan) had still accommodations for him. All this has seemed to me to bear out my supposition that he was driven back with his command by the 6th Corps upon the cavalry to which he surrendered. I see that in my report, an extract from which is with the papers submitted by you, that I name General Lee as amongst those captured by the 6th Corps. This statement may have been made on the assumption that the captures of that day were made by the 6th Corps which bore the brunt of the fighting. It would seem desirable to have a statement from General Wheaton, as some of the papers in the case claim that Lee was sent to his HQrs. If this be so, it seems singular at least that he did not turn him over to me or my Provost Marshal instead of to Gen'l Sheridan. The 6th Corps had, to the best of my recollection, some 3,000 prisoners, while the cavalry had, perhaps, twice as many. I *entirely fail to recall the incident mentioned by Gen'l Oliver Edwards, Com. 3rd brigade, 1st Division, 6th Corps, of his having turned over to me at my request the pipe and tobacco pouch taken from Gen'l Lee and of my sending them to him. I must not be understood as in anyway questioning this statement, but simply that no trace of the transaction remains in my memory. In conclusion I would say that I am found to agree with you "that the propriety of giving a medal at all for this incident would seem to be questionable at least. The papers in the case are returned herewith.*

Very Respectfully, Your Obt Servt

From: H. G. Wright, Brig & Bvt Maj Gen'l U.S.A. (Retired)

[Source: 37TH Massachusetts Protest Case file at the National Archives: AGO Record & Pension Office, Document File #476510, File for David D. White, 37th Massachusetts, Volume 8W3 ROW16 COM17, Shelf F, Box #699] Manuscript 24****

Comments & Supporting Evidence:

1. It is important to note that as of this George W. Davis letter dated July 23, 1897, the War Department is starting to form an opinion on the possible resolution to this perplexing matter by stating the following: "I also enclose a copy of recent regulations issued by the President respecting awards of medals, and in this connection I will say that the propriety of giving a medal at all for this incident would seem to be questionable at least."

2. It would appear that General H. G. Wright has very little recollection of this event which happened over 32 years ago. This is most likely due to several factors: (1) this event was not that important to him given his overall responsibilities, (2) this event was not observed by him directly, (3) this act, performed on a regimental level, was far removed from the Corps level, (4) the huge passage of time to have vivid recollections of this small event, and (5) he was 77 years old at the time of this writing and died two years later. His age could have impaired his ability to recall these events.

3. Initially, General Wright only remembered seeing Custis Lee at General Sheridan's headquarters as stated in his July 17, 1897 letter. Upon review of the Case, he remembered a little more. The one area that General Wright did remember well is meeting General Custis Lee at General Sheridan's headquarters and General Sheridan suggesting that he (Wright) take General Custis Lee back to his headquarters since, "he was an old friend of mine." This account raises six important points:

    A. General Wright raises a very interesting question. If the 6th Corps Infantry captured General Custis Lee, why was he not turned over to General Wright and his Provost Marshal instead of to General Sheridan? David White's account is relatively silent on the turnover of Custis Lee. In White's own testimony, he states that he "afterwards delivered him to the Provost Marshall in the rear." Did White turn Custis Lee over to Wright's or Sheridan's Provost Marshall? John Grace in his testimony states "White ordered him to the rear." Jerome King in his testimony states that White handed off General Custis Lee to a commissioned officer of the Regiment. David White's statement that he delivered Custis Lee to a Provost Marshall is consistent with Wright's idea that Lee should have been taken to a Provost Marshall. It is highly probable that White was not actively engaged in taking General Custis Lee to any headquarters. As stated in the testimonies of John Grace and Jonas Champney as contained in White's pension file, right after the capture of Custis Lee, White was detailed with others to the rear to bring more ammunition to the front. This would seem to indicate that White spent little time turning over General Custis Lee to anyone if the battle was still active and he was bringing more ammunition to the front.

    B. The Hawthorn account, as given by T. J. Hassett, is extremely detailed with regard to the facts centered on the "turn over" of General Custis Lee. General Wright's recollection of meeting General Custis Lee at General Sheridan's headquarters corroborates the Hassett account that he, Hawthorn, and a staff officer were trying to deliver Custis Lee to Sheridan's headquarters before turning him over to a Major of the 121st New York. It is unclear whether or not this Major was successful in taking Custis Lee to Sheridan's headquarters. It is a mystery why they were delivering Custis Lee to Sheridan's headquarters and not to Wright's headquarters, or his Provost Marshall, as suggested by General Wright.

C. The first Hawthorn account as found in the Official Records, as outlined in Exhibit H-OR-1, states that he, Hawthorn, "was one of the men detailed by Colonel Olcott on account of such capture, to conduct General Custis Lee to the headquarters of General Wheaton, commander of the 1st Division, 6th Army Corps." In addition, the second Hawthorn account, as given by him and contained in Exhibit H-MR-3, states that "Colonel Egbert Olcott, commanding the Regiment, detailed Hawthorn as one of the men to conduct the noted rebel general to the headquarters of General Wheaton." Both of these accounts for Hawthorn can not support Custis Lee being in Sheridan's headquarters.

D. General Custis Lee being at General Sheridan's headquarters after his capture does support the account given by Miles L. Butterfield in Exhibit B-MR-1 when Butterfield stated: "I took charge of them and one of their numbers asked to whom he had the honor of surrendering. When told, he said that he was General Custis Lee, son of General Robert E. Lee, and would like to be taken to General Sheridan. With two men of the 37th Massachusetts, I took them to the rear where Generals Sheridan and Wright were found, and turned them over to General Sheridan. General Wright had been Lee's tutor at West Point, and recognizing General Wright, Lee extended his hand to the General, who did not take it, but turning to Colonel Franklin, Chief of Staff, said, "Colonel, take these men to the rear."

E. General Wright's recollection that General Sheridan suggested that General Custis Lee go back with General Wright (presumably back to his headquarters), because Wright and Custis Lee were old friends, is an important recollection. This statement corroborates General Edwards' account of the pipe, and General Wright's desire to send it back to General Custis Lee because Custis Lee was Wright's pupil at West Point. The fact that General Wright would have to "send back" the pipe and tobacco pouch to General Custis Lee would indicate that General Custis Lee was not in Wright's headquarters when this pipe exchange took place between Edwards and Wright. This could be further proof that General Custis Lee was in fact with General Sheridan as recalled by Wright. The following two points should be noted:

- If General Wright recollected the pipe incident cited by General Edwards, this would have been powerful corroborating evidence for the account of David White. This recollection did not happen. General Wright was very clear when he stated, "However, I must not be understood as in any way questioning this statement by General Edwards, but simply that no trace of the transaction remains in my memory."

- It is interesting that General Wright remembers and then adopts the preliminary resolution to this perplexing Case offered by George W. Davis of the War Department by stating that he agrees with Davis' assessment, "that the propriety of giving a medal at all for this incident would seem to be questionable at least."

F. General Wright was over 77 years old when he was answering this inquiry. He passed away two years later. General Wright's memory might have been fragile at this advanced age of his life. This might explain why he did not recollect the pipe incident that was so well recollected and articulated by a General of a younger age, Oliver Edwards.

EXHIBIT-W-PF-20

Introduction:

(1) A letter from George W. Davis of the War Department dated August 2, 1897, to General G. W. C. Lee, President, Washington and Lee University, asking General Custis Lee the following question posed by General Alger, Secretary of the War Department, "Was any particularly distinguished gallantry shown by any enlisted man in the Union force in your immediate presence at the time of your capture?"
(2) This is followed by a letter from R. E. Lee Jr., nephew of Custis Lee, dated August 13, 1897, writing for his uncle Custis Lee, and answering the above question posed by General Alger.

Evidence:

(1) *August 2, 1897, To: General G. W. C. Lee, President Washington and Lee University*
I have the honor to request, by direction of the Secretary of War, that you will kindly supply if possible certain information desired by the War Department. More than two years ago the Department authorized the presentation of a Medal of Honor to a soldier of the 121st New York Regiment for your capture at Sailor's Creek, April 6, 1865. The proof of service seemed ample and of course the act was deemed to be of sufficient gallantry to warrant such recognition or it would not have been given. The fact of this presentation becoming known, a rival claimant for the honor appeared, and asserted with what would ordinarily be regarded as conclusive testimony that the award to the actual recipient was at least of questionable propriety. The papers in the case are voluminous. Among them is found a letter from you, through your private Secretary, to Colonel Archibald Hopkins of this city, giving your recollections of the occurrence. Since the filing of the counter claim, the incident itself as described in the official records and the testimony filed, has been quite carefully examined and this suggests a question to you which General Alger desires me to ask. Was any <u>particularly distinguished gallantry</u> shown by any enlisted man in the Union force in your immediate presence at the time of your capture? That the defense of your division was most gallant is known to all, and that the attack was most creditable is also an undisputed fact in history, but wherein any particular enlisted man could justly claim special merit for your capture is not clear from the records, and if such credit is due to any one, you would be certain to know the fact and possibly be able to describe the man. It appears officially that there were two regiments of the 6th Corps present at the moment you surrendered. The medalist belongs to one and the claimant to the other. The losses of each at Sailor's Creek were 39 killed and wounded in one of these regiments and 23 in the other. The Secretary will be very glad to have the benefit of your knowledge in deciding this perplexing case. A copy of regulations recently made by the President and now in force is enclosed.
Yours very sincerely,
From: George W. Davis, Major, U.S.A.

[INCLOSURE]
WAR DEPARTMENT, Washington, June 26, 1897:

By direction of the President, the following regulations are promulgated respecting the award of Medals of Honor, and paragraph 177 of the Regulations is amended to read as follows:

177: Medals of Honor, authorized by the Act of Congress, approved March 3, 1863, are awarded to officers and enlisted men in the name of The Congress, for particular deeds of most distinguished gallantry in action.

1. *In order that the Congressional Medal of Honor may be deserved, service must have been performed in action of such a conspicuous character as to clearly distinguish the man for gallantry and intrepidity above his comrades—service that involved extreme jeopardy of life or the performance of extraordinarily hazardous duty. Recommendations for the decoration will be judged by this standard of extraordinary merit, and incontestable proof of performance of the service will be exacted.*

2. *Soldiers of the Union have ever displayed bravery in battle, else victories could not have been gained; but as courage and self-sacrifice are the characteristics of every true soldier, such a badge of distinction as the Congressional Medal is not to be expected as the reward of conduct that does not clearly distinguish the soldier above other men, whose bravery and gallantry have been proved in battle.*

3. *Recommendations for medals on account of services rendered in the Volunteer Army during the late war, and in the Regular Army previous to January 1, 1890, will, if practicable, be submitted by some person other than the proposed recipient, one who is personally familiar with all the facts and circumstances claimed as justifying the award, but the application may be made by the one claiming to have earned the decoration, in which case it will be in the form of a deposition, reciting a narrative description of the distinguished service performed. If official records are relied on as evidence proving the personal service, the reports of the action must be submitted or cited; but if*

these records are lacking the testimony must embrace that of one or more eyewitnesses, who, under oath, describe specifically the act or acts they saw, wherein the person recommended or applying clearly distinguished himself above his fellows for most distinguished gallantry in action.

4. *Recommendations for medals on account of service rendered subsequent to January 1, 1890, will be made by the Commanding Officer at the time of the action or by an officer or soldier having personal cognizance of the act for which the badge of honor is claimed, and the recommendation will embrace a detailed recital of all the facts and circumstances. Certificates of officers or the affidavits of enlisted men who were eyewitnesses of the act will also be submitted if practicable.*

5. *In cases that may arise for service performed hereafter, recommendations for award of medals must be forwarded within one year after the performance of the act for which the award is claimed. Commanding officers will thoroughly investigate all cases of recommendations for Congressional Medals arising in their commands, and indorse their opinion upon the papers, which will be forwarded to the Adjutant General of the Army through regular channels.*

From: R. A. ALGER, Secretary of War.
Washington, August 13th, 1897

(2) *To: Maj. Geo. W. Davis, War Department, Washington, D.C.*

Dear Sir:
My uncle, G. W. C. Lee, who is still prevented from writing by illness, desires me to answer the special question contained in your letter of the 2nd Inst., as follows: There was no particularly distinguished gallantry shown by any enlisted man in the Union force in his immediate presence at the time of his capture. I have the honor to be, Very respectfully:
From: R. E. Lee, Jr.

[Source: 37TH Massachusetts Protest Case file at the National Archives: AGO Record & Pension Office, Document File #476510, File for David D. White, 37th Massachusetts, Volume 8W3 ROW16 COM17, Shelf F, Box #699]**Manuscript 24**

Comments & Supporting Evidence:

1. This is a very interesting set of documents. It would appear that the War Department was "stumped" at this point in the process in determining who definitively captured General George Washington Custis Lee at the Battle of Sailor's Creek, VA, April 6, 1865. It would also appear that the War Department wanted to avoid making a decision on who definitively captured Custis Lee. Instead, the War Department wanted to make a decision on a much easier question concerning the capture of Custis Lee, that being, "was any particularly distinguished gallantry shown by any enlisted man in the Union forces in your presence at the time of your capture?" In addition, the War Department now wanted the "particularly distinguished gallantry" standard, a new regulation made by the President on June 26, 1897, to be the standard for which this 37th Massachusetts Protest Case should now be judged.

2. The two fundamental points put to General Custis Lee on August 2, 1897, were:
   A. "Was any particularly distinguished gallantry shown by any enlisted man in the Union force in your immediate presence at the time of your capture?"
   B. "Wherein any particular enlisted man could justify claim special merit for your capture is not clear from the records, and if such credit is due to any one, you would be certain to know the fact and possibly be able to describe the man."

3. The War Department must have surely recognized that this matter would have been painfully sensitive for Custis Lee to recollect and offered him the following platitude: "That the defense of your division was most gallant is known to all, and that the attack was most creditable is also an undisputed fact in history."

4. The War Department's question was very clever because if Custis Lee could not answer the first question, which was to identify and describe the man who captured him over 32 years ago, then Custis Lee would only have to answer the easier and more subjective second question which was, "was any particularly distinguished gallantry shown by any enlisted man in your capture?" As one

might expect, Custis Lee was not able to answer the first question as to the identity or description of the man who captured him. Custis Lee's response to the second question as to any gallantry shown by a Federal soldier during his capture was very predictable. The reasons it was predictable are:

A. <u>First reason,</u>

George Washington Custis Lee (circa April, 1865):

Custis Lee simply did not like the Northerners as a result of the War. This is exemplified in the following three examples: **First:** Christiana Bond, a friend of Custis Lee, records a conversation that she had with Custis. Ms. Yates, the author who discovered this entry, offers a commentary at the end of Christiana Bond's remarks. *"In the moonlight we had hours of talk on the deck, in the midst of which I said, "Is it true that your father would never use the word "Yankee," but said, "Charge those people?" "Yes," he said, "it is true; but, he said, I did not share his feelings." Again in answer to my rather inane question, "why did the South so suddenly give up?" General Custis Lee said, "I can only answer for my command; for four days we had nothing to eat but the corn the men carried in their pockets".... General Custis Lee had none of his father's acceptance of the South's defeat and the wrecking of all his hopes. He seemed broken and disheartened, perhaps because life was still before him; while with General Robert E. Lee there was the resignation of a Christian and calm consciousness of fulfilled duty as a soldier and patriot.* **[Source: "The Perfect Gentleman, The Life and Letters of George Washington Custis Lee, Volume 2, Bernice-Marie Yates, 2003]**Manuscript 143**** <u>Second</u>: Ms. Yates also makes the following observations of Custis Lee: *"Custis was constantly receiving letters from strangers both North and South for a memento of his father. It was Custis' habit to reply politely but with a curt edge to the Northerners' request."... "It is interesting to note that late in Custis Lee's life he was still receiving requests for his autograph and those of other members of his family. Though always polite, when the request came from a Northerner, his response was short and curt."* **Third**: Ms. Yates gives a very good account of the long battle that Custis Lee had over his confiscated Arlington, VA, estate. She offers the following assessment about a settlement that was reached: *"This was a bittersweet triumph for Custis Lee. He obtained financial compensation for the Arlington Estate as well as closure to this chapter of his life but he had lost his home irrevocably and the foes of his father retained their hateful position on his most beloved property."* **[Source: "The Perfect Gentleman, The Life and Letters of George Washington Custis Lee, Volume 2, Bernice-Marie Yates, 2003]**Manuscript 143**** Custis Lee's bitterness toward Northerners would make it very difficult for Custis Lee to give any Northerner credit of "distinguished gallantry" for his capture. Custis Lee most likely viewed his capture by the Federal forces with contempt and a direct result of the Confederates being overwhelmingly out numbered.

B. <u>Second reason,</u> as noted in Exhibit W–PF–12, Custis Lee suffered from severe depression which was particularly acute during this August 2, 1897 time period. Custis Lee was finally successful in resigning from Washington College just prior to this date. Given his melancholy state of mind at this difficult period in his life, it is unlikely that Custis Lee would have thought positively about any Union enlisted man involved in his capture at the Battle of Sailor's Creek.

C. <u>Third reason,</u> on February 3, 1865, Custis Lee was promoted to Major-General without having served in any active field action. He served during most of the Civil War as an aide to President Jefferson Davis **[Source: Generals in Gray]**Manuscript 50****. Many scholars believe that Custis Lee was extremely sensitive about his promotions, believing that others thought it was due to the powerful influence of his famous father. Custis Lee was especially sensitive about his promotion to Major-General without having distinguished himself in a single battle. Though scholars agree that his promotions were probably not the result of his father's influence, public perception around this matter was probably viewed as fact by Custis Lee. Being captured as a new Major General along with his entire command at the Battle of Sailor's Creek, his first and only active engagement of the Civil War, was probably viewed by him as somewhat frustrating if not humiliating. He most likely viewed the whole episode as a low point in his life and military career. Surely he was not going to give credit to anyone in the Union Army for "distinguished gallantry" for his capture. It should be noted that Custis Lee often sought to persuade his superiors that he was not worthy of a promotion. This is evidenced in the writings of W. Gordon McCabe in his paper read at the Annual Meeting of the Virginia Historical Society which reads:

… For the rank he cared no whit; for we have Mr. Davis's explicit statement that he repeatedly offered him promotion (long before he finally consented to accept it), and that he as steadily refused it. "The only obstacle to be overcome," writes Mr. Davis, "was his own objection to receiving promotion. With a refined delicacy, he shrank from the idea of superseding men who had been actually serving in the field." It was said at the time, and is constantly repeated, that he spoke to his father on the subject, requesting most earnestly field-assignment, and that the latter told him that his highest duty was obedience to the will of his superior.

[Source: W. Gordon McCabe "Major General George Washington Custis Lee"; Southern Historical Society Papers, Volume 39; February 24, 1914]**Manuscript 45**

In addition, Major Stiles, a close associate of Custis Lee, writes the following concerning Custis Lee and his feelings about being a Major General:

Gen. Custis Lee, eldest son on Gen. Robert E. Lee, a man of the very highest character and an officer of the finest culture and a very high order of ability. He did not have a fair opportunity during the war, President Davis, of whose staff he was a member, refusing to permit him to go to the field, though he plead earnestly to do so. He was a most sensitive and modest gentleman, and would have rejoiced to command even a regiment in his father's army. After he was sent to the field, in the modified way in which he was sent near the close of the war, he more than once told me that every time he met one of his father's veteran fighting colonels he felt compromised at having the stars and wreath of a major-general on his collar.

[Source: "Four Years under Marse Robert" by Major Robert Stiles]**Manuscript 2**

This reluctance to be promoted was probably due, in part, to his feelings that he was not distinguished in battle and hence not worthy of promotion like his compatriots who were tested in the field of battle. This reluctance could also be due, in part, to his depression manifesting itself at this stage in his life. If Custis Lee did not have a positive impression of himself and his own military career during the War, it would be difficult for him to have a positive impression about any Federal soldier who captured him and the manner in which he was captured.

5. Col. Joseph Warren Keifer, commanding the 2nd Brigade in General Truman Seymour's 3rd Division at the Battle of Sailor's Creek, wrote the following letter to General Horatio G. Wright (Infantry commander at the Battle of Sailor's Creek) on October 22, 1888:

Springfield, Ohio, October 22, 1888, General Horatio G. Wright, Washington, D.C.:
My Dear Friend: -- After expressing to you that high regard I have always had for you, and also expressing the hope that your health is good, also that of your family, I have the honor to call your attention to the following matter, of some interest to you no doubt. General R. S. Ewell, of date of December 20, 1865, in the form of a report addressed to General R. E. Lee, to be found in Vol. 13, Southern Historical Papers, page 247, in speaking of the Battle of Sailor's Creek, after having concluded his general report of that battle, says: "I was informed at General Wright's headquarters, whither I was carried after my capture, that 30,000 men were engaged with us when we surrendered, viz., two infantry corps and Custer's and Merritt's divisions of cavalry, the whole under command of General Sheridan." On page 257, same book, in a note appended to a report of the same battle, by General G. W. C. Lee, he says: "I was told after my capture, that the enemy had two corps of infantry and three divisions of cavalry opposed to us at Sailor's Creek." Now, as I know you commanded the infantry engaged on the Union side in that battle from first to last, and that no infantry troops, save of

your corps, there fought under you, that only a portion of the Third Division (in which I was then serving) was present, and General Frank Wheaton's division of the Sixth Corps was the only other infantry division there, though I am not quite sure that his entire division was up and engaged in the battle at the time of the assault, overthrow, and destruction of General Ewell's forces, and my recollection is quite clear that General G. W. Getty's division of your corps did not arrive on the field in the time for the battle, I am certain Generals Ewell and G. W. C. Lee have fallen into a grave error. We certainly captured more men in the Sailor's Creek battle than Ewell and G. W. C. Lee say were engaged on the Confederate side. Since the war, there seems to be a disposition to disparage the Northern soldiers by representing a small number of Confederate troops engaged with a very large number of Union troops. The above is to my mind simply an illustration of what I find running through the reports, letters, and speeches of Southern officers. As I am writing something from time to time in a fugitive way, and may some time write with a view to a more connected history of the war, in so far as it came under my personal observation, I should be very much obliged to you if you will write me a letter on this subject as full as you feel that you have time, and allow me to make such use of it as I may think best. I wish I had a copy of your report of this battle, etc. Where can I get it?

Believe me yours, with the highest esteem,

J. Warren Keifer

[Source: The Battle of Sailor's Creek by J. Warren Keifer, late Brevet Major General, MOLLUS, OH, pages 1-20; 1879]**Manuscript 54**

This letter is interesting because in 1888, Colonel Keifer feels that the former "Southern Officers" are disparaging the former "Northern Soldiers." He cites, by way of example, the reference to troop sizes and how the Confederates state they were so greatly outnumbered by the Federals. This begs the question; did Custis Lee feel disparagingly in any way toward the Northern soldiers who were involved in the Battle of Sailor's Creek? Did he still feel this way in 1897, when he was asked to respond to the question, "was any particularly distinguished gallantry shown by any enlisted man in your capture?"

6. The author finds this statement by George W. Davis interesting, "the act was deemed to be of sufficient gallantry to warrant such recognition or it would not have been given." If the act was already judged by the War Department as being deemed worthy "to warrant such recognition", why then was its worthiness being reexamined now?

EXHIBIT-W-PF-21

Introduction:

This is a document containing handwritten notes by Major George W. Davis of the War Department, who was handling this Case for Secretary of War Alger from July 15, 1897, to August 13, 1897.

Evidence:

Medal of Honor Case of Harris S. Hawthorn

Letter to Gen. Wright asking whether he will give Secy benefit of his opinion; if so, will fwd papers. G. W. D. July 15/97
Reply G. W. – Will be in Washington on 26
Letter Transm Papers to Gen. W at 1203 N St Wash July 23 G. W. D
Papers returned by Gen. Wright July 31, 1897
Letter to Gen G. W. C. Lee Aug 2
Aug 5th Mr. R. E. Lee nephew of Gen. Custis Lee called to say that the Genl was quite ill but he would call as soon as he was able - That the General told him a [unable to determine 2 words], that his actual capture was expected without any struggle whatever. When the fighting had ended then came the man to whom he surrendered, remarked that by surrendering to him he would receive a furlough. G. W. D.

Aug 13, 1897-Gen Lee – further replied to inquiry from the Aug 1 that there was no particular gallantry shown by any enlisted soldier at the time of his capture. G. W. D.

[Source: 37TH Massachusetts Protest Case file at the National Archives: AGO Record & Pension Office, Document File #476510, File for David D. White, 37th Massachusetts, Volume 8W3 ROW16 COM17, Shelf F, Box #699]**Manuscript 24**

Comments & Supporting Evidence:
1. This document appears to be various handwritten notes written by Major George W. Davis (G. W. D), working in the Office of the Secretary of War, who was the person doing most of the investigative "leg work" in the 37th Massachusetts Protest Case.
2. The August 5th entry is insightful and the author made an attempt to translate this entry in its entirety through the use of a professional paleographer, but two words were unable to be interpreted.

EXHIBIT-W-PF-22

Introduction:
This is a letter from Major George W. Davis, of the War Department, dated August 9, 1897, to Harris S. Hawthorn, Esq., in care of Mr. S. D. Locke, Hoosick Falls, NY, asking Hawthorn to return his Medal of Honor to the War Department until the merits of the 37th Massachusetts Protest Case can be decided.

Evidence:

From: War Department, Washington D.C., August 9, 1897
To: Harris S. Hawthorn, Esq.
In care of: S. D. Locke, Hoosick Falls, N.Y.

By direction of the Secretary of War I call your attention to the following. On the 17th of April, 1897, a letter was received in the Department from Mr. Jas L. Bowen, Historian of the 37th Massachusetts Volunteers, calling attention to what he stated to be a fact–that General Custis Lee at Sailor's Creek, April 6, 1865, surrendered to Corporal David White, formerly of Co. E, 37th Massachusetts Volunteers. This contention is supported by the affidavits of five officers and enlisted men of the 37th Massachusetts, by a letter of the Adjutant of the Regiment, another from its Colonel and by a letter from General Oliver Edwards, who commanded the Brigade to which the 37th Massachusetts belonged. These communications have but recently been brought to the attention of the Secretary of War. In view of the doubt that the protest creates, the Secretary directs me to make to you this communication, and to say that pending an investigation of the controversy, he thinks the Medal awarded to you on the 12th of December 1894, ought to be returned to the Department, until the merits of the case are determined. As you can not possibly wish to retain a decoration of this kind without a clear and uncontested title, he has no doubt that you will gladly carry out his suggestion. General H. G. Wright, who commanded the 6th Army Corps, in the action in question, has seen all the papers and confesses his inability to give an opinion in the case, beyond the remark, "that the propriety of giving a medal at all for this incident would seem to be questionable at least."
Respectfully,
From: George W. Davis, Major, U.S.A.

[Source: 37TH Massachusetts Protest Case file at the National Archives: AGO Record & Pension Office, Document File #476510, File for David D. White, 37th Massachusetts, Volume 8W3 ROW16 COM17, Shelf F, Box #699]**Manuscript 24**

Comments & Supporting Evidence:
1. At this point in time, the Secretary of War has accumulated a substantial amount of testimonies and evidence in the Protest Case file from the 37th Massachusetts.
2. It is interesting to note that the Secretary of War is asking for the return of the Medal of Honor from Harris Hawthorn before he rendered his decision in this matter. One would have to assume by this

request that Secretary Alger believed that the 37th Massachusetts presented a very compelling, if not convincing, case.

3. The cited quote from General Wright is also interesting, "that the propriety of giving a medal at all for this incident would seem to be questionable at least." It should be noted that this quote did not originate with General Wright, but was offered to him by Major George Davis, of the War Department. This quote was in Davis' his first communication to General Wright on this matter. General Wright simply agreed with the quote originated by George Davis and incorporated it into his response back to the War Department.

4. It is surprising that General Wright should take such a definitive position on this matter. He had no direct observation of the capture of Custis Lee and had no recollection of the matter whatsoever other than seeing General Custis Lee at General Sheridan's headquarters at the end of the battle. One has to ask, how would Wright know if any distinguish gallantry was displayed in the capture of Custis Lee?

5. By including General Wright's quote to Harris Hawthorn in this letter of August 9, 1897, this act continues to demonstrate that the Secretary of War was already developing an easy resolution to this very difficult and perplexing case. Instead of deciding who captured Custis Lee, the Secretary of War was directing the decision to be one of whether or not this act was worthy of the Medal.

EXHIBIT-W-PF-23

Introduction:

This is a letter from a John P. Locke, son of the late S. D. Locke of Hoosick Falls, NY, dated August 17, 1897, providing extracts of two letters that his father S.D. Locke allegedly received from Custis Lee, which were dated December 29, 1894, and January 11, 1895. **[See addendum on page 281]**

Evidence:

Sylvanus D. Locke Automatic Binding Harvester, Hoosick Falls, NY, Aug. 17th, 1897.
The following are correct extracts taken from letters received by my father, the late S. D. Locke, of Hoosick Falls, N. Y., from Genl & Prest. G. W. C. Lee on the 29th of Dec., 1894 and the 11th of Jan., 1895.
From: John P. Locke
"It is true that I was unarmed, but it is also true that there were enough of my own people about me to protect me, if necessary." "Major Stiles was near me when I was taken Prisoner. He was assisting me to protect the men on the opposing sides from shooting one another unnecessarily." "I accompanied a private soldier, who told me, I believe, that he belonged to the 6th Corps, commanded by Genl. H. G. Wright, across Sailor's Creek on a log, and went with him a short distance to the top of the hills, where I met an officer of the old army. This place may have been the Head Quarters of Genl Wheaton."
Very truly,
G. W. C. Lee
Sworn and subscribed before me this 9th day of September, 1897
By Lyman G. Willer, Notary Public, For: John P. Locke
[Source: 37TH Massachusetts Protest Case file at the National Archives: AGO Record & Pension Office, Document File #476510, File for David D. White, 37th Massachusetts, Volume 8W3 ROW16 COM17, Shelf F, Box #699]**Manuscript 24**

Comment & Supporting Evidence:

1. It would appear from this letter that Sylvanus D. Locke, who was instrumental in helping Harris Hawthorn obtain the Medal of Honor in 1894, died between 1894 and 1897.

2. It would also appear that Sylvanus D. Locke's son, John P. Locke, is now taking up the cause for Harris Hawthorn. John Locke's letter is, most likely, in direct response to the letter that was sent to Harris Hawthorn by the Secretary of War dated August 9, 1897, requesting the return of the Medal of Honor from Hawthorn.

3. John Locke states that these letters were received from Custis Lee by his father, Sylvanus Locke, on the December 29, 1894, and January 11, 1895. Why did these important letters not become a part of Hawthorn's initial Medal of Honor application? The answer appears to be that they were received by Sylvanus Locke after Hawthorn was approved for the Medal of Honor which occurred on December 12, 1894. The question this now creates is why was Sylvanus Locke still communicating with Custis Lee on this matter well after Hawthorn received his medal? Surely Locke must have known that Hawthorn got his medal approved on December 12, 1894. Letters from Custis Lee on December 29, 1894, and then again on January 11, 1895, would indicate a continued correspondence with Custis Lee by Locke after the medal approval. Was S. D. Locke concerned with the strength of Hawthorn's original application file? Was S. D. Locke still seeking additional proof?

4. The author has attempted, but has not been able to locate the original letters sent by Sylvanus Locke to Custis Lee. The author wished to examine Locke's line of questioning to Custis Lee and determine the amount of prompting Custis Lee might have received from Locke. The author is bothered by the fact that John Locke only submitted "correct extracts" of the two Custis Lee letters. It is doubtful that Custis Lee was very verbose in his response back to Sylvanus Locke given his well documented fragile health condition and his probable distaste for this topic. Why then did John Locke not provide entire transcripts of these important Custis Lee letters? One would have to assume that John Locke only provided elements that he felt would be helpful to Hawthorn's case and omitted elements that he thought might be harmful. This is the only instance that the Locke family submitted just extracts of letters that they received from others in this matter, and which they then submitted as evidence for Hawthorn.

5. The author has never been able to ascertain the nature of the strong relationship between the Locke family and Harris Hawthorn.

6. It is interesting to note that Custis Lee did respond to Sylvanus Locke's line of questioning. It is well documented that Custis Lee was a man who felt a strong sense of duty. Perhaps he considered it his duty to respond to Locke's letters though he found the topic distasteful and personally would have preferred not to respond.

7. An examination of each extract produces the following observations and comments:

A. "It is true that I was unarmed, but it is also true that there were enough of my own people about me to protect me, if necessary." Custis Lee's statements, "It is true," and "it is also true," would indicate that S. D. Locke proposed to Custis Lee a scenario of his capture and Custis Lee was now commenting on Locke's scenario. This statement by Custis Lee that he was unarmed at the time of his capture is a powerful piece of testimony for the Hawthorn case. One would have to interpret the meaning "unarmed" as not carrying any weapon whatsoever, including a sword. The 37th Massachusetts Protest Case relies heavily on physical evidence, particular the sword of Custis Lee. Custis Lee's testimony directly contradicts, however, the testimony of Charles Dwight, who specifically saw Custis Lee with his sword at the Battle of Sailor's Creek (see Exhibit W–PF–12) Custis Lee's statement raises several interesting questions. Did Custis Lee choose to be unarmed because "there were enough of my own people about me to protect me if necessary"? Or, did Custis Lee's arms remain in the Confederate wagon train and he was separated from them at the time of the Battle of Sailor's Creek? The author feels that it is highly unlikely that Custis Lee did not carry a sword and was not wearing it at Sailor's Creek. A sword had little value on the battlefield; however, it was a significant display of rank. One that Custis Lee, given his military training for exactness, felt required by regulations to wear. The author also feels that there is a high probability that Custis Lee also carried a side arm, specifically a revolver, for his own protection given the perilous situation he was constantly in such as having to quickly evacuate Richmond and then on a dangerous march with the Union troops in active pursuit of his forces. Lastly, it makes for a much better story for Custis Lee to state that he was unarmed during his capture. This is a much better story than stating he was fully armed and in a position to shoot it out with the enemy to avoid his capture, but did not do so. What gallantry could the Federal troops claim for capturing an unarmed man? In addition, if David White's version is true and Custis Lee remembered being stripped of his sword, belt, haversack, etc., this must have been a painful and humiliating memory for him. It is very possible that Custis Lee was trying to put his capture in the best possible light for himself and his command by stating that he was completely unarmed at the time of his capture.

B. "Major Stiles was near me when I was taken prisoner. He was assisting me to protect the men on the opposing sides from shooting one another unnecessarily." In order to adequately evaluate this comment, it is necessary to revisit the Stiles account that was highlighted earlier. In this Major Stiles' account of the Battle of Sailor's Creek, he states the following, after lining up his men and awaiting the approach of the Federals:

"I had continued to walk along their front for the very purpose of preventing them from opening fire; but now I stepped through the line, and, stationing myself about the middle of it, called out my orders deliberately—the enemy, I am satisfied, hearing every word. "Ready!" To my great delight the men rose, all together, like a piece of mechanism, kneeling on their right knees and their faces set with an expression that meant—everything. "Aim!" The musket barrels fell to an almost perfect horizontal line leveled about the knees of the advancing front line. "Fire!" I have never seen such an effect, physical and moral, produced by the utterance of one word. The enemy seemed to have been totally unprepared for it, and, as the sequel showed, my own men scarcely less so. The earth appeared to have swallowed up the first line of the Federal force in our front. There was a rattling supplement to the volley and the second line wavered and broke. The revulsion was too sudden. On the instant every man in my battalion sprang to his feet and, without orders, rushed, bareheaded and with unloaded muskets, down the slope after the retreating Federals. I tried to stop them, but in vain, although I actually got ahead of a good many of them. They simply bore me on with the flood…. I therefore jammed the color staff down through a thick bush, which supported it in an upright position, and turned my attention to my battalion, which was scattered over the face of the hill firing irregularly at the Federals, who seemed to be reforming to renew the attack. I managed to get my men into some sort of formation and their guns loaded, and then charged the federal line, driving it back across the creek, and forming my command behind a little ridge, which protected it somewhat. I ran back up the hill and had a brief conversation with General Custis Lee—commanding the division, our brigade commander having been killed—explaining to him that I had not ordered the advance and that we would be cut off if we remained long where we were, but that I was satisfied I could bring the battalion back through a ravine, which would protect them largely from the fire of the enemy's artillery, and reform them on the old line, on the right of the naval battalion, which had remained in position. He expressed his doubts as to this, but I told him I believed my battalion would follow me anywhere, and with his permission I would try it. I ran down the hill again and explained to my men that when I got to the left of the line and shouted to them they were to get up and follow me, on a run and without special formation, through a ravine that led back to the top of the hill. Just because these simple-hearted fellows knew only enough to trust me, and because the enemy was not so far recovered as to take advantage of our exposure while executing the movement to the rear and reforming, we were back in the original lines in a few moments—that is, all who were left of us. It was of no avail. By the time we had well settled into our old position we were attacked simultaneously, front and rear, by overwhelming numbers, and quicker than I can tell it the battle degenerated into a butchery and a confused melee of brutal personal conflicts."

[Source: Four Years under Marse Robert, Neale Publishing Co., New York, 1903, pages 329-335 by Robert Stiles]Manuscript 2****

From Stiles' account, he was down hill from General Custis Lee trying to regroup his men who charged the Federals. It would appear that Custis Lee and Stiles were separated by some distance until Stiles could get his men back to their original position on top of the hill. One would assume that once Stiles successfully executed this maneuver, he was back in very close proximity to Custis Lee. What he now states about the circumstances surrounding his capture is most interesting and quite important. We continue to revisit Major Stiles account:

"I could not let myself degenerate into a mere fighting brute or devil, because the lives of these poor fellows were, in some sense, in my hand, though there was nothing I could do just then to shield or

save them. Suddenly, by one of those inexplicable shiftings which take place on a battle-field, the fighting around me almost entirely ceased, and whereas the moment before the whole environment seemed to be crowded with the enemy, there were now few or none of them on the spot, and as the slaughter and the firing seemed to be pretty well over, I concluded I would try to make my escape. By the way, I had always considered it likely I should be killed, but had never anticipated or contemplated capture. I think it was at the junction I encountered General Custis Lee, but it may have been after I was picked up. At all events, selecting the direction which seemed to be most free from Federal soldiers and to offer the best chance of escape, I started first at a walk and then broke into a run; but in a short distance ran into a fresh Federal force, and it seemed the most natural and easy thing in the world to be simply arrested and taken in. My recollection is that General Lee asked to be carried before the Federal general commanding on that part of the line, who, at his request, gave orders putting a stop to the firing, there being no organized Confederate force on the field. Thus ended my active life as a Confederate soldier, my four years' service under Marse Robert, and I was not sorry to end it thus, in red-hot battle, and to be spared the pain, I will not say humiliation, of Appomattox."

[Source: Four Years under Marse Robert, Neale Publishing Co., New York, 1903, pages 329-335, by Robert Stiles]**Manuscript 2**

> If Custis Lee is correct in his statement that, "Major Stiles was near me when I was taken prisoner," then Custis Lee must have been trying to escape just like Major Stiles was. This would strongly support the version given by David White in his newspaper articles, as found in Exhibit W–MR–4, which describes White spotting and then pursuing Custis Lee who was heading for the Creek. Custis Lee's statement does not support the T. J. Hassett account given for Hawthorn as found in Exhibit H–AF–1, where Hassett states that Hawthorn charged the Confederate line and captured Custis Lee at the point of his bayonet while Custis Lee was in the front of his line. It would also not support Hassett's account where Custis Lee wanted to go back to his Confederate troops and obtain the surrender of his other men. The author is convinced that both Custis Lee and Major Stiles were actively engaged in the battle and tried to escape in the very final moments of the active battle.

> C. "I accompanied private soldier, who told me, I believe, that he belonged to the 6th Corps, commanded by Genl. H. G. Wright, across Sailor's Creek on a log, and went with him a short distance to the top of the hills, where I met an officer of the old army. This place may have been the Head Quarters of Genl. Wheaton." This statement is not helpful to the Miles L. Butterfield account in that Butterfield states, "With two men of the 37th Massachusetts, I took them (Custis Lee) to the rear where Generals Sheridan and Wright were found and turned them over to General Sheridan." Custis Lee should have remembered that he was accompanied by a Major (the rank of Butterfield at the time), particularly given the following statement by Butterfield where he discloses his identity to Custis Lee: "I took charge of them and one of their number asked to whom he had the honor of surrendering. When told, he said that he was General Custis Lee, son of General Robert E. Lee, and would like to be taken to General Sheridan." This statement is also not helpful to the T.J. Hassett account given for Harris Hawthorn. Hassett states: "The Colonel (Olcott) then ordered me (Hassett) to take charge of the prisoner. With orderly Tom Smith and Private H. S. Hawthorn, we conducted the prisoner (Custis Lee) to where we supposed General Sheridan's headquarters to be but found that they had been removed two miles to the front." Custis Lee most likely would have remembered that he was accompanied by a captain, the rank of T. J. Hassett at the time. This statement by Custis Lee, however, is helpful to Hawthorn's own account where Hawthorn states that he was ordered by his commanding officer, Colonel Olcott, to bring General Custis Lee to the headquarters of General Wheaton. Once again David White's accounts have very little to say on how Custis Lee was conducted to the rear. White states that he turned Custis Lee over to the Provost Marshall in the rear. White was evidently not involved in conducting Custis Lee to the headquarters of either Wheaton or Sheridan. He was, instead, assigned to bring ammunition from the rear to the front shortly after his capture of Custis Lee. This is the moment when David White sustained a rupture injury (see Exhibits W–PR–1 & 2).

EXHIBIT-W-PF-24

Introduction:

Joseph H. Heath:

This is a letter from John P. Locke dated August 17, 1897, providing a copy of a letter received by his father, the late S. D. Locke of Hoosick Falls, NY, from Captain Jos. Heath, late of Little Falls, NY. The letter from Jos. Heath is dated December 25, 1894. **[See addendum on page 281]**

Evidence:

Sylvanus D. Locke, Automatic Binding Harvester, Hoosick Falls, NY
This is a copy of a letter received by my father, the late S. D. Locke of Hoosick Falls from Capt. Jos. Heath, late of Little Falls, N.Y.,
From: John P. Locke

Little Falls, NY, Dec. 25th; 94, To: S. D. Locke, Esq.,
Sergt. Hawthorn had Gen. Custis Lee and Chief of Staff and had a hard tussle to keep them as Col. Olcott was just at my left when I lost five men and 1st Lieut. Getting the flag of the Savannah Guards, the most beautiful flag of the Confederacy. Wishing Sergt. Hawthorn all the glory of one of the old Upton Guards & 121st Regt. Men, god-speed and my best respects for him I remain in F. C. & L.
From: Capt. Josh. Heath, U.S. Pension Attorney, Office 539 E. Jefferson St., Little Falls, N.Y.
Sworn and subscribed before me this the 9th day of September, 1897
Lyman G. Willer, Notary Public, For: John P. Locke

[Source: 37TH Massachusetts Protest Case file at the National Archives: AGO Record & Pension Office, Document File #476510, File for David D. White, 37th Massachusetts, Volume 8W3 ROW16 COM17, Shelf F, Box #699]Manuscript 24****

Comments & Supporting Evidence:

1. It would appear that John Locke submitted this August 17, 1897; letter in response to the letter sent by the Secretary of War to Harris Hawthorn dated August 9, 1897, requesting the return of the Medal of Honor from Hawthorn.

2. It would also appear that Sylvanus D. Locke received two letters from Captain Josh Heath, one dated December 14, 1894, and this one dated December 25, 1894. Due to the confusing nature of this letter dated December 25, 1894, the author believes that this letter was actually the first letter created by Josh Heath and should have been dated December 14, 1894. Conversely, the letter dated December 14, 1894, as found in Exhibit W–PF–25, should have been dated December 25, 1894, and was most likely the second letter created by Heath which was much more coherent.

3. It is uncertain what questions Sylvanus Locke asked of Josh Heath in his initial inquiry to him. It is also uncertain what Josh Heath meant by, "Sergt Hawthorn had Genl. Custis Lee and Chief of Staff and had a hard tussle to keep them as Col. Olcott was just at my left when I lost five men and 1st Lieut....." This would seem to indicate that Hawthorn was guarding Custis Lee and probably Major Stiles (Chief of Staff?) when a dispute arose with the 37th Massachusetts.

4. It is interesting that Josh Heath would take the time to write this letter on Christmas Day.

5. Like the extracts of the two Custis Lee letters as found in Exhibit W–PF–23, it is surprising that S. D. Locke is still gathering documentation after Harris Hawthorn received his medal. Once again, did he feel that Hawthorn's application was weak and needed more substantial evidence and proof?

6. One has to question why John Locke provided a complete transcription of this Josh Heath letter and only extracts of the two important Custis Lee letters. Surely the Custis Lee letters would have been more important than the Heath letters, and thus worthy of complete transcriptions.

7. From Joseph H. Heath's military service record it appears that he received a severe gun shot wound to the face and shoulder at the battle of Winchester, VA, September 19, 1864. He was

hospitalized and returned to duty November 1864. He was in command of Company I, 121st New York from December 11, 1864 to February 1, 1865. From that point he was transferred to Company H, but does not appear to be in command of the company. Other than being reduced to 2nd Sergeant in January 1864, there is nothing atypical in Joseph H. Heath's military service record.

[Source: Military Service Record of Joseph H. Heath's, National Archives, Washington, DC]**Manuscript 128**

EXHIBIT-W-PF-25

Introduction:
This is a letter from John P. Locke, dated August 17, 1897, providing another copy of a letter received by his father, the late S. D. Locke, of Hoosick Falls, NY, from Capt. Jos. Heath, "late of Little Falls, NY." The letter from Jos. Heath is dated December 14, 1894. **[See addendum on page 281]**

Evidence:
Sylvanus D. Locke, Automatic Binding Harvester, Hoosick Falls, NY
This is a correct copy of a letter received by my father, the late S. D. Locke of Hoosick Falls from Capt. Jos. Heath, late of Little Falls, N.Y.,
From: John P. Locke

Little Falls, NY, Dec. 14th; 94.
To: Sylvanus D. Locke, Esq.,
I was an eyewitness of Harris S. Hawthorn of Co. F. 121st at Little Sailor's Creek, as we had crossed the creek and made the rise of ground ahead we descended in a small wood where the enemy lay behind the roadsides and small works thrown up. This between 4 & 5 P.M., and as we advanced I captured a dying Colonel with a Mason's Pin on his neck tye. I took that off and put it in pocket when Sergt. Hawthorn came to me and said Capt. There comes some of the Rebel Cavalry and I am going for them & off he went double quick up the road and I was keeping my Co. H. 121st. N.Y. Vol. firing to our front to keep the enemy down so we could capture a handsome battle flag & we got it & Sergt. H.- got Gen. Custus Lee and brought him in, as Custus General I mean, was coming with his cavalry in the rear; of course, we had the advantage chance to gain our advantage. Our flag is in Albany, N.Y. & can be seen by calling on Sergt. Brayton G. Priest, Late Co. A. 121st N.Y. Vol. Inf. Sergt. H.—is entitled to all the badges the Govt. can give him as he halted Gen. Custus Lee & had him dismount & surrender to him alone & was a good soldier as ever carried a gun.
Yours respectfully,
From: Capt. Josh. Heath, No. 539 E. Jefferson St., Little Falls, N.Y.
Anything more you may want, write.
Sworn and subscribed to before me this 9th day of September, 1897
Lyman G. Willer, Notary Public, For: John P. Locke

[Source: 37TH Massachusetts Protest Case file at the National Archives: AGO Record & Pension Office, Document File #476510, File for David D. White, 37th Massachusetts, Volume 8W3 ROW16 COM17, Shelf F, Box #699]**Manuscript 24**

Comments & Supporting Evidence:
1. This letter is much more coherent than the other letter sent by Josh Heath, which leads the author to believe this is Heath's second letter. Sylvanus Locke most likely gave Mr. Heath a framework from which to work so Heath could make a better response during a second go-around.
2. This account differs significantly from the account given by T. J. Hassett. This account has Captain Heath, commanding Company H of the 121st New York, firing to the front to keep the enemy down so that his troops could capture a handsome enemy flag. Then along comes Hawthorn (who is a Private at the time and not a Sergeant as stated by Heath) and tells a Captain of a different company (Heath was commanding Company H and Hawthorn belonged to Company F), that he spotted rebel cavalry and he is going off after them. Then Hawthorn goes double quick up the road in pursuit of the rebel Cavalry. Then somehow Hawthorn manages to capture General Custis Lee

and bring him in to the Union lines. In this process, Hawthorn manages to have Custis Lee dismount and surrender to Hawthorn alone.

3. This account has serious flaws. For example, General Custis Lee was not a Cavalry officer. In addition, it is just too unbelievable. Since it cannot be reconciled with the T. J. Hassett account, the more believable Hassett account should stand as the official Hawthorn version and this Heath account dismissed.

4. This Heath account is interesting in the respect that he places Custis Lee with a horse, something Custis Lee denies having in Exhibit W–PF–12.

5. A review of Joseph H. Heath's military pension reveals the following interesting points. First, it appears that Heath was a baker by trade all his adult life. It is puzzling why the two letters he wrote for Harris Hawthorn give the appearance that Heath is a U.S. pension attorney. Perhaps a Pension Office attorney wrote the letters as Heath dictated them. Second, Heath passed away approximately one month after writing the two letters for Hawthorn. Third and perhaps most important, Heath was a very ill man when he was writing these letters. He was suffering severely with rheumatism, organic heart disease, advanced diabetes, and gangrene. He states as early as 1890, that he is totally incapacitated, confined to bed, and the only work he can do is writing. In 1892, he stated that, "I suffer every thing but death, my hands, arms, legs, feet, and shoulders swell to twice their natural size." Given Heath's extremely poor health condition when he wrote the Hawthorn letters, one has to question their accuracy. In addition, one would have to question if they were actually written by him given the condition of his hands as described above. This may account for their confusing nature and why two letters were written while one could have sufficed.

[Source: Joseph H. Heath Pension File, certificate number 155762, National Archives, Washington, DC]**Manuscript 129**

6. The author came in contact with Mr. David Krutz of Little Falls, NY. Mr. Krutz has studied the 121st New York and the various Civil War era letters that Joseph Heath sent home to his local newspaper, "The Herkimer County Journal & Courier." The author sent these two 1894 Heath letters to Mr. Krutz for examination. The following letter from Mr. Krutz provides valuable insight into these two 1894 Heath letters, comparing them to Heath's war time letters.

March 21, 2006

Frank, The letters written by Joe Heath in 1894 do not seem to me to be consistent with his war time correspondence. All of his letters that were published during the war by the local newspaper, "The Herkimer County Journal & Courier," appear to come from a fairly well educated individual. The spelling, grammar, phraseology, etc. are much different than that evidenced in his 1894 letters. But, I believe a good explanation can be found for this discrepancy. (1) If the 1894 letters were written by Joe Heath, they were written by a man at death's door. At the time, Joe was suffering from diabetes, rheumatism, a "carbuncle," and heaven knows what else. He would die a short time later, and I can't believe his mind was very lucid. A fair comparison between a healthy "Big Joe," and a failing man, literally on his death bed, can not be made. (2) All of the "Joe Heath" letters that I have read were printed up in the local newspaper. I have to believe that the editor, Jean Stebbins, corrected any spelling, grammatical errors, etc. that may have existed, prior to publication. Of the hundreds and hundreds of soldier's letters that I have read in the "Journal's" pages, only one may have been printed verbatim, and that one as a laugh. Again, a comparison can not be made. Sorry that I couldn't give you a more definitive response. It is my belief that Joseph Heath, late of the 121st NY, probably wrote the 1894 letters. The facts seem to fit the case, and I have a hard time believing that someone else wrote the 1894 letters as a ruse. Unfortunately, the character of the war time letters and the 1894 letters are too different to add weight to my supposition. I have enclosed a copy of one of "Big Joe's" letters for you to do your own comparison. Also enclosed is a description of the Savannah Guard's flag that you might find interesting. If I can be of any help, please let me know. In any regard, stay in touch.
Good luck, David Krutz

[Source: Letter in the possession of the author]**Manuscript 159**

The author did compare the 1894 Heath letters with the one sent and referenced above by Mr. Krutz, and the author fully agrees with Mr. Krutz that the differences in the letters are substantial. Mr. Heath died on January 29, 1895 at the young age 52, and enjoyed good health until he was taken ill in the fall of 1894, according to his obituary.

[Source: "The Herkimer County Journal & Courier," January 29, 1895 edition]**Manuscript 160**

7. As with the T. J. Hassett account, where T. J. Hassett of Company K of the 121st New York eye witnessed Hawthorn capturing Custis Lee, Joseph Heath of Company H of the 121st New York also eye witnessed Hawthorn capturing Custis Lee, though both accounts differ significantly on the actual events. It would have seemed more logical for soldiers from Company F, Hawthorn's Company, who should have been eyewitnesses to the event, to provide evidence as opposed to soldiers from Companies H (Heath) and K (Hassett) of the 121st New York.

BIOGRAPHY:

Heath, Joseph H.: Age, 20 years. Enrolled, July 25 1862, at Little Falls to serve three years; mustered in as first sergeant, Co. A, August 23, 1862; promoted to sergeant-major, May 1, 1864; second lieutenant, no date; mustered in as first lieutenant, Co. C, July 25, 1864; wounded in action, September 19, 1864, at Opequon, VA; transferred to Co. I, December 21, 1864; to Co. H, February 17, 1865; mustered out with company, June 25, 1865 near Hall's Hill, VA. Comm. second lieutenant, May 23, 1864, with rank from March 15, 1864, vice H. C. Van Scoy promoted; first lieutenant, July 13, 1864, with rank from June 1, 1864, vice S. E. Pierce died of wounds.
[Source: Annual Report of the Adjutant-General of the State of New York for the Year 1903, Serial No. 36, Albany, NY, Oliver A. Quayle; 1904]**Manuscript 127**

EXHIBIT-W-PF-26

Introduction:

This is an unsigned, typewritten, letter from Harris Hawthorn dated September, 1897, to General W. Davis, Assistant Secretary of War (probably George W. Davis).

Evidence:

Hoosick Falls, N. Y., Sept., 1897, To: Gen. W. Davis, Ass't Secretary of War

In reply to your communication of August 9th with regard to the claim of officer and men of the 37th Massachusetts Volunteers "That Gen Custis Lee surrendered to Corporal David White, formerly of Co. E, at Sailor's Creek, April 6th, 1865," I wish to respectfully reply. General Custis Lee surrendered to me and me alone at Sailor's Creek on April 6th, 1865. I wish to call your attention, as proof of the above, to the Records of the Union and Confederate Armies, Vol. 46, Series 1, Part First, Page 925, wherein Major General F. Wheaton, commanding 1s Division, 6th Corps, reports,--Brig. Gen. G. W. Custis Lee captured by Harris S. Hawthorn Co. F. 121st N. Y. Vols." I would say in connection with the capture of Gen. Custis Lee that an attempt was made at the time by two men of another regiment to take Gen. Custis away from me, but my Col. And Lieutenant Hassett came to my help and I conducted him to and delivered him to Gen. Wheaton. A claim was made by members of the 37th Mass. to the credit of Gen. Custis Lee's capture and at an investigation before Judge Advocate, H. E. Hindmarsh their claim was proven false. I would refer you in this connection to page 937 for a record of my sworn testimony, also to a certificate of character given me by my chaplain on that occasion, found on page 938. I might here say that as a reward for the capture of Gen. Lee I was promoted to Sergeant and given a furlough for twenty days. Also please notice by page 927 report of Brig. Gen. Wm. H. Penrose that the 37th Mass had a habit of trying to rob others, preferring to steal glory rather than earn it. I enclose herewith copies of letters from General G. W. Custis Lee and Capt. Josh Heath written to the late Hon. S. D. Locke with regard to the capture of Gen. Lee by me. As to the medal awarded me and "my wish to retain a decoration of this kind without a clear and uncontested title," I feel that my title according to the record of reports made by my commanding officers to the War Department immediately after the capture of

Gen. Lee is clear. Whether the act in question was deserving of such recognition, I am hardly qualified to judge. My claim is now as it was April 6th, 1865, that I demanded and compelled the surrender of General G. W. Custis Lee and that the official record is true.

Very respectfully yours,

No signature

[Source: 37th Massachusetts Protest Case file at the National Archives: AGO Record & Pension Office, Document File #476510, File for David D. White, 37th Massachusetts, Volume 8W3 ROW16 COM17, Shelf F, Box #699]**Manuscript 24**

<u>Comments & Supporting Evidence:</u>

1. This unsigned letter dated September, 1897, would appear to be Harris Hawthorn's detailed and official rebuttal to the letter sent to him by the Secretary of War dated August 9, 1897, which asked Hawthorn to return his Medal of Honor.

2. Since this is an important rebuttal, a paragraph by paragraph analysis follows:

3. In the first and second paragraphs, Hawthorn asserts that General Custis Lee surrendered to him and him alone. This is a consistent theme that Hawthorn has always asserted.

4. In the third paragraph, Hawthorn is offering as proof that he captured Custis Lee the Official Report of General Wheaton, commanding 1st Division of the 6th Corps. In fact, the roll-up to General Wheaton's Official Report states, "Private Harris S. Hawthorn, Company F, One Hundred and Twenty-first New York Volunteers, captured Brig. Gen. (G. W.) Custis Lee, on the 6th instant." As explained in Exhibits H–OR–1, H–OR–2 and H–OR–3, this statement is merely a "roll-up" of a report initially generated by Brevet Colonel Olcott commanding the 121st New York. From Olcott it was rolled up by Brevet Brigadier General Joseph E. Hamblin, commanding the 2nd Brigade, of which the 121st N Y was a part. It was ultimately rolled up to the General Frank Wheaton report, commanding the 1st Division of the 6th Corps, of which the 2nd Brigade and 121st N Y were a part. This all goes to say that the statement, made by General Wheaton that Harris Hawthorn captured Custis Lee, was originally authored by Olcott or a member of Olcott's staff. Hamblin and Wheaton merely adopted Olcott's initial statement for their respective Official Reports. It is obvious that Harris Hawthorn was well versed in the Official Records, having the ability to cite specific series, volumes, and pages. It would appear that Hawthorn researched the Official Records thoroughly to substantiate his claim to the capture of Custis Lee.

5. The fourth paragraph by Hawthorn corroborates T. J. Hassett's account to a certain degree. The Hassett account states:

Colonel Olcott who was also on foot refused the request but ordered comrade Hawthorn to conduct General Lee to Sheridan's headquarters. No sooner had he started, however, when an officer of the other regiment [37th Mass.] referred to attempted to take charge of the prisoner. My orderly sergeant Tom Smith reported the fact to me and I called Colonel Olcott's attention to it when the Colonel raised his sword as if to strike the officer down when the latter quickly got away. [See Exhibit H-AF-1]

Hawthorn states in this letter that two men of another regiment tried to take Custis Lee away and, his Colonel and Lieutenant Hassett came to his aid and that he delivered Custis Lee to General Wheaton. Hawthorn's statement that he conducted and delivered Custis Lee to General Wheaton directly contradicts, however, T. J. Hassett's detailed account which states that they conducted Custis Lee to General Sheridan's headquarters, not Wheaton's.

6. In the fifth paragraph, Hawthorn states that Judge Advocate H. E. Hindmarsh conducted an investigation and proved false the claim by members of the 37th Massachusetts. If Judge Advocate Hindmarsh conducted an investigation and came to an official determination, the Official Records would have contained a definitive statement directly from Hindmarsh outlining his determination. All that appears in the Official Records, however, is Hawthorn's own sworn statement and a certificate of character given by Hawthorn's chaplain of the 121st New York. Please see the following from the Official Records:

CAMP IN THE FIELD, VA, April 14, 1865

Private Harris S. Hawthorn, Company F, One hundred and twenty-first New York Volunteers, being duly sworn, says that he knows of his own knowledge that he is the first person (officer or enlisted man) who seized or captured General Custis Lee, of the Confederate Army, in the engagement of the 6th of April; and that he never lost sight or control of said General Custis Lee until he delivered him up to Colonel Olcott, commanding One hundred and twenty-first New York Volunteers; and that he, Hawthorn, was one of the men detailed by Colonel Olcott, on account of such capture, to conduct General Custis Lee to the headquarters of General Wheaton, commanding First Division, Sixth Army Corps.

H. S. HAWTHORN.

Subscribed and sworn to, at Malvern, near Burkeville, VA, this 14th day of April, 1865, before me.

H. E. HINDMARSH, *Lieutenant, Judge-Advocate, First Division, Sixth Army Corps.*

CAMP OF 121ST NEW YORK REGIMENT, April 14, 1865

I hereby certify that for more than two years I have well known Harris S. Hawthorn, Company F, One hundred twenty-first New York Regiment, as a professed Christian, and have always regarded him worthy of confidence, by the uniform consistency of his religious life. I regard his testimony on any subject as unimpeachable, and that no assurance can be stronger than his affirmation under the sanctity of an oath.

JOHN R. ADAMS, *Chaplain of 121st New York Regiment.*

[Source: Official Records: "The Appomattox Campaign," Volume 46, Series 1, Folio 111]**Manuscript 3**

It is most probable that Judge Advocate Hindmarsh came to the camp of the 121st New York just to take Hawthorn's sworn statement and nothing more. The following tells a little bit more about Judge Advocate Hindmarsh. Lieutenant Henry E. Hindmarsh, of the 95th Pennsylvania, was promoted to Captain by Brevet May 12, 1864 for meritorious services in the battles of the Wilderness and at Spotsylvania Court House, VA. He was severely wounded. On October 19, 1864, he was recognized for gallantry at the battles of Winchester, Fisher's Hill and Cedar Creek, VA. Henry E. Hindmarsh served as the Judge Advocate in the 1st Division of the 6th Corps commanded by Brevet Major General Frank Wheaton.

[Source: Official Records, Volume 42, Series 1, Part III, page 1030]**Manuscript 55**

In addition, the author made an investigation at the National Archives to determine if the Archives had any records of this Hawthorn alleged investigation/tribunal by Hindmarsh, which perhaps might not have made its way into the Official Records. The following reply was received:

National Archives and Records Administration
December 24, 2003

Dear Mr. White:
The following is in reply to your inquiry concerning the capture of General Custis Lee by Private Harris S. Hawthorn of Company F, 121st NY Infantry Regiment. We have examined the War Department records in our custody including the Register of Letters Sent by the Judge Advocate of the 1st Division, 6th Army Corps (RG 393, Part 2, Entry 4508), but did not locate evidence of a military tribunal concerning this matter. We have enclosed a copy of the original affidavit which was published in the "Official Records of the War of the Rebellion" for use in your research.
From: David H. Wallace, Old Military and Civil Records, Textual Achieves Services Division

[Source: Letter and photocopies in the possession of the author]**Manuscript 141**

As an interesting side note, after carefully reviewing a photocopy of the original sworn statement given by Hawthorn concerning his capture of Custis Lee, which photocopy was sent to the author with this December 24, 2003, letter from the National Archives, it is certain that the writer of the Official Report for the 121st New York on the Battle of Sailor's Creek is the exact same writer of the Hawthorn sworn statement. Harris Hawthorn merely signed what had already been written for him. Perhaps Hawthorn was a poor writer and dictated his thoughts to the writer of the 121st New York's

Official Report. Hawthorn was not an illiterate man and given the importance of his sworn testimony in this matter, he really should have penned his own thoughts. Hindmarsh penned the "subscribed and sworn to" language in the document together with his original signature and Adams penned the character testimonial together with his original signature. This "pre-written" sworn testimony created for Hawthorn is an unusual approach for documenting in the Official Records Hawthorn's strong assertion that he alone captured Custis Lee.

7. Hawthorn also states in the fifth paragraph, "I might here say that as a reward for the capture of General Lee, I was promoted to Sergeant and given a furlough for twenty days." This is not exactly true. On April 20, 1865, at the headquarters of the 121st New York, Colonel Olcott issued Special Order #29 which among many other items, stated that Private Harris Hawthorn was promoted to Corporal, Corporal Metcalf having been promoted. Hawthorn's promotion, along with many others given on the 20th of April 1865, by Special Order No. 29, was retroactive back to March 1, 1865. On April 24, 1865, Harris Hawthorn was furloughed with many others for gallantry for 20 days. On June 11, 1865, at the headquarters of the 121st New York, Special Order #39 promoted Corporal Harris Hawthorn of Company F to the rank of Sergeant, when Sergeant J. S. Scott was discharged.

[Source: Harris Hawthorn's Military Service Record, National Archives, Washington, DC and 121st New York Regimental Books, National Archives, Washington, DC: R6 No. 94, Stack Area 9W3, Row 9, Compartment 30, Shelf A]**Manuscripts 48 & 49**

It should be noted that David D. White was also promoted to Corporal by his 37th Massachusetts on May 19, 1865, Corporal Tanner having died of his wounds.

[Source: David White's Military Record, National Archives, Washington, DC]**Manuscript 47**

Like Hawthorn's promotion, David White was promoted to Corporal for the capture of General Custis Lee and his gallantry at the Battle of Sailor's Creek.

8. In the sixth paragraph, Harris Hawthorn sounds somewhat embittered when he states, "the 37th Massachusetts had a habit of trying to rob others, preferring to steal glory rather than earn it." The reference that Hawthorn gives for this statement is found in the Official Records, a report given by Bvt. Brig. Gen. William H. Penrose, commanding the 15th New Jersey Infantry, which states:

No. 107
Report of Bvt. Brig. Gen. William H. Penrose, Fifteenth New Jersey, Infantry, April 5, 1865
Sir: I have the honor to submit the following partial report of the part taken by my command—First Brigade, First Division, Sixth Corps—in the assault on the enemy's lines, and subsequent engagements of the same day: On the morning of the 2d instant the brigade was formed in four lines, its left in rear and right of the Third Brigade, First Division, Sixth Corps. Just before daylight the signal was given to advance, when the lines moved forward. They had gone but a short distance before the first and second lines became one, owing to the fact that the pickets which were to have advanced simultaneously with us did not, and the first line received the fire of the enemy's pickets, which was very severe. The entire command pushed on, and in a few moments parts of each regiment had possession of the enemy's lines. From some cause the entire lines took direction 200 yards to the left of the points designated, and I found my men had entered the works on the front intended to have been taken by the Third Brigade. At this point two pieces of artillery (Rodman's ordnance) were captured by Brevet Major Paul, acting assistant adjutant-general, and Capt. James W. Penrose, acting aide-de-camp, of my staff, with a few men. A guard was placed upon the guns. Some time after two companies of the Thirty-seventh Massachusetts Volunteers came up to the guns and wished to remove them, which Captain Penrose refused to allow them to do. They then formed around the platforms. Before those two companies came up Captain Penrose had loaded the guns, but could not find primers with which to fire them. In the meantime, his attention was directed elsewhere, when the men of the Thirty-seventh Massachusetts drove my guard from the guns, claiming them as their capture. As this has occurred once before I am not disposed to allow it to pass this time without notice, as the command is entitled to the credit of the capture.

[Source: Official Records, "The Appomattox Campaign," Volume 46, Series 1, page 927]**Manuscript 3**

It is apparent that Harris Hawthorn was putting his own spin on this incident, trying to paint the 37th Massachusetts as a credit-robbing regiment. Once again, the author is surprised at the level of detail that Harris Hawthorn researched the Official Records in order to justify his own position, as to be able to come up with this unrelated uncomplimentary entry on the 37th Massachusetts in a Penrose New Jersey regimental report. As a counter point to this uncomplimentary entry by Penrose, one must examine the entry made by Archibald Hopkins in his Official Report shortly after the Battle of Sailor's Creek.

HDQRS. Thirty-Seventh Massachusetts Volunteers, March [April] 7, 1865
Sir: I have the honor to state that there were 3 officers and 28 men wounded and 8 men killed in the engagement of yesterday. The officers were Capt. Walter B. Smith, First. Lieut. And Adjt. John S. Bradley, and Second Lieut. Harrie A. Cushman. There were 360 officers and men, and General C. Lee, captured by my command. General Lee was captured by Private D. D. White, Company E, of this regiment, and he formally surrendered his sword to Lieut. W. C. Morrill, of this regiment, who now wears it. At least one battle-flag was captured by the Thirty-seventh Regiment, and another one is claimed, although the capture is claimed by another command.
Very Respectfully,
A. Hopkins, Captain, Commanding Regiment.

[Source: Official Records, "The Appomattox Campaign, Volume 46, Series 1, page 948]**Manuscript 4**

Hopkins' accounting of the capture of battle flags the day after the battle is extremely fair and well balanced, not at all written by a man that, "had a habit of trying to rob others, preferring to steal glory rather than earn it," as was asserted by Hawthorn. Hopkins' statement, "and another one is claimed, although the capture is claimed by another command," demonstrates the integrity at which Archibald Hopkins objectively reported on this matter concerning a dispute with another command. The author's research has found Archibald Hopkins to have been a man of the highest integrity, with nothing surfacing in his background or actions to indicate otherwise. It must also be mentioned that the author found no claim by the 37th Massachusetts to the capture of the two pieces of Rodman's artillery referenced by Penrose in his report above. Penrose might have over reacted. The 37th Massachusetts did claim the capture of three guns, and Richard Welch of Company E was awarded the Medal of Honor for capturing the battle flag of the gun bearers of this squadron.

9. In the seventh paragraph, Hawthorn states that he is submitting copies of G. W. Lee letters. In fact, John Locke submitted only extracts of these letters. John Locke submitted full copies of two Josh Heath letters. [See Exhibit W–PF–23 for John Locke's extracts of the Custis Lee letters and Exhibits W–PF–24 and W–PF–25 for the copies of the Josh Heath letters.] Once again, why did John Locke not submit complete copies of the original Custis Lee letters like he did the Heath letters? Given their potential importance in this matter, this is unexplainable and casts suspicion.

10. In the eighth paragraph, Harris Hawthorn re-asserts his claim to the Medal of Honor by saying that he has a clear title to the capture of General Custis Lee, "according to the record of reports made by my commanding officers to the War Department immediately after the capture of General Lee." These reports do, in fact, state that Hawthorn captured Custis Lee, but by no means do they state that he has a clear and uncontested title to the capture. In fact, they state that there is a controversy concerning the matter.

11. In the ninth and concluding paragraph, Harris Hawthorn states that he "demanded and compelled the surrender of General G. W. Lee." This statement would indicate that Hawthorn had an "active battlefield" capture of Custis Lee. Though Hawthorn next makes reference to the Official Record being true as a way to substantiate his claim, the Official Record does not contain the language of Hawthorn's claim that Hawthorn "demanded and compelled the surrender of General G. W. Lee." The Official Record simply states in Colonel Olcott's report that Hawthorn captured Custis Lee.

EXHIBIT-W-PF-27

Introduction:

The last piece of testimony in the 37th Massachusetts Protest Case file is an undated, handwritten, and signed letter from Harris Hawthorn stating the physical condition that Custis Lee was in when he, Hawthorn, captured him. This letter is of paramount importance in this Case and the reader is encouraged to examine it carefully. A photograph of this letter follows to allow for this examination of the original document. A precise transcription follows below:

Evidence:

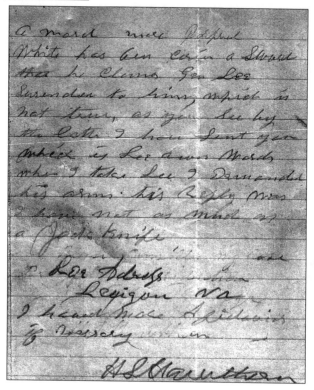

Harris S. Hawthorn Note:

A word more. Corporal White has ben carin a sword that he claims Gen Lee surrendered to him which is not true, as you see by the letter I have sent you which is Lee own words. When I take Lee I demanded his arms his reply was I have not as much as a jack knife.
Lee Adress Lexigon VA
I have more Afidavis if necesry within
H. S. Hawthorn

[Source: 37TH Massachusetts Protest Case file at the National Archives: AGO Record and Pension Office, Document File #476510, File for David D. White, 37th Massachusetts, Volume 8W3 ROW16 COM17, Shelf F, Box #699]Manuscript 24****

Comments & Supporting Evidence:

1. This undated letter signed by Harris Hawthorn was in the 37th Massachusetts Protest Case file. Since this document is in the Protest Case file, one would have to assume it was created after Hawthorn's initial rebuttal letter which is dated September 1897, since he starts this letter off with the words, "a word more."
2. This is the most defining and differentiating piece of evidence found in the Protest Case. The reason being is that this document makes a very clear distinction between Hawthorn and White with regard to physical evidence taken from General Custis Lee at the time of his capture.
3. The 37th Massachusetts Protest Case states that when David White captured General Custis Lee, Custis Lee had in his possession, and subsequently surrendered, his sword, haversack, belt and various miscellaneous items that, most likely, were in his haversack.
4. Harris Hawthorn states in this letter, "When I take Lee I demanded his arms his reply was I have not as much as a jack knife." In support of this statement, Hawthorn references Lee's statements as contained in the extracts of Custis Lee's letters to Sylvanus Locke dated December 29, 1894, and January 11, 1895, made by John P. Locke, which alleges Custis Lee to state, "It is true that I was unarmed, but it is also true that there were enough of my own people about me to protect me, if necessary."

5. With this letter, there is now a clear method to decide who captured General Custis Lee at the Battle of Sailor's Creek, April 6, 1865.
   A. If General Lee was armed and had a sword, belt, haversack, etc., and this fact could be proven, then the David D. White version of the Custis Lee capture would be true.
   B. If General Custis Lee didn't have as much as a jack knife at the time of his capture and this could be proven, then Hawthorn's version would be true.
6. With this important document that was created by Harris Hawthorn himself, physical evidence now becomes of ultimate importance in deciding this perplexing case. If physical evidence can be found today (sword, belt, haversack, sidearm, etc.), and this physical evidence can be proven to have been in the possession of the 37th Massachusetts and can also be proven to have been in the possession of General Custis Lee at the time of his capture, then, this will indisputably prove the truth of the counterclaim of the 37th Massachusetts, namely that David White/William Morrill captured General George Washington Custis Lee at the Battle of Sailor's Creek, VA, April 6, 1865.
7. A search was initiated by the author for this physical evidence, and the results will appear as various items of evidence cited in Exhibits labeled W–CT and W–BN.

EXHIBIT-W-PF-28

Introduction:

Russell A. Alger:

This is the decision rendered in the 37th Massachusetts Protest Case by Secretary of War R. A. Alger, dated September 20, 1897.

Evidence:

War Department, Office of the Secretary, September 20, 1897
After a very careful consideration of the Official Records relating to the capture of Gen. G. W. C. Lee at Sailor's Creek on April 6, 1865, and of the evidence filed in support of the claim to a Medal of Honor by Harris S. Hawthorn, formerly a private, Co. F. 121st New York Infantry Volunteers, and also that filed in support of a counter claim for a medal for David White, formerly a Corporal, Co. E. 37th Massachusetts Volunteers, the incident of service in each case being the same, to wit,—the capture of General Lee—I am fully convinced that there was no opportunity for the display of any action by any individual soldier, that could, under law and regulations, earn the Congressional Medal of Honor. Messrs. Hawthorn and White will be notified of this action.
From: R. A. Alger, Secretary of War
[Source: 37TH Massachusetts Protest Case file at the National Archives: AGO Record & Pension Office, Document File #476510, File for David D. White, 37th Massachusetts, Volume 8W3 ROW16 COM17, Shelf F, Box #699]**Manuscript 24**

Comments & Supporting Evidence:

1. The decision in the Protest Case by Secretary of War R. A. Alger was very predictable and not surprising at all.
2. Secretary Alger's letter referring to Hawthorn as formerly a Private and White as formerly a Corporal, shows that Alger was not well versed in the facts of this Protest Case. Hawthorn was formerly a Sergeant and White was formerly a Corporal.
3. It is useful to have a complete chronology of the thinking that was behind this decision:

A. On July 23, 1897, Major George W. Davis of the War Department wrote General H. G. Wright and in that letter Davis stated, "I also enclose a copy of recent regulations issued by the President respecting awards of medals and in this connection I will say that the propriety of giving a medal at all for this incident would seem to be questionable at least."

B. On July 30, 1897, General H. G. Wright wrote back to Major George W. Davis, and in his letter stated, "In conclusion I would say that I am found to agree with you that the propriety of giving a medal at all for this incident would seem to be questionable at least."

C. On August 2, 1897, Major George W. Davis wrote Custis Lee and posed to him the following question from General Alger, Secretary of War, "Was any particularly distinguished gallantry shown by any enlisted man in the Union force in your immediate presence at the time of your capture?"

D. On August 9, 1897, George W. Davis wrote Harris Hawthorn to ask for the return of his Medal of Honor and in his letter stated, "General H. G. Wright, who commanded the 6th Army Corps, in the action in question, has seen all the papers and confesses his inability to give an opinion in the Case, beyond the remark, "that the propriety of giving a medal at all for this incident would seem to be questionable at least." It must be noted that this was not General Wright's original opinion, but General Wright was agreeing with an opinion fed to him by Major Davis of the War Department back on July 23, 1897.

4. The decision of who really captured Major General Custis Lee at the Battle of Sailor's Creek would have been extremely difficult decision for Secretary R. A. Alger to make. Difficult, yes, impossible, no. Instead, R. A. Alger decided to follow the course of least resistance, armed with a "no gallantry" statement by Custis Lee and a "no gallantry" statement by General Wright which statement General Wright adopted from Major Davis. Alger's decision, "I am fully convinced that there was no opportunity for the display of any action by any individual soldier, that could, under law and regulations, earn the Congressional Medal of Honor," allowed him to completely avoid having to make the difficult decision of who actually captured Custis Lee.

5. Alger's decision begs the following question; if Harris Hawthorn qualified for a Medal of Honor in December 1894, for the capture of Custis Lee at the Battle of Sailor's Creek, then why does Hawthorn (or White) not qualify for it in September 1897? This question will be addressed later.

6. This was clearly the easiest way out for the Secretary of War to make a decision in this Protest Case, but what did Alger's decision really mean? Obviously, it meant that David White would not receive a Medal of Honor for the capture of Custis Lee. Did it also mean that Harris Hawthorn's Medal of Honor would be revoked and stripped away because Hawthorn did not earn it under Alger's new determination that there was "no gallantry" involved in the capture of Custis Lee?

EXHIBIT-W-PF-29

Introduction:

This is a letter from Col. F. C. Ainsworth, Chief of the Record and Pension Office, dated September 22, 1897, to James L. Bowen and Harris S. Hawthorn, informing them of the decision by the Secretary of War.

Evidence:

War Department, Washington City, September 22, 1897.
To: Mr. James L. Bowen

Referring to the claim, advanced by you in April last, in behalf of David D. White, late corporal, Company E, 37st Massachusetts Infantry Volunteers, at that time a resident of Charlemont, Massachusetts, for the honor of having captured General G. W. Custis Lee, of the Confederate Army, at Sailor's Creek, Virginia, April 6, 1865, for which capture a medal or honor had been previously awarded to Harris S. Hawthorn, formerly a sergeant, Company F, 121st New York Infantry Volunteers, I have the honor to inform you that the papers in the case, having been submitted to the Secretary of War, were returned by him to this office, under date of the 20th instant, with remarks as follows: After a very careful consideration of the Official Records relating to the capture of Gen. G. W. C. Lee at Sailor's

Creek on April 6, 1865, and of the evidence filed in support of the claim to a Medal of Honor by Harris S. Hawthorn, formerly a private, Co. F, 121st New York Infantry Volunteers, and also that filed in support of a counter claim for a Medal for David White, formerly a Corporal, Co. E, 37th Massachusetts, the incident of service in each case being the same, to wit,—the capture of General Lee,—I am fully convinced that there was no opportunity for the display of any action by any individual soldier, that could, under law and regulation, earn the Congressional Medal of Honor. Messrs. Hawthorn and White will be notified of this action."

Very respectfully,

From: F. C. Ainsworth, Chief, Record and Pension Office.

[Source: 37TH Massachusetts Protest Case file at the National Archives: AGO Record & Pension Office, Document File #476510, File for David D. White, 37th Massachusetts, Volume 8W3 ROW16 COM17, Shelf F, Box #699]**Manuscript 24**

<u>Comments & Supporting Evidence:</u>

1. This letter was sent out to James Bowen and Harris Hawthorn on September 22, 1897. This was the end of the Protest Case and any further action by the Secretary of War concerning this protest filed by the 37th Massachusetts.

2. The author is baffled why the Secretary of War did not undertake strong measures to immediately revoke the Medal of Honor that was issued to Hawthorn if Alger now determined that Hawthorn did not earn it "under law and regulation." One would think that the War Department would have demanded that Hawthorn immediately surrender his Medal of Honor. For some unexplainable reason, this did not happen.

3. Russell A. Alger was appointed as Secretary of War by President McKinley on March 4, 1897. In late September 1898, President McKinley appointed a presidential commission, headed by General Grenville Dodge, to investigate allegations of the War Department's mismanagement. Though the commission cleared Alger of all corruption charges, it did find that the War Department lacked efficient administration and discipline. Russell A. Alger resigned as the Secretary of War at President McKinley's request, submitting his resignation letter to President McKinley on July 19, 1899. Perhaps the unorthodox way this Case was handled and the lack of follow up on the decision on 37th Massachusetts Protest Case made by Secretary Alger and the War Department can be attributed to these findings of mismanagement uncovered by this Dodge Commission.

<u>EVIDENCE OVERVIEW</u>
<u>EXHIBITS-W-CT-(1-4)</u>

The purpose of introducing this line of evidence is to bring to light important unpublished evidence that is currently in the possession of Charles W. Thayer, a collateral relative of Lt. William Morrill of the 37th Massachusetts. Charles W. Thayer is a retired professor from the University of Pennsylvania, Philadelphia, PA, and is currently residing in Manchester Center, VT.

<u>EXHIBIT-W-CT-1</u>

<u>Introduction:</u>

<u>Charles W. Thayer:</u> (PHOTO: COURTESY CHARLES W. THAYER)

The author has managed to contact and interview a collateral relative of William C. Morrill. William C. Morrill was a Lieutenant at the Battle of Sailor's Creek and commanded Company E of the 37th Massachusetts. The David White account states that General Custis Lee "officially" surrendered to Morrill, with Custis Lee not wanting to surrender to a private like David White but to an officer like William Morrill. The Official

Records state that William Morrill was wearing Custis Lee's sword after the capture of Custis Lee. At the time of this interview, Charles W. Thayer was living in Parkesburg, PA. He is a retired professor of Earth Sciences of the Department of Geology at the University of Pennsylvania in Philadelphia, PA. This is an "in-person" interview of Charles Walter Thayer which the author recorded and later transcribed. Mr. Thayer is currently residing in Manchester Center, VT. This interview was conducted on December 8, 1995.

Evidence:

An interview conducted with Charles W. Thayer on December 8, 1995, by the author:

Frank White: *Charles, could you tell me how you are a descendant of Captain William C. Morrill of the 37th Massachusetts Regiment and Harriett Richardson, whose letter to James S. Bowen of Springfield, Massachusetts, dated at Hadley, Massachusetts, May 26, 1897, is attached hereto?*

Charles Thayer: *Actually, I'm not a descendant of William Morrill. Morrill was a cousin and he was a cousin of the various Richardson girls and the Richardson's then married Thayers, who currently occupy the old homestead where Morrill returned very briefly and left his Civil War relics.*

Frank White: *Charles, you're in possession of various handwritten letters by William C. Morrill that he wrote during the Civil War and sent back to various family members. The reason why you are in possession of these letters and believe them to be authentic is…?*

Charles Thayer: *Well, as I was growing up, my grandfather's house, which was not the same as the Richardson's house, in which the relics were originally returned by Morrill, there was always the Lee pistol sitting on the window sill and I was always very interested in its history. My grandfather also had the documents relating to its history and the original letters, and fairly early on I urged my father to urge my grandfather to put all these things in order so that all the rest of the descendants could have the benefit of his knowledge. So I guess part of my early contribution was to get the historical record in order. The documents were always around, the history was always part of the family tradition and eventually I did go to the original homestead, the Richardson homestead in which my grandfather had grown up, and retrieved other of the Civil War relics including Morrill's Spencer rifle and the Springfield rifle musket that had presumably belonged to the black farm helper who had gone off to fight the war.*

Frank White: *Charles, could you tell me a little bit about the family tradition surrounding William Morrill and his participation in the Battle of Sailor's Creek?*

Charles Thayer: *I guess there's not really much family tradition, it's a matter of documentation in the letter that Morrill wound up with the sword and revolver that had belonged to Major General George Washington Custis Lee because a private in his regiment had captured the worthy general and by means, which I guess at this point will never know how, Morrill wound up in possession of many of these relics, brought them home to visit his charming young female cousin at the Richardson homestead and left all of his relics there. Then his home was in Maine, I guess he must have gone back to Maine before he then moved to Pennsylvania to pursue his oil interests.*

Frank White: *Charles, can you tell me about the tradition with regard to the horse?*

Charles Thayer: *Okay, again, it's a matter of what my grandfather wrote down in the family memoirs. The horse, I believe, was a gray; and the horse was brought back to the family farm at Hockanum, Massachusetts, and the story goes, that to show off the horse's gait, he rode this thing around the field and wound up putting a leg in a woodchuck hole, breaking a leg and having to shoot the horse. But the reason they liked to display the gait was that this was an unusual sort of horse, it was probably a Tennessee walking horse or something of that nature which had a gait beyond the normal walk, trot, canter that most northern horses would have had. This would have been something that you would want to show off to a northerner who wasn't familiar with the smooth riding variety of a southern horse. So that at least is consistent with the fact that this horse did have a southern origin.*

Frank White: *Charles, are there any family traditions with regard to how the Custis Lee sword got out of the possession of your family?*

Charles Thayer: *Yes, the tradition here pretty much documents the Harriett Richardson letter or the Harriett Richardson's letter documents the tradition. I was not aware of Harriett's letter until you dug it out of the archives. But the story my grandfather told was that a couple of men from Morrill's regiment showed up at the farm one day and wanted to take the sword for some sort of reunion and that it wound up in some museum somewhere. As I was questing for the sword, I tried all the possibilities I could think of, the Southern White House in Richmond, the Smithsonian, they knew nothing and I asked collectors and so forth. And now, of course, we know that the museum in question was the one you would expect, the GAR Museum right there in Northampton.*

Frank White: *Charles, with regard to any of the other relics that were supposed to be captured from General Custis Lee, like the saddle and the revolver. Can you talk a little more about the family tradition of how they were handed down and also the legend behind it?*

Charles Thayer: *Well, all these things just stayed in the Richardson's house at Hockanum, and so my grandfather grew up and needed to go set up housekeeping because only one of the sons could continue to occupy the family house; so I guess he moved most of the stuff with him to his new home in Amherst where he taught at the University of Massachusetts and was an Agronomist. The pistol itself, as I remember from very early in my childhood, sat on the window sill on the south window of the old brick house, one of those deep window sills, and in my youth I didn't know how to handle guns and I played with it as a toy like a cap gun snapping at the birds in the bird feeder outside on winter days, but it was always a big attraction when I got to my grandfather's. I would run in immediately and handle the Lee revolver and I hate to admit it that I played with it.*

This concludes the interview of Charles W. Thayer by Frank Everett White.
The answers to the above questions are true and correct to the best of my knowledge and recollection.
Signed Charles W. Thayer, Dated 16 Dec '95
[Source: Transcription of interview in the possession of the author]**Manuscript 25**

Comments & Supporting Evidence:

Comments are necessary for each of Charles Thayer's answers. These comments are contained below:

1. Answer (1) – Charles W. Thayer states that William Morrill was a cousin to the Richardson family and that his Thayer family married into this Richardson family. For a more detailed description of the relationships between the Morrills, Richardsons and Thayers, please see Exhibit W–CT–2.

2. Answer (2) – Charles W. Thayer is currently in possession of various letters written by William Morrill during his service in the Civil War. These letters were sent to various Richardson family members when they were living at the old Richardson family homestead in Hockanum, MA (see Exhibit W–CT–4). These Morrill letters were originally in the possession of Charles W. Thayer's grandfather, Charles Hiram Thayer. Charles W. Thayer is also in possession of a Confederate revolver alleged to be the revolver of General Custis Lee, which was taken by Morrill during Custis Lee's capture. This Confederate revolver was originally in the possession of Charles W. Thayer's grandfather. Charles W. Thayer is also in possession of a 140-page typescript entitled, "The Old Pomroy House at Hockanum and the Civil War," written in 1962 in Amherst, MA, by Charles W. Thayer's grandfather, Charles Hiram Thayer (see Exhibit W–CT–3). This typescript is the product of Charles W. Thayer's urging his father and grandfather as described in his statement: "My grandfather also had the documents relating to its history (the Custis Lee revolver) and the original letters (Morrill's) and fairly early on I urged by father to urge my grandfather to put all these things in order so that the rest of the descendants could have the benefit of his knowledge. So I guess part of my early contribution was to get the historical record in order." It would appear, as stated by Charles W. Thayer in this interview, that he collected other Civil War relics from the Richardson homestead as well.

3. Answer (3) – This family knowledge from Charles W. Thayer is insightful. He references a Morrill letter that explains how Morrill took possession of the Custis Lee sword and revolver. Thayer's family tradition also states that Morrill returned home from the Civil War to the Richardson homestead and left "his Civil War relics there." Family tradition then has Morrill returning to the home of his parents in ME before moving out to PA to pursue his oil interests. This family tradition corroborates events documented in Morrill's military service record. **[Source: Military Service Record William C. Morrill, #1466-US-1865, National Archives, Washington, DC]**Manuscript 57****

4. Answer (4) – The Thayer family tradition as documented on page 61 in Charles Hiram Thayer's 1962 typescript, describes Morrill bringing back a horse with a saddle to the Hockanum farm while on a short furlough after the Battle of Sailor's Creek. This statement is corroborated by Morrill's military service record which shows that Morrill was furloughed for 20 days starting April 23, 1865. In fact, Morrill's military service record contains a letter from Morrill stating, *"I respectfully ask twenty five (25) days leave of absence to go to my home in Massachusetts and visit my sister* [cousin] *who is dangerously ill."* This Thayer family account corroborates the horse account given May 11, 1897, by Samuel E. Nichols as found in Exhibit W–PF–9. It can also explain why Archibald Hopkins was questioning Custis Lee about a sorrel horse as found in Exhibit W–PF–12. The Thayer family tradition is that Morrill brought back from the Civil War to the Hockanum farm a southern horse, perhaps Custis Lee's horse or a horse from another Confederate officer taken at the Battle of Sailor's Creek.
[Source: Military Service Record William C. Morrill #1466-US-1865 National Archives] **Manuscript 57**

5. Answer (5) – The Thayer family tradition corroborates the account given by Harriett Richardson, who was William Morrill's first cousin living on the Hockanum homestead, concerning the Custis Lee sword no longer being in the possession of the Richardson family and the Custis Lee sword being removed from the Hockanum homestead location.

6. Answer (6) – As Charles W. Thayer's grandfather, Charles Hiram Thayer, moved out of the Hockanum homestead into his own home in Amherst, MA, he must have taken the pistol, which

was always referred to by the Thayers as the Custis Lee pistol, with him. Charles W. Thayer clearly remembers playing with it at his grandfather's house when he was a young boy.

7. In conclusion, Charles W. Thayer's family documents, traditions, and relics offer strong substantiation to the David D. White claim by providing the following pieces of new evidence:

   A. William Morrill's letter relating, firsthand, the capture of Custis Lee (see Exhibit W–CT–4)

   B. The family tradition concerning a revolver or pistol alleged to have been Custis Lee's.

   C. The family tradition concerning the Custis Lee sword and its removal from the Richardson family and the Hockanum homestead.

   D. The documented Thayer family traditions as contained in Charles Hiram Thayer's 1962 transcript entitled, "The Old Pomroy House at Hockanum and the Civil War," as contained in Exhibit W–CT–3.

EXHIBIT-W-CT-2

Introduction:

The author conducted another interview with Charles Walter Thayer on June 14, 2000. The purpose of this interview was to:

1. Clearly document the family relationships of the Morrill, Richardson and Thayer families, and to precisely show how Charles Walter Thayer was related to William C. Morrill.

2. Clearly document how Charles Walter Thayer came in possession of the Custis Lee revolver, the Civil War William Morrill letters, the typescript written by his grandfather entitled the, "Old Pomroy House at Hockanum and the Civil War," and other Civil War relics. This transcribed telephone interview was signed by Charles W. Thayer on August 25, 2000, with Mr. Thayer attesting to the accuracy of his statements.

Evidence:

Telephone Interview with Charles Walter Thayer dated June 14, 2000

(1) Family Tree:

- *Jeddediah Morrill and Mable Richardson married in the year 1836 in Williamsburg, Maine.*
- *They had three children, Harriett born 1838, William born 1841, and Anna born 1843.*
- *Mable Richardson was a sister to William Richardson, who was referred to as uncle by William Morrill in his Civil War letters. William Richardson lived in Hockanum, Massachusetts.*
- *William Richardson and first wife, Sarah Clark, had the following children: Abbie Clark Richardson, Lucy Richardson, Mary Richardson (died 1867 age 22), Harriett Richardson (that wrote to James Bowen concerning the Custis Lee sword), Henry "the rebel" Richardson, Martha Richardson and Mable Richardson.*
- *William and Sarah Richardson and their children lived in the "old Pomroy house" at Hockanum, Massachusetts.*
- *Charles Stiles Thayer married Abbie Clark Richardson on November 24, 1864.*
- *Charles Stiles and Abbie Richardson Thayer had five children: Henry, Lucy, Laura, Charles Hiram, and Richard.*
- *Charles Stiles and Abbie Richardson Thayer and their children lived in the Hockanum home for a period of time.*
- *Charles Hiram Thayer was born in 1884 and married in 1939.*
- *Charles Hiram Thayer had a son, Charles Vallentine Thayer and a daughter, Kasha, deceased – no children.*
- *Charles Vallentine Thayer had a son, Charles Walter Thayer, the interviewee, and another son.*

(2) TRAIL OF REVOLVER POSSESSION:

- *Charles Hiram Thayer grew up in the old William Richardson homestead at Hockanum, Massachusetts.*

- *About the time he married (1939), Charles Hiram Thayer moved out of the Hockanum home into his own home in Amherst, Massachusetts.*
- *Charles Hiram Thayer took the Lee pistol and Morrill letters with him when he moved out of the Hockanum home. He always referred to the pistol as "The Lee Pistol" based on family knowledge.*
- *When Charles Walter Thayer visited with his grandfather, Charles Hiram Thayer, he used to play with the Lee pistol, which was always in his grandfather's Amherst, Massachusetts, home.*
- *The Lee pistol was always by itself, no holster or belt.*
- *Charles Hiram Thayer was a professor of agronomy at the University or Massachusetts in Amherst, Massachusetts.*
- *Charles Hiram Thayer's brother, Richard Thayer, retained ownership of the old William Richardson Hockanum homestead.*
- *When Charles Walter Thayer was a teenager, he asked his grand uncle, Richard Thayer, if he could have other Civil War relics from the Hockanum home. Charles Walter Thayer got Morrill's Spencer rifle, Morrill's ammunition box (received from Charles H. Thayer before other relics–could possibly give exact date from inventory in Philadelphia office), and a Springfield rifle musket that had presumably belonged to a black farm helper who enlisted in the war.*
- *Charles Walter Thayer did not get the saddle that was brought back by Morrill from the Civil War with the "southern" horse. A branch of the Richard Thayer family (the grandson of Richard Thayer, also Richard), still owns the Richardson homestead and Charles Walter Thayer believes the saddle is still in the attic of this Hockanum homestead.*
- *Charles Walter Thayer inherited from his grandfather, Charles Hiram Thayer, the Lee pistol/revolver, the Morrill letters, the family write-up entitled, "The Old Pomroy House at Hockanum and the Civil War' (1962) and bars from Morrill's uniform, and several 7-packs of Spencer cartridges.*

(3)MISCELLANEOUS:

- *Charles Hiram Thayer documented the family history, created the family write-up entitled "The Old Pomroy House at Hockanum and the Civil War" – 140 pages (1962) and transcribed the Morrill letters, all of which are now in the possession of Charles Walter Thayer as of the date of this interview.*

June 20, 2000
Signed by Charles W. Thayer, August 25, 2000 - to attest to the accuracy.
[Source: Transcription of interview in the possession of the author]**Manuscript 26**

Comments & Supporting Evidence:

Comments are necessary for each of Charles Thayer's points. These comments are contained below:
1. Family Tree:
   A. This shows that William Morrill's mother was Mable Richardson.
   B. William Morrill's uncle was a William Richardson (brother to Morrill's mother, Mable Richardson), and he owned the farm in Hockanum, MA.
   C. William Richardson had a large family and they all lived at the Hockanum farm. William Morrill's Civil War letters were to various members of this Richardson family, particularly his female Richardson cousins.
   D. Charles Stiles Thayer married into this Richardson family (Abbie Richardson). He had a son, Charles Hiram Thayer (who authored "The Old Pomroy House at Hockanum and the Civil War," the 1962 transcript, and originally had the Custis Lee pistol and other Civil War relics), who had a son, Charles Vallentine Thayer, who had a son, Charles Walter Thayer (the interviewee).
   E. From this family tree, it is easy to see how Charles Walter Thayer (the interviewee) would have come into the possession of William Morrill's Civil War relics and Thayer family documents.

2. Trail of the Revolver Possession:
    A. This section precisely describes how Charles Walter Thayer came in possession of William Morrill's Civil War relics, particularly the Custis Lee revolver, and Thayer family documents.
3. Miscellaneous:
    A. Charles Walter Thayer urged his grandfather, Charles Hiram Thayer, to document the Thayer family oral traditions. This was done by Charles Hiram Thayer as found in his typescript, "The Old Pomroy House at Hockanum and the Civil War," (see Exhibit W–CT–3) and a typescript of all the original William Morrill Civil War letters (see Exhibit W–CT–4).

EXHIBIT-W-CT-3

Introduction:

Charles H. Thayer: (PHOTO: COURTESY CHARLES W. THAYER)

A typescript entitled, "The Old Pomroy House at Hockanum and the Civil War," which was written by Charles Hiram Thayer in 1962 at Amherst, MA. This typescript was created by Charles Hiram Thayer to document his family knowledge at the urging of his grandson, Charles Walter Thayer. This document is currently in the possession of Charles Walter Thayer. Charles Walter Thayer has the complete 140-page typescript with the exception of page 31, which is missing. For the purpose of this Exhibit, only page 51 and pages 58 through 63 of the typescript are included as they describe William Morrill's actions and the capture of General G. W. Custis Lee.

Evidence:

Richardson Farm, Hockanum, MA:
(PHOTO: COURTESY CHARLES W. THAYER)

***THE OLD POMROY HOUSE AT HOCKANUM
AND THE CIVIL WAR,
BY: CHARLES HIRAM THAYER, 1962, (140
pp, bound typescript, Amherst, MA)***

***Page 51** THE 37ᵀᴴ MASS. VOL. INF. The 37th went into camp at Pittsfield in the late summer of 1862 and were mustered into the U.S. service on September 4. The boys from Hockanum Village who enlisted in this regiment were William Morrill, Theodore Church and William Champney. William Morrill had come down from Williamsburg, Maine, in the spring of 1860 when he was just past 19, to work on the Hockanum farm for his maternal uncle, William Richardson. Theodore Church lived in South Hadley, but had worked in Hockanum Village a good deal. He was engaged to Julia Johnson of the village, sister of Herbert Johnson, who had enlisted in the 27th Mass. William Champney had lived and worked in Hockanum a good deal and was known to everyone there. He was one of these little, dark, wiry and very active men. He had to stretch himself for three days before the army would accept him. He served as hospital steward all through the war. **Page 58:** Trench warfare in the Petersburg lines continued for month after month while Grant made repeated efforts to cut the railroads behind the*

Confederate right that supplied Richmond. On Oct 27, 1864, an attack on the railroads was repulsed at Hatchers Run. Both armies extended their intrenchments further west. The regiments in the Army of the Potomac had by this time been so much reduced by losses that very often colonels were in command of brigades, captains of regiments, and lieutenants of companies. On Feb. 17, 1865, Wm. Morrill was made 1st Lieutenant and given command of Co. E of the 37th. By the middle of March Sherman had driven Johnston's army north across both Carolinas and defeated him at Bentonville, NC. On March 25, Lee made a desperate attempt to break Grant's lines at Ft. Stedman but was defeated with the loss of 4,000 men. On March 27 Sheridan brought his cavalry back from the Shenandoah to the Army of the Potomac and Grant put him in charge of the spring campaign. On April 1 Sheridan turned Lee's flank and captured Pickett's whole division of 5,000 men at Five Forks. Grant figured these losses must have left Lee's intrenchments undermanned and ordered an assault along the whole line on the morning of April 2. **Page 59:** The 6th Corps charged just before daylight and made the first breakthrough in the Confederate entrenchments. The other corps followed and by the end of the day the whole 35-mile line was taken. The 37th Mass. went forward against a 3-gun fort through 5 lines of abatis. Wm. Morrill snagged his belt in scrambling through this and lost his sword and pistol. Co. E. of the 37th was first over the parapet. A corporal in Co. E. seized the rebel flag and won the Congressional Medal of Honor. The regiment lost 3 men killed and 32 wounded. After a day spent in clearing the lines the 6th Corps started in the pursuit of Lee. Lee's effort, when he evacuated Petersburg and Richmond, was to get west and south, either to join Johnston or to make a stand at Lynchburg; Grant's was to head him off and bring him to battle. With Sheridan's cavalry in the lead, the infantry of Grant's army followed, marching to the limit of endurance. On April 6 Sheridan sent word back that he had the rebel rear-guard cut off and wanted the 6th Corps in a hurry to finish them. The 6th Corps had already marched 20 miles that day but they put in another 3 miles at the double and were sent into the Battle of Sailor's Creek against Ewell's Corps. The 37th Mass. came up against a battalion of artillerymen who had left their big guns in the forts of Richmond and another of marines who had helped to sink the Confederate Navy in the James River when Richmond fell. The 37th held its ground against a rebel charge when the rest of the Union line fell back at short distance. This left the 37th almost surrounded. The rebel marines proved as tough as their name; **Page 60:** the fight became desperate and hand-to-hand; the 37th lost 9 killed and 31 wounded. Some men were killed with the bayonet; one man of the 37th was thrust through the breast and pinned to the ground, yet he shot his assailant, pulled out the bayonet and walked to the rear. He survived the war for over 20 years. The rebels could not stand up against the Spencer seven-shooters of the 37th and when the cavalry came in on their rear they were forced to surrender. A corporal of Co. E. captured Maj. Genl. G. W. C. Lee (Custis Lee, eldest son of Genl. Robert E. Lee) at the muzzle of his Spencer. Custis Lee refused to surrender to a non-com, when Lt. Morrill came up and told him to surrender, or else. He did, and Morrill took his sword and pistol to replace his own that he had lost in the abatis of the Petersburg lines. Ewell himself and 5 other generals, with thousands of their men, surrendered to the 6th Corps and the cavalry. The 6th Corps camped on the battlefield that night and the next day joined the pursuit again. After Lee's army surrendered at Appomattox on April 9, the 6th Corps marched back in the direction of Petersburg 35 miles to Burkeville where it camped for 10 days and then marched 75 miles south to Danville on the North Carolina line. Danville had been the last seat of the Confederate government, and Johnston's army, not far away, had not surrendered yet, though it did so before the 6th Corps reached Danville. After a week in Danville the 6th Corps was sent north by rail, to camp for two weeks near Petersburg. During this time Lt. Morrill got a short furlough home to Hockanum. He brought with him a dog, said to be half bloodhound and half mastiff, who, as Old Mack, became a character in the farm **Page 61:** family. He also brought a mare, beautifully gaited but rather old, with a Confederate cavalry saddle. After his discharge he took the mare down on Hockanum Flats to show her gaits; she stepped in a woodchuck hole, broke her leg and had to be shot, but the saddle still (1962) hangs in the Hockanum barn, a McClellan type saddle covered with rawhide. Lt. Morrill was back with the regiment at Petersburg when the 6th Corps began its march to Washington and home. He said they had to march 100 extra miles because a railroad bridge had been wrecked near Alexandria. They marched through mud and dust, grouching over the hard marches, through Richmond and Fredericksburg to camp just outside Arlington, across the Potomac from Washington. As they marched through Richmond on May 24, they passed in review before Generals Ord and Halleck. The Grand Review of the Armies of the United States took place in Washington before President Johnson, Grant, Sherman, and all the high generals. All day on May 23, Grant's army marched in review, in spit-and-polish precision. Sherman's army couldn't match that and didn't want to try; on the 24th they marched through just as they had come from their campaigns in Georgia and the Carolinas, in most effective contrast. On June 8, the 6th Corps paraded through enthusiastic Washington crowds who remembered how it had marched through the streets just a year before to drive Early away from the city. The 37th Mass. had fewer men than the other regiments of its brigade, and the narrow company fronts, only 18 men in K, the color company, told of its battle losses. **Page 62:** Lt. Morrill was given the rank of Brevet Captain in recognition of his service at Petersburg and Sailor's Creek. The brevet was an honorary promotion that gave its holder no increase in command nor in pay. The 37th now discharged from Federal service, left Washington for home by steamer and train. It had taken 27 cars to carry the regiment away from Pittsfield when it left for the war, and how it came back to that town in six. A big reception for the regiment in Pittsfield on the morning of June 24 was followed by a banquet in Springfield that afternoon. Then the regiment went on to the State Camp at Readville for final discharge and pay. Wm. Morrill came back to the old farmhouse at Hockanum and hung up his Spencer; his belt with the sword and pistol; his knapsack and his ammunition-box (with some 25 live Spencer cartridges in it), all in Abbie Richardson Thayer's half of the attic. They remained there for over 50 years. Morrill got interested in the oil boom in Pennsylvania, moved out there, married and spent the rest of his life. He came back on a visit to Hockanum some time in the early '80s to see his cousins at the farm and his friends of the 37th. As Wm. Champney was driving by one day, Morrill hailed him, Champney hitched his horse, and the two old soldiers talked their heads off for the rest of the day. In 1888 two friends of Morrill from the 37th who lived in Northampton, probably Abbott and Nichols, came to Hockanum with a letter for Abbie Richardson Thayer from Morrill asking that she give them the Custis Lee sword, which they would take to a Grand Army celebration and then put in some museum. No one in the family now knows of its present whereabouts. **Page 63:** The Custis Lee pistol is now (1962) in the hands of Charles Hiram Thayer. His grandson, Charles W. Thayer, has proved by some pretty good research, that it is a Rigdon-Ansley, caliber 36, serial number 1763, made in Augusta, Georgia, in 1864. Less than 1000 of these were made and only 22 other specimens of this pistol are known. Burke Davis, author of <u>Appomattox: Nine April Days</u>, in a letter to Charles Hiram Thayer, says, "This pistol is one of the really fine relics of the War." See <u>Confederate Arms</u>, by William A. Albaugh and Edward N. Simmons. Published 1957 by The Stackpole Company, Harrisburg, Penn.

[Source: "The Old Pomroy House at Hockanum" by Charles Hiram Thayer, Amherst, MA; 1962]**Manuscript 27**

Comments & Supporting Evidence:

There is much information contained in this typescript and a page by page commentary is necessary:

1. Page 51 – This page is insightful because it tells how William Morrill came from his home in Williamsburg, ME, in the spring of 1860 at the age of 19, to work on the farm of his maternal uncle, William Richardson. It would appear that William Morrill stayed on the Richardson farm from the spring of 1860 to his enlistment in the Civil War on September 4, 1862. This would account for his close relationship with the Richardson family (his uncle, aunt and female cousins) and would explain why he sent letters to them from the Civil War. In fact, there is Thayer family tradition that hints that William Morrill had a romantic interest in one of his cousins, Mary Richardson.

2. Page 58 – This page states that Morrill was promoted to 1st Lieutenant and given command of Co. E of the 37th Massachusetts. This statement is corroborated by Morrill's military service record which states he was "promoted to 1st Lieut. Co. E. Feb 17, 1865." Prior to this, Morrill was promoted from Sergt. Co. G. to 2nd Lieut. This would validate the David D. White claim that Custis Lee "officially" surrendered to White's commanding officer; with White also being in Company E. **[Source: Military Service Record William C. Morrill #1466-1865, National Archives, Washington, DC]**Manuscripts 57****

3. Page 58 – The statement, "The regiments in the Army of the Potomac had by this time been so much reduced by losses that very often colonels were in command of brigades, captains of regiments and lieutenants of companies." This would explain why Captain Archibald Hopkins was commanding the 37th Massachusetts, and Lt. Morrill was commanding Company E of the 37th Massachusetts at the Battle of Sailor's Creek. (Also, see Exhibit W–OR–1 for the promotions received by both Hopkins and Morrill.)

4. Page 59 – This statement is most important: "The 37th Mass. went forward against a three-gun fort through five lines of abatis. Wm. Morrill snagged his belt in scrambling through this and lost his sword and pistol." This incident described by Thayer was the Federal assault on Petersburg, VA, on April 2, 1865. Thayer states an important fact, that Morrill lost his belt, sword and pistol in the abatis. This event is corroborated by four pieces of documentation and evidence as outlined below:

    A. This write-up gives the following account on the assault on Fort Fisher, Petersburg, VA, on April 2, 1865, by the 37th Massachusetts:

As soon as it was light enough for the soldiers to see the ground upon which they were to step two guns from Fort Fisher boomed out the signal and in an instant the dark lines swept forward. The forlorn hope of skirmishers and pioneers reached the abatis in a few moments. It was not only firmly secured by earth thrown over the trunks, but was strengthened by a double row of sharpened stakes firmly fixed in the ground. A destructive fire was opened upon the exposed line, which the skirmishers returned with interest from their Spencer rifles while the pioneers chopped and wrenched away the obstructions with desperate energy. Captain Robinson was wounded in the arm while striving to force his way through the obstructions; Sergeant Charles H. Tracy of Company A, on duty with the pioneers, was severely wounded, and while lying on the ground encouraging his comrades, received a second shot in the knee joint causing the loss of his leg. Fortunately in the gloom most of the enemy's fire went over the attacking forces and the loss was but a fraction of what it would have been a few minutes later. Meantime the line of battle sprang forward with a rush and a cheer. It gave little heed to the pioneers or the obstructions on which they were engaged; into and through them it went some how, no one could tell in the wild excitement just how, and straight forward to the enemy's works. A three-gun fort was the objective of the Thirty-seventh, a strong work protected by a ditch. Company E led in the scramble up the parapet.

[Source: "History of the Thirty-Seventh Regiment Massachusetts Volunteers," by James L. Bowen, pages 410 – 411, 1884]**Manuscript 58**

    Captain Archibald Hopkins commanded this assault for the 37th Massachusetts and Morrill's Company E would appear to be the lead company in the advance for the Federal forces. If Morrill's Company was the lead Company, it could explain his excitement leading an assault and not wanting to stop and turn back to retrieve his lost belt.

    B. Col. Oliver Edwards, commanding the 3rd Brigade, gives the following report of this event:

The command moved from its camp on the night of the 1st, at 10.30 o'clock, and massed in front of Fort Fisher, where the brigade remained some time waiting for the Second Division to get into position. I then moved outside the works, marching left in front, and formed on the right of the First Brigade, Second Division, twenty-five paces echelon, in three lines, with an interval of 300 paces between each line, in the following order, from right to left; First line, Thirty-seventh Massachusetts and Fifth Wisconsin Volunteers; second line, One hundred and nineteenth Pennsylvania, Forty-ninth Pennsylvania, and Second Rhode Island Volunteers; third line, Eighty-second Pennsylvania Volunteers. I caused a skirmish line of seventy-five Spencer rifles (all volunteers) to be deployed along my brigade front, and twenty axmen, selected from the pioneer corps. I also distributed a sufficient quantity of axes along the first line, to be used in case the axmen had trouble in removing the obstructions. The command was severely harassed by the fire of the enemy's skirmishers while forming. At 4 a.m. the line moved forward, taking up the double-quick after passing the ravine in my front, and stormed the fort in my front, together with a portion of the works on its left, successfully carrying them, capturing 10 guns, 3 battle-flags and a large number of prisoners.

[Source: Official Records, "The Appomattox Campaign," Volume 46, Series 1, Folio 114, page 941]Manuscript 4****

    C. Captain Archibald Hopkins, commanding the 37th Massachusetts as part of Edwards' 3rd Brigade, gives the following report of this event:

In the assault on the enemy's works at Petersburg on the morning of April 2 this regiment was in the front line of the brigade on the right of the Fifth Wisconsin. In advance of the line of battle were deployed as skirmishers seventy-five picked men and volunteers from this regiment, who covered the entire brigade front and were commanded by Capt. J.C. Robinson, assisted by Second Lieut. H. A. Cushman. At the word of command the regiment advanced rapidly, with a cheer, forced their way through two lines of abatis, over the ditch into the enemy's fort, where (after a brief but sharp conflict, the enemy's gunners, standing to their pieces and firing them two or three times after some of us, were in the fort) we captured 3 guns, about 40 prisoners, and a battle-flag.

[Source: Official Records, "The Appomattox Campaign," Volume 46, Series 1, Folio 115, page 945]Manuscript 4****

    D. The following affidavit was discovered by the author at the Massachusetts National Guard Archives in Worcester, MA.

I certify on honor that on the 2nd day of April, 1865, at or near Petersburg, VA, the ordinance stores enumerated below were lost under the following circumstances: The Regiment to which my company belongs was ordered to advance under fire of the enemy to assault their works in so doing 1 Non Commissioned officer and 3 Privates were severely wounded. The arms and equipment carried by these men were unavoidable lost as after gaining their works we continued to advance and did not again visit that part of the field.
A Hopkins, Capt 37th Company C
The undersigned being duly sworn deposes and says that he is cognizant of the facts as above stated and that they are true to the best of his knowledge and belief.
E. E. Stanard, 1st Segt. Co C 37th Mass Vols.
Sworn and subscribed before me this 26th day of June 1865 at Readville Mass
Samuel E. Nichols, 1st Lieut and Actg Adgt 37th Mass.
I attest that this is an accurate transcription of a document located at Massachusetts National Guard Archives, Worcester, MA 37th MV1 Collection
Leonid Kondratiuc, Col, USA (ret), Director, March 28, 2001

[Source: Affidavit by Archibald Hopkins, a true transcription in the possession of the author, National Guard Archives, Worcester, MA, 37th Massachusetts Regiment, M. V. I. Collection]Manuscript 101****

    This "lost ordinance" affidavit by Archibald Hopkins who commanded the 37th Massachusetts at Petersburg, VA, underscored the possibility of losing equipment and arms by soldiers pushing through the enemy abatis at Petersburg. Specifically, this affidavit shows how William Morrill could have lost his belt on the enemy abatis at Petersburg and why he did not return again to that part of the field to reclaim it.

    Page 60 – The following statement concerning the Battle of Sailor's Creek corroborates the David D. White account with its description concerning the Custis Lee sword:

"The rebels could not stand up against the Spencer seven-shooters of the 37th and when the cavalry came in on their rear they were forced to surrender. A corporal of Co. E. captured Maj. Genl. G. W. C. Lee (Custis Lee, eldest son of Genl. Robert E. Lee) at the muzzle of his Spencer. Custis Lee refused to surrender to a non-com, when Lt. Morrill came up and told him to surrender, or else. He did, and Morrill took his sword and pistol to replace his own that he had lost in the abatis of the Petersburg lines."

The Corporal referred to by Thayer was most likely Private David D. White. David was a private at the Battle of Sailor's Creek, but soon became a corporal thereafter.

5. Pages 60 and 61 – This account about a southern horse corroborates the horse story given by Samuel E. Nichols on May 11, 1897, as found in Exhibit W–PF–9 and supports Archibald Hopkins' question to Custis Lee about a horse as found in Exhibit W–PF–12.

6. Page 62 – This page states that William Morrill came back to the old Hockanum farm after the Civil War and left all his Civil War "relics" at this farm. It also states that they remained in the Richardson attic for over 50 years. From there these relics came into the possession of Charles Hiram Thayer and then to his son Charles Walter Thayer.

7. Page 62 – The statement about the Custis Lee sword corroborates nicely the account given by Harriett Richardson (cousin to William Morrill) on May 26, 1897, as found in Exhibit W–PF–14. In addition, the reference made here to two of William Morrill's friends coming to the Hockanum home in 1888 to pick up the sword of Custis Lee for a Grand Army celebration is an interesting one. The following article can establish the start of these 37th Massachusetts "Grand Army" reunions.

The 43rd annual reunion of the 37th Massachusetts Regiment Volunteers' Association was held in Memorial Hall today on the 49th anniversary of the battle of Winchester, in which the 37th rendered distinguished service. Rev. H. L. Fisher of the Carew Street Baptist church and Chaplin R. R. McGregor of the E. K. Wilcox Grand Army Post addressed the members of the association.

[Source: "Looking Backward 50 Years Ago," Springfield Daily News, Sept 21, 1963]**Manuscript 100**

This article would place the start date of these 37th Massachusetts reunions at Memorial Hall in Northampton, MA in 1870 (1963 – 50 years ago – 43rd reunion = 1870). This helps validate the integrity of the 1888 Grand Army celebration date as cited by Charles Thayer. It should also be noted that the finish date of these 37th Massachusetts reunions can be pegged to the year 1931 (1961-30 years ago = 1931) at Memorial Hall by the title of this newspaper article below:

"When the 37th Massachusetts Regiment held its final reunion here 30 years ago at Memorial Hall"

[Source: Springfield Daily News, March 30, 1961]**Manuscript 100**

37th Massachusetts Veterans Reunion (undated): (PHOTO: COURTESY HISTORIC NORTHAMPTON)

8. Page 63 – The Custis Lee pistol referenced on this page, if Thayer family tradition is correct, provides extremely valuable physical evidence for the David D. White claim that Custis Lee was armed and surrendered his arms and personal property to White/Morrill at the time of his capture. This would directly contradict Harris Hawthorn's claim that Custis Lee didn't have as much as a "jack knife" at the time Hawthorn captured him, as was recorded by Hawthorn in his own hand writing as contained in the document found in Exhibit W–PF–27.

9. Since the claim has been raised by these Thayer family documents that Lee was wearing a belt that contained a sword and revolver at the time of his capture, the author investigated the likelihood of this Thayer claim by researching expert sources which yielded the following results:

A. The uniform and dress of the (Confederate) army pursuant to General Order No. 9–Adjutant and Inspector General's Office, Richmond, VA, June 6, 1861, is as follows:

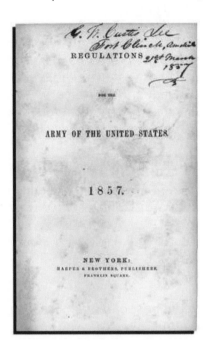

Custis Lee's (signed) 1857 Army Regulations Book:

SWORD BELT:

(44) *For all officers—a waist belt, not less than one and one-half inches, nor more than two inches wide; to be worn over the sash; the sword to be suspended from it by slings of the same material as the belt, with a hook attached to the belt upon which the sword may be hung.*

(45) *For General Officers—Russian leather, with three stripes of gold embroidery; the slings embroidered on both sides.*

(46) *For all other officers—black leather, plain.*

(47) *For all non-commissioned officers—black leather, plain.*

SWORD BELT PLATE:

(48) *For all officers and enlisted men—gilt, rectangular; two inches wide, with a raised bright rim; a silver wreath of laurel encircling the "arms of the Confederate States."*

SWORD AND SCABBARD:

(49) *For all officers—according to patterns to be deposited in the Ordinance Bureau.*

SWORD KNOT:

(50) *For all officers—of plaited leather, with tassels.*

[Source: "Uniform and Dress of the Army of the Confederate States," Richmond, VA: Chas. H. Wynne, Printer, 94 Main Street, 1861, as contained in the modern "Uniform and Dress of the Army and Navy of the Confederate States of America" introduction by Richard Harwell, St. Martin's Press]**Manuscript 59**

This uniform and dress code, though explicit on a belt and sword, is silent on a revolver. The most probable explanation is that a belt and sword were considered as dress and not an arm, while a revolver was considered an arm. It is highly probable that General Custis Lee, given his keen attention to military regulations as outlined and mandated in his personal military regulations book depicted above, was completely compliant with Confederate uniform and dress code. On the converse side, it is just about imaginable to think that Custis Lee would have been "out of uniform" at any time during active duty. This is particularly true during an active battle, like Sailor's Creek, where being dressed in full uniform was an essential display of rank.

B. Mr. Chris Calkins, with the National Parks Service and a leading authority on Civil War history and the Battle of Sailor's Creek, expressed his opinion in the following letter that General Custis Lee wore the full dress of a Confederate officer. To substantiate his opinion, Calkins cites the famous photograph taken by Bradley of Robert E. Lee, Custis Lee, and Col. Walter Taylor on April 16, 1865, at Robert E. Lee's Franklin Street home in Richmond, VA.

[Source: William A. Frassanito "Grant and Lee, the Virginia Campaigns, 1864-1865," pages 416-418]**Manuscript 60**

United States Department of the Interior, National Park Service
June 19, 2000

Dear Mr. White:

As per our phone conversation concerning the possible dress of Major General George Washington Custis Lee upon surrendering himself during the Battle of Little Sailor's Creek, April 6, 1865: I would assume that he, like most other high officers in the Army of Northern Virginia, wore a standard battle garb consisting of a sword, sword belt, and a revolver for personal protection. That General Lee wore

the full dress of a Confederate officer is proven by the photograph of he and his father in Richmond, just ten days after his surrender at Sailor's Creek. That General Lee gave up his sword and associated regalia, and possibly personal belongings such as a haversack, is highly likely, as it was a custom to turn these items over to the individual you are surrendering to. The fact that Harris Hawthorn, 121st N.Y. is given credit for Lee's capture has me wondering. Could David White have taken the general at gun point (as the regimental history says), removed him of his belt and equipment, then eventually the general was handed over to Hawthorn who officially took him to the rear and was given the Medal of Honor for his "capture"? You probably need to check what Hawthorn's Medal of Honor records say in the National Archives and compare them against what you know about White's story. Good luck with your research and keep me informed of your progress.
Sincerely, Chris Calkins, Historian
[Source: Personal letter with photo in the possession of the author]**Manuscript 60**

It is also interesting to note Chris Calkins' opinion regarding items that are turned over during a surrendered and his opinion and conclusion concerning the capture of General G. W. Custis Lee.
C. Custis Lee took command of the troops defending Richmond pursuant to the following order:

HEADQUARTERS DEPARTMENT OF RICHMOND,
Near Bottom's Bridge, June 13, 1864.
Brig. Gen. G. W. C. Lee will take command of the troops in this department east of the fortifications of the city of Richmond, and including those at and near Chaffin's Bluff and farm.
By command of Major-General Ransom:
T. O. Chestney, Assistant Adjutant-General.
[Source: Official Records, Volume 40, Series 1, Part 2, page 646.]**Manuscript 61**

It would appear that Custis Lee was engaged in active wartime duty which carried very real risks and dangers as the following write up indicates:

Chaffin's Bluff, June 21—1864 – 7 p.m.
General G. W. C. Lee:
Your dispatch of 5.30 p.m. received. You have been notified that General Heth with two brigades has been ordered north of James River. You must judge of the essential points to hold in order to thwart the enemy in his approach to Richmond. Whatever operations you may decide upon I advise that you use all your available force for the purpose. I should hope your force with Carter's artillery could drive the enemy back.
R. E. Lee.
[Source: Official Records, Volume 40, Series 1, Part 2, page 674]**Manuscript 61**

It would seem very probable, given the risky position that Custis Lee was continually in prior to the Battle of Sailor's Creek, that he secured a revolver for his own personal protection. The Richmond Armory was still well supplied in 1864 and the purchase of a revolver for his own personal use from this armory would have been easy for General Custis Lee to accomplish.
D. In Baltimore on October, 1865, Howard McHenry wrote about the evacuation of Richmond, VA, in an article entitled, "Retreat of Custis Lee's Division and the Battle of Sailor's Creek." This article contains the following statement:

Although all the wagons were loaded almost beyond the ability of the miserable animals to start them, still piles of baggage remained lying by the roadside. There was no help for it, and no time for selection even; and many an officer and man found himself about to start on an indefinite campaign without a single article except what he wore upon his back, and with a very dim prospect indeed of being able to get a new supply."
[Source: Southern Historical Society Transactions, "Retreat of Custis Lee's Division and the Battle of Sailor's Creek," Volume One, 1874]**Manuscript 62**

It would appear that General Custis Lee had to carry what he needed "upon his back," lending support that he had his sword, revolver and particularly a haversack containing his personal items as described in the various testimonies in the 37th Massachusetts accounts. These items, most likely, would have been on his person during the Battle of Sailor's Creek.

E. Howard McHenry also writes the following concerning the troops commanded by Custis Lee:

They were all armed with the musket, however, and formed a splendid body of men, fine material, excellently officered and disciplined. Their long inactivity had enabled them to keep their uniforms in better plight than usual, and their scarlet caps and trimmings lent a little more of the pomp and circumstance of war than was to be seen elsewhere in the Army of Northern Virginia. They numbered about 1400 men in line. Truly the Confederacy never witnessed such a patched-up organization as this division, but nevertheless each component part was in a high state of efficiency, and the whole worked harmoniously together, deriving from its very peculiarities something of an esprit de corps.
[Source: Southern Historical Society Transactions (ditto), Volume One; 1874]**Manuscript 62**

It would appear from this writing that Custis Lee's troops were well equipped and outfitted. One would have to suppose that Custis Lee was well outfitted as well. This article suggests that their equipment and arms were in a "new" state given their long inactivity from battle. This could explain the excellent, like new, condition of the alleged Custis Lee revolver in the possession of Charles W. Thayer. As an interesting aside, Howard McHenry states in this article, "My horse started violently at seeing Major Frank Smith's dead horse in the road." Both McHenry and Smith were a part of Custis Lee's troops during the march from Richmond, and if they were riding horses, surely Custis Lee, being their commander, must have been riding a horse as well.

F. J. Warren Keifer, Brevet Major General, wrote an article in 1879 entitled, "Sketches of War History – The Battle of Sailor's Creek." In this article he talks about some of the Confederate troops captured at Sailor's Creek. The article states, *"The fact that when disarmed there was found to be a large wagon load of pistols of all patterns and manufacturers, collected from all the civilized countries of the world, afforded much true soldier merriment."* **[Source: Mollus-OH, III, "Sketches of War History, The Battle of Sailor's Creek," pages 1-20]**Manuscript 54**** It would appear from this statement that the Confederate troops at the Battle of Sailor's Creek were well armed with pistols, as a large wagon load was collected by the Federals after their surrender. The author was able to uncover the following two accounts that show that at least two Confederate officers had pistols at the Battle of Sailor's Creek.

"There were several incidents of this fight at Sailor's Creek which I would like to mention … I had a pistol, a large colt…."
[Source: Southern Historical Collection, University of North Carolina, Chapel Hill, NC, "Personal Reminiscences of William Starr Basinger"]** Manuscript 77**

"The adjutant, John S. Bradey, a gallant soldier, always at the front, as the musketry lulled, demanded a sword of a Confederate officer near whom he was standing when the officer, without a word, put his pistol to the adjutant's breast."
[Source: "The Military Engineer" May/June 1927, Article entitled "The Battle of Sailor's Creek" by Archibald Hopkins]**Manuscript 85**

Given these two examples of Confederate officers who were subordinates to Custis Lee at the Battle of Sailor's Creek, and were in possession of pistols during this battle, it is not unreasonable to think that General Custis Lee was also armed with a pistol during the Battle of Sailor's Creek.

G. Charles Hiram Thayer's transcript states that the Custis Lee revolver is a Rigdon-Ansley, 36 caliber, serial number 1763, made in Augusta, GA, in 1864. From the two books cited below, we learn the following important facts about this type of Rigdon-Ansley revolver:

(1) "Charles H. Rigdon became the ace revolver manufacturer of the Confederacy. His revolvers were the best made within the borders of the Confederacy. If he did not manufacture more revolvers for the Confederacy than any other Southern maker, he was a close second in the quantity of his products."
[Source: Firearms of the Confederacy]**Manuscript 63** (2) these Rigdon-Ansley 12 stop revolvers were produced *"on or about March 13, 1864"* under a CSA government contract (3) they started with serial number 1500 (these revolvers were a continuation of a prior CSA government contract to produce 1500 6 stop revolvers with the Leech & Rigdon company, Rigdon-Ansley's predecessor (4) the production of these revolvers ended on or about *"January 27, 1865* (5) the highest known serial number is *"# 2359"* (6) *"all the Rigdon-Ansley's were made in Augusta, Georgia"* (7) most all these revolvers were stamped with *"CSA on the barrel top,"* like Thayer's revolver cited above and (8) *"under Confederate Army regulations, officers were not issued side-arms or equipment. They were required to purchase their own. This was done either privately or through Confederate States Armories. They were purchasable by any officer from any armory or arsenal that happened to have one on hand."*
[Source: "The Original Confederate Colt, The Story of the Leech & Rigdon and Rigdon-Ansley Revolvers," by William Albaugh 111, Greenberg Publisher, NY; 1953]**Manuscript 189**

> This revolver is a perfect fit by way of date, quality and make with the type of revolver that Custis Lee could have purchased from the armory in Richmond in 1864. Overlaying the serial numbers with the start and stop dates of production, Thayer's revolver with serial number 1763 was most likely manufactured between May-June, 1864. This date range coincides nicely with the start of the only active field service that Custis Lee saw during the entire course of the war. Being an aide to Jefferson David for most of the war, he did not need a revolver until now, when he became responsible for the defense of the City of Richmond from the encroaching enemy.

10. In conclusion, it is the author's opinion that it is highly probable that General Custis Lee was wearing a belt (see Exhibit W–PF–18 by Hubbard M. Abbott attesting to this fact), a sword (see Exhibit W–PF–12 by Confederate Captain Charles Stevens Dwight attesting to this fact), a revolver and a haversack during the Battle of Sailor's Creek. It seems highly improbable that Custis Lee was totally unarmed during the Battle of Sailor's Creek as was claimed by Harris Hawthorn.

EXHIBIT-W-CT-4

Introduction:
These Civil War letters have been handed down to Charles W. Thayer from his grandfather, Charles Hiram Thayer. They were originally stored in the old Richardson family farm in Hockanum, and all were written by William Morrill to Richardson family members living on the Hockanum, MA, farm.

Charles W. Thayer has the following original William C. Morrill letters in his possession:
1. William Morrill to cousin, Mary Richardson–Union, VA, and White Plains, VA, dated <u>5 November, 1862</u>.
2. William Morrill to cousin, Lucy Richardson–near Falmouth, VA, dated <u>20 December, 1862</u>.
3. William Morrill to cousin, Lucy Richardson–Co. G., 37th Mass. Vols., camp near Falmouth, VA, dated <u>25 January, 1863</u>.
4. William Morrill to cousin, Lucy Richardson–camp near Falmouth, VA, dated <u>12 February, 1863</u>.
5. William Morrill to cousin, Mary Richardson–camp near Falmouth, VA, dated <u>6 March, 1863</u>.
6. William Morrill to cousin, Mary Richardson–camp near White Oak Church, VA, dated <u>17 May, 1863</u>.
7. William Morrill to cousin, Mary Richardson–camp near White Oak Church, VA, dated <u>25 May, 1863</u>.
8. William A. Champney to friend, Mary Richardson – Fairfax Court House, VA, dated <u>21 June, 1863</u>.
9. William Morrill to cousin, Lucy Richardson–in the field five miles south of Petersburg, VA, dated <u>25 June, 1864</u>.
10. William Morrill to cousin, Mary Richardson–in the field near Reams Station, VA, dated <u>1 July, 1864</u>.
11. William Morrill to Lucy Richardson–in the field, dated <u>5 August, 1864</u>.
12. Samuel E. Nichols, 37th Mass. Vols. to Mr. William Richardson–Headquarters, 37th Mass. Vols. Adjutant Office, opposite Court House, Winchester, VA, dated <u>22 September, 1864</u>.

13. William Morrill to cousin, Mary Richardson–Satterlee Hospital, West Philadelphia, dated <u>30 September, 1864</u>.
14. William Morrill to cousin, Mary Richardson–Satterlee Hospital, West Philadelphia, dated <u>9 October, 1864</u>.

William C. Morrill: (PHOTO: COURTESY CHARLES W. THAYER)

15. William Morrill to cousin, Mary Richardson–Satterlee Hospital, West Philadelphia, dated <u>22 October, 1864</u>.
16. William Morrill to cousin, Lucy Richardson–camp 37th Mass. Vols., Winchester, VA, dated <u>8 December, 1864</u>.
17. William Morrill to cousin, Mary Richardson–camp of the 37th Mass. Vols., Warren Station, VA, dated <u>9 February, 1865</u>.
18. William Morrill to uncle, William Richardson–camp of the 37th Mass. Vols., Warren Station, VA, dated <u>18 March, 1865</u>.
19. William Morrill to cousin, Mary Richardson–camp of the 37th Mass. Vols., Burkes Station, VA, dated <u>13 April, 1865</u>.
20. Samuel E. Nichols to William R. Richardson–headquarters 37th Mass. Vols., dated <u>18 April, 1865</u>.
21. William Morrill to uncle, William Richardson–camp of the 37th Mass. Vols., near Alexandria, VA, dated <u>7 June, 1865</u>.

Author note: The letter of primary interest is #19, William C. Morrill to cousin, Mary Richardson, camp of the 37th Mass. Vols., Burkes Station, VA, dated April 13, 1865. The following is a typescript of this original letter with some ending editorial comments by the transcriber, Charles Hiram Thayer. The author has a photocopy of both this original letter and the typescript transcription by Charles Hiram Thayer. The author has carefully compared these two documents. They are identical in word content.

Evidence:

Camp of the 37th Mass. Vols, Burkes Station, VA, Apr. 13, 1865
From Wm. C. Morrill to Mary,

Dear Mary,
 After a series of hard marches and quite a good deal of fighting we have a day of leisure. Since I last wrote you we have been on the go most of the time. The last week we were in camp we were stirring nearly every day to make the Rebs think there was something going on with us. We had been under orders to be ready to move at a moments notice for some time. In night of the 31st of March we were ordered to pack up soon after dark. Tin cups and plates were to be put inside the haversacks so they could make no noise and we were to leave camp with loaded guns and bayonets fixed. This we all thought looked very much like charging the enemy's works. But the order was countermanded and we went back to quarters at midnight. But the night of the 1st of April (SA 360) got the same orders and go we did. The result of the charge made by the 6th Corps was the most glorious of the war. The 37th charged a Fort, took two guns and a stand of colors. Lost three officers and forty enlisted men killed and wounded. After forming our lines we moved down to the left inside the Reb works driving everything before us. They left in a great hurry. (SA 362) We found in passing one tent hot biscuits just cooked but they had not eaten them so several of us officers had a Reb lunch after our mornings work. After sweeping down to the left some three or four miles we faced about and shaped our course for Petersburg. After some skirmishing the darkness of night found two Divisions of the 6th Corps in the rear of the city while the 9th Corps and part of the 6th was knocking on the front door–such was the state of things at dark. During the night the Rebs evacuated and Petersburg was ours. I was on the skirmish line all night and among the first to advance in the morning. When we got up to the line occupied by the enemy the night before we were met by the mayor of the city under flag of truce who wished to surrender the city to some general officer. Had it not been for this delay our line would have been the

first to enter the city. As it was the 9th Corps men were first in. By order of Genl. Edwards, Capt. Gray and myself took what men we had out with us and went into the city and done patrol duty for a while. Soon after the Regt. Joined us. Soon got orders to join the Corps and night found us far away after Genl. Lee's retreating army. The 4th and 5th had good evidence that we were hard after him—heard that Genl. Sheridan had captured quite a number of guns, also a large wagon train. The morning of the 6th could hear the booming of our cannon said to be shelling the wagon train as it retreated. (SA 370) Soon after noon we could see them on the go near Rice's Station. We engaged their rear-guard and took some of their wagons. Then we formed a line of battle and advanced. After going half a mile or more found the Rebl Genl. Ewell with his corps massed in some pines. Our cannon got into position and shelled them a while, when we got orders to move forward. We all knew what was before us but went in with a steady step and fixed determination to conquer or die. This was the most desperate fighting the Regt. Ever had—some of our men were killed with the bayonet—indeed it could be called hand to hand fighting. But the day was won by the brave men of the 6th Corps. Our loss in this engagement was three officers and forty men. We were able to keep such a murderous fire with our Spencer rifles that those in our front could not stand up and fight us much. One great reason why our loss was so light—those who got up to fight the seven shooters were soon cut down. After the fight I had some conversation with a Reb Capt. He was very much surprised to find that we had but one line of battle—said he had never been under such a fire in his life. His leg was mangled by one of our shells before our infty got engaged so he was on the ground during the whole fight. During the fight one of my men captured Major Genl. Custis Lee, a son of R. E. Lee's. I presume if Henry Richardson is back with Genl. Ewell he is a prisoner as Ewell and staff was captured by the 5th Wisconsin of our Brigade. The morning of the 2d when we took the Fort I lost my sword and revolver which cost me forty two (42) dollars. I now wear the one which I took from Maj. Genl. Lee—am quite well pleased with the exchange. Have been quite well since left camp, but a little cold. Could write more had I time to do so. Write soon.

W. C. Morrill, 1st Lt. Co. E., 37th Mass.

P.S. I think we shall start for Danville soon, as we are to draw eight days rations. W. C. M.

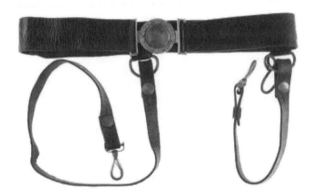

Morrill's quote, "I now wear the one which I took from Maj. Genl. Lee, am quite well pleased with the exchange," could be referring to William Morrill taking Custis Lee's single (one) sword belt, like the confederate example to the left, which could have had attached two items, Custis Lee's sword with a scabbard and his revolver in a leather holster.

Author Note: Custis Lee had at least one experience of being armed with a revolver during the Civil War. In her diary entry dated September 10, 1863, Mary Boykin Chesnut recorded the following; *"Custis Lee and my husband [James Chesnut Jr.] loaded their pistols, and the President [Jefferson Davis] drove off in Dr. Garnett's carriage, my husband and Custis Lee on horseback alongside him."* **[Source: "A Diary from Dixie, as written by Mary Boykin Chesnut, wife of James Chesnut Jr., United States Senator from South Carolina, 1859-1861, and afterward an Aide to Jefferson Davis and a Brigadier General in the Confederate Army", edited by Isabella D. Martin and Myrta Lockett Avary; D. Appleton and Company, NY, 1905]**Manuscript 197**** It can be inferred from this diary entry that Custis Lee was accustomed to carrying his revolver when he was engaged in a military operation or a hazardous mission, such as the one mentioned above. If he was accustomed to carrying his revolver, then it is highly likely that Custis Lee was armed with it when he was captured by David White and William C. Morrill at the Battle of Sailor's Creek.

William C. Morrill Letter Dated April 13, 1865 to his cousin Mary Richardson:

(PHOTOS: COURTESY CHARLES W. THAYER)

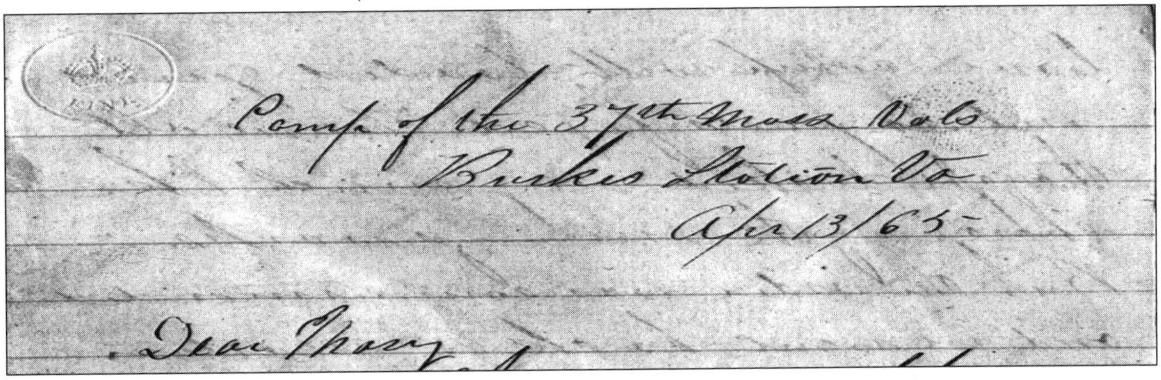

Camp of the 37th Mass Vols
Burkes Station Va
Apr 13/65

Dear Mary

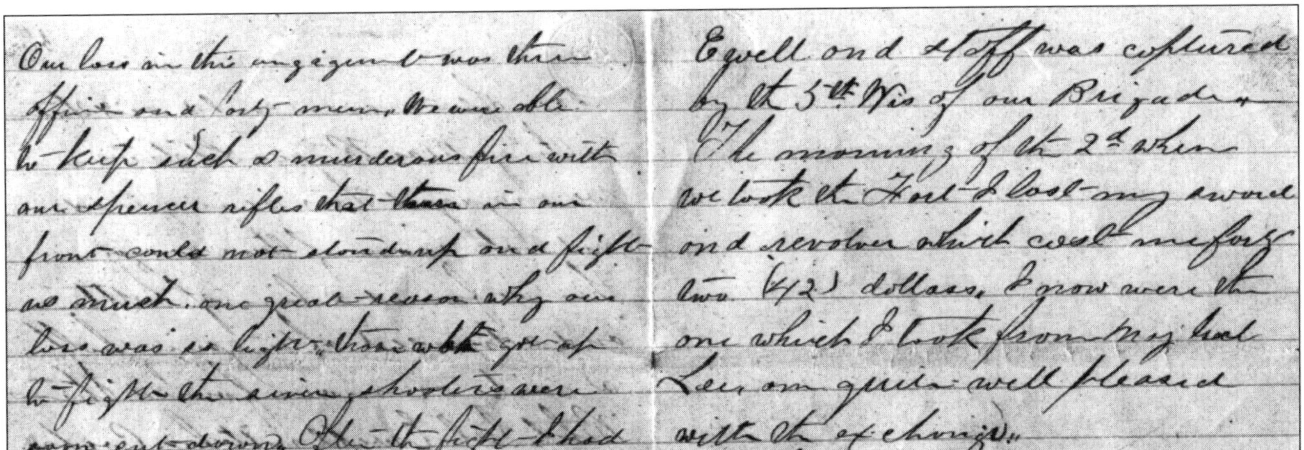

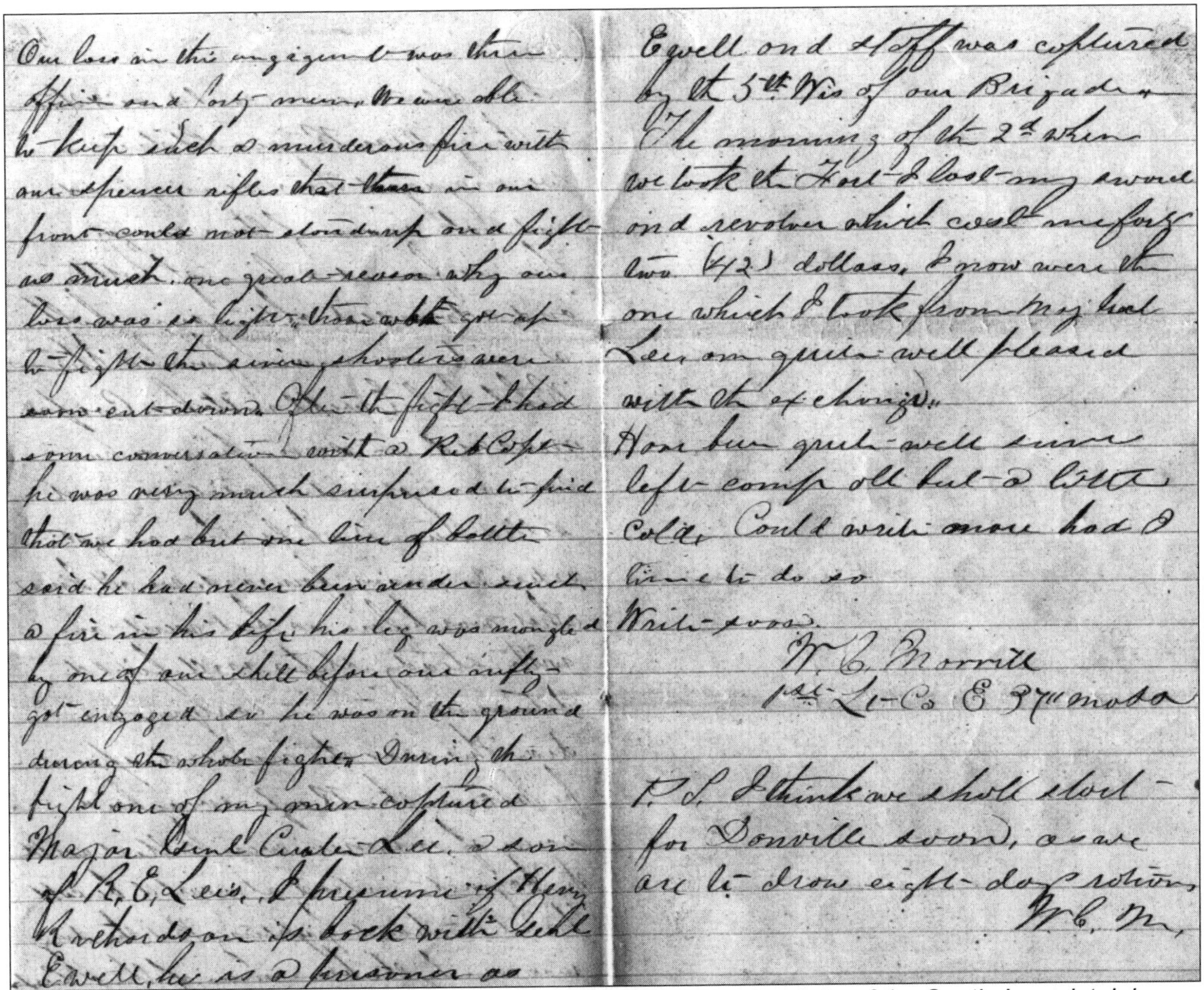

Our loss in this engagement was three officers and forty men. We were able to keep such a murderous fire with our Spencer rifles that those in our front could not stand up and fight as much. one great reason why our loss was so light, those who got up to fight the rising shooters were soon cut down. After the fight I had some conversation with a Reb Capt. he was very much surprised to find that we had but one line of battle said he had never been under such a fire in his life. his leg was mangled by one of our shells before our infantry got engaged so he was on the ground during the whole fight. During the fight one of my men captured Major Genl Custis Lee, a son of R. E. Lee's. I presume if Henry Richardson is back with Genl Ewell, he is a prisoner as Ewell and staff was captured by the 5th Wis of our Brigade.

The morning of the 2d when we took the Fort I lost my sword and revolver which cost me forty two (42) dollars, I now wear the one which I took from Maj Genl Lee. am quite well pleased with the exchange.

Have been quite well since I left camp all but a little cold. Could write more had I time to do so.

Write soon.

W. C. Morrill
1st Lt Co E 37th Mass

P.S. I think we shall start for Danville soon, as we are to draw eight days rations
W. C. M.

*****The original of the foregoing letter, which establishes the authenticity of the Custis Lee pistol, is now (1962) in our safe deposit box at the First National Bank of Amherst. There are 5 photographic copies of this letter in our home safe. Dr. C. H. Toll of Amherst College said on reading the letter: "Strange! Here he was within four days and a few miles of Appomattox, and he does not mention Lee's surrender." It would appear from the letter that Morrill's writing time was cut short. The best understanding of the Battle of Sailor's Creek, the last and fiercest battle of the 37th Mass., will be obtained from Burke Davis' book, TO APPOMATTOX: NINE APRIL DAYS. The story of April 6 gives* *details of the fight and makes clear (page 225) why, though he was captured by a corporal of Co. E, 37th Mass., Custis Lee surrendered to the company commander, Lieut. Morrill.*

From: Burke Davis To: C. H. T.
Colonial Williamsburg, Williamsburg, VA, 11 Nov. 1960.

Dear Mr. Thayer:
I was thrilled to get the copy of the letter from you; I only wish it had come to me before I turned loose my Appomattox manuscript. It's a fine letter…. The pistol you have, which must mean much to you, is one of the really fine relics of the war. I wonder that your family doesn't plan to deposit it some day in some appropriate museum

[Source: Original handwritten letters by William C. Morrill in the possession of Charles W. Thayer]**Manuscript 28**

Comments & Supporting Evidence:

1. The author discovered this concise write-up on the nature of Civil War letters. This write-up gives a good background on Civil War letters and provides a good context for the William Morrill Civil War letters contained in this section.

Letters Home:

Most Civil War soldiers were not widely traveled before they joined the army. Leaving their families behind, they entered a strange new life far from home and loved ones. Homesickness was a common ailment for blue and gray soldiers throughout the war, and the only direct contact with home available to most men was through letter writing. The Civil War caused the largest outpouring of letter writing in American history. Each day, 90,000 letters passed through Washington, DC, with twice that number going through Louisville, KY, for the Union armies in the West. The newly formed Confederate postal service appropriated existing federal routes and offices and utilized many of the same postmasters. Service was uncertain in the North as well as in the South, but grew especially bad in the South near the end of the war. Stationery also became scarce in the South, and soldiers wrote letters on almost any type of paper, but they preferred proper writing paper. Many varieties of stationery were marketed to the Union and Confederate soldiers; most were decorated with eagles, flags, or other patriotic symbols.

2. William Morrill's letter dated April 13, 1865, is extremely important and offers independent corroboration of the David White account by the soldier (Morrill) most directly involved in the incident. The statement in Morrill's letter, "During the fight one of my men captured Major Genl. Custis Lee, a son of R. E. Lee's," surely is a reference to David Dunnells White as the man responsible for the capture. It is very important to note that Morrill himself does not claim the capture of Major General Custis Lee, but credits it to one of his men.

3. The next statement in William Morrill's letter to his cousin, Mary Richardson, is of equal importance: "The morning of the 2d when we took the fort (Fisher at Petersburg, VA), I lost my sword and revolver which cost me forty two (42) dollars. I now wear the one which I took from Maj. Genl. Lee—am quite well pleased with the exchange." This event is validated by Captain Archibald Hopkins, commanding the 37th Massachusetts, in his Official Report dated April 2, 1865, where he states, "At the word of command the regiment advanced rapidly with a cheer, forced their way through two (2) lines of abatis over the ditch and into the enemy's fort … the rapid advance through the abatis facing a brief but sharp conflict." This is the exact spot where Morrill must have snagged his belt and lost his sword and revolver. Where Morrill states that he lost two items (his sword and revolver), he also states, "I now wear the one which I took from Maj. Genl. Lee." The most probable explanation to reconcile this "two to one" language discrepancy is that Morrill lost his "one belt" containing his sword and revolver and now wears the "one belt" of Custis Lee's, which also contained Custis Lee's sword and revolver. If this is true, it substantiates the Thayer family claim that Charles W. Thayer is now in the possession of the Custis Lee revolver and corroborates nicely the David White account of the capture of Custis Lee and Lt. William Morrill's involvement in that capture.

4. The following are photographs of the revolver in the possession of Charles W. Thayer, which is claimed by the Thayer family to be the revolver of General C. W. Custis Lee taken by Morrill at the Battle of Sailor's Creek. It is worth noting that this Rigdon-Ansley revolver has the serial number 1763, which is a perfect match both by way of date of manufacture and the manufacturer itself, with a revolver that Custis Lee could have had in his possession on April 6, 1865.

REVOLVER OF MAJOR GENERAL CUSTIS LEE:
(PHOTOS: COURTESY CHARLES W. THAYER)

Author Note: It should be noted that the author is aware of one other revolver that is alleged to belong to Custis Lee. It is a Model 1851 Colt Navy and legend has it that it was given to Custis Lee by his father after Custis graduated West Point. [**Source: "The Colt Engraving Book"; V-1, by R. L. Wilson, Bannerman's Publishing, NY]**Manuscript 190** This was probably Custis Lee's "dress" pistol. Custis Lee's father, Robert E. Lee, also had a Model 1851 Colt Navy and this is currently in the Museum of the Confederacy." The pistol depicted here was probably Custis Lee's Confederate made "field pistol," purchased in 1864 during his field command in the defense of Richmond.

EVIDENCE OVERVIEW
EXHIBITS-W-BN-(1-5)

The purpose of introducing this line of evidence is to bring to light some important eyewitness testimony from Mr. Buzz Newell, deceased, and formally of Leeds, MA. In addition, testimony is provided by Mr. Jim Parsons of Leeds, MA, concerning the factual nature and reliability of Buzz Newell's eye-witness testimony.

EXHIBIT-W-BN-1

Introduction:

Buzz Newell:
(PHOTO: COURTESY THE LATE JIM PARSONS)

The author came in contact with a Mr. Buzz Newell in 1995, having been referred to him as a Civil War authority and an expert on Northampton, MA, local history. While the author was inquiring about the role of Northampton, MA, troops in the Civil War, Mr. Newell related to the author that he personally observed the Custis Lee sword in the "old" G. A. R. Museum in Northampton, MA. Shortly after this telephone conversation with Mr. Newell, he was diagnosed to be terminally ill with cancer. The author created response letters for Mr. Newell so that his observations of the Custis Lee sword could be documented for this work. It should be noted that the following response letters were completed by Mr. Newell when he was ill and battling the disease. The author created a checklist format for these response letters to facilitate an easy reply by Mr. Newell given his delicate health condition. His statements are attested to be true and accurate, to the best of his knowledge, by his own signature.

Evidence:

LETTER ONE: *May 18, 1995, To: Mr. Buzz Newell, Leeds, MA*

Dear Buzz,

I hope that this letter is finding you well and in good spirits. Buzz, I am about to publish an article entitled, "The Battle of Sailor's Creek: The Capture of George Washington Custis Lee." I believe that it will be a very informative and interesting article and I plan on sending you a copy when it is finished.

I would like to use information that you provided me over the telephone in the article. I am hoping that I have the major points correct and I have listed them below:

1. *When you were a young man, you used to regularly visit a G. A. R. Hall in Northampton, Massachusetts.*
2. *While visiting this G. A. R. Hall on its many occasions, you observed the sword of George Washington Custis Lee.*
3. *The sword was in a glass case with many other swords from the Civil War period.*
4. *You knew that it was the sword of George Washington Custis Lee because it was labeled as such.*
5. *At this time, you were developing an active interest in the Civil War so you were paying keen interest to such detail.*
6. *When the G. A. R. Hall closed, the exact location of the Custis Lee sword became unknown to you.*

Buzz, I would be <u>deeply appreciate</u> if you would acknowledge that I have these facts correct. It is these facts that I would like to use in my article. If you feel up to it, Buzz, could you please sign this letter below acknowledging these facts to be true and return it to me in the self-addressed, stamped envelope. I will be going to "press" shortly.

<u>Thank you</u> for your time and consideration of this matter, Buzz.

Warmest Regards,

From: Frank White

Signed: <u>Buzz Newell </u>(Original Signature)

LETTER TWO: *May 31, 1995, To: Mr. Buzz Newell, Leeds, MA*

Dear Buzz,

Thank you so <u>very</u> much for responding to my last letter, it was deeply appreciated! Buzz, this is the <u>last time</u> that I will trouble you with this matter. I could, however, use your help to clarify my last letter. Please put a check next to each box that is true and correct:

RECOLLECTION OF SWORD: *(check one that applies)*

- ☐   *I can recall "<u>exactly and precisely</u>" what the Custis Lee sword looked like.*
- ☒   *I can recall "<u>somewhat</u>" what the Custis Lee sword looked like.*
- ☐   *I can recall "<u>vaguely</u>" what the Custis Lee sword looked like.*

NATURE OF SWORD: *(check one that applies)*

- ☒   *The Custis Lee sword <u>was</u> a presentation sword.*
- ☐   *The Custis Lee sword <u>was not</u> a presentation sword.*
- ☐   *Not sure.*

MODEL AND/OR MANUFACTURER OF SWORD: *(check one that applies)*

- ☐   *I <u>can recall</u> the exact model and/or manufacturer of the Custis Lee sword.*
- ☐   *I <u>cannot recall</u> the exact model and/or manufacturer of the Custis Lee sword.*
- ☒   *I never committed this information to memory.*

SWORD INSCRIPTION: *(check one that applies)*

- ☐   *The sword <u>was</u> inscribed with the name of Custis Lee.*
- ☐   *The sword <u>was</u> inscribed with the name of Custis Lee <u>and</u> I can <u>recall</u> the exact location of the inscription on the sword.*
- ☐   *The sword <u>was not</u> inscribed with the name of Custis Lee.*
- ☒   *Not sure.*

SCABBARD: (check one that applies)

- ☐ *When in the G. A. R. Hall, the sword <u>was with</u> a scabbard <u>which was</u> inscribed with the name of Custis Lee.*
- ☐ *When in the G. A. R. Hall, the sword <u>was with</u> a scabbard <u>which was not</u> inscribed with the name of Custis Lee.*
- ☐ *When in the G. A. R. Hall, the sword <u>was not with</u> a scabbard.*
- ☒ *Not sure.*

CERTAINTY: (check one that applies)

- ☒ *I am <u>100%</u> certain that I saw the actual sword of General George Washington Custis Lee in the G. A. R. Hall in Northampton, Massachusetts.*
- ☐ *I am <u>somewhat</u> certain that I saw the actual sword of General George Washington Custis Lee in the G. A. R. Hall in Northampton, Massachusetts.*

YEAR: (Please fill in)

The approximate year I observed the Custis Lee sword in the Northampton, Massachusetts, G. A. R. Hall was <u>last time 1947</u> (**Author note:** filled in by Buzz Newell)

Thank you, Buzz, for taking the time to complete the checklist. Your knowledge in this area will be of great historical importance. My very warmest regards.

Sincerely, From: Frank White

Acknowledged to be true and correct:

Signed: <u>Buzz Newell</u> (Original Signature)

[Source: An affidavit and letter signed by the late Mr. Buzz Newell of Leeds, MA]**Manuscript 29**

Comments & Supporting Evidence:

1. If Mr. Buzz Newell did in fact see the Custis Lee sword in the "old" G. A. R. Museum in Northampton, MA, this most likely would indicate a strong connection to the 37th Massachusetts which had many soldiers who enlisted from this area and perhaps the Abbott family of Northampton, MA.

2. According to Harriett Richardson's letter dated May 26, 1897, as found in Exhibit W–PF–14, she states that some years earlier William Morrill authorized that the Custis Lee sword be given to Frank Abbott, brother of Hubbard Abbott of Northampton, MA. By the tone of this letter, it would sound like Harriett Richardson was familiar with Hubbard Abbott, but not necessarily Frank Abbott. This could be explained by the fact that William Frank Abbott moved from the Northampton/Hockanum area a few years after the Civil War according to his pension file. William Frank Abbott lived in the following areas: 1865–1869: South Hadley, MA; 1869–1874: Andover, MA; 1874–1879: Chelsea, MA; 1879–1844: Neponset, MA; 1884–1886: Milton Lower Mills, MA; 1886–1889: Lynn, MA; and 1889–1912: Boston, MA **[Source: Military Pension File of William Frank Abbott, National Archives, Washington, DC]**Manuscript 52**** Hubbard Abbott, however, lived in Northampton, MA, all of his life after returning from the Civil War. Since Harriett was living in Hockanum, MA, which is in close proximity to Northampton, Hubbard Abbott could have been familiar to her, hence her language, "Frank Abbott, brother of Hubbard Abbott of Northampton, Mass."

3. Thayer family tradition, as relayed by Charles Hiram Thayer, has two of Morrill's Civil War buddies visiting the Hockanum farm in the year 1888 to pick up the Custis Lee sword from the Richardson family. One of these buddies could have been William Frank Abbott. If the year 1888 is correct, William Frank Abbott would have been living in Lynn or Boston, MA, according to his pension record, when he visited Hockanum to pick up the Custis Lee sword. Since the sword was never returned to the Richardson family, one would assume that William Frank Abbott held on to it. Even though the intent was to donate it to a museum when it was given to William Frank Abbott, according to Thayer family tradition, it must not have made its way into the G. A. R. Northampton Museum before 1897. If it had, Hubbard Abbott, in his testimony dated July 9, 1897, as found in Exhibit W–PF–18, surely would have mentioned this fact. Being a prominent citizen of Northampton and a member of the 37th Massachusetts Volunteers Association (Treasurer, 1896–

1897), surely he would have belonged to the local Northampton G. A. R. He would have known if his brother had deposited the Custis Lee sword in this local Northampton G. A. R. Museum between the years 1888–1897. All that Hubbard Abbott states about the sword and belt in his July 9, 1897, testimony is, "The sword and belt were in the possession of Lt. Morrill until his death." William Morrill died on January, 29 1892, at the age of 51 in Rochester, NY. This statement made by Hubbard Abbott would indicate that he was not aware that his brother, William Frank Abbott, picked up the Custis Lee sword from the Richardson family in the year 1888 for a Grand Army celebration (this is assuming that this 1888 date is accurate as recorded in the Thayer family documents).

4. If Buzz Newell did see the Custis Lee sword in the "old" G. A. R. Museum in Northampton, MA, he would have seen it starting somewhere in the 1930's ending with the year 1947. Buzz Newell was born on January 27, 1922 and he states that he took an active interest in the holdings of the museum when he was a young boy, most likely in the 1930's. He also states that the last time he saw the Custis Lee sword was in 1947. This would mean that the Custis Lee sword could have been donated to the "old" G. A. R. Museum in Northampton between 1897 (when Hubbard Abbott of Northampton, MA, testified in the 37th Massachusetts Protest Case and apparently did not know where the Custis Lee sword was) and the 1930's when Buzz Newell allegedly began to observe it. Perhaps it was given to the Northampton "old" G. A. R. Museum at the death of William Frank Abbott in Boston in 1914, with William Frank Abbott most likely being in possession of it after he obtained it from Harriett Richardson in 1888. **[Source: William F. Abbott Probate File, # 167460, Suffolk County, MA]**Manuscript 53**** This could have been done directly by his heirs; or it could have been given to his brother Hubbard Abbott of Northampton, who then donated it to the Northampton G. A. R. at some point in time before his death. Hubbard Abbott died in Northampton, MA, on September 20, 1929, according to his death record on file at the Northampton, MA, City Clerk's office.

EXHIBIT-W-BN-2

Introduction:

Jim Parsons:
(PHOTO: COURTESY THE LATE JIM PARSONS)

The late Mr. Jim Parsons was a renowned local historian of the Northampton, MA, area and was a life-long resident of the Leeds, MA, area. Mr. Parsons was born July 14, 1930, and passed away July 4, 2006. Mr. Parsons had a close personal relationship with Buzz Newell for many years. Mr. Newell was also a long time resident of the Leeds, MA, area. The following are notes from a telephone interview with Mr. Parsons conducted by the author after making Jim's acquaintance in the year 1996.

Evidence:

March 12, 1997
Telephone Interview with Jim Parsons:

- *Memorial Hall in Northampton, Massachusetts, was built as a tribute to Civil War veterans*

- *First occupied by the G. A. R. and the G. A. R. occupied the meeting rooms. Then by the Clark Library (first real library of Northampton—Clark got absorbed by the Forbes Library when it was built in 1896)*
- *Northampton Historical Society came into existence 1910–1920 and shared Memorial Hall with the dwindling G. A. R.*
- *G. A. R. most likely had their own military collection but it was slowly but surely turned over to the Historical Society Museum when the G. A. R. dwindled away. The Historical Society also collected a lot of World War I and II stuff.*
- *Mrs. Shepherd was the director of the Historical Society while Mary Persis Crafts worked it day to day*
- *The Historical Society also came into the ownership of the Historical houses they have today*
- *In the 1970's, when Mary Persis Crafts passed way, the museum collections were moved from Memorial Hall into the current historic houses; a lot of stuff got legs at this time—the historic houses now have a very minor Civil War collection*
- *The Forbes Library also has some Civil War stuff donated but turned it over to the Historical Society*
- *Buzz would have seen the George Washington Custis Lee sword in the Historical Society Museum*

[Source: A telephone interview conducted with Mr. Jim Parsons of Leeds, MA, by the author dated March 12, 1997]**Manuscript 30**

Comments & Supporting Evidence:

Mr. Parsons' interview notes have several important points as follows:

1. Jim Parsons provides a detailed lineage of the museum in which Buzz Newell claims to have seen the Custis Lee sword.
2. A quick summary of this museum lineage is:
   A. Memorial Hall was built in the 1800's after the Civil War as a tribute to the veterans of that war
   B. It was shared by the G. A. R. and Northampton Historical Society in the years 1910's – 1920's
   C. The G. A. R. Museum got absorbed by the Northampton Historical Society Museum when the G. A. R. members started to dwindle and pass away
   D. Buzz would have seen the George Washington Custis Lee sword in the Memorial Hall Northampton Historical Society Museum in the 1930's–1947 (which was formally the "old" G. A. R. Museum).

EXHIBIT-W-BN-3

Introduction:

This is another interview conducted by the author with Mr. Jim Parsons of Leeds, MA. This interview is insightful and substantiates the fact that Mr. Buzz Newell claimed to have seen the sword of Custis Lee in Northampton, MA.

Evidence:

An Interview Conducted with Jims Parsons of Leeds, MA, on May 30, 1996, by the Author

Frank
White:
Jim, I understand that you have a knowledge of the Custis Lee sword at one time being in Northampton, Massachusetts. I recognize that your knowledge comes from conversations that you had with Mr. Raymond "Buzz" Newell, also of your town of Leeds, Massachusetts. Would you mind telling me about your conversations, your knowledge of the Custis Lee sword, where it was in Northampton and anything more about it?

| Jim Parsons: | Sure, Frank. In Northampton we had and still do have a very extensive museum. But at the time of the Custis Lee sword being here, it was located in Memorial Hall in a very hard-to-access museum on the third floor, a place I want to show you sometime and test what kind of shape you're in. But that place was once very popular with high schoolers, and I went in there regularly with friends just to see some of the variety of materials that were there. I was familiar with the various Civil War artifacts, but not sufficiently educated at the time as to the importance of individuals. So, if the Custis Lee sword was there, I certainly saw it, but I wasn't aware of its significance at the time. Well, in recent years I have become great friends with Buzz Newell. Buzz Newell has been regarded for many, many years as the individual who knows the most about the Civil War in our area. He was one of those who was responsible for the creation of various reenactment groups here. He was once with the 10th Massachusetts and then he formed a complete regiment made up of Masons and former Masons, because there were Masonic regiments as well. He did a great deal of lecturing around in his full regalia; he had an extensive collection himself in weaponry of all kinds, though not limited to the Civil War, but he was a weapons collector for many, many years and had a diversified collection of weapons. Well, Buzz used to have the answer whenever I had a question. I'd like to think of myself as a student, not an expert, but a student of the Civil War. I enjoy it. Whenever I had a question that seems to be unanswerable in my immediate sources, I'd go to Buzz and I could always be sure that Buzz would be able (1) to answer the question or (2) point me in the right direction and (3) possibly give me the material to look it up in. All those things. In the case of the Custis Lee sword (do you want me to just ramble on). In the case of the Custis Lee sword, when I first heard of the fact that it was indeed taken by a member of the 37th Mass., I have a special interest in the 37th Mass. because it had more of the young men from Northampton than even the 10th, which is referred to as Northampton's "own" regiment. And I have friends whose ancestors fought in the Civil War with the 37th. So when I heard the story of the capture of the Custis Lee sword, it was of particular interest to me and I wanted to get the details as I could from Buzz Newell. I sat down with Buzz and Buzz's memory has been as near infallible as most of us are ever likely to be. When it comes to issues regarding the Civil War, it would be a rare instance when I would look up a fact that had been conveyed to me by Buzz and find it would be inaccurate in some way. He's very, very good. Regarding his memory of the Custis Lee sword, he was, first of all, a young man very much interested in history in general. As an example of that I want to repeat what I said to you earlier, that he used to go to the area of the Quabbin Reservoir where towns of Enfield and three or four towns there were destroyed to become the Quabbin Reservoir. He went there and talked with people as they were dismantling the buildings; and he accumulated swords and weapons and special kinds of furniture, things that people were simply pitching out and he ended up with a large cache of all these items. His father then drove him over with their hearse, and he picked up all these items and brought them back to Northampton where he collected them. At any rate, that gives you an idea that his interest was not simply a flash in the pan, but something he was always involved with. One of the items that he did do related to the 37th Mass., he was the driving force behind the Samuel Eddy reenactment that we had here back in '82 when Samuel Eddy, also of the 37th, was recognized for having been given the Medal of Honor. Well, getting back to Custis Lee, Buzz explained to me that he used to be a regular visitor to the museum in |

Northampton and in there they had a very special collection from the Civil War period, including the sword of Custis Lee. And he remembered it in detail, its specific location and the various special display cases that were there. I know, I recall these and after all these years, where these swords were, but <u>what</u> they were and the <u>significance</u> of them I really didn't know at that time. But the area where they were located, Buzz confirmed as the spot where, indeed, the Custis Lee sword was located. And what happened to it, Buzz seems to feel that the Custis Lee sword left when we lost some other artifacts. It was one of the things that happened during the time when the lady who administered the museum at Memorial Hall passed on and there was a period of no security whatsoever and things disappeared. And it may have been at that time, but at any rate that sword, as well as others disappeared. For example I just showed you a picture of Col. Parsons up here. His sword suddenly surfaced in Hartford, Connecticut. I think I mentioned to you that another sword that was there surfaced in a catalog in New York. Buzz has the actual ad for the sword that belonged to the Reverend Enoch Hale, who was Nathan Hale's brother and lived just a few miles from where we are sitting. So, that seems to be the circumstance of its leaving there. From my point of view, I'm going to be giving some time to trying to find the actual card that Mary Persis Craft had.

Accession Cards and Museum Exhibit Labels by Mary Persis Crafts:
Ms. Crafts created these as curator of the now defunct museum that was
in Memorial Hall, Northampton, MA.

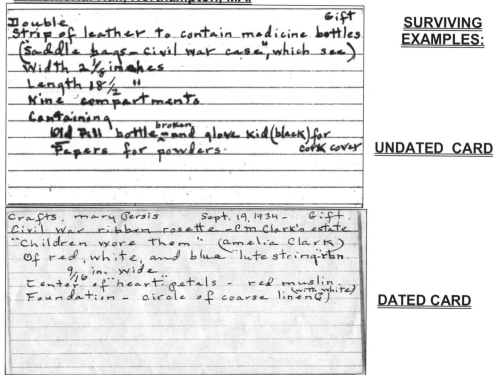

SURVIVING EXAMPLES:

UNDATED CARD

DATED CARD

Author note (2007): Marie Panik, curator for the Northampton Historical Society, Northampton, Massachusetts, also known today as Historic Northampton, has identified this handwriting as belonging to Mary Persis Crafts. Ms. Panik is unable, in most cases, to determine the exact date that Ms. Crafts created these cards and labels. According to Ms. Panik, they have only a few cards and labels that survive today from the Civil War period.

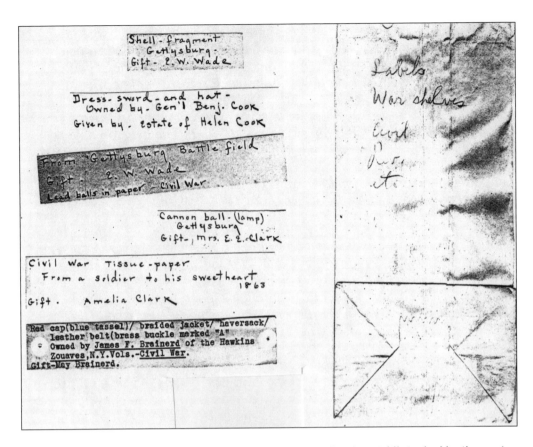

Shell - fragment
Gettysburg.
Gift - E. W. Wade

Dress - sword - and - hat -
Owned by - Gen'l Benj. Cook
Given by - Estate of Helen Cook

From Gettysburg Battle field
Gift - E. W. Wade
Lead balls in paper - Civil War

Cannon ball - (lamp)
Gettysburg
Gift - mrs. E. E. Clark

Civil War Tissue - paper
From a soldier to his sweetheart
1863
Gift - Amelia Clark

Red cap(blue tassel)/ braided jacket/ haversack/
leather belt(brass buckle marked "A"
Owned by James F. Brainerd of the Hawkins
Zouaves, N.Y.Vols.—Civil War.
Gift-May Brainerd.

Labels
War shelves
Civil
War
etc

We have a large collection still of wonderful militaria at Historic Northampton including "Fighting Joe" Hooker's sword, much to the dismay of the Hadley people, but the Custis Lee sword is not there. What I'm hoping is that the cards are still among the records which were transferred from the Memorial Hall to our present location, among those original accession cards of Mary Persis Crafts.

Frank White:
I think that kind of brings it up to date. Jim, why would Buzz Newell be so interested in the Custis Lee sword that he would commit this fact to memory and be able to remember it in such a vivid fashion many years later?

Jim Parsons:
It's his nature. First of all, there are certain areas I have strength in terms of memory. One of them is not in recalling dates, and specific numbers associated with regiments, certain groups or phases of battles and that's not like him; he does like facts. And, consequently, when he talks about a specific activity in the Civil War, you'll hear a sprinkling of dates and numbers and it is just something he is innately interested in. An advance indication was when they were building the Quabbin, that he would go over there at that time and it was just his nature to be interested in military items of all sorts. And, again by way of his credibility; I should mention once again that his military collection includes a pistol, a presentation pistol to James Braman of the 10th Massachusetts, Company C, who was killed at Fair Oaks, and he was the first man killed in the Northampton group of the 10th. Buzz was at a collector's show in Long Island at least 25 years ago when he heard of a Northampton pistol being there. He went over to look at it and sure enough, it was the one presented to James Braman, the very weapon that had been presented to James before he went off to the war. He did acquire it. He still has it. He has taken its provenance beyond imagination; the detail he has on it. He has fired

it over James Braman's grave; he has dismantled it and restored it so it is in perfect working condition. He is very precise. His other activities include being a nationally recognized judge in antique automobiles. I have an antique car out in the garage here. When I had trouble with the motor, Buzz came down, took the book, glanced through it, and overhauled the motor to get that thing working like the clock it is today. So, he is a very precise, very accurate with an incredibly retentive mind when he is committed. As he put it, when he was restoring his Cadillac, it very nearly gained him a Cadillac and lost him a wife!

Frank White: *Jim, can you address the fact of why we are unable to interview Buzz Newell on the Custis Lee sword directly today, which is May 30, 1996?*

Jim Parsons: *Yes, unfortunately, I am able to tell you why. Buzz was always a man who enjoyed robust health which allowed him to pursue the many, many interests he had; whether it be the weaponry, the Civil War, or antique autos. He was stricken with cancer a couple years ago, and he has been waging a battle against it ever since. And it seems to go through a period of remission when things are going fine and then, bang, he's hit with another resurgence of it and it really demoralizes him. He thinks he has it licked, and what has happened here since this thing resurfaces, he feels so defeated by it. He's really lost a great deal of his interest in the Civil War, in fact, in virtually all the activities he enjoyed before. And he talks about giving away or getting rid of all those things that were part of his interest. I hope it's not a sign that he's giving up, but he just in the past couple of weeks called me to tell me that he had some material for me and that he had to go in for some more work because there had been some bad results from some blood tests that he had. So, essentially, that's it. I wouldn't approach him today on any area where he, I think, feels a little regretful about it, regretful in a sense that he no longer has the same interest. It's almost as if there is a preliminary lost.*

Frank White: *Great. Thank you. This concludes the interview with Jim Parsons.*

Attested to be true and correct to the best of my knowledge and recollections.
Signed: Jim Parsons (original signature)   *Dated June 12, 1996*

[Source: An "in-person" interview with Mr. Jim Parsons of Leeds, MA, by the author dated May 30, 1996, with the original transcription currently in the possession of the author]**Manuscript 31**

Comments & Supporting Evidence:

The important points from this interview are as follows:

1. This piece of evidence goes to substantiating the credibility of Mr. Buzz Newell and his assertion that he saw the sword of General Custis Lee in the "old" G. A. R. or Northampton Historical Society museum in Memorial Hall, Northampton, MA.
2. Not only has Mr. Buzz Newell made the assertion of seeing the Custis Lee sword to the author, but he has also made the same assertion, for many years, to his close and long time friend, Mr. Jim Parsons.
3. Mr. Buzz Newell passed away on October 15, 1998, after fighting a long battle with cancer.
4. The author examined what currently survives of the Mary Persis Craft's accession cards and exhibit labels collected from the defunct museum that was in Memorial Hall, Northampton, MA. These extant cards and labels are archived at the Northampton Historical Society, Northampton, MA. The author was not able to find a card or label for the sword of Custis Lee.

EXHIBIT-W-BN-4

Introduction:

This is a letter from Jim Parsons of Leeds, MA, attesting again to the credibility of Mr. Buzz Newell and Buzz's knowledge of the Civil War and his interest in collecting Civil War arms.

Evidence:

May 12, 1997, To Whom It May Concern:

Raymond D. "Buzz" Newell is a life-long resident of Northampton, Massachusetts, where he has been a successful businessman in several enterprises. These include the operation of the largest funeral home in the community, an ambulance/limousine service, and a hardware business. Buzz is now 75 and been suffering with cancer for some years. As a consequence, he has had to curtail many of the activities related to his diverse interests and his business enterprises. Let me summarize areas where his expertise is recognized not only in this region but nationally. History was one of his loves from his earliest years. As a teenager he was attracted to the towns which were then being dismantled and now lie beneath the Quabbin Reservoir in western Massachusetts. He even rode his bicycle on occasion to the area where he acquired a wide variety of historical objects. These were stored in the home of a cooperative neighbor of the area until his father could drive there to retrieve the items. Among the artifacts collected during this period were ancient firearms and swords. It must have inspired Buzz because he developed a major collection of both, and an expertise in the field that brought him wide recognition. Concurrent with this teenage experience in the lost towns was his fascination with the splendid collections of the Northampton Historical Society which were housed in Memorial Hall whose main entrance is guarded by life-sized bronze statues of a soldier and sailor of the Civil War. The Memorial Hall Museum, which I also remember well, had a great military collection ranging from the Revolution to World War I. Buzz is nine years older than I so his visits there were in the 1930's while my visits were in the war and post-war years of the 40's. Unfortunately, the museum was the victim of losses due to theft after the death of its long-time curator, Mary Persis Crafts. Many irreplaceable items had disappeared by the time the collections were moved in their entirety to the present home of Historic Northampton, a complex of three contiguous historic houses on Bridge Street in Northampton. In the meantime, Buzz's interests continued to grow. He became a collector and expert in the field of antique automobiles with skills ranging the entire gamut from engine rebuilding to the restoration of bodies and interiors. His accomplishments in this area would be a lengthy report on its own. Buzz's great love was the study of the Civil War throughout his life. He was involved with the founding of the Tenth Mass. Volunteers re-enactment group in Northampton and as a leader in its activities for some years. He then formed the 39th Massachusetts Masonic Civil War Regiment which had forty members while Buzz was there to lead and inspire. He was also a frequent speaker in full Civil War uniform at schools, civic convocations, and patriotic events. Buzz Newell has served as my personal ultimate source in many of my activities as a local historian. My activities include numerous published articles, a book IMAGES OF AMERICA: Northampton published in the fall of 1996 by Arcadia Press, my role in the producing of the book WHEN THIS CRUEL WAR IS OVER (University of Massachusetts, 1992) and my several radio series. Some of my projects were the subject of a feature article in the March/April edition of Historic Preservation titled: "Every Town Needs a Jim Parsons." I cite my own background only to emphasize the special role as a resource that Buzz Newell has served for me and so many others in his knowledge of the Civil War and the regional regiments that took part. Among Buzz's most memorable achievement was the commemoration he organized in honor of Congressional Medal of Honor recipient Samuel E. Eddy of Chesterfield, Massachusetts. The event was held in September of 1982 in Eddy's home town. It should be mentioned at the outset that Sam Eddy received his medal for his courageous actions as a member of the 37th Mass. Volunteers in the Battle of Sayler's Creek, the Union victory in which Custis Lee surrendered his sword. Some highlights of this commemorative weekend: This event in 1982 brought together over fifty Congressional Medal of Honor winners, the largest grouping of medal winners to that time. Some important points are:

1. At Sayler's Creek, the Savannah Volunteer Guards surrendered their flag. Over forty members of the present day Savannah Guards attended this weekend. Their original flag from Sayler's Creek as returned to them at this time.
2. Some 600 members of artillery, cavalry and infantry units, representing seven states, took part in the battle re-enactment. Other highlights included a period ball and a memorial service in the Chesterfield Congregational Church. Two of the Medal of Honor winners group took a direct part in the impressive service.
3. Several descendants of Samuel Eddy were present and his actual Medal of Honor was on display.

This brief highlighting in no way does justice to the event which was two years in the planning but it was typical of the dedication that Buzz brought to every venture. It was also reflective of his incredible knowledge of the Civil War in general and Sayler's Creek in particular. Buzz has related to me on several occasions how he had been attracted to the Custis Lee sword in the displays of the Northampton Historical Society's Museum as a young man. His memory is keen; his recollections of facts have been flawless in all of my discussions with him. He is a striver for perfection in all of his activities whether it be the restoration of his 1928 Cadillac or in his breadth of Civil War knowledge. There is no doubt in my mind that Buzz Newell's recollection of the Custis Lee sword being in Northampton is accurate. His record of a lifetime speaks for itself.
James M. Parsons (original signature)

[Source: Letter from Jim Parsons to the author, dated May 12, 1997, the original letter is currently in the possession of the author]**Manuscript 32**

Comments & Supporting Evidence:

The important points are as follows:
1. This is a well-written and insightful letter by Mr. Jim Parsons. It demonstrates his close personal relationship with Buzz Newell through out the years.
2. This letter again underscores the fact that Buzz Newell would have visited the Northampton Historical Society Museum (the old G. A. R. Museum) in the 1930's in Memorial Hall.
3. This letter seeks to establish the credibility of Buzz Newell and his assertion that he saw the sword of George Washington Custis Lee.
4. It would appear that Buzz Newell was very knowledgeable and interested in the 37th Massachusetts and the Battle of Sailor's Creek. This is evidenced by his Herculean effort to organize, manage and promote the Samuel Eddy commemoration. This would explain his keen interest and steadfast memory of the Custis Lee sword being displayed in the Northampton, MA, Memorial Hall Museum. The author believes that Buzz Newell had no other motive for asserting that he saw the sword of Custis Lee, other than he was just stating what he knew to be true in an area that he had an extreme interest.

EXHIBIT-W-BN-5

Introduction:

This is a letter and photograph to show the depth of the holdings of the Northampton Historical Society, MA. The photograph and caption entitled, "Civil War Mementos on Exhibition," was printed in the Springfield, MA Daily News on January 23, 1961, for the Northampton Historical Society, MA.

Evidence: *August 3, 1932*

Dear Mrs. Shepherd:

I have many times been an interested visitor at your Historical Society. Having a large collection of Civil War relics, naturally I am most interested in your military exhibit. Now I have relics of all the wars our country has been engaged in—but am most interested in the Civil War and noticed that you have many duplicates as follows: Many bullets, two knapsacks, two wooden canteens. I have some cap boxes – bayonets, caps, etc. all of which your collection is lacking. I think it would be profitable, if we could make exchanges. Of course I would benefit—but the public would see a greater variety of the sort our grandfathers carried in the War of '61–'65. Yours Sincerely, Francis Lord

Civil War Mementos on Exhibition

NORTHAMPTON—Pictured are uniforms worn by Union soldiers during the Civil War, 1861-1865, on display in the rooms of the Northampton Historical Society in Memorial Hall. Mary Persis Crafts, curator of the society's collections, claims that the rifle shown was made at Harper's Ferry in 1833 and used by a Union soldier in the great war between the States. The rifle bears the insignia of the U. S. Army of the Potomac, consisting of an eagle. During the centennial anniversary of the Civil War this year, the society will have on display numerous relics and mementos given to it by relatives of men who served with the North.

Spfld. Daily News, Jan. 23, 1961

Northampton—Pictured are uniforms worn by Union soldiers during the Civil War, 1861-1865, on display in the rooms of the Northampton Historical Society in Memorial Hall. Mary Persis Crafts, curator of the society's collections, claims that the rifle shown was made at Harper's Ferry in 1833 and used by a Union soldier in the Great War between the States. The rifle bears the insignia of the U.S. Army of the Potomac, consisting of an eagle. During the centennial anniversary of the Civil War this year, the society will have on display numerous relics and mementos given to it by relatives of men who served with the North.
Springfield Daily News, January 23, 1961

[Source: A letter dated August 3, 1932, from Francis Lord to Mrs. Shepherd, curator of the Northampton Historical Society, and the Springfield Daily News Edition, January 23, 1961, both on file at the Northampton Historical Society, Northampton, MA]**Manuscript 33**

Comments & Supporting Evidence:

There are several important points to be gained from this, which are:

1. Both pieces of evidence, the letter and the newspaper caption with the photograph, indicate that the Northampton Historical Society Museum in Memorial Hall had a very large and extensive collection of Civil War relics. As the caption states, these Civil War relics and mementos were given to the Northampton Historical Society by "relatives of men who served with the North."

2. According to the documented Thayer family tradition, William Morrill's two Civil War buddies wanted the Custis Lee sword for an event and then were going to deposit it in a museum. This G. A. R. Museum or Northampton Historical Society Museum would seem like a very logical choice for several reasons: (1) the size of the museum's exhibit with respect to the amount of Civil War relics,

(2) its original affiliation with the old G. A. R., (3) its close proximity to the old Richardson Hockanum farm where Morrill allegedly deposited the sword after the Civil War, and (4) it was the Abbott brothers enlistment town when entering the Civil War and signing up for service in the 37th Massachusetts.

3. Due to the depth of the Civil War era artifact collection at this museum, it is not unreasonable to think that the Custis Lee sword could have been deposited here after leaving the Richardson home and was then observed by Mr. Buzz Newell during his youth.

EXHIBIT W-BN-6

Introduction:

In June, 1994, the author placed an advertisement in a Civil War periodical asking for any information concerning the capture of Major General George Washington Custis Lee at the Battle of Sailor's Creek, VA, April 6, 1865. Charles W. Thayer, who has been previously cited in this work in Exhibits W-CT-1-4, responded to the author's advertisement. After our initial contact, we soon began to compare notes on the topic of the capture of Custis Lee and his sword which was of great interest to the both of us, albeit for different reasons. When the author came in contact with Charles W. Thayer, Charles was, and still is, a well respected consultant and professional collector of military arms. After initially comparing notes, Charles W. Thayer began to conduct his own research, delving into the sword of Custis Lee that was captured at the Battle of Sailor's Creek, VA. Charles conducted this research totally independent of any research that the author was conducting at the time. In fact, until recently the author was completely unaware that Charles Thayer conducted any research on the sword of Custis Lee. While the author's motivation for his research on the sword of Custis Lee was to find additional material to support this work, Charles W. Thayer's motivation was to find the current owner of the Custis Lee sword. If Charles W. Thayer was able to locate the Custis Lee sword and purchase it from its current owner, he would add it to his collection which contains the purported revolver of Custis Lee. The combination of these two items, with their documented provenance as belonging to Custis Lee at the time of his capture at Sailor's Creek, would have created a very valuable asset for Charles. The Thayer family tradition as documented by Charles W. Thayer's grandfather, and which is found in Exhibit W-CT-3, states that the Custis Lee sword was in the possession of Charles Thayer's collateral relative, William Morrill, immediately after the Civil War. The Thayer family tradition also states that in the year 1888, the Custis Lee sword was given by Morrill's cousin, Harriet Richardson, to a couple of 37th Massachusetts veterans for display at a Grand Army celebration. After this celebration, the sword was then to be donated to a local museum. Relying on this information, Charles Thayer began his search for the Custis Lee sword in Northampton, MA, the city closest to the old Richardson farm in Hockanum, MA. The Thayer family tradition states that Morrill returned to this Richardson farm in Hockanum, MA, immediately after his service in the Civil War. Combining all this information, Charles speculated that the Custis Lee sword might still be in a Northampton, MA, local area museum. After placing a few phone calls, Charles was directed to contact Mr. Buzz Newell, a highly regarded local historian of the Northampton, MA, area. Buzz was reputed to have in-depth expertise on local soldiers and regiments that fought in the Civil War. Once again, it is very important to note that all this research activity by Charles W. Thayer was done independent of any similar research that was being conducted, or was soon to be conducted, by the author. Charles W. Thayer contacted Mr. Buzz Newell on August 14, 1994, and he was able to have an in-depth telephone conversation with Buzz. Fortunately, Charles W. Thayer was able to have another follow-up telephone conversation with Buzz shortly after their first telephone conversation. In addition to these two telephone conversations, in the summer of 1994 Charles W. Thayer was able to personally visit Buzz Newell in Buzz's Leeds, MA, home. It is important to note that these three interactions between Charles W. Thayer and Buzz Newell occurred in the year 1994, well before the author's first contact with Buzz Newell in May, 1995. When Charles W. Thayer interacted with Buzz Newell, Buzz Newell's cancer was in a state of remission and Buzz was in relatively good spirits and receptive to Civil War discussions. Buzz appeared to be very coherent, quite articulate and knowledgeable about the facts when discussing with Charles Thayer the sword of Custis Lee. The author encountered a very different situation when he first contacted Buzz Newell in May

1995. The author's first contact with Buzz Newell came just after Buzz received the news that his cancer had reoccurred and he was now diagnosed as being terminally ill. After receiving this news, Buzz Newell completely "shut down" as to all matters relating to his interest in the Civil War, including any continuation of discussions about the Custis Lee sword. During this difficult time not even Jim Parsons, Buzz's good friend, could initiate a discussion with Buzz about the Custis Lee sword. The author was elated when he recently discovered that Charles W. Thayer had these three interactions with Buzz Newell in the year 1994, when Buzz was still in remission and in good spirits. Charles W. Thayer took comprehensive notes during his two telephone conversations with Buzz Newell, and these notes record, in detail, Buzz Newell's observations and testimony. The following letter from Charles W. Thayer to the author, dated December 17, 2006, summarizes all the facts that Charles W. Thayer was able to harvest from Buzz Newell during their interactions. They primarily relate to the Custis Lee sword with some additional information on related topics. This letter was created and then signed by Charles Thayer. It is based on Charles W. Thayer's hand written notes at the time of his two telephone conversations with Buzz. It is also based on Charles' current recollections of the information that Buzz shared with him during their two telephone conversations and personal visit together. There was some information shared by Buzz that Charles did not have time to record in his notes, but Charles did commit this information to his memory. Charles has verbally shared these unrecorded facts with the author, as well as imbedding most of them in his letter to the author. It should be mentioned here that Charles W. Thayer did not take any notes while personally visiting with Buzz at his home, believing it was rude to do so. Vouching for the strength of Charles W. Thayer's memory and his ability to recall, the author has always found Charles W. Thayer's recollections to be meticulously accurate and very well balanced. Charles will not hesitate to state that he does not remember something or that his recollection of a particular point is vague and should be treated with caution. This attention to accuracy and balance is indicative of Professor Charles W. Thayer's innate "scientific" nature. The information contained in this Charles W. Thayer's letter is an invaluable piece of evidence because it corroborates the information that the author was able to independently harvest from Buzz Newell by way of letters on May 18th and 31st, 1995. These May 18th and 31st Buzz Newell letters can be found in Exhibit W-BN-1. The value of Charles W. Thayer's letter is that it brings to light Buzz's observations and testimony in the year 1994 in much more detail than the author was able to derive from a terminally ill Buzz Newell in the year 1995. This unique information from Buzz Newell, which has been preserved through the efforts of Charles Thayer in the year 1994, can not be derived from any other source today. Though the author has diligently searched, it would appear that Buzz Newell does not have any surviving contemporaries who possess any knowledge of the Custis Lee sword. Thankfully, Buzz Newell shared his observations and testimony about the Custis Lee sword with Charles W. Thayer in the year 1994, and to a lesser degree with the author in the year 1995, before Buzz Newell took this unique and important information to his grave. The letter of Charles W. Thayer to the author dated December 17, 2006, follows in its entirety:

Evidence:

17 December 2006

Dear Frank,

You have posed a central question: Was the Custis Lee sword in the North Hampton GAR Museum? I have reviewed my file (C. W. T.'s search for Lee Sword in Northampton, a sub file in the Lt. Wm. Morrill file), which includes the notes on my phone conversations with Buzz Newell that I have already sent to you. I conclude that Buzz Newell was a highly regarded local historian whose testimony as to the Lee sword's presence must be taken seriously. Sometime in August, 1994, probably in response to a communication from you, I called the Northampton (MA) Historical Society. My female informant advised that they had only 2 swords there; the provenance of both was known and they definitely did not include the Lee sword. But there had been some thefts before her tenure began, five years before. She said that the Forbes Library had a collection, but most of it had gone to the Historical Society. I called the Forbes Library, and spoke to Luanne. She advised me to call Louise Knox, who was a descendant of H. Abbott, he being a brother of Frank Abbott who took the Lee sword from the

Richardson/Thayer home in Hockanum in 1888. It was evidently Louise Knox (the name Elise Feeley also appears in my notes) who told me to contact the two local Civil War researchers: Buzz (Raymond) Newell and Jim Parsons. Both specialized in the local regiments, the 10th and 37th and both lived in Leeds. On 14 August, 1994, I called Buzz. You have the notes from this conversation. He informed me that the flags of the local Civil War regiments, the 10th, 37th, and 52nd had been in the GAR Museum (Memorial Hall) in Northampton, its charter was "turned in" in 1933. There were two brass cannons, scrapped for $25 each. He last saw the Lee sword in 1946. The "goodies" went to the Forbes Library, but there were only two swords. Buzz continued, relating the story of "inside" thefts that removed the Lee sword; the sword of Lt. Joseph K. Newell of the 10th Regiment, presented to him by the town, and so inscribed; and the Col. Parsons sword. Buzz mentioned another Newell sword, presented to then Captain Newell by his company, which was evidently not in the museum. The stolen swords were still in Northampton, in the hands of an otherwise legitimate private "closet" collector. Buzz had spearheaded a 1982 posthumous presentation of the Medal of Honor to Samuel Eddy of the 37th Mass. Eddy had returned the original because it was mailed to him in a "paper bag." For some reason, Buzz needed a Medal of Honor "temporarily" in his preparation for the Eddy presentation, and sought the loan of one from the "closet" collector, whose response was a hostile "No!" Said collector was then about 62, retired from government employment, and collected guns, swords, and uniforms. From my notes, it appears that the original Eddy medal was purchased for "big bucks" from someone in Michigan and shipped 48 hours before the 1982 presentation. Buzz stated the following about the Lee sword: It was inscribed on the guard, where the thumb touches it, "Presented to Lieut. G. W. C. Lee." He remembered it because it was inscribed in a relatively unusual location. For some reason, I concluded it was a pre-Civil War inscription. Buzz was not clear about the sword's details. My notes say the scabbard was "leather and brass," which was crossed out by me and replaced by "iron." I had to prompt him with choices, just as I would a non-expert auction staffer. My goal was to distinguish among the frail, straight-bladed M1860 Field and Staff Officer's sword, which did not see wide use in the Civil War, the leather-scabbard M1850 Foot Officer's sword with curved blade and semi-basket hilt, and the M1850 Field and Staff Officer's sword, with curved blade, larger basket hilt and iron (metal) scabbard. When I asked if it had a "basket hilt," he said yes, which told me it was not the M1860. Also, that model has such a narrow guard there would be little space for an inscription thereon. Buzz went on to talk about the ceremony that returned the captured flag of the Savannah Guards on Sept 12, 1982 (part of the Eddy event) [Note from the enclosed Official Program that he got he date right], the Colt in his collection that belonged to James H. Brayman of the 10th (KIA Fair Oaks, VA), and a book of letters from the 37th by Mason Whiting Tyler, late Bvt. Colonel of the 37th. The day after my call to Buzz Newell, I called Jim Parsons. It must have been Jim who told me of Buzz's bout with cancer, and that it was then in remission. That is not in my notes, but the following is. The Col. Parsons sword, stolen from Memorial Hall, was found at a tag sale and was then owned by Larry Tatro, a postman in Northampton. At some later time, I called Buzz again. I did not date the notes at the time, but they are on different paper, and relate only to the sword. As I recall, that small tablet of colored paper was at home on the farm in PA, whereas I had first called Buzz from my U. of Penn office. After the fact, I dated those "colored" notes as before my 1994 visit to Buzz. It appears I had my reprint of Schuler, Hartley, and Graham's 1864 Illustrated Catalog of Arms & Military Goods in front of me (I kept it at home, so this is consistent with my memory of the paper). When I quizzed Buzz by phone, I was frustrated because he did not know his sword "models." I thought "basket" hilt would convey the M1850 F&S, but then, in a sense, it applies to the enlisted men Cavalry sabers as well. I though "half-basket" was a good layman's term for the M-1850 Foot officers. I was not then aware that the M1850 Foot came in a metal scabbard. So at the time, I thought "iron" vs. "leather and brass" would distinguish Staff and Field vs. Foot, respectively. (The iron vs. steel issue is irrelevant, neither Buzz nor I could tell the difference). So his positive response to metal scabbard left me confused, because at the time, I thought any Lt. Should have the Foot Officer's sword. So out of all this, I think we can be confident only of the fact that the G. W. C. Lee sword was an Officer's sword, not the straight bladed frail M1860 Field and staff, and it had a metal scabbard. A perfect fit for what we are now learning a Lt. Of Engineers should have carried. That this came through despite my attempt to "shoehorn" Buzz's recollections into *my erroneous pigeon-holes of the time is remarkable. This phone conversation, Buzz described how the Lee sword was lying next to the Luke Lyman and Parson's swords in the GAR Museum. He went on to tell me of a book by Christopher M. Caulkins, 1980, "Thirty-Six Hours before Appomattox." In the first interview, he had said the Lee sword was stolen along with the Lt. Newell and Parson's swords. My 15 August 1994 call to Jim Parson's confirmed the theft and recovery of the Col. Parson's sword. Buzz mentioned the Luke Lyman sword only in the second interview. Is this a significant inconsistency? A legitimate addition? An error in my notes? In the summer of 1994, with classes over, I visited Buzz Newell in Leeds, MA He seemed to be in good health. I remember he had a packet of artillery projectile fuses on the bookshelf in his living room, wrapped in brown paper and stenciled in large black characters with the burning time, and the stamp of the Confederate arsenal that made them. No other weaponry was evident (or if so, it was not memorable). Perhaps he had liquidated it in view of his health problem. He did show me papers, images and documents, etc, relating to local Civil War history. And there was of course discussion of the Eddy commemorative event. Buzz asked me if my cousin Wm. Morrill of the 37th had gotten along with the rest of the regiment. Buzz had noticed that Morrill had not participated in the veteran's activities of the 37th! So Buzz was clearly still an astute observer of the historical record. (Morrill was not from Mass, but ME, and lived in PA after the War, hence his non-participation). As you read the enclosed copy of the Eddy Commemorative program (which Buzz must have given me when I visited him), note that the 1982 event was held because the original medal was mailed to Eddy, and not properly presented. It makes no mention of Eddy himself returning the medal, as Buzz had told me over the phone in 1994. Is this an inconsistency? Or diplomacy in the printed program? You will recall that when Leonard Day told me of Buzz's practical joke, namely his alleged discovery of an Indian tomahawk in an implausible local context, I began to wonder if Buzz had simply been telling me what I wanted to hear when I grilled him about the Lee sword. As I review the record, I now reject that possibility for three reasons:*

1) *Buzz gave me the same description of the sword (an unlikely variant of the M1850 Foot Officer's sword in an iron (metal) scabbard) on two different occasions. I now know that Buzz was describing to me a M-1850 F&S sword with a metal scabbard and the unlikely Lieut. inscription.*
2) *Buzz was too serious about Civil War history to play any conscious role in falsifying it. The Eddy Commemorative proves that.*
3) *Buzz was not looking for attention. Although he was the chairman and motivating force behind the Eddy Commemoration, he did not broadcast the fact. The committee members are listed on the last page of the program in alphabetical order. The officers are not first.*

I have included "extraneous" material from my notes on Buzz's conversations to demonstrate that his recollection of detail was unimpaired.
Merry Christmas,
Charles W. Thayer
Source: [Signed letter from Charles Thayer to the author dated December 17, 2006, with e-mail clarification dated January 19, 2007, in the possession of the author]**Manuscript 163**

Comments and Supporting Evidence:

There are many important points that come to light as a result of Charles W. Thayer's letter. Given the importance of the various items raised by Charles W. Thayer, these points are commented on and expanded below. Where appropriate, Thayer's documented points are also supplemented with information the author has acquired from Charles Thayer during our many discussions, in which Charles was recalling his two telephone conversations and personal visit with Buzz Newell. Many of Charles' points are substantiated by specific research performed by the author. These research results are clearly noted with the source material from which they were derived.

1. The most important point in the Charles Thayer letter is that Buzz Newell verbally told Charles W. Thayer in two telephone calls and one face to face meeting that he (Buzz) saw the Custis Lee sword in the Northampton, MA, Memorial Hall Museum. As mentioned earlier, these discussions between Charles Thayer and Buzz Newell were in the year 1994 and were separate and distinct

from the author's own attempts to uncover the same type of information from Buzz Newell in the year 1995. The author was not aware that Charles W. Thayer had these discussions with Buzz Newell in year 1994 until Charles Thayer informed the author of these discussions in the year 2006. It is also important to note that Buzz Newell told Charles Thayer in the year 1994 that the last time he saw the Custis Lee sword in the Memorial Hall Museum was the year 1946. When Buzz Newell responded to the author in writing in the year 1995, Buzz stated that the last time that he saw the Custis Lee sword in the Memorial Hall Museum was the year 1947. So Buzz Newell was relatively consistent about when he last saw the Custis Lee sword. Buzz Newell was able to describe the Custis Lee sword to Charles Thayer in some of detail. Charles Thayer was a professional military arms collector and consultant at the time of Charles' interviews with Buzz Newell. Charles Thayer was able to question Buzz Newell in such a way as to be able to harvest as much recollected facts from Buzz as possible. Buzz testified that the Custis Lee sword that he saw in the Memorial Hall Museum had a "basket hilt" and a scabbard made of "iron" (metal). This description is a perfect match with a Model 1850 Staff and Field Officer Sword, which had a government regulation "basket hilt" and a steel (metal) scabbard. **Source: [E-mails from John Thillmann to the author dated January 9, 2007]**Manuscript 164** On the surface, this type of sword might appear to be completely inconsistent with the type of sword that Custis Lee, a 2nd Lieutenant after graduating from West Point, would have been required to purchase and wear on duty. As a 2nd Lieutenant, the Custis Lee sword was inscribed: "Presented to Lieut. G. W. C. Lee." As a 2nd Lieutenant, one would think that Custis Lee would have been required to purchase and wear a Model 1850 Foot Officer sword given his rank of 2nd Lieutenant. A deeper examination of this point, however, justifies the Model 1850 Staff and Field Officer Sword as being the type of sword belonging to Lt. Custis Lee, and adds strong credibility to Buzz Newell's testimony about his observation. If Buzz Newell was fictitiously manufacturing a story about seeing the Custis Lee sword, he most likely would have described the sword as a Model 1850 Foot Officer sword which had, with very rare exceptions, a leather and brass scabbard. This is the type of sword that would have belonged, by Army regulations, to a company grade officer such as a 2nd Lieutenant. This was the rank of Custis Lee when he purchased his sword and it was inscribed with the words, "Presented to Lieut. G. W. C. Lee." This is the inscription that Buzz Newell said he observed on the Custis Lee sword when it was in the Memorial Hall Museum. Staff and Field Officer Swords were to be worn by officers of the rank of Major and higher, not 2nd Lieutenants. A deeper examination, however, yielded the following expert testimony from Francis L McGrane, Director of the US Army Engineer Museum in Fort Leonard Wood, MO. All members of the US Army Corps of Engineers during the time of Custis Lee's graduation from West Point were Staff Officers, regardless of their rank. Pursuant to US Army regulation at the time, all US Army Corps of Engineer members were required to purchase and wear the Model 1850 Staff and Field Officer Sword. **Source: [E-mail from Francis McGrane to the author dated January 9, 2007 and an e-mail from John Thillmann to the author dated January 9, 2007]**Manuscript 165** A brief examination of Custis Lee's military career yields the following facts. Custis Lee graduated from the West Point Military Academy in June 1854, and was commissioned a Brevet Second Lieutenant in the Army Corps of Engineers. He was promoted to 2nd Lieutenant on March 3rd, 1855. On October 20th, 1859, Custis Lee was promoted to 1st Lieutenant, US Army Corps of Engineers, and was assigned to the Engineering Bureau in Washington, DC. On April 17, 1861, Virginia succeeded from the Union. In May 1861, Custis Lee resigned his US Army commission and became a "Major of Engineers" in the Provisional Army of Virginia. One would expect that Custis Lee would still have been required to wear his Model 1850 Staff and Field Officer Sword with this new position. Shortly thereafter, now with the Confederate States of America, Custis Lee was reduced in rank to a Captain in the Corps of Engineers. With this new position, Custis Lee still would have been required to wear his Model 1850 Staff and Field Officer Sword. In August, 1861, Custis Lee was promoted to the rank of "Colonel of Cavalry" and an Aide-de-Camp to Confederate President Jefferson Davis. As an Aide-de-Camp to President Jefferson Davis, Army regulations still required Custis Lee to wear a Model 1850 or Model 1860 Staff and Field Officer Sword. In June 1863, Custis Lee was promoted to Brigadier General and was still serving as Aide-de-Camp to President Jefferson Davis. In October 1864, Custis Lee was promoted to Major General and was assigned to his first field duty in the defenses of Richmond. Given Custis Lee's erratic promotion path, 2nd Lieutenant, 1st Lieutenant, Major in the Provisional Army of Virginia, Captain in the Corps of Engineers in the Confederacy, Colonel of Cavalry and Aide-de-Camp to President Jefferson Davis in the Confederacy, and then ultimately to Generalship within the Confederacy, it is understandable that Custis Lee could have retained, throughout his entire Civil War military service, his Model 1850 Staff and Field Officer sword that he acquired when he was a 2nd Lieutenant in the US Army Corps of Engineers. He served as a Staff Officer, both as an Engineer and then as Aide-de-Camp, until the very end of the Civil War. Custis Lee was promoted to a Major General and given a field command shortly before the Battle of Sailor's Creek. Should Custis Lee have traded his Federal Staff and Field Officer Sword for a Confederate Staff and Field Officer sword when he resigned from the US Army to join the Confederacy? Because there were few factories in the South, new edged weapons were hard to come by in the Confederacy. Some new edged weapons were made by blacksmiths or were brought through the blockade, but most Confederate swords had been used by the militia or had been taken from Federal armories. Most arms experts agree that swords manufactured by the Confederacy were of inferior quality to the swords manufactured in the North. So Custis Lee might not have had any great desire to abandon his trusty, quality made, Ames Model 1850 Staff and Field Officer Sword for a Confederate manufactured Model 1850 or Model 1860 Staff and Field Officer Sword of an inferior quality and difficult to obtain. As the Civil War progressed into the later part of 1864, Custis Lee became a Field Major General and was "released" from being an Aide-de-Camp to President Jefferson Davis. Not having the position of an Aide-de-Camp, and as a new Field General, Custis Lee had every right, by way of Army regulation, to "upgrade" his Model 1850 Staff and Field Officer sword to a new, separate and distinct, "General's" sword. Confederate manufactured swords were even more difficult to acquire at this late stage in the Civil War and their quality was further diminished. Custis Lee might not have felt any great need to upgrade his Model 1850 Staff and Field Officer sword to a "General's" sword given these difficult conditions. In addition, Custis Lee felt very sensitive about his promotion to the rank of General, feeling he did not earn it by being tested in the hot field of battle like most of his peers who were promoted to this rank. This fact could have also had a bearing on his decision not to upgrade the Staff and Field Officer Sword that he acquired when he was a 2nd Lieutenant in the US Army Corps of Engineers. Lastly, Custis Lee could have grown very fond of his M-1850 Staff and Field Officer sword, having had it in his possession since 1855. It was presented to him and inscribed, which would have only increased its sentimental value. Listing all the factors above we have the following, (1) Custis Lee was a Staff Officer for most of his Civil War military service; (2) Confederate manufactured swords were hard to come by and were of inferior quality when compared to Federal manufactured swords during most of the time that Custis Lee served in the Confederacy; (3) he was highly sensitive and quite reserved about his promotion to General, which promotion would have allowed him to "upgrade" his sword to a "General's" sword, and (4) Custis Lee might have been sentimentally attached to his old sword. Taking all these factors into consideration, it is probable that Buzz Newell could have seen a Model 1850 Staff and Field Officer Sword inscribed with the words, "Presented to Lieut. G. W. Custis Lee," in the Northampton, MA, Museum. This is the type of sword that Buzz Newell described to Charles Thayer, one that had a basket hilt and an iron (metal) scabbard. The author feels that this description of a Model 1850 Staff and Field sword with a Lieutenant's inscription adds to the credibility of Buzz Newell's story. This is an odd and highly improbable combination. Only under a unique circumstance, like the one described above with Custis Lee being a <u>Lieutenant</u> Engineer and also a <u>staff officer</u> who was required to wear a M-1850 Staff and Field Officer sword, can this odd combination occur. Buzz Newell could not have spontaneously put this odd combination together correctly. Buzz Newell was simply telling Charles Thayer exactly what he observed, not the perfect combination that Charles wanted to hear, which was a standard Lieutenant's sword with a leather and brass scabbard (the M-1850 Foot Officer Sword). It must be noted, for complete accuracy, that the M-1850 Foot Officer Sword was also made with a steel scabbard, but under rare circumstances as compared to the standard leather and brass scabbard. Civil War sword authority John Thillmann states the following, *"These swords were either an Ames or Horstmann Model-1850 Foot in a steel scabbard. They are fairly rare as the steel scabbard was manufactured for junior (Lt and Capt.) officers who rode on horseback as the leather scabbard was too stressed to withstand the rigors of horseback on a sword."* **Source: [E-mail from John Thillmann to the author dated January 1, 2007]**Manuscript 166**** Even though the M-1850 Foot Officer sword did come in a rare metal scabbard, Buzz most assuredly saw a M-1850 Staff and Field Officer Sword with the standard metal (steel) scabbard because Custis Lee was required to have this type of sword as a staff officer in the US Army Corps of Engineers.

2. A very important statement made by Buzz Newell, that has already been mentioned in point number one above, was that one of the swords in the Northampton, MA, Memorial Hall Museum was inscribed with the words, <u>"PRESENTED TO LIEUT. G. W. C. LEE.</u>" Buzz was able to link this inscription to the history of the 37th Massachusetts and the Battle of Sailor's Creek and determine that this was the sword of George Washington Custis Lee. According to Buzz Newell, this sword was inscribed in such an unusual place that this inscription became indelibly burned into his memory. Buzz stated that the inscription was on the inside of the guard, where the thumb rests on the guard while holding the sword in the right hand. When the author learned of this, he consulted a variety of Civil War sword experts, and was informed that even though this location is somewhat rare for an inscription, it is not without precedent. Approximately 2% of Civil War swords that are inscribed have the inscription in this exact location (see the photograph below, showing the flat metal area on the inside the guard that provides adequate surface area for an inscription).

<u>Model 1850 Staff and Field Officer Sword manufactured by Ames:</u>
(PHOTO: COURTESY JOHN THILLMANN)

A careful examination of the inside of the guard of a M-1850 Staff and Field Officer sword shows that there is a flat area of metal exactly where the right hand thumb rests on the guard, where an inscription like, "Presented to Lieut. G. W. C. Lee," could have been placed. The part of the guard where the other four fingers of the right hand rest is primarily decorative metal work and impractical to inscribe. Buzz Newell's testimony that the Custis Lee sword had an inscription on this area of the sword, which fact has been independently validated that a Model 1850 Staff and Field Officer Sword could accommodate an inscription in this area, adds to the credibility of Buzz Newell's testimony. It would be difficult for Buzz Newell to correctly fabricate all these interrelated points during a spontaneous telephone conversation with Charles Thayer.

3. Since Buzz Newell vividly recollected three items about the Custis Lee sword, (1) the inscription, (2) the basket hilt and (3) the iron (metal) scabbard, it is worth expanding on the iron scabbard. The following are the specifications for the Model 1850 Staff and Field Officer sword:

The Regulation for the Model 1850 Staff & Field Officers' Sword

BLADE: *Shoulder, back rounded, edge, bevel, point, tapering nearly equal from edge and back, curvature slight; large groove, small groove; <u>tang</u>, riveting; etched vine on back; letters "U.S." guns, drums, colors and rays on left side; eagle, guns, colors, and rays on right side.*

HILT: <u>Pommel</u>, [brass, gilded,] notch for guard, scrolled back, rivet-cap, hole for the tang of the blade; <u>gripe,</u> wooden body, [birch or maple,] seal skin covering, [blackened,] wire, [fine brass, richly gilded,] notch for guard, ridges, shoulder, hole for the tang of the blade.

GUARD: *Front branch, hook; back branch; middle branch; letters "U.S." and open scroll-work between branches; plate [brass, gilded,] bead, flange, scroll, lip, mortised for tang of blade and for strap of sword knot.*

SCABBARD: [sheet steel, browned] *Interior lining well-seasoned bass-wood; body back, front, sides, holes for screws; mouth piece, [brass, gilded,] rim; 2 bands, [brass, gilded,] knob, eye for the ring, screws, and screw-holes; 2 rings, [gilded;] tip, [gilded,] screw, screw-hole, front and back branch.*

Source: [E-mail to the author from John Thillmann dated January 9, 2007]Manuscript 167****

By way of contrast, the specifications for the Model 1850 Foot Officer Sword is as follows:

The Regulation for the Model 1850 Foot Officer's Sword

The nomenclature is the same as for the staff officer's sword, except as follows:

BLADE: *Etched, guns, colors, and rays on the left side; shield, colors, and rays on the right side.*

GUARD: *It has neither middle branch nor letters.*

SCABBARD: [sole leather, jacked, fluted, blackened, and varnished]

Body, back, front, sides, holes for screws; mouth-piece and top band united, [brass, gilded,] rim, band, knob, eye for ring, screw, and screw-hole; band, [brass, gilded,] knob, eye for ring, screw, and screw-hole; 2 rings, [gilded;] tip [brass, gilded,] fluted, screw and screw-hole, front and back branches.

The following description of the Uniform for the Army of the United States, having been approved by the Secretary of War, is published for general information, and will be strictly conformed to. Colonels of Regiments and Corps will rigidly enforce this order; and Generals and other Inspecting Officers will notice all deviations from it. Every departure from the established dress will subject the offender to trial by Court-Martial for disobedience of orders.

Source: [E-mail to the author from John Thillmann dated January 9, 2007]Manuscript 167****

This is a significant point. Buzz Newell consistently told Charles Thayer that the Custis Lee sword that he observed in the Memorial Hall Museum had a scabbard of iron (metal). This would mean that Buzz saw a Model 1850 Staff and Field Officer sword with a standard steel (metal) scabbard and not a Model 1850 Foot Officer sword with a standard leather and brass scabbard. This is extremely consistent with the type of sword Custis Lee would have had based on the points above. As to the iron versus steel discrepancy, the Model 1850 Staff and Field Officer Sword was made with a steel scabbard. The Government would not accept iron, and specifically specified browned sheet steel. This browned sheet steel, when aged, gives the appearance of a dark metal like iron. Many Model 1850 Staff and Field Officer Swords auctioned today carry the erroneous description of an iron scabbard. This mistake is based on the appearance of the metal as opposed to the auction houses evaluating the actual metal. The author is certain that this is what happened to Buzz Newell. While observing the Custis Lee sword and looking at the darkened metal scabbard, Buzz assumed it was iron, not having the expertise to know otherwise. The author believes this adds to the credibility of the testimony of Buzz Newell. Buzz Newell was not telling Charles Thayer what Charles wanted to hear; instead Buzz was simply giving Charles his eyewitness testimony. Buzz was able to distinguish between a metal versus leather scabbard, but he made the common mistake of stating that the metal for the scabbard was iron instead of browned sheet steel, which was the actual metal that the scabbard was manufactured from.

3. Combining both telephone conversations with Buzz Newell, Charles documented in his notes Buzz's assertion that at least four Civil War swords were stolen from the museum in Memorial Hall.

Memorial Hall, Northampton, MA:

These four swords were no longer in the possession of the Northampton, MA, Historical Society, today known as Historic Northampton. Memorial Hall in Northampton, MA, was opened in the year 1887. It was built as a tribute to local Northampton, MA, area veterans, particularly the veterans of the Civil War. A local GAR post, the W. L. Baker Post, maintained a museum on the third floor of Memorial Hall from the time of Memorial Hall's opening until the year 1937, when the GAR Post disbanded with only two of its members still living. The Northampton, MA, Historical Society was formed in the year in 1904. There is evidence that this historical society took over the care of the GAR Museum artifacts in the early 1930's, under the direction of two primary curators, Edith Shepherd and Mary Persis Crafts. Mary Persis Crafts developed an extensive artifact collection for the museum during her stewardship, which ended with her passing in the year 1966. Buzz Newell used to visit this museum frequently when he was growing up. During his freshman and sophomore years of high school, Buzz attended the D.A. Sullivan School, which was in close proximity to Memorial Hall. The museum was thriving during these years when Buzz Newell would have visited it. According to the following article, the museum was encouraging visits by young people. *"Because of the educational value, the Historical Society is especially desirous that the younger people visit the exhibit. Quite a number of the young people have already attended, but it is planned to have them attend in groups and also to have talks on the displays so their significance in the history of the city may be better understood."* **Source: ["Relics of the Past Here," Daily Hampshire Gazette, October 1, 1930]**Manuscript 188****In the Northampton Historical Society annual report for the year ending October 1, 1934, Mrs. Shepherd reported that the museum had over one thousand people sign the visitors' log. A check of this visitors' log for the years 1937-1942, records the following: <u>39</u> visits to the museum by an individual boy or group of boys in the year 1937, incomplete logs in 1938/9, <u>28</u> in 1940, <u>23</u> in 1941. **Source: [E-mails from Marie Panik, curator of Historic Northampton, to the author dated February 1 & 6, 2007]**Manuscript 168**** Buzz Newell as a young teenager, then as a high school student and finally as a recent high school graduate, was most likely included in these 1937-1942 visitor log statistics. As related by Buzz Newell himself, it was during this time, all the way to the year 1947 when he got married, that he developed a keen interest in the Civil War artifact collection housed in the Memorial Hall Museum. Buzz stated that during his many visits he memorized in detail each noteworthy sword in this collection. The last time Buzz claims that he saw the four swords that were stolen, which included the Custis Lee sword, was the year 1946/7. This is not to say that Buzz was claiming that the swords were stolen in the year 1946/7. Buzz Newell got married in April 1947 and was perhaps unable to visit the museum after that date given his new family obligations. This most likely is the reason that Buzz stated that the last time he saw the four stolen swords was in the year 1946/7. Buzz's first child was born in the year 1948 which would have increased the demands on his time, leaving little time for his past hobbies and interests. Another important fact related to the stolen swords is that Buzz Newell, in the year 1987, informed Jim Parson about two of the four swords that were missing. These two missing swords belonged to two Northampton Civil War veterans. Jim Parsons then notified the Northampton Historical Society. There is a note in the possession of the Northampton Historical Society which documents Jim Parsons' conversation with a Northampton Historical Society employee about these two missing swords which belonged to Northampton soldiers. **Source: [Photocopy of this document is in the possession of the author and is contained in the files of Historic Northampton]**Manuscript 169**** This note indicates that Buzz Newell has been consistent with his stolen sword testimony for a long period of time, at least since the year 1987. This indicates that Buzz truly believed this situation to be true. According to Buzz, the four stolen swords, including the two swords belonging to the Northampton, MA, veterans, were all inscribed. This allowed Buzz to know with certainty the soldiers to whom these swords belonged. If these swords were inscribed, they would have been of greater value than the swords in the collection that were not inscribed, making them more susceptible to theft. According to Buzz Newell, the four stolen swords that were inscribed are: (1) George Washington Custis Lee (a Confederate Major General who yielded up his sword to a Lieutenant in the 37th Massachusetts from Hockanum, MA), (2) Joseph B. Parsons (a Northampton soldier mentioned in the 1987 Parsons/Newell/Historical Society memo), (3) Joseph K. Newell and (4) Luke Lyman (a Northampton soldier also mentioned in the 1987 Parsons/Newell/Historical Society memo). Joseph B. Parsons was a Lieutenant Colonel in the 10th Massachusetts. He was a resident of Northampton before and after the Civil War. Joseph K. Newell was a 1st Lieutenant in Company I in the 10th Massachusetts. He was a resident of Springfield, MA, before and after the Civil War. Buzz claimed that the Newell sword was presented to Newell by, "the town," and was so inscribed. Luke Lyman was a Brevet Brig. General in the 27th Massachusetts. He was a resident of Northampton before and after the Civil War.

4. Buzz attributed the thefts, in part, to corrupt Northampton, MA, police officers. It is well documented that the Northampton, MA, Police Department suffered a major scandal when two of its officers were convicted of 28 thefts at various establishments in the Northampton, MA, area. The thefts occurred while these officers were on duty. This string of thefts occurred in the late 1960's to the mid 1970's, according to State Police investigative reports on these two officers. **Source: [The Commonwealth of Massachusetts, Department of Public Safety, Division of State Police, Case Number 77-109-2200-0216, Criminal Records Section, Framingham, MA]**Manuscript 170**** Though these officers never volunteered a confession of a theft of Civil War swords from the Memorial Hall Museum during their various plea bargain arrangements and State's evidence against one another, the possibility exists that these police officers did commit this crime as strongly alleged by Buzz Newell. Buzz shared some more specific points with Charles W. Thayer on exactly how he believed the swords were stolen. Buzz believed that with the passing of Mary Persis Crafts, and with the museum in a state of decay, these policemen were given access to the museum by a Northampton City employee and together they stole the most valuable swords, the ones that were inscribed. It is common knowledge amongst many of the long time residents of Northampton, MA, that the Memorial Hall Museum was the target of theft. This is best stated by a local Northampton, MA, author writing about Memorial Hall where she states; *"The third, or top, floor of Memorial Hall, designed to serve as a museum and art gallery, was reached by a handsome double staircase ascending from the library level. The museum did not open until 1887 when cases, paid for with money raised by private subscriptions, were installed by Smith and Levermore's shop, according to the Gazette. It housed much Civil War memorabilia donated by the veterans themselves, including swords, sidearms, uniforms, cannonballs, flags, books and regimental records. Under the care of the Northampton Historical Society, the collection remained in Memorial Hall until the 1970's, when a number of items disappeared, apparently stolen. Some years after the death in 1966 of Mary Persis Crafts, who oversaw the collection beginning in the 1930's, the remaining contents were taken down to the Society's headquarter on Bridge Street."* **Source: ["For Those Who Fought and Died, the Creation of Northampton's Memorial Hall," by Allison Lockwood, Hampshire Life Magazine, May 22-28, 1992]**Manuscript 171**** The following excerpts from a Daily Hampshire Gazette article dated December 30, 1968, show the state of disrepair into which the museum fell after the death of Mary Persis Crafts in 1966 and how prone it was to theft. *'The museum, tucked away in relative obscurity, is open two days per week during the summer months only. But a visit to view the vast collection of Northampton historical artifacts is well worth the wait and the climb. Hundreds of visitors used to tour the museum when it was opened and cared for by the late Mary Persis Crafts. The museum was dear to her and she gave the exhibits tender care. She kept it open as a public service, preserving the history of the city for future generations. "We haven't been able to replace this dedicated and knowledgeable curator," a spokesman for the society says today.... Since the death of Miss Crafts the museum hasn't had enough care. Many items are now unlabeled and other labels have become loosened and are falling off. James Parsons, director of federal-state funded projects for city's schools was concerned about the future of the artifacts at the museum after viewing the disarray and the danger of loss of labels from the exhibits. He is interested in having an inventory made of the material and having this material made easily accessible to the general public, especially students at the city's schools. For the past two summers, the museum has been open two afternoons a week, manned by the Neighborhood Youth Corp. This was a good project and worthwhile, but some feel the museum needs far more care than it has been getting. Hours and hours of labor went into creating the museum and the many meticulously hand written labels, probably done by Miss Crafts. Mrs. Richard Holden, vice president of the Historical Society, said that the museum and material housed there is a "very real concern" of that group. Efforts are*

being made to do something about the situation, perhaps as apart of the program of Total Community Development. The Historical Society has done what it could with limited funds and little help. **Source: ["City Museum Lingers In Obscurity In Memorial Hall," Daily Hampshire Gazette, Northampton, MA, December 30, 1968]**Manuscript 172**** This article paints a picture of a museum that was ripe for theft, exactly the situation and the environment that existed when the inscribed swords were stolen by the policemen and others as relayed by Buzz Newell to Charles Thayer. **Source: [Charles Thayer's original handwritten notes of the 1994 telephone conversations with Buzz Newell, a copy of these notes are in the possession of the author]**Manuscript 173****

5. As stated before, Buzz Newell said that he used to visit the Memorial Hall Museum often while he was a young man. These frequent visits, combined with his interest, allowed him to study and memorized many of the artifacts including the four inscribed Civil War swords. To add credence to Buzz's story that he frequently visited the museum, the author again refers to the article in the Daily Hampshire Gazette dated December 30, 1968, which states, *"Even the most casual glance at the visitors' roster reveals how often students of another generation visited the museum. The list includes an amazingly high percentage of young people who are now the city's teachers, attorneys and leading citizens."* **Source: ["City Museum Lingers in Obscurity in Memorial Hall": Daily Hampshire Gazette, Northampton, MA, December 30, 1968]**Manuscript 172**** This statement in the newspaper article is consistent with Buzz Newell's description of himself and his early interest in the museum. Buzz Newell said that this museum was a gathering spot for the young people in town. This statement is supported by the facts presented in this article. Once again, the museum visitors' log shows many visits by "boy(s)" throughout the course of many years. This is particularly true for the years of 1937-1942, when Buzz was a young man and a high school student, in close proximity to the museum.

6. The author finds it astounding that Buzz Newell had such a command of facts that he would know that William Morrill of the 37th Massachusetts did not participate in any of the local 37th Massachusetts' veteran activities. This is true because Morrill moved to PA shortly after the Civil War. Buzz Newell did not know that Morrill moved, and speculated Morrill's inactivity was due to not getting along with the rest of the regiment. Knowing that Morrill did not participate in 37th Massachusetts' veteran activities underscores the credibility of Buzz Newell and shows that he was a man deeply immersed in the details of the local regiments.

7. Charles W. Thayer mentions an incident described by a long time Northampton, MA, resident, Leonard Day. Buzz Newell played a practical joke on some of his friends and got them tromping through mud looking for a Native American tomahawk that was not to be found. Buzz got a big laugh out of this event. On a more serious note, however, Buzz Newell's son, David Newell, told the author that, "my father's tale spinning feats were somewhat legendary in the community." **Source: [E-mail from David Newell to the author dated November 23, 2006, in the possession of the author]**Manuscript 174**** The author had several conversations with Len Day about Buzz's practical jokes. Len felt they were all done in good fun, with no deliberate or malicious attempt to deceive. Len Day believes that Buzz Newell was completely (100%) reliable when it came to testimony concerning anything to do with the Civil War and local Northampton regiments. David Newell, on the other hand, provided this caution to the author; "make no mistake, in terms of what I am trying to share with you. I am confident that what my father shared with you includes considerable factual detail, and at least an equal dose of fiction …unfortunately, you'll have to sort the fact from the fiction on your own." **Source: [Same e-mail from David Newell as cited above].** The author acknowledged this caution and accepted the challenge to "sort the fact from the fiction." The author is convinced that Buzz Newell's account of the Custis Lee sword is factual because it would have been near impossible for Buzz Newell to have fabricated these points "on the spot" when called "out of the blue" by Charles W. Thayer on August 14, 1994. It would have been difficult for Buzz to have repeated these points with exact correctness during a second phone call and a personal visit with Charles Thayer, if these points were fabricated by Buzz. The author is satisfied, by the facts, that Buzz Newell was giving a factual account of his observations of the Custis Lee

sword to Charles Thayer in 1994, to the author in 1995, and to his long time friend, Jim Parsons, over the course of many years.

8. Given the amount of information contained in this exhibit, a summary of key events and dates will be helpful to put Buzz Newell's testimony in proper perspective. The W. L. Baker Post of the Grand Army Republic was installed in the year 1885. **Source: [Hampshire Gazette, January 6, 1885]**Manuscript 175**** In April, 1885, this new GAR Post asked for an appropriation to rent space in Memorial Hall. **Source: [Hampshire Gazette, "GAR Asks for Appropriation for Hall Rent" April 7, 1885]**Manuscript 175**** In a newspaper article dated May 25, 1886, it mentions in a single paragraph the donation of three items to the W. L. Baker G. A. R. Post, a State flag, two guerdons and a set of State records of the Massachusetts Volunteers. **Source: [Hampshire Gazette, "Gifts to GAR," May 25, 1886]**Manuscript 176**** In a newspaper article dated July 12, 1887, it states, *"The museum room in Memorial Hall is now finished with four cases for displaying any articles which may be left there…. Many people who have been waiting for cases before making donations, may now bring forward their relics."* **Source: [Hampshire Gazette, "The Museum Ready," July 12, 1887]**Manuscript 177**** One would have to assume that the museum referenced in this article as "being in Memorial Hall" was a GAR Museum. This is due to the fact that the Northampton Historical Society was not incorporated until the year 1905. This next point independently validates the documented Thayer family tradition as contained in Exhibit W-CT-3. On Thursday, September 20, 1888, the W. L. Baker Post of Northampton, MA, held a huge "Grand Army celebration field day." Over 25 GAR Posts from western MA were in attendance, and over 1200 Civil War veterans participated in the celebration. There was a huge dress parade on Main Street in downtown Northampton with over 15 bands and drum corps. This parade was witnessed by thousands of spectators. A dinner and "gala/camp fire" occurred that evening for the Civil War veterans at City Hall. All the downtown businesses and mills closed that day to allow their employees to view this major event. All the buildings along the parade route were draped in flags and bunting. The newspaper covering this event stated, *"Not in recent years has the city had a better planned or more capably extended public event . . . the gathering of 1200 veterans from western Massachusetts was a great success in every way."* **Source; [Hampshire Gazette, "Grand Army Field Day," September 25, 1888]**Manuscript 178**** As stated earlier, this GAR field day celebration sounds a lot like a GAR celebration mentioned in the writings of Charles H. Thayer as contained in Exhibit W-CT-3. In documenting the Thayer family oral history, Charles H Thayer described the following; *"In 1888, two friends of Morrill from the 37th who lived in Northampton, probably Abbott and Nichols, came to Hockanum with a letter for Abbie Richardson Thayer from Morrill asking that she give them the Custis Lee sword, which they would take to a Grand Army celebration and then put in some museum."* As previously stated, on July 12, 1887, the Baker GAR Post had a museum "ready to receive relics" on the third floor of Memorial Hall in Northampton, MA. Could this be the same museum referred to in Charles H. Thayer's documentation of Thayer family history where the Custis Lee sword was to be placed after the Grand Army celebration? This match seems more than coincidental. The article describing this Grand Army celebration in the year 1888 independently validates the 1888 Grand Army celebration account referenced in the documented Thayer family history created by Charles H. Thayer. There does not appear to have been a similar type of GAR celebration in Northampton, MA, either before or after this 1888 grand affair. In the year 1905 the Northampton Historical Society was formed. **Source: [E-mail to from Marie Panik, curator of Historic Northampton, to the author dated October 3, 2006]**Manuscript 179**** According to the annual reports of Northampton Historical Society; *"from 1917 to 1922 or so, the Northampton Historical Society needed to vacate Memorial Hall and store its collection at the Northampton Institution for Savings so that the registration board could utilize the rooms. They returned circa 1922 and were allotted an additional room in 1924. Mary Persis Crafts apparently joined in 1930 and began cataloguing work right away-a card index file has been started, October 7, 1930 Annual report."* **Source: [E-mail from Marie Panik to the author dated September 20, 2006]**Manuscript 176**** It would appear from this information that the Northampton Historical Society started a museum in Memorial Hall in the 1920's, or perhaps earlier (1917?). In 1930, Mary

Persis Crafts was hired as the curator of this museum and started her cataloguing work of the artifacts. In the year 1937, the W. L. Baker Post of the G. A. R. vacated their rooms in Memorial Hall with the passing of all but two of their members. **Source: [Northampton Gazette, "Grand Army Rooms Have Been Vacated," June 4, 1937]**Manuscript 180**** There is every indication that the Historical Society Museum acquired care of the GAR Museum artifacts by this time, and most likely several years earlier. The following newspaper article states, *"As the veterans of the Civil War dropped from the scene, one by one, the Northampton Historical Society made a specialty of preserving mementoes of Northampton's role in the conflict."* **Source: [Daily News, Springfield, MA, "Northampton, Civil War Centennial Committee at Work," January 16, 1961]**Manuscript 181**** Buzz Newell visited the Memorial Hall Museum during his high school years, 1937-1941. Perhaps he visited the Memorial Hall Museum before this time period. For sure he visited after this time period up to the year 1947. The years of 1937-1941 is the approximate time period that Buzz would have seen the Custis Lee sword in the Memorial Hall Museum, along with the Parsons, Newell and Lyman swords. Buzz Newell married in the year 1947 and this is the last time he claims to have seen the four swords mentioned above. Mary Persis Crafts died in the year 1966 and the museum degenerated into a state of decay with minimal security and no accountability for the artifacts. A new curator for the museum was hired in the year 1972, which was Mrs. Ruth Wilbur. Buzz Newell claimed that the Custis Lee, Parsons, Newell and Lyman swords were stolen from the Memorial Hall Museum by corrupt Northampton, MA, policemen sometime between the late 60's and early 70's. Coincidentally, two Northampton, MA, policemen were indicted and convicted of 28 thefts of various establishments in the Northampton, MA, area. In 1987 Buzz Newell informed Mr. Jim Parsons that the Parsons and Lyman swords, two swords belonging to local Northampton, MA, Civil War veterans, were missing from the Northampton Historical Society Museum collection. Jim Parsons immediately informed the Historical Society of Buzz Newell's story. In 1994 Buzz Newell informed Charles W. Thayer of the four stolen swords, including the sword of Custis Lee. In 1995, a terminally ill Buzz Newell also informed the author of the stolen Custis Lee sword. Consistently and without any wavering or discrepancy, Buzz Newell claimed to have personally seen these four swords in the Memorial Hall Museum, including the sword of Custis Lee.

9. Lastly, in an attempt to further validate the credibility of Buzz Newell's story, the author has attempted to establish an audit trail of the Civil War swords that were in museum in Memorial Hall, under the care of either the GAR or Northampton Historical Society. This analysis was greatly aided by the discovery of the following statement made in the 1938 annual report of the Northampton Historical Society: *"the Metropolitan Museum, New York, sent out a questionnaire asking for a list of the American powder horns, arms and armor which were in our Museum. Miss Crafts made a careful list of these and handed it to Mr. Tucker to be sent to the Metropolitan Museum."* **Source: [E-mail from Marie Panik to the author dated September 20, 2006]**Manuscript 176**** In the year 1938, if Mary Persis Crafts made a careful listing of the powder horns, arms and armor in the collection of the Memorial Hall Museum for the Metropolitan Museum of Art in New York, NY, which museum was then conducting a national survey of local museums under the direction of their then current curator Stephen Grancsay, perhaps Mary Persis Crafts would have a line item in her listing for the sword of Lieut. G. W. C. Lee. The year 1938 is in the time period that Buzz Newell would have seen the Custis Lee sword in the Memorial Hall Museum. If this entry was found, this would be the ultimate "smoking gun," or in this case "smoking sword," to prove once and for all that the sword of Custis Lee was at one time in the Memorial Hall Museum in Northampton, MA. With the Herculean efforts of the Metropolitan Museum of Art staff, the author was able to unearth this Mary Persis Crafts listing from the depths of the archives of the Metropolitan Museum of Art. Extreme excitement ran through the author's veins as the listing was carefully examined, line by line, for the long hoped for line item entry declaring the sword of Custis Lee. But it was not meant to be. Mary Persis Crafts started her listing with meticulous descriptions of powder horns, arms and armor in her Memorial Hall Museum collection. Then, for some completely unexplainable reason, in the middle of her listing, she wrote the following generic entry, *"**Dress-swords-10 Gift History: Civil War.**"* After this entry, she resumed her meticulous descriptions of the arms and armor in the

remainder of her Memorial Hall Museum collection. The author can not explain this. The only possible explanation was that these ten Civil War swords came from the old GAR Museum collection. Given the early "pre-Historical Society" date that these swords were probably donated, she was unable to ascribe donors to these ten Civil War swords as she did for most of the other items in her listing. This fact might have prompted Mary Persis Crafts to create this one "lump sum" generic entry for the ten Civil War swords. This generic "lump sum" entry only occurred for the Civil War swords, as she made meticulously detailed entries for swords of an earlier and later date in her Memorial Hall Museum collection. Being extremely disappointed, the author decided to put aside his disappointment and make the best use of this still valuable data. In the year 1938, Mary Persis Crafts had ten Civil War "Dress Swords" in her collection. Mary Persis Crafts use of the term "Dress Sword" is interesting and requires a careful examination. The author fully recognizes that scholars of swords, particularly Civil War swords, will strenuously argue the precise definition of a "Dress Sword." One definition of a "Dress Sword" is found in the widely referenced internet encyclopedia Wikipedia. This internet encyclopedia, which is based on public input, classifies a standard regulation Model 1850 Staff and Field Officer sword as a "Dress Sword" (please see the Wikipedia

chart to the right). The Wikipedia author based this definition on the fact that in accordance with the "Revised United States Army Regulations of 1861, Uniform Dress Regulations," a regulation sword was a required part of the uniform, or "dress" of an officer. This fact lead the author to conclude that a Model 1850 Staff and Field Officer sword must be classified as a "Dress Sword." This Model 1850 Staff and Field Officer Sword was a standard regulation sword worn extensively by officers in the Civil War. On the other hand, John H. Thillmann, an internationally recognized authority on Civil War swords, does not even use the classification of a "Dress Sword" in his book entitled, "Civil War Cavalry & Artillery Sabers, 2001." He uses only two classifications, *campaign grade,*" which are regulation swords made for active use in the battlefield, and *"presentation grade,"* which are

Model 1850 Staff and Field Officers' Sword	
Type	Dress sword
Place of origin	USA
In service	1850-1872
Used by	USA
Wars	American Civil War

swords made exclusively for show. There is no standard and universally accepted definition of the term "Dress Sword." This lack of a universally accepted definition can cause a sword to be classified as a "Dress Sword" based solely upon the definition that a classifier prefers to use at the time of a sword's evaluation and subsequent classification. The author is firmly convinced that this is exactly what Mary Persis Crafts did in her 1938 listing. **Source: [Photocopy of the original Mary Persis Crafts listing of 1938, and various other correspondence from the Metropolitan Museum of Art in New York, NY]**Manuscript 186**** Mary Persis Crafts was not a Civil War arms expert or professional evaluator. She was a diligent amateur. She used the term "Dress Sword" in its most generic form, to refer to any sword of quality that perhaps was carried by an officer. This is underscored by the fact that Mary Persis Crafts did not use any model citations to describe any of the arms in her Memorial Hall Museum collection. This fact is an indication that she was not well versed in proper arms naming conventions as a professional evaluator would be. The Northampton, MA, Historical Society, also known today as Historic Northampton, currently has an inventory of their Civil War swords. This inventory is now recorded in a computerized data base. This inventory was first started by curator Ruth Wilbur in the 1970's. Ms. Wilbur was the successor to Mary Persis Crafts. This inventory was further refined by Suzanne Stone-Duncan in the 1980's, and then further updated and validated by Dr. George Snook in 2006. The author has taken the current computerized inventory of the Civil War swords at Historic Northampton and has attempted to cross reference these swords to notes produced for the Civil War swords that were inventoried by Ruth Wilbur and Suzanne Stone-Duncan in the 1970's and 1980's respectfully. In addition, Marie Panik, current curator of Historic Northampton, has conducted an exhaustive search for any extant archived accession index cards and exhibit labels created by Mary Persis Crafts for Civil War swords. Where Marie Panik has found accession cards or exhibit labels created by Mary Persis Crafts for Civil War swords, the author has cross referenced these cards and/or labels as well. The goal of this comprehensive exercise was to identify the Civil War swords that are currently in the possession of Historic Northampton, and tie these swords to those that were in the possession of Historic Northampton during the Wilbur and Stone-Duncan administrations (1970's and 1980's), and then ultimately tie these swords back to cards and labels created for them during the Mary Persis Crafts administration (1930-1966). Mary Persis Crafts had ten Civil War swords in her collection in 1938, as she noted in her arms and armor listing to the Metropolitan Museum of Art. The table below will attempt to answer the question, "of the Civil War swords currently in the computerized inventory of the Historic Northampton collection, can any of them be traced back to the ten Civil War swords that Mary Persis Crafts identified in her collection in the year 1938? Or, are there some swords that are missing or unaccounted for, that might have occurred sometime between the Crafts' listing in 1938 and the current computerized inventory in 2007. If there are at least four swords missing or unaccounted for, then this fact can add credence to Buzz Newell's account that the inscribed swords of Custis Lee, Joseph B. Parsons, Joseph K. Newell and Luke Lyman were stolen from the Memorial Hall Museum. The table below shows the Civil War swords that are currently in the computerized inventory of Historic Northampton, and the Civil War swords that are currently in the collection of Historic Northampton that still need to be added to the computerized data base. The author added up all the Civil War swords currently at Historic Northampton and totaled them. Then the author deleted swords from the current Historic Northampton inventory that were donated after the Mary Persis Crafts listing of 1938. In addition, the author also deleted swords from the current Historic Northampton inventory that the author believes Mary Persis Crafts would not have classified as Civil War swords when she developed her listing in 1938. A new total was calculated after these deletions and then compared with the total of 10 Civil War swords that Mary Persis crafts had in 1938. If this analysis yielded a disparity in these two totals, and Mary Persis Crafts had at least four more swords in 1938 than can be accounted for today in the current Historic Northampton collection, this could add credibility to Buzz Newell's testimony that four inscribed swords were stolen from the collection of the Northampton Historical Society. **Source: [Photocopy of sword analysis by Charles Thayer/George Snook, 2006-2007]**Manuscript 187****

HISTORIC NORTHAMPTON CIVIL WAR SWORD "INVENTORY" DATA BASE TABLE:

COMPUTERIZED INVENTORY 2007 (with accession #'s-in bold)
1. **No accession number and not in the computerized data base, due to it being in a display case:** Light Cavalry saber, Model 1860.
2. **54.4**-A non-regulation militia sword labeled a ceremonial "musician's sword," made by the Ames Sword Company. Made with out knuckle bow and has a six ball cross guard.
3. **54.12**-Model 1860 Cavalry saber. Outer markings on hilt, US/DR/1863.
4. **54.13**-Model 1850 Foot Officer Sword. Brown steel scabbard* but too tight for blade so an obvious mismatch. Ames on scabbard. * Most likely there was an original leather and brass scabbard.
5. **54.14**-A non commissioned officer's sword, Model 1840, with an early turned down guard. No markings and this sword is known as the Romeo Fortier sword. Romeo Fortier, a local Northampton, MA, resident, likely donated this sword to the Northampton Historical Society after 1938.
6. **54.19**-Model 1850 Foot Officer Sword belonging to General Joseph Hooker. Original gilt, leather and brass scabbard and Ames manufacturer.
7. **1985.47.13**-Model 1860 Cavalry saber (Roby manufacturer). US/1865/A. G. M.
8. **1985.47.14 (not in computerized data base)**-Model 1860 Officer Calvary saber, believed to be the sword of William Baker for whom the local GAR Post was named. Metal scabbard.
9. **54.7, 54.8, 54.9 & 54.10**-A group of <u>four</u> similar swords. William Baker Post GAR ceremonial swords. Distinguishing GAR markings on all four swords.
POSSIBLE 12 CIVIL WAR SWORDS CURRENTLY AT HISTORIC NORTHAMPTON

DELETIONS:

(1)-NO NUMBER: (Deleted): Marie Panik was able to find an accession card that states "SWORD, OLD CAVALRY, gift of September 1947, Bertha and Charles Marsh" **Source: [Accession card at Historic Northampton, photocopy in the possession of the author]**Manuscript 182**** Though this might not be the exact sword donated by the Marsh family, it needs to be accounted for and the author attributed it to this M-1860 Light Cavalry saber. It is deleted from the Mary Persis Crafts 1938 listing because it was donated to the Northampton Historical Society in the year 1947.

(2)-54.4: (Deleted): It would appear from the following entry in her listing in the year 1938 that Mary Persis Crafts could distinguish between earlier militia swords and Civil War swords: *"Sword: The Helen Cook estate (Dress Sword) History-Mass. State Militia-circa 1845-1848, Owned by Gen Benj. E. Cook."* If Mary Persis Crafts could make this distinction, she most likely would have listed this earlier militia (labeled musicians) sword separately from the Civil War swords, if it was donated before 1938. Since this sword does not appear as a separate entry in her 1938 listing, the author has concluded this sword was donated after the year 1938. There is the possibility that this sword, labeled a musicians sword, could have been donated by Frank Pelton in 1951, like number (3) below. Frank Pelton's father Timothy originally entered the Civil War as a musician.

(3)-54.12: (Deleted): Marie Panik was able to find an accession card that states: *"FATHER'S SWORD AND BELT CARRIED IN THE CIVIL WAR, Mr. Fred Pelton, gift 1951"* **Source: [Accession card at Historic Northampton, photocopy in the possession of the author]**Manuscript 183**** According to Ancestry. COM, Fred Pelton's father was a Timothy R. Pelton of Northampton, MA. Timothy died in 1877. Timothy enlisted in the 37th Massachusetts as a musician, then in the 1st Massachusetts Cavalry and then 5th Massachusetts Cavalry. Though this might not be the exact sword donated by the Pelton family, it needs to be accounted for and the author attributed it to this M-1860 Cavalry saber with its belt, since Timothy Pelton's service was primarily in the Cavalry and the donation was with a belt. **Source: [E-mail from E. Stanard-Ancestry. Com, dated December 15, 2006]**Manuscript 183****

(4)-54.13: (Retained): No other information about this sword is available and it could have been donated on or before 1938 for inclusion into Mary Persis Craft's listing. It might have, however, been donated after the 1938 listing. No one knows. For the purpose of this analysis and to be conservative, the author assumed it was donated on or before the 1938 listing, and has retained it.

(5)-54.14: (Deleted): This is an early non-commissioned officer's sword. The author believes that Mary Persis Crafts would have been able to distinguish this early sword and listed it separately from the Civil War swords (see 2 above), if it was donated before she made her 1938 listing. Since this sword does not appear as a separate entry in her listing, the author has concluded it was donated after 1938.

(6)-54.19: (Deleted): There is clear evidence that this General Joseph Hooker sword was donated to the Northampton Historical Society on December 20, 1939, well after the Mary Persis Crafts 1938 listing. As such, it can not be counted in Mary Persis Crafts listing of the ten Civil War swords. **Source: [Letters (December 20, 1939) on the Hooker sword donation, on file at Historic Northampton, photocopies in the possession of the author]**Manuscript 184****

(7)-1985.47.13: (Retained): There is evidence that this Civil War sword, with a "1985 accession number," came from the old GAR Museum to Forbes Library when the GAR disbanded in the year 1937. The following newspaper article states that when the W. L. Baker Post of the GAR vacated their rooms in Memorial Hall in the year 1937, some of their belongings were given to the George S. Bliss Camp of the Sons of Union Veterans in Florence, MA. The rest of the articles went to the Forbes Library. **Source: [Northampton Gazette, "Grand Army Rooms Have Been Vacated, June 4, 1937]**Manuscript 180**** In 1985, this sword was removed from the Forbes Library and placed with Historic Northampton and given a 1985 accession number. There is a high probability that this sword, with a "1985" accession number, which came to Historic Northampton from the Forbes Library, was in the original Mary Persis Crafts listing of 1938.

(8)-1985.47.14: (Retained): This sword followed the same path as number 7 above and was retained by the author.

(9)-54.7, 8, 9, and 10: (Retained): The author struggled with these swords. Mary Persis Crafts would have known that these ceremonial GAR swords were not really swords used during the Civil War. In fact, most were manufactured many years later, most likely in the 1880's and 1890's when the GAR was at its peak membership. It is also uncertain when these swords were donated to Historic Northampton. Since they have some tie to the Civil War, the author was conservative and decided to retain all four of these swords in this analysis. Also to be conservative, the author decided to assume that all four GAR swords were donated before Mary Persis Crafts' 1938 listing.

Author Note: Marie Panik, the current curator at Historic Northampton, has preformed a detail search of Historic Northampton's/Northampton Historical Society's de-accession records. She was not able to find a single entry for the de-accessioning of any swords, particularly swords that could have been associated with the Civil War. **Source: [Photocopies of the listings of complete de-accession records at Historic Northampton]**Manuscript 185****

Conclusion: Taking the most conservative approach, which is including all four GAR swords, and assuming that all <u>retained</u> swords were donated before the Mary Persis Crafts listing of 1938, the number of Civil War swords listed by Mary Persis Crafts in the year 1938 that survive today and are currently in the Historic Northampton collection is **seven out of ten**. Taking the most aggressive approach, which is assuming that none of the four GAR swords are included, and that all <u>retained</u> swords were donated after the Mary Persis Crafts listing of 1938, with the exception of the two 1985.47.13 and 14 Forbes Library swords, the number of Civil War swords listed by Mary Persis Crafts in the year 1938 that survive today and are currently in the Historic Northampton collection is **two out of ten**. The final total most likely resides somewhere **between two and seven out of the ten** Civil War Swords that were in the original Mary Persis Crafts listing of 1938, are in the Historic Northampton collection today. This analysis, though not flawless, is surely compelling enough to leave open the possibility to support Buzz Newell's testimony. That testimony being that four inscribed Civil War swords, namely the swords of Custis Lee, Joseph Parsons, Joseph Newell and Luke Lyman, were stolen from the Memorial Hall Museum. Of the ten Civil War swords listed by Mary Persis Crafts in the year 1938, these four swords that were included in that 1938 listing are now missing and are no longer in the current collection of Historic Northampton. This could suggest that the sword of Custis Lee went from Custis Lee to William Morrill, then to the 37th Massachusetts veterans for a Grand Army celebration, and then to the Memorial Hall Museum in Northampton, MA, where it was stolen. The current location of the Custis Lee sword is unknown.

10. The most fitting conclusion to this section, after the many pieces of evidence that have been presented, is the actual testimony of Buzz Newell, penned in his own hand while terminally ill. The author firmly believes that Mr. Buzz Newell saw the sword of Custis Lee in the Northampton, MA, museum which was once located in Memorial Hall.

CERTAINTY: (check one that applies)

☑ I am <u>100%</u> certain that I saw the actual sword of General George Washington Custis Lee in the G.A.R. Hall in Northampton, Massachusetts.

☐ I am <u>somewhat</u> certain that I saw the actual sword of General George Washington Custis Lee in the G.A.R. Hall in Northampton, Massachusetts.

YEAR: (please fill in)

The approximate year I observed the Custis Lee sword in the Northampton, Massachusetts G.A.R. Hall was _____ (print year) *Last time 1947*

Acknowledged to be true and correct:

Buz Newell

Buz Newell

EVIDENCE OVERVIEW
EXHIBIT-W-MF-(1)

The purpose of introducing this line of evidence is to introduce to the reader another source, completely independent from any of the sources associated with the 37th Massachusetts Protest Case, that claims that a Lieutenant of the 37th Massachusetts, most probably Lt. William Morrill, was in possession of Custis Lee's sword and belt after Custis Lee's capture at the Battle of Sailor's Creek on April 6, 1865. This evidence is in the form of Mahogany family papers, namely a Civil War letter written by Edward A. Mahogany of the 37th Massachusetts. The Mahogany family papers also include a Civil War photograph of Edward A. Mahogany which the author has included in this section with the permission of the Mahogany family.

EXHIBIT-W-MF-1

Introduction:

Edward A. Mahogany: (PHOTO: COURTESY MAHOGANY FAMILY)

A letter written by Edward A. Mahogany, dated April 16, 1865, to his mother Mrs. Cordelia Mahogany of North Hadley, MA. Mahogany was a Private in the 37th Massachusetts at the time of the Battle of Sailor's Creek and belonged to Company F. He is writing about events in April 1865.

Evidence:

The Battle of the 6th was quite a smart little fight & they came so near that the Bayonet was used pretty freely. Most of the men that were hurt at all were kill[ed] or wounded badly. Co F was very fortunate & only had one man killed & two wounded. W. Leggett was killed and Foster & Dunbar lost their arms. I was with the Color Guard & came out safe. The man that stood to my right had his leg broke. The man that carried the State Colors & stood in front of me was wounded the 2nd. I stood close to Gen Custis Lee when he was captured & one of our Lieuts has got his Sword and belt.

Edward A. Mahogany Letter to his Mother Dated April 16, 1865:
(PHOTOS: COURTESY MAHOGANY FAMILY)

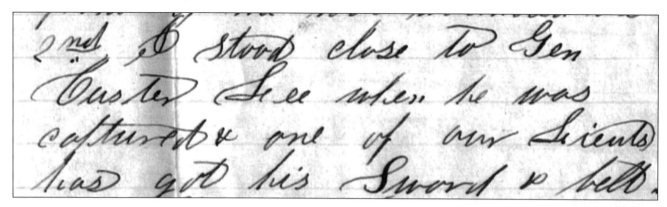

[Source: Civil War letter of Private Edward A. Mahogany currently in the possession of the Mahogany family, with a photocopy and a photograph copy of the letter currently in the possession of the author]**Manuscript 112**

Comments and Supporting Evidence:

1. This letter was written at Burkesville Junction, VA, on April 16, 1865. The letter appears to be authentic in all respects and a photograph of key portions of the original letter is displayed above:

2. Though not a part of the 37th Massachusetts Protest Case, this is one of the most compelling pieces of evidence to support the 37th Massachusetts Protest Case. Here is a 37th Massachusetts Private, writing his mother ten days after the Battle of Sailor's Creek, stating that he stood close to General Custis Lee "when he was captured" and that one of the 37th Massachusetts' lieutenants, most certainly Lt. William Morrill, "has got his sword and belt." This is extremely strong independent corroboration of the various 37th Massachusetts accounts concerning the physical evidence of a sword belonging to Custis Lee. This letter was written in the year 1865 by a common soldier who had no knowledge that the 37th Massachusetts Protest Case was to occur in the year of 1897. Mahogany witnessed this event and then recorded it ten days after it happened, so it had to be very fresh in his mind. Mahogany would have had no motive for making these statements to his mother in his letter other than just simply describing his activities as a soldier in the Civil War.

3. From this independent eyewitness account, it would appear that Lt. William Morrill had Custis Lee's sword, belt, and perhaps other items after the capture of Custis Lee.

BIOGRAPHY:

Mahogany, Edward A, Priv. - Res Sutherland; 20; farmer; enl. Aug 1, 1862; must. Aug 20, 1862; must. out June 21, 1865 as Corpl.
[Source: Massachusetts Soldiers, Sailors, and Marines in the Civil War, Volume 3, Compiled and Published by the Adjutant General, Norwood Press; 1932]Manuscript 112****

4. The author received the following letter attesting to the authenticity of this April 16th, 1865, Edward A. Mahogany letter, signed by its current owner Eve Mahogany.

From: Eve Mahogany, Burlington, Massachusetts, March 20, 2001

Dear Mr. White,
This is to attest to the fact that I am in the possession of a letter dated April 16th, 1865, written at Burkesville Junction, Virginia by Edward A. Mahogany. This is just one of several Civil War letters written by Edward A. Mahogany that are currently in my possession. Since they are family heirlooms, having been passed down to me through various generations of Mahogany family members, I have a sure knowledge of their authenticity. In addition, I made a photograph of this April 16, 1865, Edward A. Mahogany letter for Frank White. This photograph was taken of the original letter. I attest to these facts.
Very truly yours,
Signed: Eve Mahogany (Original Signature)
[Source: Original letter in possession of the author]Manuscript 112**

EVIDENCE OVERVIEW
EXHIBITS-W-BA-(1-10 CONFEDERATE)
EXHIBITS-W-BA-(1-21 FEDERAL)

This line of evidence contains many battlefield accounts of the Battle of Sailor's Creek written by many different authors. Some accounts are written shortly after the battle while most are written many years later. The primary purpose of this line of evidence is to establish, to the extent possible, the whereabouts of Major General Custis Lee, Private Harris Hawthorn and Private David White during the final moments of this battle. The final moments would have been the time that Custis Lee was captured by either Hawthorn or White. A secondary purpose is to accurately recreate, in text and photographs, the various troop positions and movements within the battlefield of Sailor's Creek, to see if this re-creation supports either the Hawthorn or 37th Massachusetts accounts. To effectively accomplish these two purposes, these battlefield accounts are divided into two sections as described below:

Section One: W-BA-Confederate 1-10: Confederate accounts primarily from Lt. General Ewell's troops, of which Custis Lee's Division was a part. Particular attention is given to Major William S. Basinger's account, who was commanding the 18th Georgia Battalion, which was a part of Custis Lee's Division. The 18th Georgia Battalion directly opposed the 121st New York. Particular attention is also given to Major Robert Stiles' account, who was commanding the Chaffin's Bluff Battalion, which was also a part of Custis Lee's Division. The Chaffin's Bluff Battalion primarily opposed the 37th Massachusetts.

Section Two: W-BA-Federal 1-21: Federal accounts primarily from Major General Wheaton's Division of which Hamblin's 2nd and Edwards' 3rd Brigades were a part. Particular attention is given to Col. Olcott's account, who was commanding the 121st New York, which was a part of Hamblin's Brigade. The 121st New York directly opposed the 18th Georgia Battalion. Particular attention is also given to Capt. Hopkins' account, who was commanding the 37th Massachusetts, which was a part of Edwards' Brigade. The 37th Massachusetts primarily opposed the Chaffin's Bluff Battalion.

This line of evidence shows that Custis Lee's most probable whereabouts during the final moments of the Battle of Sailor's Creek was much closer to the battle line of the 37th Massachusetts fighting against the Chaffin's Bluff Battalion than it was to the battle line of the more distant 121st New York fighting against the 18th Georgia Battalion. If this interpretation is true, this would place David White in a much more favorable battlefield location to have captured Custis Lee when compared to the battlefield location of Harris Hawthorn.

EXHIBIT-W-BA-1 CONFEDERATE

Introduction:

William S. Basinger:

Several accounts given by William S. Basinger, Major, Commanding the 18th Georgia Battalion at Sailor's Creek, which was a component of Colonel Stapleton Crutchfield Artillery Brigade, which was a component of General Custis Lee's Division. The author chose to include several accounts from Basinger, written at different times in his life, because Basinger's account is so very important. He describes how he halted, charged and drove back the initial advance of the 121st New York. This could indicate that Harris Hawthorn of the 121st New York was also pushed back with his regiment as well, impeding his chances to get to the battlefield location of Custis Lee in a timely manner.

Evidence:

Crutchfield's Artillery Brigade

Report of its Operations, April 3–6, 1865, when it was captured with Lee's Division at Sailor's Creek. This, printed from the original manuscript, was recently supplied by General G. W. Custis Lee, late President Washington and Lee University:, Savannah, March 3, 1866.

Major-General G. W. C. Lee, Commanding Lee's Division, Ewell's Corps, Army Northern Virginia.

GENERAL:

In compliance with your request that I would communicate in an official form such information as I may possess of the operations of Crutchfield's Brigade, from the evacuation of the lines on the north of the James River to the capture of the Division at Sailors' Creek, on the 6th April, 1865, I have the honor to report as follows: The Brigade consisted of the 10th, 18th, 19th and 20th Virginia Battalions of artillery, the Chaffin's Bluff garrison composed of five unattached Virginia companies of artillery, temporarily organized as a battalion, and the 18th Georgia battalion. These battalions were organized in pairs, and commanded as follows: The Chaffin's Bluff battalion and the 18th Georgia by major W. H. Gibbes; the 18th and 19th Virginia by Lieutenant-Colonel Howard; the 10th and 20th Virginia by Lieutenant-Colonel Atkinson . After crossing Sailor's Creek, and while halted near the crest of the hill beyond it, the enemy was discovered advancing in heavy force towards our left and rear. His artillery came up rapidly and took position on the summit of the hill we had recently passed over, on the other side of the creek, near the houses of Hillsman's farm, and not more that 350 and 400 yards from us, as I have ascertained by a subsequent careful examination of the ground. The division immediately formed line, faced to the rear, about one-third of the distance down the hill, Crutchfield's Brigade on the right. The 18th Georgia was on the extreme right of the brigade; next stood the Chaffin's Bluff troops, Major Robert Stiles. In consequence of the transfer of Major Gibbes on the day previous, to Hardaway's Battalion of Artillery, the command of these two battalions had devolved on myself. The conformation of the ground was such that I could see distinctly only these two battalions after getting into position. Consequently, whatever I have to state further relates to them alone. The different battalions moved up successively from right to left. No sooner were the colors of the 18th Georgia and Chaffin's Bluff troops established, than the enemy directed his fire upon those commands with great rapidity and accuracy. But both battalions dressed up to their colors with as much steadiness and formality as if on parade. I observed particularly the Chaffin's Bluff companies, as I was told they had never before been engaged. There was something surprising in their perfect steadiness and order. By this time many causalities having occurred, and the enemy's fire becoming remarkably accurate and severe, the troops were directed to lie down in their places. But notwithstanding this precaution, many of Major Stiles' command were killed and wounded. The 18th Georgia suffered not at all, as they lay in a slight depression of the ground. I do not think I had a man hurt by artillery during the engagement. Covered by his artillery the enemy moved up his infantry in three lines of battle, preceded by skirmishers. As soon as our own skirmishers had retired, they were received with a general discharge from our whole line, which speedily threw their first line into confusion, killing and wounding considerable numbers. Unable to face our fire, that line fell back in disorder, which, as I was afterwards told, they communicated to their second line. Such was the eagerness of Major Stiles' men, that upon perceiving the enemy's hesitation, they sprang up from their recumbent attitude and rushed upon them, fixing bayonets as they advanced; and it was with difficulty that Major Stiles and I could check them and restore the line. I was also afterwards informed, by other officers of the brigade that the enemy's second line was broken in a similar manner by our fire, and that his third line was met by ours in a general advance with the bayonet, and driven back beyond the creek, when the flag of truce appeared announcing the surrender of the whole corps by General Ewell. I communicate information received from others of what did not fall under my own observation, for the sake of the corroboration it may give to statements from other quarters. After the restoration of our line, broken, as just stated, by the precipitate charge of Major Stiles' command, my attention was confined to what took place on our extreme right, and I saw no more of the general engagement. I have before stated that my battalion was on the extreme right of the brigade. Its right rested on the road by which we had marched after crossing the creek. On the other side of the road was a dense pine ticket, which concealed all beyond from view. Perhaps you will recollect passing the command early in the engagement, and telling me I might feel secure about my flank, as Kershaw's Division was beyond the ticket; as I understood matters, with his extreme left covering our flank, his line being at right angles to ours. After re-establishing Major Stiles' Battalion, I passed up to our right. I had scarcely got there, when I perceived a large body of the enemy advancing through the thicket diagonally upon our flank, and already within about forty yards. They could not have been seen at a greater distance, so close were the trees. I had but eighty-five men, but I could not leave the spot, nor was there a moment to spare. I changed front instantly (receiving, as the movement was made, a volley which proved fatal to several), and took position in a wide and shallow gully at the road-side. Perceiving that the superior numbers of the enemy would enable him to destroy us by his fire, I ordered bayonets fixed and attacked. Through the extraordinary gallantry of the men, the attack was entirely successful. Many of the enemy were killed with the bayonet, and the rest were driven off in disorder, after a desperate struggle, distinguished by many acts of individual heroism. Lieutenant G. M. Turner, though previously wounded on the skirmish line, joined in the charge, and was shot down in the act of saving the life of a comrade. Lieutenant W. D. Grant took a regimental flag from the hands of its bearer, and was prostrated by mortal wounds immediately after delivering it to me. Sergeant George James is reported to have taken another, and fell shortly after. Captain G. C. Rice was overpowered by an officer of the enemy of greatly superior size and strength, in Confederate uniform, and was shot by him on the ground, after he had surrendered. Lieutenant W. H. King revenged him, and was himself killed on the instant. Sergeant C. B. Postell, with three or four others, was surrounded by a party of the enemy, and refusing to yield, was killed with all his comrades. Lieutenant F. Tupper, pursuing too far, fell mortally wounded on the bank of the creek, about 300 yards from our position. I hope I did not commit an error in taking this course. The safety of the brigade was at stake. If my brave fellows had flinched or given way, the enemy would have thrown himself on our flank, and the general loss must have been much greater than it was. I had scarcely reassembled the remnant of the battalion in its original position, with but one officer unwounded besides myself, when you passed by and reassured me as to my apprehensions of further molestation from that quarter by the information that other troops had been sent to guard that approach. They probably never reached their destination; for in a very few minutes another but smaller body of the enemy came on over the same ground. Supposing them to be some of our own troops giving way, I took my men out to rally them and discovered that they were enemies only when within a few paces. I attempted, as our only recourse, to repeat the attack which had just terminated so well; but overpowered by superior numbers, though fighting to the last, all the rest of the command were killed, wounded or taken. Sergeants R. Millen and S. Morton stood to the last before their colors, keeping at bay a party of about fifty men, and were the last to fall. Seeing then but one officer and the non-commissioned staff remaining, I displayed my handkerchief in token of surrender. As I did so, the enemy, hitherto sheltering themselves behind the trees, rushed into the road, and fired upon my wounded who lay in the gully before mentioned. It was with the greatest difficulty they could be induced to cease from this barbarity. I mention this closing incident as one more numerous atrocities which indicated the relentless spirit in which the war was waged against us. Having subsequently re-visited the field and passed some days in its immediate vicinity, I was informed by one of the neighboring residents that the troops encountered by my battalion were Hamblin's Brigade of the 6th Corps, consisting of three regiments, of which one-half were ordered forward at each time. The information was obtained from General Hamblin himself, who further admitted that he suffered very severely and lost six colors.

Very respectfully, your obedient servant,

Wm. S. Basinger, Major Com'd'g 18th Georgia Battalion.

[Source: "Crutchfield's Artillery Brigade" by William S. Basinger, Southern Historical Society Papers, Volume XXV, pages 38-44]Manuscript 1****

Comments and Supporting Evidence:

1. The author discovered another account given by William Starr Basinger. This account is as follows:

... With the colors of these two battalions (18th Georgia and Chaffin's Bluff), I established the line of battle for the division, and every command moved into its place with perfect regularity, allowing for the roughness and irregularity of the ground.... As their first line advanced, a body of the enemy advanced through that thicket. As I saw them coming, I called the Guards to their feet, and marched them by the right flank so as to place them directly in front of the enemy's advance, fixing bayonets as the movement was made. There was a gully along this side of the road by which we had come to that point, and my design was to get the Guards into that gully, so as not only to face the enemy, but to use that road as a sort of rampart. Having got them into the gully, as the enemy continued to approach, I ordered a charge with the bayonet.... The attack was successful, and we drove them back.... Supposing we had nothing more to apprehend from that quarter, I recalled my men, and marched them back to their original position in the line.

In additional writings in this Basinger Reminiscences, the account goes to add:

*... At one time during this battle the enemy appeared on the right flank of the Guards, who were lying down awaiting orders. Major Bassinger called the command quickly to its feet and changed direction by its right, almost perpendicularly to its original line, so as to face the enemy, ordering bayonets to be fixed during the progress of the movement. It was apparent to the commanding officer that, outnumbered as the Guards were, it would never do to rely on their fire alone or to await attack, so he gave the command at once to charge. Major Bassinger states in his report of this action: "Never did such command meet with more willing or more magnificent response. Every officer and man in his place, with every nerve at its utmost tension, in perfect silence, without the shout which often accompanies a charge, the battalion sprang forward against the foe. It was a thrilling and inspiring spectacle, that line of leveled steel as it rushed forward to the attack. The enemy were so near that it reached them unbroken. The shock was irresistible. Surprised by the promptness and violence of the charge, and somewhat disordered by their passage through the trees, the leading ranks of the enemy went down as if struck by a thunderbolt. The Guards rushed on. Rank after rank fell before them. But the same trees which had disordered the enemy's advance broke up the line of the Guards into separate parties. Now the rear ranks of the enemy, which had not yet been reached by the bayonet, began to fire. But the indomitable spirit, energy and activity of the Guards prevailed, and the enemy were fairly routed and driven out of the wood and back across the creek." **Second Charge:** Later on, on the same day, resort had to be made with the bayonet to a second charge on the enemy, which was made with the same spirit as before, but the enemy were too many and the Guards too few. It was impossible to drive them back. The remaining members of the corps then rallied on the side of the road determined to fight to the last, the colors being planted on the road-side. The enemy were behind trees and fired from shelter. Major Bassinger, standing near when several of the command were shot down, was unarmed, his sword having been shattered by a bullet, in one hand, and his pistol in the other. Further resistance was obviously impossible. Major Bassinger, desirous of saving the lives of those few that remained, waved his handkerchief in token of surrender.*

In more writings in this Basinger Reminiscences, the account goes on to further say:

...The Battle of Sailor's Creek took place on April 6, 1865. My friends, Genl Custis Lee and Major Robt Stiles, who were also taken prisoners, were entertained in Genl Sheridan's tent that night. Major Stiles told me the next day that he heard Sheridan say that our division had killed and wounded over 5000 of his men. We had only 2250 in the division.

[Source: "Personal Reminiscences to 1896," Southern Historical Collection, University of North Carolina, Chapel Hill, NC]**Manuscript 77**

2. There are many important points to be learned from Basinger's two accounts.
   A. Basinger was in command of the 18th Georgia and the Chaffin's Bluff Battalions.
   B. Being in the rear of the Division during the march to Sailor's Creek, the 18th Georgia, followed by the Chaffin's Bluff troops, set the battle line for the rest of the Division.
   C. Basinger's 18th Georgia was the extreme right Battalion of Custis Lee's Division, with the 18th Georgia's right resting on the road.

D. Major Stiles' Chaffin's Bluff Battalion was on the left of the 18th Georgia.

E. Because of the conformation of the terrain, Basinger could only see and carefully observe the 18th Georgia and Chaffin's Bluff Battalions.

F. Basinger had eighty-five men in the 18th Georgia Battalion.

G. The Chaffin's Bluff garrison consisted of five unattached Virginia companies of artillery, temporarily organized as a Battalion.

H. During the initial Federal artillery barrage, the 18th Georgia was sheltered by lying in a "slight depression of the ground."

I. The Chaffin's Bluff garrison did not have the shelter of this depression in the ground, and "many in Major Stiles command were killed or wounded."

J. On the other side of the road, on the right flank on the 18th Georgia was a "dense pine thicket, which concealed all beyond from view."

K. Custis Lee passed by (presumably on horseback) early in the engagement and told Basinger that Kershaw's troops were on the other side of the road and thicket, with Kershaw's extreme left flank covering Basinger's extreme right flank with the two troops being nearly at right angles to each other.

L. As the Federals advanced on Major Stiles' Chaffin's Bluff battle line, they were met with a rifle discharge from the whole of the Chaffin's Bluff line. Stiles' men charged the retreating Federals.

M. Major Stiles and Major Basinger checked and then restored the Chaffin's Bluff line.

N. After restoring Stiles' Battalion to its original position, Basinger himself moved to the right flank of the 18th Georgia. He observed the enemy coming through the pine thicket on the other side of the road diagonally upon the right flank of the 18th Georgia.

O. With the Federals about 40 yards away, Basinger changed the front of the 18th Georgia's to be along a gully which was along side the road. This position was almost perpendicular to Basinger's original battle line formation.

P. Once having his troops in the gully, Basinger ordered a charge with the bayonet. This charge halted the Federal advance and drove the Federals back to the Creek and beyond.

Q. After pushing this Federal advance back to the Creek, Basinger recalled his 18th Georgia troops to re-form along the gully at road side.

R. At this time, Custis Lee passed this way again (presumably on horseback) and reassured Basinger that he would not get assaulted by the enemy from that direction again. Custis Lee was sending additional troops to guard that approach.

S. Basinger was assaulted a second time by the Federals through the same approach. He ordered a second charge, like the first, but was overpowered by the superior numbers of the Federals.

T. Basinger regrouped in the roadside gully after this second charge. The Federals shot at his Battalion from behind the trees of the pine thicket.

U. Basinger surrendered his troops, most likely on the road. Basinger's original line in the gully was approximately 300 yards from the creek.

V. Basinger was told shortly after the battle that his 18th Georgia Battalion encountered regiments from General Hamblin's Federal Brigade [Note: This was primarily the 121st New York, with Warren C. Dockun of the 121st New York capturing the 18th Georgia's flag.]

W. It would appear that General Custis Lee and Major Robert Stiles were together after they were captured. This is due to the fact that Custis Lee and Major Stiles were being entertained in General Sheridan's tent according to Basinger. If this is true, this could be a good indication that Custis Lee and Robert Stiles were captured together by the same Federal command and were sent to the Federal rear together. This may also indicate that Custis Lee and Robert Stiles were in the close proximity during the final moments of the battle.

3. On April 14, 1865, William Starr Basinger wrote the following letter to his mother:

My Dear Mother,
On our way, a sad train of captives from the unfortunate field of Sailor's Creek of Apl 6, to I know not whither, I seize an opportunity to let you know what has befallen me. I lost everything, the most

common necessities. As soon as I am sure of a permanent place of confinement, I will draw on you for a little money. I know how embarrassed you all are in that way. But I will make the draft as small as possible. I cannot think of the splendid conduct & of the losses of my noble little command without mingled emotions of admiration & grief, of 85 engaged, I lost 24 killed, 28 wounded, & the rest prisoners. Rice, Turner & King were killed. Tupper mortally wounded. Smith, Dillon & Blois severely wounded. Starr painfully, but doing well. I escaped with a slight wound, but was grazed many times. My coat was pierced; my sword belt struck, my pistol shattered in one hand, my sword in the other. We drove a regiment with the bayonet, & took their colors. But I cannot give you particulars now. For the conduct of command, let it suffice to say, that every one I meet, from Ewell down to the privates, congratulates me upon it. Tell the Stiles that their cousin, Major Robt. Stiles, was under my immediate command, behaved himself more like a hero than any man I ever saw, & is with me, a prisoner. I have prepared a list of casualties for the N Y Herald, & will write fully as soon as I get a chance. Thank God for his wonderful preservation of my life & Believe me ever your affte son, & my sisters affte brother.
Wm S Basinger.

[Source: Basinger Papers, Southern Historical Collection, University of North Carolina Library, Chapel Hill, NC]**Manuscript 130**

The valuable fact about this letter is that Basinger is recounting some important points about his command's actions at the Battle of Sailor's Creek just 8 days after the event, while his memory is still very fresh. He validates the items in his more detailed writings, such as, "we drove a regiment with the bayonet, & took their colors." This is an obvious reference to their fight with the 121st New York. This reference, once again, is written just 8 days after the battle in the form of a simple, private letter to his mother. One would have to assume that Basinger is being totally factual and not motivated by any other agenda, when he was writing this personal letter to his mother.

4. On April 16, 1865, William Starr Basinger wrote another more descriptive letter home to his mother:

My Dear Mother,

I write on board a steamer on our way from City Point to Washington, a train of prisoners. We were taken with Ewell's command on the 6th, at the battle of Harper's farm. The Batlln was nearly destroyed. I lost 25 killed, 27 wounded, & all prisoners. Rice King, Turner killed. Grant very dangerously wounded. Smith wounded in thigh, Starr in shoulder, Dillon, Thigh; Blois, foot. These last were doing very well. Pearson's wound not serious. Dillon was paroled & left with some Amelia friends. I have a very slight wound in my left hand. A ball shattered my pistol, which was held in that hand. Another my sword in my right. Another hit my belt buckle; & another pierced my coat just above the belt. I saw my life preserved many times. The command behaved most nobly. Made 2 attacks with the bayonet. The first drove a regiment & took their colors. Grant took them. Percy Elliott is severely wounded. Wm Bennett Killed; also Dick Millen. Will send you from prison a complete account. I lost everything, & have not had a change of clothes. Will have to draw on you for a little money. I write now as a paroled prisoner to let you know I am well. But my grief for my men & for the misfortunes of our country have made the last 10 days the most wretched of my life. Tell the Stiles their cousin, Maj. Rob. Stiles, was under my immediate command, & behaved like a hero. Indeed, I am saluted on all sides, from the Genl down, with compliments on the splendid conduct of the troops under my command. Be of good courage, & don't give up. God will not abandon us. It is on Him only now that we can rely.
My love to my sister. Yrs affly
Wm S Basinger

[Source: Basinger Papers, Southern Historical Collection, University of North Carolina, Chapel Hill, NC]**Manuscript 131**

Ten days after the Battle of Sailor's Creek, Basinger describes his command's two attacks on the enemy with the bayonet, with the first attack driving a regiment (the 121st New York) and the capturing of their colors. He also describes Major Stiles being under his command. These events are all consistent with his writings of April 14, 1865, which were all documented in letters to his mother shortly after their occurrences. The author believes that this evidence adds credibly to

Basinger's assertions that he drove the 121st New York back when the 121st New York made their initial advance upon the flank of Basinger's 18th Georgia Battalion.

5. As supporting evidence to Basinger's claim that he charged the Federals and drove them to the Creek, and then unsuccessfully charged them a second time once the Federals regrouped, the author introduces the following description of the battlefield of Sailor's Creek the day after the battle from Union Quartermaster Horatio C. King:

Horatio C. King:

One incident of this field is as fresh in memory as if it occurred yesterday. Near the edge of the creek on the right of the road leading to Farmville was a natural rifle-pit formed by the wash of heavy rains. It was covered by an enfilading fire from our batteries on the opposite hills. Passing by this road the morning after the fight, the gulch was almost filled with rebel dead, which were also thickly strewn along the road and through the woods on the left. Kneeling on the body of a fallen comrade, with his hands uplifted as if in prayer, his eyes open and a placid smile on his face, was a handsome Confederate soldier. Approaching to give him succor if wounded, and willing to accept his surrender, we were shocked to find him dead. It impressed us greatly and there was silence for a while as our reluctant horses picked their way through the harvest of death.

[Source: "Rifle Shots and Bugle Notes" by Joe A. Joel & Lewis R. Stegman, Grand Army Gazette Publishing Company, 1884, article by Colonel Horatio C. King entitled "Five Forks and Lee's Surrender," page 92]**Manuscript 138**

There are four important facts to be gained from this account given by Horatio C. King:

A. It would appear that Mr. King observed and then later described the scene where Basinger's 18th Georgia fought Olcott's 121st New York. The description includes the gully on the right side of the road facing south toward Farmville, where Basinger's 18th Georgia positioned their troops to meet the initial Federal advance. The critical point in this writing is that King not only saw many rebel dead in the gully and in the road, he also saw them thickly strewn in the woods on the left side of the road facing south toward Farmville. King's observation physically validates Basinger's account that Basinger charged the Federals from the gully which was on the right side of the road facing toward Farmville. Basinger's troops then crossed the road and charged into the woods on the left side of the road facing toward Farmville, pushing the Federals troops back to Sailor's Creek. Basinger's troops incurred many fatal casualties as a result of this charge. These Confederate dead soldiers in the woods on the left side of the road facing toward Farmville were the dead soldiers that King was observing the day after the Battle of Sailor's Creek. This Basinger charge on the Federals is the only explanation to account for rebel dead being "thickly" strewn in the woods on the left side of the road facing south toward Farmville, as observed by King. If Basinger did not charge and push the 121st New York back, Basinger's Confederate dead would have been confined exclusively to the gully and perhaps to a lesser degree on the road itself. But there were Confederate dead "thickly" strewn in the woods on the left side of the road facing Farmville, exactly where Basinger stated his charge on the 121st New York occurred. Strangely, Olcott, commanding the 121st New York, does not indicate in his Official Report that his 121st New York was pushed back by the 18th Georgia during a charge by Basinger's troops.

B. The charge of the 18th Georgia and the resulting push back of the 121st New York would indicate that the 121st New York was involved in a lengthy back and forth struggle with Basinger's 18th Georgia Battalion before finally over powering them. The 18th Georgia surrendered at their original battlefield position on the road where they tried to regroup and reassemble after their charges. This would, most probably, indicate that Harris Hawthorn of the 121st New York was also held up for a considerable length of time before being able to break through the 18th Georgia line to pursue other battlefield activities.

C. The September 1, 1865, diary entry of Horatio King concerning the Battle of Sailor's Creek is insightful:

… After the battle Genl Sheridan ordered me, being the ranking Q. M., to take charge of the train. My duties became most [?] and I made every endeavor to be relieved from the irksome duty but without success. Immediately after the battle at Sailor's Creek I took a portion of my train to the field for wounded….

[Source: The Library Cap Website, Dickinson College Library, by Laura Detloff, "The Voices Now that Answer Not," Section: Horatio Collins King "The Role of the Veteran in Remembrance," printout in the possession of the author]**Manuscript 114**

This diary entry would explain why Horatio C. King would pay special attention to the strewn path of the dead on the battlefield. King was the ranking Quartermaster in charge of the ambulance train. He was trying to harvest survivors among the dead on the battlefield of Sailor's Creek. The author believes that his description of the gulch on the right side of the road facing south and the strewn Confederate dead through the woods on the left side of the road facing south, are extremely accurate observations and factually documented by King. It is also worth noting that Horatio C. King's military service record indicates that for the month beginning April 1, 1865, he was "in the field" and "on duty as the chief Quartermaster of the 1st Calvary Division."

[Source: Military Service Record of Horatio C. King at the National Archives, Washington, DC, "General and Staff Officers, Union Quartermasters," file number 43042982]**Manuscript 132**

D. The following paragraph in the preface of "Rifle Shots and Bugle Notes" is insightful:

In presenting our work to the former soldiers and sailors, and the people of the United States, we feel that it is due to them to say that many of the articles published were written years ago; that they then presented the ideas of the writers, fresh from the conflict, and that we have printed them as they were written, setting down "naught in malice, but with charity for all."

[Source: "Rifle Shots and Bugle Notes," by Joe A. Joel & Lewis R. Stegman–Grand Army Gazette Publishing Company, 1884]**Manuscript 138**

This preface leaves open the possibility that Horatio C. King wrote his article in "Rifle Shots and Bugle Notes" much earlier than the publishing date of 1884, which leaves open the additional possibility that this write up could have been written by Horatio King from recollections that were more fresh in his mind and closer to the War's end than the 1884 date would indicate.

EXHIBIT-W-BA-2 CONFEDERATE

Introduction:

Robert Stiles:

An account given by Robert Stiles, Major, Commanding the Chaffin's Bluff Battalion at Sailor's Creek, which was a component of Colonel Stapleton Crutchfield Artillery Brigade, which was a component of General Custis Lee's Division.

Evidence:

… The enemy was coming on and everything was still as the grave. My battalion was formed upon and around a swell of the hill, which threw it further to the front than any other command in the division, so that I was compelled to shape my own course, as I had received no special orders…. The earth appeared to have swallowed up the first line of the Federal force in our front. There was a rattling supplement to the volley and the second line wavered and broke. The revulsion was too sudden. On the instant every man in my battalion sprang to his feet and, without orders, rushed, bareheaded and with unloaded muskets, down the slope after the retreating Federals. I tried to stop them, but in vain,

although I actually got ahead of a good many of them. They simply bore me on with the flood…. My battalion was scattered over the face of the hill firing irregularly at the Federals, who seemed to be reforming to renew the attack. I managed to get my men in some sort of formation and their guns loaded, and then charged the Federal line, driving it back across the creek, and forming my command behind a little ridge, which protected it somewhat…. I ran back up the hill and had a brief conversation with General Custis Lee, commanding the division, our brigade commander having been killed, explaining to him that I had not ordered the advance and that we would be cut off if we remained long where we were, but that I was satisfied I could bring the battalion back through a ravine, which would protect them largely from the fire of the enemy's artillery, and reform them on the old line, on the right of the naval battalion, which had remained in position. He expressed his doubts as to this, but I told him I believed my battalion would follow me anywhere, and with his permission I would try it. I ran down the hill again and explained to my men that when I got to the left of the line and shouted to them they were to get up and follow me, on a run and without special formation, through a ravine that led back to the top of the hill. Just because these simple-hearted fellows knew only enough to trust me, and because the enemy was not so far recovered as to take advantage of our exposure while executing the movement to the rear and reforming, we were back in the original lines in a few moments—that is, all who were left of us. It was of no avail. By the time we had well settled into our old position we were attacked simultaneously, front and rear, by overwhelming numbers, and quicker than I can tell it the battle degenerated into a butchery and a confused melee of brutal personal conflicts. I saw numbers of men kill each other with bayonets and the butts of muskets, and even bite each others' throats and ears and noses, rolling on the ground like wild beasts. Suddenly, by one of those inexplicable shiftings which take place on a battlefield, the fighting around me almost entirely ceased, and whereas the moment before the whole environment seemed to be crowded with the enemy, there were now few or none of them on the spot, and as the slaughter and the firing seemed to be pretty well over, I concluded I would try to make my escape. By the way, I had always considered it likely I should be killed, but had never anticipated or contemplated capture. I think it was at this juncture I encountered General Custis Lee, but it may have been after I was picked up. At all events, selecting the direction which seemed to be most free from Federal soldiers and to offer the best chance of escape. I started first at a walk and then broke into a run; but in a short distance ran into a fresh Federal force, and it seemed the most natural and easy thing in the world to be simply arrested and taken in.

[Source: Four Years under Marse Robert, Neale Publishing Company, NY, 1903, pages 329-335]**Manuscript 2**

Comments and Supporting Evidence:

1. There are many important points to be learned from Major Stiles' account.
    A. Major Stiles' Chaffin's Bluff Battalion was formed upon and around a swell (or knoll) of a hill. This would explain why Major Basinger could see only his command (18th Georgia) and Stiles command (Chaffin's Bluff) because of the contour of this swell in the battlefield.
    B. Stiles' men seemed to be in front of the rest of the Division's battle line as a result of being on this swell.
    C. The Federal line broke in their front, and the Chaffin's Bluff troops ran after the retreating Federals. This charge was unauthorized by Stiles.
    D. Stiles' men were scattered on the open field after the first charge, and a second charge drove the Federals across the creek. Stiles' men then hid behind a small ridge.
    E. Stiles ran up the hill to confer with Custis Lee, who presumably was at the knoll in Stiles' original position.
    F. Stiles ran back down the hill after conversing with Custis Lee, got to the left of his line which was still behind the small ridge, and led them left into a ravine.
    G. Stiles, and what was left of his Chaffin's Bluff troops, followed the ravine up the hill to the knoll, this being their original position. This was on the right of the Naval Battalion, and where Custis Lee and Stiles conferred about regrouping the Confederate troops that charged.

H. Stiles thought he could re-form his men using this ravine because the Federals had not yet recovered from the charge by his troops.

I. As soon as Stiles' Chaffin's Bluff troops reformed on the knoll on the right of the Naval Battalion, the Federals attacked again. The fighting at this important point evolved into a very brutal hand to hand combat.

J. Though Stiles is not definitive in his recollections, it may be that Major Stiles and General Custis Lee tried to make their escape around this same point in time in the battle, during the hand to hand combat fight. It would appear from the evidence that Custis Lee was surrounded by Major Stiles' men in the final moments of the battle (Custis Lee states this fact in Exhibit W–PF–23, that plenty of Stiles' men were protecting him and that Major Stiles was near when he was captured). In addition, other evidence supports that Custis Lee and Major Stiles were captured almost together (Hawthorn stated that he took both of them to General Wheaton's headquarters and Basinger stated that both Custis Lee and Major Stiles were entertained at General Sheridan's headquarters after their capture). It is interesting to note from Stiles' account that Major Stiles decided to escape by himself. He did so by "selecting the direction which seemed to be the most free from Federal soldiers." David White's account, as contained in his local newspaper article, describes Custis Lee in a similar situation when White encountered him, with Custis Lee being somewhat separated from his command and making his way toward Sailor's Creek. There is, however, a significant difference between the accounts of Custis Lee and Major Stiles during the final moments of the battle. Where Stiles initiated his escape attempt while he was temporarily caught in an "inexplicable" lull of the battle immediately around him, Custis Lee must have initiated his escape attempt from the heart of the hand to hand combat zone. This is strongly surmised because Custis Lee was almost captured by Lieut. Harry A. Cushman of the 37th Massachusetts during the final hand to hand combat of the battle (see Exhibit W-PF-4). Lieut. Cushman was severely wounded in this attempt. Immediately after being almost captured by Cushman, Custis Lee must have withdrawn himself a short distance behind his own line to make his escape attempt. At this point he was then spotted and pursued by David White.

EXHIBIT-W-BA-3 CONFEDERATE

Introduction:

Major General G. W. Custis Lee, commanding a Confederate Division during the Battle of Sailor's Creek, which was a part of Lieutenant General Richard Ewell's Corps, states the following in his Official Report of the battle.

Evidence:

Custis Lee (circa 1864/5):

REPORT OF GENERAL G. W. C. LEE, From 2d to 6th April, 1865
Richmond, VA, April 25, 1865
… To meet this movement General Kershaw's division formed on the right and mine on the left of the road upon which we were moving, our line of battle being across the road facing Sailor's Creek, which we had not long passed. Before my troops got into position, the enemy opened a heavy fire of artillery upon our lines, which was continued up to the time of our capture. After shelling our lines and skirmishing for some time, an hour or more, the enemy's infantry advanced and were repulsed, and that portion which attacked the artillery brigade was charged by it and driven back across Sailor's Creek. This brigade was then brought back to its original position in line of battle under a heavy fire of artillery. Finding that Kershaw's division, which was on my right, had been obliged to retire in consequence of the enemy having turned his right flank, and that my command was entirely surrounded, to prevent useless sacrifice of life the firing was

stopped by some of my officers aided by some of the enemy's, and the officers and men taken as prisoners of war.

[Source: Southern Historical Society Transactions, volume 1, pages 118-121; 1883]**Manuscript 64**

Comments and Supporting Evidence:

1. There are a few points to be learned from this Custis Lee account of the battle.
    A. Custis Lee corroborates the fact that his Division formed on the left of the road and General Kershaw's Division formed on the right of the road, all facing north.
    B. Only Crutchfield's (Stiles') Artillery Brigade of Custis Lee's Division charged the Federals and drove them back across Sailor's Creek.
    C. Custis Lee corroborates Stiles' account that the charging Stiles Brigade was brought back to its original position which was their original line of battle.
    D. Custis Lee corroborates Kershaw's account that Kershaw's Division was forced to retire and that the Federals turned his right flank (see Exhibit W–BA–4-Confederate)
    E. It would appear that Custis Lee had nothing to do with ordering any cease fire to prevent the "useless sacrifice of life." This action was undertaken by some of Custis Lee's officers aided by some of the Federal officers. It is highly probable that Custis Lee and Major Stiles were attempting their escapes during the final active stages of the battle.

EXHIBIT-W-BA-4 CONFEDERATE

Introduction:

Joseph B. Kershaw:

Major General Joseph B. Kershaw, commanding a Confederate Division during the Battle of Sailor's Creek, which was a part of Lieut. General Richard S. Ewell's Corps, states the following in his Official Report of the battle.

Evidence:

Report of Maj. Gen. Joseph B. Kershaw, C. S. Army, CAMDEN, S. C., October 9, 1865

… As the troops in my front had halted, I detached Humphreys' brigade, commanded by Colonel Fitz Gerald, and Gary's dismounted battalion, under Lieutenant-Colonial Barham, to take position near the house occupied as a hospital by Pickett's division, to cover my crossing Sailor's Creek. Upon arriving at the top of the hill on the south side of the creek, I was informed by General Ewell that the enemy had possession of the road in front of General Anderson, and that we were to hold the enemy in check while that officer attempted to open the way. My command then consisted of only three brigades— Humphreys', Simms' (Brig. Gen. J. P. Simms commanding), and Du Bose's brigade (Brig. Gen. D. M. Du Bose commanding)—and the dismounted cavalry already mentioned; the whole at that time amounted to less than 2,000 effective men. Du Bose was placed in the edge of the wood, with his right resting on the road; Simms, on the left of the road, a little in advance. General Lee's division was on the left of the road, his right occupying a line in front of Du Bose, his left on the same line, or nearly so. In the meantime the enemy attacked and overpowered Humphreys and the dismounted cavalry, forcing them back to my position. They were formed at once on the left of the road, and Simms was moved farther to the right. The enemy made his appearance in rear of Simms' brigade at the same time he was engaged in front and flank. That officer attempted to extricate his command, but found it impossible to do so without confusion, as he was attacked on all sides. This condition of things being discovered by the other troops, all fell back toward the rear and left. I kept up something of a skirmish as the

command retreated; but after moving some 400 yards I discovered that all who had preceded me had been taken by the Yankee cavalry, who were in line of battle across the road. I then directed the men about me and the members of my staff to make their escape in any way possible.
J. B. Kershaw

[Source: Official Records, "The Appomattox Campaign," Volume 46, Series 1, pages 1283 and 1284]**Manuscript 70**

Comments and Supporting Evidence:

1. There are many important points to be learned from Joseph B. Kershaw's account.
   A. His Division consisted of only three Brigades, Humphreys', Simms' and Du Bose's.
   B. Du Bose was placed on the right side of the road facing north, with his left "in the edge of the wood" and his right resting on the road. Du Bose's Brigade was behind the battle line formed by Custis Lee's Division, most likely forming a near-right angle to the extreme right of Custis Lee's Division, which was the 18th Georgia Battalion. This description of Du Bose's formation would explain a gap between the right flank of the 18th Georgia Battalion and the left flank of the Du Bose Brigade. This gap could have occurred in the woods and could explain why Basinger's right flank was diagonally attacked by the 121st New York through this gap while the Federals approached through these woods from Sailor's Creek.
   C. Simms' Brigade was placed at the right of Du Bose's Brigade, on the left side of the road facing north, a little in front of Du Bose's right.
   D. Humphreys' Brigade remained behind to guard the Confederate crossing of the creek. When Humphreys' Brigade was attacked and overpowered by the Federals, they were inserted between Du Bose's and Simms' Brigades, with Simms' Brigade being moved further to the right to accommodate this insertion of Humphreys' Brigade.
   E. It would appear that Simms' Brigade, which was now on the right of Kershaw's Division, collapsed first, being attacked in the right flank and rear (most likely by the Federal Cavalry troops).
   F. After Simms' Brigade collapsed, the Humphrey and Du Bose Brigades continued to fight, retiring toward the rear and to the left of the Division for about 400 yards until they were captured or surrendered.
2. Another account by Kershaw is as follows:

"The wings of Sheridan's infantry united to his cavalry to the right and left of us, the circle of fire was complete. At length, my right gave back, and a fire from the rear announced Anderson's fate. I [g]ave the order to fall back, firing, and slowly moved with the retreating line, through the dense woods as near as I could guess toward Appomattox"

[Source: "Black Day of the Army, April 6, 1865," Greg Eanes, E&H Publishing Company, Inc., pages 199-204]**Manuscript 98**

The important point here is that Kershaw's Divisions were hit from three angles. Kershaw's right was hit by Custer's Calvary, his front was hit by Stagg's Cavalry Brigade, and Kershaw's left was hit by Hamblin's 2nd Brigade of Infantry.

EXHIBIT-W-BA-5 CONFEDERATE

Introduction:
An account of the Battle of Sailor's Creek given by McHenry Howard, A. A. I. G. Custis Lee's Division, Baltimore, October 1865.

Evidence:
... Custis Lee's division, which thus took the field for its first and last campaign, was organized as follows: Barton's brigade was composed of five regiments or battalions, some of which were veteran, while others, known as "Richmond Locals," had no experience in the field beyond service in the trenches. Altogether they numbered about 1300 for line of battle. The so-called "Heavy Artillery

Brigade" was anomalously constituted, being composed of six battalions, each commanded by a Major, with a Lieutenant-Colonel over two Majors. In command of the whole was Colonel S. Crutchfield, formerly chief of artillery to General Stonewall Jackson, and who was just recovering from a wound received when that hero fell so unhappily. Only the Georgia battalion, Major Basinger, and one or two other companies had seen field service—and they not a great deal; the rest had, for over two years, manned the guns and works around Richmond and at Chaffin's Bluff. Most of the companies were heavy artillery by enlistment, but several were light artillery, and one was even, properly, a cavalry company…. At Amelia Court-House our division received a large and efficient accession, but one which also added yet more to its heterogeneous character. This consisted, in the first place, of the so-called "Naval Brigade," formed of the officers and men who had been stationed at Drewry's Bluff, now organized into something like a regiment, the tars being armed with Minnie muskets. They numbered about 1500 (?) and were commanded by Commodore Tucker. There were also four or five companies of "Richmond Locals," which were incorporated with Barton's brigade, and two or three companies of light artillery, armed with muskets, which were added to the heavy artillery brigade. Infantry, cavalry, light and heavy artillery, and sailors, "Locals," "Richmond Defenses," &c., we had thus in our small division all the elements of a complete army and navy…. The morning (April 6th) was damp, and the ground in bad condition for marching…. Barton's brigade now showed not more than 500 men in line, the heavy artillery but few more, and the Naval Brigade was reduced to not over 600. These calculations, however, are made from memory (October 1865)…. Under this fire the two divisions were faced about and formed in the line of battle, with Kershaw on the (now) right of the road, Custis Lee on the left. In Custis Lee's division, Lieutenant-Colonel John Atkinson's two battalions, 10th and 19 Virginia, the Chaffin's Bluff battalion, and the 18th Georgia, Major Basinger, all of the heavy artillery brigade, were on the right and a little thrown forward; next on the left was the Naval Brigade, Commodore Tucker, then Barton's, and finally Lieut.-Colonel James Howard's command, 18th and 20th Virginia. Majors M. B. Hardin and Jas E. Robertson, being the remainder of the heavy artillery brigade, held the extreme left…. After shelling us with impunity as long as they pleased, the Federals engaged us with musketry, their cavalry being armed with the repeating carbine. Thinking to overwhelm us by numbers, they made a charge which resulted in some close fighting, particularly at the road. Here, it is said, the Chaffin's Bluff and Basinger's (Georgia) battalions had a desperate hand-to-hand encounter with them, in which the Federals were worsted. The assailants thus met with a much more stubborn resistance than they anticipated, and were everywhere driven back in confusion, leaving many dead and wounded on the ground. Colonel Atkinson's command and, I believe, the two battalions above named, even made a spirited counter-charge as far as the creek, driving the enemy sheer across…. I saw a number of men in blue uniforms, where Kershaw's line had been, but supposing them to be prisoners, no attention was paid to their appearance. I presume now they were engaged in receiving the surrender of his men. Along Custis Lee's line the firing was still continued, and we had no idea the battle was so nearly ended. I thought we were endeavoring to hold our ground until night might enable us to draw off, but from what I saw afterwards we were so surrounded that escape was impossible, and to have prolonged the contest would have been a useless sacrifice of life. There being an intermission in the fire presently, I passed along the line toward the left to inspect the condition of affairs. The line was at every point unbroken and the men in excellent spirits, exulting in their success so far, and confident of their ability to hold out. But, alas! There was nothing to hold out for.

[Source: "Retreat of Custis Lee's Division and the Battle of Sailor's Creek" by McHenry Howard, Southern Historical Society Transactions, Volume One, pages 61-72; 1874]Manuscript 62****

Comments and Supporting Evidence:

1. We learn many important points from McHenry Howard's account:
   A. This gives us the most detailed and perhaps accurate description of the battlefield line-up of Custis Lee's Division, since this was written in October, 1865, while Howard had a fresh recollection. Howard's recollections would have still been very fresh in October 1865. From left to right facing Sailor's Creek was: Lieut. Colonel James Howard's Command, 18th and 20th

Virginia; next Barton's Brigade; next Commodore Tucker's Command, Naval Brigade; next and a little forward Lieut. Colonel John Atkinson's Command, 10th and 19th Virginia; next Major Stiles Command, Chaffin's Bluff Battalion; next and finally, Major Basinger's Command, 18th Georgia.

B. At the time of battle, Barton's Brigade numbered about 500, the Heavy Artillery Brigade consisting of the 10th, 18th, 19th and 20th Virginia, Chaffin's Bluff and the 18th Georgia numbered a little over 500 and the Naval Battalion numbered not over 600 (revised downward by Howard in his second account which follows later in this report).

C. The Federals charged, which initially resulted in hand to hand combat with the Chaffin's Bluff and 18th Georgia Battalions.

D. Atkinson's 10th and 19th Virginia, Stiles' Chaffin's Bluff and Basinger's 18th Georgia made a countercharge, driving the Federals across the Creek. It would appear that Tucker's Naval Battalion, Barton's Brigade and James Howard's 18th and 20th Virginia stayed in position and did not countercharge the Federals.

E. Kershaw's line was possibly collapsing at this point.

F. The left of Custis Lee's line, presumably Tucker, Barton and James Howard, were maintaining an unbroken line to the end of the battle.

2. Another account given by McHenry Howard provides some additional important details.

… Under this fire the two divisions were formed in line of battle facing to the rear, with Kershaw on the (now) right of the road and Custis Lee on the left or west side. In Custis Lee's Division Lieutenant-Colonel John Atkinson's two battalions-the 10th and 19th Virginia-the Chaffin's Bluff Battalion and the 18th Georgia, Major Basinger (all of the Heavy Artillery brigade, with muskets), were on the right and a little thrown forward (to our late rear) on account of the nature of the ground. Next on the left was the Naval Battalion under Commodore Tucker, then Barton's Brigade, and finally Lieutenant-Colonel James Howard's command, 18th and 20th Virginia, Majors M. B. Hardin and James E. Robertson, being the rest of the heavy artillery brigade, held the extreme left…. I have used expressions implying a want of certainty in my own knowledge of the identity of the particular troops which had this hand to hand fighting and went as far as the creek in the countercharge, because in this fighting my horse was struck behind the saddle by a musket ball which sounded like a stone thrown against a fence. I was at the time with General Custis Lee and his staff on the road and, I think, with the front line. I had ridden this horse—or mare rather—ever since the battle of Gaines' Mill in 1862 where we captured General John F. Reynolds, to whom she was said to belong. My horse appearing to be mortally, or badly, wounded, I took her back fifty or a hundred yards and left her tied to a tree. When I got back our troops which had gone forward had returned, or were returning, to their original position and both artillery and musketry open a deadly fire on us again…. My observation of the latter part of the battle, after the shooting of my horse prevented my getting about well, was chiefly limited to the center of the line-on the left (west) of the road. I noticed the naval brigade, which had been standing firm as a rock, apparently beginning to fall back but in a perfectly regular formation and I hurried over and asked Commodore Tucker the cause…. "General Humphreys (commanding the 2nd Corps of the Army of the Potomac) in his History of the Virginia Campaign of 1864-1865, page 383, puts Ewell's strength on the ground (being Custis Lee's and Kershaw's Divisions), at about 3600. And he estimates, taking my published account of 1865, Custis Lee's Division at about 1600. But I undoubtedly overestimated the naval battalion, as explained hereinbefore."

[Source: "Recollections of a Maryland Confederate Soldier and Staff Officer," reprinted in 1975 from the 1914 edition, Morningside Bookshop, by McHenry Howard]**Manuscript 80**

Several additional points to be learned from McHenry Howard's "Recollections" are:

A. Howard was with Custis Lee in the road when the Confederates initiated their countercharge on the Federals.

B. Howard went to the center of Custis Lee's line when the Confederates were returning from their countercharge and the Federal artillery opened fire on the Confederate positions again. Since Howard was staff of Custis Lee, it can be assumed that Custis Lee also went to the center of his line at this point in the battle.

C. This center position in Custis Lee's line had to be in close proximity to the Naval Battalion since they came under the direct observation of Howard. Howard most likely was positioned between the Naval and Chaffin's Bluff Battalions.

D. Since Howard was a staff officer in Custis Lee's Division, he would have been concentrating on the "big picture" of the overall battlefield. That is why the author has a high degree of confidence in Howard's description of the Confederate troop positions on the battlefield.

EXHIBIT-W-BA-6 CONFEDERATE

Introduction:
An account given by W. L. Timberlake of the 2nd Virginia Battalion, Company D, which was a component of General Custis Lee's Division and Barton's Brigade.

Evidence:
...He faced Custis Lee about and formed along the open brow of the sassafras and pine tufted hill, Kershaw on the right and Lee on the left. There, with flags over them, they lay, from the road down into the ravine and up its northern bank, and every man in that line knew that a crisis was coming, for Anderson, behind them to the west, was engaged, and in full view of the valley's eastern brink the 6th Corps was massing into the fields double quick, the battle lines blooming with colors, growing longer and deeper with every moment, the batteries at a gallop coming into action front. We knew what it all meant....The sun was more than half way down, the oak and pine woods behind them crowning the hill and laying evening's peaceful shadows on Ewell's line, and on Sheridan's its long afternoon beams glinted warmly and sparkled on the steel barrels of the shouldered arms of the moving infantry, for they were getting under way. Seymour's and Wheaton's men were approaching the creek-but let us hurry over to Custis Lee's lines to a spot on the open, rounded eastward knoll, where Major Stiles' battalion lay....Until the Federal Infantry had reached the creek the artillery fire had been fast and dreadfully fatal; then it stopped, and all was still as the grave as the men made their way through the thickety banks and formed on the farther side. I'll not try to give all the details of that bloody engagement, but our men, under orders, reserved their fire until their lines were close up, then they let go a crashing volley. The execution was frightful, and at once they charged their center with fury and drove it back in confusion cross the creek. But meanwhile the enemy's troops on the left and right have been successfully crowding our flanks into the bowlike hollow of the ravine's head and the 37th Massachusetts had the fiercest, most hand-to-hand, and literally savage encounter of the war with the remnant of Stiles' battalion and the marines from ships that had lain in the James River. I was next to these marines and saw them fight. They clubbed their muskets, fired pistols into each other's faces, and used the bayonets savagely. Pretty soon a flag of truce came in sight, the officer bearing it coming bravely up to our line under fire.... Gen. H. C. Wright, who commanded the 6th Corps of the Federal Army, in his official report of this battle, says: "The 1st and 3rd Divisions of this Corps charged the enemy's position, carrying it handsomely, except at a point on our right of the road crossing the creek, where a column, said to be composed exclusively of the Marine Brigade and other troops which had held the lines of Richmond previous to the evacuation, made a counter charge upon that part of our lines in their front. I was never more astonished. These troops were surrounded. The 1st and 3rd Divisions of this Corps were on either flank, my artillery and a fresh division in their front, and some three divisions of Major General Sheridan's cavalry in their rear.

[Source: "In the Siege of Richmond and After" by W. L. Timberlake, Confederate Veteran, Volume 29, pages 412-414]**Manuscript 65**

Comments and Supporting Evidence:
1. There are several important points to be learned from W. L. Timberlake's account:
    A. He gives a very nice description of Custis Lee's battle line, starting from the road, down into the ravine and back up its northern bank.
    B. Timberlake validates that Major Stiles' Battalion lay on an open, rounded, eastward knoll.
    C. The Confederates charged driving some of the Federals across the creek.

D. The Federals on the left and right were crowding the Confederate flanks into the bowl-like hollow of the ravine's head.
E. The 37th Massachusetts had a brutal hand-to-hand clash with the remnant of Stiles' Battalion, and the Marines, presumably with Commodore Tucker's command.

EXHIBIT-W-BA-7 CONFEDERATE

Introduction:

An account given by Capt. Thomas B. Blake of the 10th Virginia Battalion of Heavy Artillery.

Evidence:

…The 10th Battalion and 19th Virginia Battalion of Artillery (also of five companies) were under command of Col. John Wilder Atkinson, of Richmond, a son of the Bishop of North Carolina, with Lieut. Johnny Cowarden, of Richmond, as adjutant. These two battalions, together with the 18th and 20th Virginia Battalions of Artillery, commanded by Col. James Howard, of Baltimore, formed the "Artillery Brigade," under the command of Col. Stapleton Crutchfield, acting brigadier general, and Capt. W. N. Worthington, of Richmond, adjutant general. The Artillery Brigade and Barton's Brigade formed Gen. G. W. Custis Lee's division, which was attached to Lieutenant General Ewell's corps. The Artillery Brigade was thoroughly drilled in artillery practice and manned the heavy guns on the line of the Richmond defenses. It was also armed with rifles and was well drilled in infantry tactics. This was the only body of fully equipped and disciplined troops for the immediate defense of Richmond and on several occasions demonstrated great efficiency in protecting the city…. Thursday, April 6, when we reached Sailor's Creek, a small stream which at that time had overflowed its banks from the continuous rains of the past few days, giving the appearance of a small river. We halted a few minutes, then waded across this stream and took our position on the rising ground about one hundred yards beyond…. We threw ourselves prone upon the ground, which was covered with a growth of broom sedge and a few small bushes, mostly pine. Our line of battle was long drawn out; exceedingly thin…. When they had advanced to within thirty or forty paces of our line, the order was given to charge. In a moment we were all on our feet, yelling like demons and rushing at them…. They broke just before we reached them, after pouring a deadly fire into our ranks. A part of our line on the right engaged in a hand-to-hand bayonet fight. We followed them to the edge of the stream, into which they plunged, and kept up a merciless fire on them at short range as they crossed…. After the enemy had been driven back across the creek; we gathered up our handful of men and fell back to our original position…. We had scarcely reached our former position when Custer's Brigade, of Sheridan's Cavalry, came down on us from the rear. A young cavalry officer rode in among us and begged us to surrender; telling us that we were entirely surrounded and that further resistance would be useless. It was so brave and gallant an act that no one attempted to molest him. In the meanwhile the infantry which had been driven back across Sailor's Creek re-formed and was advancing on us in greater force. We now realized that we were utterly powerless and were forced to surrender.

[Source: "The Artillery Brigade at Sailor's Creek," by Capt Thomas S. Blake, Confederate Veteran, Vol. 28 (1920), pages 213-216]**Manuscript 79**

Comments and Supporting Evidence:

1. The points to be learned from Capt. Thomas B. Blake's account are as follows:
   A. The 10th, 19th, 18th and 20th Virginia Battalions formed the Artillery Brigade under Colonel Stapleton Crutchfield.
   B. This Artillery Brigade and Barton's Brigade formed the majority of Custis Lee's Division.
   C. Crutchfield's Artillery Brigade was armed with rifles and was well drilled in infantry tactics.
   D. Custis Lee's Division battle line was exceedingly thin, long and drawn out.
   E. He corroborates the Confederate charge, indicating that the right of Custis Lee's line engaged in a hand-to-hand bayonet fight.
   F. He also corroborates that the Confederates drove the Federals across the creek.
   G. The Confederates regrouped back to their original positions with a handful of men that were left.

H. It would appear in the final moments of the battle that the Federal Cavalry descended on the rear of the 10th Virginia at the same time the Federal Infantry re-formed and began a new attack on their front.

EXHIBIT-W-BA-8 CONFEDERATE

Introduction:
An account given by General Ewell as found in the writings of Walter C. Watson.

Evidence:

...What happened to Ewell has been told by himself and other survivors. His report continues: "My line ran across a little ravine, which leads nearly at right angles towards Sailor's Creek. Gen. G. W. C. Lee was on the left, with the Naval Battalion under Commodore Tucker behind his right. All of Lee's and part of Kershaw's Division were posted behind a rising ground that afforded some shelter from artillery. The creek was perhaps three hundred yards in their front, with brush pines between and a clear field beyond it.
[Source: "Sailor's Creek," by Walter C. Watson, Southern Historical Society Papers, Volume XLII (1917), pages 136-51]**Manuscript 78**

Comments and Supporting Evidence:
1. The important note here is Ewell states that his line ran across a little ravine, which was at a right angle to Sailor's Creek. This ravine is an important landmark, together with the knoll, in identifying the whereabouts of Major Stiles and General Custis Lee in the final moments of the battle. Ewell states that his battle line front was approximately 300 yards from Sailor's Creek. It would appear that brush pines were between his troops and the advancing Federals
2. The following account by Morris Schaff places the ravine approximately in the center of Custis Lee's division:

Kershaw having been driven across the creek, Ewell faced Custis Lee about and formed along the open brow of the sassafras-and pine-tufted hill, Kershaw on the right, and Lee on the left; the ravine scoured out of the face of the hill was about the center of his line.
[Source: "The Sunset of the Confederacy" by Morris Schaff, 1912]**Manuscript 89**

The author places the 18th Georgia, Chaffin's Bluff troops, the Naval/Marine troops at Atkinson's 10th and 19th Virginia troops between the road and the right of the ravine facing toward Sailor's Creek. The author places Barton's Brigade and James Howard's 18th and 20th Virginia troops to the left of the ravine, once again facing toward Sailor's Creek.

EXHIBIT-W-BA-9 CONFEDERATE

Introduction:
An account of R. T. W. Duke–Lieut. Colonel of the 2nd Battalion of Virginia Reserves–which was in Barton's Brigade.

Evidence:

... In a few minutes we were moved to the right, and as the ground was rough, hilly and thick with trees and undergrowth, I dismounted and turned my horse over to my orderly. We proceeded a half mile or more and were halted a little below the crest of a steep ridge, with a deep ravine in front of us, and another ridge opposite us as high, if not higher than our ridge. From our position the opposite crest was distant some 200 to 300 yards.... Soon after we took our position the artillery of the enemy opened upon us, but the range was too high and did no damage, except to the tree tops. After the artillery had ceased firing a line of skirmishes appeared on the crest of the opposite ridge, but soon retired from a brisk fire opened by our line. After they retired a long line of infantry appeared on the opposite ridge. Our men opened on them and for a time there was brisk musketry fire on both sides. We had the advantage of position; the enemy were shooting below a point blank-range, while our men were

shooting above that range. I believe it is the general observation of military men that troops usually shoot a little too high. After some half hour, more or less, the enemy in our front retired, but a large body, at least a brigade, was observed moving around our left. FLAG OF TRUCE: All things were quiet for a time; then I observed a flag of truce on the opposite ridge. General Barton directed me to meet it. I did so, and proceeded to the bottom of the ravine, where I met a mounted officer, who proved to be General (or Colonel) Oliver Edwards. He informed me that Generals Ewell, Lee, and all of the command who were not killed, had surrendered, and he desired us to surrender in order to prevent further useless effusion of blood. This proposition I declined, on the ground that we had received no orders from our commanders to surrender. I reported the interview to General Barton and about that time squadron of cavalry rode up from the rear and we surrendered.

[Source: "Burning of Richmond"; by R. T. W. Duke; Southern Historical Society Papers; Volume 25]**Manuscript 38**

Comments and Supporting Evidence:

1. It would appear from Duke's account that Barton's Brigade did not charge the Federals. Barton's Brigade was positioned with a large ravine at their front while facing toward Sailor's Creek. Barton's Brigade held off a frontal assault by the Federals, but they were getting flanked by the Federals on their left and ultimately surrendered to the Federal Cavalry who came on their rear.

2. Another more detailed account by R. T. W. Duke is as follows:

We immediately formed a line of battle on the hills nearly parallel to Sailor's Creek, we being almost on the extreme left, which was somewhat retired from the creek, our position being on the slope of a high ridge, with a deep ravine in front of us and a steep, high hill behind. I think the only command to the left of us was the marines from the gunboats under the command of Captain Semmes, and on our right was a battalion from the fortification around Richmond under the command of Colonel Crutchfield. We had hardly taken our position in line of battle when the enemy commenced a furious cannonade on our positions, and in a short time the Federal infantry appeared on the opposite ridge, and the musketry became pretty sharp. Our loss was trifling, our position being on the slope of the hill and the enemy firing over us. I remember that Colonel Crutchfield; who was not very far from me, was mortally wounded and borne from the field. I think here should be mentioned the fact worthy of remembrance. During the action I had stepped back a few paces to communicate with General Barton. As I returned to my command I found that they had faced about and were moving to the rear, but in pretty good order. I halted them, pointed to the marines on our left who were standing firm, about faced the command, and they marched back, every man, and resumed their position in line, although under a regular fire. These were boys and old men who had seen very little of war, and I do not think regulars could have done better. After the firing had continued for perhaps more than an hour, the enemy in our front fell back on the ridge out of sight. Soon thereafter a Federal officer approached our line with a flag of truce. He was halted about a hundred yards off. I was ordered by General Barton to see what it meant, so I went down and met him. I think he gave his name as General Edwards. He informed me that we were entirely surrounded and that our extreme right, which was out of our sight, had been cut to pieces; that General Ewell, Gen. Custis Lee, and all the right of the command had surrendered. Mark you, we were in the woods and somewhat separated from the right of the division. I replied that his command had certainly retired from our front, and I saw no cause for our surrendering. We then parted, he retiring toward where his command had last been seen; and I returned to my command, then went back to General Barton, about thirty steps in the rear, and was making my report when a squadron of Sheridan's Cavalry dashed from the rear immediately upon us. There was nothing for us to do but to surrender. General Barton, being satisfied that the enemy were on our front, flank, and rear, surrendered his command.

[Source: "With the Confederate Reserves"; by R. T. W. Duke, Confederate Veteran, Volume 26, pages 486 and 487]**Manuscript 103**

There are three important points to be learned from this account by Duke:

A. This gives the best description of the position of Barton's Brigade, aligned on a slope.

B. Duke is mistaken when he states that he "thinks" the Marines were on the left of Barton's Brigade. The Marines and Crutchfield's troops were on Barton's right flank, and Howard, commanding the 18th and 20th Virginia Heavy Artillery, was on Barton's left flank.

C. Barton's Brigade was in the woods and somewhat separated from the rest of the troops making up the right of Custis Lee's Division. This could explain, in part, why they did not get caught up in the charge of Stiles' Chaffin's Bluff and Atkinson's Virginia Heavy Artillery troops. Another factor that might have prevented Barton's troops from participating in the Confederate charge that was done by their fellow troops to their right would have been the large and deep ravine (west branch) that was in their immediate front.

3. The following is an account from the Regimental history of the 47th Virginia Infantry, which was a part of Barton's Brigade:

… The brigade started marching again at dawn on April 6 and crossed Sayler's Creek about 3:00 p.m. There was a burst of firing up ahead of the men and more firing to their rear. Ewell's Corps had been cutoff by pursuing Union troops. To meet the threat, Custis Lee's division was deployed to the left of the road with its front protected by the swampy bottomland of Sayler's Creek. The 47th Virginia and the rest of Barton's Brigade were in the center of the division's line. Union artillery fired at the Confederate line and then the enemy charged. The Union charge was met with a tremendous volley from the Confederate line that hurled it back. Some inexperienced men under Major Robert Stiles pursued the retreating Yankees, but the 47th Virginia veterans held their place in the line. Stiles' men were recalled and the line was stabilized again. The Union troops rallied, resumed the artillery fire, and struck again in overwhelming numbers, this time from the front and flank. There was a brief burst of hand-to-hand fighting and it was all over.

[Source: "47th Virginia Infantry," H. E. Howard, Inc, 1991]**Manuscript 104**

The important point to be gained from this write-up is that Barton's Brigade held their position and did not charge like Stiles' and Atkinson's men.

EXHIBIT-W-BA-10 CONFEDERATE

Introduction:
An account by Charles Stevens Dwight, Captain and Staff of General Kershaw.

Evidence:
… Let me say here that I am trying to describe only what occurred on the front held by Kershaw's Division. I saw something of Gen. Lee's Division on our immediate left, but scarcely anything that happened on our right. Gen. Kershaw formed his line only one deep, the men several feet apart; sometimes the spaces were greater, and as the brave fellows fell, how many a one did fall! The intervals became painfully and dangerously wider. Strict orders had been given to hold our fire until the enemy got within about fifty yards, and also to aim low. There was a thrilling moment, the opposing lines presented a grand sight. Then a flash-and-roar. Few bullets missed a mark. The great column, stunned and shattered, hesitated. Then came the rush of our long thin line and, of course, that rebel yell. The attacking column broke and fled in wild confusion, closely pressed by our yelling and firing line. But here came the supporting column in splendid order. Retiring slowly our division resumed its first position, awaiting the oncoming enemy. The broken first line having passed through their supports was quickly re-formed. I need only say that the second attack resulted exactly like the first. The casualties were considerable to us, very heavy to the enemy. This routine of attack and repulse continued, with occasional intervals, during several hours. It must be said that the enemy showed admirable pluck and discipline in keeping up so long their futile and costly attacks…. But, comrades, the end is at hand. Why repeat the story of our last and one of our best fights? The constantly increasing infantry and artillery fire far to the right and the evidently approaching [enemy] gave warning that the right had been turned and driven in. The cavalry poured in behind our line and at once surrounded and captured Gen. Kershaw and those of the staff who were with him, his three brigadiers, and Gen. W. C. Lee and all the line officers and men who could not slip through.

[Source: "A South Carolina Rebel's Recollections, Personal Reminiscences of the Evacuation of Richmond and the Battle of Sailor's Creek, April 6, 1865," by Charles Stevens Dwight, the State Company, Columbia, SC; 1917]**Manuscript 40**

Comments and Supporting Evidence:

1. The important point to be learned from Dwight's account is that the Kershaw line held off the frontal assaults of the Federals for quite some time by Kershaw's troops launching several charges against the Federals. It is important to note that the 121st New York not only went against the 18th Georgia, but presumably went against some portion of Kershaw's left flank as well. If this is true, then the 121st New York would surely have been involved in these "attack and repulse" actions as described by Dwight. The 121st New York would have had a difficult time breaking through Kershaw's left flank, just as they would have had a difficult time breaking through the 18th Georgia, with these various charges initiated by the Confederates. Kershaw's troops were ultimately defeated by having their right flank turned, allowing the Federal Calvary to pour in behind their line.

EXHIBIT-W-BA-1 FEDERAL

Introduction:

Brevet Colonel Egbert Olcott, commanding the 121st New York during the Battle of Sailor's Creek, describes the following events in his Official Report concerning the Battle of Sailor's Creek.

Evidence:

Report of the part taken by the One hundred and twenty-first New York Volunteers in the Battle of Sailor's Creek, April 6, 1865

The brigade being in two lines, the One hundred and Twenty-First New York formed the right of the first, the Ninety-fifth Pennsylvania being on the left. About 4 pm advanced across Sailor's Creek. Remained a short time under the crest of the hill to reform, the creek being quite deep and the crossing difficult. Charged with the rest of the line, drove the enemy, capturing a large number of prisoners. Pressing forward, the enemy were found to be on the right flank of the brigade, the troops on the immediate right having been repulsed. The regiment, by order of Colonel Olcott, rapidly changed front, forming on the road that, crossing the creek, runs nearly perpendicular to the original line of battle. Farther down the road, near the creek, a portion of the Thirty-seventh Massachusetts were striving to hold their ground. The One hundred and Twenty-First New York having checked the enemy, who were endeavoring to get into the rear of the brigade, was ordered to charge, which it did, driving the enemy in confusion, capturing General Custis Lee and several other officers of high rank, together with two stand of colors.

[Source: Official Records, "The Appomattox Campaign," Volume 46, Series 1, page 937]**Manuscript 3**

Comments and Supporting Evidence:

1. There are several important points to be learned from Egbert Olcott's account of the battle.
    A. The 121st New York was on the front line of Hamblin's Brigade, forming the right portion of this front line, with the 95th Pennsylvania on the left of the 121st New York, which formed the left portion of this front line.
    B. After crossing the creek and re-forming, the 121st New York charged forward, going up the hill presumably on the left side of the road.
    C. The 121st New York found that Confederate troops were pressing forward on the right flank of their Regiment and Hamblin's Brigade, "endeavoring to get to the rear of the Brigade." These Confederates were undoubtedly the 18th Georgia, ordered by Major Basinger to charge the 121st New York when the 121st New York first made their initial attack on the diagonal right flank of Basinger's 18th Georgia. The 121st New York's initial attack on the right flank of the 18th Georgia was through the woods and into a gap between the right flank of the 18th Georgia and the left flank of Du Bose's Brigade which was positioned at the "edge of the wood."

D. The 121st New York, discovering some Confederates on their right flank, changed front to parallel the road, eventually forming a battle line on the road. By this time, Major Basinger most likely reassembled his Battalion from their initial charge on the 121st New York and re-formed in the gully at road-side. One has to question why Olcott did not describe having been initially driven back by a charge from the 18th Georgia, as described by Basinger and supported by the observations of the battlefield pattern of the Confederate dead by Horatio C. King.

E. With the 121st New York and the 18th Georgia now having their battle lines formed on each side of the road, Olcott ordered the 121st New York to charge. This final charge overpowered Basinger's troops and the 18th Georgia was forced to surrender. The final moments of the battle between the 121st New York and the 18th Georgia appear to have been fought on this road. It is interesting to note that Col. Olcott did not mention in his Official Report a fierce hand-to-hand combat as described by Major Stiles. This is a good indication that the 121st New York did not fight with the Chaffin's Bluff troops at all, having been confined to fight solely the 18th Georgia and possibly some of Du Bose's Brigade in Kershaw's Division. This is understandable given the fact that the road on which the 121st New York and the 18th Georgia fought their final battle is a considerable distance, about 300 yards, from the head of the ravine where Major Stiles regrouped his men and brought them back to their original positions at the top of the hill to ultimately fight their final hand to hand battle with the 37th Massachusetts.

F. The two stands of colors captured by the 121st New York were: (1) the flag of the Savannah Guards also known as the 18th Georgia; which was captured by Warren Dockun, and (2) a flag of an unknown Confederate regiment, which was captured by Benjamin Gifford.

[Source: File # AAK-534-EB, 1869, National Archives, Washington, DC] Manuscript 109**

EXHIBIT-W-BA-2 FEDERAL

Introduction:
An account of the 121st New York given by Isaac O. Best, author of their regimental history.

Evidence
Colonel Olcott, finding the ground in front of him clear and the enemy holding on to the works on the right, half wheeled the 121st to the right and moved lengthwise and partly in the rear of the enemy's line and they immediately abandoned their works and surrendered. These last troops we encountered were Marines, or land sailors, and had never before been in battle.
[Source: "History of the 121st New York State Infantry," by Isaac Best, 1921]Manuscript 12**

Comments and Supporting Evidence:
1. The two important points to be learned from Best's account are:
   A. The 121st New York partially got in the rear of the 18th Georgia, indicating the possibility that some of the 121st New York marched straight to the road and high enough to be partially on the right flank and rear of the charging 18th Georgia.
   B. Only after tangling severely with the 18th Georgia and compelling their surrender did the 121st New York move on to fighting the Marines, who were the last Confederate fighting force on the field. The Marines were fighting until nightfall, when they eventually surrendered to Kiefer. This would indicate that the 121st New York first fought the 18th Georgia, and then much later, fought Tucker's Naval/Marine Battalion. This would also indicate that the 121st New York did not fight against Stiles' Chaffin's Bluff troops.

EXHIBIT-W-BA-3 FEDERAL

Introduction:
Brevet Brigadier-General Joseph E. Hamblin, commanding the 2nd Brigade of the 1st Division of the Federal 6th Army Corps, states the following in his Official Report concerning the Battle of Sailor's Creek.

Evidence:

Reports of Bvt. Brig. Gen. Joseph E. Hamblin. Sixty-fifth New York, Infantry, April 15, 1865
Report of operations of Second Brigade in the Battle of Sailor's Creek, April 6, 1865:

… the Second Connecticut Heavy Artillery, Colonel Hubbard commanding, on right, and the left wing of Sixty-fifth New York Volunteers on left of second line. Advanced across a broad swamp traversed by a deep creek; rallied the line on the opposite side preparatory to a charge. Finding a wide interval in the front of Third Brigade, on my right, moved the brigade by right flank about fifty yards…. the Second Connecticut Heavy Artillery, Colonel Hubbard commanding, turned to the left, pushing half a mile up the road, capturing wagons, forges, battery wagons, &c.

[Source: Official Records, "The Appomattox Campaign," Volume 46, Series 1, pages 932 and 933]**Manuscript 3**

Comments and Supporting Evidence:

1. We learn two important points from this account of Joseph Hamblin.
    A. He corroborates the "wide interval" between his Brigade and Oliver Edwards' 3rd Brigade. As mentioned previously, this gap was penetrated by Basinger's 18th Georgia troops during their initial charge of the Federal line.
    B. The 2nd Connecticut Heavy Artillery was on the right of the 2nd Brigade's second line of their battle formation, with the left wing of the 65th New York being on the left side of this second line. During the battle, the 2nd Connecticut Heavy Artillery "turned to the left, pushing a half mile up the road, capturing wagons, forges, & battery wagons." It is very difficult to see how Private Dennis Moore of Company K of the 2nd Connecticut Heavy Artillery assisted in the capture of Custis Lee, given this account of the 2nd Connecticut Heavy Artillery's movements during the battle. With the 2nd Connecticut Heavy Artillery pushing a half mile up the road, and Custis Lee being, most probably, at the head of the ravine with Major Stiles, Moore would have been a considerable distance from Custis Lee. This sizeable distance would have been a very difficult route for Moore to transverse in an open, active battlefield in order to get to where Custis Lee was positioned to assist Hawthorn in Custis Lee's capture.

EXHIBIT-W-BA-4 FEDERAL

Introduction:

An account of the Battle of Sailor's Creek given by a member of the 2nd Connecticut Heavy Artillery, a Lieutenant Curtis.

Evidence:

When formed, the line was advanced—sometimes by brigade front and sometimes by a flank—but always on, until we crossed Sailor's Creek and came to a halt under a steep bank, from the crest of which the rebels poured down a murderous fire. Two lines were formed, the Second Connecticut Volunteer Artillery and Sixty-Fifth New York in the second line. Everything being ready, "Forward!" sounded along the whole line, and away we went up the hill, under a very hot fire. It was tough work to get over the crest, but at last we got the Johnnies started, and made good time after them. The Second Heavies captured Mahone's Head-quarters train, and many prisoners, besides one battle flag. We were badly broken, but after running on for some distance were finally halted and re-formed. Colonel Hubbard and Major Jones came up in time to present us to Generals Sheridan, Wright, Wheaton and Hamblin, who all rode along to the front. We also advanced soon after, and found things in a promising condition. General Ewell and staff and several thousand other prisoners had been taken, together with wagon trains, guns, caissons, and small arms without number.

[Source: "History of the Second Connecticut Volunteer Heavy Artillery, Originally the Nineteenth Connecticut Volunteers" by Theodore F. Vaill 1868]**Manuscript 87**

Comments and Supporting Evidence:

1. This account states two important facts:
   A. It was "tough work" to get over the crest held by the Confederates. Once they did, the 2nd Connecticut Heavy Artillery was badly broken. This would indicate that the 2nd Connecticut Heavy Artillery had a difficult time penetrating both Basinger's and Kershaw's line. It could also indicate that the 2nd Connecticut Heavy Artillery was affected by the charge of Basinger's 18th Georgia troops which came upon them, and upon the 121st New York.
   B. The 2nd Connecticut Heavy Artillery captured Mahone's Headquarters train, validating the Official Report that the 2nd Connecticut Heavy Artillery went up the road where the Union Cavalry was fighting with Confederate General Anderson's troops. Mahone's Headquarters train would have been located with Anderson's troops. Given this account, it continues to be very difficult to see how Private Moore was anywhere near the vicinity of Custis Lee during the battle. [Note: the 2nd Connecticut Heavy Artillery does not have a surviving battle report for Sailor's Creek in the Official Records]

EXHIBIT-W-BA-5 FEDERAL

Introduction:

Warren J. Keifer reports on the Naval/Marine Battalion, which was under the overall command of Gen. Custis Lee at the Battle of Sailor's Creek.

Evidence:

As the gloom of approaching night settled over the field, covered with dead and dying, the fire of artillery and musketry ceased, and General Ewell, together with eleven of his general officers, and about all his gallant army that survived, were prisoners. Commodore Tucker and his Marine Brigade, numbering about 2,000, surrendered to me a little later. They were under cover of a dense forest, and had been passed by in the first onset of the assault. Most of the officers (about thirty-five in number) of this Marine Brigade had served in the United States navy before the war, and prior to the evacuation of Richmond, served in and about Richmond on gunboats and river batteries. As infantrymen they cut a sorry figure in maneuvers, but they were brave, stood to their assigned position after all others of their army had been overthrown, and then knew nothing about flight or retreat, so were taken captive as a body. By reason of their first position, they suffered heavily in killed and wounded.
[Source: "The Battle of Sailor's Creek," MOLLUS, OH, III, pages 1-20] **Manuscript 54**

In Noah Andre Trudeau's book, "An End to Valor" on page 112 he states the following:

...Among the last of the surrounded Confederate units to capitulate was the dry-docked Naval Battalion. "They fought better and longer than any other troops upon the field," wrote Keifer to his wife afterward. The Union officer, believing that the sailors were ready to give up the fight, rode into their ranks to accept their surrender. The navel men began to follow his instructions, not recognizing him as a Yankee officer. When they understood what he was attempting to do, several leveled their Muskets at the intruder. Said Keifer, "Commander Tucker, who commanded the Brigade, knocked up the muzzles of the guns nearest to me and saved my life. I succeeded in escaping to my lines unhurt. I at once bore down upon them and in a few moments captured the Brigade entire." Quipped one of Keifer's men, "Although sailors themselves, yet Sailor's Creek had no charms for them."
[Author Note: Trudeau's source for Keifer is: "J. Warren Keifer, Letters from his Papers housed in the Library of Congress' Manuscript Division," personal letter to the author.]

Comments and Supporting Evidence:

1. Three important points are to be learned from J. W. Keifer's account.
   A. This Naval/Marine Brigade under Commodore Tucker was the last Confederate fighting battalion left on the field, which was "under cover of a dense forest and had been passed by in the first onset of the assault."

B. This Naval/Marine Brigade was still fighting into the approaching night fall despite the fact that all the Confederate Generals (including Custis Lee) were already captured.

C. Commodore Tucker surrendered to Keifer at the very end of the battle.

EXHIBIT-W-BA-6 FEDERAL

Introduction:

Miles L. Butterfield, staff of General Wheaton and one of the claimants to the capture of Custis Lee, recounts his recollections of the Battle of Sailor's Creek.

Evidence:

…When our division arrived at the creek, and found that they could not cross at that point, (the water being very deep and running very swift) they were obliged to march a mile to the left, as before stated. General Wheaton, in command of our division, was stationed about the center of the division and in rear of it, on somewhat elevated ground, so as to see the whole battlefield. I was the only officer of his staff left with him, the others having been sent with orders to the different brigade commanders. When the bugle sounded the advance, General Hamblin, being on the extreme left, with a thicket of small timber between his brigade and the 3rd, did not see the movements of the troops to his right, and did not move his brigade with the rest of the corps, which had a big gap between the two brigades, and the left flank of our regiment (37th Mass.) exposed to a cross fire from the enemy. As General Wheaton saw this, he turned to me and said, "Major, for God's sake, start General Hamblin's brigade." I dismounted, and, leaving my horse with the orderly, plunged into the stream which was about to my waist and running very swift. By the aid of the willows and witch hazel, I managed to reach the other side of the creek, where General Hamblin's brigade was awaiting orders. On receiving the order, the brigade was immediately put into motion and I joined the 37th Massachusetts in the charge.

[Source: Miles L. Butterfield, "Personal Reminiscences with the Sixth Corps, 1864–1865, MOLLUS-WI, Volume IV, pages 85-93; 1905]**Manuscript 5**

Comments and Supporting Evidence:

1. There are three important points that can be learned from Miles Butterfield's account.
    A. Butterfield corroborates the fact that was stated by Basinger who commanded the 18th Georgia, that there was a thicket of woods between Hamblin's 2nd Brigade with the 121st New York on the right of that Brigade and Edwards' 3rd Brigade with the 37th Massachusetts on the left of that Brigade. This thicket initially shielded the attacking 121st New York from the view of the 18th Georgia as stated by Basinger.
    B. A large gap formed between the 2nd Brigade and the 121st New York and the 3rd Brigade and the 37th Massachusetts. This gap served as a natural battlefield thoroughfare into which some of Basinger's 18th Georgia troops plunged during their authorized charge to repulse the advancing 121st New York.
    C. The 2nd Brigade, with the 121st New York, "did not see the movement of the troops to their right (3rd Brigade with the 37th Massachusetts) and did not move their Brigade with the rest of the Corps." This further widened the distance between these two Brigades.

EXHIBIT-W-BA-7 FEDERAL

Introduction:

This is an account given by General Frank Wheaton, who was an important Federal Infantry Division commander at the Battle of Sailor's Creek.

Evidence:

The Second Brigade was ordered to charge at once up the steep hills and into the enemy's line in the woods. This movement was brilliantly executed under a galling fire, and the Third Brigade at the same time advancing against the strong lines in its front, and the Battle of Sailor's Creek was won. A brigade of Southern marines stubbornly continued the fight, but the movements of the One hundred and twenty-

first New York and Thirty-seventh Massachusetts Volunteers, which were admirably handled, compelled them to speedily recognize our victory.
[Source: Official Records, "The Appomattox Campaign," Volume 46, Series 1, pages 914-915]**Manuscript 6**

Comments and Supporting Evidence:
1. Two important points can be learned from General Wheaton's account.
   A. Hamblin's 2nd Brigade had to go through the woods to confront the Confederates. This supports Basinger's account that the 121st New York initially approached the flank of the 18th Georgia through dense woods.
   B. The 121st New York and the 37th Massachusetts both fought with the Confederate Marines who were holding out to the very last moments of the battle (around nightfall). It is interesting to note that Wheaton does not mention in his Official Report Keifer's attack on the Confederate Naval/Marine Brigade.

EXHIBIT-W-BA-8 FEDERAL

Introduction:
Captain Archibald Hopkins, commanding the 37 Massachusetts at the Battle of Sailor's Creek, states the following in his Official Report concerning the Battle of Sailor's Creek.

Evidence:

At the Battle of Sailor's Creek the regiment [37th Mass.], after severe double-quicking, which greatly exhausted the men, was put in position in column of wings, right in front, rear of the Second Rhode Island. When the order to advance was given I deployed the regiment into line of battle and moved to left, so that my right joined the left of the Second Rhode Island. Just before reaching the swamp, which protected the enemy's position, I ordered the right company (C) to deploy so as to cover our front. They executed this movement with admirable rapidity and precision considering the nature of the ground, crossed the swamp, moved up the hill, and were soon exchanging shots with the enemy. The line was halted and reformed after crossing the swamp under cover of the hill, the crest of which was held by the enemy. We were then moved a short distance by the right flank, when the order "forward" was given. The men reserved their fire with noteworthy coolness until we were within a few rods of the enemy, who were formed in two lines of battle on the crest of the hill. They then opened with rapid volleys, advancing all the while with a yell. The enemy, unable to withstand our fire, gave back slowly at first, and soon disappeared from our front, leaving several prisoners and a caisson in our hands. I now found that we were entirely unsupported on either flank, and was about to take measures to connect with the Second Brigade, which had been on our left, when I noticed what seemed to be a heavy column of the enemy moving by the flank around our left. I hastened to that part of the line and caused it to be thrown back, after which a few well directed volleys drove them out of sight again. At this juncture of affairs it was discovered that the enemy had moved a column through a ravine, which served to partly conceal the movement, around our right and about half the length of the regiment in our rear. We had barely time to face about when they charged us and a desperate hand-to-hand fight with swords, pistols, and bayonets ensued. Several men were wounded with the bayonet. We did not give them an inch of ground and they were finally forced back into the ravine, where we swept the whole length of their line with such a terrible raking fire that they were unable to reply, and soon gave token of surrender. We accordingly ceased firing, when they opened fire on us, wounding Adjutant Bradley and some others. We immediately opened again with redoubled energy, and in a few moments they surrendered in earnest.... Over eighty rebel dead were afterward counted in the ravine I have mentioned.... After the severest fighting was over the One hundred and twenty-first New York formed with their colors and a few men on our right.
[Source: Official Records, "The Appomattox Campaign," Volume 46, Series 1, pages 946-947]**Manuscript 4**

Comments and Supporting Evidence:

1. There are many important points to be learned from Archibald Hopkins' account of the battle.

    A. Hopkins attempted to form a tight connection with the 2nd Rhode Island on his right, as shown by this statement, "we were then moved a short distance by the right flank, when the order forward was given." This movement to his right flank must have widened the already large gap that existed on Hopkins' left, between his regiment and the 121st New York.

    B. Hopkins corroborates the fact that Major Stiles' Chaffin's Bluff troops, "opened with rapid volleys, advancing all the while with a yell."

    C. The 37th Massachusetts, due to the firepower of their Spencer repeating rifles, was able to repulse the Chaffin's Bluff charge on their front.

    D. At this point in the battle, the 37th Massachusetts was now entirely unsupported on either flank. Though Hopkins tried to connect his Regiment to the 2nd Brigade and the 121st New York on his left, Basinger's 18th Georgia charge now filled this gap between the 37th Massachusetts and 121st New York. Both Olcott's 121st New York and Hopkins' 37th Massachusetts faced their line to meet this threat on their right and left flanks respectively, and drove Basinger's men back to their original position, which was at a gully along the side of the road.

    E. After assisting in the repulse of Basinger's charge which was on his left flank, Hopkins now had to deal with the charge of Stiles Chaffin's Bluff men on his right flank. Hopkins mentions that he faced his troops toward the ravine to deal with Stiles' charging men. Hopkins' account, together with Stiles' account, would place the charging Chaffin's Bluff troops between the 37th Massachusetts' right flank and a natural ravine.

    F. It would appear from this Hopkins' account, that as Major Stiles was attempting to bring his troops to their original positions on the top of the hill by using the ravine for cover, some of his troops in the ravine attacked the 37th Massachusetts. It is more probable; however, that the 37th Massachusetts attacked the Chaffin's Bluff troops in their original reformed position at the top of the hill together with troops stranded in the ravine after the charge. In addition, the Chaffin's Bluff troops most likely counter attacked the 37th Massachusetts from these two positions as well. This is when the deadly hand to hand combat occurred between Stiles' and Hopkins' men, as described in detail by Stiles and documented by many others. It should be noted that the 37th Massachusetts now had their front parallel with the ravine when this final hand to hand combat occurred.

    G. The 37th Massachusetts was equipped with Spencer repeating rifles. This prompted Hopkins to write, "we swept the whole length of their line with such a terrible raking fire that they were unable to reply."

    H. It is interesting to note that over eighty Confederate dead were counted in the ravine. This would indicate that this ravine was wide and deep enough to hold this amount of dead soldiers.

    I. Lastly, only after the most severe fighting was over did the 121st New York form on the right side of the 37th Massachusetts, on the battle ground next to the ravine. This was the battle ground on which the 37th Massachusetts had just completed fighting.

2. Another account of the Battle of Sailor's Creek given by Archibald Hopkins is as follows:

… Sheridan's cavalry had cut off the principal wagon train of Lee's army, and Stonewall Jackson's old corps, now commanded by Ewell, had been put in position to check our pursuit and to save the train if possible. General Kershaw was on the right of the Confederate line, Custis Lee on the left and the naval battalion, made up of picked men from the abandoned gunboats at Richmond and clothed and equipped in the best English fashion, was in the rear of Lee's right in reserve.

Contact

We began to move down the hill in column of wings, but deployed into line of battle and threw our skirmishers before we reached the creek, which was barely fordable, being up to our armpits. After crossing, line was reformed and the regiment moved by the flank a short distance to the right, and then the order was brought up by Colonel Tom Colt, riding as jauntily and coolly as on parade, to charge up the hill. The growth of young pines was so dense that is was impossible to see more than the length of the regimental line or to tell whether our connection on the right or left was maintained. Just here, Chaplain Morse, whose place was in the rear with the ambulances, appeared in front of the line, and it took a peremptory order to send him back. He was a Methodist minister, whom we had chosen from the ranks as our chaplain, and though always faithful in the duty to which he had been unexpectedly called, he could never forget that he had come out to fight. We were now moving steadily up the hill, and stray bullets began to fly too plentifully to be pleasant. As we pushed on I saw Sergeant Cowles, as he fell, shot through the body, wave his hand and cheer on the men with his last breath. Instinctively, we felt that a few steps more would precipitate a bloody fight, but the line did not waver, nor was there any flinching or skulking, the soldierly discipline and steadiness which had been infused into the regiment standing it in good stead as often before. In a moment, as we rose to the crest, a crashing volley from an enemy, still invisible, tore through the pines over our heads. The misdirected aim was most fortunate for us, for our men held their fire like the veterans they were and, before the enemy could reload, we were close upon them, with few vacancies in our ranks. Then, at the word, every man poured in seven shots from his Spencer at easy speaking distance and with deadly effect. Large numbers fell, killed and wounded, many came in and gave themselves up, some escaped, and all semblance of organization or opposition melted away from our front and disappeared.

Hand-to-Hand

Flushed with success, we moved steadily to the front, a distance of probably 300 yards, when, the growth becoming less dense, it appeared that we had no support on either flank. Just at this juncture, Custis Lee moved part of his command, comprising the naval battalion, through one of the deep gulches around our right, and about half the length of regiment in our rear. We discovered the movement just in time to face about and, in a moment, it was hand to hand, and a brief, fierce struggle for the mastery ensued with musketry at arm's length, officers fighting with clubbed muskets and pistols, and the bayonet and the cutlasses of the sailors coming into free use for the first time in our experience. Clouds of sulphurous smoke soon obscured everything not close at hand, and it was as these opened and shifted, that I had glimpses of battle groups and scenes which will always remain in my memory. One, just a momentary glimpse seen and lost too soon to know the result, of a powerful officer in gray, with clubbed musket raised to strike down Captain Chandley, who had a Spencer rifle himself and was cocking it to fire. Another, of a flaming Southern battle flag planted in the ground a few feet away, the center of a desperate struggle. A blue-coated sergeant seized it with determined grasp, only to fall desperately wounded beneath its folds, when a plucky little fellow, whom I recognized through the smoke as Private Taggert, of Company B, wrested it from its hold and carried it safe to the rear. The battle was now at its height. Blue and gray mingled in a confused mass, swayed back and forth in the eddying smoke, and fierce cries of "Down with 'em!" Give 'em h--l!" and the crashing of crossed bayonets could be heard rising above the sound of the musketry. The intense excitement swallowed up all sense of danger, and every man fought most valorously, almost with savage fury. Meanwhile, our Spencers had again given us the advantage, and the enemy's force, broken into confused groups, was driven back in a huddled mass into the little ravine through which they had come. We gathered at its mouth and gave them such a terrible raking fire that they soon began to show white handkerchiefs in token of surrender, and our firing ceased. The adjutant, John S. Bradley, a gallant soldier, always at the front, as the musketry lulled, demanded the sword of a Confederate officer near whom he was standing, when the officer, without a word, put his pistol to the adjutant's breast. He saw the movement just in time to knock the pistol aside, then they grappled, and rolled over each other down into the ravine, the officer discharging his pistol into the adjutant's shoulder as they went. A Confederate also shot him through the thigh and, in an instant more, his antagonist would have dispatched him with another pistol shot, when Private Eddy, of Company B, who had been watching his chance, as Bradley's assailant came uppermost, shot him dead. He had hardly fired, when a powerful "greyback" thrust him through the body with a bayonet, the point coming out near the spine, and he was thrown down and pinned to the ground. His antagonist then tried to wrest his Spencer from him, but he clung to it desperately and, in spite of the terrible disadvantage of his position, succeeded in firing another shot, which was fatal to his brave and determined enemy. The rebel fell upon him as he lay, but Eddy thrust the body aside, pulled out the bayonet which transfixed him, and staggered to the rear, *where he was cared for and finally recovered. After this, of course, we opened fire again, with deadly effect, and they gave up this time in earnest. General Custis Lee surrendered at the muzzle of Corporal David White's rifle, and we sent to the rear with him, his staff and nearly three hundred prisoners, and a silk flag belonging to a crack Savannah battalion, besides the battle flag already spoken of…. It was past three o'clock when we struck the enemy and, as the shadows fell, and the evening breeze rose and sighed a requiem through the swaying pines, all sounds of conflict had died away, and we made our bivouac close at hand.*

[Source: "The Battle of Sailor's Creek" by Archibald Hopkins, late Colonel, 37th Massachusetts Volunteers, "The Military Engineer," Volume XIX, May-June, 1927 No. 105]**Manuscript 85**

There are many important points that we learn from this version of Archibald Hopkins' account of the Battle of Sailor's Creek. This account contains important observations due to Archibald Hopkins' immediate proximity to the active field of battle:

A. Facing north, Kershaw was on the right, Custis Lee was on the left, and the Naval Battalion was in the rear (in reserve) in the line up of the Confederate battle line.

B. After crossing the creek, Hopkins moved the 37th Massachusetts a short distance to his right flank, making the gap with the 121st New York on his left even wider.

C. Due to the thick pine growth, Hopkins could not tell if he was connected at his right or left during his advance up the heights to attack the Confederates.

D. After the Confederates' crashing volley that went over the heads of the 37th Massachusetts, the 37th Massachusetts opened fire with their Spencer rifles and melted away any Confederate opposition from their front.

E. The Confederates, part of Custis Lee's command, moved their troops through one of the deep gulches to the right of the 37th Massachusetts. This portion of Custis Lee's troops moved about half the length of the 37th Massachusetts toward the rear of the 37th Massachusetts.

F. After the hand to hand combat, the 37th Massachusetts drove the Confederates into the ravine.

G. The 37th Massachusetts gathered at the "mouth of the ravine" and gave the Confederate troops that lay in the ravine a raking fire.

H. Bradley rolled into the ravine during his fight with a Confederate officer, indicating that the ravine was both large and deep.

I. Custis Lee was captured after the 37th Massachusetts opened fire again on the Confederates in the ravine. The 37th Massachusetts opened fire again on the Confederates only after the Confederates made an initial gesture of surrender, which they then subsequently revoked.

J. This version by Hopkins states that he sent the Savannah Guard's silk flag to the rear. He stated in his Official Report, however, that this flag was in dispute with regard to which Federal unit had actually captured it. Charles Taggart of the 37th Massachusetts did capture a Confederate flag during the Battle of Sailor's Creek; however, the Confederate regiment is unknown. It is now quite certain that the 121st New York captured this flag from Basinger's 18th Georgia troops.

[Source: File # AAK-534-EB, 1869, National Archives, Washington, DC]**Manuscript 109**

<u>EXHIBIT-W-BA-9-FEDERAL</u>

<u>Introduction:</u>

An account given on the Battle of Sailor's Creek by Harrie A. Cushman, originally a member of the 7th Massachusetts who subsequently became a 2nd Lieutenant of Company E, 37th Massachusetts. Cushman was deeply involved in the action at the Battle of Sailor's Creek.

<u>Evidence:</u>

On the 6th moved following Sheridan until "Sailor's Creek" was reached. Here the enemy under Ewell, which was composed of nearly a third of Lee's army, was making a desperate stand to protect their wagon-trains. The order, "Double-quick," was received, and for three miles the men went forward at a pace which nothing but the intense excitement enabled them to sustain. On they pressed, and passing

Generals Sheridan and Wright, Gen. Edwards pausing for a moment to receive their welcome and directions for placing his command, led the brigade straight for the battle-field at quick speed. Crossing the creek, the lines were deployed, the Thirty-seventh on the left of the brigade; the skirmishers advanced up the slope, a scattering fire was encountered from the enemy's skirmishers, and as the regiment advanced scrambling through the woods a terrific crash of musketry burst from the Confederate lines. But the aim was high, and mostly went over the heads of the Thirty-seventh. Here again the Spencer did its annihilating work by tearing the opposing line into demoralized fragments. While some surrendered, and many fell, the rest broke away and ran through the forest pursued by the elated Thirty-seventh. Soon a heavy column was seen passing the left flank of the regiment. It was Gen. Custis Lee, who had moved his brigade (including the famous Seventh regiment of Savannah and a battalion of marines from the gunboats which had been destroyed at the evacuation of Richmond,) through a ravine to the rear of the regiment, which had become isolated and unsupported in its advance. The command was "Change front to the rear!" and Lee's brigade burst from the cover of the gulch and ferociously charged upon the thin line of the Thirty-seventh. It was the severest test the regiment had ever been subjected to, but was most magnificently met. Lee's wave of chivalry struck the rock of Massachusetts' manhood only to recoil. Both sides fought with desperate courage, hand to hand with bayonets, clubbing each other with muskets, pistols, and even knives, and the blue end gray mingled in one mass as the line swayed to and fro, the blue not gaining an inch. At last the repeating rifles proved superior, and the enemy were pushed back in a broken rout into the gorge from which they had emerged, and made signals of surrender. At this time Lieut. Cushman was wounded, while Gen. Custis Lee was in the act of surrendering to him, by a marine who had thrown down his gun, the rebel thinking that he was about to shoot the general, having him covered by a revolver near his left cheek. Corporal White of Lieut. Cushman's company afterwards captured the general…. Three hundred prisoners were captured by the Thirty-seventh, and Generals Ewell and Kershaw were captured elsewhere in the line, with about all that remained of Ewell's corps. There was little attempt to count, scarcely to guard, the captures made. Everywhere the shout was, "Forward!"—onward to strike the final blows. Private Taggart of Co. B (after an unsuccessful attempt was made by 1st Sergt. Warner of Co. E, he being wounded) captured a rebel color, for which act of bravery he received a Medal of Honor.

[Source: "History of the Seventh Massachusetts Volunteer Infantry in the War of the Rebellion of the Southern States Against Constitutional Authority 1861-1865," by Nelson V. Hutchinson, Taunton, MA, Published by Authority of the Regimental Association, 1890, Chapter "Veterans and Recruits, 7th Massachusetts Volunteers, transferred to the 37th Massachusetts Volunteers," compiled by Harrie A. Cushman]**Manuscript 83**

Comments and Supporting Evidence:

1. There are several interesting points that can be learned from the Harrie A. Cushman account. It is worthy to note that several soldiers from the 7th Massachusetts transferred to the 37th Massachusetts shortly after June 14, 1864, when their term of service with the 7th Massachusetts expired. Harrie A. Cushman was one of those who transferred.

    A. The 37th Massachusetts was the regiment on the left of Edwards' 3rd Brigade after crossing Sailor's Creek

    B. A burst of musketry came from the Confederate lines as the Federals started their climb up the hill. This burst was largely over the heads of the 37th Massachusetts and did little damage to their Regiment.

    C. The author believes that Cushman is describing the Confederate charge by Stiles' troops that was on the right flank of the 37th Massachusetts and not on the left flank as he has stated here. From Hopkins' battle report we know there was an initial charge by Basinger's 18th Georgia troops to the left of the 37th Massachusetts, which was also on the right of the 121st New York. Perhaps Cushman is blending and confusing the two Confederate charges, the one by Basinger's troops to the left of the 37th Massachusetts and the one by Stiles' troops to the right of the 37th Massachusetts.

D. The Confederate charge to the right of the 37th Massachusetts was alongside and down a ravine, which description is consistent with other reports. This Confederate charge went almost to the rear of the 37th Massachusetts, which had become isolated from other Federal regiments and was totally unsupported in its advance.

E. When the 37th Massachusetts changed its front to the right and to the rear, the Confederates charged them from the ravine and the terrible hand to hand combat ensued.

F. Cushman places Custis Lee directly at the spot of this hand to hand battle, when the Federals were in the process of pushing the Confederates back into the ravine, the same ravine from which the Confederates originally made a charge.

G. Cushman's statement that, "There was little attempt to count, scarcely to guard, the captures made," is an extremely important statement and will be discussed in more detail in the conclusion section of this report.

H. He correctly credits other parts of the Federal line, not the 37th Massachusetts, with capturing Generals Ewell and Kershaw.

2. Harrie E. Cushman, 2nd Lieutenant of Company E of the 37th Massachusetts, gives another valuable account of the Battle of Sailor's Creek as found in the 37th Massachusetts Protest Case file.

… April 6th 1865: On said day – my company E of the 37th Mass Vols was on the left of the regiment. The 121st New York was, when the advance was made, more than 4 companies distance from me, just before I was shot.
[Source: 37th Massachusetts Protest Case file, # 476510, National Archives, Washington, DC]**Manuscript 24**

Two important points are to be learned from this account by Cushman:

A. It would appear that Company E of the 37th Massachusetts, of which Cushman was a member, was the Company on the extreme left of the 37th Massachusetts line. In addition, the 37th Massachusetts was on the extreme left of Edwards' Brigade.

B. There was a considerable distance, more than four companies in length, between Company E of the 37th Massachusetts, which was on the extreme left of the 37th Massachusetts line and its entire Brigade, and the 121st New York line and its entire Brigade. If Cushman's recollections are accurate, and he stated them correctly, this can quantify the size of the gap between the 121st New York and 37th Massachusetts as being the length of more than four companies in distance.

EXHIBIT-W-BA-10 FEDERAL

Introduction:
Samuel E. Nichols, Adjutant and Lieutenant of the 37th Massachusetts, gives an account of the Battle of Sailor's Creek.

Evidence:
… Company "E," 37th Mass. Vols. was thrown to the left of Edwards' brigade, of which it was a part, at the ending portion of the fight on that day, April 6, 1865, in order to preserve the connection as closely as possible with the next brigade. Yet considerable space intervened.
[Source: 37th Massachusetts Protest Case file, # 476510, National Archives, Washington, DC]**Manuscript 24**

Comments and Supporting Evidence:
1. The important point to be learned from this Nichols' account is that Company E of the 37th Massachusetts was on the extreme left of Edwards' Brigade and was trying to preserve a connection with the 121st New York, which was on the right of Hamblin's Brigade. This connection was not successfully maintained as a "considerable space intervened" between the two Regiments. This gap also means that Harris Hawthorn in the 121st New York and David White in the 37th Massachusetts were separated by a considerable distance on the battlefield.

EXHIBIT-W-BA-11 FEDERAL

Introduction:
An account of the Battle of Sailor's Creek given by Hazard Stevens.

Evidence:
It was now late in the afternoon. While Anderson was forming across and along the main road, facing west and south, to resist the cavalry attacks, Ewell was forming his lines upon the crest overlooking the stream, facing east and northwest to resist the impending onset of the infantry corps. His lines extended from Anderson's left almost in a semicircle around the brow of the plateau, across the road, and some distance into the woods north of it. General Kershaw held his right, Custis Lee his left, the Naval Brigade, a fine body of men from abandoned gunboats in the James, the center, where it crossed the open field on the main road near the summit of the hill, and was the only part of the line exposed to view from the high ground north of the creek.

[Source: "Battle of Sailor's Creek," Papers of the Military Historical Society of Massachusetts, the Appomattox Campaign of 1865, printed Boston, MA, 1907, Volume 6, by Hazard Stevens, read before the Society December 8, 1884]**Manuscript 88**

Comments and Supporting Evidence:
1. The important fact that can be gained from this account is the description of Ewell's battle line. Ewell's line extended from Anderson's left in a semicircle fashion around the brow of a plateau, across the road and them some distance into the woods.

EXHIBIT-W-BA-12 FEDERAL

Introduction:
Colonel Oliver Edwards, commanding the 3rd Brigade of the 1st Division of the Federal 6th Corps, states the following in his Official Report concerning the Battle of Sailor's Creek.

Evidence:
Report of Col. Oliver Edwards, Thirty-seventh Massachusetts Infantry, Commanding Third Brigade, Hdqrs. Third Brig., First Div., Sixth Army Corps, April 17, 1865

… After passing the creek I halted the line, which had become somewhat broken by the passage of the creek, and reformed it under the crest of the hill in my front. As soon as the line was reformed the brigade moved rapidly forward and soon became heavily engaged with the enemy. At this time I was deprived of the Thirty-seventh Massachusetts, on which I depended for holding my left; the Second Rhode Island Volunteers, losing its connection with the Thirty-seventh and being exposed to a severe fire from the left flank and our own batteries, were thrown into disorder and obliged to fall back, and by so doing partially exposing the left flank of the Forty-ninth, which was also thrown into disorder, but soon rallied…. Thirty-seventh Massachusetts advanced at the same time with the brigade, driving the enemy slowly, but soon found both flanks exposed and a column of the enemy coming in on their left. Their left was thrown back to meet this attack, which they admirably repulsed. By this time they discovered the enemy on their right flank and some 100 yards in the rear. The regiment faced about, and a desperate hand-to-hand fight ensued. The enemy were finally forced back and they taken in flank; their line being swept by the fire of the Spencers they surrendered.

[Source: Official Records, "The Appomattox Campaign," Volume 46, Series 1, pages 941 and 942]**Manuscript 4**

Comments and Supporting Evidence:
1. There are several important points that can be learned from Oliver Edwards' account:
   A. Edwards corroborates the fact that the 37th Massachusetts became exposed on both flanks after their advance.

B. The 37th Massachusetts first encountered the charging Confederates on their left flank. This was Basinger's charging 18th Georgia. It would seem from this Edwards' account that the 37th Massachusetts helped repulse Basinger's troops that were charging between the 37th Massachusetts and the 121st New York.

C. The 37th Massachusetts' right flank became exposed when the 2nd Rhode Island and 49th Pennsylvania, which where connected to the 37th Massachusetts' right flank, broke and retreated as the Chaffin's Bluff troops charged.

D. The Chaffin's Bluff troops, "got some 100 yards in the rear" of the right flank of the 37th Massachusetts. The 37th Massachusetts then changed their front to be along their initial right flank position.

E. Edwards states, "The regiment faced about, and a desperate hand to hand fight ensued, the enemy were finally forced back and they taken in flank; their line being swept by the fire of the Spencers they surrendered." It would appear from this statement that the new front of the 37th Massachusetts clashed with the Confederate troops, which now extended from the top of the hill, which was their original position, all the way down the hill along the ravine. The Chaffin's Bluff troops were extended in this precarious manner because of their earlier unauthorized charge downhill.

2. In the year 1897, Oliver Edwards gave another account of the Battle of Sailor's Creek and the role of his Command in the battle:

In the Battle of Sailor's Creek April 6th, 1865 commanded my brigade the 3rd of the 1st Div 6th Corps and the 37th Mass Vols was my left regiment. Major General Custis Lee, commanding Gen Ewell's left division, formed in two lines with the left and center in my front resisting my attack, and formed in one line without supports. As my brigade advanced up the heights the 49th Penna. Vols. connecting with the right of the 37th Mass Vols came under fire of canister from our own batteries posted on the heights in our rear, and by the unauthorized orders of its Colonel Hickman fell back to the base of the hill, and the regiment on its right conformed to the movement. Though these regiments obeyed my orders with alacrity and charged up the hill again, yet for some minutes there was a gap in my line on the right of the 37th Mass Vols--of the front of the two regiments. General Custis Lee charged with one of his brigades into this gap: his lines being closed en masse. The 37th Mass. were armed with Spencer magazine rifles which made them equal in fighting strength to a good brigade, and they seeing the coming charge changed front forward on their right, which brought them in contact with the right flank of Gen Lee's charging column and the bayonet was used freely. It was right here and then that Corporal David White Co E 37th Mass Vols Inft captured Major General Custis Lee…. The 37th Mass Vols in contact with Gen Lees charging column, and on their right flank with their bayonets and the terrible fire of their repeating rifles enfilading Lee's lines en masse: killed, wounded or captured the entire charging column. No other regiment or command had anything to do with this part of the fight or with the capture of Major Gen Custis Lee.

[Source: 37th Massachusetts Protest Case file, # 476510, National Archives, Washington, DC]**Manuscript 24**

There are several important points to be learned from this account offered by General Oliver Edwards in the year 1897:

A. The 37th Massachusetts was the left regiment in his Brigade (3rd Brigade – 1st Division, 6th Corps).

B. Custis Lee commanded the left of Ewell's troops, which were facing toward Sailor's Creek, and formed his troops in two lines. Custis Lee's center and left (Chaffin's Bluff, Naval, Barton and Howard troops) most likely formed directly opposite Edwards' Brigade.

C. Edwards' troops were in one line of formation with no second line for support.

D. It would appear from Edwards that the 49th Pennsylvania and 2nd Rhode Island fell back, unauthorized, as a result of being bombarded by their own Federal artillery fire.

E. Though the 49th Pennsylvania and 2nd Rhode Island charged up the hill again against the Confederates, a gap formed on the right of the 37th Massachusetts, leaving the

37th Massachusetts unsupported. Custis Lee's troops charged through this gap created by the 49th Pennsylvania's and the 2nd Rhode Island's retreat.

F. The 37th Massachusetts changed front forward toward their right flank, coming upon the right flank of the charging Custis Lee troops.

G. This is when the hand to hand combat occurred between the 37th Massachusetts and Custis Lee's troops, with the 37th Massachusetts prevailing with their bayonets and the enfilading fire from their Spencer repeating rifles.

H. The important statement that Edwards made in this account is that no other regiment took part in this aspect of the battle, just the 37th Massachusetts.

3. Another valuable account of the Battle of Sailor's Creek is given by Oliver Edwards. It is as follows:

*… Gen. Sheridan pointed to the heights covered with pine across Sailor's Creek and said, "The enemy, are there, I want you to form your brigade in one line, cross the creek and carry the heights." I asked him if my flanks would be covered, and he said, "never mind your flanks, go through them, they are demoralized as h---." We charged across the stream-with mud and water up to the waist of my lads-under a hot "point blank" fire, and we carried the first rise bringing us to the foot of the heights held by the enemy in two strong lines of battle in close order. The ground in front, and to my right was covered with a second growth of pine so close that it was difficult to see but a few yards. I sent Seargent Cameron, and ten men of the 5th Wisconsin, as a post of observation . . . 200 yards to my right, and front, Lt. Gen. Ewell in command of the enemy, was worried about his exposed left, as was I as to my exposed right, and he was reconnoitering to his left, and front accompanied only by his staff. Seargent Cameron from his post of observation-saw the approach of Ewell and staff; Cameron ordered his men to lie low, and Ewell rode up close when Cameron, and his men unmasked, and with their guns pointed demanded the surrender of Ewell and staff. Ewell replied, "I am Lieut General Ewell, I desire to surrender to a commissioned officer," to which Sergt Cameron responded, "I am Sergt Cameron get off that horse," and Ewell explained that he had but one leg and was fastened by a strap to his horse. Sergt Cameron sent in his prisoners and they spent the night at Gen Wrights head quarters, meantime, in advancing up the heights, the 49 Penna, and 2nd R. I. came under heavy fire from our own batteries, posted on the opposite heights and Lieut Col Hickman of the 49th ordered his regiment to retreat down the hill. The 49th and 2nd R. I. understanding this to be an order from competent authority fell back to the foot of the heights, and Gen Custis Lee, lead one of his brigades closed en masse in a charge through the gap in my lines, this left the 37th Mass Inftry cut off on my extreme left. The 37th was commanded by Major Archibald Hopkins, and numbered but little over 300 men; this fine regiment with perfect confidence in themselves and in their Spencer repeaters-charged front forward to their right, coming directly in contact with the right flank of Lees brigade, so close that the sword, and the bayonet, were both in use. Maj. Hopkins killed an officer with his sword. The flank fire of the 37th from their magazine guns, at close quarters cut down the mass of Lee's men, Gen Custis Lee (**Author Note:** Right here, Edwards wrote, "surrendered to C" and then crossed it out and continued with the following) was really captured by Corporal David White of Co E though his reply to the demand for his surrender was "tut tut man I wish to surrender to a commissioned officer. The Colonel next in command was in act of handing his sword to adjutant Bradley, when, seeing how small was the command opposed to him, he drew back his sword, and attacked the adjutant with his pistol. Bradley grappled with his foe, though wounded by his pistol shot-and they rolled into a hollow, where surrounded by rebels, Bradley was shot through the thigh, when Samuel B. Eddy, private Co. D, shot the rebel Colonel as he was about to shoot Bradley, through the head with his pistol: a rebel who saw the man who killed his Colonel put his bayonet through private Eddy's body, the bayonet passing through his lung, and coming out near his spine. Eddy dropped his gun, and tore the bayonet out from his body, then in a hand to hand struggle with his foe temporarily disabled him and crawled to his gun, and with it killed his antagonist. The thick smoke covered this desperate hand to hand fight which ended in the surrender of all that was left of Lee's changing column. The annals of the "War of the Rebellion" will hardly show the parallel of this heroic fight of Major Hopkins, and his 37th Massachusetts regiment of 300 men, this struggle lasted but a few minutes, and the 49 Penna and 2nd R. I. advanced at once-on orders up the heights, which they never would have abandoned had it not have been for the unauthorized orders of Col Hickman. The*

enemy in front of the 5th Wis, and 82nd Penna now waved white handkerchiefs, which I believed meant surrender; and ordered these regiments to cease firing, while I, accompanied by Major E. A. Landell, and orderly Beers, rode in front, when we reached the point where the white signals were, we were within a few yards of the enemy's extreme left of two lines of battle; the front line was kneeling down, and the second lying down, with their left resting on a deep ravine or gully that angled down the heights passing through my line near my left. We were too close to the enemy's line to have any chance to get away by direct retreat, and our only chance was to go ahead, and bluff it out, if we could, or jump our horses into the ravine (which was deep enough to cover horse and man), and make a dash down it for the left of our line. Riding up to the enemy's left, I asked for the commanding officer when a manly fine looking officer stepped to the front. I introduced myself, stating that I had come over to receive his surrender; he refused, introducing himself as, Colonel R. T. W. Duke, on the grounds that they had no orders to surrender. I told him he had better surrender to avoid useless effusion of blood, that I had Genls. Ewell and Custis Lee prisoners, that Sheridan's cavalry was in their rear, and the 6th Corps in their front, that they were surrounded, but Col Duke still declined to surrender, then I demanded time to return to my line, which he denied, demanding my surrender, which I answered by saying we did not know what that meant, just then-over our way, and asking if he intended firing on me while I was returning to my lines, Col Duke said I will not give you any definite time, when I bid him good bye saying I hoped we would meet under pleasanter circumstances, and slowly re-crossed the ravine, and returned to my lines having seen the enemy's left, and ascertained that it was entirely exposed-as the ravine afforded no real protection-and that there was no enemy in front of the 3rd division on my right. I requested Col Treux, commanding the left brigade of the 3rd Div., to change front forward to his left, and charge on Col Dukes left and rear, while I, charged his front. Col Traux objected to this wanting the orders of his division Commander, Gen Seymour; there was no time to get such orders, and I asked Col Traux to take my position, and I would make the flank attack. Col Traux finally agreed to accept my orders, and make the flank attack, provided I would promise to assume all responsibility therefore, if he got in to trouble. This I readily agreed to, and he made the flank attack while I charged in front, and this closed the battle of Sailors Creek with the surrender of the last of Ewell's Corps. Hamblin's brigade of the 1st Div, and the 2nd Div of the 6th Corps had some fighting to my left which I did not see, and am not posted on, but the main fight fell on my brigade as the loss of more than half of the killed and wounded of the 6th Corps showed.

[Source: "My Recollections of the Civil War" by General Oliver Edwards, pages 228-247, a loose undated typescript housed in the Illinois State Historical Library, Old State Capitol, Springfield, IL. Author Note: For the purpose of generally dating this document, it should be noted that Oliver Edwards' life span was 1835-1904]**Manuscript 84**

There are many important points that we glean from this version of Edwards' account of the Battle of Sailor's Creek:

A. After crossing the creek, his Division carried the first rise bringing them to the foot of the heights held by the Confederates.

B. The ground in front and to the right of his Division was covered with a secondary growth of pine that was so close that it was difficult to see beyond a few yards.

C. He gives a detailed account on how Ewell was captured by Sergeant Cameron of the 5th Wisconsin while General Ewell was out observing his exposed left flank. It is interesting to note that Ewell desired to surrender to a commissioned officer and not to a Sergeant. This has similarities to David White's account where Custis Lee did not want to surrender to a Federal Private or a Federal non-commissioned officer.

D. The 49th Pennsylvania and the 2nd Rhode Island came under fire by their own Federal artillery, and Col. Hickman gave unauthorized orders to retreat. Custis Lee's Confederate troops also charged them.

E. The 37th Massachusetts was cut off from the rest of Edwards' Division.

F. The 37th Massachusetts had a little over 300 men and they changed their front to their right flank to meet Custis Lee's charging troops.

G. A hand to hand fight ensued and Hopkins killed a Confederate officer with his sword. This is interesting in that it shows that Hopkins, a Captain, had a sword during the Battle of Sailor's Creek.

H. In the fight, Bradley rolled into the ravine where the Confederates were positioned.

I. The 49th Pennsylvania and the 2nd Rhode Island regrouped and charged up the heights during the time of the 37th Massachusetts' hand to hand fight.

J. The 5th Wisconsin and the 82nd Pennsylvania were going up against the extreme left of Custis Lee's Confederate line, which were waving handkerchiefs as a token of surrender.

K. This is the best description of the ravine found by the author. The Confederates' extreme left rested on the ravine, and the ravine angled down the heights passing through Edwards' line near the left of his line (where the 37th Massachusetts was positioned). The ravine was deep enough to cover a horse and a man.

L. Edwards thought he could make an escape from the Confederate left line by doing the following: "jump our horses into the ravine and make a dash down it for the left of our line."

M. Edwards encountered Colonel Duke of Barton's Brigade which apparently formed the left of Custis Lee's Confederate line facing toward Sailor's Creek (see Duke's report for collaboration of this event).

N. Custis Lee and General Ewell were apparently already prisoners of Edwards' Division when this exchange between Edwards and Duke occurred.

O. Edwards re-crossed the ravine when returning to his line after his conversation with Col. Duke.

P. The right Federal Brigade (facing toward Sailor's Creek) of the 3rd Division, commanded by a Col. Truex, attacked the left flank of the Confederate line, commanded by Col. Duke. There were no Confederate troops in the front of this Federal 3rd Division to oppose them.

Q. Edwards acknowledges that Hamblin's Brigade of the 1st Division had some fighting; however, he was not posted on the particulars of this fighting due to the fact that Hamblin was far to his left. According to Edwards, the main fight fell on his Brigade. He cites as proof of this fact the statistics that over half of the killed and wounded in the 6th Corps were from his Brigade.

EXHIBIT-W-BA-13 FEDERAL

Introduction:
This is an account given by B. F. Johns, a Corporal of Company A of the 49th Pennsylvania, concerning his own capture at the Battle of Sailor's Creek.

Evidence:
The bugle sounded "attention" and the old Eighth [Sixth] Corps went forward down a steep hill and lined up along a quicksand swamp. As soon as I put my foot on the edge of the swamp I knew what it was, and if we all attempted to go over at once some of us would be submerged: so to be sure it would not be me, I went forward, amid a scattering of volley of musketry, from one bunch of grass to another, and got over dry shod, and lay down and waited for the rest to follow. It was laughable to see the boys floundering through the mud and water. After the line was reformed my Captain ordered me to take five men and go out on the skirmish line. I called for five volunteers, but there were but four came forward. I then picked one little fellow that was noted for his cowardice. He came forward with tears running down his cheeks, saying, "I will go, and let these other fellows know I am not afraid." I deployed my men, keeping the gun-shy boy alongside me. There was no rebel line of skirmishers: they had fired on us while crossing the swamp, killing one man and wounding several others, and then fallen back to their line of battle, less than 200 yards in our front. As soon as we discovered their position my gun-shy boy fired into their ranks. I tried to keep him from firing, but there was too much big game there for him to hold his fire. I was still in easy speaking distance of my regiment, and I called out that the rebel line of battle was about 200 yards in front, prone on the ground, and almost obscured by scrub-pine and other undergrowth. While the boy was reloading his musket our whole line advanced, and we fell into our places and the command went forward with a yell. The rebels gave us one volley and ran. We drove them out of the pine thicket into big timber. At the edge of the big timber my Captain ordered me to

advance with my skirmishes. I had advanced about 100 yards when I saw the rebels all going toward our left. I turned around to call the attention of the other skirmishers to the movements of the rebels, but there was no skirmisher to be seen. I walked back a few steps, wondering what had become of everybody, when I chanced to see my regimental flag down near the swamp, where we had crossed. I then surmised that the movements of the rebels were to flank us on the left, and our line had been withdrawn to prevent an enfilading fire. I started back to where I saw our flag. When I got into the pines, I saw a man off to my left whom I took to be one of our own men, and called to him to come this way, that I believed the rebels were trying to flank us on the left. He did come, and when he was in reach of me he raised his gun and said to me, "Drop that gun, you Yankee------, or I'll blow your heart out." Had I known who he was when I first saw him I could have shot him, or at least escaped, but he was dressed in blue, and I had believed him one of our own men. As he had the "drop" on me I concluded that the best thing to do was to obey orders. He took my haversack, but he didn't get much; all I had in it was a small piece of fresh beef, which he gulped down like a hungry dog. After I had thrown down my gun and cartridges, and handed over my haversack my captor ordered me to double-quick to the rear. We had gone only a few yards when our three batteries on the hill opened up with a double canister, and such a sight I never saw before, except at Spotsylvania Court-House. The first round drove the rebels back to where we were, and my captor ordered me to lie down in a deep ravine in the old field. This order I obeyed very promptly: we were scarcely down when the rebels came tumbling in and filled the ditch, nearly smothering me. In a few moments the artillery ceased firing, and a musketry fire commenced. The rebels crawled out of the ditch and moved to the left, and my captor undertook to march me to the rear. I then saw a sight I will never forget: men were lying in every direction, heads shot off and arms and legs scattered and bleeding. I had not long to view this scene of carnage, as I was hustled back into the big timber and down into a ravine, where was a stream of water. We stopped to get a drink. A rebel on horseback came along and snatched a temperance badge from my coat. I suppose he thought he had something valuable, but it was only a cheap, soft-metal badge, and cost only 25 cents. My captor tried to prevent him taking it, but the cavalryman was too quick, and was off before he could be reached. I was soon ordered up through the wood, but we did not go far until we came in sight of a line of skirmishers. My captor asked me who they were. I said, "They are our cavalry skirmishers." He made me about-face and took me back to the ravine, and while we were there our infantry line was pushed forward.

B. F. JOHNS, Corporal, Co A, 49th PA, Chambersburg, PA

[Source: "Closing Scenes, the Capture of Ewell's Command and the Exhausting March to Burkesville with the Prisoners" by B. F. Johns, Corporal, Co A, 49th Pennsylvania, "The National Tribune," Washington, DC, Thursday, February 13, 1902]**Manuscript 81**

Comments and Supporting Evidence:

1. There are some important points to be learned from this account by B. F. Johns of the 49th Pennsylvania. It should be remembered that the 49th Pennsylvania was on the immediate right of the 37th Massachusetts at the Battle of Sailor's Creek when the Federal advance was initiated.

    A. This part of the Confederate line was separated by about 200 yards from the Federals who had advanced, and the Confederates were positioned on ground that was almost obscured by scrub-pine and other undergrowth.

    B. With the Federal advance, the Confederate troops in front of the 49th Pennsylvania retreated to the tall timbers.

    C. Johns observed that the 49th Pennsylvania troops had retreated to prevent what he thought would be an enfilading fire. The Confederate troops were now flanking the 49th Pennsylvania on their left. This is consistent with other accounts that depict Stiles' men charging to the right of the 37th Massachusetts and the left of the 49th Pennsylvania. While the 49th Pennsylvania retreated in the face of this Confederate charge, the 37th Massachusetts held firm in their original position.

    D. With the retreat of the 49th Pennsylvania and the capture of Johns, the Federal artillery opened up and the Confederates attempted to retreat back to their original positions.

E. Johns and the 49th Pennsylvania had to be in very close proximity to the ravine, as Johns was ordered by his captor to lie down in this ravine while the Federal artillery fire was occurring.

F. When the Federal artillery fire stopped, the Confederates crawled out of this ravine and moved to go against the approaching 37th Massachusetts.

G. It would appear that when Johns was brought to the rear of the Confederate lines by his captors, he followed the ravine which went into the big timbers.

EXHIBIT-W-BA-14 FEDERAL

Introduction:
This account on the Battle of Sailor's Creek, given by the 2nd Rhode Island, was found by the author in their Regimental history.

Evidence:
...But across the men went with the rest, now under Seymour, and; gaining the bank, immediately reformed and pushed up the slope beyond, the enemy retiring into the woods upon the ridge. But here was a large force of the enemy, lying concealed and awaiting the approach of our troops. A scathing and murderous fire was opened, and the enemy charged down upon the command. It was a hand to hand fight, the combatants mingling together and freely using bayonets and musket butts. Here fell Captain Gleason of G and Lieutenant Perry of F, for the fighting was severe. Indeed Seymour had nearly the entire weight of the enemy upon him, while Wheaton was moving around to his support to strike the foe upon his flank. Conspicuous in this contest, among the enemy's troops, was a battalion of marines from Richmond, disdainful of fear and eager for the fray. They fought with such impetuosity as to throw our lines into dire confusion, and almost before he was aware of it Seymour and his division -a part of the Second with them-were tumbled back into and across the creek, the enemy following and planting his flags upon the bank. But brief was his triumph. Edwards formed his brigade upon the enemy's flank and poured in a deadly fire. A few rounds of canister, from a battery which was opportunity sent to the relief of our troops, cleared the way for their return. The men of the Second who had been forced across the creek rushed back again. The rest of Wheaton's division now came gallantly into action. Our artillery, on the hither side of the creek, opened on the mass of the clustering enemy on the further bank. There was no escape for the daring marines, and they were actually forced across the creek to surrender themselves to Seymour and his command. General Getty was now sent across, and Wheaton turned his attention to the ridge. The Sixth Corps, in the new formation, made its advance, subjected to a heavy fire, but still pressing the enemy hard and gaining an advantage at every step. Down through the woods then came our cavalry, having got into the enemy's rear, and, in a few minutes after, the battle was over. General Ewell, with his subordinate commanders, Kershaw, Barton, Corse and others, 8000 or 10,000 prisoners—there was not time to count them—14 guns and the trains, were the prizes of that day's struggle. Colonel Rhodes, in his manuscript narrative, says, that Sergeant Cameron of the 5th Wisconsin took Ewell's horse by the bridle, and delivered his distinguished prisoner over to General Wright. General C. E. Lee and staff, Commodore Tucker and staff, and the men of their respective commands, and a wagon train with its contents, were also among the captures made by Edwards' brigade.

[Source: "The Second Rhode Island Regiment" a Narrative of Military Operations in which the Regiment was Engaged" by Augustus Woodbury; 1875]Manuscript 90****

Comments and Supporting Evidence:
1. There are three points to be learned from Woodbury's account.
    A. Though Woodbury mistakenly states that the 2nd Rhode Island was a part of Seymour's Division, he credits Edwards' Brigade as the brigade that captured Custis Lee.
    B. He gives a good account of the manner in which the 2nd Rhode Island broke after the Confederate charge, and it would appear that the 2nd Rhode Island might have been chased by some charging Confederate Marines as well.

C. He writes an interesting statement that, "there was not time to count them," referring to the Federals' Confederate prisoners. This would indicate that the Confederate prisoners were pouring in fast and furious toward the rear of the Federal lines during the course of the battle.

EXHIBIT-W-BA-15 FEDERAL

Introduction:
Lieutenant George Peck of the 2nd Rhode Island tells about his experiences at the Battle of Sailor's Creek.

Evidence:

… At the word "FORWARD!" the men sprang to their feet, fired into the woods, and with a cheer dashed forward on the run. Gaining a few rods, they fell, loaded (officers meanwhile simply stooping), rose again, fired, and made a second dash. With the third dash came the words: "Now close on them— Go for them!"… At length I imagined I had about reached the summit, and must be ready to close on the hostiles, so I looked up; but lo! no one was before me. Surprised and perplexed, I turned to the left and no one was there. The colors were already half way down the hill and moving deliberately to the rear; the soldiers on the extreme left had already reached the creek…. In taking my rapid survey, I noticed thirty or fourty "secesh" on a projecting knoll, enjoying a comfortable target practice.
[Source: "Great Campaigns, the Appomattox Campaign March 29-April 9, 1865" by Chris Calkins, inclusion entitled: "A Recruit before Petersburg," by George Peck, pages 119-122; 1880]**Manuscript 35**

Comments and Supporting Evidence:
1. There are two important points that can be learned from this account by George Peck.
    A. Being on the extreme right of his Regiment, he witnessed the entire retreat of his 2nd Rhode Island when the Confederate troops charged his unit.
    B. He was within eyeshot of the grassy knoll where Stiles' men were originally positioned. This would place the advancing 2nd Rhode Island just to the right of this knoll while advancing up the hill from Sailor's Creek.

EXHIBIT-W-BA-16 FEDERAL

Introduction:

Fredrick Moody:

It would appear from many battle accounts that the 37th Massachusetts also tangled with some element of the Confederate Marine/Naval Brigade. Sergt. Fredrick Moody of the 37th Massachusetts has an entry in his diary that illustrates this point.

Evidence:
… charged on the enemy across a swamp and up a steep hill at the top of which were the enemy. We had a hard fight, our regt. being hotly engaged by a brigade of marines.
[Source: Civil War diary of Frederick A. Moody, Sergt., Co. D, 37th Massachusetts, currently in the possession of Charles W. Thayer (originally purchased from a Mr. Gordon, antique dealer]**Manuscript 108**

Comments and Supporting Evidence:
1. This shows that the 37th Massachusetts not only engaged Stiles' Chaffin's Bluff and Atkinson's 10th and 19th Virginia Heavy Artillery troops along the ravine, but they also engaged some element of the Marine/Naval Battalion as well. Perhaps this engagement with the Marine/Naval Battalion occurred after the 37th Massachusetts' fight with the Stiles' and Atkinson's troops.

2. The following account will attempt to show the battlefield position of the Marine/Naval battalion.
Daniel B. Sanford, Milledgeville, Ga: "Permit me to ask through your columns who commanded the battalion of marines in the Battle of Sailor's Creek, VA, and where did they come from? Their line of battle was just in front of Phillips's Georgia Legion of Infantry, of which I was a member.
[Source: Daniel B Sanford, "Confederate Veteran," Volume 8, Number 4, April 1900, pg 170]**Manuscript 105**

The important point from Sanford's account is that the right flank of the Marine/Naval Battalion was just in front of Phillip's George Legion, which was a part of Du Bose's Brigade, Kershaw's Division.
3. The following account elaborates further on the battlefield position of the Marines:

… Mr. Daniel B. Sanford, of Milledgeville, GA, wishes to know who commanded the marine battalion at the Battle of Sailor's Creek on April 6, 1865. Commodore John R. Tucker commanded the naval brigade in that fight, not the marine battalion, although there was a company of marines in the brigade commanded by Capt. Sims, of the Marine Corps…. I belonged to the naval brigade, and was in that fight. DuBose's Brigade was on our right, and the Eighteenth and Nineteenth Virginia Battalions of Artillery on the left.
[Source: B. S. Johnston, "Battle of Sailor's Creek," Confederate Veteran, Volume 8, number 4, page 538]**Manuscript 106**

This account provides more details on the position of the Marine/Naval Battalion. On their right was Kershaw's Division, specifically Du Bose's Brigade and on their left was Atkinson's 10th and 19th Virginia Heavy Artillery (not the 18th and 19th as was stated by Johnson since these units were not paired together during the Battle of Sailor's Creek). This would place the Marine/Naval Battalion behind the Chaffin's Bluff troops and perhaps to some degree behind the 18th Georgia. They were also somewhat behind and to the right of the 10th and 19th Virginia Heavy Artillery as well.
4. The following account describes who, from the Federal side, opposed the direct front line of the Confederate Marine/Naval Battalion.

… Amid this scene of destruction the naval brigade marched forth with Commodore Tucker in command, and Major Simms, of the marine corp, in command of the marines ... were ordered to take position across the creek, and to hold our position until relieved. Custer relieved us. During the day's fight our brigade was opposed in an almost hand-to-hand fight with the Sixth army corps (Hancock's) in our immediate front.
[Source: R. A. Camm, Lieut. C. S. Navy, "A Naval Officers Recollection of Lee's Retreat," Southern Bivouac, May 1884, Volume 2, Number 9]**Manuscript 107**

This interesting account, which references a hand-to-hand fight with the 6th Army Corps, most likely is referencing some element of the Confederate Marine/Naval Battalion tangling with the 37th Massachusetts. This occurred during the final moments of the Battle of Sailor's Creek.

EXHIBIT-W-BA-17 FEDERAL

Introduction:
The Adjutant-General of Massachusetts is reporting on the 37th Massachusetts' involvement in the Battle of Sailor's Creek. The Adjutant-General is quoting an unknown author.

Evidence:

… Beyond the stream for a quarter of a mile we advanced through a thick growth of underbrush, fighting as we went. The firing waxed hotter and hotter, until suddenly we found to our dismay that the regiment on our right had given way, and the brigade on our left had broken the connection, and halted some distance back. We were lost to our friends. Our nearest neighbor was our foe. The rebels came pouring down upon us, and within a few seconds had attacked and enveloped both flanks of the

regiment. A hand-to-hand combat ensued. Many men were wounded with the bayonet, and pistol-shots were freely exchanged…. Meanwhile the Spencer rifle was working the havoc for which it was intended. All down the front of our regiment, the gaps that our fire opened in the enemy's ranks were fearful. They had started to attack us massed in heavy columns. Scattered fragments only reached us. They came throwing down their guns, raising their hands, and imploring the cessation of the fire.
[Source: "Annual Report of the Adjutant-General of the Commonwealth of Massachusetts for the Year Ending December 31, 1865," Boston, MA, 1866]**Manuscript 133**

Comments and Supporting Evidence:

1. The important point to be learned from this account is that the 37th Massachusetts was enveloped on both flanks by the attacking enemy due to the fact that the regiment on their right had given way and the Brigade on their left had broken the connection and halted some distance back. This could give credence to the Miles Butterfield account that states that Hamblin's Brigade did not start their advance with Edwards' Brigade; hence Hamblin's Brigade was some distance back. Another plausible explanation for Hamblin's Brigade being "some distance back" is that the 121st New York (on the right of Hamblin's Brigade) became bitterly engaged with Basinger's 18th Georgia troops and were initially pushed back by them to Sailor's Creek. In addition, the gaps that were created in the Confederate line near the end of the battle by the firepower of the 37th Massachusetts' Spencer rifles could have been one of those gaps through which David White got in front of his own Federal line to pursue and capture Custis Lee. This would be consistent with White's own account of the capture of Custis Lee that is contained in the North Adams, MA, newspaper articles.

EXHIBIT-W-BA-18 FEDERAL

Introduction:
This account of the Battle of Sailor's Creek is given by a Union Cavalry officer, F. C. Robinson, of the 1st West Virginia Cavalry.

Evidence:
… In pursuing up the hill through the field we came to the summit of the ridge overlooking Big Sailor's Creek, where we could see the rebel lines down at the foot of the hill, some 400 yards away, hotly engaged with the Sixth Corps; and they were having a warm time down there. Suddenly the Sixth Corps batteries from the opposite hilltops opened from the rear of their line of battle and their shells flew about us uncomfortably close.
[Source: The National Tribune, Washington, DC August 18, 1877, "Sailor's Creek, the Capture of Gen. Ewell and His Corps," by F. C. Robinson]**Manuscript 134***

Comments and Supporting Evidence:
1. The important point in this account is that the Federal Cavalry broke through the Confederate Cavalry lines and was coming upon the rear of Custis Lee's Infantry Division, which Division was some 400 yards from the summit of the ridge overlooking Sailor's Creek.

EXHIBIT-W-BA-19 FEDERAL

Introduction:
This account of the Battle of Sailor's Creek is given by James Dean, the Chief of Staff for the 2nd Connecticut Heavy Artillery.

Evidence:

… At about 4 o'clock we came out on a rise of ground that showed us a little of the fun that was going on with the cavalry charging off to our right, and a brigade of our own division just going in also. We were thrown into a line at once—121st N. Y. and 95th Penn. for our front line, with 65th N. Y. deployed as

skirmishers on our left flank, and the 2ⁿᵈ Co. H. A. (for the first time in all its service) forming our second line. We advanced in this formation into heavy open timber and halted, while our General Hamblin rode out to our right to report to General Sheridan. Very soon an orderly galloped back from our General with instructions to myself as Chief of Staff to move our command by the right flank until clear of the timber. Doing so, we came out upon a thrifty looking piece of growing corn. Clear of the woods, we again faced to the front. General Hamblin swung up his saber and gave the order to charge, and away we went, down the slope of the cornfield, across forty yards of swampy ground, and struck "Little Sailor's Creek," a narrow stream but deep in spots, and with banks tangled by bushes and vines. Crossing the field I had noticed a farm road or cart track leading diagonally to the left, and turned my horse into it, as I was riding between our two lines, knowing that it probably crossed the creek in front of us at a favorable place, as it proved to do. But our lines of course took the creek as they came to it to get through as best they might, while the enemy on the hill before us poured in their musketry fire. I was across quickly, and helped to straighten our first line, and send it ahead, the hill before us rising so abruptly from the bottom land that we were protected from the enemy's fire. As quickly as we saw the second line getting over and through the creek, we raised our cheer, faithfully echoed by the second line, and up we went, meeting the men of our 3ʳᵈ Brigade, who had been repulsed, as we fortunately were not, for we swept everything in front of us, capturing 2200 prisoners and several battle flags…. We lost but few men in the charge, though the place of it looked dubious at first. We captured Generals Ewell, Fitz Hugh Lee and several others of similar rank eight in all…. We found among the Rebels immediately opposed to us, the men of two commands that had never seen any fields fighting as such before, the 51ˢᵗ Georgia Inf'y and Semmes' Naval Battalion. They fought well, but we were too much for them.

[Source: James Dean, typescript at the Connecticut Historical Society, Hartford, CT]**Manuscript 139**

Comments and Supporting Evidence:

1. This account is important due to the fact that Dennis Moore of the 2ⁿᵈ Connecticut Heavy Artillery is credited by Hamblin as assisting in the capture of Custis Lee. It is also important in that the 2ⁿᵈ Connecticut Heavy Artillery does not have an existing Official Report for the Battle of Sailor's Creek, so this Dean typescript serves as a good substitute.

2. Dean does not mention Dennis Moore assisting in the capture of Custis Lee, but makes a general reference to all the Confederate Generals captured by the Federal forces.

3. It is likely that the 2ⁿᵈ Connecticut Heavy Artillery was "rocked and then set back" during their initial charge of the Confederate troops, just like the 121ˢᵗ New York was, by the 18ᵗʰ Georgia (2ⁿᵈ Connecticut Heavy Artillery was in the second line behind the 121ˢᵗ New York). This possibility can be inferred from Dean's comment, "We lost but few men in the charge, though the place of it looked dubious at first." This dubious nature could have been referring to their push back.

4. It would appear that as the 121ˢᵗ New York was contending against the 18ᵗʰ Georgia at the road, and after the 121ˢᵗ New York regrouped after the 18ᵗʰ Georgia's charge, the 2ⁿᵈ Connecticut Heavy Artillery moved to their left to contend with the 51ˢᵗ Georgia Infantry of Kershaw's Division line. After prevailing against them, they moved onto Semmes' Naval Battalion, one of the last Confederate fighting forces left on the battlefield. As stated before, it is very difficult to see how Dennis Moore was in the vicinity of Custis Lee on the battlefield to assist Hawthorn in the capture of Custis Lee if Moore followed the movements of his Regiment. Perhaps Moore did not.

EXHIBIT-W-BA-20 FEDERAL

Introduction:

This account in the Official Records of the Battle of Sailor's Creek is given by Lieutenant Colonel John Harper, commanding the 95ᵗʰ Pennsylvania Infantry at the Battle of Sailor's Creek.

Evidence:

Report of Lieut. Col. John Harper, Ninety-fifth Pennsylvania Infantry.
HDQRS NINETH-FIFTH REGIMENT PENNSYLVANIA VOLS., April 13, 1865

SIR: In obedience to orders, I have the honor of making the following report of the part taken by my command in the action of the 6th instant, Sailor's Creek. My command was placed upon the left of the One hundred and twenty-first Regiment New York Volunteers, forming, with that regiment, the front line of the brigade. At the command "forward" we proceeded steadily (not withstanding a severe fire of musketry, by which I sustained some loss) across the open ground until we arrived at the creek, where some little delay took place, it being difficult to cross in some parts. After crossing, however, the line was reformed, and advanced to the foot of the hill upon which the enemy were posted; here we halted, by order, for a short time, during which the line was put in good shape for the charge. Very soon the order to advance was given, when we advanced to the top of the hill, where we were met by a terrific fire of musketry which, momentarily, staggered the line (I may here mention the gallant conduct of Bvt. Col E. Olcott, commanding the One Hundred and twenty-first New York Volunteers, who, by his example, did much to gain the victory which soon followed); with a cheer, however, the men pressed forward, and after a stubborn contest forced the enemy to retire in confusion, capturing many prisoners, who were ordered to the rear. Upon gaining the woods in which the enemy had been posted I found that a number of them had made a stand upon our left flank, and were becoming very annoying. I advanced upon them with my colors and fifteen or twenty of the men in my regiment and some of the One hundred and twenty-first New York Volunteers

I am, sir, very respectfully,

JOHN HARPER, Lieutenant-Colonel Ninety-fifth Pennsylvania Vols., Commanding.

[Source: Official Records, "The Appomattox Campaign," Volume 46, Series 1, in three parts, Part 1, Reports, pages 938-939]Manuscript 140****

Comments and Supporting Evidence:

1. It is interesting to note that Harper also mentions being "momentarily staggered," with the 95th Pennsylvania being on the front line with the 121st New York in Hamblin's assault of the Confederate line. Once again, this could be attributed to Basinger's 18th Georgia charge of the Federals which momentarily staggered Hamblin's Brigade, including Harper's troops.

2. After contending with and prevailing against the Confederate line in their immediate front, it would appear that some, if not most, of the 95th Pennsylvania and the 121st New York moved to their left flank to contend with flanking Confederate troops there. Hawthorn, however, could not have followed this leftward movement of his 121st New York. Instead, he would have had to quickly move straight ahead through the surrendering 18th Georgia to be anywhere in the vicinity of Custis Lee on the active battlefield to capture him.

EXHIBIT-W-BA-21 FEDERAL

Introduction:

This account of the Battle of Sailor's Creek is given by Horace Clement Russell of Company F of the 37th Massachusetts Infantry. This account was written in March, 1918, from his memory.

Evidence:

Col. Edwards was mad–he was in command of the brigade and had ordered the 37th regiment to be held in reserve, but through some misunderstanding of orders our regiment went in with the rest on the right of the line. "Let me have my old 37th regiment and I'll find out whether those devils will surrender or not," and coming down to where he supposed we were, found that we had gone in with the rest. There was a lull in the firing and as there was an opening that was unprotected, D. L. Westmore, a member of my company, said he guessed he would go into the woods and see if the skirmishers needed any help, and he walked right into the rebel lines. He was disarmed and questioned as to our

forces and numbers as is always the case at such times to get information. *Gen. Custis Lee, a nephew of Gen. Robert E. Lee, commanding a brigade of rebels, asked him some questions and he says, "You Johnnies had better be getting out of here or we will have every one of you." Presently the firing began again and they told him to get back to the rear where the guard would take care of him, but he <u>scooted</u> into the brush, and going around he made his way back inside our lines again in half an hour, minus his rifle which the rebels had taken away from him. Our company was on the right of the regiment and we discovered that we were being flanked. To save ourselves we were obliged to "refuse our right," that is, fall back a little and face toward the right–the next company had to do the same thing. Sergt. Lewis ordered this change of front and told us to "go for 'em," and we went for them, pushing them back until they took refuge in some shallow gullies that the rains had washed out on sloping ground. We steadily advanced, firing as fast as possible with our Spencer repeating rifles which (the rebels said) we loaded Sundays and fired all the week, when the rebels began to wave handkerchiefs and rags in token of surrender. We stopped firing and advanced within about five rods when they gave us a volley in our faces. We thought if they wanted more of that same kind we would give them all they wanted and a little more for full measure, and we went for them for business and poured the bullets into them until they could not fire a shot. The gullies were not deep and they could not protect their heads and the upper part of their bodies very much, consequently most of them were shot in the head or chest and the gullies were full of dead bodies. Gen. Custis Lee with his brigade surrendered to our regiment. D. L. Wetmore, the member of my company taken prisoner as before related, walked up to Gen. Lee and says, "I told you a little while ago that you fellers had better get away, or we would have every dog of you, and now you see if you had taken my advice you might have saved your skins." About six o'clock we re-formed our lines, got off on the road as if nothing had happened, and proceeded toward Farmville. We lost thirty men in this affair, and it proved to be the last engagement of twenty two battles and skirmishes in which the regiment participated while in the service.*
[Source: "Memoirs of Horace Clement Russell, Company F, 37th Massachusetts Infantry," Gettysburg National Military Park Library, Gettysburg, PA]**Manuscript 142**

Comments and Supporting Evidence:

1. The most important aspect of this account is the story surrounding the battlefield activities of D. L. Wetmore of Company F of the 37th Massachusetts. If this story is true, it would place the location of Custis Lee directly in front of the 37th Massachusetts during the heat and final moments of the battle.
2. Russell validates the many accounts of the 37th Massachusetts facing toward their right to avoid a Confederate flank and then confronting the Confederates who took refuge in a gully or ravine.
3. He definitively claims that Custis Lee and his brigade surrendered to the 37th Massachusetts.
4. Horace Russell validates Edward Mahogany's (37th Massachusetts, Company F) account when Mahogany wrote in his letter home that Custis Lee was within their midst after the 37th Massachusetts captured him. Horace Russell does this by stating that D. L. Wetmore walked up to Custis Lee shortly after his capture and said, "I told you a little while ago that you fellers had better get away, or we would have every dog of you, and now you see if you had taken my advice you might have saved your skins."

EVIDENCE OVERVIEW
EXHIBIT-W-BT-(1)

The purpose of introducing this line of evidence is to show the current landmarks and features of the Sailor's Creek battlefield. This includes the ravine, head of the ravine, grassy knoll, gully at the side of the road and other features. Using these current landmarks and features, the author has attempted to map the most probable locations of the 121st New York vs. the 18th Georgia fight and the 37th Massachusetts vs. the Chaffin's Bluff troops fight. This mapping will show the battlefield distance between these two fights. It can then be extrapolated the distances between Harris Hawthorn, David White and Custis Lee.

EXHIBIT-W-BT-1

Introduction:

The following photographs show the important landmarks and geographic features of the Sailor's Creek battlefield as they currently exist:

Evidence: [Seven photographs as follows:]

Photograph one: On top of the grassy knoll looking over the battlefield northward toward Sailor's Creek. This is the path that the Chaffin's Bluff troops and the 10th and 19th Virginia Heavy Artillery would have charged down to push back the advancing Federal troops coming up from Sailor's Creek.

(WEST)-RAVINE   **(NORTH)-ON GRASSY KNOLL OVERLOOKING BATTLEFIELD**   **(EAST)**

Photograph two: The gully along the side of the road where the 18th Georgia Battalion positioned themselves to meet the advancing 121st New York. This is where they would also surrender.

(EAST)-ROAD   **(SOUTH)-GULLY AT THE SIDE OF THE ROAD**   **(WEST)-GRASSY KNOLL**

Photograph three: The ravine where the Chaffin's Bluff troops tried to regroup after their charge of the Federals. This is also where they fought the 37th Massachusetts. Chris Calkins points to the head of the ravine where Custis Lee was most likely positioned during the final moments of the battle.

(EAST)-GRASSY KNOLL   **(SOUTH)-RAVINE-POINTING TOWARD HEAD OF THE RAVINE**   **(WEST)**

Photograph four: Facing southward at the bottom of the hill looking at the grassy knoll. The 37th Massachusetts made this climb to confront the Confederates positioned on the grassy knoll.

(EAST)-ROAD   **(SOUTH)-GRASSY KNOLL**   **(WEST)-RAVINE**

Photograph five: On top of the grassy knoll, where there is currently a footpath to a Civil War monument. The Confederate troops, particularly those of Major Robert Stiles, formed on and around this grassy knoll at the start of the battle. The head of the ravine lay just to the west side of this grassy knoll, where Custis Lee was positioned.

(SOUTH)   **(WEST)-ON TOP OF GRASSY KNOLL**   **(NORTH)-SAILOR'S CREEK**

Photograph six: An aerial photograph of the Sailor's Creek battlefield highlighting various landmarks and features that are in existence today, and to a large degree, were in existence on April 6, 1865.

NORTHWARD

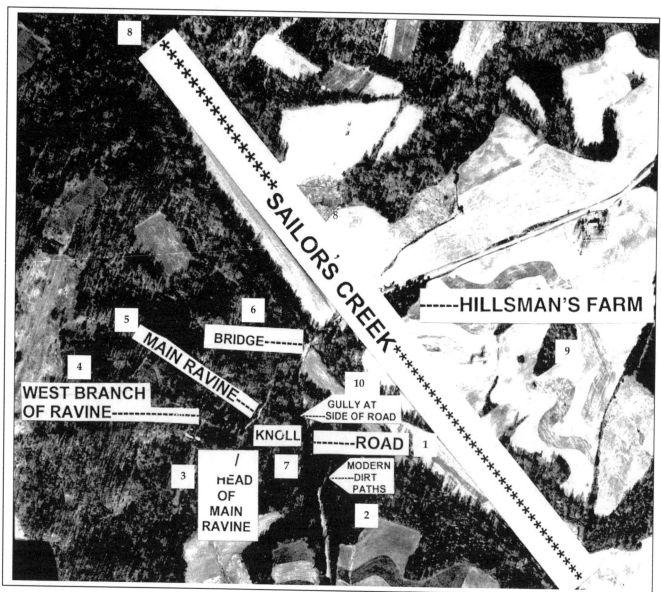

SOUTHWARD

LEGEND:

[1] ROAD: This is the road that the troops followed and where battle lines were drawn
[2] MODERN DIRT PATH: To the left of the box is a faint image of a modern dirt path
[3] HEAD OF THE RAVINE: Where Custis Lee was positioned for most of the battle
[4] WEST BRANCH RAVINE: Where Confederate troops positioned themselves to await Federals
[5] MAIN BRANCH RAVINE: Where Stiles' troops charged and attempted to re-group
[6] BRIDGE: Crossing Sailor's Creek
[7] GRASSY KNOLL: Where Stiles' troops were originally positioned at the start of the battle
[8] SAILOR'S CREEK: Nice image to the left and bottom of the bottom [8] box
[9] HILLSMAN FARM HOUSE: Battlefield landmark
[10] GULLY: Roadside gully where Basinger formed the 18th Georgia

Photograph seven: A battlefield map (circa 1880's) that depicts the positions of the battles between the 37th Massachusetts vs. the Chaffin's Bluff troops, and the 121st New York vs. the 18th Georgia.

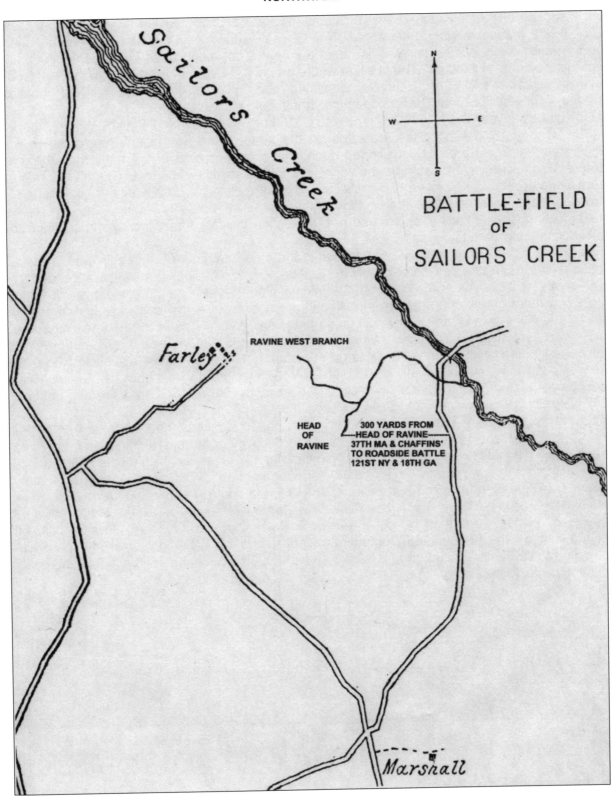

Comments and Supporting Evidence:

1. The grassy knoll in which Major Stiles originally assembled his Chaffin's Bluff troops "on and around," is very identifiable today and has a Civil War monument at its center.

2. The north-south facing ravine, with its western branch, is very identifiable today and surely is the ravine spoken of in the various battle accounts. The head of this ravine is also very identifiable today. It is a gradual sloping area, about 15 to 20 feet wide at its mouth, which gradually funnels into the north-south facing ravine. This head is surely a collection point for rainwater running off from the top of the sloping hill. The position where the 121st New York clashed with the 18th Georgia Battalion on the road can be accurately estimated today given the troop line-ups and geographic landmarks (grassy knoll, etc.) described in the various battle accounts.

3. The distance between the following two points: (1) the point where the 121st New York clashed with the 18th Georgia Battalion on the road and (2) the head of the north-south facing ravine where Custis Lee was most probably positioned during the final moments of the battle right before his capture; was accurately measured to be very close to 300 yards or 900 feet. Though this might not seem like a great distance in every day life, this is a huge distance for any Infantry soldier to travel across on an open battlefield, particularly when an active battle is raging. The risk of being intentionally or accidentally shot is great, not to mention the fact that there was intensive Federal Artillery fire going on in this area as well.

4. Given the fact that David White's position during the final moments of the battle was in the exact location where Custis Lee's most probable location was, which location was at the head of the north-south facing ravine at the center of the original Confederate line, and also given the fact that Harris Hawthorn had to sprint approximately 300 yards over an active battlefield just to get to that probable location, would lead one to conclude that David White was in a much better geographic position on the battlefield to have captured Custis Lee than Hawthorn was. It must not be forgotten that not only did Hawthorn have to run a great distance across an active battlefield where Custis Lee was positioned, his Regiment, the 121st New York, was greatly held back by the stubborn fight and charge of the 18th Georgia. In fact, this charge by the 18th Georgia initially pushed the 121st New York all the way back to Sailor's Creek.

5. In summary, in order for Harris Hawthorn to have captured Custis Lee on the battlefield of Sailor's Creek, Hawthorn would have had to; (1) initially fight his way up to the 18th Georgia from the creek under a hail of bullets,(2) recover from the charge of the 18th Georgia which pushed him back to the creek, (3) claw his way back to the road and engage the 18th Georgia again to force their surrender,(4) break through the surrendering 18th Georgia line, (5) sprint 300 yards over an active battlefield, (6) stumble upon Custis Lee behind his Confederate lines within the context of a raging hand to hand battle and then (7) get the draw on Custis Lee to force his surrender, all without getting shot by the surrounding Confederate troops who were fiercely loyal and dedicated to protecting their Major General and Division commander. This scenario seems highly improbable, if not impossible, to the author.

CHAPTER SIX:

VERDICT:

After analyzing all the evidence contained in this report, the author is now prepared to present to the reader a conclusive verdict, and definitively answer the question posed in the introduction of this report: "Who, within the Federal forces, was responsible for the capture of Confederate Major General George Washington Custis Lee at the Battle of Sailor's Creek, VA, on April 6, 1865; and in what manner was he captured?" The author has dismissed the Miles L. Butterfield account. This is because of the fact that the author was unable to find, through an exhaustive search, any additional evidence to support Butterfield's self initiated claim that he captured Custis Lee. The author has also dismissed the J. Warren Keifer account. A careful analysis of his claim would indicate that Keifer never intended to claim that either he, or his troops he commanded, captured Custis Lee. His intention was to state that General Wright's 6th Army Corps, of which Keifer's Brigade was just a part, captured Custis Lee. This leaves two primary claimants to be considered, Harris S. Hawthorn of the 121st New York and David D. White of the 37th Massachusetts. As with any court case, there are summations and closing arguments. For the Harris Hawthorn case, the author submits as a closing argument a newspaper article written by a Washington, DC, reporter or correspondent working for the "New York Sun." This article was written on September 18, 1897, two days before Secretary of War Alger made public his decision in the 37th Massachusetts Protest Case, on September 20, 1897.

WHO CAPTURED GEN. CUSTIS LEE?
The Records Show That It Was Sergeant Hawthorn
of the 121st New York

Washington, Sept. 18: *An argument has arisen between the members of the Thirty-seventh Massachusetts and the 121st New York Volunteers over the capture of Gen. Custis Lee at the battle of Little Sailor Creek, April 6, 1865. According to the War Department records, Sergeant Harris S. Hawthorn of the 121st New York was the captor of Gen. Lee and a medal was awarded him for the part he took in the capture. The Thirty-seventh Massachusetts disputed the capture by Hawthorn, and wants the credit given to Corporal White of their regiment. The War Department recently wrote for information on the subject, and a reply was recently received from Mr. Hawthorn. He says that Gen. Lee surrendered to him alone at Sailor's Creek, and refers for corroboration to the record of the department in which is a report from Maj. Gen. F. Wheaton, commanding the First Division, Sixth Corps. An attempt was made by others to take his prisoner from him, he says, but his Colonel and Lieut. Hassett came to his rescue. An investigation made before Judge Advocate H. E. Hindmarsh proved the claim of the Thirty-seventh Massachusetts to be without foundation. For the capture of Lee a furlough of twenty days was given Hawthorn, and he was promoted to sergeantcy. He incloses letters from G. W. C. Lee and Capt. Josh Heath, written to the late Hon. S. D. Locke of Hoosick Falls, N.Y. The letter from Gen. Lee says it is true that he was unarmed when he was captured, but enough of his own people were present to protect him if necessary. He said he surrendered to a private soldier, who told him he belonged to the Sixth Corps, commanded by Gen. H. G. Wright, and was taken to a place where he met an officer. It might have been to Gen. Wheaton's headquarters. Capt. Heath says that he was an eyewitness to the capture. He says that while his company was engaged in capturing the beautiful battle flag of the Savannah Guards, in which they lost five men and a Lieutenant, Sergeant Hawthorn went down the road and came back with Gen. Lee. Capt. Heath says that Hawthorn was one of the best soldiers that ever shouldered a gun. Hawthorn adds: "Corporal White has been carrying a sword which he claims was surrendered to him by Gen. Lee. This is not true, as you can see by Gen. Lee's letter. When I took Gen. Lee I demanded his arms. His reply was, I have not as much as a jackknife. I can furnish affidavits if necessary."*

[Source: "The Sun," by the Sun Printing and Publishing Association, New York, NY; Newspaper Edition: Sunday, September 19, 1897, page 7, Volume LXV-No. 19, five cents]Manuscript 154****

It should be noted that in the year 1897, "The New York Sun" was New York City's largest circulating newspaper, and they found this Case to be newsworthy. This New York Sun article was also carried by the Otsego Republican newspaper in their October 27, 1897, edition. As an introduction to a reprint of this New York Sun article, this Otsego, NY, newspaper states the following which the author would like to use as the final closing statement for the position of Harris Hawthorn and the 121st New York Case.

The following appeared in the New York Sun, Sept. 19, and will prove interesting reading to the many friends of Mr. H. S. Hawthorn, as it definitively settled his right to the badge of honor awarded him by the Government for the capture of Gen. Custis Lee at the battle of Little Sailor Creek, April 6, 1865.

[Source: "The Otsego Republican," Edition: Wednesday, October 27, 1897]Manuscript 155****

As a summation and closing argument for the 37th Massachusetts, the author simply submits the entire collection of evidence amassed in this report, allowing this body of evidence to speak for itself. With this, it is now time for this report to render a verdict. The reader is encouraged to now do the same. With all the evidence that the author could possibly find in this case now presented, the author respectfully submits a verdict that firmly concludes that Private David D. White captured Confederate Major General George Washington Custis Lee at the Battle of Sailor's Creek, VA, April 6, 1865. Harris S. Hawthorn may have participated in bringing Custis Lee to the rear of the Federal lines sometime after Custis Lee's capture, but Hawthorn did not capture Major General G. W. Custis Lee on the field of battle. Based on the body of evidence, the author has attempted to reconstruct the events surrounding the capture of Major General George Washington Custis Lee. This reconstruction will focus on the actions and movements of General Custis Lee during the battle, along with the movements and actions of Harris S. Hawthorn and David D. White. For reasons stated above, the movements and actions for Butterfield and Keifer are not considered in this "reconstruction of events." This reconstruction is as follows.

RECONSTRUCTION OF EVENTS

At the start of the battle, having crossed Sailor's Creek, Major General George Washington Custis Lee faced his Confederate Division north toward Sailor's Creek in preparation to meet the advancing Federal army. He was riding on his horse to the various positions of his battalion commanders, conferring with them and preparing them for the upcoming battle. On the Federal side, having also crossed Sailor's Creek, Harris Hawthorn lined up within his Company F of the 121st New York. His Regiment was on the front line of Hamblin's 2nd Brigade. His Regiment was lined up on the left side of the road facing south, with their backs toward Sailor's Creek. David White lined up within his Company E of the 37th Massachusetts. His Regiment was on the front left line of Edwards' 3rd Brigade. His Regiment lined up on the right side the road facing south, with their backs also toward Sailor's Creek. When the Federals initiated their advance up the hill toward the Confederate positions, General Custis Lee was still on horseback directing his various Battalion commanders. When Harris Hawthorn advanced forward with his Regiment, he encountered the diagonal right flank of Major Basinger's 18th Georgia Battalion. When David White advanced forward with his Regiment he encountered the direct front of Major Stiles' Chaffin's Bluff Garrison. When the 37th Massachusetts was very close, the Chaffin's Bluff troops fired an initial volley into this advancing Federal line. Immediately after this volley, the Chaffin's Bluff troops charged without the orders of their commander, Major Stiles. The 10th and 19th Virginia Heavy Artillery troops, which were on the left of the Chaffin's Bluff troops, also participated in this charge. The 37th Massachusetts held firm against this charge. The 2nd Rhode Island and the 49th Pennsylvania, however, which were on the right flank of the 37th Massachusetts, broke from their advancing line and spontaneously retreated down the hill away from the charging Confederate troops. On another area of the battlefield, when the advancing 121st New York came upon the diagonal right flank of the 18th Georgia, the 18th Georgia immediately changed their front to be alongside the road. This created a new front for the 18th Georgia which now paralleled the front of the approaching 121st New York. The 18th Georgia, which was commanded by William Star Basinger, soon recognized that they were severely outnumbered by the approaching 121st New York and the supporting second line of Hamblin's Brigade. Coming quickly to this realization, Basinger took the offensive and ordered his troops to charge with fixed bayonets against the advancing 121st New York. This charge temporarily halted the advance of the 121st New York, causing the 121st New York to spontaneously fall back all the way to Sailor's Creek. During this charge, some of Basinger's troops also filled a large gap between the advancing 37th Massachusetts and the 121st New York. The 121st New York began to regroup from their spontaneous retreat when Basinger's troops ran into the second line of Hamblin's Brigade. With this regrouping, the 121st New York changed their original front to now be along their original right flank so that they could combat Basinger's men that were in the gap between the 121st New York and the 37th Massachusetts. The 37th Massachusetts also changed their original front to now be along their original left flank to combat Basinger's men in this gap. The dual attacks by the regrouped 121st New York and the 37th Massachusetts were successful in driving Basinger's troops from this gap and their attacking position on the 121st New York in the woods. Basinger's troops now fell back to their original battlefield position in a gully alongside the road. The 121st New York now fronted themselves on this road, directly across and parallel to the reassembled front of the 18th Georgia. The 121st New York was now positioned for a new attack on the 18th Georgia. The 18th Georgia braced for this upcoming attack. The 37th Massachusetts, having held their original front against the initial Chaffin's Bluff charge due to the repeating firepower of their Spencer rifles, and also having repulsed the 18th Georgia charge on their original left flank, now had to defend their right flank against a rush of two major movements. They were the Chaffin's Bluff troop, which initially bounced off the front of the 37th Massachusetts, together with the charging 10th and 19th Virginia Heavy Artillery troops, which were positioned directly in front of the advancing 2nd Rhode Island and 49th Pennsylvania. All these Confederate troops were now running downhill to their left, alongside the 37th Massachusetts, in a battlefield void caused by the retreating 2nd Rhode Island and 49th Pennsylvania. This flow of Confederate troops occurred precisely between the 37th Massachusetts' extreme right flank and a natural ravine or gully that existed on the battlefield. To address this Confederate movement, the 37th Massachusetts changed their original front toward their extreme right flank, so as to now be parallel to this ravine. The Confederate Chaffin's Bluff and 10th and 19th Virginia Heavy Artillery troops found themselves in the precarious position of now being sandwiched between this natural ravine and the new front of the 37th Massachusetts. Company E of the 37th Massachusetts, with David White as a member of this Company, was on the extreme left of the 37th Massachusetts. With this new "ravine facing" front created by the 37th Massachusetts, Company E was now the 37th Massachusetts' company farthest uphill and would have been located somewhere near the head of this ravine. About the time the Federal advance came within close proximity of the Confederate positions, General Custis Lee dismounted his horse and positioned himself at the center of his Division. His central location was, in all probability, according to the various battlefield accounts contained in this report, near or at the head of the ravine. Major Stiles, trying to regroup his troops from their spontaneous charge, ran uphill to confer with General Custis Lee. Stiles told General Custis Lee that he thought he could reassemble his men to their original battlefield position at the top of the hill by bringing them up through the ravine. The ravine would offer his troops some protection from enemy fire. Custis Lee was doubtful that this could effectively be done. When this conference took place, both Stiles and Custis Lee were positioned near or at the head of the ravine. Custis Lee gave Stiles his permission to attempt to reassemble of his troops using the ravine. Major Stiles then ran downhill and moved his troops from the open battlefield, to their left and then into this ravine. He then tried to bring them uphill to their original battlefield position where General Custis Lee was now stationed. When Stiles completed this action to the best of his ability, some of his troops were now re-positioned back into their original battle line at the top of the hill around the head of the ravine. Most of Stiles' men, however, never made it back to the top of the hill and remained in the ravine. It is worth mentioning here a well documented fact concerning the Battle of Sailor's Creek. When Stiles' Chaffin's Bluff and 10th and 19th Virginia Heavy Artillery troops charged and caused the retreat of 2nd Rhode Island and 49th Pennsylvania, the Federal artillery which was positioned on the other side (north) of Sailor's Creek, resumed their artillery assault on the Confederate positions again, similar to what the Federals did at the start of the battle. So Stiles not only had the difficult task of getting his men off an open battlefield into a ravine, he had to do it under a pounding Federal artillery assault. This could explain while Stiles' was only partially successful in getting his troops back to their original battlefield position at the top of the hill at or near the head of the ravine. At this time on the other battle front, the 121st New York, with Harris Hawthorn, attacked the 18th Georgia on the road and completely overpowered them. The 121st New York captured two of the 18th Georgia's battle flags, with Warren Dockun and Benjamin Gifford of the 121st New York receiving the credit. This last clash between the 121st New York and the 18th Georgia Battalion resulted in Major Basinger unconditionally surrendering his troops. While the 18th Georgia was surrendering to the 121st New York, the 37th Massachusetts became engaged in a brutal hand to hand combat with Stiles' Chaffin's Bluff troops and members of the 10th and 19th Virginia Heavy Artillery. The 37th Massachusetts line was still parallel to the ravine. The "Chaffin's Bluff and 10th and 19th Virginia Heavy Artillery" line was now parallel with this 37th Massachusetts front, extending from its original position at the top of the hill and at the head of the ravine, and going downhill following the ravine. General Custis Lee and Major Stiles were now at the top of the hill, in the original position of Stiles' troops. When the 37th Massachusetts changed fronts to be parallel with the ravine, this swing movement placed Company E, which was always on the extreme left the 37th Massachusetts, at the top of the hill and near the head of the ravine. This now positioned David White of Company E to be in very close proximity to General Custis Lee and Major Stiles, who were monitoring the final moments of the battle from the top of this hill, "head of the ravine," vantage point. At this point in the battle, the whole battle line of the 37th Massachusetts and the Chaffin's Bluff and the 10th and 19th Virginia Heavy Artillery engaged in a brutal hand to hand combat. This action must have enveloped Custis Lee at his vantage point, because Custis Lee was almost captured at this point in time by the aimed revolver of Lieut. Harrie A. Cushman of the 37th Massachusetts. Lieut. Cushman was severely wounded in this attempt and fell back to the rear of his line. At this point, Custis Lee withdrew from this hand to hand combat zone to be a short distance behind his desperately engaged troops. Determining that the defeat of his Division was imminent, he decided to make his escape. General Custis Lee moved toward Sailor's Creek by going behind his line which was battling the 37th Massachusetts. This decision to head for the creek might sound unusual given the fact that the Federal troops had just come from that direction; however, it can be explained. The Federal Cavalry was quickly coming upon Custis Lee's rear, and his flanks were being turned inward by Hamblin attacking his right and Keifer attacking his left. Going straight ahead toward the creek for his escape while the Federals were now up hill might have seemed to Custis Lee, at the moment, to be the only avenue temporarily free of the enemy. David White, in the middle of this hand to hand combat zone, spotted a high ranking Confederate officer making his way toward the creek. White then advanced through the hand to hand combat line and pursued this officer. When White overtook the officer, White halted him at gunpoint and demanded his surrender. General Custis Lee refused to surrender to Private White, but was compelled to do so when he felt that his life was in jeopardy by White's determination to bring him in at gun point. At this point, others of the 37th Massachusetts were close by to witness this interaction between Custis Lee and Private White. General Custis Lee then demanded that Private White take him to commissioned officer so that he, Custis Lee, could officially surrender. David White then brought Custis Lee to his commanding officer, Lt. William Morrill, who was near by. It was at this point in time that Lt. Morrill made White aware of the fact that the Confederate officer that White had just captured was Major General George Washington Custis Lee, son of the famed Robert E. Lee. Custis Lee then surrendered his sword, his belt containing a revolver and his haversack containing many personal items to Lt. William Morrill. If it really happened, General Custis Lee now engaged Lieutenant William Morrill in a brief discussion about obtaining a furlough to avoid becoming a prisoner of war. It is important to note that the battle was still very active when Custis Lee was captured, with the hand to hand combat raging on in the foreground. The following two statements most likely depict the frenzied conditions that occurred on the battlefield at the time of Custis Lee's capture. General Hamblin gave this report concerning the battle of Petersburg; however, the conditions depicted in this Petersburg report could have easily applied to the conditions at the Battle of Sailor's Creek. The report states, *"Officers and men were so enthusiastic in the pursuit that little attention was paid to guarding or getting receipts for captured prisoners or property.* [Source: **Official Records, "The Appomattox Campaign," Volume 46, Series 1, page 932]**Manuscript 72**** James Bowen of the 37th Massachusetts records the following account concerning the Battle of Sailor's Creek, *"No less than six confederate generals were secured, including Ewell, Kershaw and Custis Lee, with about all that remained of Ewell's corps. There was little attempt to count, scarcely to guard the captures made; everywhere the shout was FORWARD! ONWARD! To strike the final blows and destroy everything that remained to Lee as an organized army."* [Source: **"History of the 37th Regiment Massachusetts Volunteers," by James L. Bowen. 1884, page 419]**Manuscript 73****

With the Federal forces pressing forward with the excitement of achieving a victorious battle, General Custis Lee was temporarily left unguarded by the 37th Massachusetts who captured him. After the capture of Custis Lee, White was immediately detailed with others of the 37th Massachusetts to bring ammunition from the rear to the battlefront for use in the continued fight. So David White was definitely not guarding his captured General, Custis Lee. It is at this moment that Harris Hawthorn, having penetrated the line of the surrendering 18th Georgia Battalion on the road, proceeded beyond that line into the ravine area of the battlefield where the 37th Massachusetts was engaged. This is where Hawthorn came upon the already captured, but temporarily unguarded, General Custis Lee. Harris Hawthorn demanded that Custis Lee surrender and yield up his side arms. It is at this point that Custis Lee uttered his defining words to Hawthorn as recorded by Hawthorn himself, "I don't have as much as a jack knife." As far as Hawthorn knew, he captured General Custis Lee. The reality was, Custis Lee had already been captured, disarmed, stripped of his personal belongings and left temporarily unguarded by the 37th Massachusetts when Hawthorn came upon him. Hawthorn then sought to take firm control of Custis Lee as his prisoner of war. When the 37th Massachusetts became aware of this, they became involved again with the captured Custis Lee. A dispute broke out between the 121st New York involving Hawthorn, Col. Olcott, Hassett and perhaps others and some unidentified members of the 37th Massachusetts (we can rule out White because he was getting ammunition from the rear and got seriously injured in the process). Hawthorn, Hassett, Moore, Butterfield and perhaps members of the 37th Massachusetts all brought General Custis Lee to the rear for processing. Custis Lee was initially brought to General Wheaton's headquarters but eventually wound up at General Sheridan's headquarters. While all this was taking place, different members of the 37th Massachusetts divided up the personal belongings that were taken from Custis Lee's haversack. Lt. Morrill got Custis Lee's belt containing Custis Lee's sword and revolver. This combination nicely replaced Morrill's own sword and revolver which he lost in the abatis during the assault on Fort Fisher, Petersburg, VA, on April 2, 1865. Lt. William Morrill also took Custis Lee's horse. General Oliver Edwards got Custis Lee's Meerschaum pipe and his embroidered tobacco pouch. David White got Custis Lee's empty haversack. Custis Lee's other personal items that were in the haversack, like his dictionary, hairbrush, stamps, etc., were distributed amongst various members of the 37th Massachusetts. Col. Olcott, who commanded the 121st New York at the Battle of Sailor's Creek, stated in his Official Report that there was, "some controversy concerning the matter," about who really captured Custis Lee. Given this controversy, on April 14, 1865, Harris Hawthorn took the initiative by issuing a sworn statement to field Judge Advocate Hindmarsh stating that he alone captured Custis Lee. David D. White took no such action. David White was still injured and quite incapacitated during this mid-April time period and would not have been in a position to make a counter statement even if he wanted to. Given the evidence, it is doubtful that White even felt inclined to do so. It would appear that neither David White nor the 37th Massachusetts desired to take any special action on this matter, believing that the capture of Custis Lee was just a part of their overall well performed military action at the battle. In addition, the 37th Massachusetts probably had no idea that Hawthorn even made a sworn statement to Judge Hindmarsh claiming the capture of Custis Lee. If they had, the 37th Massachusetts might have taken an aggressive stand to "set the record straight" according to their own knowledge of the events. This suggestion is substantiated by the fact that Bowen received an overwhelming response from the veterans of 37th Massachusetts in the year 1897 when Bowen initiated his Protest Case. It is worth mentioning again that both Hawthorn and White were promoted to Corporals by their respective superiors for the capture of Custis Lee at the Battle of Sailor's Creek. After an exhaustive examination of all of the evidence presented in this report, this "reconstruction of events" is the only plausible conclusion that the author could reach. It answers in detail the question, "who within the Union forces was responsible for, and in what manner was Confederate Major General George Washington Custis Lee captured at the Battle of Sailor's Creek, VA, on April 6, 1865"? To a large degree, this "reconstruction of events" as outlined above reconciles the account of the capture of Custis Lee offered by the 37th Massachusetts with the account offered by Harris Hawthorn. The author sincerely welcomes the introduction of any new evidence that might alter this "reconstruction of events" and the conclusion reached by the author. This conclusion, or verdict, being that Private David D. White is the real soldier that definitively captured Major General Custis Lee at the Battle of Sailor's Creek. Unless any new evidence comes forth challenging the conclusion made in this report, and given the exhaustive nature of the research performed, the author respectfully suggests that the conclusion reached in this report be treated as a historical fact by scholars of both the Civil War and the Battle of Sailor's Creek.

Battle Reconstruction Using Aerial Photographs:

To better visualize the "reconstruction of events" described above, the following aerial photographs of the battlefield of Sailor's Creek have been superimposed with the positions of the Confederate and Federal troops. These aerial photographs also have been superimposed with the positions of Harris Hawthorn, David White and Custis Lee. Photographs one through five, with their corresponding descriptions, should be treated as, "snapshots in time," as the Battle of Sailor's Creek was unfolding.

PHOTO ONE
NORTHWARD

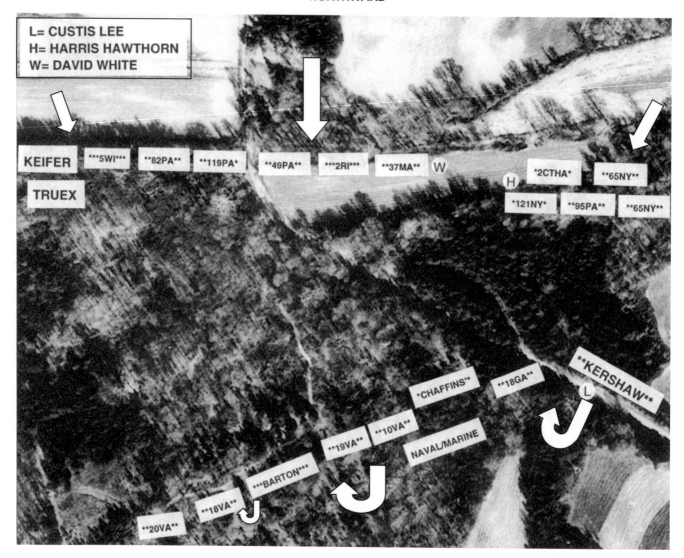

SOUTHWARD

- **Photograph one** is a depiction of the actual start of the Hillsman Farm fight at the Battle of Sailor's Creek. Prior to this snapshot, the Federals organized their troops on the north side of Sailor's Creek to prepare these forces to be able to cross Sailor's Creek in an efficient manner. On the south side of Sailor's Creek, the Confederate forces were now stopped and positioning themselves to meet the advancing Federal forces that would soon be crossing Sailor's Creek.

- Once Sailor's Creek was crossed by the Federals, which occurred with some difficulty due to the muddy and swollen nature of the creek, combined with the heavy skirmish fire by the Confederates on the Federals while the Federals were crossing the creek, the Federals realigned themselves on the south side of Sailor's Creek as depicted above.
- Joseph Hamblin aligned his 2nd Brigade of the 1st Division facing southward toward the hill where the Confederate troops were now positioned awaiting the Federal assault. Hamblin's Brigade was formed in two lines. Facing in the direction of the Confederates, the 121st New York was on the right of Hamblin's first line and the 95th Pennsylvania Regiment was on the left of Hamblin's first line. The 2nd Connecticut Heavy Artillery was on the right of Hamblin's second line and the 65th New York Regiment, as skirmishers, was on the left of Hamblin's lines.
- Oliver Edwards aligned his 3rd Brigade of the 1st Division facing southward toward the hill where the Confederate troops were positioned awaiting the Federal assault. Facing the Confederates, Edwards' Brigade was loosely connected on his left with the right flank of Hamblin's 2nd Brigade. Unlike Hamblin's Brigade, Edwards' Brigade was formed in a single line of battle. Facing the Confederates and starting from the extreme left flank of Edwards' Brigade was the 37th Massachusetts, followed by the 2nd Rhode Island, followed by the 49th Pennsylvania, followed by the 119th Pennsylvania, followed by the 82nd Pennsylvania and finally followed by the 5th Wisconsin on the extreme right flank of the Brigade. The 1st Brigade of the 3rd Division was commanded by Col. William Truex and this Division was positioned on the right flank of Edwards' Brigade facing the Confederates.
- Confederate Major General Custis Lee's Division was now stopped. He positioned his troops in a defensive battle line to meet the advancing Federals that had crossed Sailor's Creek.
- Custis Lee's Division was positioned on the left side of the road facing northward toward Sailor's Creek. On his Division's extreme right flank facing the advancing Federals was the 18th Georgia Battalion. The right flank of this 18th Georgia Battalion rested slightly on the road. Starting at the extreme right flank of Custis Lee's Division was the 18th Georgia Battalion, followed by the, Chaffin's Bluff Garrison, followed by the 10th Virginia Heavy Artillery, followed by 19th Virginia Heavy Artillery, followed by Barton's Brigade (which had their front resting on the west branch of the ravine) and finally followed by the troops of the 18th and 20th Virginia Heavy Artillery on the Division's extreme left flank, (which also had their front resting on the west branch of the ravine).
- A Naval/Marine Brigade was in position a little behind the Chaffin's Bluff Garrison and the 10th Virginia Heavy Artillery, to serve as a secondary support force for Custis Lee's single line of battle.
- Major Stiles' Chaffin's Bluff Garrison, though initially positioned in a straight alignment with the Custis Lee's single line of battle, was actually located a little forward from the rest of Custis Lee's battle line. This was due to the topology of the battlefield. They were positioned on and around a grassy knoll that caused them to jut out a little as they tried to conform to this terrain. Confederate General Kershaw lined his Division on the right side of the road facing northward, almost perpendicular or at a right angle to Custis Lee's Division. As with Custis Lee's Division, Kershaw's Division was also stopped and lined up in a defensive position awaiting the Federals to advance upon their battle line. Kershaw was watching both the Federal Infantry and Calvary.
- An important point to note is that the extreme right flank of Custis Lee's Division and the extreme left flank of Kershaw's Division were not well connected. A large gap existed. This was due to the fact that this area of intersection was wooded, which would have visually hindered the two Divisions from forming the desired tight connection. In addition, the Confederates were forming their battle lines in haste which could have impaired their forming this tight connection.
- Custis Lee was on horseback at this early point, conferring with other leaders on the road. White was with his 37th Massachusetts Regiment and Hawthorn with his 121st New York Regiment.

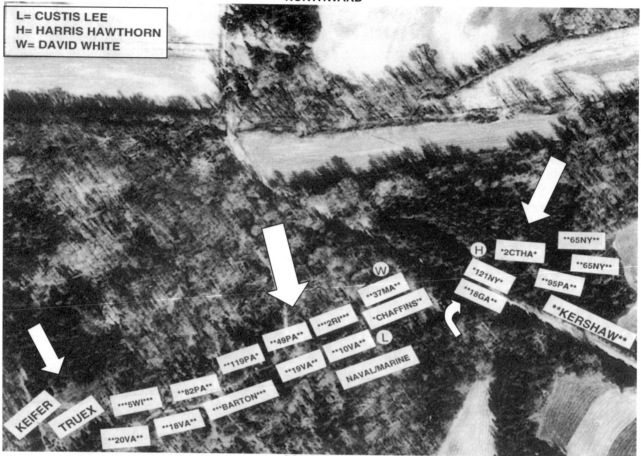

L= CUSTIS LEE
H= HARRIS HAWTHORN
W= DAVID WHITE

SOUTHWARD

- **Photograph two** is the next snap shot in time. This is when the Federals advanced up the hill and came in contact with the Confederates in their defensive battle lines near the top of the hill.

- As Hamblin's Brigade advanced up the hill toward the Confederate positions, a large gap developed between the extreme right flank of his brigade and the extreme left flank of Edwards' Brigade, as shown above. The 121st New York was on the extreme right of Hamblin's Brigade and the 37th Massachusetts was on the extreme left of Edwards' Brigade.

- The 121st New York advanced through dense woods and came diagonally upon the right flank of the 18th Georgia Battalion. Once again, the left flank of Kershaw's Division was not well connected to the right flank of Custis Lee's Division, with the 18th Georgia being on Custis Lee's extreme right flank. This loose connection allowed the 121st New York to come diagonally upon the right flank of the 18th Georgia relatively unmolested. Spotting this Federal advance, Basinger and his 18th Georgia Battalion quickly changed their front to parallel the road. This also allowed them to directly parallel the oncoming front of the 121st New York.

- The 37th Massachusetts advanced up the hill toward the Confederate positions and became directly opposed to the Confederate Chaffin's Bluff troops. The Chaffin's Bluff troops observed the 37th Massachusetts coming directly at them. The Chaffin's Bluff troops were fully loaded and patiently waiting for the opportunity to fire a deadly volley into their ranks as soon as the 37th Massachusetts came within close enough range.

- The 2nd Rhode Island and the 49th Pennsylvania advanced up the hill toward the Confederate positions and became directly fronted with 10th and 19th Virginia Heavy Artillery troops. These positions were in, and immediately around, the vicinity of the ravine that ran in a north-south direction throughout the entire length of this section of the battlefield.

- The 119th Pennsylvania, 82nd Pennsylvania and the 5th Wisconsin, on the right of Edwards' Brigade facing the Confederates, advanced up the hill toward the Confederate positions and fronted with Barton's Brigade and the 18th and 20th Virginia Heavy Artillery troops.
- Barton's Brigade and the 18th and 20th Virginia Heavy Artillery formed the left part of Custis Lee's Division's battle line facing the approaching Federals. Barton's Brigade and the 18th and 20th Virginia Heavy Artillery had in their immediate front, a fairly deep divide in the terrain belonging to an east-west branch of the main ravine. This branch shows up nicely in the aerial photograph.
- The main segment of this natural ravine ran in a north-south direction. The branch to this main ravine ran in a somewhat diagonal east-west direction across the battlefield. Barton's Brigade, together with the 18th and 20th Virginia Heavy Artillery, with the 20th Virginia Heavy Artillery forming the extreme left flank of Custis Lee's Division facing the approaching Federals, rested on the south side of the divide in the terrain belonging to this east-west branch of the ravine.
- The 119th Pennsylvania, 82nd Pennsylvania and the 5th Wisconsin, with the 5th Wisconsin forming the extreme right flank of Edwards' Brigade facing the Confederates, rested on the north side of this divide in the terrain belonging to this east-west branch of the main ravine.
- As Hamblin's and Edwards' Brigades advanced up the heights toward the Confederate defensive positions, both of these Brigades were fired upon by Confederate skirmishers that were deployed at various locations downhill throughout the battlefield.
- As the Federals continued their advance up the heights, these Confederate skirmishers slowly began to withdraw southward to join the main body of the Confederate troops.
- Federal Brig. General Truman Seymour's 3rd Division, which contained Col. William S. Truex's 1st Brigade, advanced southward through the woods upon the unguarded left flank of Custis Lee's Division. Custis Lee's Division did not have any more troops remaining to confront the advance of Seymour's Division. All indications are that Seymour's and Truex's advance went completely unimpeded with no Confederates to oppose them. There are indications; however, that Seymour temporarily halted his advance in order to maintain a tight connection with the right flank of Edwards' Brigade. This was done when Edwards' Brigade halted when they fronted the Confederate lines of Barton's Brigade and the 18th and 20th Virginia Heavy Artillery.
- There are also some indications at this early stage of the battle that when Seymour's Division containing Treux's 1st Brigade, saw that there were no Confederate forces directly opposed to them, they began to reposition their advance slightly to their left flank facing the Confederates. This maneuver was initiated in order to advance directly upon the unguarded extreme left flank of Custis Lee's Division and turn it inward toward the Confederate center. If Seymour and Treux were successful in turning Custis Lee's left flank inward, this would spell disaster for Custis Lee's Division and the entire Confederate army positioned in this area of the battle.
- It must be noted that prior to this alignment by the Federals, which was created to facilitate their advance up the heights toward the Confederate defensive positions, the Federals severely bombarded the Confederate defensive positions with heavy artillery fire. The Federal artillery was positioned on the north side of Sailor's Creek near the Hillsman farm house. This Federal artillery fire had mixed success in causing damage to the Confederate lines. By in large, the Confederates held to their defensive positions despite this heavy Federal artillery fire. The Confederate Infantry had no artillery ordinance to fire back at the Federals, due to the fact that their artillery ordinance was with their wagon train which had traveled off in a different direction.
- Hawthorn remained with his 121st New York. The 121st New York was now fronted on the road and positioned directly opposite Basinger's 18th Georgia Battalion.
- White remained with his 37th Massachusetts. The 37th Massachusetts was now fronted directly opposite Stiles' Chaffin's Bluff Garrison.
- Custis Lee, seeing the threat of the approaching Federals and the ensuing battle, positioned himself at a vantage point at the center of his line, near the head of the north-south facing main ravine. His position was behind and between the Chaffin's Bluff Garrison and the 10th Virginia Heavy Artillery. This central area allowed Custis Lee to direct the efforts for most of his Division.
- Kershaw maintained his original position along the road and awaited the approaching Federals.

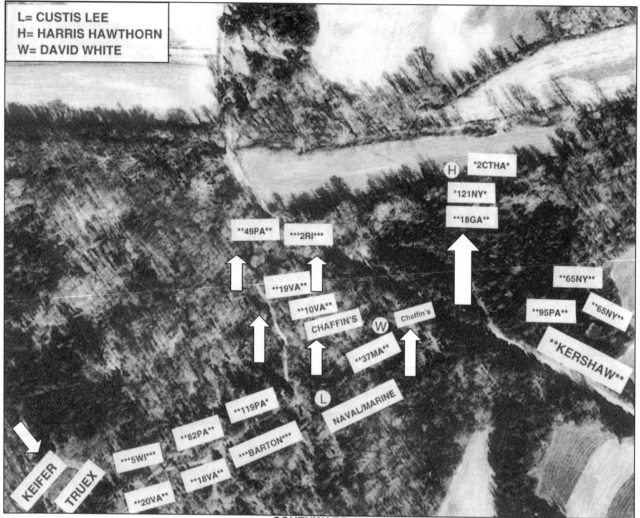

L= CUSTIS LEE
H= HARRIS HAWTHORN
W= DAVID WHITE

2CTHA

121NY

18GA

49PA ***2RI***

19VA

10VA

CHAFFIN'S

Chaffin's

65NY

95PA **65NY**

KERSHAW

37MA

NAVAL/MARINE

119PA

82PA

BARTON

5WI

18VA

KEIFER

TRUEX

20VA

SOUTHWARD

- **Photograph three** is the next snapshot in time. This is when the battle started to become fully engaged, with various elements of combat occurring within many locations of the battlefield.
- The 121st New York assaulted the 18th Georgia Battalion on the road. Basinger, seeing that his troops were severely outnumbered by the Federals, ordered his 18th Georgia Battalion to fix their bayonets and charge the 121st New York. This initial charge was successful. The 18th Georgia Battalion pushed the 121st New York back a considerable distance, probably to Sailor's Creek. Harris Hawthorn would have also been pushed back to Sailor's Creek with his 121st New York. The 2nd Connecticut Heavy Artillery, which was in a second line behind the 121st New York within Hamblin's Brigade, was also affected and pushed backward by this charge of the 18th Georgia Battalion. Their troops, however, added much needed support and critical manpower to the 121st New York. The 2nd Connecticut Heavy Artillery was finally able to stabilize the retreating 121st New York, and together stopped the charge of the 18th Georgia Battalion. This halting of the 18th Georgia Battalion's charge occurred at or near Sailor's Creek. Dennis Moore would have also been pushed back with his 2nd Connecticut Heavy Artillery, and like Hawthorn of the 121st New York, would have wound up close to Sailor's Creek at this point in the battle. Hawthorn and Moore, with their Regiments, would have been dazed by this charge from the 18th Georgia Battalion and would have required some time to reorganize.

- The 95th Pennsylvania now moved to the left of their original battlefield position facing the Confederates. The 95th Pennsylvania did not get involved or affected in the charge of the 18th Georgia Battalion upon the 121st New York and 2nd Connecticut Heavy Artillery. Instead, the 95th Pennsylvania moved directly toward the extreme left flank of Kershaw's Division which was on the road, and prepared to attack them.

- The troops of the 65th New York of Hamblin's Brigade, which were initially deployed as skirmishers, remained in their original position as skirmishers at this point in the battle.

- Confederate Major Stiles' Chaffin's Bluff troops patiently waited and then fired a deadly volley into the advancing Federals. After this, they charged the advancing 37th Massachusetts. The 37th Massachusetts was able to hold firm to their original position on the battlefield because of the rapid firepower of their repeating Spencer rifles. They did not retreat as a result of the charge by Stiles' troops. The Chaffin's Bluff troops "bounced" off the immediate front of the 37th Massachusetts and flowed on both sides of the 37th Massachusetts. On the left flank of the 37th Massachusetts facing the Confederates, a small number of Chaffin's Bluff troops combined with the charging 18th Georgia Battalion to push the 121st New York and 2nd Connecticut Heavy Artillery back to Sailor's Creek. On the right flank of the 37th Massachusetts facing the Confederates, most of the Chaffin's Bluff troops combined with the 10th and 19th Virginia Heavy Artillery to initiate a charge on the 2nd Rhode Island and 49th Pennsylvania. This Confederate charge caused the 2nd Rhode Island and 49th Pennsylvania to retreat backward toward Sailor's Creek. This Confederate charge by most of Stiles' troops and the 10th and 19th Virginia Heavy Artillery, and the resulting Federal retreat by the 2nd Rhode Island and 49th Pennsylvania, occurred in the location between the extreme right flank of the 37th Massachusetts facing the Confederates, and the north-south facing branch of the main ravine on the battlefield.

- The 119th Pennsylvania, 82nd Pennsylvania and 5th Wisconsin, at this point in time, had a musketry battle across the divide of the east-west branch of the ravine with Barton's Brigade and the 18th and 20th Virginia Heavy Artillery. Due to this deep divide in this branch of the ravine, which separated the Confederate lines from the Federal lines, Barton's Brigade and the 18th and 20th Virginia Heavy Artillery did not charge the advancing Federals in their front as did their fellow 18th Georgia, Chaffin's Bluff and 10th and 19th Virginia Heavy Artillery troops.

- Kershaw's Division was still in their original position and started to be attacked by the Federals.

- Seymour's Division, containing the commands of Truex and Keifer, continued to advance diagonally upon the unguarded extreme left flank of Custis Lee's Division; however, Seymour's Division did not become actively engaged at this time. They were simply moving forward.

- Custis Lee remained in the center of his battle line at the head of the main branch of the north-south facing ravine. He was observing the charge of his Chaffin's Bluff and 10th and 19th Virginia Heavy Artillery troops upon the Federals. He was in somewhat of an exposed position at this time, with his troops that were directly in front of him all downhill now chasing the retreating Federals. Being dismounted at this point in the battle, and given that he could only be in one place at one time, he had no opportunity to mange the efforts at his right flank, (Basinger's 18th Georgia), or at his left flank, (Barton's Brigade and the 18th and 20th Virginia Heavy Artillery).

- White was with his 37th Massachusetts fending off the charge of the Chaffin's Bluff troops. It should be noted that at this point in the battle, White's Company E of the 37th Massachusetts was the Company that formed the extreme left flank (facing the Confederates) of both the 37th Massachusetts and Edwards' Brigade.

- Also at this point in the battle, the Confederates were on the offensive and appeared to have the upper hand. Basinger, with his 18th Georgia Battalion, was able to push the 121st New York and the 2nd Connecticut Heavy Artillery back to Sailor's Creek with a charge using their fixed bayonets. Stiles' Chaffin's Bluff troops, with the 10th and 19th Virginia Heavy Artillery, were able to push the 2nd Rhode Island and 49th Pennsylvania back to Sailor's Creek as well. The Federal commanders, viewing these precarious developments from their Hillsman Farm vantage point, ordered a new round of cannonade to blast these charging Confederates.

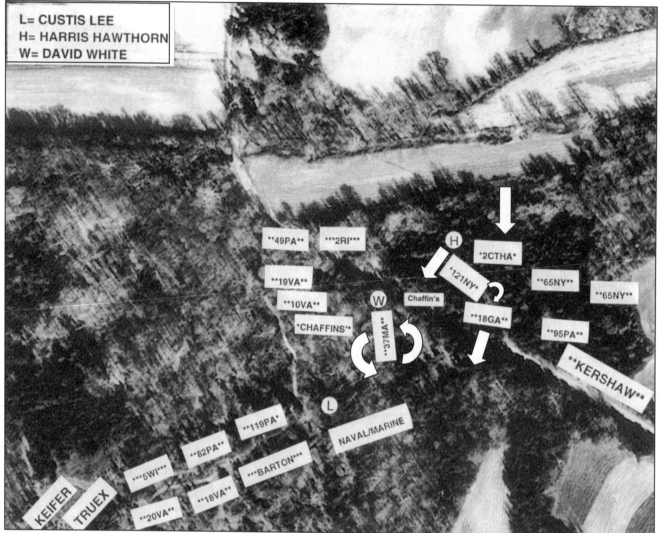

L= CUSTIS LEE
H= HARRIS HAWTHORN
W= DAVID WHITE

SOUTHWARD

- **Photograph four** is the next snapshot in time. Determining that the Federals were starting to regroup, Basinger began to move his 18th Georgia Battalion uphill from their downhill position which was caused by their charge. This was done to bring them back to a gully along the road.
- The regrouped 121st New York, with the 2nd Connecticut Heavy Artillery in a second line of battle behind them, started their advance back up the hill after the retreating 18th Georgia Battalion. As this advance was being made, Olcott, the commander of the 121st New York, noticed on his right flank a small contingent of soldiers which were from the Chaffin's Bluff troops combined with a remaining element of troops from the 18th Georgia Battalion. This small contingent of Confederate troops was located between Olcott's 121st New York's right flank and Edwards' 37th Massachusetts' left flank. This small contingent was created by a portion of the Chaffin's Bluff and 18th Georgia troops, both running downhill in the gap that existed between the 37th Massachusetts and 121st New York. Olcott ordered his 121st New York to make a 45 degree turn to their right flank in order to confront and chase away this small contingent of Confederate troops.
- Hopkins, the commander of the 37th Massachusetts, also noticed this small contingent of Confederate troops on his left flank in the gap that existed between his 37th Massachusetts and the 121st New York. In a move similar to Olcott's, Hopkins ordered his 37th Massachusetts to fall

back slightly and make a 45 degree turn to their left flank to front this small contingent of charging Confederate troops. With Olcott's 121st New York firing on one side, and Hopkins' 37th Massachusetts firing on the other side, the Federals were soon able to chase away this small contingent of Confederate forces that charged into this gap between these two Federal Regiments.

- The remainder of Hamblin's Brigade, consisting of the 95th Pennsylvania and to some extent the 65th New York, attacked in earnest the left flank of Kershaw's Division.
- The Chaffin's Bluff troops, together with the 10th and 19th Virginia Heavy Artillery, ceased their charge on the 2nd Rhode Island and 49th Pennsylvania. This occurred when these Confederate troops pushed these Federals back to Sailor's Creek. This also occurred when the Federals opened fire again with their artillery cannonade upon the Chaffin's Bluff and 10th and 19th Virginia Heavy Artillery troops which were now strewn haphazardly on the open battlefield.
- The Naval/Marine Battalion stayed in place in their original position as a secondary line and did not participate in the charge on the Federals by the Chaffin's Bluff and 10th and 19th Virginia Heavy Artillery troops. They were positioned in the immediate vicinity, with them being somewhat behind and slightly to the south, of the head of the north-south facing natural ravine.
- Barton's Brigade and the 18th and 20th Virginia Heavy Artillery did not participate in the charge of the Chaffin's Bluff and 10th and 19th Heavy Artillery troops. They remained in place in their original position on the south side of the east-west branch of the ravine.
- Barton's Brigade and the 18th and 20th Virginia Heavy Artillery continued to be engaged in a musketry battle with the 119th Pennsylvania, 82nd Pennsylvania and 5th Wisconsin. Once again, these troops were separated by a fairly deep terrain divide in the east-west branch of the natural ravine. This divide discouraged closer combat between these Confederate and Federal troops, so they just continued to fire at one another across the divide of the ravine.
- Seymour's Division, with Truex's and Keifer's troops, actively advanced upon the unguarded left flank of Custis Lee's Division. At this point in the battle, they still did not become engaged with any Confederate forces. There were just not any Confederate forces available to oppose them.
- Kershaw's Division was still positioned on the road and they were now actively battling the Federals forces. Kershaw had a portion of Hamblin's Brigade coming upon their left flank facing the Federals. They now also had the Federal Calvary forces coming upon their front and right flanks. Kershaw's Division was now engaged in a serious fight, threatening their entire force.
- Hawthorn and Moore, with their 121st New York and 2nd Connecticut Heavy Artillery Regiments respectfully, recovered from being pushed back by the charge of the 18th Georgia Battalion. Both Hawthorn and Moore were now making their way back up the hill to confront the 18th Georgia Battalion, who were now attempting to reposition themselves in their original battle line within a gully along side the road.
- White continued to be within the lines of the 37th Massachusetts. When Hopkins ordered the 37th Massachusetts to change their front to their left flank by executing a 45 degree movement to check the Confederate threat on their left flank, White's Company E which was on the extreme left flank of the 37th Massachusetts also got moved down hill toward Sailor's Creek. Naturally, White also moved downhill with his Company E.
- Custis Lee's position remained the same, in the center of his battle line at the head of the north-south branch of the natural ravine. Once again, Custis Lee was still in an exposed position with the Chaffin's Bluff and 10th and 19th Virginia Heavy Artillery troops now absent from his front as a result of their charge downhill after the retreating Federals. Behind him and slightly off to the side was his secondary line consisting of the Naval/Marine Battalion.
- With this snapshot in time, the Hillsman Farm fight of the Battle of Sailor's Creek was actively in motion. The Confederates initially positioned themselves defensively, however, some units took the offensive with charges. The Federals were always on the offensive, looking to crush the Confederate resistance if at all possible. The Federals were clearly taken by surprise by the Confederate charges. At this point in the battle, it was still uncertain what the final outcome would be.

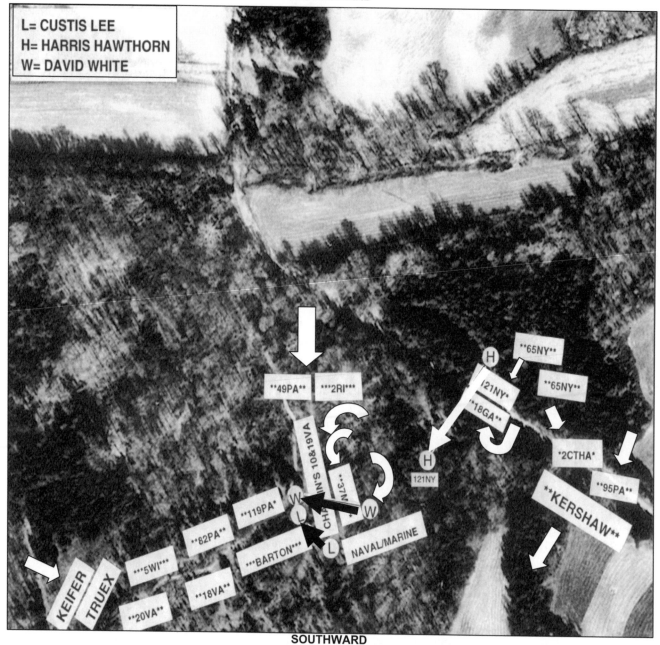

L= CUSTIS LEE
H= HARRIS HAWTHORN
W= DAVID WHITE

65NY
65NY
49PA ***2RI***
121NY*
18GA
CHAPIN'S 10&19VA
2CTHA
**37N*
H
121NY
95PA
**119PA*
KERSHAW
82PA
W
L
NAVAL/MARINE
BARTON
5WI
L
18VA
KEIFER
TRUEX
20VA

SOUTHWARD

- **Photograph five is the last snapshot in time.** The regrouped 121st New York attacked the 18th Georgia Battalion which had managed to firmly reposition themselves at a gully alongside the road after their initial charge. The 18th Georgia Battalion attempted another charge on the 121st New York, but they were simply overpowered by the shear number of Federal troops. Basinger and his 18th Georgia Battalion, seeing that further resistance was useless, surrendered to the 121st New York on the road.

- The 2nd Connecticut Heavy Artillery, after stabilizing the 121st New York from the charge of the 18th Georgia Battalion, moved toward their left flank to join the 95th Pennsylvania and 65th New York in attacking the left flank of Kershaw's Division. The 2nd Connecticut Heavy Artillery then followed the road south to Marshall's Crossroads in pursuit of the enemy. This placed the 2nd Connecticut Heavy Artillery far from the troops of Custis Lee.

- Kershaw's Division was attacked by a portion of Hamblin's Brigade on their left flank and the Federal Calvary on their front and right flank. As a result, Kershaw's Division was forced backward and their flanks were turned inward. Kershaw and his Division surrendered to the Federals as the Federals poured into their two flanks and then ultimately into their rear.
- After charging the Federals, Stiles conferred with Custis Lee, who was still positioned at the head of the north-south ravine. It was decided at this time to try to regroup the Chaffin's Bluff and 10th and 19th Virginia Heavy Artillery troops that were strewn downhill on the battlefield. Stiles gathered his men and then lead them into the north-south ravine with the intent of using the ravine as shelter to bring his men back up the hill to their original position at the head of the north-south ravine. This maneuver by Stiles was only partially successful because of the quick movement of the 37th Massachusetts to now confront Stiles' troops on their right flank.
- The 37th Massachusetts, after chasing away the small contingent of Confederates on their left flank noticed the Chaffin's Bluff and 10th and 19th Virginia Heavy Artillery troops on their original right flank, chasing after the retreating 2nd Rhode Island and 49th Pennsylvania. As Stiles was regrouping the Chaffin's Bluff and 10th and 19th Virginia Heavy Artillery troops into the north-south ravine, the 37th Massachusetts immediately changed their front by moving toward the ravine, and then pivoting and rotating their line 180 degrees uphill so that they could now parallel the head of the ravine area and be directly in front of the bulk of Stiles' troops who were making their way up the hill to their original battlefield position.
- With the 37th Massachusetts now fronted parallel to this ravine, they became engaged in a brutal hand-to-hand combat with the Chaffin's Bluff troops and the 10th and 19th Virginia Heavy Artillery when they emerged from the ravine to fight. This hand-to-hand fight occurred uphill, along the top of the hill portion of the north-south facing ravine. It also occurred at the head of the ravine area where Custis Lee and Major Stiles were now positioned, the head of the ravine being the center of the original Confederate line prior to the charge. At the head of this ravine area, a small number of the men from the Confederate Naval/Marine Brigade joined the Chaffin's Bluff and the 10th and 19th Virginia Heavy Artillery troops to hand-to-hand fight the 37th Massachusetts. Due to the firepower strength of their Spencer repeating rifles, the 37th Massachusetts was able to over power Stiles' troops and compel their surrender at the head of the ravine, and the top of the hill area of the north-south facing ravine.
- Barton's Brigade and the 18th and 20th Virginia Heavy Artillery troops were attacked on three fronts; the Federal Infantry in their front (Edwards' Brigade), the Federal Infantry on their left flank (Seymour's troops) and the Federal Cavalry in their rear (Custer's troops). They ultimately surrendered to the Federal Calvary that poured into their rear from Marshall's Crossroads.
- The majority of the Naval/Marine Brigade, being nestled in a secluded pocket of woods, was initially overlooked by most of the advancing Federal troops. They remained the last active Confederate fighting force on the Battlefield of Sailor's Creek. Around nightfall, Keifer's troops, which were a part of Seymour's Division, advanced on the extreme left flank of this Naval/Marine Brigade and compelled their surrender. This was done after the battle was over.
- David White and his Company E of the 37th Massachusetts were on the extreme left flank of his Regiment. When the 37th Massachusetts wheeled 180 degrees uphill to have their front parallel with the top of the hill portion of the north-south ravine and Stiles' troops which were making their way uphill using the ravine, White and his Company E were now placed at the head of the ravine area. Company E was now in a position to directly oppose the soldiers of the Chaffin's Bluff and the 10th and 19th Virginia Heavy Artillery troops that were able to make their way back to the top of the hill. This also placed David White in close proximity to Custis Lee, who was observing the battle from the center of the original Confederate line, which was located at the head of the north-south ravine. David White then advanced beyond his Regiment's line, which was still fronted parallel to the ravine. By doing so, White broke through the hand-to-hand combat line of fighting occurring between his Regiment and the Confederate troops. Once behind this line, White then spotted, pursued, overtook and captured a Confederate officer who turned out to be Major General Custis Lee. Custis Lee had moved from his head of the ravine

position and was trying to make his escape from the hand-to-hand combat which had enveloped him at his position at the head of the ravine. Custis Lee was making his way toward Sailor's Creek, behind and to the west of his Confederate troops that were still engaged in this brutal hand-to-hand combat with the 37th Massachusetts.

- Dennis Moore, of the 2nd Connecticut Heavy Artillery, did not follow his Regiment's movement southward along the road toward Marshall's Crossroads to continue the attack on Kershaw's Division. Instead, Dennis Moore followed the path of Harris Hawthorn.

- Harris Hawthorn and Dennis Moore, of the 121st New York and 2nd Connecticut Heavy Artillery respectfully, participated in causing the surrender of the 18th Georgia Battalion on the road. Once this surrender was secured, Hawthorn advanced past the surrendering 18th Georgia Battalion and moved toward the Naval/Marine Battalion, which remained largely in place in their original battlefield position behind the Chaffin's Bluff troops. At this point in time, this forward movement put Hawthorn and Moore in the rear and to the east of the 37th Massachusetts, which was still fronted parallel to the ravine and fighting the Confederates. As a result of Hawthorn's and Moore's movement into this area of the battlefield, Harris Hawthorn and Dennis Moore spotted and laid hold of a temporarily unguarded Confederate officer who happened to be Custis Lee. Custis Lee had already been captured and stripped of his side arms and personal belongings by the 37th Massachusetts and was standing in the rear of the 37th Massachusetts line. When Hawthorn and Moore seized Custis Lee they demanded his surrender and arms. This is when Custis Lee informed them that he did not have as much as a jack knife. This was because Custis Lee had already turned over his arms to the 37th Massachusetts when he was captured. Hawthorn and Moore attempted to usher Custis Lee to the headquarters of General Wheaton, when a dispute broke out between the 121st New York and 37th Massachusetts. At this point in time, White was in the rear of the Federal lines retrieving ammunition and was not involved in ushering Custis Lee to any headquarters. White was injured in this retrieval process.

As an interesting aside, the author would like to call the reader's attention to the following account which describes Charles A. Taggart's capture of a Confederate flag during the Battle of Sailor's Creek. Taggart was a member of the 37th Massachusetts. Taggart's account of the capture of a Confederate flag is very similar to White's account found in the newspaper articles of his capture of the Confederate Major General Custis Lee. Taggart's account is as follows:

Charles A. Taggart:

During a lull in the desperate hand to hand struggle of this memorable day, Private Charles A. Taggart, of Company B, Thirty-seventh Massachusetts Infantry, stepped out about twenty paces to the front of his regiment and up a slight rise of ground, from which place he saw a squad of about twenty rebels in a low, protected spot firing on the men to his right. Taking shelter behind a tree near by he fired several shots into their midst, when to his surprise he observed a rebel flag among them. Immediately he started for their color-bearer, demanding the surrender of the flag, which he grasped, and in the struggle for its possession he found himself assisted by another Union man, who had also seen the colors and who was intent upon their capture. The two wrested them from the rebel, but Taggart's comrade was shot down, while he, taking advantage of an opening, rushed back with the colors into the Union lines. Unfortunately the Federals took him for a leader of a rebel charge and it was miraculous that he escaped with but one slight wound on his right leg.

[Source: "Deeds of Valor, How America's Civil War Heroes Won the Congressional Medal of Honor," edited by W. F. Beyer and O. F. Keydel, Longmeadow Press, 1992]Manuscript 135****

It would appear that both Taggart and White achieved battlefield prizes. Taggart captured a Confederate flag and White a General when they both advanced through their 37th Massachusetts' battle line which was engaged in the brutal hand-to-hand combat with the Confederates. Both men spotted and then pursued their respective targets behind this hand-to-hand battle line.

CHAPTER SEVEN:

CALL TO ACTION:

Given the verdict that was reached as expressed in Chapter six of this report, chapter seven will now attempt to answer a critical question, "What, if anything, should be done concerning the Medal of Honor that was awarded to Harris S. Hawthorn for the capture of Major General George Washington Custis Lee?" To completely answer this question, one must answer the following **four questions** first:

1. The **first question** that must be answered is, "was the feat of capturing Confederate Major General George Washington Custis Lee at the Battle of Sailor's Creek by a Private within the opposing Union forces worthy of a Medal of Honor"? To accurately answer this question, one must review the evolving legislation governing the Medal of Honor and the criteria for its award. The initial legislation creating the Medal of Honor is described by the following essay:

On December 9, 186,1 Iowa Senator James W. Grimes introduced S. No. 82 in the United States Senate, a bill designed to "promote the efficiency of the Navy" by authorizing the production and distribution of "medals of honor." On December 21st the bill was passed, authorizing 200 such medals be produced "which shall be bestowed upon such petty officers, seamen, landsmen and marines as shall distinguish themselves by their gallantry in action and other seamanlike qualities during the present war (Civil War)." President Lincoln signed the bill and the (Navy) Medal of Honor was born. Two months later on February 17, 1862, Massachusetts Senator Henry Wilson introduced a similar bill, this one to authorize "the President to distribute medals to privates in the Army of the United States who shall distinguish themselves in battle." Over the following months wording changed slightly as the bill made its way through Congress. When President Abraham Lincoln signed S. J. R. No. 82 into law as 12 Stat. 623-624 on July 14, 1862, the Army Medal of Honor was born. It read in part:

... Resolved by the Senate and House of Representatives of the United States of America in Congress assembled, That the President of the United States be, and he is hereby authorized, to cause two thousand 'medals of honor" to be prepared with suitable emblematic devices, and to direct that the same be presented, in the name of the Congress, to such non—commissioned officers and privates as shall most distinguish themselves by their gallantry in action, and other soldier-like qualities, during the present insurrection (Civil War)."

[Source: Congressional Medal of Honor Society Web Site, "The Medal's History," 2001]**Manuscript 74**

This would have been the criteria that Harris S. Hawthorn fulfilled when he was awarded the Medal of Honor on December 29, 1894. The following essay describes the continuing evolution of the legislation governing the Medal of Honor and the criteria for its award:

The 1890s were, in the words of one medal historian, "the Dark Ages in the history of the Medal of Honor. The old veterans of the Civil War were on the march, storming the halls of Congress in their black slouch hats and pestering the overworked clerks at the War Department." In person or by mail, they sought their own Medals of Honor. Since there was no time limit on awards, a constant stream of requests flowed into the capital. "I believe I am entitled to a medal" was a common line, followed by a brief description of an act from years before. There was usually no extensive review or verification of the action; in some cases, the applicant's word was sufficient. The Secretary of War would then direct that a medal be engraved and sent to the veteran. From 1891 to 1897 over 500 Medals of Honor were awarded for Civil War actions. The Medal of Honor Legion, a newly formed organization of medal recipients, expressed concern that the generous bestowal of the award was weakening its intended prestige. By the middle of the decade many army officials agreed. On June 26, 1897, Secretary of War Russell A. Alger announced a more uniform method of determining Medal of Honor eligibility, stating that a deed must demonstrate "most distinguished gallantry in action" based on "incontestable proof" of the action.

[Source: "Above and Beyond, Congressional Medal of Honor Society," Boston Publishing Company, 1985, page 122]**Manuscript 13**

It would appear that the first major change to the initial legislation governing the Medal of Honor legislation occurred with the June 26, 1897, legislation cited above. This change occurred after Harris Hawthorn received his Medal of Honor on December 29, 1894, and before the determination by Secretary Alger of the 37th Massachusetts Protest Case on September 20, 1897. This new legislation in its entirety reads as follows:

War Department, Washington, June 26. 1897

By direction of the President, the following regulations are promulgated respecting the award of Medals of Honor, and paragraph 177 of the Regulations is amended to read as follows:

177. Medals of Honor, authorized by the Act of Congress, approved March 3, 1863, are awarded to officers and enlisted men in the name of the Congress, for particular deeds of most distinguished gallantry in action.

1. *In order that the Congressional Medal of Honor be deserved, service must have been performed in action of such a conspicuous character as to clearly distinguish the man for gallantry and intrepidity above his comrades-service that involved extreme jeopardy of life or the performance of extraordinarily hazardous duty. Recommendations for the decoration will be judged by this standard of extraordinary merit, and incontestable proof of performance of the service will be exacted.*

2. *Soldiers of the Union have ever displayed bravery in battle, else victories could not have been gained; but as courage and self-sacrifice are the characteristics of every true soldier, such a badge of distinction as the Congressional Medal is not to be expected as the reward of conduct that does not clearly distinguish the soldier above other men, whose bravery and gallantry have been proved in battle.*

3. *Recommendations for medals on account of services rendered in the Volunteer Army during the late war, and in the Regular Army previous to January 1, 1890, will, if practicable, be submitted by some person other than the proposed recipient, one who is personally familiar with all the facts and circumstances claimed as justifying the award, but the application may be made by the one claiming to have earned the decoration, in which case it will be in the form of a deposition, reciting a narrative description of the distinguished service performed. If official records are relied on as evidence proving the personal service, the reports of the action must be submitted or cited; but if these records are lacking the testimony must embrace that of one or more eyewitnesses, who, under oath, describe specifically the act or acts they saw, wherein the person recommended or applying clearly distinguished himself above his fellows for most distinguished gallantry in action.*

4. *Recommendations for medals on account of service rendered subsequent to January 1, 1890, will be made by the Commanding Officer at the time of action or by an officer or soldier having personal cognizance of the act for which the badge of honor is claimed, and the recommendation will embrace a detailed recital of all the facts and circumstances. Certificates of officers or the affidavits of enlisted men who were eyewitnesses of the act will also be submitted if practicable.*

5. *In cases that may arise for service performed hereafter, recommendations for award of medals must be forwarded within one year after the performance of the act for which the award is claimed. Commanding officers will thoroughly investigate all cases of recommendations for Congressional Medals arising in their commands, and indorse their opinion upon the papers, which will be forwarded to the Adjutant General of the Army through regular channels.*

R. A. ALGER, Secretary of War.

[Source: 37th Massachusetts Protest Case File at the National Archives: AGO Record & Pension Office, Document File #476510, File for David D. White, 37th Massachusetts, Volume 8W3 Row 16 Com 17, Shelf F Box # 699]**Manuscript 24**

It is quite evident that this new legislation "raised the bar" for the criteria for awarding a Medal of Honor. It is this new criterion that Secretary of War Russell A. Alger used when deciding the 37th Massachusetts Protest Case. Alger's decision on September 20, 1897, was as follows, "I am fully convinced there was no opportunity for the display of any action by any individual soldier that could, under law and regulations, earn the Congressional Medal of Honor, Messrs. Hawthorne and

White will be notified of this action." It is apparent from this statement that Russell Alger did not believe that the act of capturing General Custis Lee at the Battle of Sailor's Creek met this new June 26, 1897, criterion for awarding a Medal of Honor. It should be noted, once again, that even though White and Hawthorn were indeed notified of Alger's decision, no other action was taken by Secretary of War Alger in this matter. Harris Hawthorn continued to retain the Medal of Honor that was awarded him in 1894. The following story is relevant and brings to light the frame of mind of Secretary of War Russell A. Alger when he was deliberating the 37th Massachusetts Protest Case:

One of the great ironies of the era of American expansion is that its most enduring figure was recommended for a Medal of Honor but was denied the award. Years later the rejection would still rankle Theodore Roosevelt, Rough Rider and President. After the Rough Riders' legendary charge up San Juan Hill on July 1, 1898, Lieutenant Colonel Roosevelt became a hero back in America. He was praised for his actions and later recommended for the Medal of Honor. The wave of popularity that greeted him on his return to the U. S. led to the governorship of New York, the vice-presidency, and, upon the assassination of William McKinley, the White House. But while he would gain the presidency, Teddy Roosevelt was denied the other prize he coveted. In the fall of 1898 the War Decorations Board prepared to reject Roosevelt's case due to a lack of eyewitness statements vouching for his actions on the hill. Roosevelt, elected governor that November, was livid. He quickly asked his friend Senator Henry Cabot Lodge of Massachusetts to look into the matter on his behalf. "The War Department does not intend that I shall have the Medal of Honor," he wrote Lodge in November. "If I didn't earn it, then no commissioned officer can ever earn it." Lodge reported that the War Department offered a retroactive brevet promotion in lieu of the medal, but Roosevelt was adamant. "Don't bother about the brevet," he replied. "It is the medal for which I care." The governor asked his former comrades to verify his actions, and soon written statements from other Rough Riders arrived in Washington. Major General Leonard Wood, a Medal of Honor recipient from the Indian Wars, stated that Roosevelt was one of the first up San Juan Hill and that "his services on the day in question were of great value and of a most distinguished character." Captain Robert Howze, another recipient, noted two occasions on which Roosevelt had displayed "the most conspicuous gallantry" on the hill. But while the Decorations Board may have looked favorably on the evidence, the Secretary of War, Russell A. Alger, was offended by Roosevelt's pressure tactics toward the panel. The former Rough Rider was convinced that Alger was bitter over his complaints that the War Department had mismanaged the American logistical effort in Cuba. The conflict came to a head in early 1899 when Alger announced at a White House dinner that Roosevelt would not receive the medal. Roosevelt and Lodge, in attendance that night, were humiliated. By the end of January, Roosevelt had given up on his quest. "As for that infernal Medal of Honor," he wrote Lodge, "I really wish and ask that you do nothing more about it at all." Amid mounting charges of mismanagement during the war, Alger was dismissed in July. Teddy Roosevelt's Medal of Honor was forgotten.

[Source: "Above and Beyond" by Congressional Medal of Honor Society, Boston Publishing Company, 1985]Manuscript 13****

It would appear from the narrative above that Secretary of War Russell A. Alger was tired and perhaps even angry with the whole Medal of Honor process. Alger loathed the intense political lobbying for Medals of Honor that was occurring during this 1897-1899 timeframe. The following write-up also gives an account of Russell A. Alger's probable frame of mind when he was deliberating the 37th Massachusetts Protest Case in the year 1897.

Between 1890 and 1894, the AGO received a near-geometrically growing number of applications for the Medal of Honor. In 1890, 33 medals were awarded, which doubled the following year to 67, and mushroomed to 127 in 1894. More than five hundred medals were awarded between 1891 and 1897 for actions performed during the Civil War. Because the army had not established a system for applying for the medal (as the navy had done in 1862), some medals were awarded based on scant evidence. As word spread of the availability of the medal, veterans all over the country sought to secure a piece of glory for themselves. Because many of these honorees were not required to provide hard evidence of their heroics, some critics of the AGO felt the integrity of the medal was in jeopardy. Further depreciating the value of the medal, the Grand Army of the Republic and other veterans groups began giving out their own medals, some of which looked conspicuously similar to the Medal of Honor. On April 23, 1890, a group of U. S. veterans founded the Medal of Honor Legion to protect the medal and the principles upon which the medal had been established. The organization included many powerful former members of the U. S. military (Langbein later served as the legion's commander) and lobbied for measures that would preserve the medal's reputation. Faced with the growing onslaught of requests, and spurred on by groups such as the legion, the army and the War Department looked for a solution. On June 26, 1897, Secretary of War Russell A. Alger announced that future Medals of Honor would be awarded based on "incontestable proof of the most distinguished gallantry in action." Alger also stipulated that future recommendations would have to be submitted to the AGO within one year of the act.

[Source: "The Army Medal of Honor," by Mark C. Mollan, National Archives Prologue Magazine, summer 2001, Vol. 33, No. 2]Manuscript 146****

The 37th Massachusetts Protest Case was initiated by Mr. Bowen on April 15, 1897. As cited above, this was at the height of the unrelenting pressure that Secretary of War Alger was receiving concerning the over issuance and the basic integrity of the Medal of Honor. One would have to assume that Secretary of War Alger was very much bothered by this matter, and would have preferred to be working on more pressing areas in his opinion. As a result, and to rid himself of this annoyance, Alger might have been very determined to single-handedly close down the flood gates to new applicants seeking "to secure a piece of glory for themselves." The 37th Massachusetts could not have picked a worse time, from their perspective, to have their case in front of Secretary of War Russell A. Alger for consideration. The following essay is helpful in that it describes the continuing evolution of the legislation governing the Medal of Honor:

Though medal policy had been clarified somewhat, [by this June 26, 1897, legislation] the liberality of many past awards still vexed some lawmakers and officers. In April 1916, President Wilson signed a law that not only revised the medal standards but also allowed the army to atone for past indiscretions. The bill provided for the establishment of an "Army and Navy Medal of Honor Roll" and directed that a pension of ten dollars per month starting at age sixty-five be paid to each person who had "been awarded a medal of honor for having distinguished himself conspicuously by gallantry or intrepidity, at the risk of his life, above and beyond the call of duty." This last phrase would set the tone for later Medal of Honor awards for all armed services. Some veterans were bound to be ineligible for the roll because of the tougher requirements for the medal. The War Department was ready to take a drastic step to correct what some viewed as unwarranted past awards. The opportunity came about in June 1916 when Congress authorized the department to appoint a board of five retired general officers to review every one of the 2,625 army Medals of Honor awarded up to that time. Chosen to head the panel was Lieutenant General Nelson A. Miles, a medal recipient from Chancellorsville, a commander during the Indian Wars, and a past commander of the Medal of Honor Legion. Though Miles and his fellow officers later expressed uneasiness at being asked to rescind awards years after they were given, their concern over the dilution of the medal's prestige apparently superseded those feelings. In a report filed on February 15, 1917, the army board removed from the rolls the names of 911 recipients, more than one-third of the previous total. Included was an entire regiment, the 27th Maine, numbering 864 men, and the 29 members of the honor guard that had escorted President Lincoln's body to Illinois in April 1865. All these men were judged not to have merited the medal because they did not distinguish themselves in combat and at the risk of life. The other eighteen were expunged for either lack of supporting evidence or failure to meet statutory requirements.

[Source: "Above and Beyond," Congressional Medal of Honor Society, Boston Publishing Company; 1985]Manuscript 13****

The following essay provides a more detailed description of this important 1916 act which created the Medal of Honor Review Board cited above:

Act provided for the appointment by Secretary of War of a board of five retired general officers for the purpose of "investigating and reporting upon past awards or issue of the so-called congressional medal *of honor by or through the War Department; this with a view to ascertain what medals of honor, if any, have been awarded or issued for any cause other that distinguished conduct ... involving actual conflict with an enemy." "And in any case, this act continued, "in which said board shall find and report that said medal was issued for any cause other than that hereinbefore specified, the name of the recipient of the medal so issued shall be stricken permanently from the official Medal of Honor list. It shall be a misdemeanor for him to wear or publicly display such medal, and, if he shall be in the Army, he shall be required to return said medal to the War Department for cancellation." By October 16, 1916, the Board created by this act had met, gathered all Medal of Honor records, prepared statistics, classified cases and organized evidence which might be needed in its deliberations. Between October 16, 1916, and January 17, 1917, all of the 2,625 Medals of Honor which had been awarded up to that time were considered by the Board, and on February 15, 1917, 911 names were stricken from the list.... In its final report, the Board indicated that in the large majority of cases "the medals have been awarded for distinguished conduct in action, measuring that term by the highest standard, and there can be no question as to the propriety of the award. In some cases, the Board reported, the rewards the men received were "greater than would now be given for the same acts," but in the absence of evidence to the contrary, "and because there has been no high judicial interpretation of the Medal of Honor laws" the Board found that there were "but few instances where the medal has not been awarded for distinguished services."*

[Source: "United States of America's Congressional Medal of Honor Recipients and their Official Citations," by Bob Proft, Highland House II, Inc., 1994]Manuscript 71****

It is extremely important to recognize that this Medal of Honor Review Board cited above did in fact thoroughly review the Harris Hawthorn Medal of Honor application file. Hawthorn's Medal of Honor application file has the following chronological stamps on the front cover of the file folder:

Medal of Honor Board – Rec'd Oct. 14, 1916
Loaned to the Medal of Honor Board
Medal of Honor Board – Considered Dec. 12, 1916
Medal of Honor Board – Returned Dec. 12, 1916

[Source: Medal of Honor Application file for Harris S. Hawthorn, file number, 401677, National Archives, Washington, DC]Manuscript 15****

The author was fortunate to find at the National Archives the minutes of the Medal of Honor Review Board. The following information was discovered for the Board's review of the Harris S. Hawthorn case # 2134:

December 12, 1916

- *The Board met at 10:20 AM in room 231, all members present*
- *The following cases were considered: 2154, 2151, 2129, 2131, 2126, 2124, 2120, 2122, 2119, 2153, 2139, 2138, 2106, 2118, 2104, 2109, 2103, 1926, 2100, 2099, 2134, 1932, 1942, 1927, 1937, 1938, 1039, 1923, 1921, 1922, 2479, 2389, 1919, 1904, 1910, 1907, 1916, 1909, 2496, 1903*
- *Flies of 2,625 cases showing synopsis and basis of award in each case*
- *Case 2134 (401673) Hawthorne, Harris S., considered December 12, 1916*
- *Sailor's Creek, VA, April 6, 1865-Captured the Confederate General G. W. Custis Lee*
- *Nov.26/94 Congressman C. D. Haines requests medal for 2134*
- *Sept.9/94 letter of Capt. T. J. Hassett K 121 N. Y. V.*
- *Specifically mentioned April 18/65 by F. Wheaton, Maj. Gen. Vols. and Apl. 15/65 Gen. Hamblin, Brig. Comdr.*
- *Apl. 14/65 affidavit by 2134*
- *Apl. 29/65 Gen. H. G. Wright reports surrender to 6th Corps of Gen. Custis Lee*
- *Dec. 12/94 Asst. Sec. Doe awards*

- *Apl. 15/97 Historian Bowen, 37th Mass. Protests award, and Sept. 20/97 Secy. Alger, after considering evidence files in case and counter-claim of David White, decides there was no display of action by either entitling to medal under law and regulations.*
- *1 medal issued Dec. 29, 1894*

[Source: "Minutes of Meetings of Medal Of Honor Board," Convened Pursuant to G. O. No. 136, Par. 14, War Department, July 16, 1916, Record Group 94 "Records of the Adj. General's Office, Oversized Document File 1805-1917, File No. 2411162 AGO, National Archives, Washington, DC] **Manuscript 151**

A careful examination of these Medal of Honor Review Board minutes and the Harris S. Hawthorn Medal of Honor application file yielded an important fact. The Medal of Honor Review Board only reviewed the documents in the Harris S. Hawthorn Medal of Honor application file (file number 401673). The Medal of Honor Review Board did not review the documents in the 37th Massachusetts Protest Case file (file number (476510). This is substantiated by the fact that only the Hawthorn application file (401673) was borrowed and stamped by the Medal of Honor Review Board. The 37th Massachusetts Protest Case file (476510) was not borrowed and was not stamped by the Medal of Honor Review Board. In addition, the Bowen and Alger letters referenced in the board minutes above are copies of two documents originally in the 37th Massachusetts Protest Case file (476510). These two letters are the only documents that were copied from the 37th Massachusetts Protest Case file (476510) and then filed in the Hawthorn application file (401673). This is an extremely important fact. The Medal of Honor Review Board only used the Hawthorn application file (401673) to decide if the act of capturing Custis Lee at the Battle of Sailor's Creek by a Federal private was worthy of the Medal of Honor. The Medal of Honor Review Board did not decide the merits of the 37th Massachusetts Protest Case file (476510) and the Board did not attempt to answer the question of who actually captured Custis Lee, Hawthorn or White. Historians agree that this Medal of Honor Review Board did an extremely comprehensive job in reviewing all existing Medals of Honor. This is highlighted in the following statement: *"The Board of Generals authorized in the previous legislation convened under Lt. General Nelson Miles, a medal recipient from the Civil War. General Miles took an active role in promoting legislation to protect the medal as commander of the Medal of Honor Legion and approached the work of his committee with determination and dedication. Every award of the Army Medal of Honor since the Civil War was reviewed. The recipients were anonymous to the board, represented only by a number."* **[Source: The Timeline of the Medal of Honor and its History: homeofheros.com/moh/history_ timeline_html]**Manuscript 145**** When the Medal of Honor Review Board concluded their analysis, they issued an in-depth report of their findings and determinations. The Board prefaced their report with several preamble paragraphs, of which the following three are important:

ONE:

"The records of all persons on the medal of honor list, numbering 2,625, have been carefully examined by the board. In a large majority of cases the medals have been awarded for distinguished conduct in action, measuring that term by the highest standard, and there can be no question as to the propriety of the award. In some cases the papers are missing and those on file do not furnish evidence, which of itself would be satisfactory to this board, except for the corroborative evidence contained in the action of the proper authorities at the time. The evidence was satisfactory to them and should not be questioned now, after a lapse of so many years, and death of important witnesses, and of the recipients of the medals, and loss of valuable papers. In some cases also the term "distinguished conduct in action," is defined by the authorities making the award, as well as by applicants for the medal, with much greater liberality than is now exercised under the regulations of the War Department in awarding medals of honor. With but few exceptions these cases set forth the acts of brave men under trying circumstances. The reward which these men received were greater than would now be given for the same acts, but the acts were highly meritorious nevertheless and, in the absence of adverse evidence and because there has been no high judicial interpretation of the medal of honor laws, the board has felt bound to measure the act by the standard established by the authorities at the time of the award,

rather than by that now observed, thus avoiding as far as practicable, retroactive judgment on the course of the War Department in a matter lawfully within its discretion, and so closely affecting the honor of so many patriotic citizens living and dead."

TWO:

"The report also sets forth that the board found but few instances where the medal has not been awarded for distinguished service specifying, in this connection, the award to 555 members of the Twenty-seventh Maine. Reference is made to awards to 309 other members of the Twenty-seventh Maine; to five members of the Twenty-seventh New Jersey; and to one member of the Twenty-second New York State Militia. The board then refers to certain other instances where medals were awarded for causes which it did not consider as distinguished conduct in action, viz, to one John B. Lynch, for carrying dispatches; to one Thomas Gilbert, for picking up shells and extinguishing burning fuses; to one John C. Hesse and Joseph K. Wilson, for bringing off colors of the Eighth United States Infantry concealed about their persons while quartered at San Antonio when that post was surrendered to the Confederates; to 29 officers and men comprising the 'so called" Lincoln body guard; to one Robert Storr, a British subject who enlisted in the Union Army and died in service; to Dr. Mary E. Walker, a female contract surgeon, concerning whom there is no evidence of distinguished gallantry, and to one James M. Hawken, for extinguishing a fire in a Government storehouse. Reference is made in the report to awards to five civilians, among them being William F. Cody, the board expressing the opinion that they rendered distinguished service in action and fully earned their medals, and expressing also the hope that a modification of the law will permit them to retain the medals."

THREE:

"In the opinion of this office (Judge Advocate General), the act (Section 122 of the National Defense Act of June 3, 1916) confers no authority upon the Secretary of War to review the report of the board by carrying out certain of its findings and refusing to carry out others. It is expressly provided in the language above quoted that "in any case in which said board shall find and report" that the medal was issued for any cause other than that specified in the statute "the name of the recipient of the medal so issued shall be stricken permanently from the medal-of-honor list." There is no discretion vested in the Secretary of War to review the report of the board, but the statute enjoins that the action shall be taken in any case in which the board "shall find and report" that the award was issued for a cause other than that specified by statute. I am clearly of the opinion that the Secretary of War is bound by the report of the board in executing the terms of the law."

[Source: Final Report of the Medal of Honor Review Board "In Response to a Senate Resolution of July 14, 1919, Certain Documents in Relation to the Interpretation and Execution of Sections 5 and 122 of the National Defense Act Approved June 3, 1916, 66th Congress, 1st Session, Senate Document No. 58]**Manuscript 152**

> This Medal of Honor Review Board, in its review of the Harris Hawthorn application file, determined that the act of capturing Major General George Washington Custis Lee at the Battle of Sailor's Creek by a Federal private was indeed worthy of a Medal of Honor. This is underscored by the fact that Hawthorn's Medal of Honor application file was thoroughly reviewed by this Medal of Honor Review Board and this Review Board did not revoke Hawthorn's Medal of Honor, operating under the guiding principles articulated in preamble number one (1) above. It should be noted that several Medals of Honor were revoked by this Board after going through their detailed review as summarized in preamble number two (2) above. What this in essences means is that this Medal of Honor Review Board effectively "overturned" Russell A. Alger's decision that Alger rendered on September 20, 1897, in the 37th Massachusetts Protest Case where he stated that, "I am fully convinced there was no opportunity for the display of any action by any individual soldier that could, under law and regulations, earn the Congressional Medal of Honor." This "overturning" of Alger's decision by the Board is very real. This is because of the fact that the Board reviewed Alger's decision letter found in the 37th Massachusetts Protest Case file (476510), and then copied and filed it in the original Hawthorn Medal of Honor Application file (401673). The Board then chose to do something directly opposite of Alger's decision, that being the upholding of a Medal of Honor for the

capture of Custis Lee at the Battle of Sailor's Creek. Finally, it is quite clear in preamble three (3) above that the decision rendered by the Medal of Honor Review Board in upholding the Medal of Honor for the capture of Custis Lee at the Battle of Sailor's Creek by a Federal Private is final and binding on all parties involved. Just in case there is an opinion rendered today that the Medal of Honor Review Board was too liberal in upholding the Medal of Honor for the capture of Custis Lee on an active Sailor's Creek battlefield, please note again the language contained in preamble one (1) above. The Review Board stated that, "the board has felt bound to measure the act by the standard established by the authorities at the time of the award, rather than by that now observed, thus avoiding as far as practicable, retroactive judgment on the course of the War Department in a matter lawfully within its discretion, and so closely affecting the honor of so many patriotic citizens living and dead." If one looks closely at the following representative sample of Medals of Honor reviewed and upheld by the Review Board, and notes their similarities to the act of capturing Major General Custis Lee on the active battlefield of Sailor's Creek, one will understand why the Board, working under the guiding principle stated above, upheld the Medal of Honor for the capture of Custis Lee. If the Board was to revoke the Medal of Honor for the capture of Custis Lee, the Board would have had to revoke Medals of Honor for many hundreds of similar acts like these below. It should be noted that many of the following Medals of Honor were issued to recipients many years after the feat, and many of the recipients were not initially recommended by their superior officers to receive a medal as recorded in the Official Reports:

NAME/RANK/ORGANIZATION:	*DATES, PLACES AND DESCRIPTION OF ACT:*
Everett Anderson Sergeant 15th PA Cavalry	Jan 14, 1864................................(Date of act) Crosby Creek, TN...............................(Place of act) Dec 3, 1894......................................(Date MoH award) Captured single-handed, a Confederate...(Description act) General, during a charge upon the enemy
James Clancy Sergeant 1st NJ Cavalry	Oct 1, 1864 Vaughn Road, VA July 3, 1865 Shot the Confederate Gen. Dunovant dead during a charge, thus confusing the enemy and greatly aiding the repulse
Robert Coffey Sergeant 4th VT Infantry	May 4, 1863 Banks Ford, VA May 13, 1892 Single-handedly captured 2 officers and 5 privates of the Eighth LA (CSA)
John Curtis Sergeant major 9th CT Infantry	Aug 5, 1862 Baton Rouge, LA Dec 16, 1896 Voluntarily sought the line of battle, and alone and unaided captured 2 prisoners, driving them before him, to regimental headquarters at the point of the bayonet
James Dunlavy Private 3rd IA	Oct 25, 1864 Osage, KS April 4, 1865 Gallantry in capturing Gen. Marmaduke
Russell Elliott Sergeant 3rd MA Cavalry	Apl 19, 1864 Natchitoches, LA Nov 20, 1896 Seeing a Confederate officer in advance of his command, charged on him alone and unaided and captured him

Arthur Ferguson...........................Sept 28, 1899
1st Lieut   Luzon, PI
36th US Vol Infantry   Mar 8, 1902
                                           Charged alone a body of enemy and captured a captain

Harris Hawthorne..........................April 6, 1865
Corporal   Sailor's Creek, VA
121st NY Infantry   Dec 29, 1894
                                           Captured the Confederate General G. W. Custis Lee

George Healy................................July 29, 1864
Private   Newman, GA
5th IA Cavalry   Jan 13, 1899
                                           Although nearly surrounded by the enemy, captured a
                                           Confederate soldier, and with the aid a comrade who
                                           joined him later, captured 4 other Confederates, then
                                           disarmed the 5, and brought them all into the Union lines

Leonidas Inscho...........................Sept 14, 1862
Corporal   South Mountain, MD
12th OH Infantry   Jan 31, 1894
                                           Alone and unaided and with his left hand disabled,
                                           captured a Confederate captain and 4 men

Leverett Kelly.............................Nov 25, 1863
Sergeant   Missionary Ridge, TN
36th IL Infantry   Apr 4, 1900
                                           Sprang over the works just captured from the enemy, and
                                           calling to his comrades to follow, rushed forward in the
                                           face of a deadly fire and was among the first over the
                                           works on the summit, where he compelled the surrender
                                           of a Confederate officer and received his sword

Theodore Kramer...........................Sept 29, 1864
Private   Chapin's farm
188th PA Infantry   April 6, 1865
                                           Took one of the first prisoners, a Captain

George Lucas..............................July 25, 1864
Private   Benton, AR
3rd MI Cavalry   Dec, 1864
                                           Pursued and killed the Confederate Brig. Gen. George M.
                                           Holt, Arkansas Militia, capturing his arms and horse

Joel Lyman................................Sept 19, 1864
Sergeant   Winchester, VA
9th NY Cavalry   Aug 20, 1894
                                           In an attempt to capture a Confederate flag, he captured
                                           one of the enemy's officers and brought him within the
                                           lines

Patrick Pentzer............................Apr 9, 1865
Captain   Blakely, AL
97th IL Infantry   Oct 9, 1879
                                           Among the first to enter the enemy's entrenchments, he
                                           received the surrender of a Confederate general officer
                                           and his headquarters flag **Author note:** This Medal of Honor
                                           is significant in that it occurred at the end of the war, like the
                                           Custis Lee capture, when some might say that the capture of
                                           the Confederate enemy was relatively easy or inevitable.

William Richney............................ Sept 19, 1863
Corporal   Chickamauga, GA
15th OH Infantry   Nov 9, 1893
                                            While on the extreme front, between the lines of the
                                            combatants, single-handed he captured a Confederate
                                            Major who was armed and mounted

John Rutherford.......................... May 27, 1864
First-Lieut   Hanovertown, VA
9th NY Cavalry   Mar 22, 1892
                                            In a gallant dash on a superior force of the enemy, and in a
                                            personal encounter, captured his opponent

Richard Smith ....Aug 21, 1864
Private   Weldon Railroad
95th NY Infantry   Mar 13, 1865
                                             Captured 2 officers and 20 men of Hagood's Brigade while
                                             they were endeavoring to make their way through the
                                             woods

James Sturgeon............................June 15, 1864
Private   Kennesaw Mountain, GA
46th OH Infantry   Jan 2, 1895
                                             Advanced beyond the lines, and in an encounter with 3
                                             Confederates, shot 2 and took the other prisoner

Harlan Swift....................................July 30, 1864
Second-Lieut   Petersburg, VA
2nd NY Mounted Rifles   July 20, 1897
                                             Having advanced with his regiment and captured the
                                             enemy's line, saw 4 of the enemy retiring toward their
                                             second line of works. He advanced upon them alone,
                                             compelled their surrender, and regained his regiment with
                                             the 4 prisoners

Joseph Taylor.................................Aug 18, 1864
Private   Weldon railroad, VA
7th RI Infantry   July 20, 1897
                                             While acting as an orderly to a general officer, on the field
                                             and alone, encountered a picket of 3 of the enemy and
                                             compelled their surrender

Calvary Young................................Oct 25, 1864
Sergeant   Osage, KS
3rd IA Cavalry   Apl 4, 1865 **Author note:** (Another "end or war" capture)
                                             Gallantry in capturing Gen. Cabell

[Source: Final Report of the Medal of Honor Review Board-"In Response to a Senate resolution of July 14, 1919, Certain Documents in Relation to the Interpretation and Execution of Section 5 and 122 of the National Defense Act Approved June 3, 1916, 66th Congress, 1st Session, Senate Document No. 58]Manuscript 152****

A careful review of the acts listed above clearly shows that there was no more gallantry associated with these acts than the act performed by David White in breaking through the hand-to-hand battle line to pursue and single-handedly capture Major General Custis Lee at Sailor's Creek. The act performed by David White was indeed "distinguished service in action, measuring that term by the highest standard." So, this Medal of Honor Review Board has answered the question posed at the beginning of this chapter which was, "was the act of capturing Major General George Washington Custis at the Battle of Sailor's Creek, VA, by a private in the opposing Union forces worthy of a Medal of Honor." The answer rendered by this Medal of Honor Review Board was **yes.**

2. The **second question** that must be answered is, "should the Medal of Honor that was awarded to Hawthorn for the capture of Custis Lee have a recipient name correction from Harris S. Hawthorn to David D. White?" The answer based on the evidence and corresponding verdict rendered in this report is a resounding, **yes**. Once again, the evidence presented in this report overwhelmingly supports the fact that Private David D. White captured Major General Custis Lee during the Battle of Sailor's Creek. The evidence simply does not support Harris S. Hawthorn being the first soldier to capture Custis Lee.

3. The **third question** that must be answered is, "can David D. White receive a Medal of Honor, if his commanding officers at the Battle of Sailor's Creek did not recommend in writing that he receive one in their Official Records?" It must be remembered that this "absent recommendation" for David White was caused by a reporting "roll up" oversight as described earlier in this report. The answer is definitively **yes**. There is clear precedent for this. James Bowen, the 37th Massachusetts' secretary and historian, applied for and received a Medal of Honor for a 37th Massachusetts soldier, Samuel E. Eddy, who was not initially recommended to receive one in the Official Reports by his commanding officers at the Battle of Sailor's Creek. Bowen received the following correspondence.

Medal of Honor, Record and Pension Office, War Department, Washington City
June 12, 1894
To: Mr. James L. Bowen, Springfield, Massachusetts
In reply to your communication of the 9th instant, in which you request that a medal of honor be awarded to Samuel E. Eddy, late private, 37th Massachusetts Volunteers, for bravery in action, I am directed by the Secretary of War to inform you that the act of Congress approved March 3, 1863, under which medals of honor are issued, provides for their presentation "to such officers, non-commissioned officers and privates as have most distinguished or may hereafter most distinguish themselves in action, and that, as the law is viewed in this Department, these medals were intended as rewards for conspicuous acts of personal bravery or self-sacrifice rather beyond the mere call of duty and not for acts wholly within the line of official duty however nobly performed. Applications for medals, therefore, should clearly set forth the conspicuous act of gallantry by which the soldier distinguished himself above his comrades and the particular action in which it was performed, and should be accompanied, if possible, by the recommendation of his former commanding officer and by the statements or affidavits of at least two eye-witnesses
Very respectfully,
F. C. Ainsworth, Colonel, U.S. Army, Chief, Record and Pension Office
[Source: Samuel E. Eddy Medal of Honor file, Eak, 492, 1867, # 391014 and 408333, National Archives, Washington, DC]**Manuscript 113**

Samuel E. Eddy: (PHOTO: COURTESY FORBES LIBRARY)

The last paragraph describes how Samuel Eddy could be awarded a Medal of Honor even though he was not recommended for one in the Official Records by his battlefield commanding officers. James Bowen did exactly what was stated in the letter cited above and with much persistence, was able to secure a Medal of Honor for Samuel Eddy on September 10, 1897. So as this case demonstrates, a soldier can be awarded a Medal of Honor even though he was not recommended for receiving a medal in the Official Records by his battlefield commanding officers.

4. The **fourth and last question** that must now be answered has two facets: (1) will current law allow for a posthumous award of a Medal of Honor to David D. White as the soldier that actually captured Confederate Major General Custis Lee at the Battle of Sailor's Creek, VA? (2) Alternatively, will current law allow for some type of "recipient name change" to be made to the existing Medal of Honor that is officially on record with the government for the capture of Custis Lee at the Battle of Sailor's Creek? Specifically, removing from this Medal of Honor the name of Harris Hawthorn as the soldier who captured Major General Custis Lee and replacing it with the name of David D. White as

the soldier who truly captured Custis Lee. The single answer to the two facets of this last question lies in the evolving legislation governing the Medal of Honor and the determination of what legislation will be used to measure the attributes of David White's act performed in 1865. The evolution of the legislation defining the attributes of the act to qualify for a Medal of Honor is as follows:

- **July 17, 1862** (original and the one Hawthorn was measured against in 1894) GALLANTRY IN ACTION AND OTHER SOLDIER LIKE QUALITIES
- **June 26, 1897** (the one Alger used to decide the 37th Massachusetts Protest Case) PARTICULAR DEEDS OF MOST DISTINGUISHED GALLANTRY IN ACTION
- **June 3, 1916** (the one that the Medal of Honor Review Board used to decide all Medal of Honor cases awarded up to that point, for acceptance or revocation) DISTINGUISHED SERVICE IN ACTION, MEASURING THAT TERM BY THE HIGHEST STANDARDS
- **July 9, 1918** (the following essay puts this important 1918 legislation into an informative perspective)

*This (Medal of Honor Review) Board had few legal definitions to guide it in its work. It had to work with a quantity of regulations and precedents in making its decisions, and this mass of information was uncoordinated and even, in some cases, conflicting. For example, the act of April 27, 1916, provided for a "Medal of Honor Roll" for those who met the definition of valor above and beyond the call of duty; whereas the original act creating the Medal on July 12, 1862, specified only gallantry in action and "other soldier like qualities" as the basis for award. In 1918, Congress decided to clear away any inconsistencies of the legislation which had grown around the Army medal and make a set of perfectly clear rules for its award. On July 9, 1918, an act was approved which stated as follow: "the provisions of existing law relating to the award of Medals of Honor are amended so that the President is authorized to present, in the name of the Congress, a Medal of Honor only to each person, who, while an officer or enlisted man of the Army, shall hereafter, in action involving actual conflict with an enemy, distinguish himself conspicuously by gallantry and intrepidity at risk of his life above and beyond the call of duty." At one stroke, by use of the word "**hereafter**," this legislation wiped out of existence the War Department's problem of acting on numerous ancient and complicated claims for medals originating as far back as the Civil War.*

[Source: "United States of America's Congressional Medal of Honor Recipients and their Official Citations" by Bob Proft, Highland House 11, Inc. 1994]**Manuscript 71**

The author suggests that the act of David White, performed in the year 1865, be evaluated against the same legislative standard that the act of Harris Hawthorn, which was also performed in the year 1865, and which was evaluated in the year 1894. This is when the Medal of Honor was issued for this act of capturing Custis Lee at the Battle of Sailor's Creek. The author also suggests that the same 1916 Medal of Honor Review Board analysis of the case be used for measuring the act of the capture of Custis Lee in action. The same standard used by the Board to judge the Hawthorn Case, that being, "distinguished service in action, measuring that term by the highest standard," should be the same standard used to judge the David White Case. In addition, the same peer to peer comparison of all the cases that was used by the Board to judge the Hawthorn matter in 1916 should also be used for David White. If this suggestion is adopted, then a path might be possible for awarding a Medal of Honor to David White. If this suggestion is rejected, then the 1918 "hereafter" legislation makes it quite clear that David D. White cannot be awarded a Medal of Honor, either a new medal or a recipient name change of an existing medal, for the capture of Custis Lee at the battle Sailor's Creek. The author was quite certain of this fact until the author read a newspaper article and contacted the Congressional Medal of Honor Society. The author learned that on or about January 17, 2001, then President Bill Clinton posthumously awarded Medals of Honor to Theodore Roosevelt (in the Spanish American War) and Corporal Andrew Jackson Smith (in the Civil War). The following letter from the Congressional Medal of Honor Society Headquarters explains the circumstances surrounding these two posthumous awards.

Dear Frank,

So far, here's what I've got. We found it in the "On Point" Newsletter of the Army Historical Foundation. Roosevelt was recommended for the Medal of Honor after San Juan Hill, but Army officials decided not to award him the medal (seems that Roosevelt vigorously campaigned for the medal and offended many high-ranking officers). Others have attributed the refusal to the Army's bias against volunteer units. Still others believed that Roosevelt's actions at San Juan Hill simply did not demonstrate a level of gallantry worthy of the MOH). In 1997, Roosevelt supporters, including the Theodore Roosevelt Association and Rep. Rick Lazio (R-NY) began a campaign asking the Army to reevaluate its decision to deny Roosevelt the MOH. Rep. Steve Buyer (R-IN) also expressed support for awarding Roosevelt the medal. As for CPL Andrew Jackson Smith, he served with the 55th Massachusetts Infantry at the Battle of Honey Hill, S.C., 30 November 1864. He was originally nominated in 1916, but no official report documenting his actions was discovered until recently. We'll keep digging, but at least this is a start!

Sincerely,
Carol Cepregi, C. M. O. H. S.

[Source: Personal letter in the possession of the author]**Manuscript 110**

The following press release was issued concerning these posthumously awarded Medals of Honor.

Civil War Hero, Roosevelt, Awarded Medal of Honor
By Jesse J. Holland, the Associated Press

Washington – A former president best known for his charge up San Juan Hill during the Spanish-American War and a former slave whose courage during the Civil War was ignored by the Army for almost a century got posthumous Medals of Honor from President Clinton. "May we continue to live up to the ideals for which both Andrew Jackson Smith and Theodore Roosevelt risked their lives," Clinton said Tuesday as he presented the medals to the Smith and Roosevelt families in a ceremony in the Roosevelt Room of the White House.

Larger than life:

"TR was a larger-than-life figure, who gave our nation a larger-than-life vision of our place in the world," Clinton said. "Part of that vision was formed on San Juan Hill." Roosevelt led his regiment of volunteers, the Rough Riders, into action alongside Army regulars up Kettle Hill, one of two hills comprising San Juan Heights. The Rough Riders then advanced up San Juan Hill with as few as four men but arrived after regulars had taken it. The Roosevelt family will donate the award back to the White House, Roosevelt's 58-year-old great-grandson, Tweed Roosevelt, said.

Finally honored:

Alongside the Roosevelt family was the family of Cpl. Andrew Jackson Smith of the 55th Massachusetts Volunteer Infantry, a former slave who joined the Union Army during the Civil War. "In one five-minute span, the 55th alone is said to have lost over 100 men, but they never lost their colors because Corporal Smith carried them through the battle, exposing himself as the lead target," Clinton said. Although Smith was first nominated in 1916, he was rejected for the Medal of Honor even though 80 other soldiers who saved their unit's colors were awarded the honor after the Civil War. Smith's family thanked Clinton for finally coming through for their ancestor. His 93-year-old daughter, Caruth Smith Washington, came to the White House to see her father's dream of winning the Medal of Honor finally come true. "I am very proud to be his daughter," she told reporters.

[Source: New Jersey Courier News, January 17, 2001, page A-7]**Manuscript 111**

The following letter from the Congressional Medal of Honor Society attempts to answer the question that must now be asked concerning the posthumous awarding of these Medals of Honor. This question is, "what legal authority did President Clinton operate under when he awarded these posthumous Medals of Honor"?

Society Headquarters, 02/07/2002

Dear Frank,

I am attaching a document which explains the way in which Medals can be awarded beyond the time limits. A great example of this is currently in legislation. The House Bill has passed and it is now in the Senate. The bill is #2561. It waves the time limit for 3 possible recipients. You can check the progress of this bill at www.thomas.loc.gov. If you still have more questions, please let us know.
Sincerely,
Carol Cepregi

Current Policy and Benefits – Re: Recommendation for MOH
(the following is from the DoD Manual of Military Decorations and Awards)
"Procedures Involving Recommendation for the MoH"

1. *The Secretary concerned shall establish procedures for processing recommendations for the award of the MoH within his or her department. However, as a minimum, these recommendations shall contain the endorsement of the subordinate Unified Commander or JTF [Joint Task Force] Commander, if involved; the Unified or Specified Commander concerned; and the CJCS [Chairman of the Joint Chiefs of Staff]. After endorsement by the CJCS, the recommendation shall be referred to the Secretary for appropriate action.*

2. *Except as provided in 10 U. S. C. 3744 or 8744 … recommendations for the Army and Air Force MoH must be entered formally into official channels within 2 years of the act warranting the recommendation, and awarded within 3 years. Recommendation of the Navy-Marine Corps MoH, excepted as provided in Section 6248 … must be formally entered into official channels within 3 years of the act warranting the recommendation, and awarded within 5 years.*

3. *Recommendations for the award of the MoH disapproved by a Service Secretary, or the Secretary of Defense, may only be resubmitted if new, substantive and material information is provided within the time limits contained in 10 U.S. C. 3744, 6248, and 8744…. The information forming the basis must have been previously unknown and not considered by the recommending and disapproving officials. The determination of the existence of the new material and substantive information being a basis for reconsideration may not be delegated below the Service Secretary.*

4. *The remaining bases for reconsideration are instances in which a Service Secretary or the Secretary of Defense determines there is evidence of **material error** or impropriety in the original processing of or decision on a recommendation for award of the Medal of Honor. Examples of such instances might be loss of accompanying and/or substantiating documents to the recommendation, or proven racial or gender discrimination. Determination of the existence of material error or impropriety in the original processing and decision shall not be delegated below the Service Secretary. In such cases, the Secretary of Defense shall determine the need for legislation.*

5. *All other instances of reconsideration shall be limited to those in which the formal recommendation was submitted within statutory time limits, the recommendation was lost or inadvertently not acted upon, and when these facts are conclusively established by the respective Service Secretary or other official delegated appropriate authority. These provisions are to protect the integrity and purity of purpose of the MoH by ensuring that all relevant information is submitted and considered while the actions are fresh in the minds of the witnesses."*

[The process for restoration of a rescinded Medal of Honor is different. Since the rescissions during World War I, no other MoH awards have been rescinded. However, if a request for a restoration of a MoH were made, the process would be different than the procedures noted above. For those seeking restoration of the Medal of Honor, an appeal must be considered by the appropriate Board for Correction of Military Records. This appeal is requested via the President, a Member of Congress or the Secretary of Defense. If the Board recommends reinstatement, the decision is passed to the service Secretary and then, ultimately to the President.]
[Source: Personal letter in the possession of the author]**Manuscript 110**

It would appear from these two posthumously awarded Medals of Honor and all the supporting legal and legislative actions that allowed President Clinton to present them, that there is a path whereby David D. White can be posthumously awarded a Medal of Honor. The fourth provision above allowing for reconsideration based on "material error" in the original processing of a Medal of Honor would be the applicable provision for the 37th Massachusetts Protest Case and David D. White. The author firmly believes that **"material error"** occurred with Russell A. Alger's handling and decision of the 37th Massachusetts Protest Case. In addition to "material error" which would open the door for reconsideration, the 37th Massachusetts Protest Case would also need to meet all the requirements set forth by current legislation. At a minimum, there would need to be legislative bills passed that would read something like this:

- Be it enacted by the Senate and House of Representatives of the United States of America assembled, that the time limitation specified in sections 6248(a) and 3744(b) of title 10, United States Code, shall not apply with respect to the posthumous award on the Medal of Honor under section 6241 of such title to David Dunnells White (service number xxx) for acts of distinguished service in action during the Civil War while a member of the United States Army.
- Notwithstanding the time limitations specified in sections 6248(a) and 3744(b) of title 10, United States Code, or any other time limitations, the President may award the Medal of Honor posthumously to David Dunnells White of Berkshire County, MA, for acts of distinguished service in action during the Civil War while serving in the 37th Massachusetts for the Federal Army.

It is clear, however, that both the Roosevelt and Smith cases had strong political champions to usher their cases through all the necessary halls of the Federal Government and put forth the necessary legislative bills like the ones noted above. As of the writing of this report, the David D. White Case is unknown to any one but the author and does not yet have a political champion. Putting this matter aside for a moment, let's answer the question posed at the beginning of this chapter; "what, if anything, should be done concerning the Medal of Honor that was awarded to Harris S. Hawthorn for the capture of Major General George Washington Custis Lee?" Let's also answer a natural extension to this question; "should a new Medal of Honor or a recipient name change to an existing Medal of Honor be awarded to David D. White?" The answer is **absolutely!** Absolutely, to correct an injustice to the Commonwealth of Massachusetts that was caused by the "material error" in the processing of the 37th Massachusetts' Protest Case by the Federal Government. Absolutely, to appropriately recognize and pay honor to David D. White for his act of courage after so many years of failing to do so by the Federal Government. Absolutely, to set the historical record straight on this important aspect of United States history for future generations of historical scholars to come. Absolutely and probably most important, to preserve the firm integrity and unquestionable accuracy of the esteemed Medal of Honor. Not to do so, would mock the sacred nature of this pinnacle of military achievement and honor. It is the author's sincere hope that a champion will come forth after reading this report and "set things right" in this important matter. But for the author, who lacks the legal, political and legislative expertise to do this himself, discovering the truth in this matter has been reward enough. Major General George Washington Custis Lee was indeed captured by Private David Dunnells White of the 37th Massachusetts at the Battle of Sailor's Creek, VA, on April 6th, 1865. This act was positively deemed by the Federal Government as qualifying for a Medal of Honor. David D. White should be awarded a Medal of Honor. The author sincerely hopes, and would be immensely grateful, to be able to witness this award sometime during the remainder of his mortal lifetime. Only time will tell.

THE END

A CLOSING TRIBUTE:

"TESTIMONIAL CERTIFICATE" JOHN GRACE, COMPANY E, 37TH MASSACHUSETTS

In the year 1869, the General Court of Massachusetts passed the following Resolve: *CHAPTER 53: Resolved To Provide For Testimonials To Soldiers And Sailors—Resolved, that the governor appoint three suitable persons, who, together with the lieutenant governor and the adjutant-general, shall be commissioners, without pay, to cause to be engraved and printed a suitable testimonial for each officer, soldier or sailor who served on the quota of Massachusetts during the war of the rebellion, and was honorably discharged from, or died in the service; and that the adjutant-general deliver such testimonials, on application, to such persons as he may deem entitled to receive the same...approved May 10, 1869* **[Source: "Acts and Resolves Passed by the General Court of Massachusetts in the Year 1869, Published by the Secretary of the Commonwealth of Massachusetts, Wright & Potter, State Printers, 79 Milk Street, Boston, MA; 1869]**Manuscript 162 **** This Resolve, and its resulting tribute, as illustrated by the certificate above, was a nice attempt by the Commonwealth of Massachusetts to recognize its veterans that served in the Civil War. Perhaps other states did something similar. When the author concluded this work, he was awaken to the fact that this War, particularly the Battle of Sailor's Creek, came at the steep cost of extreme human sacrifice. In many cases, this was manifested by soldiers giving their "last full measure of devotion." I am sure that the Massachusetts lawmakers felt that their tribute in 1869 was woefully inadequate to sufficiently thank their veterans for their service and sacrifice. In a similar manner, the author feels woefully inadequate to add to this tribute now. But what needed to be said in 1869 needs to be said again today, lest we forget. Thank you! Thank you veterans for what you have done and the legacy you have left behind.

ADDENDUM
"Sylvanus D. Locke Papers"

This addendum was created as a result of an important discovery that the author found just prior to the publication of this book. The Yale University Library, Manuscript and Archives Division, has an obscure manuscript collection known as the Sylvanus D. Locke Papers. Buried within these Papers are the original letters that Sylvanus D. Locke exchanged with Custis Lee and Joseph H. Heath in December 1894 and January 1895, while Sylvanus D. Locke was involved in Harris Hawthorn's Medal of Honor process.

SYLVANUS D. LOCKE

These letters within the Sylvanus D. Locke Papers supplement the evidence found in **W-PF-23** (which contains two Custis Lee letters, one dated December 29, 1894, and the other dated January 11, 1895); **W-PF-24** (which contains a Joseph Heath letter, dated December 25, 1894); and **W-PF-25** (which contains a Joseph Heath letter dated December 14, 1894). Sylvanus D. Locke settled in Hoosick Falls, New York (which is Harris S. Hawthorn's hometown), in the year 1869 and became a very prosperous business man, patenting and manufacturing farming equipment. Sylvanus D. Locke passed away in Hoosick Falls on September 27, 1896. Harris S. Hawthorn secured the help of the influential Sylvanus D. Locke in the years of 1894 and 1895 while applying for his Medal of Honor. In order to gain the most benefit from this addendum, the reader is encouraged to refer back to, and re-read, the various exhibits cited in this addendum. This addendum contains new information that sheds valuable light on the evidence found in the original exhibits.

Exhibit W-PF-23-Addendum (SUPPLEMENTARY EVIDENCE 1 OF 4)

Introduction:
This is a letter dated December 24, 1894, that Sylvanus D. Locke wrote to Custis Lee. Sylvanus D. Locke is requesting information about the capture of Major Stiles. This letter was not found in the 37th Massachusetts Protest Case file (Exhibits W-PF 1-29), and is being introduced now as new evidence in this addendum. It is a typescript and is signed by Sylvanus D. Locke in his own handwriting.

Evidence:
Sylvanus D. Locke's Automatic Binding Harvester
Hoosick Falls, N. Y. Dec 24, 1894

Maj. Gen. Custes Lee, Prest.,
Washington & Lee University,
Lexington, Va.

My Dear General:

Between 4 and 5 P. M. of Apr. 6, 1865, at the battle of Sailors Creek, Va., you were taken prisoner. Will you kindly inform me whether any other officer was taken with you? It is said that one of your staff officers, Major Stiles (?), was with you. Believing that you will pardon me for asking the question and hoping to hear from you soon or by return mail, I beg to subscribe myself with distinguished consideration.
Most Sincerely Yours,
S. D. Locke

Comments & Supporting Evidence:

1. Sylvanus D. Locke's motive behind writing this letter will become clear when the reader reads Exhibit W-PF-24 and 25-Addendum which is documented below. As of the writing of this letter (December 24, 1894), Sylvanus D. Locke was fully aware that Harris S. Hawthorn was awarded a Medal of Honor. The author was initially puzzled as to why Sylvanus D. Locke was writing to Custis Lee for additional information, when Hawthorn was already awarded a Medal of Honor (please see comments in Exhibit W-PF-23). The answer is now known. Sylvanus D. Locke was not seeking additional information for Harris S. Hawthorn's Medal of Honor application. Instead, he was trying to obtain information on the capture of Major Stiles which could have led to additional honors for Harris S. Hawthorn given by the War Department.

Exhibit W-PF-23-Addendum (SUPPLEMENTARY EVIDENCE 2 OF 4)

Introduction:

This letter dated December 27, 1894, was written by Custis Lee to Sylvanus D. Locke. It was in response to Sylvanus D. Locke's letter to Custis Lee dated December 24, 1894. This Custis Lee letter was not found in the 37th Massachusetts Protest Case file (Exhibit W-PF-23), and is being introduced now as new evidence in this addendum. This is a copy of the original letter, and is written in the handwriting of John P. Locke, son of Sylvanus D. Locke.

Evidence:

Lexington, Va.
27 Dec., 1894

Mr. S. D. Locke,
Hoosic Falls, N. Y.

Dear Sir:
Major Stiles was near me when I was taken prisoner and was taken prisoner also, I presume, although we were there separated.
Very truly yours,
G. W. C. Lee
Copy of letter rec'd by S. D. Locke Dec. 29, 1894 & answered Jan. 6, 1895
J. P. L.

Comments & Supporting Evidence:

1. The author is impressed that Custis Lee responded to Sylvanus D. Locke's letter, and that he did so in a very timely manner.
2. In this letter, Custis Lee is stating that Major Stiles was near him when he was taken prisoner, but that they were separated after being taken prisoner. The reader will see below that this was not the response Sylvanus D. Locke was hoping for when he wrote to Custis Lee.

Exhibit W-PF-23-Addendum (SUPPLEMENTARY EVIDENCE 3 OF 4)

Introduction:

This second letter that Sylvanus D. Locke wrote to Custis Lee is dated January 5, 1895. It provides descriptions of several events as well as requesting additional information from Custis Lee. This second letter from Sylvanus D. Locke was not found in the 37th Massachusetts Protest Case file (Exhibits W-PF-1-29), and is being introduced now as new evidence in this addendum. It is a typescript and is signed by Sylvanus D. Locke in his own handwriting.

Evidence:

Sylvanus D. Locke's Automatic Binding Harvester, Hoosick Falls, N. Y. Jan. 5, 1895

Gen. G. W. Custis Lee, Prest. of Washington & Lee University, Lexington, Va.

General:
Your esteemed favor of the 27th ultimo is received. You are undoubtedly correct in your reference to Maj. Stiles. In connection with your capture, allow me to mention a few incidents that will undoubtedly refresh your memory. Both yourself and the Major were entirely unarmed. The only appearance of an arm was possesed [sic] by Maj. S Stiles in the form of a broken scabbard. Unarmed and defenseless, a soldierly surrender to Sergt. Hawthorne, who suddenly presented his bayonet, was inevitable and the better part of valor. After the surrender, you were taken back across Sailors Creek into the Union lines and to Gen. Wheaton's headquarters that were then in the field. During this time, two incidents happened that you will recall. First: when you reached the Creek, which was muddy and waist deep, you siggested [sic] to Sergt. Hawthorne that wading the stream might be avoided if he would allow you to lead the way. Upon his assenting, you lead down the stream a short distance and pointed out a log which you and the Sergt. safely crossed without getting wet. Maj. Stiles, however, refusing to follow any d____ Yankee, declined the friendly log and plunged through the mud and water to the opposite bank. Second: when private, or sergt., Hawthorne had conducted you and Maj. Stiles to Gen. Wheaton's headquarters, you found Gen. Wheaton (commander of the Div., 6th Army Corps) absent. He returned in a short time and greeted you pleasantly. While conversing with you, his servant spread a light repast on the ground, of which the Gen. cordially invited you to partake. This invitation you most courteously [sic] accepted. Whereupon you followed Gen. Wheaton and, sitting upon the ground, indulged in pleasant conversation. Maj. Stiles, however, would have none of it and sullenly remained standing. Upon arising, Gen. Wheaton, turning and noticing the soldier (Sergt. Hawthorne) still waitingly standing, said "soldier you may report to your regiment."
The above seems to be a correct statement, General, of two incidents that occurred that day. I hope that the statements of them recalls the fact that Maj. Stiles was captured at the same time as yourself and by the same partye. I write in behalf of Sergt. Hawthorne, now an old white-haired man, who speaks of Gen. Custis Lee as a manly soldier, one of the grandest he ever met, and hope that you can and will find it in your heart to confirm his general statement that at the battle of Sailor's Creek, on the 6th of Apr., 1865, by the strange and unexpected fortune of war, he took Maj. Stiles and yourself prisoners and conducted you to Gen. Wheaton's headquarters. Sergt. Hawthorne's story is discredited here. If possible, I hope that you will do the old man a world of good by writing me a word of confirmation. Believing you will do this, I am my dear General, with an appreciation of your noble, manly and magnanimous character.
Most Sincerely Yours,
Sylvanus D. Locke

Comments & Supporting Evidence:

1. This Sylvanus D. Locke letter is very insightful because it offers excellent descriptions of some of the claims made by Harris S. Hawthorn concerning his capture of Custis Lee and Major Stiles. It is surmised that Harris S. Hawthorn must have relayed this information to Sylvanus D. Locke during their local hometown associations.

2. Sylvanus D. Locke is acknowledging, as a correct fact, Custis Lee's assertion that Custis Lee and Major Stiles were near each other when they were taken prisoner on the battlefield, but were separated after their capture.

3. As the author originally suspected and documented in the comments section of Exhibit W-PF-23, Sylvanus D. Locke asked Custis Lee many "leading" questions in his letter. Sylvanus D. Locke presented Custis Lee many of Harris Hawthorn's descriptions of key events surrounding the capture of Custis Lee and Major Stiles. Sylvanus D. Locke then asked Custis Lee to confirm the accuracy of these events. In a court of law, this technique is referred to as "leading the witness", and is not permitted.

4. First, Sylvanus D. Locke begins by assertively stating that Custis Lee and Major Stiles were unarmed when Sergt. Hawthorn captured them. Immediately after this assertion Hawthorn (through Sylvanus D. Locke) makes the assertion that he (Hawthorn) captured Custis Lee and Major Stiles together. The point made by Hawthorn that both Custis Lee and Major Stiles were unarmed when he captured them is very important. This "unarmed (Hawthorn) vs. armed (37th Massachusetts)" issue is the primary differentiator between the Hawthorn account and the 37th Massachusetts account (please see Chapter Six-Verdict). The author has found throughout his research that whenever Hawthorne provides an account of his actual capture of Custis Lee, the account is always on the sparse side, providing very few details on the exact manner in which he captured Custis Lee. The account contained in this letter is no exception. It simply states that Hawthorn, "suddenly presented his bayonet", and compelled their surrender. For the author, it is unbelievable that Hawthorn could have "suddenly presented his bayonet" on an active battlefield, compelling the capture of both Custis Lee and Major Stiles together. This is especially true when one considers the fact that both Custis Lee (in Exhibit W-PF-23-Addendum) and Major Stiles (in Exhibit W-BA-2-Confederate) independently state that they were not together in the final moments of the battle. If they were not together, they could not have been captured together. For the author, it is much more plausible that Hawthorn took control of Custis Lee and Major Stiles when they were standing together on the battlefield, having already been captured and customarily disarmed, and having been left temporarily unguarded within the Federal line when Hawthorn happened upon them and took control of them at the point of his bayonet (please see Chapter Six-Verdict).

5. Sylvanus D. Locke then describes a scenario of how Hawthorn conducted Custis Lee and Major Stiles across Sailor's Creek after their capture. The act of "conducting Custis Lee into the Federal lines after his capture" is where Hawthorn always spends energy articulating his account and offering specific details. It must be noted that Hawthorn's account found in this letter, which explains how he crossed Sailor's Creek with Custis Lee, is totally opposed to the account offered by T. J. Hassett as found in Exhibit H-AF-1. If Hawthorn's account in this letter is correct, then it casts serious doubt on the veracity of the contents of T. J. Hassett's account found in Exhibit H-AF-1.

6. Sylvanus D. Locke then describes the scenarios of Hawthorn conducting Custis Lee and Major Stiles to General Wheaton's headquarters, Custis Lee and General Wheaton dining on the ground and Hawthorn being dismissed by General Wheaton to return to his regiment. Once again, in typical Hawthorn style, this part of the account is full of details. It must be noted that these scenarios are diametrically opposed to T. J. Hassett's account found in Exhibit H-AF-1. Once again, this casts serious doubt on the veracity of the entire T. J. Hassett account.

7. Sylvanus D. Locke states again, that Custis Lee and Major Stiles were captured together by Harris Hawthorn. It must be noted that this statement of a duel capture is something that Custis Lee did not concur with in his December 27, 1894, letter (see Exhibit W-PF-23-Addendum-2 of 4).

8. Lastly, in addition to the flattering platitudes that Sylvanus D. Locke offers to Custis Lee in his concluding paragraph, it is interesting to note that Sylvanus D. Locke states that at the time of this letter, January 5, 1895, that "Sergt. Hawthorne's story is discredited here." This statement by Sylvanus D. Locke was made more than two years before the 37th Massachusetts filed their Protest Case. The author is curious about who might be the parties actively trying to discredit Hawthorn's account in January, 1895.

9. The author is amazed that Sylvanus D. Locke never informed Custis Lee in either of the two letters that he sent to Custis Lee that Harris S. Hawthorn was awarded the Medal of Honor for his capture. It would appear that Sylvanus D. Locke was executing his own specific agenda when corresponding with Custis Lee, and that agenda did not, for whatever reason, include informing Custis Lee of Hawthorn's Medal of Honor.

10. Stiles had a revolver while serving at Chaffin's Bluff in the winter of 1864/1865. In his book, Four Years under Marse Robert, on page 315, he states, "I ordered them to halt, impressing the order with my revolver." Stiles also states in the same book, page 334, while fighting with his men at the Battle of Sailor's Creek, "but alas, my sword had broken in the clash." It is unlikely that Stiles was

totally unarmed, without his revolver or his broken sword, when he was captured at Sailor's Creek. This calls into question Locke's words that Stiles and Custis Lee were, "unarmed and defenseless."

Exhibit W-PF-23-Addendum (SUPPLEMENTARY EVIDENCE 4 OF 4)

Introduction:

This letter dated January 9, 1895, is Custis Lee's response to Sylvanus D. Locke's letter dated January 5, 1895. Only an abbreviated "extract" of this letter was in the 37th Massachusetts Protest Case file (see Exhibit W-PF-23). This "abbreviated extract" was created by Sylvanus D. Locke's son, John P. Locke, in the year 1897. The complete and non-abbreviated Custis Lee letter is being introduced now as new evidence in this addendum. The letter is a copy of the original Custis Lee letter, and is written in the handwriting John P. Locke.

Evidence:

Lexington, Va.
9 Jany, 1895
Mr. Sylvanus D. Locke,
Hoosick Falls, N. Y.

Dear Sir:
I have just rec'd your letter of the 5th Inst., and should be glad to confirm Sergt. Hawthorne's statement as given by yourself, but that my recollections of the affair at Sailor's Creek does not altogether coincide with his own. I gave myself up to a non-commissioned officer in preference to a commissioned officer because, as the former said to me, it would be the means of procuring him a furlough. It is true that I was unarmed, but it is also true that there were enough of my own people about me to protect me if necessary. I remember that Major Stiles was near me when I gave myself up, because he was assisting me to prevent the men on opposing sides from shooting one another unnecessarily, but I do not recollect I have seen him again for a long time afterwards. The incident you relate in regard to him, is so unlike him that I think there must be some mistake about it. I accompanied Sgt. ~, who told me, I believe, that he belonged to the 6th Corps, commanded by Genl. H. G. Wright, across Sailor's Creek on a log. I suppose though I did not before know of it's existence, as when I crossed the creek earlier in the day I was on horseback and took the ford of the main road and went with him a short distance to the top of the hills, where I met an officer of the old army, whom I never met before but of whom I had often heard. This place may have been the Hd. Qts. of Genl. Wheaton, but I have no recollection of meeting him or of taking a meal with him. I passed that night at the camp of Genl. Sheridan whom I had known at the U. S. Military Academy West Point, N. Y. At this Camp Genl. H. G. Wright, with whom I had served in the Engineer Bureau of the War Dept., Washington D. C. came to see me and met then & there and afterwards several other old army acquaintances, but to the best of my knowledge and belief, I did not see Genl. Wheaton at all. I have given all the confirmation in my power to the statement of Segt. Hawthorne, & hope it may be satisfactory to him.
Very truly,
G. W. C. Lee
Copy of a letter rec'd Jan. 11, 1895, by S. D. Locke
J. P. L.

Comments & Supporting Evidence:

1. As stated before, the author is impressed that Custis Lee would take the time to respond to Sylvanus D. Locke's letter, and to do so in a timely fashion. Custis Lee was truly a honor-bound gentleman when it came to responding to letters that he received.
2. The author has compared Custis Lee's response in this letter with the various responses that he gave during the 37th Massachusetts Protest Case in the year 1897 (see Exhibits in W-PF). In the year 1897, some of Custis Lee's responses came through his personal secretary. The response in

this letter is cordial, somewhat lengthy and appears to be written with a helpful tone. In contrast, Custis Lee's responses during the 37th Massachusetts Protest Case were generally abrupt and with a certain tone of indignation. This observation might be explained in two ways. First, Custis Lee was in much better physical and mental health in 1894 when he wrote this letter than he was in 1897 during the 37th Massachusetts Protest case. Second, Custis Lee could have been angered during the 37th Massachusetts Protest Case when he learned that a Medal of Honor was awarded to Harris S. Hawthorn for his capture at the Battle of Sailor's Creek. Particularly in light of the fact that this information was withheld from Custis Lee by Sylvanus D. Locke during their exchange of letters.

3. With this Custis Lee letter now available in its entirety, it is easy to see why John P. Locke, son of the late Sylvanus D. Locke, created only an abbreviated "extract" of this letter for submission to the 37th Massachusetts Protest Case in the year 1897. As was strongly suspected by the author in his comments in Exhibit W-PF-23, John P. Locke extracted only those items that had the potential of being helpful to Hawthorn's case. John P. Locke deliberately did not extract those items that had the potential of being adverse to Hawthorn's case. Unfortunately, this was not a very honest thing for John P. Locke to do. He must have thought that he had the best interest of his good friend Harris Hawthorn in mind when he was doing so.

4. It was honest of Custis Lee to state in the beginning of his letter that his recollection of events did not "altogether coincide" with the recollections of Hawthorn.

5. The language that Custis Lee used to describe "giving himself up" to a non-commissioned vs. commissioned officer is much more in line with 37th Massachusetts accounts than it is with Hawthorn's account. Hawthorn's account contains no mention of Custis Lee surrendering to an officer. It simply states that Hawthorn compelled Custis Lee to surrender at the point of his bayonet.

6. The author was initially confused by a Custis Lee statement found in Exhibit W-PF-12, which seemed to indicate that Custis Lee surrendered to a Federal soldier because this Federal soldier would ensure that he (Custis Lee) received a furlough. According to this letter, however, Custis Lee is stating that he surrendered to a Federal non-commissioned officer, as opposed to a Federal commissioned officer, because the former would receive a furlough. The author finds this assertion difficult to comprehend. It is hard to believe that Custis Lee, with his troops engaged in a vicious hand to hand battle with the enemy, would have the presence of mind during this type of struggle to be concerned with a Federal non-commissioned officer receiving a furlough for his surrender. One would logically think that this would be the last thing on Custis Lee's mind during this difficult time.

7. Custis Lee recounts several interesting items in this letter. It should be noted again that John P. Locke extracted only selected points from Custis Lee's letter, which he then incorporated into his letter that he sent to the 37th Massachusetts Protest Case in 1897. The points from Custis Lee's letter that John P. Locke extracted for use in his Massachusetts Protest letter were items that would either be neutral or favorable to Harris Hawthorn's account, such as: (1) Custis Lee was "unarmed" (which unarmed notion was suggested to Custis Lee by John Locke's father, Sylvanus D. Locke), (2) Custis Lee had people around him to protect him (3) Major Stiles was near to Custis Lee during the battle (4) Custis Lee's captor mentioned that he was a member of the 6th Corp (5) Custis Lee and Major Stiles were trying to prevent the men on opposing sides from shooting one another unnecessarily (6) Custis Lee was taken to the top of the hills, which was believed to be the headquarters of General Wheaton (7) and the crossing of Sailor's Creek by Custis Lee after his capture occurred on a log (see Exhibit W-PF-23 for all these extracted points). It should be noted that while reading the language in Custis Lee's letter more carefully, the author became unconvinced that Custis Lee actually remembered the log crossing story as related by Sylvanus D. Locke. It seemed like Custis Lee was just acknowledging what Sylvanus D. Locke was telling him, and then Custis Lee began to question his own recollection of the log and whether or not he had any beforehand knowledge of it.

8. John P. Locke was also careful to omit certain Custis Lee points from his letter that he submitted to the 37th Massachusetts Protest Case. Items that would have been adverse to Harris Hawthorn's account, such as: (1) Custis Lee stating that he did not see Major Stiles for a long time afterward from the time they were both captured (2) Custis Lee taking issue with Hawthorn's description of the

demeanor of Major Stile while he was crossing the creek and while he was at the headquarters of General Wheaton (3) Custis Lee having no recollection of meeting General Wheaton after his capture and (4) Custis Lee having no recollection of dining on the ground with General Wheaton after his capture (see Exhibit W-PF-23 that shows the omission of these points).

9. The fact that Custis Lee acknowledges in his letter that he was on horseback at the Battle of Sailor's Creek is very interesting. This directly contradicts his testimony that he gave in the 37th Massachusetts Protest Case in the year 1897 as found in Exhibit W-PF-12. Custis Lee's acknowledgment of being on horseback supports 37th Massachusetts claims as found in Exhibit W-PF-9 and Exhibit W-CT-1.

10. Lastly, Custis Lee's recollection that while he was at the camp of General Sheridan during the night of his capture, General H. G. Wright came to see him, is very interesting. This recollection could support General Edwards' claim that he gave General Wright Custis Lee's pipe and tobacco, which were taken from General Custis Lee during his capture by the 37th Massachusetts, so that General Wright could return it to Custis Lee (please see Exhibit W-PF-5). Maybe this pipe and tobacco exchange took place during this visit by General Wright to Custis Lee at the camp of General Sheridan. This Custis Lee recollection is also supportive of General Wright's own recollection, where he remembers meeting Custis Lee at General Sheridan's headquarters (see Exhibit W-PF-19). Naturally, John P. Locke left out all this information when he created his extract letter for the 37th Massachusetts Protest Case, because this Custis Lee recollection was contrary to Hawthorn's claim.

Exhibit W-PF-24 and 25-Addendum (SUPPLEMENTARY EVIDENCE 1 OF 1)

Introduction:

Joseph H. Heath wrote Sylvanus D. Locke a letter on December 14, 1894, concerning what he (Heath) knew about Hawthorn's capture of Custis Lee. According to Yale University, Sylvanus D. Locke's initial inquiry letter to Joseph Heath, which had to occur prior to December 14, 1894, is not in their Sylvanus D. Locke Papers. This December 14, 1894, Heath letter was submitted in its entirety to the 37th Massachusetts Protest case by John P. Locke in the year 1897 (see Exhibit W-PF-25). This letter is also in the Sylvanus D. Locke Papers. In the Sylvanus D. Locke Papers, this letter is annotated by John P. Locke with the words "received for Capt. Josh Heath December 22, 1894, answered December 22, 1894." The letter shown below dated December 24, 1894, is what Sylvanus D. Locke wrote to Joseph H. Heath in response to Heath's letter dated December 14, 1894. This letter was not found in the 37th Massachusetts Protest Case file (Exhibits W-PF-1-29). It is being introduced now as new evidence in this addendum. It is also worth noting that Heath responded back to Sylvanus D. Locke's letter with another letter dated December 25, 1894. This December 25, 1894, Heath letter is in the 37th Massachusetts Protest Case file (see Exhibit W-PF-24) and in the Sylvanus D. Papers. This December 25, 1894, letter was not annotated by John P. Locke.

Evidence:

Sylvanus D. Locke's Automatic Binding Harvester, Hoosick Falls, N. Y. Dec 24, 1894

Capt. Joseph H. Heath, Little Falls, N. Y.

My Dear Captain,
Your esteemed favor of the 14th inst giving a lucid account of the capture of Gen Lee by private Hawthorne and the capture of the flag by yourself, is just received. Hawthorne has been awarded a medal. I was only able to show his capture of Gen Lee, although, as I understand it, he captured at the same time Lee's chief of staff, Major Stiles. Hawthorne says he did, and you know he is very truthful and in every way reliable. He tells a very clear and distinct story about capturing these two officers; about the attempt of an officer in a Mass. regiment to take them from him; about the interference of Col. Olcott in his behalf, and the Colonel's order to deliver them to Maj. Gen. Wheaton, the commander of the division; and about his delivery of the prisoners to Gen. Wheaton. His story is full of details that

seem to carry confirmation. What do you know, Captain, about this matter? Did Hawthorne capture another officer with Gen. Lee? If so, he is entitled to a special acknowledgement by the War Department for his excelling distinguished gallantry. Please write me fully and soon as to your remembrance.

Truly Yours,
S. D. Locke

Comments & Supporting Evidence:

1. As stated before, Sylvanus D. Locke is not writing this letter to Joseph H. Heath to acquire information that would help Hawthorn acquire a Medal of Honor. Hawthorn had already acquired a Medal of Honor before the date of this letter.
2. Sylvanus D. Locke is looking to acquire information that would help Hawthorn receive additional recognition from the War Department for the capture Major Stiles.
3. What is telling from this letter, particularly when combined with the Custis Lee letters highlighted above, is that Hawthorn is asserting he captured both Custis Lee and Major Stiles at the same time. As mentioned before, the author believes this simultaneous capture of Custis Lee and Major Stiles by Harris Hawthorn is highly improbable. Particularly if it occurred on the active battlefield of Sailor's Creek where Custis Lee's and Major Stiles' troops were engaged in vicious hand to hand combat with the enemy. It seems much more probable that Hawthorn could have accomplished a simultaneous capture of Custis Lee and Major Stiles when Custis Lee and Major Stiles were already captured and customarily disarmed, and then left temporarily unguarded within the Federal line on the active battlefield.

[Source for all five Exhibits contained in this Addendum: "The Sylvanus D. Locke Papers" Yale University Library, Archives and Manuscripts Division, New Haven, CT]**Manuscript 195**

Box 6-Folder 62: <u>Exhibit W-PF-23-Addendum 1 and 2 of 4</u>
Box 6-Folder 63: <u>Exhibit W-PF-23-Addendum 3 and 4 of 4</u>
Box 5-Folder 44: <u>Exhibit W-PF-24/ 25-Addendum 1 of 1</u>

AUTHOR SIDE NOTE:

Another last minute discovery made by the author is the following newspaper article:

CAPTURED GEN. LEE.

There is living at Savoy Four Corners a man named David White whose name has been mentioned quite frequently of late. He is a veteran of the civil war and belonged to the 37th regiment. The reason that his name is especially noteworthy at this time is because he captured General Custis Lee during a battle at Sailor's Creek near Richmond, Va. General Custis Lee is a cousin of General Fitzhugh Lee, the present consul general at Havana.

[Source: "North Adams Transcript", North Adams, MA, April 11, 1898, edition]**Manuscript 196**

This is a peculiar article because it appeared out of nowhere. Perhaps it was published as a result of the circa 1897, 37th Massachusetts Protest Case. This could explain the statement in the article, "David White whose name has been mentioned quite frequently of late." The author surmises that veterans of the 37th Massachusetts, who were familiar with their Protest Case and the outcome rendered by Secretary of War Alger, were behind the publishing of this article. They might have desired to make a subtle public statement in the matter. The publishing of this article does not appear to be tied to the timing of Fitzhugh Lee becoming Consul General at Havana. That event occurred on April 11, 1896. The author is puzzled by the article's statement that David White's name is, "especially noteworthy at this time." Why would White's name be "especially noteworthy" in 1898, 33 years after the capture?

The author has included this article in the addendum as a last minute discovery because it adds another interesting tidbit to this fascinating, complex case.

BIBLIOGRAPHY

UNPUBLISHED SOURCES:

- 37th Massachusetts Protest Case: AGO Record and Pension File; Document File # 476510; National Archives, Washington, DC.
- 121st New York: Company Muster Rolls for March and April, 1865: Microfilm Publication: M-594, number 2702769, National Archives; Washington, DC.
- 121st New York, Regimental Books: Record Group 94; 6 volumes; National Archives, Washington, DC.
- 121st New York Infantry Books: Six Volumes, National Archives, Washington, DC.
- Abbott Family Papers: Andover Historical Society, Andover, MA
- Abbott, Hubbard M.: Civil War Pension File, #'s 313624 and 1038996; National Archives, Washington, DC.
- Abbott, William Frank: Widow Pension Record; # 1038996; National Archives, Washington, DC.
- Abbott, William Frank: Suffolk County MA Probate File # 167460.
- Abbott, William Frank: Military Service Record; National Archives, Washington, DC.
- Basinger, William Starr: Basinger Papers, Southern Historical Collection, University of North Carolina Library, Chapel Hill, NC.
- Basinger, William Starr: "Personal Reminiscences," Southern Historical Collection; University of North Carolina, Chapel Hill, NC.
- Butterfield, Miles L.: Civil War Pension Record, #545.392; National Archives, Washington, DC.
- Butterfield, Miles L.: Manuscript-"Personal War Sketches"; Typescript; Institute of Civil War Studies, Carroll College, Waukesha, IL; 1904.
- Butterfield, Miles L.: Civil War diary, Institute of Civil War Studies, Carroll College, Waukesha, IL.
- Butterfield, Miles L.: Butterfield, Miles Papers; Manuscript Collection 77, University of Wisconsin, Milwaukee, WI, 1864-1865.
- Butterfield, Miles L.: Military Service Record, National Archives, Washington, DC.
- Butterfield, Miles L.: Volunteer Service File, # 5787-VS-1884; National Archives, Washington, DC, 1884.
- Clement, Russell: Memoirs, 37th Massachusetts Infantry.
- Commonwealth of Massachusetts, Department of Public Safety, Office of the State Police: Case number 77-109-2200-0216, investigative report on thefts committed by Northampton, MA, police officers.
- Crafts, Mary, Persis: Listing of American powder horns, arms and armor in the Northampton, MA, Memorial Hall Museum in response to a survey by Mr. Stephen Grancsay, of the Metropolitan Museum of Art, New York, NY; listing dated 1938.
- Dean, James: "Following the Flag, the Three Year Story of a Veteran"; 2nd Connecticut Heavy Artillery, Connecticut Historical Society, Harford, CT; undated typescript.
- Duncan, Samuel Dr. Various family papers; Williamstown House of Local History, Williamstown, MA; various dates.
- Eddy, Samuel E.: Civil War Medal of Honor File, EAK 492-EB, Record Group 94; 1867, # 391014 and # 408333.
- Edwards, Oliver: "My Recollections of the Civil War"; Illinois State Historical Society Library; Old State Capitol, Springfield, IL; undated typescript.
- "Executive Letters of the Governor": Massachusetts State Archives, Boston, MA, bound volume 66.
- "Final Report of the Medal of Honor Review Board": 66th Congress, 1st Session, Senate Document Number 58; 1916.
- "Flags Captured": AGO file # AAK, 534-EB, 1869; National Archives, Washington, DC.

- Hampshire Gazette Newspaper, Northampton, MA: Report on the 37th Massachusetts Regiment; April 25, 1865.
- Hassett, Thomas J.: Civil War Pension File, # 1059890 and # 568455; National Archives, Washington, DC.
- Hassett, Thomas J.: Adjutant General's Office Correspondence Files, # 994910 and # 2187969; National Archives, Washington, DC.
- Hassett, Thomas J.: Military Service Record, National Archives, Washington, DC.
- Hawthorn, Harris S.: Civil War Pension File, # 724261 and # 327492; National Archives, Washington, DC.
- Hawthorn, Harris S.: Medal of Honor Application File, Record and Pension # 401673; National Archives, Washington, DC; 1894.
- Heath, Joseph H.: Military Service Record, National Archives, Washington, DC.
- Heath, Joseph D.: Pension File, # 155762; National Archives, Washington, DC.
- Historic Northampton: 1987 note on file documenting contact by Mr. Jim Parsons on missing swords, accession cards, de-accession records and December 30, 1939 letter on Hooker sword.
- Hopkins, Archibald: Affidavit in the Massachusetts National Guard Archives, Worcester, MA, 37th Massachusetts Regiment, M. V. I. Collection.
- Hopkins, Archibald: Alumni Papers; Williams College, Williamstown, MA.
- Ingraham, John J.: 121st New York; letter dated April 16, 1865.
- Keifer, J. Warren: Papers in the Library of Congress, Washington, DC.
- Kidder, John S.: 121st New York; letter dated April 10, 1865.
- King, Horatio C.: "Military Service Record; # 43042982; National Archives, Washington, DC.
- Krutz, David: Letter dealing with Joseph Heath, dated March 21, 2006.
- Lee, Custis George Washington: Military Service Record (Confederate), # 52311989; National Archives, Washington, DC.
- Locke, Sylvanus D.: "Papers", Yale University Library, New Haven, CT, Manuscript and Archives Division.
- Lord, Francis: Letter to Mrs. Shepherd, curator Northampton MA, Historical Society; dated August 3, 1932.
- Lovejoy, John M.: Letter to his mother, dated April 14, 1865, photograph in the possession of Salvatore Cilella, President Atlanta Historical Society, Atlanta, GA.
- Lovejoy, John M.: Letter to his cousin Cynthia, dated April 15, 1865, photograph in the possession of Salvatore Cilella, President Atlanta Historical Society, Atlanta, GA.
- Mahogany, Edward: Letter to his mother dated April 16, 1865, original in the possession of Charles Mahogany, Pelham, MA.
- Mahogany, Eve: Letter to author dated March 20, 2001.
- McGrane, Francis: Email on Army Corps of Engineers, staff officers and their Civil War swords, dated January 9, 2007.
- "Medals of Honor for Enlisted Men, April 2nd and 6th, 1865": Recommendation for Medals of Honor for Men in the Battles of Petersburg, April 2 and Sailor's Creek April 6, 1865: File Mark number 3963B1878; National Archives, Washington, DC.
- "Minutes of Meetings of the Medal of Honor Review Board": Records of the Adjutant General's Office; Oversized Document file 1805-1917, file # 2411162 AGO; National Archives, Washington, DC.
- Moody, Frederick: Civil War diary currently in the possession of Charles W. Thayer, originally purchased by Harold Gordon, Wellesley Hills, MA.
- Moore, Dennis: Civil War Pension File, National Archives, Washington, DC.
- "Morning Reports": 121st New York and 37th Massachusetts; Record Group 94; Records of the Adjutant General's Office; Entry 112-115; April, 1865; National Archives, Washington, DC.
- Morrill, William C: Death Record, Rochester, NY.

- Morrill, William c: Military Service Record, # 1466-US-1865, National Archives, Washington, DC
- Morrill, William C: Civil War letters, dated November 1862—June 1865, originals in the possession of Charles W. Thayer.
- Morrill, William C: Pension File, National Archives, Washington, DC.
- New York State Adjutant General: Questionnaire dated December 2, 1895 and sent to former New York State Civil War troops. Questionnaire completed by John M. Lovejoy, secretary and treasurer of the 121st New York Veterans Association.
- Newell, Buzz: Affidavit and letter with original signature; May 18 and 31, 1995.
- Newell, David: Son of Buzz Newell, e-mail sharing insights on his father and other related topics, dated November 23, 2006.
- Olcott, Egbert: Pension File # 213381; National Archives, Washington, DC.
- Panik, Marie: Curator of Historic Northampton, e-mails dated September 20, 2006, October 3, 2006 and February 1 and 6, 2007.
- Parsons, Jim: Transcription of interview; March 12, 1997 and May 30, 1996.
- Parsons, Jim: Letter to the author dated May 12, 1997.
- "Records of the U. S. Army Continental Commands, 1821-1920": Part One, Entry 4065; Volume 73/200; Army of the Potomac; List of Confederate Prisoners received by the Provost Marshal; National Archives, Washington, DC.
- "Register of Letters Sent by the Judge Advocate, 1st Division, 6th Army Corps": Record Group 393, Part 2 Entry 4508; National Archives, Washington, DC.
- Russell, Horace Clement: "Memoirs of Horace Clement Russell, Company F, 37th Massachusetts Infantry"; Gettysburg National Military Park Library, Gettysburg, PA; 1918.
- Smith, Thomas: Civil War Pension File; # 261599 and # 409897; National Archives, Washington, DC.
- Snook, George: With Charles W. Thayer, documentation relating to the current Civil War sword collection and inventory at Historic Northampton, Northampton, MA; 2006—2007.
- Thayer, Charles Hiram: "The Old Pomroy House at Hockanum and the Civil War"; Typescript; Amherst, MA; 1962.
- Thayer, Charles W.: Interview transcriptions; 1995 and 2000.
- Thayer, Charles W.: Letter and e-mail documenting his 2004 telephone conversations with Mr. Buzz Newell, letter dated December 17, 2006 and e-mail dated January 19, 2007.
- Thayer, Charles W.: Original handwritten notes of his 1994 telephone conversations with Mr. Buzz Newell.
- Thillmann, John: E-mails on Civil War swords, models, etc., dated January 1 and 9, 2007.
- White, David: Civil War Pension File; # 210739; National Archives, Washington, DC.
- White, David: Military Service Record, National Archives, Washington, DC.
- Woodcock, Philip R.: Personal diary entry dated April 6, 1865, diary archived at the U. S. Army War College, Carlisle Barracks, PA. Woodcock was a member of the 121st New York.

PERIODICALS:

- Alabama Confederate: "The "Aye, Ayes" At Sailor's Creek," Volume 17, Number 1; Jan. 1998.
- Confederate Veteran: "In the Siege of Richmond and After"; by W. L. Timberlake; Volume 29.
- Confederate Veteran: The Battle of Sailor's Creek" by B.S. Johnson; Volume 8, number 4; 1900.
- Confederate Veteran: "The Battle of Sailor's Creek" by Daniel B. Stanford; Volume 8; number 4; 1900.
- Confederate Veteran: "The Artillery Brigade at Sailor's Creek"; by Thomas S. Blake; Volume 28; 1920.
- Confederate Veteran: "With the Confederate Reserves"; by R. T. W. Duke; Volume 26.
- Confederate Veteran: "Second Dispatch from Grant to Lee"; by Capt. Marcellus French; Volume 8; 1900.

- Military Order of the Loyal Legion of the United States (ME): "How I Recovered My Sword"; by Henry S. Burrage; Lefavor Tower Company; 1902.
- Military Order of the Loyal Legion of the United States: "The Battle of Sailor's Creek."
- National Archive Prologue Magazine: "The Army Medal of Honor"; by Mark Mollan; Volume 33, Number 2; 2001.
- National Tribune: "Sailor's Creek, the Capture of Gen. Lee and his Corps," by F. C. Robinson; August 18, 1877.
- National Tribune: " Closing Scenes, the Capture of Ewell's Command and the Exhausting March to Burkesville with the Prisoners," by B. F. Johns, February 13, 1902.
- Southern Bivouac: "A Naval Officer's Recollection of Lee's Retreat," by R. A. Camm; Volume 2; Number 9; 1884.
- Southern Historical Society Transactions: "Report of G. W. C. Lee, April 2-6, 1865"; Vol. 1, pg. 118-121; 1883.
- Southern Historical Society Transactions: "Retreat of Custis Lee's Division and the Battle of Sailor's Creek," by Howard McHenry; Volume one; 1874.
- Southern Historical Collection: "Personal Reminiscences of William Starr Basinger"; University of North Carolina, Chapel Hill, NC.
- Southern Historical Society Papers: "Burning of Richmond"; R. T. W. Duke; Volume 25.
- Southern Historical Society Papers: "Crutchfield's Artillery Brigade"; William S. Basinger, Volume 25.
- Southern Historical Society Papers: "Retreat from Richmond"; by Thomas Ballard Blake; Volume 25.
- Southern Historical Society Papers: "Sailor's Creek"; by Walter C. Watson; Volume 42; 1916.
- Southern Historical Society Papers: "Major General George Washington Custis Lee; by W. Gordon McCabe; Volume 39.

PUBLISHED SOURCES:

- "Above and Beyond": A History of the Medal of Honor from the Civil War to Vietnam; Published in cooperation with the Congressional Medal of Honor Society of the United States of America; Boston Publishing Company, Boston, MA; 1985.
- Adams, John R.: "Memorial and Letters of Rev. John R. Adams," Privately printed, University Press, Cambridge, MA; 1890.
- "The Adams Transcript": North Adams, MA, Newspaper Editions, March 28, 1878 and March 2, 1882.
- Albaugh, William A.: "The Original Confederate Colt, the Story of the Leech & Rigdon and Rigdon-Ansley Revolvers"; Greenberg Publisher, New York, NY; 1953.
- Allen, T. S.: Report of the 5th Wisconsin in the Official Records, "Appomattox Campaign," Volume 46, Series 1.
- "Annual Report of the Adjutant General of the Commonwealth of Massachusetts, 1865": Boston, MA 1866.
- "Annual Report of the Adjutant General of the State of New York for 1903": Series number 36; Oliver A. Quayle State Legislative Printer; Albany, NY; 1904.
- Best, Isaac: "History of the 121st New York Infantry," published by Lieut. Jas. H. Smith; Chicago, IL; 1921.
- Bowen, James L.: "History of the 37th Massachusetts Regiment Volunteers"; Clark W. Bryan and Company Publishers, Holyoke, MA and New York City, NY, 1884.
- Burrage, Henry S.: "How I Recovered my Sword"; War Papers, Read before the Commandery of the State of Maine, MOLLUS, Volume 11; Lefavor-Tower Company, Portland, ME; 1902.
- Butterfield, Miles L.: "Personal Reminiscences with the Sixth Corps, 1864-1865"; Wisconsin MOLLUS War Papers; Volume iv; pages 85-93; 1905.

- Beyer, W.F. and O. F. Keydel: "Deeds of Valor, How Civil War Heroes Won the Congressional Medal of Honor"; Longmeadow Press; Stamford, CT; 1992, originally published 1903.
- Calkins, Chris: "Great Campaigns, the Appomattox Campaign, March 29-April 9, 1865"; Combined Books, PA; 1997.
- Calkins, Chris: "Thirty-Six Hours Before Appomattox, The Battles of Sailor's Creek, Farmville and Cumberland Church"; The Farmville [VA] Herald; 1980.
- "Camp Fire Sketches and Battlefield Echoes": "Interesting War Relic, a Sword Returned to its Owner after Twenty Two Years"; W. C. King and Company; 1887.
- Cauble, Frank: "The Proceedings Connected with the Surrender of the Army of Northern Virginia, April 1865"; Appomattox Court House National Historical Park, VA; 1962 revised 1975.
- Chesnut, Mary Boykin: "A Diary from Dixie, as written by Mary Boykin Chesnut, wife of James Chesnut Jr., United States Senator from South Carolina, 1859-1861, and afterward an Aide to Jefferson Davis and a Brigadier General in the Confederate Army", edited by Isabella D. Martin and Myrta Lockett Avary; D. Appleton and Company, 1905.
- Congressional Medal of Honor Society: "The Medal's History"; Patriots Point, SC.; 2001.
- Covais, Joseph S.: Forward in the reprint of the "History of the 121st New York State Infantry," Butternut and Blue, Baltimore, MD; 1996.
- Crenshaw, Oliver: "General Lee's College, the Rise and Growth of Washington and Lee University"; Random House, NY.
- Cushman, Harrie A.: "History of the Seventh Massachusetts Volunteers Infantry, in the War of the Rebellion of the Southern States against Constitutional Authority 1861-1865"; printed by the authority of the Regimental Association; 1890.
- "Daily News": Northampton, Civil War Centennial Committee at Work"; Springfield, MA; January 16, 1961.
- Davis, Burke: "To Appomattox-Nine April Days, 1865"; Rinehart &Co., NY; 1959.
- Dwight, Charles Stevens: "A South Carolina Rebel's Recollections, Personal Reminiscence of the Evacuation of Richmond and the battle of Sailor's Creek, April 6, 1865"; the State Company, Columbia, SC; 1917.
- Eanes, Greg: "Black Day of the Army, April 6, 1865"; E&H Publishing Company, Inc.; 2001.
- Forty-Seventh (47) Virginia Infantry: H. E. Howard, Inc.; 1991.
- Frassanito, William A.: "Grant and Lee, the Virginia Campaigns, 1864-1865"; Charles Scribner's Sons, NY; 1983.
- Fuller, Claude: "Firearms of the Confederacy"; Odysseus Editions; 1996.
- Garrison, Webb: "More Civil War Curiosities"; Rutledge Hill Press; Nashville, TN; 1994.
- "Hampshire Daily Gazette": "City Museum Lingers in Obscurity in Memorial Hall," Northampton, MA; December 30, 1968.
- "Hampshire Daily Gazette": "Relics of the Past Here"; Northampton, MA; October 1, 1930.
- "Hampshire Gazette": Northampton, MA; January 6, 1885 edition.
- "Hampshire Gazette": "GAR Asks for Appropriation for Hall Rent"; Northampton, MA; April 7, 1885.
- "Hampshire Gazette": "Gifts to the GAR"; Northampton, MA; May 25, 1886.
- "Hampshire Gazette": "Grand Army Field Day"; Northampton, MA; September 25, 1888.
- "Hampshire Gazette": "The Museum Ready"; Northampton, MA; July 12, 1887.
- "Hampshire Life Magazine": "For Those Who Fought and Died, the Creation of Northampton's Memorial Hall"; by Allison Lockwood; Northampton, MA; May 22-28, 1992.
- Harwell, Richard: "Uniform and Dress of the Army and Navy of the Confederate States of America"; Chas. H. Wynne Printer, St. Martin's Press; 1861.
- Hassett, Thomas J.: "Initiation into the Ways of Warfare," West Winfield Star, West Winfield, NY; edition February 7, 1913.
- "Herkimer County Journal & Courier: January 29, 1895 edition.
- "Herkimer Democrat": Herkimer, NY; June 6, 1894 edition.

- Hopkins, Archibald: "The Battle of Sailor's Creek"; the Military Engineer; Volume 14, no. 105; Washington, DC; 1927.
- Howard, H. E.: "The 47th Virginia Infantry"; H. E. Howard, Inc.; Lynchburg, VA; 1991.
- Howard, McHenry: "Recollections of a Maryland Confederate Soldier and Staff Officer under Johnston, Jackson and Lee"; Morningside Bookshop; 1914.
- Hutchinson, Nelson V.: "History of the Seventh Massachusetts Volunteer Infantry"; Taunton, MA; 1890.
- Keifer, J. Warren: "Sketches of War History, 1861-1865"; A Compilation of Miscellaneous Papers Compiled for the Ohio Commander of the Loyal Legion; Wilmington, OH; MOLLUS, OH; 1885-1909.
- Keifer, J Warren: "The Battle of Sailor's Creek"; MOLLUS, OH Volume III; 1879.
- Keifer, J. Warren: "A Forgotten Battle, Sailor's Creek April 6, 1865," Cincinnati, OH; 1888.
- King, Horatio C.: "Five Forks and Lee's Surrender"; Rifle Shots and Bugle Notes, Grand Army Gazette Publishing Company; NY; 1884.
- King, Horatio C.: "The Voices Now that Answer Not," Dickinson College Library; the Role of the Veteran in Remembrance; Laura Detloff; Library Cap Website.
- Maurice, Frederick: "Lee's Aide-de-Camp, Being the Papers of Colonel Charles Marshall"; University of Nebraska Press, Lincoln, NE.
- "Massachusetts in the Army and Navy during the War of 1861-1865: Wright and Potter Printing Company; Boston, MA; 1895.
- "Massachusetts Soldiers, Sailors and Marines in the Civil War": Volume 3; Compiled and Published by the Adjutant General; Norwood Press; 1932.
- McCabe, W. Gordon: "Major General George Washington Custis Lee"; paper read at the Virginia Historical Society; February 14, 1914, Southern Historical Society Papers; Volume 39
- Myers, Frank M.: "The Comanche's-A History of White's Battalion Virginia Calvary"; Continental Book Company, Marietta, GA; 1956.
- "New Jersey Courier News": Bridgewater, NJ; January 7, 2001 edition.
- "North Adams Transcript"; "Charlemont Veteran Captured a General" and Dave White Super Soldier of the Civil War Still Active"; North Adams, MA; undated.
- "Northampton Gazette": Editions; April 25, 1865 and July 18, 1865; Northampton, MA.
- "Northampton Gazette": "Grand Army Rooms Have Been Vacated"; June 4, 1937; Northampton, MA.
- "Official Records": "Appomattox Campaign"; Volume 46; Part One.
- "Official Records": "Prisoners of War"; Volume 4; Series 2.
- "Official Records": Custis Lee; Volume 40, Series 1.
- "Official Records": Judge Advocate Hindmarsh, Volume 42, Series 1, Part 111.
- "The Otsego Republican": Edition; April 29, 1865, article by Rev John Adams.
- "The Otsego Republican": Cover letter by John M. Lovejoy in the Edition; January 6, 1892; which also contains a reprint of the John Adams article of April 29, 1865.
- "The Otsego Republican": Edition; Wednesday, October 27, 1897.
- Peck, George: "A Recruit Before Petersburg."
- Proft, Bob: "United States of America's Congressional Medal of Honor Recipients and their Official Citations"; Highland House 11, Inc.; 1994.
- Schaff, Morris: "The Sunset of the Confederacy"; Cooper Square Press; 2002.
- Secretary of the Commonwealth of Massachusetts: "Acts and Resolves Passed by the General Court of Massachusetts in the Year 1869"; Wright & Potter, State Printers, 79 Milk Street, Boston, MA; 1869.
- Shaw William: A Diary as kept by Wm. H. Shaw during the Great Civil War"; by William H. Shaw.
- Spencer, James: "Civil War Generals-Categorical Listings and Biographical Directory"; Greenwood Press, NY.

- <u>Springfield, Massachusetts Daily News</u>: "Looking Backward 50 Years Ago"; September 21, 1963 and article March 30, 1961.
- <u>Stevens, Hazard</u>: "Battle of Sailor's Creek"; Papers of the Massachusetts Historical Society Magazine; Volume 6; 1884.
- <u>Stiles, Robert</u>: "Four Years under Marse Robert"; Neale Publishing Company, NY; 1903 also the Press of Morningside Bookshop version; 1977.
- <u>"The Sun"</u>: New York, NY; Edition: Sunday, September 19, 1897; Volume LXV-No. 19.
- <u>"Supplement to the Official Records"</u>: Part 11, Record of Events Series; Volumes 29 and 46; 1862-1865.
- <u>Tyler, Mason</u>: Recollections of the Civil War with Many Original Diary Entries and Letters"; G. P. Putman's Sons; NY; 1912.
- <u>Vaill, Theodore F.</u>: "History of the Second Connecticut Volunteers Heavy Artillery"; Connecticut Historical Society, Hartford, CT.
- <u>Warner, Ezra, J.</u>: "Generals in Gray: Lives of their Commanders"; Louisiana State University Press, Baton Rouge, LA; 2000.
- <u>"West Winfield Star"</u>: editions Nov. 15, and Dec. 27, 1912 and Feb. 7, 1913; West Winfield, NY.
- <u>Williams College, Williamstown, MA:</u> an undated newspaper article in a bound Volume for Williams College alumni; Archives and Special Collections; citation # 63.W 1863.
- <u>Woodbury, Augustus</u>: "The Second Rhode Island Regiment, a Narrative of Military Operations in which the Regiment was Engaged"; 1875
- <u>Yates, Bernice Marie</u>: "The Perfect Gentleman, the Life and Letters of George Washington Custis Lee"; Xulon Press; 2003

INDEX

NAMES:

AUTHOR NOTE: Because of the frequency of the entries, the names of Harris Hawthorn, Custis Lee and David White are not included in this index.

UNITS:

AUTHOR NOTE: Because of the frequency of the entries, the 37 MA Infantry and 121 NY Infantry are not included in this index.

For a complete book and price list write:

SCHROEDER PUBLICATIONS
131 Tanglewood Drive
Lynchburg, VA 24502
www.civilwar-books.com
E-mail: civilwarbooks@yahoo.com
434-525-1865

Titles Available:

* **Thirty Myths About Lee's Surrender** by Patrick A. Schroeder ISBN 1-889246-05-0

* **More Myths About Lee's Surrender** by Patrick A. Schroeder ISBN 1-889246-01-8

* **The Confederate Cemetery at Appomattox** by Patrick A. Schroeder
    ISBN 1-889246-11-5

* **Recollections & Reminiscences of Old Appomattox and Its People**
    by George T. Peers ISBN 1-889246-12-3

* **Tar Heels: Five Points in the Record of North Carolina in the Great War of 1861-5** by the
    Committee appointed by the North Carolina Literary and Historical Society ISBN 1-889246-02-6 (Soft cover) ISBN 1-889246-15-8 (Hard cover)

* **The Fighting Quakers** by A. J. H. Duganne ISBN 1-889246-03-4

* **A Duryée Zouave** by Thomas P. Southwick ISBN 1-561900-86-9 (Soft cover)
    ISBN 1-889246-24-7 (Hard cover)

* **Civil War Soldier Life: In Camp and Battle** by George F. Williams
    ISBN 1-889246-04-2

* **We Came To Fight: The History of the 5th New York Veteran Volunteer Infantry,
    Duryée's Zouaves, (1863-1865)** by Patrick A. Schroeder ISBN 1-889246-07-7

* **Campaigns of the 146th Regiment New York State Volunteers** by Mary Genevie Green Brainard
    ISBN 1-889246-08-5

* **The Bloody 85th: The Letters of Milton McJunkin, A Western Pennsylvania Soldier in the Civil
    War** Edited by Richard A. Sauers, Ronn Palm, and Patrick A. Schroeder ISBN 1-889246-13-1
    (Soft cover) ISBN 1-889246-16-6 (Hard cover)

* **The Highest Praise of Gallantry: Memorials of David T. Jenkins & James E. Jenkins of the
    146th New York Infantry & Oneida Cavalry** by A. Pierson Case (1889) with New Material by
    Patrick A. Schroeder ISBN 1-889246-17-4

* **Where Duty Called Them: The Story of the Samuel Babcock Family of Homer, New York in the
    Civil War** by Edmund Raus ISBN 1-889246-49-2

* **The Opportunity Is At Hand: Oneida County, New York, Colored Soldiers in the Civil War** by
    Donald M. Wisnoski ISBN 1-880246-20-4 (Soft cover) ISBN 1-889246-18-2 (Hard cover)

* **So You Want to Be a Soldier: How to Get Started in Civil War Re-enacting** by Shaun C. Grenan
  ISBN 1-889246-19-0

* **The Pennsylvania Bucktails: A Photographic Album of the 42nd, 149th, 150th Pennsylvania Regiments** by Patrick A. Schroeder ISBN 1-889246-14-X

* **A Summer on the Plains with Custer's 7th Cavalry: The 1870 Diary of Annie Gibson Roberts** Edited by Brian C. Pohanka ISBN 1-889246-21-2

* **The Life of Ely S. Parker: The Last Grand Sachem of the Iroquois and General Grant's Military Secretary** by Arthur C. Parker ISBN 1-889246-50-6 (Hard cover) ISBN 1-889246-52-2 (Leather bound limited edition)

* **"We Are Coming Father Abra'am" The History of the 9th Vermont Volunteer Infantry, 1862-1865** by Don Wickman ISBN 1-889246-23-9

* **A Vermont Cavalryman in War and Love: The Civil War Letters of Brevet Major General William Wells and Anna Richardson** Edited by Elliott W. Hoffman ISBN 1-889246-51-4

* **While My Country is in Danger: The Life and Letters of Lt. Col. Richard S. Thompson, 12th NJ Volunteers** by Gerry Harder Poriss & Ralph G. Poriss ISBN 0-9622393-6-4

* **No Middle Ground: Thomas Ward Osborn's Letters from Field (1862-1864)** Edited by H. S. Crumb & K. Dhalle ISBN 0-9622393-4-8

* **Unfurl the Flags: Remembrances of the American Civil War** Edited by W. E. Edmonston ISBN 0-9622393-0-5

* **Out of the Wilderness: The Civil War Memoir of Cpl. Norton C. Shepard** Edited by Raymond W. Smith ISBN 1-892059-00-2

* **A History of the 117th Regiment, New York Volunteers (Fourth Oneida)** by James A. Mowris ISBN 0-9622393-8-0

* **The Telegraph Goes to War: The Personal Diary of David Homer Bates, Lincoln's Telegraph Operator** Edited by Donald E. Markle

* **Shepherdstown: Last Clash of the Antietam Campaign September 19–20, 1862** by Thomas McGrath ISBN 1-889246-39-5

* **Charlie's Civil War: A Private's Trial by Fire in the 5th New York Volunteers, Duryée Zouaves, and the 146th New York Volunteer Infantry** Edited by Charles Brandegee Livingstone ISBN 1-889246-42-5

* **The Passing of the Armies: The Last Campaign of the Armies** by Joshua Lawrence Chamberlain (Audio Book) ISBN 1-889246-65-4

* **The Appomattox Campaign, March 29 – April 9, 1865** by Chris M. Calkins ISBN 1-889246-55-7

"HOOSICK FALLS MEDAL OF HONOR RECIPIENT HONORED"
THE EASTWICK PRESS, PETERSBURGH, NY
OCTOBER 27, 2006

By Bea Peterson

Members of the American Legion Post #40 Honor Guard were among those on hand Saturday to pay tribute to Civil War Medal of Honor awardee Harris S. Hawthorn. (Bea Peterson photo)

Way in the back of the old Maple Grove Cemetery, on the downhill side near the railroad tracks, is the grave of Harris Smith Hawthorn. He was born in Salem, NY, on February 29, 1832, and died March 23, 1911. Buried with him is his wife Adelia Brown Gill who was born December 25, 1834, and died May 8, 1920. The tall plain marker indicates Harris served in Company F, 121st New York Infantry. Except for their striking birth dates, the marker tells little about the couple. In September 2005 Norma Brenenstuhl, an officer of the Maple Grove Cemetery, received a letter from J. Donald Morfe, Field Researcher for the Medal of Honor Historical Society explaining that Harris S. Hawthorne was a Medal of Honor winner. He requested that the cemetery install a bronze plaque, supplied by the government, on Hawthorn's grave stone acknowledging he was a Medal of Honor recipient. Norma worked with Phil Leonard on the project. Ken Begin installed the plaque when it arrived and on Saturday, October 21, a short ceremony was held at his gravesite to honor him. Information gathered states "Harris S. Hawthorn (or Hawthorne) was awarded the Civil War Medal of Honor on December 29, 1894. He was a member of Company F, 121st New York Infantry. At Deatonsville (Sailor's Creek), Virginia on April 6, 1865, he captured Confederate Major General George Washington Custis Lee (son of Robert E. Lee)." His sworn statement says that "he knows of his own knowledge that he is the first person (officer or enlisted man) who seized or captured General Custis Lee of the Confederate Army, in the engagement of the 6th of April … and delivered him to Colonel Olcott." Hawthorn lived and married in Hoosick Falls. On hand for the ceremony was the Hoosick Falls American Legion honor guard, consisting of Bernie Guerard, Don St. Hilaire, Harold Nichols, Keith McCart, Fred Brenenstuhl and Walt Zwinge, Hoosick Falls Mayor Laura Reynolds, Town of Hoosick Supervisor Marilyn Douglas, Rensselaer County Legislator Lester Goodermote, Norma Brenenstuhl and Town Historian Phil Leonard. A salute was fired by the honor guard and taps was played by Tim Hayes. Mayor Reynolds said she was honored to be present at such an occasion, and Fred Brenenstuhl offered a prayer. In Morfe's letter to Norma Brenenstuhl he had a quote which stated "Poor is the Nation that has no heroes but beggared is that Nation that has and forgets them." Morfe went on to write that "Since the Revolutionary War 41 million Americans have served in the armed services with only just over 3,400 receiving the Medal of Honor. The medal is the highest honor awarded to American military personnel for gallantry in action." Hoosick Falls should be proud to have such an honored man in its history.

THIS BOOK PROVES THAT PRIVATE HAWTHORN WAS A GOOD SOLDIER, WORTHY OF HONOR, BUT NOT FOR THE CAPTURE OF MAJOR GENERAL G. W. CUSTIS LEE. THAT HONOR, WITH ITS CORRESPONDING MEDAL OF HONOR, RIGHTFULLY BELONGS TO ANOTHER SOLDIER.